Revolutions
AND
Revolutionists

Revolutions AND Revolutionists

A COMPREHENSIVE GUIDE TO THE LITERATURE

Robert Blackey

ABC-Clio, Inc.

Santa Barbara, California

Oxford, England

Copyright © 1982 by Robert Blackey

All rights reserved. No part of this publication may be reproduced, stored in a retrieval system, or transmitted, in any form or by any means, electronic, mechanical, photocopying, recording, or otherwise, except for the inclusion of brief quotations in a review, without the prior permission in writing from the publisher.

Library of Congress Cataloging in Publication Data

Blackey, Robert.
  Revolutions and revolutionists.

  (War/peace bibliography series; #17)
  Includes index.
  1. Revolutions—History—Bibliography. 2. Revolutions—History—Bibliography. 3. Revolutions—Bibliography. I. Title. II. Series.
  Z7164.R54BB55 [HM283]   016.3036s   82-6653
  ISBN 0-87436-330-6   [016.3036'4]   AACR2

10 9 8 7 6 5 4 3 2 1

ABC-Clio, Inc.
2040 Alameda Padre Serra, Box 4397
Santa Barbara, CA 93101

Clio Press Ltd.
Woodside House
Hinksey Hill
Oxford, OX1 5BE, England

Manufactured in the United States of America

Acknowledgments

The good people I would like to thank are as important as their numbers are few. Professor Richard Dean Burns of California State University, Los Angeles, is the very active and skilled editor of the War/Peace Bibliography Series; his professionalism, encouragement, and suggestions propelled this project in several important directions it might not otherwise have taken. The capable personnel of ABC-Clio Books are a joy to work with. The library staff at California State College, San Bernardino, has always provided me with gracious and efficient assistance in pleasant surroundings. Ms. Diana Church Lawson typed large parts of the first draft and saved me considerable time. Ms. Nancy Mazza also provided skilled typing assistance with the index. Finally, I thank my wife Phyllis, to whom this book is dedicated, and my sons Richard and Jeffrey for being loving, patient, and considerate, especially during those times when I devoted more of my life to this book than to them.

In preparing a bibliographic guide of this breadth it has been impossible for me actually to check and verify each of the more than 6,200 items, much less read them. Therefore, for the inevitable but, it is hoped, few errors, apologies are offered and responsibility accepted.

ROBERT BLACKEY
CALIFORNIA STATE COLLEGE
SAN BERNARDINO

THE WAR/PEACE BIBLIOGRAPHY SERIES
Richard Dean Burns, Editor

This Series has been developed in cooperation with the Center for the Study of Armament and Disarmament, California State University, Los Angeles.

#1 *Songs of Protest, War and Peace*
A Bibliography and Discography
R. S͟ERGE D͟ENISOFF

#2 *Warfare in Primitive Societies*
A Bibliography
W͟ILLIAM T͟ULIO D͟IVALE

#3 *The Vietnam Conflict*
Its Geographical Dimensions, Political Traumas and Military Developments
M͟ILTON L͟EITENBERG and R͟ICHARD D͟EAN B͟URNS

#4 *The Arab-Israeli Conflict*
A Historical, Political, Social, and Military Bibliography
R͟ONALD M. D͟EV͟ORE

#5 *Modern Revolutions and Revolutionists*
A Bibliography
R͟OBERT B͟LACKEY

#6 *Arms Control and Disarmament*
A Bibliography
R͟ICHARD D͟EAN B͟URNS

#7 *The United States in World War I*
A Selected Bibliography
R͟ONALD S͟CHAFFER

#8 *Uncertain Judgment*
A Bibliography of War Crimes Trials
J͟OHN R. L͟EWIS

#9 *The Soviet Navy, 1941–1978*
A Guide to Sources in English
MYRON J. SMITH, JR.

#10 *The Soviet Air and Strategic Rocket Forces, 1939–1980*
A Guide to Sources in English
MYRON J. SMITH, JR.

#11 *The Soviet Army, 1939–1980*
A Guide to Sources in English
MYRON J. SMITH, JR.

#12 *The Secret Wars*
A Guide to Sources in English
Volume I: Intelligence, Propaganda and Psychological Warfare, Resistance Movements, and Secret Operations, 1939–1945
MYRON J. SMITH, JR.

#13 *The Secret Wars*
A Guide to Sources in English
Volume II: Intelligence, Propaganda and Psychological Warfare, Covert Operations, 1945–1980
MYRON J. SMITH, JR.

#14 *The Secret Wars*
A Guide to Sources in English
Volume III: International Terrorism, 1968–1980
MYRON J. SMITH, JR.

#15 *World Hunger*
A Guide to the Economic and Political Dimensions
NICOLE BALL

#16 *Peace and War*
A Guide to Bibliographies
BERENICE A. CARROLL, CLINTON F. FINK & JANE E. MOHRAZ

#17 *Revolutions and Revolutionists*
A Comprehensive Guide to the Literature
ROBERT BLACKEY

About the War/Peace Bibliography Series

With this bibliographical series, the Center for the Study of Armament and Disarmament, California State University, Los Angeles, seeks to promote a wider understanding of martial violence and the alternatives to its employment. The Center, which was formed by concerned faculty and students in 1962–63, has as its primary objective the stimulation of intelligent discussion of war/peace issues. More precisely, the Center has undertaken two essential functions: (1) to collect and catalogue materials bearing on war/peace issues; and (2) to aid faculty, students, and the public in their individual and collective probing of the historical, political, economic, philosophical, technical, and psychological facts of these fundamental problems.

This bibliographical series is, obviously, one tool with which we may more effectively approach our task. Each issue in this series is intended to provide a comprehensive "working," rather than definitive, bibliography on a relatively narrow theme within the spectrum of war/peace studies. While we hope this series will prove to be a useful tool, we also solicit your comments regarding its format, contents, and topics.

RICHARD DEAN BURNS
SERIES EDITOR

Contents

Introduction   **xiii**
Chronology of Some Revolutionary Upheavals   **xxi**

1. **Concepts and Aspects of Revolution   1**
    Sociology of Revolution, **2**; Politics and Revolution, **11**; Philosophy and Revolution, **13**; Psychology of Revolution, **14**; Economics and Revolution, **15**; Ideology, **15**; Coups d'Etat, **18**; Civil Wars, **19**; Millennial Movements, **20**; War, the Military, and Guerrillas, **22**; Violence, **26**; Terrorism, **30**; Nonviolence, **35**; Counterrevolution, **37**; Peasant Revolutions, **39**; Student Rebellions, **41**; Radicalism, **44**; Anarchism, **46**; Marx and Marxism, **52**; Friedrich Engels, **60**; Socialism, **61**; Communism, **64**; Leadership and Elites, **68**; Nationalism and Revolution, **70**; Religion and Revolution, **71**; Women and Revolution, **73**; Evolution and Revolution, **74**; Literature and Revolution, **75**; Race and Revolution, **76**; Modernization and Revolution, **77**; Comparative Studies, **77**; World Revolution, **81**; Miscellaneous, **82**

2. **Ancient and Medieval   85**
    Greece, **86**; Rome, **86**; Medieval, **87**

3. **Early Modern Europe   88**
    Peasants' Revolt, 1524–1525, **91**; Revolt of the Netherlands, 1566–1609, **93**; The Fronde, 1648–1653, **94**; Puritan Revolution, 1640–1660, **95**; Oliver Cromwell, **102**; Milton and Revolution, **104**; Levellers and Diggers, **105**; Glorious Revolution, 1688–1689, **106**; Locke and Revolution, **108**; Scientific Revolution, **109**; Revolts in Spain, **110**; Rousseau and Revolution, **111**; Age of the Democratic Revolution, 1760–1815, **113**; French Revolution, 1789–1799, **115**; Robespierre and the Reign of Terror, **130**; The Vendée, 1793–1796, **132**; Edmund Burke and Revolution, **133**; Pugachev's Rebellion, 1773–1774, **134**

4. **Modern Europe   136**
    Tocqueville and Revolution, **143**; Revolutions of 1830, **144**; Revolutions of 1848, **146**; Paris Commune, 1871, **153**; Bulgarian National Revolution, 1876, **155**; Georges Sorel and Syndicalism, **156**; Revolution in Italy, **157**; Russian Revolution of 1905, **158**; Mensheviks and the February (1917) Revolution, **160**; Russian Revolution of 1917 and the Bolsheviks, **163**; Lenin and Leninism, **172**; Trotsky, **176**; Revolution in Greece, **178**; Finnish Revolution, 1917–1918, **179**; Ukrainian Revolution, 1917–1921, **179**; Hungarian Revolution, 1918–1919, **180**; German Revolution, 1918–1919, and Rosa Luxemburg, **181**; Irish Revolution, 1916–1922, **183**; Nazi Revolution, 1933, **187**; Spanish Civil War, 1936–1939, **189**;

x / Contents

Revolution in Yugoslavia, 1941–1945, **193**; Revolution in Poland, 1956, **194**; Hungarian Revolution, 1956, **194**; French Revolution, 1968, **196**; Czechoslovakian Revolution, 1968, **198**; Portuguese Revolution, 1974, **199**

5. **North America** 202

   American Revolution, 1776–1783, **204**; Samuel Adams, **223**; Thomas Jefferson, **224**; Thomas Paine, **225**; New Left, c. 1962–?1972, **226**; Herbert Marcuse, **232**; Black Revolution, c. 1954– , **233**; Quebec Revolutionary Nationalism, **236**

6. **Latin America** 238

   Latin American Independence Revolutions, **246**; Mexican Revolution, 1910, **249**; Guatemalan Revolution, 1944, **256**; Revolution in Bolivia, 1952, **257**; Cuban Revolution, 1959, **259**; Castro and Castroism, **264**; Che Guevara, **266**; Regis Debray, **267**; Chilean Revolution and Salvador Allende, 1970–1973, **268**; Revolution in Uruguay and the Tupamaros, **272**; Nicaraguan Revolution, 1978–1979, **273**; Revolutions in Argentina, **274**; Revolutions in Brazil, **276**; Revolutions in Colombia and Camilo Torres, **277**; Revolution in Peru, **278**; Revolutions in Venezuela, **280**

7. **Asia** 282

   Taiping Rebellion, 1850–1864, **292**; Boxer Rebellion, 1900, **293**; Chinese National Revolution and Sun Yat-sen, 1911–1927, **294**; Chinese Communist Revolution, 1927–1949, **297**; Mao Tse-tung and Maoism, **306**; Chinese Cultural Revolution, 1966–1969, **310**; Vietnamese Revolution, 1945–1973, **317**; Ho Chi Minh, **321**; Revolution in Laos, **322**; Revolution in Cambodia, **323**; Revolution in Thailand, **323**; Revolution in Indonesia, **324**; Revolution in Malaya, **325**; Revolution in Korea, **326**; Sepoy Mutiny, 1857, **326**; Indian Revolution and Gandhi, 1920–1949, **328**; Revolution in Afghanistan, **334**; Revolution in Turkey, **334**; Revolution in the Philippines, **335**

8. **Africa** 337

   Kwame Nkrumah, **342**; Algerian Revolution, 1954–1962, **344**; Frantz Fanon, **347**; Revolution in Zanzibar, 1964, **349**; Nyerere, Senghor, Touré, **350**; Revolutions in Portuguese Africa, **351**; Angolan Revolution, 1961–1975, **353**; Revolution in Mozambique, 1964–1975, **355**; Revolution in Guinea-Bissau, 1963–1974, **356**; Amilcar Cabral, **359**; Libyan Revolution, 1969–1970, **361**; Ethiopian Revolution, 1974–1977, **362**; Revolution in Southern Africa, **364**

9. **Other Third World Countries and the Middle East** 367

   Middle East Revolutions, **369**; Revolution in Egypt, 1952, **372**; Iranian Revolution, 1978–1979, **374**

Addendum **379**
Quotations on Revolution **399**
Author-Editor Index **419**
Subject Index **461**

To Phyllis Blackey

From the beginning . . .
        until the end.

Introduction

Given the plethora of revolutions in the history of humankind it is a wonder—and also a subject worthy of investigation—that the world has absorbed such convulsive movements. What has it meant to the past, and what will it mean for the future, to bear witness to so much unrest and dissatisfaction, to so much greed and resentment? Are revolutions merely expressions of times being out-of-joint, or are they as natural to the human condition as earthquakes and storms in the physical world, akin to growing pains of societal change?

Whatever the answers to these questions, there is no doubt that the study of revolutions is vital for an understanding of history and the modern world. But a thorough appreciation of the subject has been prevalent only during the last quarter of a century. An earlier and not uncommon academic view was—and in a few circles still is—that revolutions played only a supporting role to the more important themes, such as war, the rise of nation-states, and nationalism. Today most scholars have come to recognize revolution as a thread of history not merely central to the whole fabric, but interwoven with those more conventional themes as well. Some wars, such as the Revolt of the Netherlands and the Spanish Civil War, were also revolutions. Few nation-states have developed without a boost from a revolution, as the histories of England and France will attest. And nationalism without revolution (or its threat) would at times be a paper tiger; the truth of this statement should be evident from the history of the nineteenth and twentieth centuries.

Another obstacle to the emergence of "revolution" as a fully acceptable academic discipline is that it has been ridiculed as an intellectual toy, studied only because it is a relevant historical episode or because it is fashionable. To be sure, the English, American, French, and Russian revolutions, as well as others in the Western world, have received more than a fair amount of attention. But what of those revolutions of more current times and distant places? It appears that as members of the European-American Western world, we were insulated from events and people in faraway, esoteric lands. However, after World War II, with the final triumph of the Communist Revolution in China, with the successful and threatening revolutions in Latin America, and with the emergence—often via revolution—of independent nations in Africa, we were shaken from our cocoon of self-imposed isolation. Revolution has been recognized as a major vehicle for change in the modern world. In our nuclear age, conventional wars have often been superseded by revolutionary wars. More than ever before, revolution is seen as having played an integral part in the evolution of man. Its study cannot be relegated to the corners of academic respectability.

xiv / **Introduction**

Revolutions, then, are clearly among the most extraordinary societal phenomena. They have plagued the past and provided promise for the future. However secure and safe a society may be, the possibility of revolution cannot be completely excluded as a means for radical social change. When the essential institutions of any society fail in one or more crucial ways to meet the needs of its population, the potential for revolution is present.

Throughout modern history the dream and the reality of revolution have played a significant part in the development of civilization and the aspirations of man. The dream of revolution involves the desire of a people to control their own destinies and to construct a vastly improved if not completely new community, nation, and even world. The dream of revolution incorporates a belief in the ultimate perfection of humanity; it envisions a society in which people will be free, liberty will flourish, and equality will be a way of life. The reality of revolution is the constant companion of the dream. The reality qualifies the dream in terms of chronology, geography, and human frailty. Nevertheless, the modern idea of revolution has meant the possibility of creating a new order and a new man, the beginning of history anew. Modern revolutionists would no doubt agree that unless such a beginning can be initiated—although their stated means for getting there are obviously different—man's domination of man will continue to exist, regardless of the name we choose to call it. What we conventionally label reason and common sense are not essential to the nature of revolution simply because the new society and the new man do not need to be demonstrated rationally.

Any examination of studies concerned with the nature and idea of revolution will invariably result in considerable confusion. Whether the student is a jaded professional or an uninitiated fledgling, the experience can be intellectually traumatic. Definitions of revolutions—broad and narrow—as well as descriptions and analyses of the process run rampant on a fertile field that has sprouted stems from numerous professions and academic disciplines. What follows in the next few paragraphs is a brief exposition and guide to the nature of revolution.

Dictionary definitions can hinder more than they help. The definitions of scholars, theorists, and other writers are often not much of an improvement because they tend to cater to the particular preconceptions of their authors and adherents. In addition, the utilization of any one definition (especially narrow ones) tends to be restrictive insofar as there are invariably exceptions.

Still, we need some description, at least with which to work. Therefore, let us begin by asserting that revolutions generally have in common a variety of characteristics which can serve as a foundation for a comprehensive and functional framework:

> Revolutions are a challenge to the existing political—and perhaps social, economic, and cultural—system with an aim at redirecting and restructuring; they occur when the legitimate means for effecting changes break

down or function poorly; they often involve the use or threat of violence against some or all aspects of the status quo (that violence may be internal, external, or both). They generally disrupt society sufficiently so that after they are over, the victors, either revolutionists or status quo, must engage in a significant effort to reorder and reorganize society. Revolutions tend to include references to the past, but these are often only rhetorical tools. More often than not, revolutions tend to involve more than one country and to become international problems.[1]

From this we conclude that a good, working description/definition is as follows:

> A revolution is a political and/or social and/or economic and/or cultural upheaval which calls for a fundamental change in the existing order; it is relatively rapid and generally employs the use or threat of force; it is directed against principles and institutions, not individuals.[2]

The above description/definition is not meant to be a judgment on what is or is not a revolution. Instead, it is purposely designed to be broad enough to include a wide variety of revolutionary phenomena so as to render this bibliographic guide as useful and useable as possible. Therefore, successful or not, violent or nonviolent, grandiose or minor, much that is related to revolution is here. For example, Chapter 1 highlights the various characteristics and qualities of revolution, while the other chapters feature marginal as well as major revolutions.

Other kinds of political upheavals are often confused with the phenomenon of revolution. To be sure, there is frequently a real connection between revolutions, on the one hand, and coups d'etat, revolts, rebellions, civil wars, and secession movements, on the other; the former, in fact, may very well emerge from any of the latter. However, to keep distinctions and definitions clear and to understand where a revolt, for example, evolves into a revolution, it is important to discern the interests involved. Questions should be raised regarding the nature of the leadership (e.g., Are the leaders of an upheaval essentially any different from those in the established government? Or, are they armed with goals that seek a sudden transformation of all society?); the aim and impact upon the existing social system (e.g., Are lost privileges or rights being sought? Is recognition on the part of a minority the goal? Or, are the aims societal, national, or global in nature?); and the role of ideology (e.g., Is there any ideological background to the movement that might broaden the horizons of the participants from merely gratifying limited objectives to a vision that encompasses all of society?). Once questions are directed in this fashion, a fuller appreciation of the nature of revolution should result.

In addition, phenomena such as coups and rebellions tend to be endemic; they are often expected, frequent, and distinctive to a given geographical area. Contrarily, revolutions are essentially epidemic; their occurrence is unusual and generally unexpected, and they involve a greater area. In Latin America, for example, coups and rebellions have been endemic in the twentieth century, whereas genuine revolutions have been comparatively rare.

What ought to emerge from a study of revolutions (in the plural) is an awareness that they are complex and diverse events. Too often, however, theorists and analysts focus their attention on a limited or narrow aspect which tends to render other, though equally valid, theories innocuous. But the very diversity of past revolutions is indicative of the failure of any approach that does not acknowledge the multitude of hostilities and antagonisms that lie deeply rooted in revolution.

Similarly, there has been a conflict between those who perceive revolutions as such unique occurrences that they defy comparison and those who seek to find certain uniformities, consistencies, and broad theories in their study of revolution. Clearly, the discovery and use of uniformities is instructive, but no less so than an awareness of dissimilarities. In fact, an honest search for uniformities should illuminate an abundance of differences; no one revolution is ever a clear copy of another, and not all uniformities survive close scrutiny. For example, a number of studies have extracted uniformities from comparing the American and French Revolutions. But even such uniformities as are found (e.g., the transfer of allegiance of the intellectuals, inefficient governmental machinery) must be qualified by the fact that the two revolutions were of different types. That is, the French Revolution was civil war-like in nature and aimed at the establishment of a new system, whereas the American Revolution was anti-colonial in spirit and sought to establish the supremacy of a domestic governing elite within a system little different from the old.

A more valid approach, it appears, is to draw these extremes to a middle ground. That is, the distinctive characteristics of revolutions must be acknowledged and appreciated, and it must also be acknowledged that there is considerable value in discovering common traits among different revolutions. Study and compare revolutions and you will find a relationship between cause and effect, between combatants and the nature of the struggle, and between the plans and ideology of the victors and their subsequent policies. That, perhaps, is obvious. But such relationships should only serve to initiate investigations, revolution by revolution, not constricted beforehand by a cast-in-stone definition or time-honored precondition or characteristic. However much we may search for uniformities, as even I have done elsewhere,[3] and however much we may in fact learn from such efforts, in the final analysis there simply are no formulas for explaining all revolutions, no neat moulds into which several may be cast. After evaluating many revolutions, after becoming aware of similarities, and after satisfying—and dashing—preconceived notions, each revolution must be examined on its own, as an event unique to a given time, people, and circumstances.

In concluding the introduction to *Modern Revolutions and Revolutionists: A Bibliography* (ABC-Clio, 1976), I observed that the field of revolution was characterized by eclecticism, a probable indication of its nascent stage. As such, I noted, the works cited in that volume were perhaps no more than the tip of a literary iceberg. With this book the iceberg reveals more of its monumental size. Let us begin with some background.

In 1965 a revised and expanded edition of Crane Brinton's classic work, *The Anatomy of Revolution,* was published. Its bibliographical appendix was intended to be only "complete enough so that anyone using all the leads these books and *their* bibliographies offer would soon find himself very completely immersed in the subject."[4] Indeed, Brinton's approximately 220 entries comprised an excellent working bibliography, a starting point for a more intensive search, and the best collection to date.

Prior to the mid-1960s, the phenomenon of revolution was a subject of only limited academic and popular appeal. Revolutions within particular countries or during specific time periods were studied, but generally as part of larger geographical or chronological histories, not as a larger subject in itself. In addition to Brinton's book there were some other general studies, but the field was fractured, lacking cohesion and direction. Moreover, the value of interdisciplinary and comparative approaches was only just beginning to be appreciated on a wide scale.

Then, in the late 1960s and the 1970s, following in the wake of the American civil rights movement and the drive for freedom and independence—at various levels—in the Third World, interest in revolutions intensified. The crises faced by governments of the West, the concern over the war and revolution in Vietnam, and the vocal emergence of the New Left all contributed to a surge of interest in the study of revolutions. Scores of books and articles appeared in print as the world became a laboratory for learning. Scholars and journalists alike availed themselves of the techniques and expertise available within a variety of disciplines. And the bibliography on revolutions began to multiply.

In 1971 my book, *Why Revolution?,* was published.[5] It contained a bibliography more than twice the size of Brinton's. At the time it was probably the largest single listing on the subject. Then, in 1976, the first attempt at a comprehensive bibliography of revolutions and revolutionists appeared.[6] It included two thousand four hundred titles. The book now before you has more than six thousand entries (many of which have been published since 1976), and is an improvement over earlier efforts in several important ways, all of which are explained below.

This book does not attempt to be a font for manuscript or archival records. It is essentially a collection of published sources, most of which are available at major libraries. The only kind of primary material is that which is printed: collections of documents, government publications, and the writings of participants and eyewitnesses. Most of the works are in English or English translation, but a significant minority are in their original languages, mostly French, German, and Spanish.

The organization is designed to maximize the utility of the titles listed. Following the chronology of revolutionary upheavals, the book is divided into nine chapters, with each in turn subdivided into sections.

Aside from the first chapter, which focuses on the many aspects of revolution, the rest are based on either chronology (as in Chapters 2, 3, and 4) or geography (as in Chapters 3 through 9). The sections in Chapter 1 each treat a different characteristic or aspect of revolution. Chapter 2 is divided into sections which concentrate on ancient Greece and Rome, and medieval Europe. The sections in the remaining chapters deal directly with specific revolutions or revolutionists, with features of some of those revolutions, and with revolutionary movements in a single country.

Each chapter and most sections are launched with an introduction. Among other things, these introductions provide information about the subject in question, highlight issues of conflict or raise key questions, single out some of the more prominent works in the field, and clarify items not clearly introduced by their titles. They are designed primarily for the novice or beginning student.

Although a few of the sections are too small to be subdivided further, most are separated into two or more parts. At the very least these sections isolate articles and books, but many others have subsections for bibliographies, historiographies, documents, and/or reference works. Further, some of the larger sections are subdivided additionally into such groupings as eyewitness accounts, causes and origins, overviews, surveys, interpretations, and others that suit the specific revolution.

Finally, there are two indices, an author index and a subject index. Since many titles are applicable to more than one section alone, but are not repeated, *every* search for titles on a given subject or by a specific revolutionist should include an examination of the subject index. For example, if the "Mexican Revolution" is your subject consult the titles immediately following the introduction to Chapter 6 in addition to the obvious ones in the section "Mexican Revolution, 1910." There are among these titles works comparing the Mexican Revolution with others, and surveys of revolutionary Latin America that include discussions of Mexico. The subject index will also reveal still other titles located, for various reasons, elsewhere. Some topics, to take another example, will require a survey of more than one specific section. Therefore, when pursuing sources on, say, the "Russian Revolution of 1917 and the Bolsheviks," check the titles immediately following the introduction to Chapter 4 and those under "Mensheviks and the February (1917) Revolution," "Lenin and Leninism," "Trotsky," "Marx and Marxism," "Socialism," and "Communism." The subject index should also be consulted since, depending on the specific subject being researched, titles might be found under "Nationalism and Revolution," "Women and Revolution," "Comparative Studies," or elsewhere.

Chapter 1, "Concepts and Aspects of Revolution," is divided into thirty-three sections, most of which are really characteristics of the broader subject. Just as the language of biology classifies living things into kingdoms, phyla, classes, etc., so it might be helpful to think of "revolution" as the kingdom, and all the sections in this chapter as the

Introduction / xix

major phyla in which they may be divided; and many may be further subdivided into classes (e.g., the phylum "civil war" may be subdivided into secessionist movements, such as the American Civil War, and those fought between contending forces for control of the government, as in the Yugoslavian National Revolution, 1941–1945). The fact is that "revolution" has become so complex that dictionary definitions or simple definitions serve only to define a type of revolution, not all of them. So, "revolution" has become a broad category for a variety of revolutionary activities, including many coups d'etat, palace revolutions, rebellions, civil wars, and so on.

Thus, the first section in Chapter 1 contains titles that fit broadly under the heading of "Sociology of Revolution" (i.e., works dealing with the concept of revolution, in whole or in part, as opposed to a specific revolution or location). The student entering the field, and others interested in understanding a given revolution or revolutionist, can gain a thorough overview and a good background in fundamentals from the works in this section. The next thirty-five sections treat the phyla of revolution, or various aspects of the broad concept. The last section in Chapter 1 contains a miscellany of titles that do not fit readily into other sections, including works on utopia and revolution, success and failure, cross-continent studies, Max Weber, John Reed, and more.

Chapter 2 covers revolutions in ancient times and during the medieval world. It is divided into three brief sections: Greece, Rome, and Medieval. The works of and on Aristotle, Plato, Polybius, Thucydides, and revolts such as those by Boudicca and the Hussites are located here.

Chapters 3 and 4 deal with Europe from the sixteenth century to the present. In addition to the revolutions and revolutionists listed in the Contents, several other topics are represented among the titles following the chapter introductions, including a variety of general works and surveys, the Reformation in its revolutionary aspects, revolutionary activity in several countries over broad periods, the French Civil-Religious Wars, revolutionary activity in more than one country or in a region, the Scottish Revolution of the mid-seventeenth century, some comparative studies, the Decembrist Revolt of 1825, the Latvian Revolution of 1917, and memoirs and biographies of revolutionists and revolutionary theorists. The introductions to these two chapters, as well as to each of the others, provide amplification.

Chapter 5, "North America," focuses on the revolutionary history of the United States and Canada from the era of the American Revolution through the period of the New Left, the Black Revolution, and revolutionary nationalism in Quebec. There are separate sections for Samuel Adams, Thomas Jefferson, Thomas Paine, and Herbert Marcuse. The titles following the chapter introduction treat other subjects, such as the American revolutionary spirit, slave revolts, and the Dorr Rebellion.

Chapters 6 through 9 cover the Third World, those societies generally outside of Europe and North America. In Chapter 6, "Latin America," the Latin American independence revolutions, six major twentieth century revolutions (in Mexico, Guatemala, Bolivia, Cuba, Chile, and Nicaragua), five major revolutionists and revolutionary theorists (i.e., Castro, Guevara, Debray, Allende, and Torres), and revolutionary activity in the rest of the continent are all featured. Following the introduction to the chapter are a number of important survey histories and general items covering all or most of the continent, as well as a variety of other kinds of works.

Chapter 7, "Asia," opens with material, following the introduction, covering a broader spectrum of Chinese and Indian history than one limited to the several revolutions in those countries for which there are separate sections. Also included here are several comparative and regional studies, works on communism, nationalism, and the West, and studies of revolutionary activity in other Asian countries which are not included among the separate nineteen sections.

Chapter 8, "Africa," focuses on seven of the major revolutions (in Algeria, Zanzibar, Angola, Mozambique, Guinea-Bissau, Libya, and Ethiopia), six major revolutionists and revolutionary theorists (i.e., Nkrumah, Fanon, Nyerere, Senghor, Touré, and Cabral), and revolutionary activity in the rest of the continent, including separate sections for Portuguese Africa as a whole and Southern Africa. Following the introduction to the chapter are a number of important survey histories and general items covering all or most of the continent, as well as several other kinds of works.

The concluding chapter, "Other Third World Countries and the Middle East," treats areas of the Third World not covered in the previous three. Following the introduction are works on the Third World as a unit and those that examine specific features of its revolutionary situation. Separate sections are on revolutions in the Middle East, Egypt, and Iran.

While the twentieth century has been called an "age of revolution," this appellation is more accurately applied to the period following the end of World War II. The chronology of revolutionary upheavals indicates that since 1945 there have been more than 50 revolutions, a number greater than during any comparable time period and as many as during the previous 100 years.

This "age of revolution" has been different from earlier such ages (e.g., Age of the Democratic Revolution, era of the revolutions of 1830 and 1848) in that it has been global, with literally every inhabited continent (except Australia) being affected. Not surprisingly, most of the revolutions since 1945 have occurred among the more underdeveloped peoples of the world. Looking at the history of revolutions, therefore, it appears that revolutions are not simply an ingredient in, but an integral part of societal and world development, modernization, and maturation. However, this does not necessarily imply that all such revolutions have improved the human condition.

One thing is certain, though. After all the reading and research, all the questioning and analyzing, no one will understand revolutions who sees only the ideals and achievements, or who cannot see that side at all.

Notes

1. Robert Blackey and Clifford T. Paynton, *Revolution and the Revolutionary Ideal* (Cambridge, Massachusetts, 1976), p. 7.
2. *Ibid.*, pp. 7f.
3. *Ibid.*, pp. 262-70.
4. Crane Brinton, *The Anatomy of Revolution* (Englewood Cliffs, New Jersey, 1965), pp. 272f.
5. Clifford T. Paynton and Robert Blackey, eds., *Why Revolution? Theories and Analyses* (Cambridge, Massachusetts, 1971).
6. Robert Blackey, *Modern Revolutions and Revolutionists: A Bibliography* (Santa Barbara, California, 1976).

Chronology of Some Revolutionary Upheavals

287 B.C.	Revolt of Athens
60 A.D.	Boudicca's Revolt
1420-1433	Hussite Revolution (Holy Roman Empire)
1517	Protestant Revolution
1524-1525	Peasants' Revolt (Germany)
1562-1598	French Civil-Religious Wars
1566-1609	Revolt of the Netherlands
1640	Portuguese Revolt
1640	Revolt of the Catalans (Spain)
1640-1660	Puritan Revolution (England)
1648-1653	Fronde (France)
1688-1689	Glorious Revolution (England)
1768-1794	Revolution in Geneva
1773-1774	Pugachev Rebellion (Russia)
1776-1783	American Revolution
1780-1784	Túpac Amaru Revolt
1789-1790	Belgian Revolution
1789-1799	French Revolution
1789-1804	Haitian Revolution
1791-1794	Polish Revolution
1793-1796	The Vendée (France)
1794-1795	Dutch Revolution
1798	Rebellion of Ireland
1808-1826	Spanish-American Revolutions of Independence
1820-1823	Italian Revolution

1820–1823	Portuguese Revolution
1820–1823	Spanish Revolution
1821	Greek Revolution
1825	Russian Revolution (Decembrist Revolt)
1830	French Revolution
1830	Belgian Revolution
1830	German Revolution
1830	Italian Revolution
1830	Swiss Revolution
1830	Polish Revolution
1830	Spanish Revolution
1830	Portuguese Revolution
1848	French Revolution
1848	German Revolution
1848	Italian Revolution
1848	Austrian Revolution
1848	Hungarian Revolution
1848	Czech Revolution
1850–1864	Taiping Rebellion (China)
1854	Spanish Revolution
1857	Sepoy Mutiny (India)
1861–1865	American Civil War
1871	Paris Commune
1876	Bulgarian Revolution
1891	Chilean Revolution
1896–1901	Philippine Insurrection
1900	Boxer Rebellion (China)
1903	Panamanian Revolution
1904	Paraguayan Revolution
1905–1911	Persian Revolution
1905	Russian Revolution
1908	Young Turk Revolution
1910	Mexican Revolution
1911–1927	Chinese National Revolution
1912	Rebellion in Cuba
1916–1922	Irish Revolution
1917	Russian Revolution
1917–1921	Ukrainian Revolution
1918–1919	Hungarian Revolution
1918–1919	German Revolution
1919–1923	Turkish Revolution
1920–1947	Revolution in Indonesia
1920–1949	Revolution in India
1921	Kronstadt Revolt (Russia)

1921	Mongolian Revolution
1924	Albanian Rebellion
1927–1949	Chinese Communist Revolution
1929	Rebellion in Afghanistan
1930	Rebellion in Brazil
1930	Argentine Revolution
1931	Spanish Revolution
1931	Chilean Revolution
1933	Nazi Revolution (Germany)
1933	Honduran Rebellion
1933	Cuban Revolution
1934	Austrian Rebellion
1936–1939	Spanish Civil War
1936–1940	Paraguayan Revolution
1939–1946	Burmese Revolution
1941–1945	Yugoslav Revolution
1944	Guatemalan Revolution
1945	Venezuelan Revolution
1945–1973	Vietnamese Revolution
1948	Colombian Rebellion
1948	Costa Rican Revolution
1952	Egyptian Revolution
1952	Bolivian Revolution
1952–1959	Kenyan Mau Mau Revolution
1953	Colombian Revolution
1953	Burmese Rebellion
c. 1954–	Black Revolution (U.S.A.)
1954–1962	Algerian Revolution
1955	Argentinian Revolution
1955	Brazilian Revolution
1956	Honduran Revolution
1956	Hungarian Revolution
1956	Malayan Revolution
1956	Syrian Revolution
1957	Jordanian Revolution
1957	Colombian Revolution
1957	Guatemalan Revolution
1957–1958	Thai Revolution
1958	Iraq Revolution
1958	Burmese Revolution
1958	Pakistani Revolution
1958	Sudanese Revolution
1958	Venezuelan Revolution
1959	Cuban Revolution

1959	Tibetan Rebellion
1960–1962	Congo Civil War (Zaire)
1960–1964	Turkish Revolution
1961–1975	Angolan Revolution
c. 1962–?1972	Revolution of the New Left (U.S.A.)
1963	Dominican Republic Revolution
1963–1974	Revolution in Guinea-Bissau
1964	Revolution in Zanzibar
c. 1964–	Women's Liberation Movement
1964–1975	Revolution in Mozambique
1965–1966	Indonesian Revolution
1966–1969	Chinese Cultural Revolution
1967	Bolivian Revolution
c. 1967–	Revolution in Quebec (Canada)
1968	Peruvian Revolution
1968	Czech Revolt
1968	French Student Revolution
1969–1970	Libyan Revolution
1970–1973	Chilean Revolution
1974	Portuguese Revolution
1974–1977	Revolution in Ethiopia
1978–1979	Iranian Revolution
1978–1979	Nicaraguan Revolution
1979	Revolution in Granada

Concepts and Aspects of Revolution

> "Any people anywhere being inclined and having the power, have the right to rise up and shake off the existing government, and form a new one that suits them better. This is a most valuable and sacred right, a right we hope and believe is to liberate the world."
>
> Abraham Lincoln
> (1848)

Where the other chapters focus on revolutions and revolutionists in different parts of the world and over a chronology beginning with ancient Greece, this chapter concentrates mostly on the general and on a variety of topics that transcend any one specific revolution or period. What is here is the *stuff* of revolution.

"Revolution" is not a simple subject that can be mastered by reading a few books or studying the lives of historically prominent revolutionists. The very complexity of the topic can boggle the mind in that the more one becomes expert, the more one is aware of gaps, holes to be filled with the plaster of further study. A look at the table of contents only illustrates the point. For instance, almost three dozen sections under the heading of Chapter 1 reveal the variety of approaches and topics which contribute to a complete picture.

Even the student wishing to investigate a given revolution or revolutionist would be wise to begin here, with some of the articles and books in the first section, "Sociology of Revolution," and then onto some of the works in the other sections that deal with the features that characterize the specific subject in question. For example, if you are researching the causes of the French Revolution, your understanding of the *ancien régime* and the events leading to 1789 would be enhanced by works that examine causes in general. Some of the titles under "Historiographies" and "Articles," the collections of readings in the edited books by James C. Davies (1971) and Clifford T. Paynton and Robert Blackey (1971), and the books by Ted Robert Gurr (1970) and Chalmers Johnson (1966), all in the section "Sociology of Revolution," would be a good place to start. Then, depending on the focus of the investigation, some of the works on politics, ideology, violence, peasant revolutions, leadership and elites, and modernization would all provide a foundation and depth that merely studying the background and eve of the revolution would lack.

The many sections in this chapter are not meant to exclude others

2 / Concepts and Aspects of Revolution

not listed. An examination of the index or the "Miscellaneous" section will turn up other features (e.g., success and failure, generational problems, utopia, capitalism) that are a part of the broader subject of revolution. Comparative studies and some of the "isms" that are not indigenous to any one place (e.g., anarchism, Marxism, socialism, communism) are also highlighted in the chapter.

Sociology of Revolution

This is a catch-all section under which most of the other sections in the chapter are subsumed. Collectively the articles and books below answer the question: What is revolution? The titles in the "Historiography" subsection survey and critique some of the leading theories of revolution; Roderick Aya's (1979) piece also offers a new synthesis.

The origin of the concept of revolution is traced in the works by Arthur Hatto (1949, 1972), Eugene Kamenka (1970), Melvin J. Lasky (1970), and Karl Griewank (1969); the relevant chapter in Griewank's book appears in translation in the reader *Why Revolution?* (1971) edited by Clifford T. Paynton and Robert Blackey. The concept itself may be surveyed briefly in the article and encyclopedia length works by F. Gilbert (1973), Victor G. Kiernan (1979), William Kornhauser (1971), Walter Laqueur (1968), and Alfred Meusel (1934). Fuller treatment of the concept, its history, course, and chief proponents, is found in the books by Robert Blackey and Clifford T. Paynton (1976) and Peter Calvert (1970).

Among the most important and provocative analyses are the articles by Peter Amann (1962), James C. Davies (1962, 1967), Harry Eckstein (1965), Louis Gottschalk (1944), Rex Hopper (1950), George S. Pettee (1966), and Theda Skocpol (1973, 1976), and the books by Hannah Arendt (1963), Jean Baechler (1976), Crane Brinton (1965), Lyford P. Edwards (1929), Ted Robert Gurr (1970), Mark N. Hagopian (1974), Eric Hoffer (1951), Chalmers Johnson (1964, 1966), and Barrington Moore, Jr. (1966, 1978). More strictly sociological approaches can be found in the articles by James A. Geschwender (1968) and Raymond Tanter and Manus Midlarsky (1967), and in the books by Peter L. Berger and Richard J. Neuhaus (1970), Lewis A. Coser (1956), Rudolf Herberle (1951), Jules Monnerot (1969), Robert A. Nisbet (1969, 1970), Anthony R. Oberschall (1973), Neil J. Smelser (1962), Pitirim A. Sorokin (1925), and Ralph H. Turner and Lewis M. Killian (1957).

Historiographies

1. Aya, Roderick. "Theories of Revolution Reconsidered." *Theory and Society* 8:1 (July 1979): 39–99.

2. Blackey, Robert. "Writings on Revolution." In *Why Revolution? Theories and Analyses,* edited by C. T. Paynton and R. Blackey. Cambridge, Massachusetts: Schenkman, 1971.
3. Freeman, Michael. "Theories of Revolution" *British Journal of Political Science* 2:3 (July 1972): 339-59.
4. Kramnick, Isaac. "Reflections on Revolution: Definition and Explanation in Recent Scholarship." *History and Theory* 11:1 (1972): 26-63.
5. Larsson, Reidar. *Theories of Revolution: From Marx to the First Russian Revolution.* Stockholm: Almqvist and Wiksell, 1970.
6. Salert, Barbara. *Revolutions and Revolutionaries: Four Theories.* New York: Elsevier, 1976.
7. Stone, Lawrence. "Theories of Revolution." *World Politics* 18:2 (January 1966): 159-76.
8. Worsley, Peter M. "Revolutionary Theories." *Monthly Review* (May 1969): 30-49.
9. Yoder, Dale. "Current Definitions of Revolutions." *American Journal of Sociology* 32:3 (November 1926): 433-41.
10. Zagorin, Perez. "Theories of Revolution in Contemporary Historiography." *Political Science Quarterly* 88:1 (March 1973): 23-52.

Articles

11. Amann, Peter. "Revolution: A Redefinition." *Political Science Quarterly* 77:1 (March 1962): 36-53.
12. Arciniegas, Germán. "What's Behind Our Revolutions?" *Américas* 1 (1949): 22.
13. Arendt, Hannah. "Revolution and Public Happiness." *Commentary* (November 1960): 413-22.
14. Bascio, P. "Need for Revolution." *Catholic World* (August 1969): 207-09.
15. Binkley, Robert C. "An Anatomy of Revolution." *Virginia Quarterly Review* 10:4 (October 1934): 502-14.
16. Bunzel, John H. "The Appeal of Revolution: The Liberal's Quandary." *Antioch Review* 21 (1961): 319-27.
17. Calvert, Peter A. "Revolution: The Politics of Violence." *Political Studies* 15:1 (February 1967): 1-11.
18. Clark, Joseph. "The History and Theory of Revolutions." *Princeton Review* (April 1862): 244-76.
19. Currie, Elliott, and Jerome H. Skolnick. "A Critical Note on Conceptions of Collective Behavior." *Annals of the American Academy of Political and Social Science* 391 (September 1970): 34-45.
20. Davies, James C. "The Circumstances and Causes of Revolution." *Journal of Conflict Resolution* 11:2 (June 1967): 247-57.
21. _____. "The J-Curve of Rising and Declining Satisfactions as a Cause of Some Great Revolutions and a Contained Rebellion." In *The History of Violence in America,* edited by H. D. Graham and T. R. Gurr. New York: Praeger, 1969.
22. _____. "Toward a Theory of Revolution." *American Sociological Review* 27:1 (February 1962): 5-19.
23. Eckstein, Harry. "On the Etiology of Internal Wars." *History and Theory* 4:2 (1965): 133-63.

4 / Concepts and Aspects of Revolution

24. Edwards, Lyford P. "The Mechanics of Revolution." *St. Stephen's College Bulletin* 69:2.
25. Eisenstadt, S. N. "The Social Framework and Conditions of Revolution." In *Research in Social Movements, Conflict and Change,* edited by L. Kriesberg. Greenwich, Connecticut: J.A.I. Press, 1979.
26. Fagen, Richard R. "Revolution—for Internal Consumption Only." *Transaction* (April 1969): 10–15.
27. Feldman, Arnold S. "Violence and Volatility: The Likelihood of Revolution." In *Internal War,* edited by H. Eckstein. New York: Free Press, 1964.
28. Feuer, Lewis S. "Generations and the Theory of Revolution." *Survey* 18:3 (Summer 1972): 161–88.
29. Geschwender, James A. "Explorations in the Theory of Social Movements and Revolutions." *Social Forces* 47 (1968): 127–35.
30. Gilbert, F. "Revolution." In *Dictionary of the History of Ideas*, edited by P. Wiener. New York: Scribners, 1973.
31. Gottschalk, Louis. "Causes of Revolution." *American Journal of Sociology* 50:1 (July 1944): 1–8.
32. Goulet, Denis. "The Troubled Conscience of the Revolutionary." *Center Magazine* (May 1969): 43–50.
33. Griffith, J. A. G. "Why We Need a Revolution." *Political Quarterly* 40:4 (October-December 1969): 383–93.
34. Gurr, Ted Robert. "The Revolution—Social-Change Nexus." *Comparative Politics* 5:3 (April 1973): 359–92.
35. Halpern, Manfred. "A Redefinition of the Revolutionary Situation." *Journal of International Affairs* 23:1 (1969): 54–75.
36. Hatto, Arthur. "Revolution: An Inquiry into the Usefulness of an Historical Term." *Mind* 58:232 (October 1949): 495–517.
37. ———. "The Semantics of 'Revolution.'" In *Revolution in the Middle East,* edited by P. J. Vatikiotis. Totowa, New Jersey: Rowman and Littlefield, 1972.
38. Hoover, Calvin B. "Revolutions and Tyranny." *Virginia Quarterly Review* 36:2 (Spring 1960): 182–94.
39. Hopper, Rex. "The Revolutionary Process." *Social Forces* 28 (1950): 270–79.
40. Hutchins, Frank. "On Winning and Losing by Revolution." *Public Policy* 18:1 (Fall 1969): 1–40.
41. Illich, Ivan. "The Need for Cultural Revolution." In *The Great Ideas Today.* Chicago: Encyclopedia Britannica, 1970.
42. Jezer, Martin. "Revolution and the Generational Revolt." *Liberation* 13:3 (July-August 1968): 22–25.
43. Kaiser, Robert B. "Lessons From Revolution." *America* (28 October 1967): 469–73.
44. Kamenka, Eugene. "Revolution—The History of an Idea." In *A World in Revolution?* edited by E. Kamenka. Canberra: Australian National University, 1970.
45. Kiernan, B. "Limitations of U. S. Policy Toward the Underdeveloped World: A Note on the Sociology of Revolution." *American Scholar* 31:2 (1962): 208–19.
46. Kiernan, Victor G. "Revolution." In *The New Cambridge Modern History,* Vol. 13, edited by Peter Burke. New York: Cambridge University Press, 1979.
47. Kirchheimer, Otto. "Confining Conditions and Revolutionary Breakthroughs." *American Political Science Review* 59:4 (December 1965):964–74.

48. Kochanek, Stanley A. "Perspectives on the Study of Revolution and Social Change." *Comparative Politics* 5:3 (April 1973): 313-20.
49. Kornhauser, William. "Revolutions." In *Handbook of Military Institutions*, edited by R. W. Little. Beverly Hills, California: Sage, 1971.
50. Laqueur, Walter. "Revolution." In *International Encyclopedia of the Social Sciences*. New York: Macmillan, 1968.
51. Lasky, Melvin J. "The Birth of a Metaphor." *Encounter* (February 1970): 35-45; (March 1970): 30-42.
52. _____. "The Novelty of Revolution." In *Science et conscience de la société*, edited by J. C. Casanova. Paris: Calmann-Lévy, 1971.
53. Lederer, E. "On Revolutions." *Social Research* 3:1 (March 1936): 1-18.
54. Lowenthal, Richard. "Unreason and Revolution." *Encounter* (November 1969): 22-34.
55. Mack, Raymond W., and Richard C. Snyder. "The Analysis of Social Conflict: Toward an Overview and Synthesis." *Journal of Conflict Resolution* 1:2 (June 1957): 212-48.
56. Maravall, J. M. "Subjective Conditions and Revolutionary Conflict: Some Remarks." *British Journal of Sociology* 27:1 (March 1976): 21-34.
57. Mason, Alpheus T. "The Right to Revolt: A Last Resort in Pursuit of Happiness." *Los Angeles Times* (4 July 1976).
58. Meadows, Paul. "Sequence in Revolution." *American Sociological Review* 6:5 (October 1941): 457-59.
59. Mészáres, János. "On the Eve of Revolution." *Journal of Central European Affairs* 18 (April 1958): 48-68.
60. Meusel, Alfred. "Revolution and Counter-Revolution." In *Encyclopedia of Social Sciences*. New York: Macmillan, 1934.
61. Moore, Barrington, Jr. "On the Notions of Progress, Revolution, and Freedom." *Ethics* 72 (January 1962): 106-19.
62. Neumann, Sigmund. "The International Civil War." *World Politics* 1:3 (April 1949): 333-50.
63. Oberschall, Anthony R. "Rising Expectations and Political Turmoil." *Journal of Development Studies* 6:1 (October 1969): 5-22.
64. Overholt, William H. "Revolution." In *The Sociology of Political Organization*. Croton-on-Hudson, New York: Hudson Institute, 1972.
65. Palmer, R. R. "Generalizations about Revolution: A Case Study." In *Generalization in the Writing of History*, edited by L. Gottschalk. Chicago: University of Chicago Press, 1963.
66. Perry, Ronald W., and David F. Gillespie. "Revolution as an Approach to the History of Social Science: Exploring Theoretical Alternatives." *International Review of History and Political Science* 12 (May 1975): 76-88.
67. Pettee, George S. "Revolution—Typology and Process." In *Revolution (Nomos VII)*, edited by C. J. Friedrich. New York: Atherton, 1966.
68. Race, Jeffrey. "Toward an Exchange Theory of Revolution." In *Peasant Rebellion and Communist Revolution in Asia*, edited by J. W. Lewis. Stanford: Stanford University Press, 1974.
69. "Revolution and Social Change: Symposium." *Current* 118 (May 1970): 3-22.
70. Rothman, Stanley. "Barrington Moore and the Dialectics of Revolution: An Essay Review." *American Political Science Review* 64:1 (March 1970): 61-82.

6 / Concepts and Aspects of Revolution

71. Sathyamurthy, T. V. "Revolutions and Revolutionaries." *Transition* 5:21 (1965): 25-32.
72. Schurmann, Franz. "On Revolutionary Conflict." *Journal of International Affairs* 23:1 (1969): 36-53.
73. Schwartz, David C. "A Theory of Revolutionary Behavior." In *When Men Revolt—and Why*, edited by J. C. Davies. New York: Free Press, 1971.
74. Sewell, Elizabeth. "Coleridge on Revolution." *Studies in Romanticism* 17:4 (Fall 1972): 342-59.
75. Siegel, Jules. "Revolution." *Playboy* (March 1970): 135.
76. Simpson, Amos E. "Whither Revolution?" *Proceedings of the Symposium of French-American Studies* (March 1973): 213-22.
77. Skocpol, Theda. "A Critical Review of Barrington Moore's Social Origins of Dictatorship and Democracy." *Politics and Society* 4:1 (Fall 1973): 1-34.
78. _____. "Explaining Revolutions: In Quest of a Social-Structural Approach." In *The Uses of Controversy in Sociology*, edited by L. A. Coser and O. N. Larsen. New York: Free Press, 1976.
79. Stinchcombe, Arthur L. "Stratification Among Organizations and the Sociology of Revolution." In *Handbook of Organizations*, edited by James G. March. Chicago: Rand McNally, 1965.
80. Tanter, Raymond, and Manus Midlarsky. "A Theory of Revolution." *Journal of Conflict Resolution* 11:3 (September 1967): 264-80.
81. Tashjean, John E. "Twentieth-Century Concepts of Revolution and Casal's Constants." *Revue européenne des sciences sociales et Cahiers Vilfredo Pareto* 12:33 (1974): 187-94.
82. Toynbee, Arnold J. "Revolutionary Change." In *The Great Ideas Today*. Chicago: Encyclopedia Britannica, 1970.
83. Turner, Ralph H. "The Theme of Contemporary Social Movements." *British Journal of Sociology* 20:4 (December 1969): 390-405.
84. "Voices of Revolution." *Harvard Review* 4:1 (Summer-Fall 1966): 115-31.
85. Wigdil, W. "Addition Without Division= Revolution." *Independent* (20 June 1912).
86. Willer, David, and George K. Zollschan. "Prolegomenon to a Theory of Revolutions." In *Explorations in Social Change*, edited by G. K. Zollschan and W. Hirsch. Boston: Houghton Mifflin, 1964.
87. Wilson, George M. "Kita Ikki's Theory of Revolution." *Journal of Asian Studies* 26:1 (November 1966): 89-99.
88. Wolpe, Harold. "An Examination of Some Approaches to the Problem of the Development of Revolutionary Consciousness." *Telos* 4 (Fall 1969): 113-44.
89. Wolpert, J. F. "Myth of Revolution." *Ethics* 58 (July 1948): 245-55.
90. Worsley, Peter M. "The Analysis of Rebellion and Revolution in Modern British Social Anthropology." *Science and Society* 25:1 (Winter 1961): 26-37.
91. Yoder, Dale. "Process in Revolution." *Sociology and Social Research* 12 (1928): 253-63.

Books

92. Adams, Brooks. *The Theory of Social Revolutions*. New York: Macmillan, 1913.
93. Arendt, Hannah. *On Revolution*. New York: Viking, 1963.

94. _____ . *The Origins of Totalitarianism*. New York: World, 1958.
95. Baechler, Jean. *Revolution*. Translated by J. Vickers. Oxford: Basil Blackwell, 1976.
96. _____ . *Revolutionary Phenomena*. Paris: Presses universitaires de France, 1970.
97. Bauer, Arthur. *Essai sur les révolutions*. Paris: Giard and Brière, 1908.
98. Beals, Carleton. *The Nature of Revolution*. New York: Thomas Y. Crowell, 1970.
99. Bell, David V. J. *Resistance and Revolution*. Boston: Houghton Mifflin, 1973.
100. Bendix, Reinhard. *Nation-Building and Citizenship: Studies of Our Changing Social Order*. New York: John Wiley, 1964.
101. _____ , and Seymour Martin Lipset, eds. *Class, Status, and Power*. 2d ed. New York: Free Press, 1966.
102. Berger, Peter L., and Richard J. Neuhaus. *Movement and Revolution*. Garden City, New York: Doubleday, 1970.
103. Berle, Adolph A. *Power*. New York: Harcourt, Brace and World, 1970.
104. Beyme, K. von. *Empirishe Revolutionsforschung*. Opladen: Westdeutscher Verlag, 1973.
105. Blackey, Robert, and Clifford T. Paynton. *Revolution and the Revolutionary Ideal*. Cambridge, Massachusetts: Schenkman, 1976.
106. Brinkman, Carl. *Soziologische Theorie der Revolution*. Göttingen: Vandenhoeck and Ruprecht, 1948.
107. Brinton, Crane. *The Anatomy of Revolution*. Englewood Cliffs, New Jersey: Prentice-Hall, 1965.
108. Brogan, D. W. *The Price of Revolution*. New York: Grosset and Dunlap, 1966.
109. Brown, Stuart Gerry, ed. *Revolution, Confederation, and Constitution*. New York: Appleton-Century-Crofts, 1971.
110. Buckingham, Peter. *The Limits of Protest*. Indianapolis: Bobbs-Merrill, 1970.
111. Burns, C. D. *The Principles of Revolution*. London: Allen and Unwin, 1920.
112. Calvert, Peter. *Revolution*. New York: Praeger, 1970.
113. _____ . *A Study of Revolution*. New York: Oxford University Press, 1970.
114. Cameron, Wm. Bruce. *Modern Social Movements*. New York: Random House, 1966.
115. Camus, Albert. *The Rebel: An Essay on Man in Revolt*. New York: Alfred A. Knopf, 1956.
116. _____ . *Resistance, Rebellion & Death*. New York: Alfred A. Knopf, 1961.
117. Cheng, Ronald Ye-lin, ed. *The Sociology of Revolution*. Chicago: Henry Regnery, 1973.
118. Cohan, A. S. *Theories of Revolution: An Introduction*. New York: John Wiley, 1975.
119. Collins, Randall. *Conflict Sociology*. New York: Academic Press, 1975.
120. Colton, Ethan T. *Four Patterns of Revolution*. New York: Association Press, 1935.
121. Coser, Lewis A. *The Functions of Social Conflict*. Glencoe, Illinois: Free Press, 1956.
122. Crozier, Brian. *A Theory of Conflict*. New York: Scribners, 1975.

8 / Concepts and Aspects of Revolution

123. Davies, James C., ed. *When Men Revolt—and Why.* New York: Free Press, 1971.

124. Decouflé, André. *Sociologie des révolutions.* Paris: Presses universitaires de France, 1968.

125. DeLeon, Daniel. *Reform or Revolution.* New York: Industrial Union Party, 1936.

126. Denisoff, R. Serge, ed. *The Sociology of Dissent.* New York: Harcourt Brace Jovanovich, 1974.

127. Douglas, William O. *Points of Rebellion.* New York: Random House, 1970.

128. Dunn, John. *Modern Revolutions.* New York: Cambridge University Press, 1972.

129. Eckstein, Harry, ed. *Internal War.* New York: Free Press, 1964.

130. Edwards, Lyford P. *The Natural History of Revolution.* Chicago: University of Chicago Press, 1929.

131. Ellul, Jacques. *Autopsy of Revolution.* Translated by P. Wolf. New York: Alfred A. Knopf, 1971.

132. Friedrich, Carl J., ed. *Revolution (Nomos VIII).* New York: Atherton, 1966.

133. Gamson, William A. *The Strategy of Social Protest.* Homewood, Illinois: Dorsey Press, 1975.

134. Goodman, Paul. *New Reformation: Notes of a Neolithic Conservative.* New York: Random House, 1970.

135. Greene, Felix. *The Enemy: Notes on Imperialism and Revolution.* London: Jonathan Cape, 1971.

136. Griewank, Karl. *Der Neuzeitliche Revolutionsbegriff.* Frankfurt am Main: Europäische Verlagsanstalt, 1969.

137. Gross, Feliks, and Rex D. Hopper. *Un siglo de revolución.* Mexico City: Instituto de investigaciones sociales, Universidad Nacional, 1959.

138. Gurr, Ted Robert. *Why Men Rebel.* Princeton: Princeton University Press, 1970.

139. Gusfield, Joseph R., ed. *Protest, Reform, and Revolt: A Reader in Social Movements.* New York: John Wiley, 1970.

140. Hagopian, Mark N. *The Phenomenon of Revolution.* New York: Dodd, Mead, 1974.

141. Hartmut, T. *Die permanente Revolution.* Opladen: Westdeutscher Verlag, 1973.

142. Haskins, James. *Revolutionaries: Agent of Change.* Philadelphia: Lippincott, 1971.

143. Herberle, Rudolf. *Social Movements.* New York: Appleton-Century-Crofts, 1951.

144. Hobsbawm, Eric J. *Revolutionaries.* New York: Pantheon Books, 1973.

145. Hoffer, Eric. *First Things, Last Things.* New York: Harper and Row, 1971.

146. _____ . *The True Believer: Thoughts on the Nature of Mass Movements.* New York: Harper and Row, 1951.

147. Horowitz, David. *Containment and Revolution.* Boston: Beacon, 1967.

148. _____ . *Empire and Revolution: A Radical Interpretation of Contemporary History.* New York: Random House, 1969.

149. Hunter, Robert. *Revolution: Why, How, When?* New York: Committee for Constitutional Government, 1943.

150. Jaeggi, U., and S. Papcke, eds. *Revolution und Theorie.* Frankfort am Main: Athenäum, 1974.
151. Jessop, Bob. *Social Order, Reform and Revolution.* New York: Herder and Herder, 1972.
152. Johnson, Chalmers. *Revolution and the Social System.* Stanford: Hoover Institution, 1964.
153. _____. *Revolutionary Change.* Boston: Little, Brown, 1966.
154. Johnson, Olive M., and Arnold Peterson. *Revolution.* New York: Labor News, 1935.
155. Jones, Howard Mumford. *Revolution & Romanticism.* Cambridge, Massachusetts: Harvard University Press, Belknap Press, 1974.
156. Joussain, André. *La Loi des révolutions.* Paris: Flammarion, 1950.
157. Jouvenel, Bertrand de. *On Power: Its Nature and the History of Its Growth.* Translated by J. F. Huntington. Boston: Beacon Press, 1968.
158. Kelly, George A., and Linda B. Miller. *Internal War and International Systems: Perspectives on Method.* Cambridge, Massachusetts: Center for International Affairs, Harvard University, 1969.
159. Koepcke, C. *Revolution: Ursachen und Wirkungen.* Vienna: Günter Ozlog, 1971.
160. Kohn, Hans. *Living in a World Revolution.* New York: Simon and Schuster, 1964.
161. Kossok, M., ed. *Studien über die Revolution.* Berlin: Akademie, 1969.
162. Kumar, Krishan, ed. *Revolution: The Theory and Practice of a European Idea.* London: Weidenfeld and Nicolson, 1971.
163. Lakey, George. *Strategy for a Living Revolution.* San Francisco: W. H. Freeman, 1973.
164. Laski, Harold J. *Reflections on the Revolution of Our Time.* London: Allen and Unwin, 1913.
165. Leiden, Carl, and Karl M. Schmitt. *The Politics of Violence: Revolution in the Modern World.* Englewood Cliffs, New Jersey: Prentice-Hall, 1968.
166. Lenk, K. *Theorien der Revolution.* Munich: Wilhelm Fink, 1973.
167. Lilly, W. S. *A Century of Revolution.* London: Chapman and Hall, 1889.
168. Lindner, C. *Theorien der Revolution.* Munich: Wilhelm Goldmann, 1972.
169. Lobkowicz, Nikolaus. *Theory and Practice: History of a Concept from Aristotle to Marx.* Notre Dame, Indiana: University of Notre Dame Press, 1967.
170. London, Jack. *Revolution and Other Essays.* New York: Macmillan, 1910.
171. Luce, Paul A. *Road to Revolution.* San Diego: Viewpoint Books, 1967.
172. Lutz, William, and Harry Brent, eds. *On Revolution.* Cambridge, Massachusetts: Winthrop Publishers, 1971.
173. Mandel, Ernest. *Peaceful Coexistence and World Revolution.* New York: Pathfinder Press, n.d.
174. _____. *Revolutionary Strategy in the Imperialist Countries.* New York: Pathfinder Press, n.d.
175. _____, ed. *Fifty Years of World Revolution: An International Symposium.* New York: Pathfinder Press, 1970.
176. Mandel, Ernest, and George Novack. *On the Revolutionary Potential of the Working Class.* New York: Pathfinder Press, 1969.

10 / Concepts and Aspects of Revolution

177. Martin, Everett Dean. *Farewell to Revolution.* New York: W. W. Norton, 1935.
178. Matthews, Herbert L. *A World in Revolution: A Newspaperman's Memoir.* New York: Scribners, 1971.
179. Mazlish, Bruce; Arthur O. Kaledin; and David B. Ralston, eds. *Revolution: A Reader.* New York: Macmillan, 1971.
180. Melotti, Umberto, *Rivoluzione e Società.* Milan: Ed. La Culturale, 1965.
181. Monnerot, Jules. *Sociologie de la révolution.* Paris: Fayard, 1969.
182. Moore, Barrington, Jr. *Injustice: The Social Bases of Obedience and Revolt.* White Plains, New York: M. E. Sharpe, Pantheon Books, 1978.
183. _____ . *Social Origins of Dictatorship and Democracy: Lord and Peasant in the Making of the Modern World.* Boston: Beacon, 1966.
184. Morris, Bernard S. *Imperialism and Revolution: An Essay for Radicals.* Bloomington: Indiana University Press, 1973.
185. Neumann, Sigmund. *Permanent Revolution.* New York: Praeger, 1965.
186. *The 1962 Carolina Symposium: Today's Revolutions.* Chapel Hill: University of North Carolina Press, 1962.
187. Nisbet, Robert A. *Social Change and History.* New York: Oxford University Press, 1969.
188. _____ . *Tradition and Revolt: Historical and Sociological Essays.* New York: Random House, 1970.
189. Nomad, Max. *Apostles of Revolution.* New York: Macmillan, 1933.
190. _____ . *Rebels and Renegades.* New York: Macmillan, 1932.
191. Oberschall, Anthony R. *Social Conflict and Social Movements.* Englewood Cliffs, New Jersey: Prentice-Hall, 1973.
192. Overholt, William H. *A Theory of Revolution.* Boulder, Colorado: Westview Press, forthcoming.
193. Paul, Eden, and Cedar Paul. *Creative Revolution.* London: Allen and Unwin, 1920.
194. Paynton, Clifford T., and Robert Blackey, eds. *Why Revolution? Theories and Analyses.* Cambridge, Massachusetts: Schenkman, 1971.
195. Pellicani, L., ed. *Sociologia delle rivoluzioni.* Naples: Guide, 1976.
196. Pettee, George S. *The Process of Revolution.* New York: Harper and Row, 1938.
197. Postgate, Raymond. *How to Make a Revolution.* London: Hogarth Press, 1934.
198. Prince, J. F. T. *Creative Revolution.* Milwaukee: Bruce, 1937.
199. *Revolutionary Analysis, Strategy and Tactics Today.* New York: Pathfinder Press, n.d.
200. Riepe, Dale, et al. *Reflections on Revolution.* St. Louis: Warren H. Green, 1971.
201. Ripon Society. *Instead of Revolution.* New York: Hawthorn Books, 1971.
202. Rosenau, James N., ed. *International Aspects of Civil Strife.* Princeton: Princeton University Press, 1964.
203. Rosenstock-Hüssy, E. *Out of Revolution: Autobiography of Western Man.* New York: Morrow, 1938.
204. Rubinoff, Lionel, ed. *Tradition and Revolution.* New York: St. Martin's Press, 1971.
205. Rush, Gary, and R. Serge Denisoff, eds. *Social and Political Movements.* New York: Irvington Books, 1971.

206. Said, Abdul A., and Daniel M. Collier. *Revolutionism.* Boston: Allyn and Bacon, 1971.
207. Schieder, Teodor, ed. *Revolution und Gesellschaft.* Freiburg im Breisgau: Herder, 1973.
208. Schmalhausen, S. D., ed. *Recovery Through Revolution.* New York: Covici Friede, 1933.
209. Schwarz, Fred. *The Three Faces of Revolution.* Washington, D.C.: Capitol Hill Press, 1972.
210. Shaull, M. Richard. *Encounter With Revolution.* New York: Association Press, 1955.
211. Skinner, Tom. *Words of Revolution.* Brooklyn, New York: Tom Skinner Associates, 1970.
212. Smelser, Neil J. *Theory of Collective Behavior.* New York: Free Press, 1962.
213. Sorokin, Pitirim A. *Social and Cultural Dynamics.* Vol. 3. *Fluctuation of Social Relationships, War, and Revolution.* New York: Bedminster Press, 1962.
214. _____. *Society, Culture and Personality: Their Structure and Dynamics.* New York: Cooper Square Publishers, 1962.
215. _____. *The Sociology of Revolution.* Philadelphia: Lippincott, 1925.
216. Springer, Philip B., and Marcello Truzzi, eds. *Revolutionaries on Revolution: Participants' Perspectives on the Strategies of Seizing Power.* Pacific Palisades, California: Goodyear, 1973.
217. Talmadge, D., ed. *Whose Revolution?* New York: Howell, Soskin, 1941.
218. Turner, Ralph H., and Lewis M. Killian, eds. *Collective Behavior.* Englewood Cliffs, New Jersey: Prentice-Hall, 1957.
219. Untermann, Ernest. *The World's Revolutions.* Chicago: Charles H. Kerr, 1909.
220. Urry, John. *Reference Groups and the Theory of Revolution.* Boston: Routledge and Kegan Paul, 1973.
221. Waelder, Robert. *Progress and Revolution: A Study of the Issues of Our Age.* New York: International Universities Press, 1970.
222. Webster, Nesta. *World Revolution.* London: Constable, 1921.
223. Welch, Claude E., Jr. *Anatomy of Rebellion.* Albany: State University of New York Press, 1980.
224. Wilson, Colin. *The Outsider.* Boston: Houghton Mifflin, 1956.

Politics and Revolution

To give revolutions reasonably precise boundaries, the political conflict in the revolutionary process must be examined. Whatever the nature of a given revolution or the changes it brings about, it usually begins with a political crisis and ends with a political settlement. Even the actual course of a revolution is a protracted struggle in which the major weapons are political. Thus, to stimulate inquiry into this vital area the following titles are presented. Especially noteworthy are the articles by Carl Boogs, Jr. (1977), James C. Davies (1969), Max Handman (1933), Eugene Kamenka (1966), and Sheldon S. Wolin (1973), and the books by Feliks

12 / Concepts and Aspects of Revolution

Gross (1958), Samuel Huntington (1968), Harold D. Lasswell and A. Kaplan (1950), Barrington Moore, Jr. (1965), and Mostafa Rejai (1973).

Articles

225. Arendt, Hannah. "Thoughts on Politics and Revolution." *New York Review of Books* (22 April 1971).
226. Boogs, Carl, Jr. "Revolutionary Process, Political Strategy, and the Dilemma of Power." *Theory and Society* 4:3 (May 1977): 359–93.
227. Davies, James C. "Political Stability and Instability: Some Manifestations and Causes." *Journal of Conflict Resolution* 13:1 (March 1969): 1–17.
228. Falk, Richard A. "World Revolution and International Order." In *Revolution (Nomos VIII)*, edited by C. J. Friedrich. New York: Atherton, 1966.
229. Handman, Max. "The Bureaucratic Culture Pattern and Political Revolutions." *American Journal of Sociology* 39:3 (November 1933): 301–13.
230. Kamenka, Eugene. "The Concept of a Political Revolution." In *Revolution (Nomos VIII)*, edited by C. J. Friedrich. New York: Atherton, 1966.
231. Kenski, Henry C., Jr. "Political Revolution, Civil Violence, and Uncivil Disobedience." *Choice* 6:5-6 (July-August 1969): 619–25.
232. Kornhauser, William. "Rebellion and Political Development." In *Internal War*, edited by H. Eckstein. New York: Free Press, 1966.
233. "Political Conflict: Perspectives on Revolution." *Journal of International Affairs* 23:1 (1969): 1–118.
234. Wolin, Sheldon S. "The Politics of the Study of Revolution." *Comparative Politics* 5:3 (April 1973): 343–58.

Books

235. Aptheker, Herbert. *Nature of Democracy, Freedom & Revolution.* New York: International Publishers, 1967.
236. Cantor, Norman F. *The Age of Protest: Dissent & Rebellion in the Twentieth Century.* New York: Hawthorn Books, 1969.
237. Chomsky, Noam. *For Reasons of State.* New York: Random House, 1973.
238. Dahl, Robert A. *After the Revolution: Authority in a Good Society.* New Haven: Yale University Press, 1970.
239. Davies, James C. *Human Nature in Politics.* New York: John Wiley, 1963.
240. Douglass, James W. *Resistance and Contemplation: The Way of Liberation.* New York: Dell, 1973.
241. Gross, Feliks. *The Seizure of Political Power in a Century of Revolutions.* New York: Philosophical Library, 1958.
242. Horowitz, Irving Louis. *The Rise and Fall of Project Camelot: Studies in the Relationship Between Social Science and Practical Politics.* Cambridge, Massachusetts: M.I.T. Press, 1967.
243. Huntington, Samuel. *Political Order in Changing Societies.* New Haven: Yale University Press, 1968.
244. Kaplan, Morton A., ed. *The Revolution in World Politics.* New York: John Wiley, 1962.

245. Kent, Edward, ed. *Revolution and the Rule of Law.* Englewood Cliffs, New Jersey: Prentice-Hall, 1971.
246. Kornhauser, William. *The Politics of Mass Society.* Glencoe, Illinois: Free Press, 1959.
247. Lasswell, Harold D., and A. Kaplan. *Power and Society: A Framework for Political Inquiry.* New Haven: Yale University Press, 1950.
248. Lipset, Seymour Martin. *Political Man: The Social Bases of Politics.* Garden City, New York: Doubleday, 1960.
249. Moore, Barrington, Jr. *Political Power and Social Theory.* New York: Harper and Row, 1965.
250. Novack, George. *Democracy and Revolution.* New York: Pathfinder Press, 1971.
251. Oliver, D. *Revolution and World Politics.* Washington, D.C.: American Educational Publications, 1970.
252. Rejai, Mostafa. *The Strategy of Political Revolution.* Garden City, New York: Doubleday, 1973.
253. Skolnick, Jerome H. *Politics and Protest.* New York: Simon and Schuster, 1969.
254. Spanier, John W. *World Politics in an Age of Revolution.* New York: Praeger, 1967.
255. Wheeler, Harvey. *Democracy in a Revolutionary Era: The Political Order Today.* New York: Praeger, 1968.

Philosophy and Revolution

Articles

256. Caponigri, A. Robert. "A Philosopher's View of Revolutions and Social Change." *Proceedings of the Symposium of French-American Studies* (March 1973): 13–28.
257. Schrecker, Paul. "Revolution as a Problem in the Philosophy of History." In *Revolution (Nomos VIII),* edited by C. J. Friedrich. New York: Atherton, 1966.

Books

258. Dunayevskaya, Raya. *Philosophy and Revolution: From Hegel to Sartre, and from Marx to Mao.* New York: Dell, 1973.
259. Maguire, J. J. *The Philosophy of Modern Revolution.* Washington, D.C.: Catholic University of America Press, 1943.
260. Marek, Franz. *Philosophy of World Revolution.* New York: International Publishers, 1969.
261. Swomley, John M., Jr. *Liberation Ethics.* New York: Macmillan, 1972.

Psychology of Revolution

Ever since Aristotle wrote in his *Politics* about the importance of certain "states of mind" that contribute to favorable revolutionary conditions, the psychology of revolutions has been a significant topic. Tocqueville and Marx were concerned with psychological states as part of their larger works. At the turn of this century the works of Charles A. Ellwood (1905) and Gustave Le Bon (1913, 1921) provided provocative, though now somewhat dated, introductions. Psychologists have since been preoccupied with other matters, so that sociologists have devoted more time to the subject. Of note are the works of Hadley Cantril (1941) and Barry McLaughlin (1969). David C. Schwartz's (1972) article and Robert Jay Lifton's (1970) book are also important. Not listed here, but of related value, is *The Revolutionary Ascetic* by psychohistorian Bruce Mazlish.

Articles

262. Ellwood, Charles A. "A Psychological Theory of Revolutions." *American Journal of Sociology* 11:1 (July 1905): 49–59.

263. Riezler, Kurt. "On the Psychology of Modern Revolution." *Social Research* 10:3 (September 1943): 320–36.

264. Schwartz, David C. "Political Alienation: The Psychology of Revolution's First Stage." In *Anger, Violence, and Politics,* edited by I. K. Feierabend; R. L. Feierabend; and T. R. Gurr. Englewood Cliffs, New Jersey: Prentice-Hall, 1972.

265. Sterrenburg, Lee. "Psychoanalysis and the Iconography of Revolution." *Victorian Studies* 19 (December 1975): 241–64.

Books

266. Cantril, Hadley. *The Psychology of Social Movements.* New York: John Wiley, 1941.

267. Hopkins, P. *The Psychology of Social Movements: A Psychoanalytic View of Society.* London: Allen and Unwin, 1938.

268. Le Bon, Gustave. *The Psychology of Revolution.* London: T. Fisher Unwin, 1913.

269. _____. *The World in Revolt: A Psychological Study of Our Times.* Translated by B. Miall. London: T. Fisher Unwin, 1921.

270. Lifton, Robert Jay. *Boundaries: Psychological Man in Revolution.* New York: Random House, 1970.

271. McLaughlin, Barry, ed. *Studies in Social Movements: A Social Psychological Perspective.* New York: Free Press, 1969.

272. Toch, Hans. *The Social Psychology of Social Movements.* Indianapolis: Bobbs-Merrill, 1965.

Economics and Revolution

The importance of economic factors to revolution is probably in inverse proportion to the number of selections in this section. Most theories of revolution, from the general and abstract to the specific (e.g., Marxism), confront the subject. The paucity of titles below is merely symbolic of the extent to which economics has been integrated with other topics.

273. Dutt, R. Palme. *Fascism and Social Revolution: A Study of the Economics and Politics of the Extreme Stage of Capitalism in Decay.* New York: International Publishers, 1935.
274. Sanger, Richard H. *Insurgent Era: New Patterns of Political, Economic, and Social Revolution.* Washington, D.C.: Potomac Books, 1967.
275. Sievers, A. M. *Revolution, Evolution, and the Economic Order.* Englewood Cliffs, New Jersey: Prentice-Hall, 1962

Ideology

Ideology can play a key role in directing the behavior or changing the beliefs of a people. Therefore, its relationship to revolution should not be minimized. An ideology to which subject people are committed can undermine an existing political regime and social system. Simultaneously, an ideology offers an alternative set of values and beliefs, it provides revolutionists with a sense of unity, zeal, and devotion to principles, including a willingness to make extreme sacrifices. Ideology can mobilize a population, camouflage selfish ends, and justify and rationalize revolutionary demands and actions.

Especially valuable for launching an inquiry into this area are the articles by Erik Allardt (1971, 1973), Ernest Gellner (1969), K. Loewenstein (1953), Alasdair MacIntyre (1973), C. B. Macpherson (1966), and George Rudé (1973), and the books by David E. Apter (1964), Daniel Bell (1960), Lewis S. Feuer (1975), Mark N. Hagopian (1978), and Paul E. Sigmund, Jr. (1963).

Articles

276. Allardt, Erik. "Culture, Structure and Revolutionary Ideologies." *International Journal of Comparative Sociology* 12 (March 1971): 24–40.
277. _____ . "Revolutionary Ideologies as Agents of Cultural and Structural Change." In *Social Science and the New Societies,* edited by N. Hammond. East Lansing: Michigan State University, Social Science Research Bureau, 1973.

278. Arendt, Hannah. "Ideology and Terror: A Novel Form of Government." *Review of Politics* 15:3 (July 1953): 303–27.
279. Banerjee, D. N. "Political Ideologies and Political Behavior." *Modern Review* 92:6 (December 1952): 444–50.
280. Bergmann, G. "Ideology." *Ethics* 61 (April 1951): 205–18.
281. Brzezinski, Zbigniew. "Communist Ideology and Power: From Unity to Diversity." *Journal of Politics* 19 (1957): 549–90.
282. Gellner, Ernest. "Myth, Ideology and Revolution." *Political Quarterly* 40:4 (October-December 1969): 472–84.
283. Lively, J. F. "Power and Ideology in Soviet Politics." *Politico* 26:2 (1961): 407–18.
284. Lockwood, T. D. "A Study of French Socialist Ideology." *Review of Politics* 21:2 (April 1959): 402–16.
285. Loewenstein, K. "The Role of Ideologies in Political Change." *International Social Science Journal* 5:1 (1953): 51–74.
286. MacIntyre, Alasdair. "Ideology, Social Science and Revolution." *Comparative Politics* 5:3 (April 1973): 321–42.
287. Macpherson, C. B. "Revolution and Ideology in the Late Twentieth Century." *Revolution (Nomos VIII)*, edited by C. J. Friedrich. New York: Atherton, 1966.
288. Minar, D. W. "Ideology and Political Behavior." *Midwest Journal of Political Science* 5:4 (November 1961): 317–31.
289. Plamenatz, John. "The Communist Ideology." *Political Quarterly* 22:1 (January-March 1951), 16–26.
290. Rudé, George. "Revolution and Popular Ideology." *Proceedings of the Symposium of French-American Studies* (March 1973): 143–58.
291. Veyne, Paul. "Ideology According to Marx and According to Nietzsche." *Diogenes* 99 (Fall 1977), 80–102.
292. Winter, G. "Conception of Ideology in the Theory of Action." *Journal of Religion* 39 (January 1959): 43–49.

Books

293. Aiken, Henry David, ed. *The Age of Ideology: The Nineteenth-Century Philosophers.* New York: New American Library, 1956.
294. Albert, Michael. *What Is to Be Undone: A Modern Revolutionary Discussion of Classical Left Ideologies.* Boston: Porter Sargent, 1975.
295. Apter, David E., ed. *Ideology and Discontent.* New York: Free Press, 1964.
296. Baradat, Leon P. *Political Ideologies: Their Origins and Impact.* Englewood Cliffs, New Jersey: Prentice-Hall, forthcoming.
297. Bell, Daniel. *The End of Ideology.* New York: Free Press, 1960.
298. Bluhm, William T. *Ideologies and Attitudes: Modern Political Culture.* Englewood Cliffs, New Jersey: Prentice-Hall, 1974.
299. Bouchier, David. *Idealism and Revolution: New Ideologies of Liberation in Britain and the United States.* New York: St. Martin's Press, 1978.
300. Burns, Edward McNall. *Ideals in Conflict: The Political Theories of the Contemporary World.* New York: W.W. Norton, 1960.

301. Christenson, Reo M., et al. *Ideologies and Modern Politics.* 3d ed. New York: Harper and Row, 1981.

302. Colletti, Lucio. *From Rousseau to Lenin: Studies in Ideology and Society.* Translated by J. Merringer. New York: Monthly Review Press, 1975.

303. Connolly, William E. *Political Science and Ideology.* New York: Atherton, 1967.

304. Corbett, Patrick. *Ideologies.* New York: Harcourt, Brace and World, 1966.

305. de Crespigny, Anthony, ed. *Ideologies of Politics.* New York: Oxford University Press, 1976.

306. Drucker, H. M. *The Political Uses of Ideology.* New York: Barnes and Noble, 1974.

307. Feuer, Lewis S. *Ideology and the Ideologists.* New York: Harper and Row, 1975.

308. Fromm, Erich. *The Revolution of Hope: Toward a Humanized Technology.* New York: Harper and Row, 1968.

309. Gould, James A., and Willis H. Truitt. *Political Ideologies.* New York: Macmillan, 1973.

310. Gregor, A. James. *Contemporary Radical Ideologies: Totalitarian Thought in the Twentieth Century.* New York: Random House, 1968.

311. Grimes, Alan P., and R. H. Horowitz, eds. *Modern Political Ideologies.* New York: Oxford University Press, 1959.

312. Gross, Feliks, ed. *European Ideologies.* New York: Philosophical Library, 1948.

313. Groth, Alexander J. *Major Ideologies: An Interpretative Survey of Democracy, Socialism, and Nationalism.* New York: John Wiley, 1971.

314. Hagopian, Mark N. *Regimes, Movements, and Ideologies.* New York: Longman, 1978.

315. Halle, L. J. *The Ideological Imagination: Ideological Conflict in Our Time and its Roots in Hobbes, Rousseau and Marx.* Chicago: Quadrangle Books, 1972.

316. Kramnick, Isaac, and Frederick Watkins. *Age of Ideology: Political Thought, 1750 to Present.* Englewood Cliffs, New Jersey: Prentice-Hall, 1979.

317. Lane, Robert E. *Political Ideology.* New York: Free Press, 1967.

318. Larrain, Jorge. *The Concept of Ideology.* Athens: University of Georgia Press, 1980.

319. Mannheim, Karl. *Ideology and Utopia: An Introduction to the Sociology of Knowledge.* London: Routledge and Kegan Paul, 1954.

320. Plamenatz, John. *Ideology.* New York: Praeger, 1970.

321. Rejai, Mostafa, ed. *Decline of Ideology?* Chicago: Aldine-Atherton, 1971.

322. Seliger, Martin. *Ideology and Politics.* New York: Free Press, 1976.

323. _____. *The Marxist Conception of Ideology.* New York: Cambridge University Press, 1977.

324. Sigmund, Paul E., Jr., ed. *The Ideologies of the Developing Nations.* New York: Praeger, 1963.

325. Ulam, Adam B. *Ideologies and Illusions: Revolutionary Thought from Herzen to Solzhenitsyn.* Cambridge, Massachusetts: Harvard University Press, 1976.

326. Walsby, Harold. *The Domain of Ideologies: A Study of the Origin, Development and Structure of Ideologies.* Glasgow: W. MacLellan, 1947.

327. Ward, Barbara. *Nationalism and Ideology.* New York: W. W. Norton, 1966.

Coups d'Etat

While coups d'etat are not usually classified as revolutions, except perhaps in the popular mind, they often play a role in revolutionary activity. Thus, for some revolutions, such as many in Latin America, the coup d'etat should be studied and understood. The standard works are by D. J. Goodspeed (1961), Edward Luttwak (1969), and Curzio Malaparte (1932). The article by Auguste Blanqui (1971) is by a nineteenth century French Socialist revolutionary who was involved in the revolutions of 1830, 1848, and the Paris Commune. Also of note are the articles by David C. Rapoport (1966) and H. R. Spencer (1934), and the books by William Andrews and Uri Ra'anan (1959), Samuel Edward Finer (1962), and Eric A. Nordlinger (1977).

Articles

328. Arnade, Kurt Conrad. "The Technique of *Coup d'Etat* in Latin America." *United Nations World* 4 (1950): 21–25.

329. Blanqui, Auguste. "Instructions for an Uprising." Translated by R. Jacoby. *New Left Review,* no. 65 (January-February 1971): 30–34.

330. Jackman, R. W. "The Predictability of Coups d'Etats: A Model with African Data." *American Political Science Review* 72:4 (December 1978): 1262–75.

331. Japhet, M. "Military Coups and Military Regimes in Africa." *Militaria* 8:4 (1978): 1–12.

332. Rapoport, David C. "Coup d'Etat: The View of the Men Firing Pistols." In *Revolution (Nomos VIII),* edited by C. J. Friedrich. New York: Atherton, 1966.

333. Roberts, Adam. "Civil Resistance to Military Coups." *Journal of Peace Research* 12:1 (1975): 19–36.

334. Spencer, H. R. "Coup d'Etat." In *Encyclopedia of Social Sciences.* New York: Macmillan, 1934.

335. Thompson, William R. "Toward Explaining Arab Military Coups." *Journal of Political and Military Sociology* (Fall 1974): 237–50.

Books

336. Andrews, William, and Uri Ra'anan, eds. *The Politics of the Coup d'Etat.* New York: Van Nostrand-Reinhold Books, 1959.

337. De Grazia, Sebastian, and Livio C. Stecchini. *The Coup d'Etat: Past Significance and Modern Technique.* China Lake, California: U.S. Ordinance Test Station, 1965.

338. Finer, Samuel Edward. *The Man on Horseback: The Role of the Military in Politics.* New York: Praeger, 1962.

339. Fitch, John S., III. *The Military Coup d'Etat As a Political Process: Ecuador, 1948–1966.* Baltimore: Johns Hopkins University Press, 1977.

340. Goodspeed, D. J. *The Conspirators: A Study of the Coup d'Etat.* New York: Viking, 1961.

341. Hakes, Jay E. *Weak Parliaments and Military Coups in Africa.* Beverly Hills, California: Sage, 1973.

342. Johnson, John J., ed. *The Role of the Military in Underdeveloped Countries.* Princeton: Princeton University Press, 1962.

343. Kau, M. Y. M., ed. *The Lin Piao Affair: Power Politics and Military Coup.* White Plains, New York: International Arts and Sciences Press, 1975.

344. Luttwak, Edward. *Coup d'Etat: A Practical Handbook.* New York: Alfred A. Knopf, 1969.

345. Malaparte, Curzio. *Coup d'Etat: The Technique of Revolution.* New York: E.P. Dutton, 1932.

346. Maupas, Charlmegne Emilie De'. *The Story of the Coup d'Etat.* London: Virtue, 1884.

347. Nordlinger, Eric A. *Soldiers in Politics: Military Coups and Governments.* Englewood Cliffs, New Jersey: Prentice-Hall, 1977.

348. Thompson, William R. *The Grievances of Military Coup-Makers.* Beverly Hills, California: Sage, 1974.

Civil Wars

The extent to which civil wars are part of the revolutionary experience is debatable. Little work has been done on the subject per se, but it is given credence in the form of the works below. The American Civil War is featured in most of the selections, the most important of which is that by Emory M. Thomas (1971). In addition, it should be noted that some revolutions are characterized by civil war conflicts (e.g., Puritan Revolution, 1640–1660, and Russian Revolution, 1917). And some revolutions are secessionist movements which also have civil war characteristics (e.g., Ukrainian Revolution, 1917–1921, and Irish Revolution, 1916–1922).

Article

349. Smith, John David. "The Confederacy as a Revolutionary Experience." *Lincoln Lore* 1694 (April 1979): 1–4.

Books

350. Bond, James E. *The Rules of Riot: Internal Conflict and the Law of War.* Princeton: Princeton University Press, 1974.

351. Camejo, Peter. *Racism, Revolution, Reaction, 1861–1877: The Rise and Fall of Radical Reconstruction.* New York: Monad Press, 1976.

352. Little, Richard. *Intervention: External Involvement in Civil Wars.* Totowa, New Jersey: Rowman and Littlefield, 1975.

20 / **Concepts and Aspects of Revolution**

353. Luard, Evan, ed. *The International Regulation of Civil Wars.* New York: New York University Press, 1972.
354. Moore, John Norton, ed. *Law and Civil War in the Modern World.* Baltimore: Johns Hopkins University Press, 1974.
355. Parrish, W. E. *The Civil War: A Second American Revolution.* Huntington, New York: Robert E. Krieger, 1979.
356. Rawley, James A. *Turning Points of the Civil War.* Lincoln: University of Nebraska Press, 1974.
357. Thomas, Emory M. *The Confederacy as a Revolutionary Experience.* Englewood Cliffs, New Jersey: Prentice-Hall, 1971.
358. Wilkinson, David. *Revolutionary Civil War: The Elements of Victory and Defeat.* Palo Alto, California: Page-Ficklin, 1975.

Millennial Movements

Millenarianism is the rejection of an evil, contemporary world and the expectation of complete, radical change which will be reflected in the millennium; it foresees a world without deficiencies and salvation on earth for its adherents. Millennial movements have existed throughout history and within different cultures, both Western and non-Western, as the following titles indicate. An introductory look at the subject can be found in the article by Y. Talmon (1968), while no examination would be complete without the work of Norman Cohn (1961).

Articles

359. Allan, Graham. "A Theory of Millennialism: The Irvingite Movement as an Illustration." *British Journal of Sociology* 25:3 (September 1974): 296–311.
360. Barber, B. "Acculturation and Messianic Movements." *American Sociological Review* 6:5 (October 1941): 663–69.
361. Hills, F. "Millenarian Machines in South Vietnam." *Comparative Studies in Society and History* 13:3 (July 1971): 325–50.
362. Jacob, Margaret C. "Millenarianism and Science in the Late Seventeenth Century." *Journal of the History of Ideas* 37 (April-June 1976): 335–41.
363. Keyes, C. F. "Millennialism, Theravada Buddhism and Thai Society." *Journal of Asian Studies* 36:4 (August 1977): 283–303.
364. Miller, Glenn T. "'Fashionable to Prophesy': Presbyterians, the Millennium and the Revolution." *Amerikastudien* 21:2 (1976): 239–60.
365. Stern, T. "Ariya and the Golden Book: A Millenarian Buddhist Sect among the Karen." *Journal of Asian Studies* 27:2 (February 1968): 297–327.
366. Talmon, Y. "Millenarism." In *The International Encyclopedia of the Social Sciences.* New York: Macmillan, 1968.
367. Worsley, Peter M. "Millenarian Movements in Melanesia." *Rhodes-Livingstone Journal. Human Problems in British Central Africa* 21 (March 1957): 18–31.

Books

368. Adas, Michael. *Prophets of Rebellion: Millenarian Protest Movements against the European Colonial Order.* Chapel Hill: University of North Carolina Press, 1979.
369. Ahmed, A. S. *Millennium and Charisma among the Pathans: A Critical Essay in Social Anthropology.* London: Routledge and Kegan Paul, 1976.
370. Barkun, Michael. *Disaster and the Millennium.* New Haven: Yale University Press, 1974.
371. Braunthal, Julius. *In Search of the Millennium.* London: Victor Gollancz, 1945.
372. Burridge, Kenelm. *New Heaven, New Earth: A Study of Millenarian Activities.* New York: Schocken, 1969.
373. Capp, Bernard. *The Fifth Monarchy Men: A Study in Seventeenth-Century England Millenarianism.* Totowa, New Jersey: Rowman and Littlefield, 1972.
374. Clouse, Robert G., ed. *The Meaning of the Millennium: Four Views.* Downers Corner, Illinois: Inter-Varsity Press, 1977.
375. Cohn, Norman. *The Pursuit of the Millennium.* New York: Harper and Row, 1961.
376. Davidson, James West. *The Logic of Millennial Thought: Eighteenth-Century New England.* New Haven: Yale University Press, 1977.
377. Garrett, Clark. *Respectable Folly: Millenarians and the French Revolution in France and England.* Baltimore: Johns Hopkins University Press, 1975.
378. Gilpin, W. Clark. *The Millenarian Piety of Roger Williams.* Chicago: University of Chicago Press, 1979.
379. Gottfried, Paul. *Conservative Millenarians: The Romantic Experience in Bavaria.* Bronx, New York: Fordham University Press, 1979.
380. Harrison, J. F. C. *The Second Coming: Popular Millenarianism, 1780–1850.* New Brunswick, New Jersey: Rutgers University Press, 1979.
381. Hatch, Nathan O. *The Sacred Cause of Liberty: Republican Thought and the Millennium in Revolutionary New England.* New Haven: Yale University Press, 1977.
382. Hobsbawm, Eric J. *Primitive Rebels: Studies in Archaic Forms of Social Movements in the Nineteenth and Twentieth Centuries.* New York: Praeger, 1963.
383. Lanternari, Vittorio. *The Religions of the Oppressed: A Study of Modern Messianic Cults.* New York: Alfred A. Knopf, 1963.
384. Naquin, Susan. *Millenarian Rebellion in China: The Eight Trigrams Uprising of 1813.* New Haven: Yale University Press, 1976.
385. Obolensky, D. *The Bogomils: A Study in Balkan Neo-Manichaeism.* Cambridge: Cambridge University Press, 1948.
386. Rogers, P. G. *The Fifth Monarchy Men.* London: Oxford University Press, 1966.
387. Sandeen, Ernest R. *The Roots of Fundamentalism: British and American Millenarianism, 1800–1930.* Chicago: University of Chicago Press, 1970.
388. Thrupp, Sylvia L., ed. *Millennial Dreams in Action: Studies in Revolutionary Religious Movements.* New York: Schocken, 1970.
389. Tuveson, E. L. *Millennium and Utopia: A Study in the Background of the Idea of Progress.* Berkeley: University of California Press, 1949.
390. Wallis, W. D. *Messiahs: Their Role in Civilization.* Washington, D.C.: American Council on Public Affairs, 1943.

391. Weinstein, Donald. *Savonarola and Florence: Prophecy and Patriotism in the Renaissance.* Princeton: Princeton University Press, 1970.

392. Wilson, Bryan. *Magic and the Millennium: Religious Movements of Protest Among Tribal and Third-World Peoples.* New York: Granada Publishing, 1978.

War, the Military, and Guerrillas

Organized military conflict is a part of virtually all revolutionary activity. The role of the military, therefore, is often pivotal to the success or failure of a revolution. In fact, some scholars contend that insurrections simply cannot be successful against a professional army operating at full strength, unless an outside force intervenes. For revolutionary war see the articles of Eqbal Ahmed (1965, 1971), Jean Baechler (1971), and David A. Wilson (1963). On the military all of the following are excellent: Edwin Lieuwen (1961), Katharine Chorley (1943), John Ellis (1974), Samuel Edward Finer (1962), and D. E. H. Russell (1974).

Guerrilla warfare is non-traditional; it is less a military technique than a political condition. It is also civilian warfare, and it is as old as recorded history. In suitable terrain, cleverly coordinated and properly inspired guerrillas can, over a period of time, be invincible. But guerrilla warfare is also struggle from a point of weakness. Upon growing stronger guerrilla armies turn to more conventional means. Indispensable to understanding contemporary guerrilla warfare are *On Guerrilla Warfare* (1961) by Mao Tse-tung and *Guerrilla Warfare* (1969) by Che Guevara, both cited elsewhere in this volume. Histories of the subject can be found in the works below by Robert B. Asprey (1975) and Lewis Gann (1971). Excellent general studies are the books by J. Bowyer Bell (1971), James Eliot Cross (1963), Walter Laqueur (1976, 1977), and Robert Taber (1965). A modern development is urban guerrilla activity, and the work of Martin Oppenheimer (1969) is first-rate.

Bibliography

393. Sable, Martin H. *The Guerrilla Movement in Latin America Since 1950: A Bibliography.* Madison: University of Wisconsin Latin American Center, 1977.

Reference

394. Sutton, Antony. *Wars and Revolutions: A Comprehensive List of Conflicts, Including Fatalities. Part One: 1820 to 1900. Part Two: 1900 to 1972.* Stanford: Hoover Institution, 1971, 1973.

Documents

395. Mallin, Jay, ed. *Terror and Urban Guerrillas: A Study of Tactics and Documents.* Coral Gables, Florida: University of Miami Press, 1971.

War

Articles

396. Ahmad, Eqbal. "Revolutionary War and Counter-Insurgency." *Journal of International Affairs* 25:1 (1971): 1-47.
397. _____ . "Revolutionary Warfare: How to Tell When the Rebels Have Won." *Nation* (30 August 1965): 95-100.
398. Baechler, Jean. "Revolutionary and Counter-Revolutionary War: Some Political and Strategic Lessons From the First Indochina War and Algeria." *Journal of International Affairs* 25:1 (1971): 70-90.
399. Pye, Lucian W. "The Roots of Insurgency and Commencement of Rebellions." In *Internal War,* edited by H. Eckstein. New York: Free Press, 1964.
400. Wilson, David A. "Nation-Building and Revolutionary War." In *Nation-Building,* edited by K. Deutsch and W. J. Foltz. New York: Atherton, 1963.

Books

401. Crozier, Brian. *The Rebels: A Study of Post-War Insurrections.* London: Chatto and Windus, 1960.
402. Dennis, Lawrence. *The Dynamics of War and Revolution.* New York: Weekly Foreign Letter, 1940.
403. Elliott-Bateman, Michael; John Ellis; and Tom Bowden. *The Fourth Dimension of Warfare.* Vol. 2. *War and Revolution.* Totowa, New Jersey: Rowman and Littlefield, 1974.
404. Janos, Andrew C. *The Seizure of Power: A Study of Force and Popular Consent.* Princeton: Princeton University Press, 1964.
405. Jureidini, Paul A., et al. *Casebook on Insurgency and Revolutionary Warfare: Twenty-three Summary Accounts.* Washington, D.C.: Special Operations Office, 1962.
406. Leites, Nathan, and Charles Wolf, Jr. *Rebellion and Authority: An Analytic Essay on Insurgent Conflicts.* Chicago: Markham, 1970.
407. Momboisse, Raymond M. *Blueprint of Revolution: The Rebel, the Party, the Techniques of Revolt.* Springfield, Illinois: Charles C. Thomas, 1970.
408. Ortega y Gasset, José. *The Revolt of the Masses.* New York: W.W. Norton, 1932.
409. Paret, Peter. *French Revolutionary Warfare from Indochina to Algeria: The Analysis of a Political and Military Doctrine.* New York: Praeger, 1964.
410. Pustay, John S. *Counterinsurgency Warfare.* New York: Free Press, 1965.
411. Sullivan, David S., and Martin J. Sattler, eds. *Revolutionary War: Western Response.* New York: Columbia University Press, 1971.

412. Thompson, Robert. *Revolutionary War in World Strategy, 1945–1969.* New York: Taplinger, 1970.
413. Timasheff, Nicholas S. *War and Revolution.* New York: Sheed and Ward, 1965.

Military

Articles

414. Ferro, Marc. "The Russian Soldier in 1917: Undisciplined, Patriotic, and Revolutionary." *Slavic Review* 30:3 (September 1971): 483–512.
415. Kenez, Peter. "Russian Officer Corps Before the Revolution: The Military Mind." *Russian Review* 31:3 (July 1972): 216–25.
416. Lieuwen, Edwin. "The Military: A Revolutionary Force." *Annals of the American Academy of Political and Social Science* 334 (March 1961): 30–40.

Books

417. Adelman, Jonathan R. *The Revolutionary Armies: The Historical Development of the Soviet and the Chinese People's Liberation Armies.* Westport, Connecticut: Greenwood, 1980.
418. Chorley, Katharine. *Armies and the Art of Revolution.* London: Faber and Faber, 1943.
419. Ellis, John. *Armies in Revolution.* New York: Oxford University Press, 1974.
420. Finer, Samuel Edward. *The Man on Horseback: The Role of the Military in Politics.* New York: Praeger, 1962.
421. Haycock, Ronald, ed. *Regular Armies and Insurgency.* Totowa, New Jersey: Rowman and Littlefield, 1979.
422. Johnson, John J. *The Military and Society in Latin America.* Stanford: Stanford University Press, 1964.
423. _____ , ed. *The Role of the Military in Underdeveloped Countries.* Princeton: Princeton University Press, 1962.
424. Perlmutter, Amos. *The Military and Politics in Modern Times: On Professionals, Praetorians, and Revolutionary Soldiers.* New Haven: Yale University Press, 1979.
425. Russell, D. E. H. *Rebellion, Revolution, and Armed Force: A Comparative Study of Fifteen Countries with Special Emphasis on Cuba and South Africa.* New York: Academic Press, 1974.

Guerrillas

Articles

426. Johnson, Chalmers. "Civilian Loyalties and Guerrilla Conflict." *World Politics* 14:4 (July 1962): 646–61.

427. Marighella, Carlos. "Minimanual of the Urban Guerrilla." In *Revolutionaries on Revolution,* edited by P. B. Springer and M. Truzzi. Pacific Palisades, California: Goodyear Publishing, 1973.

428. Rejai, Mostafa. "Guerrilla Communism: China, North Vietnam, Cuba." In *Ideologies and Modern Politics,* by R. M. Christenson et al. New York: Dodd, Mead, 1971.

Books

429. Asprey, Robert B. *War in the Shadows: The Guerrilla in History.* 2 vols. Garden City, New York: Doubleday, 1975.

430. Bell, J. Bowyer. *The Myth of the Guerrilla: Revolutionary Theory and Malpractice.* New York: Alfred A. Knopf, 1971.

431. Burchett, Wilfred. *Grasshoppers and Elephants.* New York: Urizen Books, 1977.

432. Clutterbuck, Richard. *Protest and the Urban Guerrilla.* London: Cassell, 1973.

433. Cross, James Eliot. *Conflict in the Shadows: The Nature and Politics of Guerrilla War.* Garden City, New York: Doubleday, 1963.

434. Ellis, John. *A Short History of Guerrilla Warfare.* New York: St. Martin's Press, 1976.

435. El-Rayyes, Riad. *Guerrillas for Palestine.* New York: St. Martin's Press, 1976.

436. Gann, Lewis. *Guerrillas in History.* Stanford: Hoover Institution, 1971.

437. Hanrahan, Gene Z., ed. *Chinese Communist Guerrilla Tactics.* Thornwood, New York: Paladin Press, 1974.

438. Johnson, Chalmers. *Autopsy on People's War.* Berkeley: University of California Press, 1974.

439. Laqueur, Walter. *Guerrilla: A Historical and Critical Study.* Boston: Little, Brown, 1976.

440. _____ , ed. *The Guerrilla Reader: A Historical Anthology.* Philadelphia: Temple University Press, 1977.

441. Oppenheimer, Martin. *The Urban Guerrilla.* Chicago: Quadrangle Books, 1969.

442. Osanka, Franklin Mark, ed. *Modern Guerrilla Warfare: Fighting Communist Guerrilla Movements, 1941–1961.* New York: Free Press, 1962.

443. Paret, Peter, and John W. Shy. *Guerrillas in the 1960s.* New York: Praeger, 1962.

444. Pomeroy, William J., ed. *Guerrilla Warfare and Marxism.* New York: International Publishers, 1968.

445. Sarkesian, Sam C., ed. *Revolutionary Guerrilla Warfare.* Chicago: Precedent Publishing, 1975.

446. Singh, Baljit, and Ko Wang Mei. *Theory and Practice of Modern Guerrilla Warfare.* New York: Asia Publishing House, 1971.

447. Sully, François. *Age of the Guerrilla.* New York: Avon Books, 1968.

448. Taber, Robert. *The War of the Flea: A Study of Guerrilla Warfare, Theory and Practice.* New York: Lyle Stuart, 1965.

26 / Concepts and Aspects of Revolution

Violence

Violence, in the popular mind, is probably linked with revolution more than any other characteristic. Most definitions of revolution include the use or threat of violence as an integral part of the revolutionary process. During the last 100 years especially, the advocacy of violence has become evident in the writings of such prominent revolutionists as Georges Sorel, Frantz Fanon, and Che Guevara whose works are cited elsewhere in this volume; instructions detail the necessary procedures for the most effective utilization of violent tactics. This has become so because, it seems, there is no known rational alternative as effective as violence in accomplishing the goals of revolution. For example, violence can mold and preserve a national identity; it can bind a people together, dramatize their grievances, and create a new consciousness. It has even been asserted that without violence revolution is merely evolution.

A good beginning and broad based introduction to the subject may be achieved by examining the collections of readings by Ivo K. Feierabend, Rosalind L. Feierabend and Ted Robert Gurr (1972), Hugh Davis Graham and Ted Robert Gurr (1979), and James F. Short, Jr. and Marvin E. Wolfgang (1972). Excellent general commentaries, many with reflections on historical developments, include those articles by Hannah Arendt (1969), Lewis A. Coser (1972), Ivo K. Feierabend et al (1973), A. Norman Klein (1966), H. L. Nieburg (1962, 1963), Ken Southwood (1967), Charles Tilly (1975), and Eugene Victor Walter (1964), and those books by Hannah Arendt (1970), Anthony M. Burton (1978), and H. L. Nieburg (1969). Works on specific kinds of violence (e.g., mass, urban, ghetto) and violence at specific times and places can be found by examining the full list of titles.

Bibliographies

449. Bienen, Henry. *Violence and Social Change: A Review of Current Literature.* Chicago: University of Chicago Press, 1969.
450. Manheim, Jarol B., and Melanie Wallace. *Political Violence in the United States, 1875–1974. A Bibliography.* New York: Garland, 1975.

Documents

451. Brown, Richard Maxwell. "The Archives of Violence." *American Archivist* 41 (October 1978): 431–43.
452. Hofstadter, Richard, and Michael Wallace, eds. *American Violence: A Documentary History.* New York: Alfred A. Knopf, 1970.

Articles

453. Arendt, Hannah. "Reflections on Violence." *Journal of International Affairs* 23:1 (1969): 1-35.
454. Cameron, J. M. "On Violence." *New York Review of Books* (2 July 1970).
455. Clark, Ramsey. "On Violence, Peace and the Rule of Law." *Foreign Affairs* 44 (October 1970): 31-39.
456. Coser, Lewis A., ed. "Collective Violence and Civil Conflict." *Journal of Social Issues* 28:1 (1972): 1-234.
457. Feierabend, Ivo K.; Rosalind L. Feierabend; and Betty A. Nesvold. "The Comparative Study of Revolution and Violence." *Comparative Politics* 5:3 (April 1973): 393-424.
458. Flanigan, William H., and Edwin Fogelman. "Patterns of Political Violence in Comparative Historical Perspective." *Comparative Politics* 3:1 (October 1970): 1-20.
459. Galtung, Johan. "Feudal Systems, Structural Violence and the Structural Theory of Revolutions." *Proceedings of the International Peace Research Association* [Third Conference] 1 (1969): 110-88.
460. Graham, Hugh Davis. "The Paradox of American Violence: A Historical Commentary." *Annals of the American Academy of Political and Social Science.* 391 (September 1970): 74-82.
461. Grimshaw, Allen D. "Interpreting Collective Violence: An Argument for the Importance of Social Structure." *Annals of the American Academy of Political and Social Science* 391 (September 1970): 9-20.
462. Gurr, Ted Robert. "Psychological Factors in Civil Violence." *World Politics* 20:2 (January 1968): 245-79.
463. Hook, Sidney. "Violence." In *Encyclopedia of Social Sciences.* New York: Macmillan, 1934.
464. Huntington, Samuel. "Patterns of Violence in World Politics." In *Changing Patterns of Military Politics,* edited by S. Huntington. New York: Free Press, 1962.
465. Jeffreys-Jones, Rhodri. "Violence in American History: Plug-Uglies in the Progressive Era." In *Perspectives in American History,* edited by D. Fleming and B. Bailyn. Vol. 8. Cambridge, Massachusetts: Charles Warren Center for Studies in American History, Harvard University, 1974.
466. Klein, A. Norman. "On Revolutionary Violence." *Studies on the Left* 6:3 (May-June 1966): 62-82.
467. Lupsha, Peter A. "Explanation of Political Violence: Some Psychological Theories Versus Indignation." *Politics and Society* 2:1 (Fall 1971): 89-104.
468. Maier, Pauline. "Revolutionary Violence and the Relevance of History." *Journal of Interdisciplinary History* 2:3 (Winter 1972).
469. Muller, Edward N. "A Test of a Partial Theory of Potential for Political Violence." *American Political Science Review* 66:3 (September 1972): 928-49.
470. Nieburg, H. L. "The Threat of Violence and Social Change." *American Political Science Review* 56:4 (December 1962): 865-73.
471. _____. "Uses of Violence." *Journal of Conflict Resolution* 7:1 (March 1963): 43-54.
472. _____. "Violence, Law, and Informal Polity." *Journal of Conflict Resolution* 13:2 (June 1969): 192-209.

28 / Concepts and Aspects of Revolution

473. Short, James F., Jr., and Marvin E. Wolfgang. "On Collective Violence: Introduction and Overview." *Annals of the American Academy of Political and Social Science* 391 (September 1970): 1-8.
474. Shuja, Sharif M. "Political Violence in Southeast Asia: A Critical Analysis of Some Models." *Pakistan Horizon* 30:3-4 (1977): 48-64.
475. Southwood, Ken. "Riot and Revolt: Sociological Theories of Political Violence." *Peace Research Reviews* 1:3 (June 1967): 1-75.
476. Sperber, Manès. "Violence from Below." *Survey* 18:3 (Summer 1972): 189-204.
477. Tilly, Charles. "Collective Violence in European Perspective." In *Violence in America: Historical and Comparative Perspectives,* edited by H. D. Graham and T. R. Gurr. New York: Signet, 1969.
478. _____. "Revolutions and Collective Violence." In *Macropolitical Theory,* edited by F. I. Greenstein and N. W. Polsby. Reading, Massachusetts: Addison-Wesley, 1975.
479. Wada, George, and James C. Davies. "Riots and Rioters." *Western Political Quarterly* 10:4 (December 1957): 864-74.
480. Wallace, Michael. "The Uses of Violence in American History." *The American Scholar* 40:1 (Winter 1970-1971): 81-102.
481. Walter, Eugene Victor. "Power and Violence." *American Political Science Review* 58:2 (June 1964): 350-60.
482. _____. "Violence and the Process of Terror." *American Sociological Review* 29:2 (April 1964): 248-57.
483. Welch, Claude E. "Warrior, Rebel, Guerrilla and Putschist: Four Aspects of Political Violence." *Journal of Asian and African Studies* 12:3-4 (July-October 1977): 82-98.

Books

484. Anderson, William A., and Russell R. Dynes. *Social Movements, Violence, and Change: The May Movement in Curaçao.* Columbus: Ohio State University Press, 1975.
485. Arendt, Hannah. *On Violence.* New York: Harcourt, Brace and World, 1970.
486. Aron, Raymond. *History and the Dialectic of Violence.* Translated by B. Cooper. New York: Harper and Row, 1975.
487. Ben-Dak, Joseph, ed. *The Future of Collective Violence: Societal and International Perspectives.* Atlantic Highlands, New Jersey: Humanities Press, 1974.
488. Bondurant, Joan V., ed. *Conflict: Violence and Nonviolence.* New York: Lieber-Atherton, 1973.
489. Brown, Richard M. *American Violence.* Englewood Cliffs, New Jersey: Prentice-Hall, 1970.
490. _____. *Strain of Violence: Historical Studies of American Violence and Vigilantism.* New York: Oxford University Press, 1975.
491. Burton, Anthony M. *Revolutionary Violence: The Theories.* New York: Crane, Russak, 1978.
492. Caffi, A. *A Critique of Violence.* Indianapolis: Bobbs-Merrill, 1970.
493. Cohen, Norman S. *Civil Strife in America: A Historical Approach to the Study of Riots in America.* Hinsdale, Illinois: Dryden Press, 1972.

494. Conant, Ralph W. *The Prospects for Revolution: A Study of Riots, Civil Disobedience, and Insurrection in Contemporary America.* New York: Harper's Magazine Press, 1971.
495. Connery, Robert H., ed. *Urban Riots: Violence and Social Change.* New York: Random House, 1969.
496. Ellul, Jacques. *Violence.* New York: Seabury Press, 1969.
497. Engels, Friedrich. *The Role of Force in History.* New York: International Publishers, 1968.
498. Feagin, Joe R., and Harlan Hahn. *Ghetto Revolts: The Politics of Violence in American Cities.* New York: Macmillan, 1973.
499. Feierabend, Ivo K.; Rosalind L. Feierabend; and Ted Robert Gurr, eds. *Anger, Violence, and Politics: Theories and Research.* Englewood Cliffs, New Jersey: Prentice-Hall, 1972.
500. Fogelson, Robert M. *Violence as Protest: A Study of Riots and Ghettos.* Garden City, New York: Doubleday, 1971.
501. _____, and Richard Rubenstein, eds. *Mass Violence in America.* 43 vols. New York: Arno Press, 1970.
502. Graham, Hugh Davis, and Ted Robert Gurr, eds. *Violence in America: Historical and Comparative Perspectives.* Rev. ed. Beverly Hills, California: Sage, 1979.
503. Grundy, Kenneth W., and Michael A. Weinstein. *Ideologies of Violence.* Columbus, Ohio: Charles E. Merrill, 1974.
504. Gurr, Ted Robert. *The Conditions of Civil Violence.* Princeton: Center of International Studies. Princeton University, 1967.
505. _____. *Rogues, Rebels, and Reformers: A Political History of Urban Crime and Conflict.* Beverly Hills, California: Sage, 1976.
506. Hanley, J., et al. *Protest, Violence and Social Change.* Englewood Cliffs, New Jersey: Prentice-Hall, 1972.
507. Hartogs, Renatus, and E. Artzt. *Violence: Causes and Solutions.* New York: Dell, 1970.
508. Hibbs, Douglas A., Jr. *Mass Political Violence: A Cross-National Causal Analysis.* New York: Wiley-Interscience, 1973.
509. Hirsch, Herbert, and David C. Perry. *Violence As Politics.* New York: Harper and Row, 1973.
510. *The History of Violence in America: A Report to the National Commission on the Causes and Prevention of Violence.* New York: Bantam Books, 1969.
511. Honderich, Ted. *Political Violence.* Ithaca: Cornell University Press, 1977.
512. Jeffreys-Jones, Rhodri. *Violence and Reform in American History.* New York: New Viewpoints, 1978.
513. Lane, Roger, and John J. Turner, Jr., eds. *Riot, Rout and Tumult: Readings in American Social and Political Violence.* Westport, Connecticut: Greenwood, 1978.
514. Masotti, Louis H., and Don R. Bowen, eds. *Riots and Rebellion: Civil Violence in the Urban Community.* Beverly Hills, California: Sage, 1968.
515. Nardin, Terry. *Violence and the State.* Beverly Hills, California: Sage, 1971.
516. Nieburg, H. L. *Political Violence: The Behavioral Process.* New York: St. Martin's Press, 1969.
517. O'Neil, Bard E.; D. J. Alberts; and Stephan J. Rossetti, eds. *Political Violence and Insurgency.* Arvada, Colorado: Phoenix Press, 1974.

518. *Report of the National Advisory Commission on Civil Disorders.* New York: Bantam Books, 1968.

519. *Rights in Conflict: The Violent Confrontation of Demonstrators and Police in the Parks and Streets of Chicago During the Week of the Democratic National Convention of 1968.* New York: Bantam Books, 1968.

520. Rivera, Charles R., and K. A. Switzer. *Violence.* Rochelle Park, New Jersey: Hayden Book Co., 1976.

521. Rose, Thomas, ed. *Violence in America: A Historical and Contemporary Reader.* New York: Random House, 1970.

522. Sears, David O., and John B. McConahay. *The Politics of Violence: The Urban Blacks and the Watts Riot.* Boston: Houghton Mifflin, 1973.

523. Short, James F., Jr., and Marvin E. Wolfgang, eds. *Collective Violence.* Chicago: Aldine-Atherton, 1972.

524. Sorel, Georges. *Reflections on Violence.* Translated by T. E. Hulme. New York: B. W. Huebsch, 1914.

525. Von der Mehden, Fred R. *Comparative Political Violence.* Englewood Cliffs, New Jersey: Prentice-Hall, 1973.

526. Walter, Eugene Victor. *Terror and Resistance: A Study of Political Violence.* New York: Oxford University Press, 1969.

Terrorism

Terrorism is another kind of revolutionary violence that has taken on a form and meaning of its own. Although it can be used as a counter-revolutionary force (e.g., police terrorism), terrorism is typically a first step in revolutionary activity that, with success, graduates to guerrilla warfare and beyond. But by itself terrorism is an admission of political weakness. In whatever vehicle it appears, terrorism is a psychological weapon designed to use force in order to influence political behavior. It is most effective when it is indiscriminate in appearance, but in fact it is really highly discriminate. Thus, defined simply, terrorism is crime and violence for the effect it has on society or the world; it is a means to an end, not an end itself.

Political terrorism emerged as a concept during the Reign of Terror (1793–1794), in the French Revolution. But here terror was a governmental weapon. In the nineteenth century there was little effective use of terrorism. In the twentieth century it has been employed chiefly in nationalist revolutions (e.g., by the Irish against the British, by the Arabs and Jews against the British in Palestine, and by the Algerians against the French), although more recently terrorist attacks have attempted to force liberal regimes to become repressive, which in turn, would alienate the masses and initiate revolution. Terrorism seems to be most successful in colonial situations or during wars; it has been least effective in peace time.

The literature on the subject has grown rapidly, with the majority of titles below published after 1970. Most instructive for an understanding of the subject are the articles by J. Bowyer Bell (1977), Martha Crenshaw Hutchinson (1972), Walter Laqueur (1977), Flora Lewis (1978), and H. Edward Price, Jr. (1977), and the books by Yonah Alexander et al (1978), J. Bowyer Bell (1975, 1978), Frederick J. Hacker (1976), Edward Hyams (1974), Brian Jenkins (1975), and Walter Laqueur (1977, 1978). Works on terrorism throughout history and in specific locations can be identified by their titles.

Bibliography

527. Norton, Augustus R., and Martin H. Greenberg. *International Terrorism: An Annotated Bibliography and Research Guide.* Boulder, Colorado: Westview Press, 1980.
528. Smith, Myron J., Jr. *The Secret Wars: International Terrorism, 1968–1980.* Santa Barbara, California: ABC-Clio, 1980.

Documents

529. Alexander, Yonah, et al, eds. *Control of Terrorism: International Documents.* New York: Crane, Russak, 1979.

Articles

530. Alder, J. H. "The Ecology of Terrorism." *Survival* 15 (July-August 1973): 178–83.
531. Aris, Stephen. "Terror in the Land of the Basques." *The New York Times Magazine* (4 May 1980).
532. Armstrong, George. "Italy's Terrorists: Why Are They Doing It, and When Will They Stop." *Los Angeles Times* (10 August 1980).
533. Avishai, Bernard. "In Cold Blood." *New York Review of Books* (8 March 1979).
534. Bell, J. Bowyer. "Trends on Terror: The Analysis of Political Violence." *World Politics* 29:3 (April 1977): 476–88.
535. Bendiner, Robert. "Atlas' Survey: Controlling Terrorism." *Atlas World Press Review* (July 1978): 10–12.
536. Bishop, Joseph W., Jr. "Can Democracy Defend Itself against Terrorism?" *Commentary* (May 1978).
537. Bradshaw, Jon. "The Dream of Terror." *Esquire* (18 July 1978).
538. Foreign Policy Association. "International Terrorism." In *Great Decisions '79.* New York: Foreign Policy Association, 1979.
539. Goldie, L. F. E. "Combating International Terrorism: The U.N.'s Developments." *Naval War College Review* 31:3 (Winter 1979): 49–60.
540. Hutchinson, Martha Crenshaw. "The Concept of Revolutionary Terrorism." *Journal of Conflict Resolution* 16:3 (September 1972): 384–96.
541. Kopkind, Andrew. "Euro-Terror." *New Times* 10:12 (12 June 1978): 28.

542. Kramer, Jane. "A Reporter in Europe: Hamburg." *The New Yorker* (20 March 1978).
543. Laqueur, Walter. "The Truth About Terrorism." *Los Angeles Times* (1 December 1977).
544. Ledeen, Michael. "Terrorism's Explosive Myth Threatens Western Europe." *Los Angeles Times* (16 April 1978).
545. Lewis, Flora. "The Terrorists: Less a Sign of Revolution than of Decay." *The New York Times* (30 April 1978).
546. _____. "The Twisted Roots of Terrorism Run Deep." *The New York Times* (14 May 1978).
547. Menges, Constantine C. "Behind the Basque Terrorism." *New Leader* 62 (November 1979): 11-13.
548. Mohr, Charles. "A Pride of Hesitant Scholars Investigates the Emerging Discipline of Terrorism." *The New York Times* (27 May 1979).
549. Moss, Robert. "Terror: A Soviet Export." *The New York Times Magazine* (2 November 1980).
550. O'Brien, Conor Cruise. "Reflections on Terrorism." *New York Review of Books* (16 September 1976).
551. Pepper, Curtis Bill. "The Possessed." *The New York Times Magazine* (18 February 1979).
552. Pfaff, William. "Terrorism." *The New Yorker* (18 September 1978).
553. Preston, Paul. "Spain: Walking the Terrorist Tightrope." *Contemporary Review* 234 (March 1979): 119-24.
554. Price, H. Edward, Jr. "The Strategy and Tactics of Revolutionary Terrorism." *Comparative Studies in Social History* 19:1 (January 1977): 52-66.
555. Shultz, Richard. "The Limits of Terrorism in Insurgency Warfare: The Case of Viet Cong." *Polity* 11 (Fall 1978): 67-91.
556. Sterling, Claire. "Terrorism: Tracing the International Network." *The New York Times Magazine* (1 March 1981).
557. Talbott, John. "Terrorism and the Liberal Dilemma: The Case of the 'Battle of Algiers.'" *Contemporary French Civilization* 2 (Winter 1978): 177-90.
558. "Terrorism: Old Menace in New Guise." *U.S. News and World Report* (22 May 1978): 35-36.
559. "Terrorism: A Special Report." *The Washington Quarterly* (Autumn 1978): 104-30.
560. Vance, Cyrus R. "Terrorism: Scope of the Threat and Need for Effective Legislation." *Department of State Bulletin* (March 1978).
561. "War Without Boundaries." *Time* (31 October 1977).
562. Will, George F. "Terrorism Evokes a Totalitarian Past." *Los Angeles Times* (14 May 1978).

Books

563. Alexander, Yonah, ed. *International Terrorism: National, Regional, and Global Perspectives.* New York: AMS Press, 1976.
564. _____, ed. *Inter-National Terrorism: North and South America, the USSR, Europe, Asia and Africa.* New York: Praeger, 1976.
565. _____, et al. *Terrorism: Theory and Practice.* Boulder, Colorado: Westview Press, 1978.

566. _____ , and Seymour M. Finger, eds. *Terrorism: Interdisciplinary Perspectives.* New York: John Jay Press, 1977.
567. Bassiouni, M. Cherif. *International Terrorism and Political Crimes.* Springfield, Illinois: Charles C. Thomas, 1975.
568. Baumann, Carol Edler. *International Terrorism.* Milwaukee: Institute of World Affairs, University of Wisconsin, 1974.
569. Becker, Jillian. *Hitler's Children: The Story of the Baader-Meinhof Terrorist Gang.* Philadelphia: Lippincott, 1977.
570. Bell, J. Bowyer. *Terror Out of Zion: The Irgun, Lehi, Stern and the Palestine Underground.* New York: St. Martin's Press, 1977.
571. _____ . *A Time of Terror: How Democratic Societies Respond to Revolutionary Violence.* New York: Basic Books, 1978.
572. _____ . *Transnational Terrorism.* Plano, Texas: American Enterprise, 1975.
573. Burton, Anthony M. *Urban Terrorism: Theory, Practice and Response.* New York: Free Press, 1976.
574. Carlton, D., and C. Schaerf, eds. *International Terrorism and World Security.* New York: Halsted Press, 1975.
575. Clutterbuck, Richard. *Guerrillas and Terrorists.* Athens: Ohio University Press, 1980.
576. _____ . *Living With Terrorism.* New Rochelle, New York: Arlington House, 1976.
577. Committee on Internal Security, United States House of Representatives. *Terrorism.* Washington, D.C.: U.S. Government Printing Office, 1974.
578. Darrell, Trent, and Robert Kupperman. *Terrorism: Threat, Reality, Response.* Stanford: Hoover Institution, 1979.
579. Demaris, Ovid. *Brothers in Blood: The International Terrorist Network.* New York: Scribners, 1977.
580. Dobson, Christopher, and Ronald Payne. *The Terrorists: Their Weapons, Leaders and Tactics.* New York: Facts On File, 1979.
581. Evans, Alona E., and John F. Murphy, eds. *Legal Aspects of International Terrorism.* Lexington, Massachusetts: Lexington Books, 1978.
582. Evans, Ernest. *Calling a Truce to Terror: The American Response to International Terrorism.* Westport, Connecticut: Greenwood, 1979.
583. Goode, Stephen. *Guerrilla Warfare and Terrorism.* New York: Franklin Watts, 1977.
584. Green, Gil. *Terrorism—Is It Revolutionary?* New York: New Outlook, 1970.
585. Hacker, Frederick J., *Crusaders, Criminals, Crazies: Terror and Terrorism in Our Time.* New York: W. W. Norton, 1976.
586. Halperin, E. *Terrorism in Latin America.* Beverly Hills, California: Sage, 1976.
587. Hirst, David. *The Gun and the Olive Branch: The Roots of Violence in the Middle East.* New York: Harcourt Brace Jovanovich, 1979.
588. Hyams, Edward. *Terrorists and Terrorism.* New York: St. Martin's Press, 1974.
589. *International Terrorism and World Security,* edited by Carlton, David, and Carlo Schaerf. New York: John Wiley, 1975.
590. Jenkins, Brian. *International Terrorism: A New Mode of Conflict.* Los Angeles: Crescent Publications, 1975.

34 / Concepts and Aspects of Revolution

591. Katz, Robert. *Days of Wrath: The Ordeal of Aldo Moro.* Garden City, New York: Doubleday, 1980.
592. Kautsky, Karl. *Terrorism and Communism: A Contribution to the Natural History of Revolutions.* Westport, Connecticut: Hyperion Press, 1969.
593. Khrushchev, Nikita S. *The Anatomy of Terror: Khrushchev's Revelations About Stalin's Regime.* Washington, D.C.: Public Affairs Press, 1956.
594. Langguth, A. J. *Hidden Terrors.* New York: Pantheon, 1978.
595. Laqueur, Walter. *Terrorism.* Boston: Little, Brown, 1977.
596. _____, ed. *The Terrorism Reader: A Historical Anthology.* Philadelphia: Temple University Press, 1978.
597. Leach, Edward. *Custom, Law, and Terrorist Violence.* Edinburgh: University Press of Scotland, 1977.
598. Leith, James A. *Media and Revolution: Moulding a New Citizenry During the Terror.* Toronto: Canadian Broadcasting Corporation, 1968.
599. Lineberry, William P., ed. *The Struggle Against Terrorism.* New York: H. W. Wilson, 1977.
600. Liston, Robert A. *Terrorism.* Nashville, Tennessee: Thomas Nelson, 1977.
601. Livingston, Marius H., ed. *International Terrorism in the Contemporary World.* Westport, Connecticut: Greenwood, 1978.
602. McKnight, Gerald. *The Mind of the Terrorist.* London: Michael Joseph, 1974.
603. Morf, Gustave. *Terror in Quebec.* Toronto: Clark, Irwin, 1970.
604. Ochberg, Frank, ed. *Victims of Terrorism.* Boulder, Colorado: Westview Press, 1982.
605. Parry, Albert. *Terrorism: From Robespierre to Arafat.* New York: Vanguard Press, 1976.
606. Rapoport, David C. *Assassination and Terrorism.* Toronto: Canadian Broadcasting Corporation, 1971.
607. Royal United Services Institute, ed. *Ten Years of Terrorism: Collected Views.* New York: Crane, Russak, 1979.
608. Schreiber, Jan. *The Ultimate Weapon: Terrorists and World Order.* New York: Morrow, 1978.
609. Silj, Alessandro. *Never Again Without a Rifle: The Origins of Italian Terrorism.* New York: Karz Publishers, 1979.
610. Smith, Colin. *Carlos: Portrait of a Terrorist.* New York: Holt, Rinehart and Winston, 1977.
611. Sobel, Lester A., ed. *Political Terrorism.* 2 vols. New York: Facts On File, 1975, 1978.
612. Sterling, Claire. *The Terror Network.* New York: Holt, Rinehart and Winston, 1981.
613. *Terror or Love? Bommi Baumann's Own Story of His Life as a West German Urban Guerrilla.* With Statements by Heinrich Böll and Daniel Cohn-Bendit. Translated by H. Ellenbogen and W. Parker. New York: Grove Press, 1979.
614. Watson, Francis M. *Political Terrorism: The Threat and the Response.* New York: Robert B. Luce, 1976.
615. Wilkinson, Paul. *Political Terrorism.* New York: John Wiley, 1974.
616. _____. *Terrorism and the Liberal State.* New York: Halsted Press, 1978.

Nonviolence

Nonviolence, or passive resistance, is a repudiation of the use of violence to force a ruling establishment to concede reforms or revolutionary changes. Although it has historical roots in Buddhism and early Christianity, it has been developed more completely in this century by Mahatma Gandhi. (Readers would be wise to examine some of the titles in the section on Gandhi as well.) Nonviolence is the deliberate practice of civil disobedience to laws or regulations to which the resisting party objects, followed by passive obstruction of the police or military groups attempting to enforce them. It generally has its greatest chance to be effective against governments which are themselves subject to the pressure of public opinion to which, in fact, it appeals over the heads of government. It will not succeed against a totalitarian state strong enough to censor the news, or to ignore the feelings of its subjects.

Along with the works of Gandhi, those below by Henry David Thoreau (1960) and Leo Tolstoy (1948, 1960) provide excellent background. Good, brief introductions to the subject are found in the articles by Barbara Deming (1968) and Gene Sharp (1959, 1970). For further study, books by the following are especially recommended: Joan V. Bondurant (1973), David Dellinger (1970), Richard Gregg (1966), and Gene Sharp (1970, 1972, 1973).

Documents

617. Lynd, Staughton, ed. *Nonviolence in America: A Documentary History.* Indianapolis: Bobbs-Merrill, 1966.

Articles

618. Bauer, Raymond A., and Alice H. Bauer. "Day to Day Resistance to Slavery." *Journal of Negro History* 27:4 (October 1942): 388–419.
619. de Crespigny, Anthony. "The Nature and Methods of Non-Violent Coercion." *Political Studies* 12:2 (June 1964): 256–65.
620. Deming, Barbara. "On Revolution and Equilibrium." *Liberation* 12:11 (February 1968): 10–21.
621. Naess, Arne. "A Systematization of Gandhian Ethics of Conflict Resolution." *Journal of Conflict Resolution* 2:2 (June 1958): 140–55.
622. Sharp, Gene. "The Meaning of Non-Violent Resistance: A Typology." *Journal of Conflict Resolution* 3:1 (March 1959): 41–64.
623. _____. "Non-Violence: Moral Principle or Political Technique?" *Indian Political Science Review* 4:1 (October 1969-March 1970): 17–36.

Books

624. Bondurant, Joan V., ed. *Conflict: Violence and Nonviolence.* New York: Lieber-Atherton, 1973.
625. Brockway, A. Fenner. *Non-Co-operation in Other Lands.* Madras: Tagore, 1921.
626. Case, Clarence Marsh. *Nonviolent Coercion: A Study in Methods of Social Pressure.* New York: Century, 1923.
627. De Ligt, Barthelemy. *Conquest of Violence.* New York: Garland, n.d.
628. Dellinger, David. *Revolutionary Nonviolence.* Indianapolis: Bobbs-Merrill, 1970.
629. Del Vasto, Lanza. *Definitions of Nonvioience.* Weare, New Hampshire: Greenleaf Books, 1972.
630. Deming, Barbara. *Revolution and Equilibrium.* New York: Grossman Publishers, 1971.
631. Eisenberg, A., and J. Ilardo. *Argument: An Alternative to Violence.* Englewood Cliffs, New Jersey: Prentice-Hall, 1972.
632. Finn, James. *Protest: Pacifism and Politics: Some Passionate Views on War and Nonviolence.* New York: Random House, 1968.
633. Gandhi, Mohandas K. *Satyagraha in South Africa.* Translated by V. G. Desai. Rev. 2d ed. Ahmedabad: Navajivan Publishing House, 1950.
634. Gregg, Richard. *The Power of Nonviolence.* Rev. 2d ed. New York: Schocken, 1966.
635. Hope, Marjorie, and James Young. *The Struggle for Humanity: Agents of Nonviolent Change in a Violent World.* Maryknoll, New York: Orbis Books, 1977.
636. Kuper, Leo. *Passive Resistance in South Africa.* New Haven: Yale University Press, 1957.
637. Mahadevan, T. K.; Adam Roberts; and Gene Sharp, eds. *Civilian Defence: An Introduction.* New Delhi: Gandhi Peace Foundation, 1967.
638. Miller, William Robert. *Nonviolence: A Christian Interpretation.* New York: Association Press, 1964.
639. Moulton, Phillips P. *Violence, or Aggressive Nonviolent Resistance.* Wallingford, Pennsylvania: Pendle Hill, 1971.
640. Pelton, Leroy H. *The Psychology of Nonviolence.* Elmsford, New York: Pergamon, 1975.
641. Roberts, Adam. *Civilian Resistance as a National Defense: Non-Violent Action Against Aggression.* Harrisburg, Pennsylvania: Stackpole Books, 1968.
642. Seifert, Harvey. *Conquest by Suffering: The Process and Prospects of Non-Violent Resistance.* Philadelphia: Westminster Press, 1965.
643. Sharp, Gene. *An Abecedary of Nonviolent Action and Civilian Defense.* Cambridge, Massachusetts: Schenkman, 1972.
644. _____. *Exploring Nonviolent Alternatives.* Boston: Porter Sargent, 1970.
645. _____. *The Politics of Nonviolent Action.* Boston: Porter Sargent, 1973.
646. Sibley, Mulford Q. *Political Theories of Modern Pacifism.* New York: Garland, n.d.
647. _____, ed. *The Quiet Battle: Writings on the Theory and Practice of Nonviolent Resistance.* Garden City, New York: Doubleday, 1963.

648. Singer, Peter. *Democracy and Disobedience*. Oxford: Clarendon Press, 1973.
649. Templin, Ralph T. *Democracy and Nonviolence*. Boston: Porter Sargent, 1965.
650. Thoreau, Henry David. *Walden and 'Civil Disobedience'*. New York: New American Library, 1960.
651. Tolstoy, Leo. *The Kingdom of God and Peace Essays*. Translated by A. Maude. London: Oxford University Press, 1960.
652. _____ . *The Law of Violence and the Law of Love*. Translated by M. K. Tolstoy. New York: Rudolph Field, 1948.
653. Unnithan, T. K., and Y. Singh. *Sociology of Nonviolence and Peace: Behavioural and Attitudinal Dimensions*. Mystic, Connecticut: Lawrence Verry, 1969.
654. _____ , eds. *Traditions of Non Violence*. Columbia, Missouri: South Asia Books, 1973.
655. Woodcock, George. *Civil Disobedience: Seven Talks for CBC Radio*. Toronto: Canadian Broadcasting Corporation, 1966.
656. Zwiebach, Burton. *Civility and Disobedience*. New York: Cambridge University Press, 1975.

Counterrevolution

This is the other side of the coin, or the reaction to revolution, and as such, deserves a place in this volume. Counterrevolution is a confrontation whereby mass violence is intended to return to power a political group or regime that has been removed by a revolutionary movement. Perhaps the prime example is the Vendée movement of 1793–1796 in France, and that section in Chapter 3 should be consulted as well. Counterrevolution may be studied instructively in the articles by Mark Mancall (1971), Alfred Meusel (1934), and Charles Tilly (1963), and in the books by Seymour Martin Lipset (1968), John J. McCuen (1966), Herbert Marcuse (1972), and James Meisel (1966). Aside from the Vendée, specific counterrevolutionary activity can be identified in the titles of the other works listed below. The more specialized topic of counterinsurgency can be examined in the works by A. Mack (1975), David Galula (1964), Julian Paget (1967), and John S. Pustay (1965).

Articles

657. Brzezinski, Zbigniew. "Revolution and Counterrevolution." *New Republic* (1 June 1968): 23–25.
658. Buckley, William F., Jr. "The Sorry Condition of Counterrevolutionary Doctrine." In *The Great Ideas Today*. Chicago: Encyclopedia Britannica, 1970.

659. Dirlik, Arif. "The Ideological Foundations of the New Life Movement: A Study in Counterrevolution." *Journal of Asian Studies* 34:4 (August 1975): 945–80.
660. Fox, George. "Counterrevolution." *Playboy* (March 1970): 136.
661. Mack, A. "Counterinsurgency in the Third World: Theory and Practice." *British Journal of International Studies* 1:3 (1975): 226–53.
662. Mancall, Mark. "Revolution in the Counter-Revolution: A Paradigm." *Journal of Interdisciplinary History* 1:2 (Winter 1971): 339–48.
663. Martin, Benjamin F. "Albert de Mun, Charette, and the Appeal of Contre-Révolution." *Proceedings of the Western Society of French History* 4 (1976): 360–67.
664. Meusel, Alfred. "Revolution and Counter-Revolution." In *Encyclopedia of Social Sciences*. New York: Macmillan, 1934.
665. Moody, Peter R., Jr. "The Fall of the Gang of Four: Background Notes on Counterrevolution." *Asian Survey* 7:8 (August 1977): 711–23.
666. Tilly, Charles. "The Analysis of a Counter-Revolution." *History and Theory* 3:1 (1963): 30–58.
667. Weber, Eugen. "Revolution? Counterrevolution? What Revolution?" *Journal of Contemporary History* 9:2 (April 1974): 33–48.

Books

668. Blanc, Louis, and J. Crétineau-Joly. *La Contre-revolution*. Paris: Hachette, 1961.
669. Bongie, Laurence L. *David Hume: Prophet of the Counter-Revolution*. New York: Oxford University Press, 1965.
670. Doty, C. Stewart. *From Cultural Rebellion to Counterrevolution: The Politics of Maurice Barrès*. Athens: Ohio University Press, 1976.
671. Flores Caballero, Romeo. *Counterrevolution: The Role of the Spaniards in the Independence of Mexico, 1804–1838*. Translated by J. E. Rodríquez. Lincoln: University of Nebraska Press, 1974.
672. Galula, David. *Counterinsurgency Warfare: Theory and Practice*. New York: Praeger, 1964.
673. Godechot, Jacques. *The Counter-Revolution: Doctrine and Action, 1789–1804*. Translated by S. Attanasio. Princeton: Princeton University Press, 1981.
674. Kann, R. A. *The Problem of Restoration*. Berkeley: University of California Press, 1968.
675. Kohout, Pavel. *From the Diary of a Counter-Revolutionary*. Translated by G. Theiner. New York: McGraw-Hill, 1972.
676. Lipset, Seymour Martin. *Revolution and Counterrevolution*. New York: Basic Books, 1968.
677. McCuen, John J. *The Art of Counter-Revolutionary War*. Harrisburg, Pennsylvania: Stackpole Books, 1966.
678. Marcuse, Herbert. *Counterrevolution and Revolt*. Boston: Beacon, 1972.
679. Mayer, Arno J. *Dynamics of Counterrevolution in Europe, 1870–1956: An Analytic Framework*. New York: Harper and Row, 1971.
680. Meisel, James. *Counterrevolution: How Revolutions Die*. New York: Atherton, 1966.

681. Molnar, Thomas. *The Counter-Revolution.* New York: Funk and Wagnalls, 1969.
682. Paget, Julian. *Counterinsurgency Campaigning.* London: Faber and Faber, 1967.
683. Pustay, John S. *Counterinsurgency Warfare.* New York: Free Press, 1965.
684. Roy, M. N. *Revolution and Counterrevolution in China.* Calcutta: Renaissance Publishing Company, 1948.
685. Strakhovsky, Leonid I. *Intervention at Archangel: The Story of Allied Intervention and Russian Counter-Revolution in North Russia, 1918–1920.* Princeton: Princeton University Press, 1944.

Peasant Revolutions

Peasant revolts and the involvement of peasants in revolutions have characterized many periods throughout history, though attention by analysts has been relatively recent—all of the works cited below have been published since 1960. Medieval and early modern European peasant uprisings are cited in the appropriate sections in Chapters 2 and 3. Peasant involvement in revolutions in Latin America, Asia, and Africa can be seen in titles in those chapters. For a general view and survey approach, recommended are articles by Hamza Alavi (1965), Arne Disch (1979), Emmanuel Le Roy Ladurie (1979), Charles Tilly (1974), Eric Wolf (1969, 1971), and the April 1976 issue of *Comparative Politics,* and books by Gil Carl AlRoy (1966), Chalmers Johnson (1974), and Eric Wolf (1970).

Articles

686. Adeniran, Tunde. "The Dynamics of Peasant Revolt." *Ibadan* (July 1975): 9–15.
687. Alavi, Hamza. "Peasants and Revolution." *The Socialist Register* 2 (1965): 241–77.
688. Davies, Alun. "The Origins of the French Peasant Revolution of 1789." *History* 49:165 (February 1964): 24–41.
689. Disch, Arne. "Peasants and Revolts." *Theory and Society* 7:1–2 (January-March 1979): 243–52.
690. Fischer-Galati, Stephen. "The Peasants as a Revolutionary Force in the Balkans." *Journal of Central European Affairs* 23 (April 1963): 12–22.
691. Ladurie, Emmanuel Le Roy. "Peasants." In *The New Cambridge Modern History,* vol. 13, edited by Peter Burke. New York: Cambridge University Press, 1979.
692. Landsberger, Henry A. "The Role of Peasant Movements and Revolts in Development." In *Latin American Peasant Movements,* edited by Henry A. Landsberger. Ithaca: Cornell University Press, 1969.

693. Patch, Richard W. "Peasantry and National Revolution." In *Expectant Peoples: Nationalism and Development,* edited by K. H. Silvert. New York: Random House, 1963.
694. "Peasants and Revolution." *Comparative Politics* 8:3 (April 1976), special issue.
695. Redclift, Michael. "Peasants and Revolutionaries: Some Critical Comments." *Journal of Latin American Studies* 7 (May 1975): 135-44.
696. Salmon, J. H. M. "Peasant Revolt in Vivarais, 1575-1580." *French Historical Studies* 11:2 (Spring 1979): 1-28.
697. Scheiner, Irwin. "The Mindful Peasant: Sketches for a Study of Rebellion." *Journal of Asian Studies* 32:4 (August 1973): 579-91.
698. Scott, James C. "Revolution in the Revolution: Peasants and Commissars." *Theory and Society* 7:1-2 (January-March 1979): 97-134.
699. Tilly, Charles. "Town and Country in Revolution." In *Peasant Rebellion and Communist Revolution in Asia,* edited by J. W. Lewis. Stanford: Stanford University Press, 1974.
700. Wolf, Eric. "On Peasant Rebellions." *International Social Science Journal* 21:2 (1969): 286-93.
701. _____. "Peasant Rebellion and Revolution." In *National Liberation,* edited by N. Miller and R. Aya. New York: Free Press, 1971.

Books

702. AlRoy, Gil Carl. *The Involvement of Peasants in Internal War.* Princeton: Center of International Studies, Princeton University, 1966.
703. Beqiraj, Mehmet. *Peasantry in Revolution.* Cornell Research Papers in International Studies, no. 5. Ithaca: Cornell University Press, 1966.
704. Borton, Hugh. *Peasant Uprisings in Japan of the Tokugawa Period.* New York: Paragon, 1968.
705. Hobsbawn, Eric J. *Bandits.* New York: Delacorte Press, 1969.
706. Johnson, Chalmers. *Autopsy on People's War.* Berkeley: University of California Press, 1974.
707. Landsberger, Henry A., ed. *Rural Protest: Protest Movements and Social Change.* New York: Barnes and Noble, 1973.
708. Mbeki, Gowan. *The Peasants' Revolt.* Baltimore: Penguin Books, 1964.
709. Mousnier, Roland. *Peasant Uprisings in Seventeenth-Century France, Russia, and China.* Translated by B. Pearce. New York: Harper and Row, 1971.
710. Parsons, James B. *Peasant Rebellions of the Late Ming Dynasty.* Tucson: University of Arizona Press, 1970.
711. Scott, James C. *The Promise of Peasant Revolution.* New York: Free Press, forthcoming.
712. Spielberg, Joseph, and Scott Whiteford. *Forging Nations: A Comparative View of Rural Ferment and Revolt.* East Lansing: Michigan State University Press, 1976.
713. Stokes, E. T. *The Peasant and the Raj: Studies in Agrarian Society and Peasant Rebellion in Colonial India.* New York: Cambridge University Press, 1978.
714. Wolf, Eric. *Peasant Wars of the Twentieth Century.* New York: Harper and Row, 1970.
715. Woloch, Isser, ed. *The Peasantry in the Old Regime: Conditions and Protests.* New York: Holt, Rinehart and Winston, 1970.

Student Rebellions

Although student rebellions date back to the middle ages, it was primarily in the 1960s and 1970s that they increased in severity and became more revolutionary in character, a fact reflected in the publication dates of the titles in this section. In the advanced industrial countries of the West university students offered a kind of revolutionary rejection of established society in their lifestyle: long hair, sexual freedom, unconventional clothing, drugs, hard rock music, pacifism, and communal living. Students sought to transform the university as a first step toward revolutionizing society at large. This is an interesting story involving youth, affluence, privilege, ideology, and daring. It can best be explored in many of the titles below, some of the more significant of which are the articles by Philip G. Altbach and Patti Peterson (1971), Jack Douglas (1970), Richard Flacks (1967, 1970), Herbert Hendin (1971), and Kenneth Kenis- activities, including many coups d'etat, palace revolutions, rebellions, Ehrenreich and John Ehrenreich (1969), Lewis S. Feuer (1969), Julian Foster and Durwood Long (1970), Nathan Glazer (1970), and Seymour Martin Lipset and Philip G. Altbach (1969). Some of the works, as their titles indicate, concern countries other than the United States. Chapter 4 has a section dealing with the French Revolution of 1968 which had significant student involvement. Also, attention should be paid to the section on the New Left in Chapter 5; many of its titles can be used in conjunction with those below.

Bibliographies

716. Altbach, Philip G. *Student Politics and Higher Education in the United States: A Select Bibliography.* St. Louis: United Ministries in Higher Education, 1968.
717. Keniston, Kenneth, and Michael Lerner. "Selected References on Student Protest." *Annals of the American Academy of Political and Social Science* 395 (May 1971): 184-94.

Articles

718. Altbach, Philip G., and Patti Peterson. "Before Berkeley: Historical Perspectives on American Student Activism." *Annals of the American Academy of Political and Social Science* 395 (May 1971): 1-14.
719. Baird, Leonard L. "Who Protests: A Study of Student Activists." In *Protest! Student Activism in America,* edited by J. Foster and D. Long. New York: Morrow, 1970.
720. Block, J. H.; N. Haan; and M. B. Smith. "Socialization Correlates of Student Activism." *Journal of Social Issues* 25 (November 1969): 143-77.
721. Boudon, Raymond. "Sources of Student Protest in France." *Annals of the American Academy of Political and Social Science* 395 (May 1971): 139-49.

42 / Concepts and Aspects of Revolution

722. Brogan, D. W. "The Student Revolt." *Encounter* (July 1968): 20-25.
723. Douglas, Jack. "Theories of the American Student Protest Movements." In *Youth in Turmoil*, by Jack Douglas. Washington, D.C.: U.S. Government Printing Office, 1970.
724. Eisen, Jonathan, and David Steinberg. "The Student Revolt Against Liberalism." *Annals of the American Academy of Political and Social Science* 382 (March 1969): 83-94.
725. Flacks, Richard. "The Liberated Generation: An Exploration of the Roots of Student Protest." *Journal of Social Issues* 23:3 (July 1967): 52-75.
726. _____. "The Revolt of the Young Intelligentsia: Revolutionary Class-consciousness in Post-scarcity America." In *Revolution Reconsidered*, edited by N. Miller and R. Aya. New York: Free Press, 1970.
727. _____. "Social and Cultural Meanings of Student Revolt: Some Informal Comparative Observations." *Social Problems* 17:3 (1970): 340-57.
728. _____. "Who Protests: The Social Bases of the Student Movement." In *Protest! Student Activism in America*, edited by J. Foster and D. Long. New York: Morrow, 1970.
729. Garson, G. David. "The Ideology of the New Student Left." In *Protest! Student Activism in America*, edited by J. Foster and D. Long. New York: Morrow, 1970.
730. Gusfield, Joseph R. "Student Protest and University Response." *Annals of the American Academy of Political and Social Science* 395 (May 1971): 26-38.
731. Hanna, William John. "Student Protest in Independent Black Africa." *Annals of the American Academy of Political and Social Science* 395 (May 1971): 171-83.
732. Hendin, Herbert. "A Psychoanalyst Looks at Student Revolutionaries." *The New York Times Magazine* (17 January 1971).
733. Illick, Joseph E. "Perspectives of American Student Activism." *Journal of Psychohistory* 7 (Fall 1979): 175-87.
734. Keniston, Kenneth. "The Sources of Student Dissent." *Journal of Social Issues* 23:3 (July 1967): 108-37.
735. _____, and Michael Lerner. "Campus Characteristics and Campus Unrest." *Annals of the American Academy of Political and Social Science* 395 (May 1971): 39-53.
736. Kerpelman, L. C. "Student Political Activism and Ideology: Comparative Characteristics of Activists and Non-activists." *Journal of Counseling Psychology* 16 (1969): 8-13.
737. Knox, Gregory H. C. "Notes of a Young Radical." *Saturday Review* (15 August 1970): 48.
738. Laqueur, Walter. "Reflections on Youth Movements." *Commentary* (December 1969): 33-41.
739. Leggett, John. "Metamorphosis of the Campus Radical." *The New York Times Magazine* (30 January 1972).
740. Liebman, Arthur. "Student Activism in Mexico." *Annals of the American Academy of Political and Social Science* 395 (May 1971): 159-70.
741. Lipset, Seymour Martin. "The Sources of Student Activism." In *Students in Revolt*, edited by S. M. Lipset and P. G. Altbach. Boston: Houghton Mifflin, 1969.
742. Mankoff, Milton, and Richard Flacks. "The Changing Social Base of the American Student Movement." *Annals of the American Academy of Political and Social Science* 395 (May 1971): 54-67.

743. Myerhoff, Barbara G. "The Revolution as a Trip: Symbol and Paradox." *Annals of the American Academy of Political and Social Science* 395 (May 1971): 105-16.
744. Obear, Frederick W. "Student Activism in the Sixties." In *Protest! Student Activism in America,* edited by J. Foster and D. Long. New York: Morrow, 1970.
745. Pinner, Frank A. "Students—A Marginal Elite in Politics." *Annals of the American Academy of Political and Social Science.* 395 (May 1971): 127-38.
746. Sampson, E. E. "Student Activism and a Decade of Protest." *Journal of Social Issues* 23:3 (July 1967): 1-33.
747. Shimbori, Michiya. "Student Radicals in Japan." *Annals of the American Academy of Political and Social Science* 395 (May 1971): 150-58.
748. Westby, D., and R. Braungart. "The Alienation of Generations and Status Politics: Alternative Explanations of Student Political Activism." In *Learning About Politics: Studies in Political Socialization,* edited by Roberta Sigel. New York: Random House, 1968.
749. _____. "Class and Politics in the Family Backgrounds of Student Political Activists." *American Sociological Review* 31:5 (October 1966): 690-92.

Books

750. Albertson, Dean. *Student Movements of the 1960s.* New York: Monarch Press, n.d.
751. Bell, Daniel, and I. Kristol, eds. *Confrontation: The Student Rebellion and the Universities.* New York: Basic Books, 1969.
752. Califano, Joseph A., Jr. *Student Revolution: A Global Confrontation.* New York: W. W. Norton, 1970.
753. Cohen, Mitchell, and Dennis Hale, eds. *New Student Left: An Anthology.* Boston: Beacon, 1967.
754. Crough, Colin. *Student Revolt.* Levittown, New York: Transatlantic Arts, 1971.
755. Doolin, Dennis J. *Communist China: The Politics of Student Opposition.* Stanford: Hoover Institution, 1964.
756. Draper, Hal. *Berkeley: The New Student Revolt.* New York: Grove Press, 1965.
757. Editors of *The Atlantic. The Troubled Campus.* Boston: Little, Brown, 1966.
758. Ehrenreich, Barbara, and John Ehrenreich. *Long March, Short Spring: The Student Uprisings at Home and Abroad.* New York: Monthly Review Press, 1969.
759. Eichel, Lawrence, et al. *The Harvard Strike.* Boston: Houghton Mifflin, 1970.
760. Ericson, Edward E., Jr. *Radicals in the University.* Stanford: Hoover Institution, 1975.
761. Erlich, John, and Susan Erlich, eds. *Student Power, Participation and Revolution.* New York: Association Press, 1970.
762. Feuer, Lewis S. *The Conflict of Generations: The Character and Significance of Student Movements.* New York: Basic Books, 1969.
763. Foster, Julian, and Durward Long, eds. *Protest! Student Activism in America.* New York: Morrow, 1970.
764. Glazer, Nathan. *Remembering the Answers: Essays on the American Student Revolt.* New York: Basic Books, 1970.

44 / Concepts and Aspects of Revolution

765. Harris, Janet. *Students in Revolt.* New York: McGraw-Hill, 1970.
766. Kahn, Roger. *The Battle for Morningside Heights: Why Students Rebel.* New York: Morrow, 1970.
767. Kelman, Steve. *Push Comes to Shove.* Boston: Houghton Mifflin, 1970.
768. Kunen, James S. *The Strawberry Statement: Notes of a College Revolutionary.* New York: Random House, 1969.
769. Lipset, Seymour Martin. *Rebellion in the University: A History of Student Activism in America.* Brooklyn Heights, New York: Beekman Publishers, 1972.
770. _____ , and Philip G. Altbach, eds. *Students in Revolt.* Boston: Houghton Mifflin, 1969.
771. _____ , and Sheldon S. Wolin, eds. *The Berkeley Student Revolt: Facts and Interpretations.* Garden City, New York: Doubleday, 1965.
772. McEvoy, J., and A. Miller. *Black Power and Student Rebellion.* Belmont, California: Wadsworth, 1969.
773. Mandel, Ernest. *Revolutionary Student Movement: Theory and Practice.* New York: Pathfinder Press, 1969.
774. Mehnert, Klaus. *Twilight of the Young: The Radical Movements of the 1960s and Their Legacy.* New York: Holt, Rinehart and Winston, 1978.
775. Miles, Michael W. *The Radical Probe: The Logic of Student Rebellion.* New York: Atheneum, 1971.
776. Miller, Michael V., and Susan Gilmore, eds. *Revolution in Berkeley.* New York: Dell, 1965.
777. Novak, Steven J. *The Rights of Youth: American Colleges and Student Revolt, 1798–1815.* Cambridge, Massachusetts: Harvard University Press, 1977.
778. Sampson, E. E., and H. A. Korn, eds. *Student Activism and Protest.* New York: Ballantine Books, 1969.
779. Statera, Gianni. *Death of a Utopia: The Development and Decline of Student Movements in Europe.* New York: Oxford University Press, 1975.
780. Weaver, Gary R., and James H. Weaver, eds. *University and Revolution.* Englewood Cliffs, New Jersey: Prentice-Hall, 1969.

Radicalism

Radicalism is unlike the other political "isms" in that it does not encompass a philosophy. Radicals are extremists who seek to change society, from either the Left or Right. The works below, or appropriate parts of them, can be linked to other, more precise revolutionary movements. Among the more valuable are those by Egon Bittner (1963), T. H. McCormack (1950), Daniel Bell (1963), S. Bialer and S. Sluzar (1977), Leon B. Blair (1972), Daniel J. Boorstin (1969), Charles Hampden-Turner (1970), Sidney Lens (1969), and Alfred F. Young (1976).

Bibliographies

781. Goldwater, Walter. *Radical Periodicals in America, 1890-1950: A Bibliography with Brief Notes.* New York: University Place Book Shop, 1977.
782. Spahn, Theodore J., and Janet P. Spahn. *From Radical Left to Extreme Right: A Bibliography of Current Periodicals of Protest, Controversy, Advocacy, or Dissent.* Metuchen, New Jersey: Scarecrow Press 1976.

Documents

783. Bialer, S., and S. Sluzar, eds. *Sources of Contemporary Radicalism.* Boulder, Colorado: Westview Press, 1977.

Articles

784. Bettelheim, Bruno, and Richard Flacks. "The Roots of Radicalism." *Playboy* (March 1971): 106.
785. Bittner, Egon. "Radicalism and the Organization of Radical Movements." *American Sociological Review* 28:6 (December 1963): 928-40.
786. Krout, M. H., and R. Sanger. "Personality Development in Radicals." *Sociometry* 2 (1939): 31-46.
787. McCormack, T. H. "The Motivation of Radicals." *American Journal of Sociology* 56:1 (July 1950): 17-24.

Books

788. Abcarian, Gilbert, ed. *American Political Radicalism: Contemporary Issues and Orientations.* Waltham, Massachusetts: Xerox, 1971.
789. Alinsky, Saul. *Rules for Radicals.* New York: Random House, 1971.
790. Bell, Daniel, ed. *The Radical Right: The New American Right.* Garden City, New York: Doubleday, 1963.
791. Bialer, S., and S. Sluzar, eds. *Strategies and Impact of Contemporary Radicalism: Radicalism in the Contemporary Age.* Boulder, Colorado: Westview Press, 1977.
792. Blair, Leon B., ed. *Essays on Radicalism in Contemporary America.* Austin: University of Texas Press, 1972.
793. Bonwick, Colin. *English Radicals and the American Revolution.* Chapel Hill: University of North Carolina Press, 1977.
794. Boorstin, Daniel J. *The Decline of Radicalism.* New York: Random House, 1969.
795. Bottomore, T. B. *Critics of Society: Radical Thought in North America.* New York: Pantheon Books, 1968.
796. Buckman, Peter. *The Limits of Protest.* Indianapolis: Bobbs-Merrill, 1970.
797. Cantor, Milton. *The Divided Left: American Radicalism, 1900-1975.* New York: Hill and Wang, 1978.
798. Clecak, Peter. *Radical Paradoxes: Dilemmas of the American Left, 1945-1970.* New York: Harper and Row, 1973.

799. Gleason, Abbott. *Young Russia: The Genesis of Russian Radicalism in the 1860s.* New York: Viking, 1979.
800. Green, Gil. *The New Radicalism: Marxism versus Anarchism.* New York: International Publishers, 1971.
801. Gregor, A. James. *The Fascist Persuasion in Radical Politics.* Princeton: Princeton University Press, 1974.
802. Hampden-Turner, Charles. *Radical Man.* Cambridge, Massachusetts: Schenkman, 1970.
803. King, Richard. *The Party of Eros: Radical Social Thought and the Realm of Freedom.* Chapel Hill: University of North Carolina Press, 1972.
804. Kopkind, Andrew, ed. *Thoughts on Young Radicals.* New York: New Republic, Harrison-Blaine, 1966.
805. Lader, Lawrence. *Power on the Left: American Radical Movements Since 1946.* New York: W. W. Norton, 1979.
806. Lens, Sidney. *Radicalism in America.* New York: Thomas Y. Crowell, 1969.
807. MacCoby, Simon. *The English Radical Tradition, 1763-1914.* New York: New York University Press, 1957.
808. Methvin, Eugene H. *The Rise of Radicalism: The Social Psychology of Messianic Extremism.* New Rochelle, New York: Arlington House, 1973.
809. Rodnitzky, Jerome, et al. *Essays on Radicalism in Contemporary America.* Austin: University of Texas Press, 1972.
810. Silverman, Henry J., ed. *American Radical Thought: The Libertarian Tradition.* Lexington, Massachusetts: D. C. Heath, 1970.
811. Vincent, David, ed. *Testaments of Radicalism.* London: Europa Publications, 1977.
812. Walzer, Michael. *Radical Principles: Reflections of an Unreconstructed Democrat.* New York: Basic Books, 1980.
813. Young, Alfred F., ed. *The American Revolution: Explorations in the History of American Radicalism* De Kalb: Northern Illinois University Press, 1976.
814. _____ , ed. *Dissent: Explorations in the History of American Radicalism.* De Kalb: Northern Illinois University Press, 1968.

Anarchism

Anarchism, from the Greek *anarkhia,* non-rule, is a political doctrine dedicated to the abolition of formal government. A product of the industrial revolution, it had its historical roots in earlier revolutionary utopian and millenarian movements, as well as the Enlightenment and the French Revolution. It was the failure of nineteenth century revolutions and reforms that led the anarchists to challenge both their society and other revolutionists. The anarchist revolution would break the grip of authority so that the functions of life could regulate themselves; not only must the state be destroyed, but the social and economic structure must be eliminated too. Broad examinations of anarchism may be found in the articles by Paul Goodman (1970) and D. Novak (1958), and the books by

Anarchism / 47

April Carter (1971), James D. Forman (1976), Daniel Guerin (1970), James Joll (1964), Roderick Kedward (1971), Robert Nozick (1974), Gerald Runkle (1972), and George Woodcock (1962). The leading works by and about major anarchists are also listed in this section: William Godwin, the Englishman who gave the earliest literary expression to anarchism; Pierre-Joseph Proudhon, the Frenchman whose hostility to the state was implacable; Mikhail Bakunin, a Russian left-wing anarchist who preached the violent destruction of capitalism, all state authority, and formal political organization, and who wrote the infamous *Catechism of the Revolutionist*; Sergei Nechaev, the Russian follower of Bakunin who probably had a hand in the writing of the *Catechism*; Peter Kropotkin, a Russian right-wing anarchist who rejected the use of violence and believed that man's basic goodness would result in the establishment of order by voluntary cooperation; Alexander Berkman and Emma Goldman, the German and Lithuanian anarchists, respectively, who lived and agitated separately and together in America and Europe; and Daniel DeLeon, the American anarchist.

Anarchism is still alive, although it has no mass support. Anarchist parties exist on both sides of the Atlantic. There were anarchist elements in the New Left, and there are such elements among libertarians.

Articles

815. Constandse, A. L. "Anarchisme en cultuur." *Spiegel Historisch* 14:11 (1979): 617–21.
816. De Jong, Rudolf. "De ontwikkeling van het anarchisme." *Spiegel Historisch* 14:11 (1979): 579–88.
817. _____ , "Iets over de geschied schrijving van het anarchisme." *Spiegel Historisch* 14:11 (1979): 628–30.
818. Goodman, Paul. "Anarchism and Revolution." In *The Great Ideas Today.* Chicago: Encyclopedia Britannica, 1970.
819. Novak, D. "The Place of Anarchism in the History of Political Thought." *Review of Politics* 20 (July 1958): 307–29.
820. Reszler, Andr8e. "An Essay on Political Myths: Anarchist Myths of Revolt." *Diogenes* 94 (Summer 1976): 34–52.
821. Schurer, H. "Anarchism—Past and Present." *Survey* 18:3 (Summer 1972): 205–08.
822. Svoboda, George J. "Anarchism in Bohemia: The Prague Anti-Habsburg Revolutionary Society (1868–1872)." *East European Quarterly* 11:3 (1977): 267–91.
823. Woodcock, George. "Anarchism Revisited." *Commentary* (August 1968): 54–60.

Books

824. Avrich, Paul. *An American Anarchist: The Life of Voltairine de Cleyre.* Princeton: Princeton University Press, 1978.

48 / Concepts and Aspects of Revolution

825. _____. *The Modern School Movement: Anarchism and Education in the United States.* Princeton: Princeton University Press, 1980.
826. _____. *The Russian Anarchists.* Princeton: Princeton University Press, 1967.
827. Bookchin, Murray. *Post-Scarcity Anarchism.* Palo Alto, California: Ramparts Press, 1971.
828. _____. *The Spanish Anarchists: The Heroic Years, 1868–1936.* New York: Harper and Row, 1978.
829. Bose, Atindranath. *A History of Anarchism.* Calcutta: World Press Private, 1967.
830. Carlson, Andrew R. *Anarchism in Germany.* Metuchen, New Jersey: Scarecrow Press, 1972.
831. Carter, April. *The Political Theory of Anarchism.* New York: Harper and Row, 1971.
832. Confino, Michael, ed. *Daughter of a Revolutionary: Natalie Herzen and the Bakunin-Nechayev Circle.* Translated by H. Sternberg and L. Bott. La Salle, Illinois: Library Press, 1974.
833. De Leon, David. *The American as Anarchist: Reflections on Indigenous Radicalism.* Baltimore: Johns Hopkins University Press, 1978.
834. Eltzbacher, Paul. *Anarchism.* Translated by S. T. Byington. New York: Libertarian Book Club, 1960.
835. Fleming, Marie. *The Anarchist Way to Socialism: Elisée Reclus and Nineteenth-Century European Anarchism.* Totowa, New Jersey: Rowman and Littlefield, 1979.
836. Forman, James D. *Anarchism.* New York: Dell, 1976.
837. Guerin, Daniel. *Anarchism: From Theory to Practice.* New York: Monthly Review Press, 1970.
838. Hart, John M. *Anarchism and the Mexican Working Class, 1860–1931.* Austin: University of Texas Press, 1978.
839. Havel, Hippolyte. *What's Anarchism.* New York: Gordon Press, n.d.
840. Hoffman, Robert, ed. *Anarchism.* New York: Atherton, 1970.
841. Horowitz, Irving Louis, ed. *The Anarchists.* New York: Dell, 1964.
842. *Individualist Anarchist Pamphlets.* New York: Arno Press, 1972.
843. Joll, James. *The Anarchists.* London: Eyre and Spottiswoode, 1964.
844. Kedward, Roderick. *The Anarchists.* New York: McGraw-Hill, 1971.
845. Kern, Robert W. *Red Years/Black Years: A Political History of Spanish Anarchism, 1911–1937.* Philadelphia: ISHI Publications, 1978.
846. Krimerman, Leonard I., and Lewis Perry, eds. *Patterns of Anarchy.* Garden City, New York: Doubleday, 1966.
847. Labadie, Joseph A. *Anarchism.* Brooklyn, New York: Revisionist Press, n.d.
848. Latouche, P. *Anarchy.* New York: Gordon Press, n.d.
849. Mackay, John Henry. *The Anarchists: A Picture of Civilization at the Close of the Nineteenth Century.* Translated by G. Schumm. Boston: B. R. Tucker, 1891.
850. Marsh, Margaret. *Anarchist Women, 1870–1920.* Philadelphia: Temple University Press, 1980.
851. Marx, Karl, et al. *Anarchism and Anarcho-Syndicalism.* Brooklyn Heights, New York: Beekman Publishers, 1973.

852. Maurer, Charles B. *Call to Revolution: The Mystical Anarchism of Gustav Landauer.* Detroit: Wayne State University Press, 1971.
853. Nettlau, Max. *Anarchism and Social Revolution, 1880–1886.* Brooklyn, New York: Revisionist Press, 1978.
854. _____. *Anarchism from Proudhon to Kropotkin, 1859–1880.* Brooklyn, New York: Revisionist Press, 1978.
855. _____. *Anarchy Through the Times.* New York: Gordon Press, 1978.
856. _____. *History of Anarchism.* 3 vols. Brooklyn, New York: Revisionist Press, 1978.
857. _____. *The Unfolding of Anarchism: Its Origins and Historical Development to the Year 1864.* Brooklyn, New York: Revisionist Press, 1978.
858. Nozick, Robert. *Anarchy, State and Utopia.* New York: Basic Books, 1974.
859. Palij, Michael. *The Anarchism of Nestor Makhno, 1918–1921: An Aspect of the Ukrainian Revolution.* Seattle: University of Washington Press, 1977.
860. Pennock, J. Roland, and John W. Chapman, eds. *Anarchism: Nomos XIX.* New York: New York University Press, 1978.
861. Perlin, Terry M., ed. *Contemporary Anarchism.* Edison, New Jersey: Transaction Books, 1979.
862. Plekhanov, Georgi Valentinovich. *Anarchism and Socialism.* Translated by E. M. Aveling. Westport, Connecticut: Hyperion Press, 1980.
863. Read, Herbert. *Anarchy and Order.* Boston: Beacon, 1971.
864. Reichert, William O. *Partisans of Freedom: A Study in American Anarchism.* Bowling Green, Ohio: Bowling Green University Popular Press, 1976.
865. Runkle, Gerald. *Anarchism: Old and New.* New York: Dell, 1972.
866. Shatz, Marshall S., ed. *The Essential Works of Anarchism.* New York: Bantam Books, 1971.
867. Spitzer, Alan B. *Revolutionary Theories of Louis Auguste Blanqui.* Providence, Rhode Island: AMS Press, 1970.
868. Vizetelly, Ernest Alfred. *The Anarchists.* London: Lane, 1911.
869. Ward, Colin. *Anarchy in Action.* New York: Harper and Row, 1974.
870. Wolff, Robert Paul. *In Defense of Anarchism.* New York: Harper and Row, 1970.
871. Woodcock, George. *Anarchism.* Cleveland: World, 1962.
872. _____, ed. *The Anarchist Reader.* Atlantic Highlands, New Jersey: Humanities Press, 1977.
873. Zenker, E. V. *Anarchism: A Criticism and History of the Anarchist Theory.* New York: Putnam, 1897.

Mikhail Bakunin

Articles

874. Avrich, Paul. "The Legacy of Bakunin." *Russian Review* 29:2 (April 1970): 129–42.
875. Kun, Miklos. "Bakunin and Hungary (1848–1865)." *Canadian-American Slavic Studies* 10:4 (1976): 503–34.

876. Pomper, Philip. "Bakunin, Nechaev, and the 'Catechism of a Revolutionary': The Case for Joint Authorship." *Canadian-American Slavic Studies* 10:4 (1976): 535-51.

Books

877. Aldred, Guy A. *Bakunin's Writings.* New York: Gordon Press, n.d.
878. Bakunin, Mikhail. *Catechism of the Revolutionist.* In *Apostles of Revolution,* by Max Nomad. New York: Collier Books, 1933.
879. Carr, Edward H. *Michael Bakunin.* New York: Random House, 1961.
880. Dolgoff, Samuel. *Bakunin on Anarchy.* New York: Alfred A. Knopf, 1972.
881. Howes, Robert C. *The Confessions of Mikhail Bakunin.* Ithaca: Cornell University Press, 1977.
882. Masters, Anthony. *Bakunin: The Father of Anarchism.* New York: Saturday Review Press, E. P. Dutton, 1974.
883. Maximoff, G. P., ed. *The Political Philosophy of Bakunin.* New York: Free Press, 1953.

Alexander Berkman and Emma Goldman

884. Berkman, Alexander. *ABC of Anarchism.* Brooklyn, New York: Haskell House, 1979.
885. _____ . *Prison Memoirs of an Anarchist.* New York: Schocken, 1970.
886. _____ . *What Is Communist Anarchism?* Magnolia, Massachusetts: Peter Smith, n.d.
887. Drinnon, Richard. *Rebel in Paradise: A Biography of Emma Goldman.* New York: Bantam Books, 1961.
888. Goldman, Emma. *Anarchism and Other Essays.* New York: Mother Earth Publishing Association, 1910.
889. _____ . *Living My Life.* 2 vols. Magnolia, Massachusetts: Peter Smith, n.d.

Daniel DeLeon

890. Seretan, L. Glen. *Daniel DeLeon: The Odyssey of an American Marxist.* Cambridge, Massachusetts: Harvard University Press, 1979.

William Godwin

891. Clark, John P. *The Philosophical Anarchism of William Godwin.* Princeton: Princeton University Press, 1977.
892. Godwin, William. *Enquiry Concerning Political Justice.* New York: Penguin Books, 1976.

893. Kramnick, Isaac. "On Anarchism and the Real World: William Godwin and Radical England." *American Political Science Review* 66:1 (March 1972): 114-28.
894. Locke, Don. *A Fantasy of Reason: The Life and Thought of William Godwin.* Boston: Routledge and Kegan Paul, 1980.
895. Ryan, Alan. *Godwin.* New York: Hill and Wang, forthcoming.

Peter Kropotkin

896. Baldwin, Roger N., ed. *Kropotkin's Revolutionary Pamphlets.* New York: Dover, 1970.
897. Capouya, Emile, and Keitha Tompkins, eds. *The Essential Kropotkin.* New York: Liveright Publishing, 1975.
898. Kropotkin, Peter A. *Anarchism in Socialistic Evolution.* New York: Gordon Press, n.d.
899. _____. *Memoirs of a Revolutionist.* Edited by J. A. Rogers. Garden City, New York: Doubleday, 1962.
900. _____. *Revolutionary Pamphlets.* Edited by R. N. Baldwin. New York: Dover, 1970.
901. _____. *Selected Readings on Anarchism and Revolution.* Edited by M. A. Miller. Cambridge, Massachusetts: M.I.T. Press, 1970.
902. Miller, Martin A. *Kropotkin.* Chicago: University of Chicago Press, 1976.

Sergei Nechaev

903. Pomper, Philip. "Nechaev and Tsaricide: The Conspiracy within the Conspiracy." *Russian Review* 33:2 (April 1873): 123-38.
904. _____. *Sergei Nechaev.* New Brunswick, New Jersey: Rutgers University Press, 1979.

Pierre-Joseph Proudhon

Articles

905. Allen, Mary B. "P.-J. Proudhon in the Revolution of 1848." *Journal of Modern History* 24:1 (March 1952): 1-14.
906. _____. "The Solitary Revolution: Proudhon's Notebooks." *Encounter* (September 1969): 46-55.

Books

907. Brogan, D. W. *Proudhon.* London: H. Hamilton, 1934.
908. Hoffman, Robert. *Revolutionary Justice: The Social and Political Theory of P.-J. Proudhon.* Urbana: University of Illinois Press, 1972.

52 / Concepts and Aspects of Revolution

909. Lu, S. Y. *The Political Theories of P. J. Proudhon.* New York: M. R. Gray, 1922.
910. Lubac, Henri de. *The un-Marxian Socialist: A Study of Proudhon.* Translated by R. E. Scantlebury. London: Sheed and Ward, 1948.
911. Proudhon, P.-J. *General Idea of the Revolution in the Nineteenth Century.* Translated by J. B. Robinson. London: Freedom Press, 1923.
912. Ritter, Alan. *The Political Thought of Pierre-Joseph Proudhon.* Princeton: Princeton University Press, 1969.

Marx and Marxism

If there is a god to whom late nineteenth and twentieth century revolutionists have given homage, his name is Karl Marx. Although he adopted Hegel's dialectic, Marx was an aggressive, profound, and original thinker who also made time to write poetry and develop a love of Shakespeare. Never a barricade revolutionist, Marx nonetheless led an active life, much of which he spent in the major cities of Europe. More than any individual, his writings contributed to the future of revolution. Part of the controversy that pervades Marx—and Marxism—is that in writing so much (in fact, so many diverse works) over a long period of time he occasionally contradicted himself, or at least seemed to (e.g., on the question of the inevitability of violent revolution). Nonetheless, his work has become the bible to which all differing sects (e.g., revisionists, Leninists, Maoists, socialists) allude. Marx has exercised a paramount influence on working class and revolutionary movements, and on the development of capitalism as well. Among the best biographies are those by Isaiah Berlin (1959), Joel Carmichael (1967), Edward H. Carr (1934), David McLellan (1973, 1975), Saul K. Padover (1978), Robert Payne (1968), and Fritz J. Raddatz (1979).

Works on Marx are almost inseparable from those on Marxism (although Marx once said that he was *not* a Marxist), as a scanning of the titles in this section will reveal. In essence, Marxism is a theory and a program for revolution, and it is virtually synonymous with the concept of revolution. Obviously there is more to Marxism than that, but for more detail and amplification the reader should consult the bibliographies and reference books below, as well as some of the volumes by the following authors: H. B. Acton (1971), Shlomo Avineri (1970, 1977), Kostas Axelos (1976), Emile Burns (1966), G. D. H. Cole (1964), Hal Draper (1977–1978), A. James Gregor (1965), Robert L. Heilbroner (1980), Sidney Hook (1975), Robert Nigel Carew Hunt (1955), Eugene Kamenka (1972), George Lichtheim (1965), David McLellan (1971, 1974), Alfred G. Meyer (1954), and Robert C. Tucker (1969). Specialized studies related to Marxism can be gleaned from among the titles themselves.

No study of Marx or Marxism would be complete without a reading of

Marx himself. International Publishers has embarked upon the major task of publishing (in English) his collected works. McGraw-Hill has published several volumes, each covering a different theme. Many of Marx's works have been published separately, and there are good, brief collections edited by Lewis S. Feuer (1959), Arthur P. Mendel (1961), and Robert C. Tucker (1972).

Bibliographies

913. Baxandall, Lee. *Marxism and Aesthetics: An Annotated Bibliography.* New York: American Institute for Marxist Studies, 1967.
914. Bocheński, Joseph M., et al, eds. *Guide to Marxist Philosophy: An Introductory Bibliography.* Chicago: Swallow Press, 1972.
915. Eubanks, Cecil L. *Karl Marx and Friedrich Engels: An Analytical Bibliography.* New York: Garland, 1978.
916. International Mass Media Research Center. *Marxism and the Mass Media: Towards a Basic Bibliography.* New York: International General, 1978.
917. Lachs, John. *Marxist Philosophy: A Bibliographic Guide.* Chapel Hill: University of North Carolina Press, 1967.
918. Shaffer, Harry G. *Periodicals on the Socialist Countries and on Marxism: A New Annotated Index of English Language Publications.* New York: Praeger, 1977.

Reference

919. Burns, Emile, ed. *A Handbook of Marxism.* 2 vols. New York: Haskell House, 1970.
920. Stockhammer, Morris. *Karl Marx Dictionary.* New York: Philosophical Library, 1965.

Articles

921. Block, Fred. "Marxist Theories of the State in World Systems Analysis." In *Social Change in the Capitalist World Economy,* edited by B. H. Kaplan. Beverly Hills, California: Sage, 1978.
922. _____. "The Ruling Class Does Not Rule: Notes on the Marxist Theory of the State." *Socialist Revolution* 33 (May-June 1977): 6-28.
923. Braybrooke, David. "Marx on Revolutionizing the Mode of Production." In *Revolution (Nomos VIII),* edited by C. J. Friedrich. New York: Atherton, 1966.
924. Brown, H. Haines. "The Impact of Marxism." In *Problems in European History,* edited by Harold T. Parker. Durham, North Carolina: Moore Publishing, 1979.
925. Deutscher, Isaac. "Marxism and Nonviolence." *Liberation* 14:4 (July 1969): 10-16.
926. Duggett, Michael. "Marx on Peasants." *Journal of Peasant Studies* 2 (January 1975): 159-82.
927. Frankel, Boris. "On the State of the State: Marxist Theories of the State after Leninism." *Theory and Society* 7:1-2 (January-March 1979): 199-242.

928. Gregory, David. "The Influence of French Socialism on the Thought of Karl Marx, 1843–1845." *Proceedings of the Western Society on French History* 6 (1978): 242–51.
929. Kamenka, Eugene. "The Relevance—and Irrelevance— of Marxism." In *A World in Revolution?* edited by E. Kamenka. Canberra: Australian National University, 1970.
930. Kiernan, Victor G. "Marx and Marxism." *History* 64 (June 1979): 230–34.
931. Lichtheim, George. "The Origins of Marxism." *Journal of the History of Philosophy* 3:1 (April 1965): 96–105.
932. Milibrand, Ralph. "Marx and the State." *Socialist Register* 2 (1965): 278–96.
933. Riquelme, John Paul. "The Eighteenth Brumaire of Karl Marx as Symbolic Action." *History and Theory* 19:1 (1980): 58–72.
934. Spencer, Martin E. "Marx on the State: The Events in France between 1848–1850." *Theory and Society* 7:1–2 (January-March 1979): 167–98.
935. Voegelin, Eric. "The Formation of the Marxian Revolutionary Idea." *Review of Politics* 12 (July 1950): 275–302.
936. Wolfson, Murray. "Three Stages of Marx's Thought." *History of Political Economy* 11 (Spring 1979): 117–46.

Books

937. Acton, H. B. *The Illusion of the Epoch: Marxism-Leninism as a Philosophical Creed.* Boston: Routledge and Kegan Paul, 1973.
938. _____. *What Marx Really Said.* New York: Schocken, 1971.
939. Adams, H. P. *Karl Marx in His Earlier Writings.* Paterson, New Jersey: Atheneum, 1972.
940. Althusser, Louis. *For Marx.* Translated by B. R. Brewster. New York: Pantheon Books, 1970.
941. Aron, Raymond. *Marxism and the Existentialists.* New York: Harper and Row, 1969.
942. Avineri, Shlomo. *The Social and Political Thought of Karl Marx.* Cambridge: Cambridge University Press, 1970.
943. _____. *Varieties of Marxism.* Hingham, Massachusetts: Kluwer Boston, 1977.
944. Axelos, Kostas. *Alienation, Praxis, and Technē in the Thought of Karl Marx.* Translated by R. Bruzina. Austin: University of Texas Press, 1976.
945. Barzun, Jacques. *Darwin, Marx, Wagner: Critique of a Heritage.* Garden City, New York: Doubleday, 1958.
946. Bender, Frederic L. *The Betrayal of Marx.* New York: Harper and Row, 1974.
947. Berlin, Isaiah. *Karl Marx: His Life and Environment.* New York: Oxford University Press, 1959.
948. Blackburn, Robin, ed. *Revolution and Class Struggle: A Reader in Marxist Politics.* Atlantic Highlands, New Jersey: Humanities Press, 1978.
949. Bloom, Solomon F. *World of Nations: A Study of the National Implications in the Work of Karl Marx.* New York: AMS Press, n.d.
950. Blumenberg, Werner. *Portrait of Marx: An Illustrated Biography.* Translated by D. Scott. New York: McGraw-Hill, 1972.
951. Bober, M. M. *Karl Marx's Interpretation of History.* Cambridge, Massachusetts: Harvard University Press, 1950.

952. Brewer, Anthony. *Marxist Theories of Imperialism: A Critical Survey.* Boston: Routledge and Kegan Paul, 1980.
953. Brown, Bruce. *Marx, Freud, and the Critique of Everyday Life: Toward a Permanent Cultural Revolution.* New York: Monthly Review Press, 1973.
954. Bulgakov, Sergei. *Karl Marx as a Religious Type.* Belmont, Massachusetts: Nordland Publishing Co., 1979.
955. Burns, Emile. *Introduction to Marxism.* Rev. ed. New York: International Publishers, 1966.
956. Cameron, Kenneth N. *Marx and Engels Today: A Modern Dialogue on Philosophy and History.* Hicksville, New York: Exposition Press, 1976.
957. Carmichael, Joel. *Karl Marx: The Passionate Logician.* New York: Scribners, 1967.
958. Carr, Edward H. *Karl Marx: A Study in Fanaticism.* London: Dent and Sons, 1934.
959. Childs, David. *Marx and the Marxists.* New York: Barnes and Noble, 1973.
960. Cohen, G. A. *Karl Marx's Theory of History: A Defense.* Princeton: Princeton University Press, 1978.
961. Cole, G. D. H. *The Meaning of Marxism.* Ann Arbor: University of Michigan Press, 1964.
962. _____. *What Marx Really Meant.* London: Victor Gollancz, 1934.
963. Colletti, Lucio. *Marxism and Hegel.* New York: Schocken, 1979.
964. Corrigan, Philip, et al. *Socialist Construction and Marxist Theory: Bolshevism and Its Critiques.* New York: Monthly Review Press, 1978.
965. Croce, Benedetto. *Historical Materialism and the Economics of Karl Marx.* New York: Russell and Russell, 1966.
966. Davis, Horace B. *Toward a Marxist Theory of Nationalism.* New York: Monthly Review Press, 1978.
967. Drachkovitch, Milorad M., ed. *Marxism in the Modern World.* Stanford: Stanford University Press, 1965.
968. _____. *Marxist Ideology in the Contemporary World.* Stanford: Hoover Institution, 1966.
969. _____, ed. *The Revolutionary Internationals, 1864–1943.* Stanford: Stanford University Press, 1966.
970. Draper, Hal. *Karl Marx's Theory of Revolution.* 2 vols. New York: Monthly Review Press, 1977–1978.
971. Dupré, Louis. *The Philosophical Foundations of Marxism.* New York: Harcourt, Brace and World, 1966.
972. Eastman, Max. *Marxism: Is It Science?* New York: W. W. Norton, 1940.
973. Eddy, W. H. C. *Understanding Marxism.* Totowa, New Jersey: Rowman and Littlefield, 1978.
974. Evans, Michael. *Marx.* New York: Barnes and Noble, 1975.
975. Faris, Ralph M. *Revisionist Marxism: The Opposition Within.* Atlantic Highlands, New Jersey: Humanities Press, 1974.
976. Fetscher, Irving. *Marx and Marxism.* New York: Herder and Herder, 1971.
977. Fine, Ben. *Marx's Capital.* Atlantic Highlands, New Jersey: Humanities Press, 1975.
978. Fischer, Ernst. *Marx in His Own Words.* Translated by A. Bostack. New York: Herder and Herder, 1972.
979. Flakser, David. *Marxian Ideology and Myths.* New York: Philosophical Library, 1971.

56 / Concepts and Aspects of Revolution

980. Fleisher, Helmut. *Marxism and History.* London: Allen Lane, 1973.
981. Garaudy, Roger. *Karl Marx: The Evolution of His Thought.* New York: International Publishers, 1967.
982. Gemkow, Heinrich. *Karl Marx: A Biography.* Columbia, Missouri: South Asia Books, 1975.
983. Gilbert, Alan. *Marx's Politics: Communists and Citizens.* New Brunswick, New Jersey: Rutgers University Press, 1980.
984. Goldendach, David B. *Karl Marx: Man, Thinker and Revolutionist.* London: M. Lawrence, 1927.
985. Gregor, A. James. *A Survey of Marxism.* New York: Random House, 1965.
986. Heilbroner, Robert L. *Marxism: For and Against.* New York: W. W. Norton, 1980.
987. Hoeven, Johan Van Der. *Karl Marx: The Roots of His Thought.* Atlantic Highlands, New Jersey: Humanities Press, 1976.
988. Hoffman, John. *Marxism and the Theory of Praxis: A Critique of Some New Versions of Old Fallacies.* New York: International Publishers, 1976.
989. Hook, Sidney. *Marx and Marxists: The Ambiguous Legacy.* Princeton: Van Nostrand, 1955.
990. _____. *Revolution, Reform, and Social Justice: Studies in the Theory and Practice of Marxism.* New York: New York University Press, 1975.
991. _____. *Towards the Understanding of Karl Marx.* New York: John Day, 1933.
992. Howard, Dick. *The Marxian Legacy.* New York: Urizen Books, 1977.
993. Hunt, Richard N. *Marxism and Totalitarian Democracy, 1818-1850.* Vol. 1. *The Political Ideas of Marx and Engels.* Pittsburgh: University of Pittsburgh Press, 1974.
994. Hunt, Robert Nigel Carew. *Marxism Past and Present.* New York: Macmillan, 1955.
995. Johnson, Oakley C. *Marxism in United States History Before the Revolution 1876-1917.* Atlantic Highlands, New Jersey: Humanities Press, 1974.
996. Jordan, Z. A., ed. *Karl Marx: Economy, Class and Social Revolution.* New York: Scribners, 1975.
997. Kamenka, Eugene. *The Ethical Foundations of Marxism.* Rev. ed. New York: Routledge and Kegan Paul, 1972.
998. Kissin, S. F. *Farewell to Revolution: Marxist Philosophy and the Modern World.* New York: St. Martin's Press, 1978.
999. Kolakowski, Leszek. *Main Currents of Marxism: Its Rise, Growth and Dissolution.* 3 vols. Translated by P. S. Falla. New York: Oxford University Press, 1978.
1000. Korsch, Karl. *Karl Marx.* New York: John Wiley, 1938.
1001. _____. *Marxism and Philosophy.* New York: Monthly Review Press, 1972.
1002. Kubalkova, V., and A. A. Cruickshank. *Marxism-Leninism and Theory of International Relations.* Boston: Routledge and Kegan Paul, 1980.
1003. Labedz, Leopold, ed. *Revisionism: Essays in the History of Marxist Ideas.* New York: Praeger, 1962.
1004. Lefebvre, Henri. *Sociology of Marx.* Translated by N. Guterman. New York: Pantheon Books, 1968.
1005. Leff, Gordon. *The Tyranny of Concepts: A Critique of Marxism.* London: Merlin, 1961.

1006. Lenin, V. I. *Karl Marx.* San Francisco: China Books, 1976.
1007. _____. *Teaching of Karl Marx.* New York: International Publishers, 1964.
1008. Leonhard, Wolfgang. *Three Faces of Marxism: The Political Concepts of Soviet Ideology, Maoism, and Humanist Marxism.* Translated by E. Osers. New York: Holt, Rinehart and Winston, 1974.
1009. Lessner, F. *Reminiscences of Marx and Engels.* Moscow: Institute of Marxism-Leninism, n.d.
1010. Levine, Norman. *The Tragic Deception: Marx Contra Engels.* Santa Barbara, California: ABC-Clio, 1975.
1011. Lewis, John. *The Life and Thought of Karl Marx.* New York: International Publishers, 1965.
1012. _____. *The Marxism of Marx.* Brooklyn Heights, New York: Beekman Publishers, 1972.
1013. Lichtheim, George. *Marxism: An Historical and Critical Study.* New York: Praeger, 1965.
1014. Lindsay, A.D. *Karl Marx's "Capital": An Introductory Essay.* Westport, Connecticut: Greenwood, 1973.
1015. Lobkowicz, Nikolaus, ed. *Marx and the Western World.* Notre Dame, Indiana: Notre Dame University Press, 1967.
1016. Loewenstein, Julius I. *Marx Against Marxism.* Boston: Routledge and Kegan Paul, 1980.
1017. Loria, Achille. *Karl Marx.* New York: Gordon Press, n.d.
1018. Lukács, Georg. *History and Class Consciousness: Studies in Marxist Dialectics.* Translated by R. Livingstone. Cambridge, Massachusetts: M.I.T. Press, 1971.
1019. _____. *Marxism and Human Liberation: Essays on History, Culture and Revolution.* Edited by E. San Juan, Jr. New York: Dell, 1973.
1020. McLellan, David. *Karl Marx.* New York: Viking, 1975.
1021. _____. *Karl Marx: His Life and Thought.* New York: Harper and Row, 1973.
1022. _____. *Marx Before Marxism.* New York: Harper and Row, 1971.
1023. _____. *The Thought of Karl Marx.* New York: Harper and Row, 1974.
1024. _____. *The Thought of Karl Marx: An Introduction.* New York: Harper and Row, 1971.
1025. Maguire, John M. *Marx's Theory of Politics.* New York: Cambridge University Press, 1979.
1026. Mandel, Ernest. *Formation of the Economic Thought of Karl Marx.* Translated by B. Pearce. New York: Monthly Review Press, 1971.
1027. _____. *Introduction to Marxist Theory.* New York: Pathfinder Press, 1969.
1028. Marcuse, Herbert. *Soviet Marxism: A Critical Analysis.* New York: Columbia University Press, 1958.
1029. Marx, Karl. *Capital.* Translated by E. Paul and C. Paul. London: J. M. Dent, 1933.
1030. _____. *The Class Struggles in France, 1848–1850.* Moscow: Progress Publishers, 1972.
1031. _____. *A Contribution to the Critique of Political Economy.* Chicago: Charles H. Kerr, 1904.

1032. _____. *The Eighteenth Brumaire of Louis Bonaparte.* New York: International Publishers, 1963.
1033. _____. *On Revolution.* Edited and translated by S. Padover. New York: McGraw-Hill, 1971.
1034. Marx, Karl, and Friedrich Engels. *Basic Writings on Politics and Philosophy.* Edited by Lewis S. Feuer. Garden City, New York: Doubleday, 1959.
1035. _____. *Collected Works.* New York: International Publishers, 1975–.
1036. _____. *The Communist Manifesto.* New York: Appleton-Century-Crofts, 1955.
1037. _____. *The German Ideology.* New York: International Publishers, 1970.
1038. _____. *Revolution and Counter-Revolution.* Edited by Eleanor Marx Aveling. New York: Scribners, 1896.
1039. _____. *The Revolution of 1848–1849: Articles from the Neue Rheinische Zeitung.* New York: International Publishers, 1973.
1040. Mayo, Henry B. *Introduction to Marxist Theory.* New York: Oxford University Press, 1960.
1041. Mehring, Franz. *Karl Marx.* Translated by E. Fitzgerald. New York: Humanities Press, 1936.
1042. Mendel, Arthur P., ed. *Essential Works of Marxism.* New York: Bantam Books, 1961.
1043. Meszaros, Istuan. *Marx's Theory of Alienation.* New York: Harper and Row, 1972.
1044. Meyer, Alfred G. *Marxism Since the Communist Manifesto.* Washington, D.C.: American Historical Association Service Center for Teachers of History, 1961.
1045. _____. *Marxism: The Unity of Theory and Practice.* Cambridge, Massachusetts: Harvard University Press, 1954.
1046. Miliband, Ralph. *Marxism and Politics.* New York: Oxford University Press, 1977.
1047. Mills, C. Wright. *The Marxists.* New York: Dell, 1962.
1048. Nicolaievsky, Boris, and Otto Maenchen-Helfen. *Karl Marx: Man and Fighter.* Translated by G. David and E. Mosbacher. New York: Penguin Books, 1976.
1049. Ollmann, Bertell. *Alienation: Marx's Conception of Man in Capitalist Society.* New York: Cambridge University Press, 1971.
1050. Olsen, Richard. *Karl Marx.* Boston: Twayne Publishers, 1978.
1051. Padover, Saul K. *The Essential Marx.* New York: New American Library, 1979.
1052. _____. *Karl Marx: An Intimate Biography.* New York: McGraw-Hill, 1978.
1053. _____. *Karl Marx on History and People.* New York: McGraw-Hill, 1977.
1054. _____. *The Man Marx.* New York: McGraw-Hill, 1978.
1055. Parkes, Henry B. *Marxism: An Autopsy.* Chicago: University of Chicago Press, 1964.
1056. Parsons, Howard L., and John Somerville, eds. *Marxism, Revolution and Peace.* Atlantic Highlands, New Jersey: Humanities Press, 1977.
1057. Payne, Robert. *Marx.* New York: Simon and Schuster, 1968.

Marx and Marxism / 59

1058. Plamenatz, John. *Karl Marx's Philosophy of Man.* New York: Oxford University Press, 1975.
1059. Ponomarev, Boris N. *Marxism-Leninism: A Flourishing Science.* New York: International Publishers, 1980.
1060. Popper, Karl. *Open Society and Its Enemies.* 2 vols. Princeton: Princeton University Press, 1950.
1061. Prior, Andrew. *Revolution and Philosophy: The Significance of the French Revolution for Hegel and Marx.* Totowa, New Jersey: Rowman and Littlefield, 1979.
1062. Rachleff, Peter. *Marxism and Council Communism: Modern Revolutionary Thought.* Brooklyn, New York: Revisionist Press, 1974.
1063. Raddatz, Fritz J. *Karl Marx: A Political Biography.* Boston: Little, Brown, 1979.
1064. Rader, Melvin. *Marx's Interpretation of History.* New York: Oxford University Press, 1979.
1065. Raines, John C., and Thomas Dean, eds. *Marxism and Radical Religion: Essays Toward a Revolutionary Humanism.* Philadelphia: Temple University Press, 1970.
1066. Riazanov, David. *Karl Marx and Friedrich Engels.* New York: Monthly Review Press, 1974.
1067. Roberts, Paul Craig, and Matthew A. Stephenson. *Marx's Theory of Exchange, Alienation and Crisis.* Stanford: Hoover Institution, 1973.
1068. Rosdolsky, Roman. *The Making of Marx's 'Capital.'* Translated by P. Burgess. London: Pluto Press, 1977.
1069. Ross, Gandy D. *Marx and History: From Primitive Society to the Communist Future.* Austin: University of Texas Press, 1979.
1070. Sanderson, J. B. *Interpretation of the Political Ideas of Marx and Engels.* New York: Fernhill, 1969.
1071. Sayer, Derek. *Marx's Method: Ideology, Science and Critique in "Capital."* Atlantic Highlands, New Jersey: Humanities Press, 1979.
1072. Schneiderman, Jeremiah. *Sergei Zubatatov and Revolutionary Marxism: The Struggle for the Working Class in Tsarist Russia.* Ithaca: Cornell University Press, 1976.
1073. Seigel, Jerrold. *Marx's Fate: The Shape of a Life.* Princeton: Princeton University Press, 1978.
1074. Seliger, Martin. *The Marxist Conception of Ideology.* New York: Cambridge University Press, 1977.
1075. Semmel, Bernard, ed. *Marxism and the Science of War.* New York: Oxford University Press, 1981.
1076. Shaw, William H. *Marx's Theory of History.* Stanford: Stanford University Press, 1978.
1077. Singer, Peter. *Marx.* New York: Hill and Wang, 1980.
1078. Sprigge, C. J. S. *Karl Marx.* New York: Macmillan, 1962.
1079. Thomas, Paul. *Karl Marx and the Anarchists.* Boston: Routledge and Kegan Paul, 1980.
1080. Tucker, Robert C. *The Marxian Revolutionary Idea.* New York: W. W. Norton, 1969.
1081. _____ , ed. *The Marx-Engels Reader.* New York: W. W. Norton, 1972.
1082. _____ . *Philosophy and Myth in Karl Marx.* 2d ed. New York: Cambridge University Press, 1972.

1083. Ulam, Adam. *The Unfinished Revolution: An Essay on the Sources of Influence of Marxism and Communism.* New York: Random House, 1960.
1084. Vardys, V. Stanley, ed. *Karl Marx: Scientist? Revolutionary? Humanist?* Lexington, Massachusetts: D. C. Heath, 1971.
1085. Walker, Angus. *Marx: His Theory and Its Context.* New York: Longman, 1978.
1086. Wessell, Leonard P., Jr. *Karl Marx, Romantic Irony, and the Proletariat: The Mythopoetic Origins of Marxism.* Baton Rouge: Louisiana State University Press, 1979.
1087. Wesson, Robert G. *Why Marxism? The Continuing Success of a Failed Theory.* New York: Basic Books, 1976.
1088. Wolfe, Bertram D. *Marxism: One Hundred Years in the Life of a Doctrine.* New York: Dial, 1965.
1089. Wolfson, Murray. *Karl Marx.* New York: Columbia University Press, 1969.
1090. Zeitlin, Irving M. *Marxism: A Re-Examination.* New York: Van Nostrand Reinhold, 1967.

Friedrich Engels

Engels was a German communist revolutionary theorist and a co-founder with Karl Marx of modern socialism. Although he was not the original thinker Marx was, Engels' contributions were nonetheless important. He wrote jointly with Marx, researched with him, and continued their work after Marx died. Engels' contribution to Marxism is explained in the article by Donald C. Hodges (1965) and the book by Fritz Nova (1968). David McLellan's (1978) biography is one of the best.

Bibliography

1091. Eubanks, Cecil L. *Karl Marx and Friedrich Engels: An Analytical Bibliography.* New York: Garland, 1978.

Articles

1092. Berger, Martin. "Engels' Theory of the Vanishing Army: A Key to the Development of Marxist Revolutionary Tactics." *Historian* 37 (May 1975): 421–35.
1093. Hodges, Donald C. "Engels' Contribution to Marxism." *Socialist Register* 2 (1965): 297–310.
1094. Kitchen, Martin. "Friedrich Engels' Theory of War." *Military Affairs* 41 (October 1977): 119–24.

Books

1095. Berger, Martin. *Engels, Armies, and Revolution: The Revolutionary Tactics of Classical Marxism.* Hamden, Connecticut: Shoe String Press, 1977.
1096. Carlton, G. *Friedrich Engels: The Shadow Prophet.* Atlantic Highland, New Jersey: Fernhill House, 1965.
1097. Carver, Terrell. *Engels.* New York: Hill and Wang, 1980.
1098. Engels, Friedrich. *Development of Socialism from Utopia to Science.* Translated by D. DeLeon. New York: Labor News, 1934.
1099. Gemkow, Heinrich, et al. *Frederick Engels: A Biography.* Columbia, Missouri: South Asia Books, 1975.
1100. Henderson, W. O. *The Life of Friedrich Engels.* 2 vols. London: Frank Cass, 1974.
1101. Ilyichov, L. F., et al. *Frederick Engels: A Biography.* Brooklyn Heights, New York: Beekman Publishers, 1975.
1102. McLellan, David. *Friedrich Engels.* New York: Penguin Books, 1978.
1103. Marcus, Steven. *Engels, Manchester and the Working Class.* New York: Random House, 1975.
1104. Mayer, Gustav. *Friedrich Engels: A Biography.* New York: Howard Fertig, 1969.
1105. Nova, Fritz. *Friedrich Engels: His Contributions to Political Theory.* New York: Philosophical Library, 1968.
1106. Riazanov, David. *Karl Marx and Friedrich Engels.* New York: Monthly Review Press, 1974.

Socialism

Socialism is an economic system in which the means of production, distribution, and exchange are owned by the community as a whole; this may be the state or any smaller unit. Although Marx envisioned it as the stage succeeding capitalism and preceding communism, socialism is not limited to any single political form, since collective ownership theoretically can be managed by a parliamentary democracy or a political party claiming to act on behalf of the people. Socialism is a philosophy of revolution since it involves nothing less than the transformation of capitalist society into a socialist one, and that means the expropriation of the individual private owners of the means of production, distribution, and exchange. To bring about this change is what makes socialist parties revolutionary, with some dedicated to use violent means, others to use parliamentary, legal means. Since the mid-nineteenth century socialism has been a part of political movements seeking power by revolution (e.g., Russia) and parliamentary routes (e.g., Britain).

In addition to the one bibliographical citation below, those bibliographies listed under the sections "Marx and Marxism" and "Com-

62 / Concepts and Aspects of Revolution

munism" should also be consulted. Good histories of socialism can be found in the works by G. D. H. Cole (1961–1962), James D. Forman (1973), Edward Hyams (1973), Harry W. Laidler (1969), Carl Landauer (1959), George Lichtheim (1969, 1970), and Norman MacKenzie (1966). The documentary history by Albert Fried and Ronald Sanders (1964) and the collection of excerpts of the works of socialists edited by Irving Howe (1970) are useful. See also the books by revisionist socialist Eduard Bernstein (1909), turn-of-the-century French socialist leader Jean Jaurès (1906), Austrian/Czech revolutionary social democrat theorist Karl Kautsky (1909, 1913, 1971), and America's foremost socialist Norman Thomas (1963). For an introduction and analysis of socialism books by the following are recommended: Zygmunt Bauman (1976), Walter D. Connor (1978), S. N. Eisenstadt and Yael Azmon (1975), Michael Harrington (1972), Leo Huberman and Paul M. Sweezy (1968), and John Strachey (1936). For socialism in specific countries, regions, or periods the titles speak for themselves.

Bibliography

1107. Egbert, Donald Drew, and Stow Persons, eds. *Socialism and American Life.* 2 vols. Princeton: Princeton University Press, 1952.

Reference

1108. Rappoport, Angelo S. *Dictionary of Socialism.* New York: Gordon Press, 1976.

Documents

1109. Fried, Albert, and Ronald Sanders, eds. *Socialist Thought: A Documentary History.* Garden City, New York: Doubleday, 1964.

Articles

1110. Fletcher, Roger. "A Revisionist Looks at Imperialism: Eduard Bernstein's Critique of Imperialism and *Kolonialpolitik,* 1900–1914." *Central European History* 12 (September 1979): 237–71.
1111. Morgan, David W. "The Father of Revisionism Revisited: Eduard Bernstein." *Journal of Modern History* 51:3 (September 1979): 525–32.

Books

1112. Ader, Emile B. *Essentials of Socialism.* Woodbury, New York: Barron, 1966.
1113. Avineri, Shlomo, ed. *Marx's Socialism.* New York: Lieber-Atherton, 1973.
1114. Bauman, Zygmunt. *Socialism: The Active Utopia.* New York: Holmes and Meier, 1976.

Socialism / 63

1115. Beer, Max. *The General History of Socialism and Social Struggles.* New York: Russell and Russell, 1957.
1116. _____. *A History of British Socialism.* New York: Arno Press, 1979.
1117. Berki, Robert. *Socialism.* New York: St. Martin's Press, 1976.
1118. Bernal, Martin. *Chinese Socialism to 1907.* Ithaca: Cornell University Press, 1976.
1119. Bernstein, Eduard. *Evolutionary Socialism.* New York: Viking, 1909.
1120. Buttinger, Joseph. *In the Twilight of Socialism: A History of the Revolutionary Socialists in Austria.* New York: Praeger, 1953.
1121. Carr, Edward H. *Socialism in One Country, 1924–1926.* 3 vols. New York: Macmillan, 1971.
1122. Cole, G. D. H. *A History of Socialist Thought.* 5 vols. London: Macmillan, 1961–1962.
1123. Connolly, James. *Socialism and Nationalism.* Dublin: Sign of the Three Candles, 1948.
1124. Connor, Walter D. *Socialism, Politics, and Equality.* New York: Columbia University Press, 1978.
1125. Crosland, C. A. R. *The Future of Socialism.* New York: Macmillan, 1956.
1126. Crossman, R. H. S. *Politics of Socialism.* New York: Atheneum, 1965.
1127. Davis, Horace B. *Nationalism & Socialism: Marxist and Labor Theories of Nationalism to 1917.* New York: Monthly Review Press, 1967.
1128. Derfler, Leslie. *Socialism Since Marx: A Century of the European Left.* New York: St. Martin's Press, 1973.
1129. Desfosses, Helen, and Jacques Levesque, eds. *Socialism in the Third World.* New York: Praeger, 1975.
1130. Dumont, René. *Socialisms and Development.* Translated by R. Cunningham. New York: Praeger, 1973.
1131. Eastman, Max. *Reflections on the Failure of Socialism.* New York: Devin-Adair, 1955.
1132. Eisenstadt, S. N., and Yael Azmon. *Socialism and Tradition.* Atlantic Highlands, New Jersey: Humanities Press, 1975.
1133. Forman, James D. *Socialism: Its Theoretical Roots and Present-Day Development.* New York: New Viewpoints, 1973.
1134. Fraina, Louis C. *Revolutionary Socialism.* New York: Communist Press, 1918.
1135. Gay, Peter. *The Dilemma of Democratic Socialism: Eduard Bernstein's Challenge to Marx.* New York: Columbia University Press, 1962.
1136. Gorz, André. *Socialism and Revolution.* Translated by N. Denny. Garden City, New York: Doubleday, 1973.
1137. Gray, Alexander. *The Socialist Tradition.* London: Longmans, Green, 1946.
1138. Harrington, Michael. *Socialism.* New York: Saturday Review Press, 1972.
1139. Howe, Irving, ed. *Essential Works of Socialism.* New York: Bantam Books, 1970.
1140. Huberman, Leo, and Paul M. Sweezy. *Introduction to Socialism.* New York: Monthly Review Press, 1968.
1141. Hulse, James W. *Revolutionists in London: A Study of Five Unorthodox Socialists.* New York: Oxford University Press, 1970.
1142. Hyams, Edward. *The Millennium Postponed: Socialism from Sir Thomas More to Mao Tse-tung.* New York: New American Library, 1973.

64 / Concepts and Aspects of Revolution

1143. Jaurès, Jean. *Studies in Socialism.* Translated by M. Minturn. New York: Putnam, 1906.
1144. Jay, Douglas. *Socialism in the New Society.* New York: St. Martin's Press, 1963.
1145. Kautsky, Karl. *The Class Struggle.* New York: W. W. Norton, 1971.
1146. _____. *The Road to Power.* Chicago: Bloch, 1909.
1147. _____. *The Social Revolution.* Chicago: Charles H. Kerr, 1913.
1148. Kilroy-Silk, Robert. *Socialism Since Marx.* New York: Taplinger, 1972.
1149. Konrad, George, and Ivan Szelenyi. *The Intellectuals on the Road to Class Power of the Intelligentsia in Socialism.* New York: Harcourt Brace Jovanovich, 1979.
1150. Laidler, Harry W. *History of Socialism.* London: Routledge and Kegan Paul, 1969.
1151. Landauer, Carl. *European Socialism: A History of Ideas and Movements.* Berkeley: University of California Press, 1959.
1152. Lichtheim, George. *The Origins of Socialism.* New York: Praeger, 1969.
1153. _____. *A Short History of Socialism.* New York: Praeger, 1970.
1154. MacKenzie, Norman. *Socialism: A Short History.* Rev. ed. London: Hutchinson University Library, 1966.
1155. Medvedev, Roy A. *On Socialist Democracy.* Translated and edited by E. de Kadt. New York: Alfred A. Knopf, 1975.
1156. Parekh, Bhikhu, ed. *The Concept of Socialism.* New York: Holmes and Meier, 1975.
1157. Pierson, Stanley. *Marxism and the Origins of British Socialism: The Struggle for a New Consciousness.* Ithaca: Cornell University Press, 1973.
1158. Poulantzas, Nicos. *State, Power, Socialism.* New York: Schocken, 1979.
1159. Russell, Bertrand. *Roads to Freedom: Socialism, Anarchism and Syndicalism.* Edison, New Jersey: Allen Unwin, 1966.
1160. Salvadori, Massimo, ed. *Modern Socialism.* New York: Walker, 1968.
1161. Selsam, Howard. *Socialism and Ethics.* 2d ed. New York: International Publishers, 1943.
1162. Strachey, John. *The Theory and Practice of Socialism.* New York: Random House, 1936.
1163. Sweezy, Paul M., and Charles Bettelheim. *On the Transition to Socialism.* New York: Monthly Review Press, 1972.
1164. Thomas, Norman. *Socialism Re-Examined.* New York: W. W. Norton, 1963.
1165. Warren, Frank A. *An Alternative Vision: The Socialist Party in the 1930s.* Bloomington: Indiana University Press, 1974.

Communism

The lines of distinction among Marxism, socialism, and communism are finely drawn, or sometimes not drawn at all; communism is probably the most explosive of the three, at least to Americans. In one sense communism describes any society where virtually all property is held in common, with each person contributing what he is able and receiving what he needs. But communism also refers to a revolutionary movement dedicated to the overthrow of capitalism and the establishment first of socialism, then communism, and finally the classless society and stateless world. Communism also is that designation for Lenin's interpretation of Marxism as espoused by the Soviet Union. All these are related, but none are exactly the same. For a better understanding of the various shades of communism see the books by G. A. Almond et al (1954), Cyril E. Black and Thomas P. Thornton (1964), Franz Borkenau (1953, 1962), Leonard J. Cohen and Jane P. Shapiro (1974), Robert V. Daniels (1962), Isaac Deutscher (1966), Milovan Djilas (1957), James D. Forman (1973), Robert Nigel Carew Hunt (1957), Alfred G. Meyer (1967), Jules Monnerot (1977), Massimo Salvadori (1963), and Hugh Seton-Watson (1953).

Bibliographies

1166. Fund for the Republic. *Bibliography on the Communist Problem in the United States.* New York: Fund for the Republic, 1955.
1167. Hammond, Thomas T. *Soviet Relations and World Communism: A Selected Annotated Bibliography.* Princeton: Princeton University Press, 1965.
1168. Kolarz, Walter. *Books on Communism: A Bibliography.* 2d ed. London: Ampersand, 1963.
1169. Seidman, Joel I. *Communism in the United States: A Bibliography.* Ithaca: Cornell University Press, 1969.
1170. Whelan, Joseph G. *World Communism: A Selected Annotated Bibliography.* Washington, D.C.: U.S. Government Printing Office, 1964.
1171. Whetten, Lawrence L. *Current Research in Comparative Communism: An Analysis and Bibliographic Guide to the Soviet System.* New York: Praeger, 1976.

Reference

1172. Bocheński, Joseph M. *Handbook on Communism.* New York: Praeger, 1962.
1173. Sworakowski, Witold. *World Communism: A Handbook, 1918–1965.* Stanford: Hoover Institution, 1973.

Documents

1174. Gruber, Helmut. *International Communism in the Era of Lenin: A Documentary History.* Ithaca: Cornell University Press, 1967.
1175. Jacobs, Dan N., ed. *From Marx to Mao and Marchais: Documents on the Development of Communist Variations.* New York: Longman, 1979.

Books

1176. Ader, Emile B. *Communism: Classic and Contemporary.* Woodbury, New York: Barron, 1970.
1177. Almond, G. A., et al. *The Appeal of Communism.* Princeton: Princeton University Press, 1954.
1178. Berdyaev, Nicholas. *The Origins of Russian Communism.* Ann Arbor: University of Michigan Press, 1960.
1179. Black, Cyril E., and Thomas P. Thornton, eds. *Communism and Revolution: The Strategic Uses of Political Violence.* Princeton: Princeton University Press, 1964.
1180. Blackmer, Donald L. *Unity in Diversity: Italian Communism and the Communist World.* Cambridge, Massachusetts: M.I.T. Press, 1968.
1181. Borkenau, Franz. *European Communism.* New York: Harper and Brothers, 1953.
1182. _____ . *World Communism: A History of the Communist International.* Ann Arbor: University of Michigan Press, 1962.
1183. Brimmell, Jack H. *Communism in South East Asia: A Political Analysis.* London: Oxford University Press, 1959.
1184. Budenz, Louis F. *The Techniques of Communism.* New York: Arno Press, 1977.
1185. Burks, R. V. *The Dynamics of Communism in Eastern Europe.* Princeton: Princeton University Press, 1961.
1186. Cammett, John M. *Antonio Gramsci and the Origins of Italian Communism.* Stanford: Stanford University Press, 1967.
1187. Claudin, Fernando. *The Communist Movement: From Comintern to Cominform.* 2 vols. Translated by B. Pearce. New York: Monthly Review Press, 1976.
1188. Cohen, Carl, ed. *Communism, Fascism, and Democracy.* 2d ed. New York: Random House, 1972.
1189. Cohen, Leonard J., and Jane P. Shapiro, eds. *Communist Systems in Comparative Perspective.* Garden City, New York: Doubleday, 1974.
1190. Daniels, Robert V. *The Nature of Communism.* New York: Random House, 1962.
1191. Deakin, F. W.; H. Shukman; and H. T. Willetts. *A History of World Communism.* New York: Barnes and Noble, 1975.
1192. Delaney, Robert Finley. *The Literature of Communism in America.* Washington, D.C.: Catholic University of America Press, 1962.
1193. Deutscher, Isaac. *Ironies of History: Essays on Contemporary Communism.* New York: Oxford University Press, 1966.
1194. Djilas, Milovan. *The New Class: An Analysis of the Communist System.* London: Thames and Hudson, 1957.
1195. Ebenstein, William. *Communism in Theory and Practice.* New York: Holt, Rinehart and Winston, 1964.
1196. _____ . *Today's Isms: Communism, Fascism, Capitalism, Socialism.* Englewood Cliffs, New Jersey: Prentice-Hall, 1970.
1197. Fisher, Harold Henry. *The Communist Revolution: An Outline of Strategy and Tactics.* Stanford: Stanford University Press, 1955.

Communism / 67

1198. Forman, James D. *Communism: From Marx's "Manifesto" to Twentieth-Century Reality.* New York: New Viewpoints, 1973.
1199. Gyorgy, Andrew. *Communism in Perspective.* Boston: Allyn and Bacon, 1964.
1200. Hammond, Thomas T., and Robert Farrell, eds. *The Anatomy of Communist Takeovers.* New Haven: Yale University Press, 1975.
1201. Hook, Sidney. *Political Power and Personal Freedom: Critical Studies in Democracy, Communism, and Civil Rights.* New York: Criterion Books, 1959.
1202. Hudson, G. F. *Fifty Years of Communism: Theory and Practice, 1917–1967.* Baltimore: Penguin Books, 1971.
1203. Hunt, Robert Nigel Carew. *The Theory and Practice of Communism: An Introduction.* Rev. enl. ed. London: Geoffrey Bles, 1957.
1204. Kaplan, Morton A., ed. *The Many Faces of Communism.* New York: Free Press, 1979.
1205. Lane, David. *The Roots of Russian Communism: A Social and Historical Study of Russian Social Democracy, 1898–1907.* University Park: Pennsylvania State University Press, 1975.
1206. Laski, Harold J. *Communism.* Clifton, New Jersey: Augusta M. Kelley, 1927.
1207. Lunn, Alfred. *Communism and Socialism: A Study in the Technique of Revolution.* London: Eyre and Spottiswoode, 1939.
1208. Mattick, Paul. *Anti-Bolshevik Communism.* White Plains, New York: M. E. Sharpe, 1979.
1209. Mayer, Peter. *Cohesion and Conflict in International Communism: A Study of Marxist-Leninist Concepts and Their Application.* The Hague: Nijhoff, 1968.
1210. Meyer, Alfred G. *Communism.* New York: Random House, 1967.
1211. Monnerot, Jules. *Sociology of Communism.* Translated by J. Degras and R. Rees. Westport, Connecticut: Greenwood, 1977.
1212. Nollau, Günther. *International Communism and World Revolution: History and Methods.* London: Hollis and Carter, 1961.
1213. Polin, Raymond. *Marxian Foundations of Communism.* Chicago: Henry Regnery, 1966.
1214. Ponomarev, Boris N., et al. *History of the Communist Party of the Soviet Union.* Moscow: Foreign Languages Publishing House, 1960.
1215. Possony, Stefan T. *A Century of Conflict: Communist Techniques of World Revolution.* Chicago: Henry Regnery, 1953.
1216. Salvadori, Massimo. *The Rise of Modern Communism.* Rev. ed. New York: Holt, Rinehart and Winston, 1963.
1217. Schapiro, Leonard. *The Communist Party of the Soviet Union.* 2d ed. New York: Vintage Books, 1967.
1218. _____. *The Origin of the Communist Autocracy.* Cambridge, Massachusetts: Harvard University Press, 1977.
1219. Seton-Watson, Hugh. *The Imperialist Revolutionaries: Trends in World Communism in the 1960s and 1970s.* Stanford: Hoover Institution, 1978.
1220. _____. *Nationalism and Communism: Essays, 1946–1963.* London: Methuen, 1964.
1221. _____. *The Pattern of Communist Revolution.* London: Methuen, 1953.

1222. Tannahill, Neal R. *The Communist Parties of Western Europe: A Comparative Study.* Westport, Connecticut: Greenwood, 1979.
1223. Webb, Sidney, and Beatrice Webb. *Soviet Communism: A New Civilization?* 2 vols. New York: Longmans, Green, 1935.
1224. Wesson, Robert G. *Communism and Communist Systems.* Englewood Cliffs, New Jersey: Prentice-Hall, 1978.
1225. Woolsey, Theodore D. *Communism and Socialism in Their History and Theory: A Sketch.* New York: AMS Press, 1977.

Leadership and Elites

In any movement or organization, including revolutionary ones, leadership plays a crucial role; in fact, effective leadership, leadership that is able to adjust to changes in the course of a revolution, may be pivotal to success. Few leaders have made the successful transition through the various stages of revolution; Mao Tse-tung and Fidel Castro are notable exceptions. The elite among revolutionists are just as important. The article by Ellen Kay Trimberger (1972) and the books by the following are useful for further investigation: Theodore W. Adorno (1950), James MacGregor Burns (1978), William T. Daly (1972), James V. Downton (1973), Feliks Gross (1974), Alexander Groth (1966), Bruce Mazlish (1976), Mostafa Rejai (1979), and William A. Welsh (1979). The classic works in the field are by Gaetano Mosca (1939), Vilfredo Pareto (1968), and Max Weber (1964).

Articles

1226. Gouldner, Alvin W. "Prologue to a Theory of Revolutionary Intellectuals." *Telos* 26 (1975–1976): 3–36.
1227. Kautsky, John H. "Revolutionary and Managerial Elites in Modernizing Regimes." *Comparative Politics* 1:4 (July 1969): 441–67.
1228. Trimberger, Ellen Kay. "A Theory of Elite Revolutions." *Studies in Comparative International Development* 7:3 (Fall 1972): 191–207.
1229. Worsley, Peter M. "The Revolutionary Party as an Agency of Social Change (or the Politics of Mah jong)." In *Social Science and the New Societies,* edited by N. Hammond. East Lansing: Michigan State University, Social Science Research Bureau, 1973.

Books

1230. Adorno, Theodore W., et al. *The Authoritarian Personality.* New York: Harper and Row, 1950.
1231. Anderson, Donald W. *Permutations of the Revolutionary.* New York: Vantage, n.d.

1232. Beck, Carl, et al. *Comparative Communist Political Leadership.* New York: Longman, 1973.
1233. Bottomore, T. B. *Elites and Society.* New York: Penguin Books, 1966.
1234. Burns, James MacGregor. *Leadership.* New York: Harper and Row, 1978.
1235. Daly, William T. *The Revolutionary: A Review and Synthesis.* Beverly Hills, California: Sage, 1972.
1236. DePoncins, Leon V. *Secret Powers Behind the Revolution.* New York: Gordon Press, n.d.
1237. Donaldson, Robert H. *Stasis and Change in Revolutionary Elites: A Comparative Analysis of the 1956 Party Central Committee in China and the USSR.* Beverly Hills, California: Sage, 1970.
1238. Downton, James V. *Rebel Leadership: Commitment and Charisma in the Revolutionary Process.* New York: Free Press, 1973.
1239. Gross, Feliks. *The Revolutionary Party: Essays in the Sociology of Politics.* Westport, Connecticut: Greenwood, 1974.
1240. Groth, Alexander. *Revolution and Elite Access: Some Hypotheses on Aspects of Political Change.* Davis, California: Institute of Governmental Affairs, 1966.
1241. Klehr, Harvey E. *Communist Cadre: The Social Background of the American Communist Party Elites.* Stanford: Hoover Institution, 1978.
1242. Kohn, Hans. *Revolutions and Dictatorships.* Cambridge, Massachusetts: Harvard University Press, 1943.
1243. Lasswell, Harold D., and Daniel Lerner, eds. *World Revolutionary Elites: Studies in Coercive Ideological Movements.* Cambridge, Massachusetts: M.I.T. Press, 1965.
1244. Mazlish, Bruce. *The Revolutionary Ascetic: Evolution of a Political Type.* New York: Basic Books, 1976.
1245. Mosca, Gaetano. *The Ruling Class.* New York: McGraw-Hill, 1939.
1246. Pareto, Vilfredo. *The Rise and Fall of Elites.* Totowa, New Jersey: Bedminster Press, 1968.
1247. Price, Jane L. *Cadres, Commanders, and Commissars: The Training of the Chinese Communist Leadership.* Boulder, Colorado: Westview Press, 1975.
1248. Putnam, Robert D. *The Comparative Study of Political Elites.* Englewood Cliffs, New Jersey: Prentice-Hall, 1976.
1249. Randall, Margaret. *Part of the Solution: Portrait of a Revolutionary.* New York: New Directions, 1973.
1250. Rejai, Mostafa, *Leaders of Revolution.* Beverly Hills, California: Sage, 1979.
1251. Thirion, Andre. *Revolutionaries Without Revolution.* New York: Macmillan, 1975.
1252. Velli, M. *Manual for Revolutionary Leaders.* Detroit: Black and Red, 1974.
1253. Weber, Max. *The Theory of Social and Economic Organization.* Translated by Talcott Parsons. London: Collier-Macmillan, 1964.
1254. Welsh, William A. *Leaders and Elites.* New York: Holt, Rinehart and Winston, 1979.

Nationalism and Revolution

Anti-national sentiments pervade traditional Marxism. At best, Marx and Engels expected that national revolutions would merely be manifestations of the larger process of world revolution. Lenin took things further by viewing national revolutions (and the use of the forces of nationalism) as a preliminary step along the path to world revolution. The Russian Revolution, he said, was a first, not a final victory. Since then, however, talk of world, non-national revolution has been nothing more than lip service to the ideals of some theory or other, such as Marxism. The potent force of nationalism has been recognized as a worthy, justifiable vehicle, not a stop-gap. As Mao Tse-tung wrote in his *On New Democracy* (1940), "The universal truth of Marxism must be combined with specific national characteristics and acquire a definite national form if it is to be useful, and in no circumstances can it be applied subjectively as a mere formula." Thus, virtually all revolutions in this century, whatever their distinctive characteristics or political directions, have been strongly nationalistic too. And, as has been stated elsewhere, revolutionists have never made a successful revolution in a country they did not like.

Still, the relationship between nationalism and revolution is complicated and worthy of further scholarly investigation. The book by Glen St. J. Barclay (1972) is meant for the general reader, but provides an adequate introduction. Anthony D. Smith's books (1977, 1979) are probably the best recent works relating to the subject. But the reader would be wise to consult the standard works in the field by Carlton J. H. Hayes (1931), Hans Kohn (1951, 1962), Boyd C. Shafer (1965), and Louis L. Snyder (1954, 1968). A look at the index will turn up additional titles relating to nationalism and other subjects and in different countries.

Bibliographies

1255. Deutsch, Karl. *Interdisciplinary Bibliography on Nationalism.* Cambridge, Massachusetts: Technology Press of M.I.T., 1956.
1256. Pinson, Koppel S. *A Bibliographical Introduction to Nationalism.* New York: Columbia University Press, 1935.

Historiographies

1257. Shafer, Boyd C. *Nationalism: Interpreters and Interpretations.* 2d ed. Washington, D.C.: American Historical Association Service Center for Teachers of History, 1963.
1258. Wadlow, Joan K., and Leslie C. Duly. "Recent Literature on Nationalism: Some Reflections." *Canadian Review of Studies in Nationalism* 6 (1979): 1–12.

Article

1259. Geertz, Clifford. "After the Revolution: The Fate of Nationalism in the New States." In *Stability and Social Change,* edited by B. Barber and A. Inkeles. Boston: Little, Brown, 1971.

Books

1260. Barclay, Glen St. J. *Revolutions of Our Time: Twentieth-Century Nationalism.* New York: Praeger, 1972.
1261. Hayes, Carlton J. H. *The Historical Evolution of Modern Nationalism.* New York: Macmillan, 1931.
1262. Koenigsberg, Richard A. *The Psychoanalysis of Racism, Revolution and Nationalism.* New York: Library of Social Sciences, 1978.
1263. Kohn, Hans. *The Age of Nationalism.* New York: Harper and Row, 1962.
1264. _____. *The Idea of Nationalism.* New York: Macmillan, 1951.
1265. Lengyel, Emil. *Nationalism—The Last Stage of Communism.* New York: Funk and Wagnalls, 1969.
1266. Shafer, Boyd C. *Nationalism: Myth and Reality.* New York: Harcourt, Brace, 1965.
1267. Smith, Anthony D. *Nationalism in the Twentieth Century.* New York: New York University Press, 1979.
1268. _____. *Nationalist Movements.* New York: St. Martin's Press, 1977.
1269. Snyder, Louis L. *The Meaning of Nationalism.* New Brunswick, New Jersey: Rutgers University Press, 1954.
1270. _____. *The New Nationalism.* Ithaca: Cornell University Press, 1968.
1271. Symmons-Symonolewicz, Konstantin. *Nationalist Movements: A Comparative View.* Meadville, Pennsylvania: Maplewood Press, 1970.
1272. Wilson, Derek. *People, Revolutions, and Nations.* New York: International Publications Service, 1972.

Religion and Revolution

Whether the revolution has been Marxist or millennial, whether religion has been the target of revolutionists or the ideology, religion and/or religious characteristics frequently have played a role in revolutions. There is, more obviously, religion as revolutionary ideology (see Perry Miller's [1970] article on the American Revolution) during, for example, the Dutch Revolt (1555–1609), or the Irish Revolution (1916–1922), or the reaction of, say, the Catholic Church to periods of revolution (see E. E. Y. Hale's [1960] book). But there is also the parallel that exists between religion and revolution, with each having its own dogma, ideals, and even saints. Most revolutionary and religious ideologies have as a major goal the creation of the perfect human. Both are spiritual, calling upon followers to create rather than just to destroy.

Tocqueville (in his *The Old Regime and the French Revolution* [1955]) saw religious revolution as that type which eliminated one set of principles concerning the nature and destiny of man and the adoption of another set; Robespierre actually invented a new religion. Eric Hoffer (in his *The True Believer* [1951]) wrote about "religiofication," the art of turning practical purposes into holy causes. In recent times we have witnessed Islam assuming revolutionary proportions.

The best books on the subject are by Eugene C. Bianchi (1972) and Guenter Lewy (1974). Other selections below speak to more specific topics, and the index will yield further titles.

Articles

1273. Banks, Robert. "Revolution and Christian Radicalism." In *A World in Revolution?* edited by E. Kamenka. Canberra: Australian National University, 1970.

1274. Berens, John F. "Religion and Revolution Reconsidered: Recent Literature on Religion and Nationalism in Eighteenth-Century America." *Canadian Review of Studies in Nationalism* 6 (Fall 1979): 233-45.

1275. Crahan, Margaret E. "Salvation Through Christ or Marx: Religion in Revolutionary Cuba." *Journal of Interamerican Studies and World Affairs* 21 (February 1979): 156-84.

1276. Kelley, Dean M. "Guenter Lewy on Religion and Revolution: A Book Review Article." *Journal of Church and State* 16:4 (Autumn 1974): 509-15.

1277. Kent, J. H. S. "Methodism and Revolution." *Methodist History* 12 (July 1974): 136-44.

1278. Miller, Perry. "Religion as Revolutionary Ideology." In *The Role of Ideology in the American Revolution,* edited by J. R. Howe, Jr. New York: Holt, Rinehart and Winston, 1970.

1279. Moody, Joseph N. "Religion and the Democratic Revolution in Tocqueville." *Review of European History* 3 (June 1977): 282-85.

1280. Semmel, Bernard. "The Halévy Thesis: Methodism and Revolution." *Encounter* (July 1971): 44-55.

Books

1281. Bianchi, Eugene C. *The Religious Experience of Revolutionaries.* Garden City, New York: Doubleday, 1972.

1282. Billington, James H. *Fire in the Minds of Men: Origins of the Revolutionary Faith.* New York: Basic Books, 1980.

1283. Chadwick, Owen. *The Popes and European Revolution.* New York: Oxford University Press, 1981.

1284. Hales, E. E. Y. *Revolution and Papacy, 1769-1846.* Notre Dame, Indiana: University of Notre Dame Press, 1960.

1285. Hutchinson, Paul. *World Revolution and Religion*. Folcroft, Pennsylvania: Folcroft Library, 1931.
1286. Lewy, Guenter. *Religion and Revolution*. New York: Oxford University Press, 1974.
1287. Lloyd, Roger B. *Revolutionary Religion: Christianity, Fascism, and Communism*. New York: AMS Press, 1979.
1288. McFadden, Thomas, ed. *Liberation, Revolution and Freedom*. Somers, Connecticut: Seabury Press, 1975.
1289. Maier, Hans. *Revolution and Church: The Early History of Christian Democracy, 1789–1901*. Notre Dame, Indiana: University of Notre Dame Press, 1969.
1290. Raines, John C., and Thomas Dean, eds. *Marxism and Radical Religion: Essays toward a Revolutionary Humanism*. Philadelphia: Temple University Press, 1970.
1291. Semmel, Bernard. *The Methodist Revolution*. New York: Basic Books, 1973.
1292. Wilson, Colin. *Religion and the Rebel*. Westport, Connecticut: Greenwood, 1974.

Women and Revolution

The recognition of the importance of social history and the various features of the women's movement have resulted in an increase in scholarly attention to the role of women in revolution. There have been prominent female revolutionists, such as Emma Goldman and Rosa Luxemburg, but interest has spread to less obvious candidates and women in general. The best general works are by Carol R. Berkin and Clara M. Lovett (1979) and Sheila Rowbotham (1973). The other titles address specific situations, while checking the index will result in additional titles.

Articles

1293. Cobb, Richard. "The Women of the Commune." In *A Second Identity*, by R. Cobb. London: Oxford University Press, 1969.
1294. Knight, Amy. "Female Terrorists in the Russian Socialist Revolutionary Party." *Russian Review* 38:2 (April 1979): 139–59.
1295. MacCurtain, Margaret. "Women, the Vote and Revolution." In *Women in Irish Society: The Historical Dimension*, edited by M. MacCurtain and D. O'Corrain. Westport, Connecticut: Greenwood, 1979.

Books

1296. Beal, M. F. *Safe House: A Casebook Study of Revolutionary Feminism in the 1970s.* Eugene, Oregon: Northwest Matrix, 1976.
1297. Berkin, Carol R., and Clara M. Lovett, eds. *Women, War, and Revolution.* New York: Holmes and Meier, 1979.
1298. Broido, Vera. *Apostles Into Terrorists: Women and the Revolutionary Movement in the Russia of Alexander II.* New York: Viking, 1977.
1299. Clements, Barbara Evans. *Bolshevik Feminist: The Life of Aleksandra Kollontai.* Bloomington: Indiana University Press, 1980.
1300. Cook, Blanche, ed. *Crystal Eastman on Women and Revolution.* New York: Oxford University Press, 1978.
1301. _____ . *Toward the Great Change: Crystal and Max Eastman on Feminism, Anti-Militarism, and Revolution.* New York: Garland, 1974.
1302. Farnsworth, Beatrice. *Aleksandra Kollontai: Socialism, Feminism, and the Bolshevik Revolution.* Stanford: Stanford University Press, 1980.
1303. Jancar, Barbara Wolfe. *Women Under Communism.* Baltimore: Johns Hopkins University Press, 1978.
1304. Kerber, Linda K. *Women of the Republic: Intellect and Ideology in Revolutionary America.* Chapel Hill: University of North Carolina Press, 1980.
1305. Levy, Darline Gay, et al. *Women in Revolutionary Paris, 1789-1795.* Champaign: University of Illinois Press, 1979.
1306. Massell, Gregory J. *Surrogate Proletariat: Moslem Women and Revolutionary Strategies in Soviet Central Asia, 1919-1929.* Princeton: Princeton University Press, 1974.
1307. Norton, Mary Beth. *Liberty's Daughters: The Revolutionary Experience of American Women, 1750-1800.* Boston: Little, Brown, 1980.
1308. Porter, Cathy. *Alexandra Kollontai: The Lonely Struggle of the Woman Who Defied Lenin.* New York: Dial Press, 1980.
1309. Redstockings of the Women's Liberation Movement. *Feminist Revolution.* New York: Random House, 1979.
1310. Rowbotham, Sheila. *Women, Resistance & Revolution: A History of Women and Revolution in the Modern World.* New York: Pantheon Books, 1973.
1311. Stites, Richard. *The Women's Liberation Movement in Russia: Feminism, Nihilism, and Bolshevism, 1860-1930.* Princeton: Princeton University Press, 1978.

Evolution and Revolution

Article

1312. Jones, Ernest. "Evolution and Revolution." *International Journal of Psychoanalysis* 22 (1941): 193-208.

Books

1313. Boggs, James, and Grace Lee. *Revolution and Evolution in the Twentieth Century.* New York: Monthly Review Press, 1974.
1314. Buhl, W. L. *Evolution und Revolution.* Munich: Wilhelm Goldmann, 1970.
1315. Gotesky, Rubin, and Ervin Laszlo, eds. *Evolution—Revolution.* New York: Gordon, 1972.
1316. Hyndman, H. M. *The Evolution of Revolution.* London: G. Richard, 1920.
1317. Preston, Richard A., ed. *Perspectives on Revolution and Evolution.* Durham, North Carolina: Duke University Press, 1979.
1318. Wertheim, W. F. *Evolution and Revolution: The Rising Waves of Emancipation.* Baltimore: Penguin Books, 1974.

Literature and Revolution

1319. Brandes, Paul D. *The Rhetoric of Revolt.* Englewood Cliffs, New Jersey: Prentice-Hall, 1971.
1320. Dukore, Bernard F., ed. *Drama and Revolution.* New York: Irvington, 1971.
1321. Eastlake, William. *A Child's Garden of Verses for the Revolution.* New York: Grove Press, 1970.
1322. Ehrmann, Jacques, ed. *Literature and Revolution.* Boston: Beacon, 1970.
1323. Graham, Marcus, ed. *Anthology of Revolutionary Poetry.* Brooklyn, New York: Revisionist Press, 1975.
1324. Hachey, Thomas, and Ralph Weber, eds. *Voices of Revolution: Rebels and Rhetoric.* Hinsdale, Illinois: Dryden Press, 1972.
1325. Haywood, Max, and Leopold Lebedz, eds. *Literature and Revolution in Soviet Russia, 1917–62: A Symposium.* London: Oxford University Press, 1963.
1326. Katope, Christopher, and Paul Zolbrod, eds. *The Rhetoric of Revolution.* New York: Macmillan, 1970.
1327. "Literature in Revolution." *Tri Quarterly* 23–24 (Winter-Spring 1972), special issue.
1328. Lowenfels, Walter, ed. *In a Time of Revolution: Poems from Our Third World.* New York: Random House, 1970.
1329. Marquez, Robert, ed. *Latin American Revolutionary Poetry: A Bilingual Anthology.* New York: Monthly Review Press, 1975.
1330. O'Gorman, Ned, ed. *Prophetic Voices: Ideas and Words on Revolution.* New York: Random House, 1969.
1331. Rich, Andrea, and Arthur L. Smith. *Rhetoric of Revolution.* Durham, North Carolina: Moore Publishing, 1970.
1332. Sagarra, Eda. *Tradition and Revolution: German Literature and Society, 1830–1890.* New York: Basic Books, 1971.
1333. Winegarten, Renee. *Writers and Revolution: The Fatal Lure of Action.* New York: New Viewpoints, 1974.

Race and Revolution

In revolution, as in war, racial differences between contending forces are an important variable in determining or influencing the extent of the violence involved, with one group believing the other to be a threat to their own goals. The emphasis on race in revolution highlights a conflict in terms of "we-they," which is essentially a method of dehumanizing members of the opposition group; and dehumanization minimizes or even eliminates the need to justify acts of violence. Where racial differences become pronounced racial identity becomes a basis for political organization and, possibly, a source of revolution. While most theories of revolution are based upon economic and class factors, far too little attention has been paid to race and ethnic differences as variables in the revolutionary process. For further study the works of Leo Kuper (1971, 1974) are invaluable, as are the writings of black psychoanalyst and revolutionist Frantz Fanon (1966, 1967). Also especially useful are the books by Jacques Barzun (1965), Richard A. Koenigsberg (1978), and Ivar Oxaal (1971).

Article

1334. Kuper, Leo. "Theories of Revolution and Race Relations." *Comparative Studies in Society and History* 13:1 (January 1971): 87–107.

Books

1335. Barzun, Jacques. *Race: A Study in Superstition.* New York: Harper and Row, 1965.
1336. Fanon, Frantz. *Black Skin, White Masks.* Translated by C. L. Markmann. New York: Grove Press, 1967.
1337. _____. *The Wretched of the Earth.* New York: Grove Press, 1966.
1338. Gist, N. P., and A. P. Dworkin, eds. *The Blending of Races: Marginality and Identity in World Perspective.* New York: Wiley-Interscience, 1972.
1339. Isaacs, Harold. *Idols of the Tribe: Group Identity and Political Change.* New York: Harper and Row, 1975.
1340. Jenkins, Robin. *Exploitation: The World Power Structure and the Inequality of Nations.* London: MacGibbon and Kee, 1970.
1341. Koenigsberg, Richard A. *The Psychoanalysis of Racism, Revolution and Nationalism.* New York: Library of Social Sciences, 1978.
1342. Kuper, Leo. *Race, Class and Power: Ideology and Revolutionary Change in Plural Societies.* London: Duckworth, 1974.
1343. Oxaal, Ivar. *Race and Revolutionary Consciousness.* Cambridge, Massachusetts: Schenkman, 1971.
1344. Segal, Ronald. *The Race War.* London: Cape, 1966.
1345. Snyder, Louis L. *The Idea of Racialism: Its Meaning and History.* Princeton: D. Van Nostrand, 1962.

1346. Tinker, Hugh. *Race, Conflict and the International Order: From Empire to United Nations.* New York: St. Martin's Press, 1977.
1347. Van Den Berghe, P. L. *Race and Racism: A Comparative Perspective.* New York: John Wiley, 1967.

Modernization and Revolution

Here is another area in which much more work needs to be done. Modernization can be a productive or disruptive force. Rapid societal changes, modern advances, especially when seen by but not benefitting key groups, along with urbanization and other effects of modernization are often too much for a society to absorb, as has been the case in parts of Africa and Latin America. On another level, that of actively striving for modernization, each of China's revolutions in the twentieth century have been part of a drive towards modernization. In fact, most revolutions in economically backward countries have been part of efforts to overcome underdevelopment; in this sense they have been revolutions of modernization. The few titles below are a good place to begin an exploration of the subject, while checking the index will reveal several more.

Articles

1348. Halpern, Manfred. "The Revolution of Modernization in National and International Society." In *Revolution (Nomos VIII)*, edited by C. J. Friedrich. New York: Atherton, 1966.
1349. Tilly, Charles. "Does Modernization Breed Revolution?" *Comparative Politics* 5:3 (April 1973): 425–48.

Books

1350. Eisenstadt, S. N. *Modernization: Protest and Change.* Englewood Cliffs, New Jersey: Prentice-Hall, 1966.
1351. Kautsky, John H. *Patterns of Modernizing Revolutions: Mexico and the Soviet Union.* Beverly Hills, California: Sage, 1975.

Comparative Studies

The comparative study of aspects of the revolutionary process can be highly instructive and stimulating. Too often, however, two or more revolutions are discussed side by side, with the actual comparing left to the reader; such is the case with Lawrence Kaplan's edited collection (1973). There are many fine studies among the works below. Some of the more interesting and provocative are the articles by Robert Blackey (1974), Alfred Cobban (1951), Isaac Deutscher (1952), A. A. Fursenko (1976), A. James Gregor and Maria Hsia Chang (1978), Elbaki Hermassi (1976), and Theda Skocpol (1976), and the books by C. W. Cassinelli (1976), Ronald H. Chilcote (1972), Henry Steele Commager (1977), S. N. Eisenstadt (1978), F. Gentz (1959), Thomas H. Greene (1974), and Mostafa Rejai (1977). Theda Skocpol's book (1979) is not only an excellent comparison of the three revolutions in the subtitle, but also an important contribution to our understanding of the sociology of revolution. Other works of comparison can be found in the opening sections of Chapters 3 through 9.

Historiography

1352. Lipsky, William E. "Comparative Approaches to the Study of Revolution: A Historiographic Essay." *Review of Politics* 38:4 (October 1976): 494–509.

Articles

1353. Banning, Lance. "Jeffersonian Ideology and the French Revolution: A Question of Liberticide at Home." *Studies in Burke and His Time* 17:2 (Winter 1976): 5–26.
1354. Bernstein, Thomas P. "Leadership and Mass Mobilisation in the Soviet and Chinese Collectivisation Campaigns of 1929–30 and 1955–56: A Comparison." *China Quarterly* 31 (July-September 1967): 1–47.
1355. Blackey, Robert. "Fanon and Cabral: A Contrast in Theories of Revolution for Africa." *Journal of Modern African Studies* 12:2 (June 1974): 191–209.
1356. Cobban, Alfred. "Age of Revolutionary Wars: An Historical Parallel." *Review of Politics* 13:2 (April 1951): 131–41.
1357. Daniels, Robert V. "The Chinese Revolution in Russian Perspective." *World Politics* 13:2 (January 1961): 210–30.
1358. Deutscher, Isaac. "The French Revolution and the Russian Revolution: Some Suggestive Analogies." *World Politics* 4:3 (April 1952): 369–81.
1359. Ellis, Gene. "After the Revolutions: The Development Paths of Ethiopia and Peru Compared." *Ethiopianist Notes* 2:3 (1978): 19–38.
1360. Fursenko, A. A. "The American and French Revolutions Compared: The View from the U.S.S.R." Translated by Gilbert H. McArthur. *William and Mary Quarterly* 33 (July 1976): 481–500.
1361. Gabriel, Phyllis S., and Susan M. Stuart. "The Role of Health Care in Socialist Revolutions: Mozambique and Cuba." *Ufahamu* 8:2 (Fall 1978): 35–65.
1362. Gorrow, Bernard J. "The Comparative Study of Revolution." *Midwest Sociologist* 17 (1955): 54–59.
1363. Gregor, A. James, and Maria Hsia Chang. "Maoism and Marxism in Comparative Perspective." *Review of Politics* 40:3 (July 1978): 307–27.

1364. Gurr, Ted Robert. "A Causal Model of Civil Strife: A Comparative Analysis Using New Indices." *American Political Science Review* 62:4 (December 1968): 1104–24.

1365. _____. "Sources of Rebellion in Western Societies: Some Quantitative Evidence." *Annals of the American Academy of Political and Social Science* 391 (September 1970): 128–44.

1366. Halliday, Fred. "The Arc of Revolutions: Iran, Afghanistan, South Yemen, Ethiopia." *Race and Class* 20 (Spring 1979): 373–90.

1367. Hermassi, Elbaki. "Toward a Comparative Study of Revolutions." *Comparative Studies in Society and History* 18:2 (April 1976): 211–35.

1368. Kimmel, Michael. "Absolutism in Crisis: The English Civil War and the Fronde." In *The World-System of Capitalism: Past and Present*, edited by W. L. Goldfrank. Beverly Hills, California: Sage, 1979.

1369. Livingston, Donald W. "Burke, Marcuse, and the Historical Justification for Revolution." *Studies in Burke and His Time* 14:2 (Winter 1972–1973): 119–31.

1370. Mazrui, Ali A. "Gandhi, Marx and the Warrior Tradition in African Resistance: Towards Androgynous Liberation." *Journal of Asian and African Studies* 12 (January–October 1977): 179–96.

1371. Pohl, James W. "The American Revolution and the Vietnamese War: Pertinent Military Analogies." *History Teacher* 7 (February 1974): 255–65.

1372. Selden, Mark. "People's War and the Transformation of Peasant Society: China and Vietnam." In *America's Asia*, edited by E. Friedman and M. Selden. New York: Pantheon Books, 1971.

1373. Shepherd, George W. "Liberation Theology and Class Struggle in Southern Africa and Latin America." *Review of Black Political Economics* 9 (Winter 1979): 159–73.

1374. Singh, Kusum J. "Gandhi and Mao as Mass Communicators." *Journal of Communication* 29 (Summer 1979): 94–101.

1375. Skocpol, Theda. "France, Russia, China: A Structural Analysis of Social Revolutions." *Comparative Studies in Society and History* 18:2 (April 1976): 175–210.

1376. _____. "Old Regime Legacies and Communist Revolutions in Russia and China." *Social Forces* 55:2 (December 1976): 284–315.

1377. _____. "State and Revolution: Old Regimes and Revolutionary Crises in France, Russia and China." *Theory and Society* 7:1–2 (January–March 1979): 7–95.

1378. Smith, Robert Freeman. "The American Revolution and Latin America: An Essay in Imagery, Perceptions, and Ideological Influence." *Journal of Interamerican Studies and World Affairs* 20 (November 1978): 421–42.

1379. Spalding, James C. "Loyalist as Royalist, Patriot as Puritan: The American Revolution as a Repetition of the English Civil Wars." *Church History* 45 (September 1976): 329–40.

1380. Tucker, Gerald E. "Machiavelli and Fanon: Ethics, Violence, and Action." *Journal of Modern African Studies* 16:3 (September 1978): 397–415.

Books

1381. Bandyopadhyaya, Jayantanuja. *Mao Tse-Tung and Gandhi: Perspectives on Social Transformation*. New York: International Publications Service, 1974.

1382. Bowden, Tom. *The Breakdown of Public Security: The Case of Ireland, 1916–1921, and Palestine, 1936–1939*. Beverly Hills, California: Sage, 1977.

80 / Concepts and Aspects of Revolution

1383. Brutents, K. N. *National Liberation Revolutions Today: Some Questions of Theory.* 2 vols. Translated by Y. Sdobnikov; J. Bushnell; and K. Bushnell. Chicago: Progress Publishers, 1977.

1384. Cassinelli, C. W. *Total Revolution: A Comparative Study of Germany under Hitler, the Soviet Union under Stalin, and China under Mao.* Santa Barbara, California: ABC-Clio, 1976.

1385. Chilcote, Ronald H., ed. *Protest and Resistance in Angola and Brazil: Comparative Studies.* Berkeley: University of California Press, 1972.

1386. Commager, Henry Steele. *The Empire of Reason: How Europe Imagined and America Realized the Enlightenment.* Garden City, New York: Doubleday, 1977.

1387. Dahl, Robert A., ed. *Regimes and Opposition.* New Haven: Yale University Press, 1973.

1388. Detweiler, Robert, and Ramón Eduardo Ruiz, eds. *Liberation in the Americas: Comparative Aspects of the Independence Period in Mexico and the United States.* San Diego, California: Campanile Press, 1978.

1389. Eastman, Max. *Marx and Lenin: The Science of Revolution.* Westport, Connecticut: Hyperion Press, 1973.

1390. Eisenstadt, S. N. *Revolution and the Transformation of Societies: A Comparative Study of Civilizations.* New York: Free Press, 1978.

1391. *England and the Fronde: The Impact of the English Civil War and Revolution on France.* Washington, D.C.: Folger Books, 1978.

1392. Fennessy, R. R. *Burke, Paine, and the Rights of Man.* The Hague: M. Nijhoff, 1963.

1393. Fülöp-Miller, René. *Lenin and Gandhi.* New York: Garland Publishing, 1927.

1394. Gentz, F. *The French and American Revolutions Compared.* Chicago: Henry Regnery, 1959.

1395. Goodwin, Albert, ed. *The American and French Revolutions, 1763-93.* Vol. 8 in *The New Cambridge Modern History.* New York: Cambridge University Press, 1965.

1396. Greene, Thomas H. *Comparative Revolutionary Movements.* Englewood Cliffs, New Jersey: Prentice-Hall, 1974.

1397. Gurley, John G. *Challengers to Capitalism: Marx, Lenin, and Mao.* New York: W. W. Norton, 1979.

1398. Harris, Nigel. *India-China: Underdevelopment and Revolution.* Durham, North Carolina: Carolina Academic Press, 1974.

1399. Ingraham, Barton. *Political Crime in Europe: A Comparative Study of France, Germany and England.* Berkeley: University of California Press, 1979.

1400. Kaplan, Lawrence, ed. *Revolutions: A Comparative Study: From Cromwell to Castro.* New York: Random House, 1973.

1401. Nomad, Max. *Political Heretics: From Plato to Mao Tse-tung.* Ann Arbor: University of Michigan Press, 1963.

1402. Rejai, Mostafa. *The Comparative Study of Revolutionary Strategy.* New York: David McKay, 1977.

1403. Schöffer, I., ed. *Zeven Revoluties.* Amsterdam: T. H. de Bussy, n.d.

1404. Skocpol, Theda. *States and Social Revolutions: A Comparative Analysis of France, Russia, & China.* New York: Cambridge University Press, 1979.

1405. Trimberger, Ellen Kay. *Revolution From Above: Military Bureaucrats, and Development in Japan, Turkey, Egypt and Peru.* New Brunswick, New Jersey: Transaction Press, 1978.

1406. Wager, W. Warren. *World Views: A Study in Comparative History.* Hinsdale, Illinois: Dryden Press, 1977.
1407. Welch, Claude E., Jr., ed. *Soldier and State in Africa: A Comparative Analysis of Military Intervention and Political Change.* Evanston, Illinois: Northwestern University Press, 1970.
1408. Wittfogel, Karl A. *Oriental Despotism: A Comparative Study of Total Power.* New Haven: Yale University Press, 1957.
1409. Wolfstein, E. Victor. *The Revolutionary Personality: Lenin, Trotsky, Gandhi.* Princeton: Princeton University Press, 1967.

World Revolution

Whether or not the world will ever be in a state of near global-wide revolution, or in a position where revolutions have occurred over a period of time and consequently have transformed the world in some organized way is, of course, impossible to say. Some revolutionists, such as Marx and Lenin, predicted it. The scholars whose works are listed below examine aspects of the question of world revolution from a variety of perspectives. A look at the index will reveal additional titles.

Article

1410. Skocpol, Theda, and Ellen Kay Trimberger. "Revolutions and the World-Historical Development of Capitalism." In *Social Change in the Capitalist World*, edited by B. H. Kaplan. Beverly Hills, California: Sage, 1978.

Books

1411. Dawson, Christopher. *The Movement of World Revolution.* London: Sheed and Ward, 1959.
1412. Gurr, Ted Robert, et al. *World Patterns of Conflict.* Beverly Hills, California: Sage, 1979.
1413. James, Cyril L. *World Revolution, 1917–1936.* Westport, Connecticut: Hyperion Press, 1973.
1414. Kamenka, Eugene, ed. *A World in Revolution?* Canberra: Australian National University, 1970.
1415. Kelly, George A., and Clifford W. Brown, Jr., eds. *Struggles in the State: Sources and Patterns of World Revolution.* New York: John Wiley, 1970.
1416. Lasswell, Harold D., and Dorothy Blumenstock. *World Revolutionary Propaganda.* New York: Alfred A. Knopf, 1939.
1417. McKenzie, Kermit E. *Comintern and World Revolution, 1928–1943: The Shaping of Doctrine.* New York: Columbia University Press, 1964.
1418. Reissner, Will. *Dynamics of World Revolution Today.* New York: Pathfinder Press, 1974.

1419. Toynbee, Arnold J. *America and the World Revolution.* New York: Oxford University Press, 1962.

Miscellaneous

The reference works in this section are worthy of note. The book by Edward Hyams (1973) is a useful guide to many of history's revolutions, revolutionists, and related subjects. Henry C. Kenski, Jr.'s pamphlet (1974) presents the results of a survey on which books on revolution and political violence were being used in college classes, and which were considered the most important. The rest of what appears below is a mixed bag of articles and books that do not readily fit in some other section. Some of the more notable are the articles by John Dunn (1977) and Ted Robert Gurr (1970), and the books by Hannah Arendt (1972), Reinhard Bendix (1978), S. N. Eisenstadt (1968), Melvin J. Lasky (1976), Frank E. Manuel and Fritzie P. Manuel (1979), Charles Tilly (1978), and Jack Woddis (1972).

Reference

1420. Hyams, Edward. *A Dictionary of Modern Revolution.* New York: Taplinger, 1973.
1421. Kenski, Henry C., Jr. *On Teaching Courses on Revolution and Comparative Political Violence at American Colleges and Universities: A Research Note.* Institute Series, no. 21. Tucson: Institute of Government Research, University of Arizona, 1974.

Articles

1422. Davis, Richard. "India in Irish Revolutionary Propaganda, 1905-22." *Journal of Asiatic Society, Bangladesh* 22 (April 1977): 66-89.
1423. Dunn, John. "The Success and Failure of Modern Revolutions." In *Radicalism in the Contemporary Age,* edited by S. Bialer and S. Sluzar. Vol. 3. Boulder, Colorado: Westview Press, 1977.
1424. Gurr, Ted Robert. "Sources of Rebellion in Western Societies: Some Quantitative Evidence." *Annals of the American Academy of Political and Social Science* 391 (September 1970): 128-44.
1425. Partridge, P. H. "Contemporary Revolutionary Ideas." In *A World in Revolution?* edited by E. Kamenka. Canberra: Australian National University, 1970.
1426. Popper, Karl. "Reason or Revolution?" In *The Positivist Dispute in German Sociology,* edited by T. W. Adorno. New York: Harper and Row, 1976.
1427. Scheer, Robert. "Enough Already: Creating Zombies in the Name of Social Utopia." *New Times* (8 January 1979).

1428. "Symposium: Kant on Revolution." *Journal of the History of Ideas* 32 (July-September 1971).
1429. Topolski, Jerzy. "Revolutionary Consciousness in America and Europe from Mid-Eighteenth to the Early Nineteenth Century as a Methodological and Historical Problem." In *The American and European Revolutions,* edited by J. Pelenski. Iowa City: University of Iowa Press, 1980.
1430. Wandycz, Piotr S. "The American Revolution and the Partitions of Poland." In *The American and European Revolutions,* edited by J. Pelenski. Iowa City: University of Iowa Press, 1980.

Books

1431. Arendt, Hannah. *Crises of the Republic: Lying in Politics, Civil Disobedience, On Violence, Thoughts on Politics and Revolution.* New York: Harcourt Brace Jovanovich, 1972.
1432. Bendix, Reinhard. *Kings or People: Power and the Mandate to Rule.* Berkeley: University of California Press, 1978.
1433. Bukharin, Nikolai. *Historical Materialism: A System of Sociology.* Translated from 3rd Russian ed., 1921. Ann Arbor: University of Michigan, 1969.
1434. Butler, Ed. *Revolution Is My Profession.* Los Angeles: Twin Circle, 1968.
1435. Cornforth, Maurice, ed. *Rebels and Their Causes: Essays in Honour of A. L. Morton.* Atlantic Highlands, New Jersey: Humanities Press, 1979.
1436. Degrood, David H. *Dialectics and Revolution.* Atlantic Highlands, New Jersey: Humanities Press, 1978.
1437. Dunayevskaya, Raya. *Nationalism, Communism, Marxist-Humanism and the Afro-Asian Revolutions.* Cambridge: Cambridge Left Labour Club, 1961.
1438. Eisenstadt, S. N., ed. *Max Weber: On Charisma and Institution Building.* Chicago: University of Chicago Press, 1968.
1439. Gerassi, John, ed. *The Coming of the New International: A Revolutionary Anthology.* New York: World Publishing, 1971.
1440. _____ , ed. *Towards Revolution: The Revolution Reader—Writings from Contemporary Revolutionary Leaders throughout the World.* 2 vols. London: Weidenfeld and Nicolson, 1971.
1441. Girling, John L. S. *America and the Third World: Revolution and Intervention.* Boston: Routledge and Kegan Paul, 1980.
1442. Greig, Ian. *Today's Revolutionaries.* Elmsford, New York: British Book Center, 1974.
1443. Griffiths, Brian, ed. *Revolution Change?* Downers Grove, Illinois: InterVarsity Press, 1972.
1444. Hensman, C. R. *From Gandhi to Guevara: The Polemics of Revolt.* London: Penguin Books, Allen Lane, 1969.
1445. Hicks, Granville. *John Reed: The Making of a Revolutionary.* New York: Macmillan, 1936.
1446. Jackson, James. *Revolutionary Tracings.* New York: International Publishers, 1974.
1447. Kellner, Douglas, ed. *Karl Korsch: Revolutionary Theory.* Austin: University of Texas Press, 1977.
1448. Korshin, Paul J., ed. *Studies in Change and Revolution.* Elmsford, New York: British Book Center, 1975.

1449. Lasky, Melvin J. *Utopia & Revolution.* Chicago: University of Chicago Press, 1976.
1450. Lunacharsky, Anatoly V. *Revolutionary Silhouettes.* New York: Hill and Wang, 1968.
1451. MacLean, John. *In the Rapids of Revolution.* Dallas: Southwest Book Services, 1978.
1452. Manuel, Frank E., and Fritzie P. Manuel. *Utopian Thought in the Western World.* Cambridge, Massachusetts: Harvard University Press, Belknap Press, 1979.
1453. Martic, Milos. *Insurrection: Five Schools of Revolutionary Thought.* New York: Dunellen, 1975.
1454. Miller, Norman, and Roderick Aya, eds. *Revolution Reconsidered.* New York: Free Press, 1970.
1455. Nalbandian, Louise Z. *The Armenian Revolutionary Movement.* Berkeley: University of California Press, 1963.
1456. Patai, Raphael. *Myth and Modern Man.* Englewood Cliffs, New Jersey: Prentice-Hall, 1972.
1457. Pelenski, Jaroslaw, ed. *The American and European Revolutions, 1776-1848: Sociopolitical and Ideological Aspects.* Iowa City: University of Iowa Press, 1980.
1458. Revel, Jean-François. *The Totalitarian Temptation.* Garden City, New York: Doubleday, 1977.
1459. *Revolutionary Thought from Marx to Mao.* 9 vols. San Francisco: China Books, 1977.
1460. Richards, Michael. *Revolution in the Twentieth Century.* St. Louis: Forum Press, 1976.
1461. Rickards, Maurice. *Posters of Protest and Revolution.* New York: Walker, 1970.
1462. Rosenstone, Robert A. *Romantic Revolutionary: A Biography of John Reed.* New York: Alfred A. Knopf, 1975.
1463. Russell, Bertrand. *Roads to Freedom: Socialism, Anarchism and Syndicalism.* London: Allen and Unwin, 1918.
1464. Seton-Watson, Hugh. *The New Imperialism.* New York: Capricorn Books, 1967.
1465. Stampfer, Judah. *Face and Shadow: Approaches to the Modern Revolutionary Impulse.* Los Angeles: S and S Enterprises, 1971.
1466. Tilly, Charles. *From Mobilization to Revolution.* Reading, Massachusetts: Addison-Wesley, 1978.
1467. Turok, Ben, ed. *Revolutionary Thought in the 20th Century.* London: Zed Press, 1980.
1468. Walzer, Michael. *Obligations: Essays on Disobedience, War, and Citizenship.* Cambridge, Massachusetts: Harvard University Press, 1970.
1469. Winkler, Heinrich August. *Revolution, Staat, Faschismus: Zur Revision des Historischen Materialismus.* Göttingen: Vandenhoeck and Ruprecht, 1978.
1470. Wistrich, Robert S. *Revolutionary Jews From Marx to Trotsky.* New York: Barnes and Noble, 1976.
1471. Woddis, Jack. *New Theories of Revolution.* New York: International Publishers, 1972.

# Ancient and Medieval

"Revolutions . . . occurred and always will occur so long as human nature remains the same."
Thucydides
History of the Peloponnesian War

For the approximately two thousand years covered by this chapter there are precious few titles. But that should not be taken to mean that as a period for the study of revolutions it was insignificant, especially as it relates to the Greeks.

Although the Greeks had no single word for the phenomenon of revolution, it is to them that we owe the beginnings of our study. What the Greeks called "revolution"— or "uprising," or "change," or "transformation"—involved a change of rulers coupled with accompanying social changes. They were astute enough to observe that the rise and fall of states or the overthrow of rulers affected social relationships, sometimes in a startling or revolutionary way.

The works below by Thucydides, Plato, Polybius, and especially Aristotle are valuable for laying the foundations of contemporary analysis of revolutions. Thucydides said that revolutions were inevitable given the character of human nature, but each revolution was different insofar as circumstances always changed. Plato's contribution to the field is less majestic since he was more concerned with the permanence of politics than in political change. Polybius described how revolutions occurred in a cyclical pattern, with the wheel of Fortune turning and societies changing naturally from one form of government to another until they came back to where they began.

Aristotle probed the subject most deeply. He evaluated the causes of revolutions as society changed from one form of government to another; revolutions were not extraordinary, but necessary and even useful facts of political life. Aristotle gave us the concept of "state of mind," which historians and sociologists still find significant in evaluating the preconditions of revolutions. Among other things, Aristotle also noted that where political and economic power were separate, revolution was possible.

There were upheavals in Roman and medieval times, but they tended to be more rebellious than revolutionary. For revolutionary activity in ancient Greece the article by A. Fuks (1974) is useful. For revolutions in ancient Rome see the books by F. R. Cowell (1962) and Ronald Syme (1939). For revolutions in the middle ages see the books by Guy Fourquin

(1978) and M. Mollat and P. Wolff (1973); specifically, the Hussite Revolution may be explored in the books by Frederick Heymann (1955), Howard Kaminsky (1967), and John M. Klassen (1978).

1472. Petrie, W. M. Flinders. *The Revolutions of Civilisation.* New York: Haskell House, 1971.

Greece

Articles

1473. Fuks, A. "Patterns and Types of Social-Economic Revolution in Greece from the Fourth to the Second Century B.C." *Ancient Society* 5 (1974): 51-81.
1474. Kort, Fred. "The Quantification of Aristotle's Theory of Revolution." *American Political Science Review* 46:2 (June 1952): 486-93.
1475. Osborne, Michael J. "Kallias, Phaidros and the Revolt of Athens in 287 B.C." *Zeitschrift Papyrologie Epigraphy* 35 (1979): 181-94.

Books

1476. Aristotle. *The Politics of Aristotle.* Translated by B. Jowett. Oxford: Clarendon Press, 1885, especially Books II and V.
1477. De Romilly, Jacqueline. *The Rise and Fall of States According to Greek Authors.* Ann Arbor: University of Michigan Press, 1977.
1478. Gouldner, Alvin W. *Enter Plato.* New York: Basic Books, 1965.
1479. Lloyd, G. E. R. *Aristotle: The Growth and Structure of His Thought.* New York: Cambridge University Press, 1968.
1480. Luccioni, Jean. *La Pensée Politique de Platon.* New York: Arno Press, 1979.
1481. Plato. *The Republic.* Translated by B. Jowett. Garden City, New York: Doubleday, 1960, especially Books VIII and IX.
1482. Polybius. *The Histories of Polybius.* 2 vols. Translated by E. S. Shuckburgh. Bloomington: Indiana University Press, 1962, especially Book VI.
1483. Robin, Léon. *Aristote.* New York: Arno Press, 1979.
1484. Thucydides. *History of the Peloponnesian War.* Edited and translated by Sir Richard Livingstone. Oxford: Oxford University Press, 1960, especially Book III.

Rome

Articles

1485. Bernstein, Alvin H. "The Accidental Revolution (Roman Republic)." *Historian* 41 (May 1979): 513-20.
1486. Carroll, Kevin K. "The Date of Boudicca's Revolt." *Britannia* 10 (1979): 197-202.

Books

1487. Andrews, I. *Boudicca's Revolt.* New York: Cambridge University Press, 1972.
1488. Cowell, F. R. *The Revolutions of Ancient Rome.* New York: Praeger, 1962.
1489. Heaton, John Wesley. *Mob Violence in the Late Roman Republic, 133-49 B.C.* Urbana: University of Illinois Press, 1939.
1490. Syme, Ronald. *The Roman Revolution.* Oxford: Clarendon Press, 1939.
1491. Webster, Graham. *Boudicca: The British Revolt Against Rome, A.D. 60.* Totowa, New Jersey: Rowman and Littlefield, 1978.

Medieval

1492. Cosenza, Mario E. *Francesco Petrarca and the Revolution of Cola di Rienzo.* Chicago: University of Chicago Press, 1913.
1493. Fourquin, Guy. *The Anatomy of Popular Rebellion in the Middle Ages.* Translated by A. Chesters. New York: North-Holland, 1978.
1494. Heymann, Frederick. *John Zizka and the Hussite Revolution.* Princeton: Princeton University Press, 1955.
1495. Holmes, George. *Europe: Hierarchy and Revolt, 1320-1450.* New York: Harper and Row, 1976.
1496. Kaminsky, Howard. *A History of the Hussite Revolution.* Berkeley: University of California Press, 1967.
1497. Klassen, John M. *The Nobility and the Making of the Hussite Revolution.* New York: Columbia University Press, 1978.
1498. Mollat, M., and P. Wolff. *The Popular Revolutions of the Late Middle Ages.* London: Allen and Unwin, 1973.
1499. Powell, Edgar. *The Rising in East Anglia in 1381.* Cambridge: At the University Press, 1896.

 # Early Modern Europe

"Revolutions are not made; they come. A revolution is as natural a growth as an oak. It comes out of the past. Its foundations are far back."
Wendell Phillips

This is the period when revolutions began to take on their modern, familiar shape. Beginning with the Protestant Reformation/Revolution of the sixteenth century, through the English revolutions of the seventeenth century, and to the French Revolution of the late eighteenth century, what we have no difficulty labelling "revolutions" came into being. The major revolutionary upheavals of the period became turning points in the history of European nations and, in the case of 1789, in the history of the world as well. These revolutions were also points of reference for contemporaries and descendants. As such, their significance, especially for the nineteenth century, should not be underestimated.

Some of the upheavals in this chapter may be classified, at best, as marginally revolutionary. This is so for the Peasants' Revolt of 1524–1525, the Fronde, the Scientific Revolution, and Pugachev's Rebellion. But given the broad, imprecise way we have defined the term for the purposes of this volume, they are included nonetheless. As for the revolutionists (Cromwell and Robespierre) and revolutionary theorists (Milton, Locke, Rousseau, and Burke) singled out, their importance should be obvious.

There is not a separate section on the Protestant Reformation/ Revolution. Although the Reformation was a religious movement intent on saving souls and, where necessary, altering society, it had revolutionary results. A religious revolution was produced which affected all of society. The literature on the Reformation is massive. The best bibliographical source is by Roland Bainton and Eric Gritsch, *Bibliography of the Continental Reformation: Materials Available in English* (Hamden, Conn., 1972). A useful historiographical piece and list of works in English is Harold J. Grimm's *The Reformation in Recent Historical Thought* (American Historical Association Service Center for Teachers of History, Washington, D.C., 1965). Recent general histories are by G. R. Elton, *Reformation Europe, 1517–1559* (New York, 1963), Harold J. Grimm, *The Reformation Era, 1500–1650* (New York, 1965), Hans J. Hillerbrand, *Christendom Divided: The Protestant Reformation* (New York, 1971), Hajo Holborn, *A History of Modern Germany.* Vol. 1: *The Reformation* (New York, 1959), Lewis W. Spitz, *The Renaissance and the Reformation Movements* (Chicago, 1971), and Peter J. Klassen, *Europe in the Refor-*

Early Modern Europe / 89

mation (Englewood Cliffs, N.J., 1979). Specific items below on the Reformation as a revolution can be found in the article by Robert M. Kingdon (1974) and the books by W. Fred Graham (1971), Robert M. Kingdon (1974), and W. Stanford Reid (1968).

Among the other titles below dealing with the period as a whole and worth examining in some detail are the articles by J. H. Elliott (1969), M. D. Feld (1977), H. G. Koenigsberger (1974), A. Lloyd Moote (1972), and Perez Zagorin (1976), and the books by Trevor Aston (1967), Robert Forster and Jack P. Greene (1970), and H. G. Koenigsberger (1971). Works on more specific subjects are identifiable by their titles.

Bibliography

1500. Bromley, John Selwyn, and A. Goodwin. *A Selective List of Works on Europe and Europe Overseas, 1715–1815.* Oxford: Clarendon Press, 1956.

Reference

1501. Williams, E. N. *The Facts On File Dictionary of European History, 1485–1789.* New York: Facts On File, 1980.

Articles

1502. Elliott, J. H. "Revolution and Continuity in Early Modern Europe." *Past and Present,* no. 42 (February 1969): 35–56.
1503. Feld, M. D. "Revolution and Reaction in Early Modern Europe." *Journal of the History of Ideas* 38 (January-March 1977): 175–84.
1504. Greaves, Richard L. "Traditionalism and the Seeds of Revolution in the Social Principles of the Geneva Bible." *Sixteenth Century Journal* 7 (October 1976): 94–109.
1505. Kingdon, Robert M. "Was the Protestant Reformation a Revolution? The Case of Geneva." In *Transition and Revolution,* edited by R. M. Kingdon. Minneapolis: Burgess, 1974.
1506. Koenigsberger, H. G. "Early Modern Revolutions." *Journal of Modern History* 46:1 (March 1974): 99–110.
1507. _____. "Revolutionary Conclusions." *History* 57 (1972): 394–98.
1508. Kramnick, Isaac. "Religion and Radicalism: English Political Theory in the Age of Revolution." *Political Theory* 5 (November 1977): 505–34.
1509. Lewis, Theodore B. "A Revolutionary Tradition, 1689–1774: 'There Was a Revolution Here as Well as in England.'" *New England Quarterly* 46 (September 1973): 424–38.
1510. Moote, A. Lloyd. "The Preconditions of Revolution in Early Modern Europe: Did They Really Exist?" *Canadian Journal of History* 7:3 (December 1972): 207–34.
1511. Rowen, Herbert H. "The Revolution That Wasn't: The *Coup d'Etat* of 1650 in Holland." *European Studies Review* 4:2 (1974): 99–118.
1512. Skowronek, Jerzy. "The Model of Revolution in East Central European Political Thought during the Napoleonic Era." In *The American and European Revolutions,* edited by J. Pelenski. Iowa City: University of Iowa Press, 1980.

1513. Zagorin, Perez. "Prolegomena to the Comparative History of Revolution in Early Modern Europe." *Comparative Studies in Society and History* 18:2 (April 1976): 151-74.

Books

1514. Aston, Trevor, ed. *Crisis in Europe, 1560-1660.* Garden City, New York: Doubleday, 1967.

1515. Avrich, Paul. *Russian Rebels, 1600-1800.* New York: W. W. Norton, 1976.

1516. Barnes, Thomas G., and Gerald D. Feldman, eds. *Rationalism and Revolution, 1660-1815.* Waltham, Massachusetts: Little, Brown, 1972.

1517. Birn, Raymond. *Crisis, Absolutism, Revolution: Europe, 1648-1789/91.* New York: Holt, Rinehart and Winston, 1977.

1518. Blanning, T. C. W. *Reform and Revolution in Mainz, 1743-1803.* New York: Cambridge University Press, 1974.

1519. Carswell, John. *From Revolution to Revolution: England, 1688-1776.* New York: Scribners, 1973.

1520. Cornwall, Julian. *Revolt of the Peasantry, 1549.* Boston: Routledge and Kegan Paul, 1978.

1521. Fay, Bernard. *Revolution and Freemasonry, 1680-1800.* Boston: Little, Brown, 1935.

1522. Fletcher, Anthony. *Tudor Rebellions.* London: Longman, 1973.

1523. Forster, Robert, and Jack P. Greene, eds. *Preconditions of Revolution in Early Modern Europe.* Baltimore: Johns Hopkins University Press, 1970.

1524. Graham, W. Fred. *The Constructive Revolutionary: John Calvin and His Socio-Economic Impact.* Richmond, Virginia: John Knox Press, 1971.

1525. Howard, Donald D., ed. *Consortium on Revolutionary Europe: Proceedings 1974.* Gainesville: University Presses of Florida, 1978.

1526. Kelley, Donald R. *François Hotman: A Revolutionary's Ordeal.* Princeton: Princeton University Press, 1973.

1527. Kingdon, Robert M., ed. *Transition and Revolution: Problems and Issues of European Renaissance and Reformation History.* Minneapolis: Burgess, 1974.

1528. Koenigsberger, H. G. *Estates and Revolution: Essays in Early Modern European History.* Ithaca: Cornell University Press, 1971.

1529. Little, David. *Religion, Order and Law: A Study in Pre-Revolutionary England.* New York: Harper and Row, 1969.

1530. Machiavelli, Niccolo. *The Prince and the Discourses.* New York: Random House, 1950.

1531. Macpherson, C. B. *The Political Theory of Possessive Industrialism: Hobbes to Locke.* Oxford: Clarendon Press, 1962.

1532. Makey, Walter. *The Church of the Covenant, 1637-1651: Revolution and Social Change in Scotland.* Edinburgh, Scotland: John Donald, 1979.

1533. Merriman, Roger B. *Six Contemporaneous Revolutions.* Hamden, Connecticut: Archon Books, 1963.

1534. Osborn, Annie. *Rousseau and Burke: A Study of the Idea of Liberty in Eighteenth-Century Political Thought.* London: Oxford University Press, 1940.

1535. Pocock, J. G. A., ed. *Three British Revolutions, 1641, 1688, 1776.* Princeton: Princeton University Press, 1979.

1536. Reid, W. Stanford, ed. *The Reformation: Revival or Revolution?* New York: Holt, Rinehart and Winston, 1968.
1537. Ronalds, Francis Spring. *The Abortive Whig Revolution of 1678-1681.* Urbana: University of Illinois Press, 1929.
1538. Rudé, George. *Paris and London in the Eighteenth Century: Studies in Popular Protest.* New York: Viking, 1973.
1539. Salmon, J. H. M., ed. *The French Wars of Religion.* Boston: D. C. Heath, 1967.
1540. Seebohm, F. *The Era of the Protestant Revolution.* 2d ed. New York: AMS Press, 1971.
1541. Stevenson, David. *Revolution and Counter-Revolution in Scotland, 1644-1651.* London: Royal Historical Society, 1977.
1542. _____. *The Scottish Revolution 1637-44: The Triumph of the Covenanters.* New York: St. Martin's Press, 1974.
1543. Sturgill, Claude. *The Consortium on Revolutionary Europe, 1750-1850: Proceedings, 1973.* Gainesville: University Presses of Florida, 1973.

Peasants' Revolt, 1524-1525

Before the end of the first crucial decade of the Protestant Reformation another revolt erupted, one with legal, social, and economic grievances propelling it, peasants as its major warriors, and religious inspiration provided (unintentionally) by Martin Luther. Centered in southern Germany, the revolt was mostly an agrarian rebellion, though in some places urban discontent was the source for the momentum. Although the nature of the peasants' grievances was such that they did not consider themselves revolutionists, one of their self-appointed leaders was the radical priest and religious revolutionist Thomas Müntzer. Müntzer endorsed the use of violence and equated the peasants with the elect, the lords with the ungodly; Marxist historians have seen him as a proletarian revolutionist. While the revolt failed because it lacked overall unity, a complete program, and effective leadership, it remains a decisive episode, and its outcome significantly shaped the course of the Reformation.

The best places to initiate an investigation of the Peasants' Revolt are the edited collections by Janos Bak (1976), Bob Scribner and Gerhard Benecke (1979), and Kyle C. Sessions (1968); the last mentioned, for example, contains selections from leading authorities and a bibliography. The works of Günther Franz (1952, 1963) offer the most complete exposition of the revolt. The book by Friedrich Engels (1966) is an introduction to the Marxist interpretation. Other works on Luther and the Reformation should also be consulted.

Historiographies

1544. Scott, Tom. "The Peasants' War: A Historiographical Review, Part I." *Historical Journal* 22 (September 1979): 693-720.
1545. _____. "The Peasants' War: A Historiographical Review, Part II." *Historical Journal* 22 (December 1979): 953-74.

Articles

1546. Cohn, Henry J. "Anticlericalism in the German Peasants' War, 1525." *Past and Present,* no. 83 (May 1979): 3-31.
1547. Goertz, Hans-Jürgen. "The Mystic with the Hammer: Thomas Müntzer's Theological Basis for Revolution." *Mennonite Quarterly Review* 50 (April 1976): 83-113.
1548. Janzow, W. Theophil. "Background for the Peasants' Revolt of 1524." *Concordia Theological Monthly* 22:9 (September 1951).
1549. Kolb, Robert. "The Theologians and the Peasants: Conservative Evangelical Reactions to the German Peasants' Revolt." *Archäologische Reformationsgesch* 69 (1978): 103-31.
1550. Robinson, James Harvey. "The Study of the Lutheran Revolt." *American Historical Review* 7:2 (January 1903): 205-16.
1551. Scott, Tom. "Reformation and Peasants' War in Waldshut and Environs: A Structural Analysis." *Archäologische Reformationsgesch* 69 (1978): 82-102.
1552. Sea, Thomas F. "Imperial Cities and the Peasants' War in Germany." *Central European History* 12 (March 1979): 3-37.
1553. Weigand, Hermann J. "A Close-Up of the German Peasants' War." *Transactions of the Connecticut Academy of Arts and Sciences* 35 (May 1942): 1-32.

Books

1554. Bak, Janos, ed. *The German Peasant War of 1525.* Totowa, New Jersey: Biblio Distribution Centre, 1976.
1555. Bax, Ernest Belfort. *The Peasants' War in Germany.* London: Swan Sonnenschein, 1899.
1556. Engels, Friedrich. *Peasant War in Germany.* New York: International Publishers, 1966.
1557. Franz, Günther. *Der Deutsche Bauernkrieg.* 4th ed. Darmstadt: Herman Gentner Verlag, 1952.
1558. _____. *Quellen zur Geschichte des Bauernkriegs.* 2d ed. Munich: R. Oldenbourg, 1963.
1559. Hutton, William H. *The Political Disturbances Which Accompanied the Early Period of the Reformation in Germany.* Oxford: B. H. Blackwell, 1881.
1560. Kirchner, Hubert. *Luther and the Peasants' War.* Translated by D. Jodock. Philadelphia: Fortress Press, 1972.
1561. Klassen, Walter. *Michael Gaismair: Revolutionary and Reformer.* Leiden: E. J. Brill, 1978.
1562. Scribner, Bob, and Gerhard Benecke, eds. *The German Peasant War of 1525—New Viewpoints.* Boston: George Allen and Unwin, 1979.
1563. Sessions, Kyle C., ed. *Reformation and Authority: The Meaning of the Peasants' Revolt.* Lexington, Massachusetts: D. C. Heath, 1968.

Revolt of the Netherlands, 1566-1609

The Revolt of the Netherlands against the rule of Philip II and Spain was the work of a highly organized minority, led by the nobility, disciplined, inspired, and united by Calvinism, and supported by the business and working groups whose hatred of Spanish domination was probably greater than their loyalty to their own government. The revolt became akin to what the twentieth century calls an "anti-colonial revolution" when the Dutch came to realize that the only alternative to domination was independence. But this realization came about slowly, since Dutch nationalism took time to emerge, a common political ideology was lacking, the aristocracy was conservative, and economic diversity and political particularism pervaded the provinces.

The Dutch Revolt has been given considerable scholarly attention ever since the publication of the studies of John Lothrop Motley (1898). His work was superceded by that of Pieter Geyl (1958, 1961), and more recently by Geoffrey Parker (1972, 1977, 1978, 1979). Also helpful are all the articles below, and the books on Calvinism by Phyllis Mack Crew (1978), on Philip II by Edward Grierson (1969), on William the Silent by Cicely V. Wedgwood (1968), and on English assistance by Charles Wilson (1970).

Documents

1564. Kossman, E. H., and A. F. Mellink, eds. *Texts Concerning the Revolt of the Netherlands.* Cambridge: Cambridge University Press, 1974.

Articles

1565. Ellemers, J. E. "The Revolt of the Netherlands: The Part Played by Religion in the Process of Nation-Building." *Social Compass* 14:2 (1967): 93-103.

1566. Griffiths, Gordon. "The Revolutionary Character of the Revolt of the Netherlands." *Comparative Studies in Society and History* 2:4 (July 1960): 452-72.

1567. Koenigsberger, H. G. "Organization of Revolutionary Parties in France and the Netherlands During the Sixteenth Century." *Journal of Modern History* 27:4 (December 1955): 335-51.

1568. Nadal, George. "The Logic of *The Anatomy of Revolution,* with Reference to the Netherlands Revolt." *Comparative Studies in Society and History* 2:4 (July 1960): 473-84.

1569. Parker, Geoffrey. "The Dutch Revolt and the Polarization of International Politics." In *The General Crisis of the Seventeenth Century,* edited by G. Parker and L. M. Smith. Boston: Routledge and Kegan Paul, 1978.

1570. Schöffer, I. "The Dutch Revolt Anatomized: Some Comments." *Comparative Studies in Society and History* 3:4 (July 1961): 470-77.

1571. Smit, J. W. "The Netherlands Revolution." In *Preconditions of Revolution in Early Modern Europe,* edited by R. Forster and J. P. Greene. Baltimore: Johns Hopkins University Press, 1970.

Books

1572. Crew, Phyllis Mack. *Calvinist Preaching and Iconoclasm in the Netherlands, 1544–1569.* New York: Cambridge University Press, 1978.
1573. Geyl, Pieter. *The Netherlands in the Seventeenth Century, 1609–1648.* New York: Barnes and Noble, 1961.
1574. _____. *The Revolt of the Netherlands, 1555–1609.* London: Ernest Benn, 1958.
1575. Grierson, Edward. *The Fatal Inheritance: Philip II and the Spanish Netherlands.* Garden City, New York: Doubleday, 1969.
1576. Motley, John Lothrop. *The Rise of the Dutch Republic.* 4 vols. in 2. Philadelphia: Henry Altemus, 1898.
1577. Parker, Geoffrey. *The Army of Flanders and the Spanish Road, 1567–1659: The Logistics of Spanish Victory and Defeat in the Low Countries' War.* Cambridge: Cambridge University Press, 1972.
1578. _____. *The Dutch Revolt.* Ithaca: Cornell University Press, 1977.
1579. _____. *Spain and the Netherlands, 1559–1659: Ten Studies.* Short Hills, New Jersey: Enslow Publishers, 1979.
1580. Rowen, Herbert H., ed. *The Low Countries in Early Modern Times.* New York: Harper and Row, 1972.
1581. _____, and DeLamar Jensen. *The Dutch Republic: A Nation in the Making.* St. Louis: Forum Press, 1976.
1582. Wedgwood, Cicely V. *William the Silent: William of Nassau, Prince of Orange, 1533–1584.* New York: W. W. Norton, 1968.
1583. Wilson, Charles. *Queen Elizabeth and the Revolt of the Netherlands.* Berkeley: University of California Press, 1970.

The Fronde, 1648–1653

The Fronde occurred as part of one of the first periods in history seemingly characterized by revolutionary contagion, where insurrection in one place helped to spark its outbreak somewhere else. The next such period would be the Age of the Democratic Revolution (1760–1815), followed by the revolutions of 1830 and 1848. For a closer look at those revolutions contemporaneous with the Fronde (in Catalonia, Portugal, Naples, Palermo, and England), see the book by Roger B. Merriman (1963) cited in the opening section to this chapter.

The Fronde was an abortive attempt on the part of the separate, selfish segments of the French ruling elite to gain more power. The main source of discontent was the centralizing movement of the French government under Cardinals Richelieu and Mazarin. But the revolt failed to generate a new and comprehensive conception of the social and political order, however much the potential existed. In addition to the useful works listed below, the reader should consult with general histories of France in the seventeenth century, and those which concentrate on the early reign of Louis XIV and the rule of Mazarin.

Articles

1584. Bonney, Richard J. "The French Civil War, 1649-53." *European Studies Review* 8 (January 1978): 71-100.
1585. Golden, Richard M. "The Mentality of Opposition: The Jansenism of the Parisian *Curés* during the Religious *Fronde*." *Catholic Historical Review* 64:3 (October 1978): 565-80.
1586. Mousnier, Roland. "The Fronde." In *Preconditions of Revolution in Early Modern Europe,* edited by R. Forster and J. P. Greene. Baltimore: Johns Hopkins University Press, 1970.
1587. Treasure, Geoffrey. "The Fronde, Part One: The Revolt of the Lawyers, 1648." *History Today* 28 (June 1978): 353-63.
1588. _____. "The Fronde, Part Two." *History Today* 28 (July 1978): 436-45.

Books

1589. Doolin, Paul Rice. *The Fronde.* Cambridge, Massachusetts: Harvard University Press, 1935.
1590. Knachel, Paul A. *England and the Fronde.* Ithaca: Cornell University Press, 1967.
1591. Kossman, E. H. *La Fronde.* Leiden: Universitaire Pers Leiden, 1954.
1592. Moote, A. Lloyd. *Revolt of the Judges: The Parlement of Paris and the Fronde, 1643-1652.* Princeton: Princeton University Press, 1971.
1593. Westrich, Sal Alexander. *The Ormée of Bordeaux: A Revolution During the Fronde.* Baltimore: Johns Hopkins University Press, 1972.

Puritan Revolution, 1640-1660

The historiography of the Puritan Revolution, or English Civil War as it is also called, has been stimulated by a variety of interpretations and controversies. Among others there are the Whig interpretation, which emphasizes the growth of constitutional liberties, and the Marxist interpretation, which emphasizes economic evolution and class development. There are other interpretations based upon the role of individuals, politics, and religion, and there are also variations of all these themes.

Among the works below which discuss or present samples of these interpretations are the articles by Paul Christianson (1976) and Christopher Hill (1948, 1956), and the books by Roger Howell, Jr. (1975), Conrad Russell (1973), and Philip A. M. Taylor (1969). One of the most intense historiographical conflicts has revolved around the role of the gentry; this may be sampled in the articles by J. H. Hexter (1963), R. H. Tawney (1941, 1954), and Hugh Trevor-Roper (1957), and the book by B. G. Blackwood (1978).

Perhaps a good place for the novice to begin is with general histories of the period and those which concentrate on the causes of the revolution. Among the best are the books by Maurice Ashley (1979), Robert Ashton (1979), Godfrey Davies (1959), I. Deane Jones (1962), R. H. Parry (1970), Ivan Roots (1966), Conrad Russell (1973), Lawrence Stone (1972), and Perez Zagorin (1969). Not to be overlooked are some other important works, which include the series of articles in the *Journal of Modern History* (December 1977) and the books by Gerald E. Aylmer (1972), Allen P. French (1955), William Haller (1955), Paul H. Hardacre (1956), J. H. Hexter (1941), Christopher Hill (1955, 1964, 1965, 1980), Margaret A. Judson (1949), Brian Manning (1976), Valerie Pearl (1961), Leo F. Solt (1959), Lawrence Stone (1966), Michael Walzer (1965), and Cicely V. Wedgwood (1955, 1958, 1964). There is much, much more than appears here, but this should provide an adequate launching. The serious student should not fail to comb the pages of the bibliography by Godfrey Davies (1970).

Bibliography

1594. Davies, Godfrey. *Bibliography of British History: Stuart Period, 1603–1714.* 2d ed. Oxford: Clarendon Press, 1970.

Documents

1595. Gardiner, S. R. *The Constitutional Documents of the Puritan Revolution, 1625–1660.* Oxford: Oxford University Press, 1889.
1596. Haller, William, ed. *Tracts on Liberty in the Puritan Revolution, 1638–1647.* New York: Octagon Books, 1965.
1597. Kenyon, J. P., ed. *The Stuart Constitution, 1603–1688: Documents and Commentary.* Cambridge: Cambridge University Press, 1966.
1598. Prall, Stuart. *Puritan Revolution: A Documentary History.* Magnolia, Massachusetts: Peter Smith, n.d.

Contemporary Accounts

1599. Clarendon, Edward, Earl of. *The History of the Rebellion and Civil Wars in England.* 6 vols. Oxford: Clarendon Press, 1827.
1600. Hobbes, Thomas. *Behemoth: The History of the Causes of the Civil Wars in England.* Edited by W. Molesworth. New York: Burt Franklin, 1962.
1601. _____. *Leviathan.* Oxford: At the Clarendon Press, 1909.

Overviews, Surveys, Interpretations

Articles

1602. "The First English Revolution." *Journal of Modern History* 49:4 (December 1977).
1603. Hill, Christopher. "Recent Interpretations of the Civil War." *History* 41 (1956): 67-87.

Books

1604. Ashley, Maurice. *England in the Seventeenth Century.* Baltimore: Penguin Books, 1961.
1605. _____. *The English Civil War: A Concise History.* New York: Thames and Hudson, 1979.
1606. _____. *Great Britain to 1688: A Modern History.* Ann Arbor: University of Michigan Press, 1961.
1607. Ashton, Robert. *The English Civil War.* New York: W. W. Norton, 1979.
1608. Aylmer, Gerald E. *The Interregnum, 1646-1660.* London: Macmillan, 1972.
1609. Davies, Godfrey. *The Early Stuarts, 1603-1660.* 2d ed. Oxford: Oxford University Press, 1959.
1610. Firth, C. H. *The Last Years of the Protectorate.* 2 vols. London: Longmans, Green, 1909.
1611. Gardiner, S. R. *The First Two Stuarts and the Puritan Revolution.* Norwood, Pennsylvania: Norwood Editions, 1977.
1612. _____. *History of the Commonwealth and Protectorate, 1649-1656.* 4 vols. New York: Longmans, Green, 1903.
1613. _____. *A History of the Great Civil War, 1642-1649.* 4 vols. New York: AMS Press, 1965.
1614. Gush, George, and Martin Windrow. *English Civil War.* Tucson, Arizona: Aztex, 1978.
1615. Hill, Christopher. *The English Revolution.* London: Lawrence and Wishart, 1955.
1616. Ives, E. W., ed. *The English Revolution, 1600-1660.* New York: Harper and Row, 1971.
1617. Jones, I. Deane. *The English Revolution.* London: W. Heinemann, 1962.
1618. Lamont, William. *Godly Rule, Politics and Religion, 1603-1660.* London: Macmillan, 1969.
1619. Lindsay, Jack. *Civil War in England.* Atlantic Highlands, New Jersey: Humanities Press, 1967.
1620. Ollard, Richard. *This War without an Enemy.* Paterson, New Jersey: Atheneum, 1976.
1621. Parry, R. H., ed. *The English Civil War and After, 1642-1658.* Berkeley: University of California Press, 1970.
1622. Ranke, Leopold von. *A History of England, Principally in the Seventeenth Century.* 6 vols. Oxford: Clarendon Press, 1875.

1623. Roots, Ivan. *Commonwealth and Protectorate.* Westport, Connecticut: Greenwood, 1976.
1624. _____. *The Great Rebellion, 1642-1660.* London: Batsford, 1966.
1625. Trevelyan, George M. *England Under the Stuarts.* London: Methuen, 1946.
1626. Wedgwood, Cicely V. *A Coffin for King Charles.* New York: Macmillan, 1964.
1627. _____. *The King's Peace, 1637-1641.* New York: Macmillan, 1955.
1628. _____. *The King's War, 1641-1647.* New York: Macmillan, 1958.

Causes and Origins

Articles

1629. Christianson, Paul. "The Causes of the English Revolution: A Reappraisal." *Journal of British Studies* 15:2 (Spring 1976): 40-75.
1630. Hirst, Derek. "Unanimity in the Commons, Aristocratic Intrigues, and the Origins of the English Civil War." *Journal of Modern History* 50:1 (March 1978): 51-71.
1631. Zaller, Robert. "The Concept of Opposition in Early Stuart England." *Albion* 12:3 (Fall 1980): 211-34.

Books

1632. Howell, Roger, Jr. *The Origins of the English Revolution.* St. Louis: Forum Press, 1975.
1633. Jessup, F. W. *Background to the English Civil War.* Elmsford, New York: Pergamon Press, 1966.
1634. Russell, Conrad, ed. *The Origins of the English Civil War.* New York: Barnes and Noble, 1973.
1635. Stone, Lawrence. *The Causes of the English Revolution, 1529-1642.* New York: Harper and Row, 1972.
1636. Taylor, Philip A. M., ed. *The Origins of the English Civil War: Conspiracy, Crusade, or Class Conflict?* Lexington, Massachusetts: D.C. Heath, 1969.
1637. Woods, T. P. S. *Prelude to Civil War, 1642: Mr. Justice Malet and the Kentish Petitions.* Salisbury, England: Michael Russell, 1980.
1638. Zagorin, Perez. *The Court and the Country: The Beginning of the English Revolution.* New York: Atheneum, 1969.

Social Interpretations

Articles

1639. Hexter, J. H. "Storm Over the Gentry." In *Reappraisals in History,* by J. H. Hexter. New York: Harper and Row, 1963.
1640. Hill, Christopher. "The English Civil War Interpreted by Marx and Engels." *Science and Society* 12:1 (Winter 1948): 130-56.

1641. Manning, Brian. "The Peasantry and the English Revolution." *Journal of Peasant Studies* 2 (January 1975): 133-58.
1642. Tawney, R. H. "The Rise of the Gentry, 1558-1640." *Economic History Review* 11 (1941): 1-38.
1643. _____. "The Rise of the Gentry: A Postscript." *Economic History Review*, 2d ser. 7 (1954): 91-97.
1644. Trevor-Roper, Hugh. "The Social Causes of the Great Rebellion." In *Historical Essays*, edited by H. R. Trevor-Roper. London: Harper Brothers, 1957.
1645. Zagorin, Perez. "The Social Interpretation of the English Revolution." *Journal of Economic History* 19 (1959): 376-401.

Books

1646. Blackwood, B. G. *The Lancashire Gentry and the Great Rebellion, 1640-60.* Atlantic Highlands, New Jersey: Humanities Press, 1978.
1647. James, Margaret. *Social Problems and Policy During the Puritan Revolution.* Boston: Routledge and Kegan Paul, 1930.
1648. Manning, Brian. *The English People and the English Revolution, 1640-1649.* London: Heinemann, 1976.
1649. Stone, Lawrence. *Social Change and Revolution in England, 1540-1640.* New York: Oxford University Press, 1966.

Ideology

Articles

1650. Latham, R. C. "English Revolutionary Thought, 1640-1660." *History* 30 (1945): 28-59.
1651. Snow, Vernon F. "The Concept of Revolution in Seventeenth-Century England." *Historical Journal* 5:2 (1962): 167-74.
1652. Walzer, Michael. "Puritanism as a Revolutionary Ideology." *History and Theory* 3:1 (1963): 59-90. Also in *The Protestant Ethic and Modernization: A Comparative View*, edited by S. N. Eisenstadt. New York: Basic Books, 1968.
1653. _____. "Revolutionary Ideology: The Case of the Marian Exiles." *American Political Science Review* 57:3 (September 1963): 643-54.

Books

1654. Coltman, Irene. *Private Men and Public Causes: Philosophy and Politics in the English Civil War.* Naperville, Illinois: Allenson, 1962.
1655. Gooch, G. P. *English Democratic Ideas in the Seventeenth Century.* New York: Harper and Row, 1959.
1656. Haller, William. *Liberty and Reformation in the Puritan Revolution.* New York: Columbia University Press, 1955.
1657. Hill, Christopher. *Intellectual Origins of the English Revolution.* Oxford: Clarendon Press, 1965.
1658. _____. *Some Intellectual Consequences of the English Revolution.* Madison: University of Wisconsin Press, 1980.

1659. Judson, Margaret A. *From Tradition to Political Reality: A Study of the Ideas Set Forth in Support of the Commonwealth Government in England, 1649–1653.* Hamden, Connecticut: Archon Books, 1980.
1660. Walzer, Michael. *Revolution of the Saints: A Study in the Origins of Radical Politics.* Cambridge, Massachusetts: Harvard University Press, 1965.
1661. Zagorin, Perez. *A History of Political Thought in the English Revolution.* New York: Humanities Press, 1969.

Revolutionary Leaders

1662. Ashley, Maurice. *General Monck.* Totowa, New Jersey: Rowman and Littlefield, 1977.
1663. Brett, Sidney Reed. *John Pym, 1583–1643: The Statesman of the Puritan Revolution.* London: John Murray, 1940.
1664. Guizot, François. *Monk's Contemporaries: Biographical Studies on the English Revolution.* Translated by A. R. Scoble. London: H. G. Bohn, 1851.
1665. Hexter, J. H. *The Reign of King Pym.* Cambridge, Massachusetts: Harvard University Press, 1941.
1666. Keeler, Mary F. *The Long Parliament, 1640–1641: A Biographical Study of Its Members.* Philadelphia: American Philosophical Society, 1954.
1667. Pennington, Donald. *Members of the Long Parliament.* Cambridge, Massachusetts: Harvard University Press, 1954.

Puritans

Article

1668. Hughes, Richard T. "Henry Burton: The Making of a Puritan Revolutionary." *Journal of Church and State* 16 (Autumn 1974): 421–34.

Books

1669. Hill, Christopher. *Puritanism and Revolution.* New York: Schocken, 1964.
1670. Pennington, Donald, and Keith Thomas, eds. *Puritans and Revolutionaries: Essays in Honour of Christopher Hill.* New York: Oxford University Press, 1978.
1671. Yule, George S. S. *The Independents in the English Civil War.* Cambridge: Cambridge University Press, 1958.

Charles I

1672. Cowie, Leonard W. *The Trial and Execution of Charles I.* New York: Putnam, 1972.
1673. French, Allen P. *Charles I and the Puritan Upheaval.* London: Allen and Unwin, 1955.

1674. Petrie, Charles, ed. *King Charles, Prince Rupert and the Civil War.* Boston: Routledge and Kegan Paul, 1975.
1675. Wingfield-Stratford, Esmé. *Charles King of England, 1600-1637.* London: Bodley Head, 1949.
1676. _____. *King Charles and King Pym, 1637-1643.* London: Bodley Head, 1949.

Royalists

1677. Hardacre, Paul H. *The Royalists During the Puritan Revolution.* The Hague: Nijhoff, 1956.
1678. Underdown, David. *Royalist Conspiracy in England, 1649-1660.* Hamden, Connecticut: Shoe String Press, 1971.

Military

Article

1679. Kishlansky, Mark. "The Case of the Army Truly Stated: The Creation of the New Model Army." *Past and Present,* no. 81 (November 1978): 51-74.

Books

1680. Kishlansky, Mark. *The Rise of the New Model Army.* New York: Cambridge University Press, 1979.
1681. Powell, John R. *The Navy in the English Civil War.* Hamden, Connecticut: Archon Books, 1962.
1682. Solt, Leo F. *Saints in Arms.* Stanford: Stanford University Press, 1959.
1683. Woolrych, A. H. *Battles of the Civil War.* New York: Macmillan, 1961.

Miscellaneous

Articles

1684. Hill, Christopher. "John Bunyan and the English Revolution." *Marxist Perspectives* 2 (Fall 1979): 8-26.
1685. Howell, Roger, Jr. "The Structure of Urban Politics in the English Civil War." *Albion* 11:2 (Summer 1979): 111-27.
1686. Smith, Steven R. "Almost Revolutionaries: The London Apprentices during the Civil War." *Huntington Library Quarterly* 42 (Autumn 1979): 313-28.
1687. Trevor-Roper, Hugh. "Clarendon's 'History of the Rebellion.'" *History Today* 29 (February 1979): 73-79.

Books

1688. Ashley, Maurice. *Financial and Commercial Policy Under the Cromwellian Protectorate.* 2d ed. Totowa, New Jersey: Biblio Distribution Centre, 1962.
1689. Ashton, Robert. *The City and the Court, 1603-1643.* New York: Cambridge University Press, 1979.
1690. Jacob, J. R. *Robert Boyle and the English Revolution: A Study in Social and Intellectual Change.* New York: Burt Franklin, 1978.
1691. Jordan, W. K. *Men of Substance: A Study of the Thought of Two English Revolutionaries, Henry Parker and Henry Robinson.* Chicago: University of Chicago Press, 1942.
1692. Judson, Margaret A. *The Crisis of the Constitution.* New Brunswick, New Jersey: Rutgers University Press, 1949.
1693. Kaplan, Lawrence. *Politics and Religion During the English Revolution: The Scots and the Long Parliament, 1643-1645.* New York: New York University Press, 1977.
1694. Lamont, William. *Richard Baxter and the Millennium: Protestant Imperialism and the English Revolution.* Totowa, New Jersey: Rowman and Littlefield, 1979.
1695. MacCormack, John R. *Revolutionary Politics in the Long Parliament.* Cambridge, Massachusetts: Harvard University Press, 1973.
1696. Morrill, J. S., ed. *The Revolt of the Provinces: Conservatives and Radicals in the English Civil War, 1630-1650.* New York: Barnes and Noble, 1976.
1697. Morton, A. L. *The World of the Ranters: Religious Radicalism in the English Revolution.* Brooklyn Heights, New York: Beekman Publishers, 1970.
1698. Pearl, Valerie. *London and the Outbreak of the Puritan Revolution.* London: Oxford University Press, 1961.
1699. Schenk, Wilhelm. *The Concern for Social Justice in the Puritan Revolution.* Westport, Connecticut: Greenwood, 1975.
1700. Seaver, Paul, ed. *Seventeenth-Century England: Society in an Age of Revolution.* New York: New Viewpoints, 1976.

Oliver Cromwell

Cromwell was a gentleman revolutionist, the most dominating force during the Puritan Revolution. He was a soldier and politician whose religion influenced everything he did. He endeavored to reconcile most Englishmen with his regime so that both could work together to serve God. Cromwell has always had admirers and denigrators who have come from among conservative, liberal, and radical ranks. Among the paradoxes apparent in his career is the fact that the revolutionist of the 1640s became the royalist-like dictator of the 1650s.

To sample the literature dealing with Cromwell and to glimpse the changing patterns of interpretation on his life, see the first chapter in *The Greatness of Oliver Cromwell* by Maurice Ashley (1957) and the books edited by Richard E. Boyer (1966), John F. H. New (1972), and Ivan Roots (1973). Among the better biographies of Cromwell are those by Maurice Ashley (1957, 1958), Antonia Fraser (1974), Christopher Hill (1958, 1970), and Cicely V. Wedgwood (1962). Further titles can be extracted from the bibliographies by Wilbur C. Abbott (1929, 1937-1947) and Paul H. Hardacre (1961). However, the student should be on guard to the fact that Cromwell cannot be isolated from the causes of the revolution or the contending forces which emerged as the conflict progressed.

Bibliographies

1701. Abbott, Wilbur C. *A Bibliography of Oliver Cromwell.* Cambridge, Massachusetts: Harvard University Press, 1929.
1702. Hardacre, Paul H. "Writings on Oliver Cromwell Since 1929." *Journal of Modern History* 33:1 (March 1961): 1-14.

Documents

1703. Abbott, Wilbur C., ed. *Writings and Speeches of Oliver Cromwell.* 4 vols. Cambridge, Massachusetts: Harvard University Press, 1937-1947. Volume 4 contains "Addenda to Bibliography."

Books

1704. Ashley, Maurice. *Cromwell's Generals.* London: J. Cape, 1954.
1705. _____. *The Greatness of Oliver Cromwell.* New York: Macmillan, 1957.
1706. _____. *Oliver Cromwell and the Puritan Revolution.* New York: Macmillan, 1958.
1707. _____. *Oliver Cromwell, the Conservative Dictator.* London: J. Cape, 1937.
1708. Barker, Ernest. *Oliver Cromwell and the English People.* Cambridge: Cambridge University Press, 1937.
1709. Bernstein, Eduard. *Cromwell & Communism: Socialism and Democracy in the Great English Revolution.* New York: Schocken, 1963.
1710. Blauvelt, Mary Taylor. *Oliver Cromwell: A Dictator's Tragedy.* New York: G. P. Putnam's, 1937.
1711. Boyer, Richard E., ed. *Oliver Cromwell and the Puritan Revolt.* Boston: D. C. Heath, 1966.
1712. _____. *Oliver Cromwell: A Revolutionary Paradox.* St. Louis: Forum Press, 1977.
1713. Buchan, John. *Oliver Cromwell.* Boston: Houghton Mifflin, 1934.
1714. Firth, C. H. *Oliver Cromwell and the Rule of the Puritans in England.* Oxford: Oxford University Press, 1900.
1715. Fraser, Antonia. *Cromwell: The Lord Protector.* New York: Alfred A. Knopf, 1974.
1716. Gardiner, S. R. *Cromwell's Place in History.* London: Longmans, Green, 1897.
1717. _____. *Oliver Cromwell.* London: Goupil, 1899.

1718. Hill, Christopher. *God's Englishman: Oliver Cromwell and the English Revolution.* New York: Harper and Row, 1970.
1719. _____ . *Oliver Cromwell, 1658-1958.* London: Routledge and Kegan Paul, 1958.
1720. Morley, John. *Oliver Cromwell.* London: Macmillan, 1921.
1721. New, John F. H., ed. *Oliver Cromwell: Pretender, Puritan, Statesman, Paradox?* New York: Holt, Rinehart and Winston, 1972.
1722. Paul, Robert S. *The Lord Protector.* London: Lutterworth Press, 1955.
1723. Roots, Ivan, ed. *Cromwell, A Profile.* New York: Hill and Wang, 1973.
1724. Vaughan, Robert, ed. *The Protectorate of Oliver Cromwell and the State of Europe.* London: Henry Colburn, 1838.
1725. Wedgwood, Cicely V. *Oliver Cromwell.* New York: Macmillan, 1962.
1726. Young, George M. *Charles I and Cromwell, An Essay.* London: P. Davies, 1936.
1727. Young, Peter. *Oliver Cromwell and His Times.* New York: Arco Publishers, 1962.

Milton and Revolution

John Milton was not only a great poet, but also a government official under Cromwell and a defender of the Puritan Revolution. He believed in an aristocracy which would rule wisely and according to natural law. As a radical Independent he called for complete separation of church and state; toleration, he believed, was impossible as long as a state church existed. Milton also believed in the sovereignty of the people, but he did not have faith in representative government. The standard biography is the multi-volume study by David Masson (1871-1894). The books by Christopher Hill (1978), Hugh M. Richmond (1974), and Don M. Wolfe (1963) all offer different and more recent interpretations. Of course, Milton's own writing should not be overlooked.

1728. Hill, Christopher. *Milton and the English Revolution.* New York: Viking, 1978.
1729. Masson, David. *The Life of John Milton.* 7 vols. London: Macmillan, 1871-1894.
1730. Milton, John. *Complete Prose Works of John Milton.* Vol. 3. *The Tenure of Kings and Magistrates,* edited by Merritt Y. Hughes. New Haven: Yale University Press, 1962.
1731. Richmond, Hugh M. *The Christian Revolutionary: John Milton.* Berkeley: University of California Press, 1974.
1732. Wolfe, Don M. *Milton in the Puritan Revolution.* Atlantic Highlands, New Jersey: Humanities Press, 1963.

Levellers and Diggers

Among the more radical groups which emerged during the Puritan Revolution were the Levellers and the Diggers. The former expressed petit-bourgeois aims and exercised some influence over Cromwell. The latter, led by Gerrard Winstanley, expressed communist ideas, including the "free right to the land of England"; naturally, they were viewed with alarm by men of property. Christopher Hill (1973) takes a look at most of the radical groups in his book. The books by H. N. Brailsford (1961) and Joseph Frank (1955) are the standard works on the Levellers, with Gerald E. Aylmer's collection (1975) being a recent addition. The studies by T. Wilson Hayes (1979) and David W. Petegorsky (1940) are good on the Diggers.

Documents

1733. Haller, William, and Godfrey Davies, eds. *Leveller Tracts, 1647–53.* Gloucester, Massachusetts: Peter Smith, 1964.
1734. Wolfe, Don M., ed. *Leveller Manifestoes of the Puritan Revolution.* New York: T. Nelson, 1944.

Article

1735. Kishlansky, Mark. "The Army and the Levellers: The Roads to Putney." *Historical Journal* 22 (December 1979): 795–824.

Books

1736. Aylmer, Gerald E., ed. *The Levellers in the English Revolution.* Ithaca: Cornell University Press, 1975.
1737. Brailsford, H. N. *The Levellers and the English Revolution.* Stanford: Stanford University Press, 1961.
1738. Frank, Joseph. *The Levellers.* Cambridge, Massachusetts: Harvard University Press, 1955.
1739. Hayes, T. Wilson. *Winstanley the Digger: A Literary Analysis of Radical Ideas in the English Revolution.* Cambridge, Massachusetts: Harvard University Press, 1979.
1740. Hill, Christopher. *The World Turned Upside Down: Radical Ideas During the English Revolution.* New York: Viking, 1973.
1741. Holorenshaw, H. *The Levellers and the English Revolution.* London: Victor Gollancz, 1939.
1742. Pease, Theodore Calvin. *The Leveller Movement.* Washington, D.C.: American Historical Association, 1916.
1743. Petegorsky, David W. *Left-wing Democracy in the English Civil War: A Study of the Social Philosophy of Gerrard Winstanley.* London: Victor Gollancz, 1940.

Glorious Revolution, 1688-1689

The "bloodless," or Glorious Revolution culminated a century long struggle between Parliament and the Stuart kings of England over the issue of sovereignty. It was a relatively simple revolution, exhibiting none of the complexities of its predecessor of a generation earlier, the Puritan Revolution. It basically involved the forced abdication of James II and the peaceful accession of William and Mary. It was not a revolution which created a new order, but instead resulted in laws which strengthened the old. It was an aristocratic revolution engineered by the ruling classes for themselves, and not for the common people. But simple though it was, its significance lies in the fact of Parliament actually making a choice between the two kinds of rulers and their policies.

To sample the literature on the revolution see the book edited by Gerald M. Straka (1963). The best general accounts are the books by Maurice Ashley (1966), J. R. Jones (1972), David Ogg (1955), Lucile Pinkham (1954), Stuart Prall (1972), Gerald M. Straka (1962), and George M. Trevelyan (1965).

Bibliographies

1744. Davies, Godfrey. *Bibliography of British History: Stuart Period, 1603-1714.* 2d ed. Oxford: Clarendon Press, 1970.
1745. Grose, Clyde. *A Select Bibliography of British History, 1660-1760.* Chicago: University of Chicago Press, 1939.
1746. Sachse, William L. *Restoration England, 1660-1689.* Cambridge: Cambridge University Press, 1971.

Documents

1747. Browning, Andrew, ed. *English Historical Documents, 1660-1714.* New York: Oxford University Press, 1953.
1748. Kenyon, J. P., ed. *The Stuart Constitution, 1603-1688: Documents and Commentary.* Cambridge: Cambridge University Press, 1966.

Articles

1749. Cherry, George L. "The Legal and Philosophical Position of the Jacobites, 1688-1689." *Journal of Modern History* 22:4 (December 1950): 309-21.
1750. Edie, Carolyn A. "Revolution and the Rule of Law: The End of the Dispensing Power, 1689." *Eighteenth-Century Studies* 12 (Summer 1979): 434-50.
1751. Frankle, Robert. "The Formulation of the Declaration of Rights." *Historical Journal* 17 (1974): 265-79.

Glorious Revolution, 1688–1689

1752. Horowitz, H. "Parliament and the Glorious Revolution." *Bulletin of the Institute of Historical Research* 47:115 (May 1974): 36–52.

1753. Kenyon, J. P. "The Revolution of 1689: Resistance and Contract." In *Historical Perspectives,* edited by Neil McKendrick. London: Europa Publications, 1974.

1754. Mullett, Charles F. "Religion, Politics, and Oaths in the Glorious Revolution." *Review of Politics* 10:4 (October 1948): 462–74.

1755. Sachse, William L. "The Mob and the Revolution of 1688." *Journal of British Studies* 3:4 (Fall 1964): 23–40.

1756. Schwoerer, Lois G. "Propaganda in the Revolution of 1688–89." *American Historical Review* 82:4 (October 1977): 843–74.

1757. Tanner, J. R. "The Revolution of 1688." In *English Constitutional Conflicts of the Seventeenth Century, 1603–1689,* edited by J. R. Tanner. Cambridge: Cambridge University Press, 1962.

1758. Temperley, Harold W. "The Revolution and Revolution Settlement in Great Britain." In *The Cambridge Modern History,* edited by A. W. Ward et al. Cambridge: Cambridge University Press, 1908.

Books

1759. Ashley, Maurice. *The Glorious Revolution of 1688.* New York: Scribners, 1966.

1760. Bahlman, Dudley. *Moral Revolution of 1688.* New Haven: Yale University Press, 1957.

1761. Carswell, John. *The Descent on England: A Study of the English Revolution of 1688 and Its European Background.* New York: John Day, 1969.

1762. Childs, John. *The Army, James II and the Glorious Revolution.* New York: St. Martin's Press, 1981.

1763. Clark, George. *The Later Stuarts, 1660–1714.* Oxford: Clarendon Press, 1961.

1764. Hosford, David H. *Nottingham, Nobles and the North: Aspects of the Revolution of 1688.* Hamden, Connecticut: Shoe String Press, 1976.

1765. Jones, I. Deane. *The English Revolution, an Introduction to English History, 1603–1714.* London: Heinemann, 1931.

1766. Jones, J. R. *Country and Court: England, 1658–1714.* Cambridge, Massachusetts: Harvard University Press, 1978.

1767. _____. *The Restored Monarchy, 1660–1688.* Totowa, New Jersey: Rowman and Littlefield, 1979.

1768. _____. *The Revolution of 1688 in England.* New York: W. W. Norton, 1972.

1769. Kenyon, J. P. *The Nobility in the Revolution of 1688.* Hull, England: Publications Committee, the University, 1963.

1770. _____. *Revolution Principles: The Politics of Party, 1689–1720.* New York: Cambridge University Press, 1977.

1771. Landon, M. *The Triumph of the Lawyers: Their Role in English Politics, 1678–1689.* University: University of Alabama Press, 1970.

1772. Lodge, Richard. *History of England from the Restoration to the Death of William III.* London: Longmans, Green, 1910.

108 / Early Modern Europe

1773. Macaulay, Thomas Babington. *The History of England from the Accession of James II.* New York: Harper, 1856–1871.
1774. Ogg, David. *England in the Reigns of James II and William III.* Oxford: Clarendon Press, 1955.
1775. _____. *William III.* New York: Macmillan, 1967.
1776. Pinkham, Lucile. *William III and the Respectable Revolution.* Cambridge, Massachusetts: Harvard University Press, 1954.
1777. Prall, Stuart. *The Bloodless Revolution: England 1688.* Garden City, New York: Doubleday, 1972.
1778. Richardson, R. C. *The Debate on the English Revolution.* New York: St. Martin's Press, 1977.
1779. Straka, Gerald M., ed. *The Age of the Glorious Revolution of 1688.* Wilmington, Delaware: Scholarly Resources. Several volumes and dates.
1780. _____. *Anglican Reaction to the Revolution of 1688.* Madison: State Historical Society of Wisconsin, 1962.
1781. _____, ed. *The Revolution of 1688.* Lexington, Massachusetts: D. C. Heath, 1963.
1782. Trevelyan, George M. *The English Revolution, 1688–1689.* New York: Oxford University Press, 1965.
1783. Western, J. R. *Monarchy and Revolution: The English State in the 1680s.* Totowa, New Jersey: Rowman and Littlefield, 1972.

Locke and Revolution

John Locke was not only the most important theorist of the Glorious Revolution, but, indirectly, for many subsequent revolutions as well. He justified the right of revolution on the basis of natural right and the civil contract. The people, he said, are a community even after the dissolution of government, and therefore, they decide when a revolution is necessary. Revolution to Locke was not a reversal or restoration (as it had been viewed up until then), but a return to an earlier constitutional position. Not to be overlooked, and ultimately more important for the future, is Locke's opposition to the doctrine of innate ideas (in his *Essay Concerning the Human Understanding*), the belief that the human mind is miraculously foreordained and impermeable to experience. He said that human beings are products of their experience in society. This is an optimistic and monumental idea, and it has been behind the great revolutions of the next 300 years.

The two articles below, by Robert C. Grady, Jr. (1976) and Peter Laslett (1956), and the books by Maurice Cranston (1957), John M. Dunn (1969), J. H. Franklin (1978), and John Gough (1950) offer a thorough picture of Locke. And Locke, naturally, speaks for himself in his own writings.

Articles

1784. Grady, Robert C., Jr. "Obligation, Consent, and Locke's Right to Revolution: 'Who Is to Judge?'" *Canadian Journal of Political Science* 9 (June 1976): 277-92.

1785. Laslett, Peter. "The English Revolution and Locke's *Two Treatises of Government.*" *Cambridge Historical Journal* 12:1 (1956): 40-55.

Books

1786. Aaron, Richard I. *John Locke.* 3d ed. Oxford: Clarendon Press, 1971.

1787. Cranston, Maurice. *John Locke.* New York: Macmillan, 1957.

1788. Dunn, John M. *The Political Thought of John Locke.* London: Cambridge University Press, 1969.

1789. Franklin, J. H. *John Locke and the Theory of Sovereignty: Mixed Monarchy and the Right of Resistance in the Political Thought of the English Revolution.* New York: Cambridge University Press, 1978.

1790. Gough, John. *John Locke's Political Philosophy.* Oxford: Clarendon Press, 1950.

1791. Lemos, Ramon M. *Hobbes and Locke: Power and Consent.* Atlanta: University of Georgia Press, 1978.

1792. Locke, John. *Treatise of Civil Government and A Letter Concerning Toleration.* Edited by C. L. Sherman. New York: Appleton-Century-Crofts, 1937.

Scientific Revolution

The developments associated with the rise of modern science do not really comprise a revolution in the usual sense in which the word is used in this book. But since science aided significantly in helping Europe break with many of the restrictions of the past, often in a revolutionary way, these discoveries and their dissemination were vital for the course of civilization, and indirectly to the history of revolutions.

A survey of the literaure may be sampled in the edited collections of George Basalla (1968) and Vern L. Bullough (1970). A good brief overview is the article by Peter M. Heimann (1979). Excellent general surveys are by Marie Boas (1966), Herbert Butterfield (1965), and A. Rupert Hall (1966). The books by Hugh F. Kearney (1968) and Thomas S. Kuhn (1962) are also important; the former is a collection of documents and scholarly writings on the subject.

Articles

1793. Harvey, Bernard. "The Scientific Revolution and Counter-Revolution." *Proceedings of the Symposium of French-American Studies* (March 1973): 159–66

1794. Heimann, Peter M. "The Scientific Revolution." In *The New Cambridge Modern History,* vol. 13, edited by Peter Burke. New York: Cambridge University Press, 1979.

1795. Kearney, Hugh F. "Puritanism, Capitalism and the Scientific Revolution." *Past and Present,* no. 28 (1964): 81–101.

Books

1796. Basalla, George, ed. *The Rise of Modern Science.* Lexington, Massachusetts: D. C. Heath, 1968.

1797. Boas, Marie. *The Scientific Renaissance, 1450–1630.* New York: Harper and Row, 1966.

1798. Bullough, Vern L., ed. *The Scientific Revolution.* New York: Holt, Rinehart and Winston, 1970.

1799. Butterfield, Herbert. *The Origins of Modern Science, 1300–1800.* Rev. ed. New York: Free Press, 1965.

1800. Gillispie, G. C. *The Edge of Objectivity.* Princeton: Princeton University Press, 1960.

1801. Hall, A. Rupert. *The Scientific Revolution: 1500–1800.* Boston: Beacon, 1966.

1802. Haskins, Caryl. *The Scientific Revolution and World Politics.* New York: Harper and Row. 1964.

1803. Kearney, Hugh F., ed. *Origins of the Scientific Revolution.* New York: Barnes and Noble, 1968.

1804. Koyré, Alexandre. *The Astronomical Revolution.* Ithaca: Cornell University Press, 1973.

1805. Kuhn, Thomas S. *The Copernican Revolution.* Cambridge, Massachusetts: Harvard University Press, 1957.

1806. _____ . *The Structure of Scientific Revolutions.* Chicago: University of Chicago Press, 1962.

1807. Meldrum, A. N. *The Eighteenth-Century Revolution in Science—the First Phase.* Calcutta: Longmans, Green, 1930.

1808. Webster, Charles, ed. *The Intellectual Revolution of the Seventeenth Century.* Boston: Routledge and Kegan Paul, 1974.

Revolts in Spain

This section brings together works on several of the revolts in and against Spain, from the sixteenth century revolt in Castile, to the 1640 revolt in Catalonia, and to what Richard Herr calls the eighteenth century revolution in Spain.

Article

1809. Elliott, J. H. "Revolts in the Spanish Monarchy." In *Preconditions of Revolution in Early Modern Europe*, edited by R. Forster and J. P. Greene. Baltimore: Johns Hopkins University Press, 1970.

Books

1810. Elliott, J. H. *The Revolt of the Catalans.* Cambridge: Cambridge University Press, 1963.
1811. Herr, Richard. *The Eighteenth-Century Revolution in Spain.* Princeton: Princeton University Press, 1958.
1812. Seaver, Henry L. *The Great Revolt in Castile: A Study of the Comunero Movement of 1520-1521.* Boston: Houghton Mifflin, 1928.

Rousseau and Revolution

Jean Jacques Rousseau was probably the most original, profound, and permanently influential thinker of the eighteenth century. Though he was neither an active revolutionist nor consciously a revolutionary theorist, his life took the form of a revolt against society, and his influence on the French Revolution, especially through the person of Robespierre, was significant. In addition, there is controversy that has hovered around Rousseau's literary output ever since his death in 1778. His written words have been cited to show his opposition to despotism, oppression, and injustice in favor of liberty, equality, and law, on the one hand, while on the other, allusions have been made to different statements which lean in the direction of authoritarianism. As with Marx, perhaps it is some blend of profundity, contradiction, and broad appeal that makes for his level of genius. To sample this controversy see the edited collection by Guy H. Dodge (1971). Rousseau's links to the French Revolution are commented upon in many of the books below, but more specifically in the articles by G. H. McNeil (1945, 1953) and D. Williams (1933), and the book by Joan McDonald (1965). Among the better biographies are those by Frederick C. Green (1955) and Jean Guéhenno (1966).

Bibliographies

1813. Gay, Peter. "Reading about Rousseau." In *The Party of Humanity,* by Peter Gay. New York: Alfred A. Knopf, 1964.
1814. Schinz, Albert. *Etat présent des Travaux sur Jean-Jacques Rousseau.* New York: Modern Language Association, 1941.

1815. Spurlin, Paul M. "Jean-Jacques Rousseau." In *A Critical Bibliography of French Literature*. Vol. 4. *The Eighteenth Century*. Syracuse, New York: Syracuse University Press, 1951.

Articles

1816. Barber, Benjamin R., ed. "Rousseau." *Political Theory* 6:4 (November 1978), special issue.
1817. Cobban, Alfred. "New Light on the Political Thought of Rousseau." *Political Science Quarterly* 66:2 (June 1951): 272-84.
1818. Cranston, Maurice. "Remembering Rousseau: A Bicentennial Essay." *Encounter* 51:6 (1978): 38-47.
1819. McNeil, G. H. "The Anti-Revolutionary Rousseau." *American Historical Review* 58:4 (July 1953): 808-23.
1820. _____. "The Cult of Rousseau and the French Revolution." *Journal of the History of Ideas* 6 (1945): 197-212.
1821. Marshall, Terence. "Perception politique et théorie de la connaissance dans l'oeuvre de Jean-Jacques Rousseau." *Revue de français science politique* 29 (August 1979): 605-64.
1822. Williams, D. "The Influence of Rousseau on Political Opinion, 1760-1795." *English Historical Review* 48:191 (July 1933): 414-30.

Books

1823. Berman, Marshal. *The Politics of Authenticity: Radical Individualism and the Emergence of Modern Society*. New York: Atheneum, 1970.
1824. Blanchard, William H. *Rousseau and the Spirit of Revolt: A Psychological Study*. Ann Arbor: University of Michigan Press, 1967.
1825. Chapman, John W. *Rousseau: Totalitarian or Liberal?* New York: Columbia University Press, 1956.
1826. Cobban, Alfred. *Rousseau and the Modern State*. Hamden, Connecticut: Archon Books, 1961.
1827. Cohler, Anne M. *Rousseau and Nationalism*. New York: Basic Books, 1970.
1828. Crocker, Lester G. *Rousseau's Social Contract*. Cleveland: Case Western Reserve University Press, 1968.
1829. Dodge, Guy H., ed. *Jean-Jacques Rousseau: Authoritarian Libertarian?* Lexington, Massachusetts: D. C. Heath, 1971.
1830. Ellenburg, Stephen. *Rousseau's Political Philosophy*. Ithaca: Cornell University Press, 1976.
1831. Green, Frederick C. *Jean-Jacques Rousseau: A Critical Study of His Life and Writings*. Cambridge: At the University Press, 1955.
1832. Guéhenno, Jean. *Jean-Jacques Rousseau*. 2 vols. London: Routledge and Kegan Paul, 1966.
1833. Hall, J. C. *Rousseau: An Introduction to His Political Philosophy*. Cambridge: Cambridge University Press, 1973.
1834. Lemos, Ramon M. *Rousseau's Political Philosophy*. Atlanta: University of Georgia Press, 1977.
1835. McDonald, Joan. *Rousseau and the French Revolution, 1762-1791*. London: Athlone Press, 1965.

1836. McManners, John. *Rousseau.* New York: Hill and Wang, forthcoming.
1837. _____. *The Social Contract and Rousseau's Revolt against Society.* Leicester, England: Leicester University Press, 1968.
1838. Masters, Roger D. *The Political Philosophy of Rousseau.* Princeton: Princeton University Press, 1968.
1839. Morley, John. *Rousseau and His Era.* 2 vols. London: Macmillan, 1923.
1840. Plattner, Marc F. *Rousseau's State of Nature: An Interpretation of the "Discourse on Inequality."* De Kalb: Northern Illinois University Press, 1979.
1841. Rousseau, Jean Jacques. *The Social Contract and Discourses.* Translated by G. D. H. Cole. New York: E. P. Dutton, 1950.
1842. Shklar, Judith N. *Men and Citizens: A Study of Rousseau's Social Theory.* Cambridge: Cambridge University Press, 1969.
1843. Vaughan, C. E., ed. *The Political Writings of Jean-Jacques Rousseau.* 2 vols. New York: John Wiley, 1962.

Age of the Democratic Revolution, 1760-1815

Drawing upon the experience of the twentieth century as being an "age of revolutions," many historians no longer view the late eighteenth century as simply the "age of the French Revolution." Although the events in France after 1789 may be the most dramatic, other revolutionary activity, possibly reflecting a common Western or Atlantic civilization and common concerns, was underway. Needless to say, not all scholars have accepted this hypothesis. Questions have been raised as to the wisdom of studying these revolutionary movements from a Western rather than a national perspective. Also in dispute is the word "democratic"; were these revolutions indeed democratic? What is certain is that from the 1760s until the turn of the century there were a number of revolutionary upheavals on either side of the Atlantic: in Geneva, Ireland, the Netherlands, France, Hungary, the Austrian Netherlands, Poland, Italy, Switzerland, Germany, America, and Santo Domingo. To begin to understand the possibilities and problems of this hypothesis turn first to the collection of readings edited by Peter Amann (1963). Good general histories of the period are found in the books by Crane Brinton (1934), Leo Gershoy (1944), Norman Hampson (1969), and George Rudé (1966). To examine the revolutions in each of the countries mentioned above, the index along with the very titles of the articles and books should show the way. But no study of this period would be complete without a thorough reading of the pioneer work of R. R. Palmer (1959, 1964) and Jacques Godechot (1965).

Documents

1844. Williams, Merryn, ed. *Revolutions 1775–1830.* Baltimore: Penguin Books, 1971.

Articles

1845. Bienvenu, Richard T. "The Enlightenment and the Spirit of Revolution." *Proceedings of the Symposium of French-American Studies* (March 1973): 29–42.
1846. Bödy, Paul. "The Hungarian Jacobin Conspiracy of 1794–95." *Journal of Central European Affairs* 22 (1962): 3–26.
1847. Cobban, Alfred. "The Age of the Democratic Revolution." *History* 45 (1960): 234–39.
1848. Dozier, Robert R. "Democratic Revolution in England: A Possibility?" *Albion* 4:4 (Winter 1972): 183–92.
1849. Godechot, Jacques. "Revolutionary Contagion, 1770–1825." *Proceedings of the Western Society of French History* 4 (1976): 256–62.
1850. Henderson, A. J., ed. "The Irish Rebellion of 1798: Two First Hand Accounts." *Journal of the Society of Army History* 52 (Spring 1974): 34–45.
1851. Palmer, R. R. "Much in Little: The Dutch Revolution of 1795." *Journal of Modern History* 26:1 (March 1954): 15–35.
1852. _____. "World Revolution of the West: 1763–1801." *Political Science Quarterly* 69:1 (March 1954): 1–14.
1853. _____, and P. Kenez. "Two Documents of the Hungarian Revolutionary Movement of 1794." *Journal of Central European Affairs* 20 (1960): 423–44.
1854. Sugar, P. F. "The Influence of the Enlightenment and the French Revolution in Eighteenth-Century Hungary." *Journal of Central European Affairs* 17 (1957): 331–55.

Books

1855. Amann, Peter, ed. *The Eighteenth-Century Revolution.* Lexington, Massachusetts: D. C. Heath, 1963.
1856. Bourne, Henry Eldridge. *The Revolutionary Period in Europe (1763–1815).* New York: Century, 1917.
1857. Brinton, Crane. *A Decade of Revolution, 1789–1799.* New York: Harper and Row, 1934.
1858. Dippel, Horst. *Germany and the American Revolution, 1770–1800: A Sociohistorical Investigation of Late Eighteenth-Century Political Thinking.* Translated by B. A. Uhlendorf. Chapel Hill: University of North Carolina Press, 1977.
1859. Fay, Bernard. *The Revolutionary Spirit in France and America, 1763–1783.* Chapel Hill: University of North Carolina Press, 1941.
1860. Field, Henry Martyn. *The Irish Confederates and the Rebellion of 1798.* New York: Harper, 1851.
1861. Gershoy, Leo. *From Despotism to Revolution, 1763–1789.* New York: Harper and Row, 1944.
1862. Godechot, Jacques. *France and the Atlantic Revolution of the Eighteenth Century, 1770–1799.* New York: Free Press, 1965.

1863. Goodwin, Albert. *The Friends of Liberty: The English Democratic Movement in the Age of the French Revolution.* Cambridge, Massachusetts: Harvard University Press, 1979.
1864. Gottschalk, Louis. *The Place of the American Revolution in the Causal Pattern of the French Revolution.* Easton, Pennsylvania: American Friends of Lafayette, 1948.
1865. _____ , and Donald Lach. *Toward the French Revolution: Europe and America in the Eighteenth-Century World.* New York: Scribners, 1973.
1866. Hampson, Norman. *The First European Revolution, 1776-1815.* New York: Harcourt, Brace and World, 1969.
1867. Jarrett, Derek. *The Begetters of Revolution: England's Involvement with France, 1759-1789.* Totowa, New Jersey: Rowman and Littlefield, 1973.
1868. Kaiser, A. *Geschichte der Polnischen Revolution vom Jahre 1794.* Leipzig: Literarisches Museum, 1833.
1869. McDowell, R. B. *Ireland in the Age of Imperialism and Revolution, 1760-1801.* New York: Oxford University Press, 1979.
1870. Palmer, R. R. *The Age of the Democratic Revolution: A Political History of Europe and America, 1760-1800.* 2 vols. Princeton: Princeton University Press, 1959, 1964.
1871. Rudé, George. *Revolutionary Europe, 1783-1815.* New York: Harper and Row, 1966.
1872. Schama, Simon. *Patriots and Liberators: Revolution in the Netherlands, 1780-1813.* New York: Alfred A. Knopf, 1977.

French Revolution, 1789-1799

With the French Revolution of 1789 the concept and idea of revolution came of age. Revolution was now viewed as a finite process controlled by human, not supernatural forces. The events in France elevated revolution from a mere change of government (or governors) to include the more grandiose scheme of creating an entirely new social order. Revolution was to be a way to achieve perfectibility. In a proverbial nutshell, this is what gave the French Revolution its overwhelming force and international significance. For the next century and a quarter (until 1917) the French Revolution was the point of reference for virtually all revolutionary activity.

A variety of issues and controversies comprise the historiography of the French Revolution. For example, were the economic origins of the revolution rooted in poverty or prosperity? Did the Enlightenment have a positive, tragic, or no influence upon the revolution? To what extent was the American Revolution an influence? Was the revolution actually revolutionary or has a myth been perpetuated? To what extent was the revolution the result of class conflict? To what extent was the revolution a turning point in history? The titles of many of the articles and books below indicate which among them addresses which question. Useful edited collections are by William F. Church (1964), Alfred Cobban (1958), Ralph W. Greenlaw (1958, 1975), Steven T. Ross (1971), and Brian Tierney et al (1977).

Among the best general surveys and overviews are the books by François Furet and Denis Richet (1970), Pierre Gaxotte (1932), Leo Gershoy (1932, 1964), Jacques Godechot (1965), Norman Hampson (1975), Georges Lefebvre (1962, 1964), Albert Mathiez (1964), J. M. Roberts (1978), Albert Soboul (1974), and J. M. Thompson (1945). Among the many excellent specialized studies the following should not be overlooked: Elinor G. Barber (1955), Richard Cobb (1965, 1970, 1972), Alfred Cobban (1955, 1964), Franklin L. Ford (1965), Robert Forster (1960), Norman Hampson (1963), Georges Lefebvre (1924, 1947, 1963, 1973), Claude Manceron (1977, 1978), George Rudé (1959), and Albert Soboul (1964, 1972).

Historiographies

1873. Cavanaugh, Gerald J. "The Present State of French Revolutionary Historiography: Alfred Cobban and Beyond." *French Historical Studies* 7:4 (Fall 1972): 587–606.

1874. Idzerda, Stanley J. *The Background of the French Revolution.* Washington, D.C.: American Historical Association Service Center for Teachers of History, 1959.

1875. McManners, John. "The Historiography of the French Revolution." In *The New Cambridge Modern History,* Vol. 8, *The American and French Revolutions, 1763–93,* edited by A. Goodwin. Cambridge: At the University Press, 1965.

1876. Stewart, John Hall. *The French Revolution: Some Trends in Historical Writing, 1945–1965.* Washington, D.C.: American Historical Association Service Center for Teachers of History, 1967.

Documents

1877. Higgins, E. L. *The French Revolution, as Told by Contemporaries.* Boston: Houghton Mifflin, 1939.

1878. Legg, Wickham, ed. *Documents Illustrative of the History of the French Revolution.* Oxford: Clarendon Press, 1905.

1879. Stephens, Henry M., ed. *The Principal Speeches of the Statesmen and Orators of the French Revolution, 1789–1795.* 2 vols. Oxford: Clarendon Press, 1892.

1880. Stewart, John Hall. *A Documentary Survey of the French Revolution.* New York: Macmillan, 1951.

1881. Thompson, James M., ed. *French Revolution, Documents.* Oxford: Basil Blackwell, 1933.

French Revolution, 1789-1799 / 117

Eyewitness Accounts

1882. Morris, Gouverneur. *A Diary of the French Revolution.* Boston: Houghton Mifflin, 1939.
1883. Young, Arthur. *Travels in France During the Years 1787, 1788, and 1789.* Edited by C. Maxwell. Cambridge: Cambridge University Press, 1929.

Overviews, Surveys, Interpretations

Articles

1884. Ellis, Geoffrey. "The 'Marxist Interpretation' of the French Revolution." *English Historical Review* 93 (April 1978): 353-76.
1885. Ford, Franklin L. "The Revolutionary-Napoleonic Era: How Much of a Watershed?" *American Historical Review* 69:1 (October 1963): 18-29.
1886. Goodwin, Albert. "Reform and Revolution in France: October 1789-February 1793." In *The New Cambridge Modern History*, Vol. 8, *The American and French Revolutions, 1763-93*, edited by A. Goodwin. Cambridge: Cambridge University Press, 1965.
1887. Hyslop, Beatrice, et al. "The Meaning of the French Revolution: A Panel Discussion." *Proceedings of the Symposium of French-American Studies* (March 1973): 73-84.
1888. Palmer, R. R. "Reflections on the French Revolution." *Political Science Quarterly* 67:1 (March 1952): 64-80.
1889. Shulim, Joseph I. "On the Nature of the French Revolution." *Proceedings of the Consortium on Revolutionary Europe* 9 (1979): 233-38.

Books

1890. Acton, John E. *Lectures on the French Revolution.* New York: AMS Press, n.d.
1891. Aulard, Alphonse. *The French Revolution.* Translated by B. Miall. New York: Scribners, 1910.
1892. Bearman, Graham. *The French Revolution.* Exeter, New Hampshire: Heinemann Educational Books, 1977.
1893. Belloc, Hilaire. *The French Revolution.* 2d ed. London: Oxford University Press, 1948.
1894. Cairns, Trevor. *The Old Regime and the Revolution.* New York: Cambridge University Press, 1976.
1895. Carlyle, Thomas. *The French Revolution: A History.* 2 vols. New York: Dutton, 1955.
1896. Cobban, Alfred. *Aspects of the French Revolution.* New York: W. W. Norton, 1970.
1897. _____. *France Since the Revolution.* London: Jonathan Cape, 1970.
1898. _____. *The Myth of the French Revolution.* London: Lewis, 1955.
1899. Connelly, Owen. *French Revolution/Napoleonic Era.* New York: Holt, Rinehart and Winston, 1979.

118 / Early Modern Europe

1900. Dawson, Philip, ed. *The French Revolution.* Englewood Cliffs, New Jersey: Prentice-Hall, 1967.
1901. Eimerl, Sarel. *Revolution! France, 1789-1794.* Boston: Little, Brown, 1967.
1902. Ferrero, G. *The Two French Revolutions, 1789-1796.* Translated by S. J. Hurwitz. New York: Basic Books, 1968.
1903. Furet, François. *Interpreting the French Revolution.* Translated by E. Forster. New York: Cambridge University Press, 1981.
1904. _____, and Denis Richet. *The French Revolution.* Translated by S. Hardman. New York: Macmillan, 1970.
1905. Gaxotte, Pierre. *The French Revolution.* Translated by W. A. Phillips. New York: Scribners, 1932.
1906. Gershoy, Leo. *The French Revolution and Napoleon.* Englewood Cliffs, New Jersey: Prentice-Hall, 1964.
1907. _____. *The French Revolution, 1789-1799.* New York: Holt, Rinehart and Winston, 1932.
1908. Godechot, Jacques. *Les Révolutions.* 2d ed. Paris: Presses Universitaires de France, 1965.
1909. Goodwin, Albert. *The French Revolution, 1789-1794.* Rev. ed. London: Hutchinson's University Library, 1966.
1910. Gottschalk, Louis. *The Era of the French Revolution, 1715-1815.* Boston: Houghton Mifflin, 1957.
1911. Greenlaw, Ralph W., ed. *The Economic Origins of the French Revolution.* Lexington, Massachusetts: D. C. Heath, 1958.
1912. _____, ed. *The Social Origins of the French Revolution.* Lexington, Massachusetts: D. C. Heath, 1975.
1913. Hampson, Norman. *The French Revolution: A Concise History.* New York: Scribners, 1975.
1914. Hazen, Charles Downer. *The French Revolution and Napoleon.* New York: Holt, 1917.
1915. Hibbert, Christopher. *The Days of the French Revolution.* New York: Morrow, 1980.
1916. James, Cyril L. *History of the French Revolution.* New York: Gordon Press, n.d.
1917. Jaurès, Jean. *Histoire Socialiste De la Révolution Française.* 8 vols. New York: AMS Press, n.d.
1918. Johnson, Douglas. *The French Revolution.* New York: G. P. Putnam's, 1970.
1919. _____, ed. *French Society and the Revolution.* New York: Cambridge University Press, 1976.
1920. Kaplow, Jeffry, ed. *New Perspectives on the French Revolution.* New York: John Wiley, 1965.
1921. Knapton, Ernest John. *Revolutionary and Imperial France, 1750-1815.* New York: Scribners, 1972.
1922. Kropotkin, Peter. *The Great French Revolution.* New York: Schocken, 1971.
1923. Lefebvre, Georges. *Etudes sur la Révolution Française.* Paris: Presses Universitaires de France, 1963.
1924. _____. *The French Revolution.* Vol. 1. *From Its Origins to 1793.* Translated by E. M. Evanson; Vol. 2. *From 1793-1799.* Translated by J. H. Stewart and J. Friguglietti. New York: Columbia University Press, 1962, 1964.

1925. Madelin, Louis. *The French Revolution.* New York: G. P. Putnam's, 1925.
1926. Mallet du Pan, Jacques. *Considerations on the Nature of the French Revolution: And on the Causes which Prolong Its Duration.* New York: Howard Fertig, 1974.
1927. Manceron, Claude. *The French Revolution.* Vol. 1. *Twilight of the Old Order, 1774-1778.* Translated by P. Wolf. New York: Alfred A. Knopf, 1977.
1928. _____. *The French Revolution.* Vol. 2. *The Wind From America, 1778-1781.* Translated by N. Amphoux. New York: Alfred A. Knopf, 1978.
1929. Mathews, Shailer. *The French Revolution: A Sketch.* New York: Longmans, 1901.
1930. Mathiez, Albert. *The French Revolution.* New York: Grosset and Dunlap, 1964.
1931. Michelet, Jules. *History of the French Revolution.* Chicago: University of Chicago Press, 1967.
1932. Mignet, F. A. M. *History of the French Revolution from 1789 to 1814.* London: Bell, 1912.
1933. Pernoud, Georges, and Sabine Flaissier. *The French Revolution.* Translated by R. Graves. New York: Capricorn Books, 1970.
1934. Roberts, J. M. *The French Revolution.* New York: Oxford University Press, 1978.
1935. Ross, Steven T., ed. *The French Revolution: Conflict or Continuity?* New York: Holt, Rinehart and Winston, 1971.
1936. Salvemini, Gaetano. *The French Revolution: 1788-1792.* Translated by I. M. Rawson. New York: W. W. Norton, 1962.
1937. Soboul, Albert. *The French Revolution, 1787-1799.* Translated by A. Forrest and C. Jones. New York: Random House, 1974.
1938. _____. *A Short History of the French Revolution, 1789-1799.* Translated by G. Symcox. Berkeley: University of California Press, 1977.
1939. Stephens, Henry M. *A History of the French Revolution.* 2 vols. New York: Scribners, 1886-1891.
1940. Sydenham, M. J. *The French Revolution.* New York: Putnam, 1965.
1941. Thiers, M. A. *The History of the French Revolution.* Translated by F. Shoberl. Philadelphia: Carey, 1945.
1942. Thompson, James M. *The French Revolution.* New York: Oxford University Press, 1945.
1943. Tocqueville, Alexis de. *The Old Regime and the French Revolution.* Garden City, New York: Doubleday, 1955.

Causes and Origins

Articles

1944. Baszkiewicz, Jan. "La Révolution française aux yeux des révolutionnaires." *Acta Poloniae Histoire* 37 (1978): 71-93.
1945. Donaghay, Marie. "The American Revolution, Vergennes' English Policy, and the Coming of the French Revolution." *Proceedings of the Symposium of French-American Studies* (March 1973): 59-74.

1946. Eisenstein, Elizabeth L. "Who Intervened in 1788? A Commentary on *The Coming of the French Revolution.*" *American Historical Review* 71:1 (October 1965): 77–103.
1947. Hunt, Lynn A. "Committees and Communes: Local Politics and National Revolution in 1789." *Comparative Studies in Society and History* 18:3 (July 1976): 321–46.
1948. _____. "Revolution and Urban Politics in Provincial France: Troyes and Reims, 1786–1790." *Journal of Modern History* 50:4 (December 1978): abstract.
1949. Rudé, George. "The Outbreak of the French Revolution." *Past and Present*, no. 8 (November 1955): 28–42.
1950. Taylor, George V. "Noncapitalist Wealth and the Origins of the French Revolution." *American Historical Review* 72:2 (January 1967): 469–96.
1951. _____. "Revolutionary and Nonrevolutionary Content in the *Cahiers* of 1789: An Interim Report." *French Historical Studies* 7:2 (Spring 1972): 479–502.

Books

1952. Braesch, Frédéric. *1789, L'année cruciale*. Paris: Librairie Gallimard, 1941.
1953. Cobban, Alfred. *Historians and the Causes of the French Revolution*. London: University College, 1958.
1954. Doyle, William. *Origins of the French Revolution*. New York: Oxford University Press, 1981.
1955. Egret, Jean. *The French Prerevolution, 1787–1788*. Translated by W. D. Camp. Chicago: University of Chicago Press, 1978.
1956. Garrett, Mitchell B. *The Estates General of 1789*. New York: Appleton-Century, 1935.
1957. Godechot, Jacques. *The Taking of the Bastille, July 14, 1789*. New York: Scribners, 1970.
1958. Gosselin, Louis L. T. *The September Massacres*. London: Hutchinson, 1929.
1959. Kaplow, Jeffry. *France on the Eve of Revolution*. New York: John Wiley, 1971.
1960. Lefebvre, Georges. *The Coming of the French Revolution*. Translated by R. R. Palmer. Princeton: Princeton University Press, 1947.
1961. _____. *The Great Fear of 1789: Rural Panic in Revolutionary France*. Translated by J. White. New York: Pantheon Books, 1973.
1962. Lowell, Edward J. *The Eve of the French Revolution*. Boston: Houghton Mifflin, 1922.
1963. Tierney, Brian, et al, eds. *The Origins of the French Revolution*. 3d ed. New York: Random House, 1977.

Ancien Régime

Articles

1964. Behrens, C. B. A. "Nobles, Privileges and Taxes in France at the End of the Ancien Régime." *Economic History Review,* 2d ser. 15:3 (April 1963): 451-75.
1965. Doyle, William. "The Parlements of France and the Breakdown of the Old Regime, 1771-1788." *French Historical Studies* 6:4 (Fall 1970): 415-58.
1966. _____. "Was there an Aristocratic Reaction in Pre-Revolutionary France?" *Past and Present,* no. 57 (November 1972): 97-122.

Books

1967. Behrens, C. B. A. *The Ancien Régime.* New York: Harcourt, Brace, World, 1967.
1968. Dakin, Douglas. *Turgot and the Ancient Regime in France.* London: Methuen, 1939.
1969. Funck-Brentano, Frantz. *The Old Regime in France.* Translated by H. Wilson. London: Edward Arnold, 1929.
1970. Sagnac, P. *La fin de l'Ancien Régime et la Révolution américaine.* 3d ed. Paris: Presses Universitaires de France, 1952.
1971. Taine, Hippolyte. *The Ancient Regime.* Translated by J. Durand. New York: Henry Holt, 1876.

Economic and Social Considerations

1972. Balsama, George D. *The Social Impact of the French Revolution.* St. Charles, Missouri: Forum Press, 1974.
1973. Bosher, J. F. *French Finances, 1770-1795: From Business to Bureaucracy.* Cambridge: Cambridge University Press, 1970.
1974. Cobban, Alfred. *The Social Interpretation of the French Revolution.* London: Cambridge University Press, 1964.
1975. Forrest, Alan. *Society and Politics in Revolutionary Bordeaux.* New York: Oxford University Press, 1975.
1976. Hampson, Norman. *A Social History of the French Revolution.* Toronto: University of Toronto Press, 1963.
1977. Labrousse, C. E. *La Crise de l'Economie Française à la Fin de l'Ancien Régime et au Début de la Révolution.* Paris: Presses Universitaires de France, 1943.
1978. Rudé, George. *The Crowd in the French Revolution.* Oxford: Clarendon Press, 1959.
1979. Sée, Henri. *Economic and Social Conditions in France During the Eighteenth Century.* Translated by E. H. Zeydel. New York: F. S. Crofts, 1927.
1980. Soboul, Albert. *La France à la Veille de la Révolution: Economie et Société.* Paris: Centre de Documentation Universitaire, 1960.

Participation, Democracy, Legitimacy

Articles

1981. Applewhite, Harriet B. "Political Legitimacy in Revolutionary France, 1788-91." *Journal of Interdisciplinary History* 9 (Autumn 1978): 245-76.
1982. Hunt, Lynn A. "Symbolic Legitimation and Popular Politics in Revolutionary France." *Proceedings of the Consortium on Revolutionary Europe* 9 (1979): 281-88.
1983. Palmer, R. R. "Popular Democracy in the French Revolution: Review Article." *French Historical Studies* 1:4 (December 1960): 445-69.
1984. Rudé, George. "The French Revolution and 'Participation'." In *A World in Revolution?* edited by E. Kamenka. Canberra: Australian National University, 1970.

Book

1985. Webster, Nesta. *The French Revolution: A Study in Democracy.* London: Constable, 1922.

Ideology

Article

1986. Banning, Lance. "Jefferson, Ideology and the French Revolution: A Question of Liberticide at Home." *Studies in Burke and His Time* 17:2 (Winter 1976): 5-26.

Books

1987. Elton, Godfrey. *The Revolutionary Idea in France, 1789-1871.* New York: Longmans, Green, 1923.
1988. Van Duzer, Charles Hunter. *Contribution of the Ideologues to French Revolutionary Thought.* Baltimore: Johns Hopkins University Press, 1935.

Enlightenment

Articles

1989. Lougee, Carolyn C. "The Enlightenment and the French Revolution." *Eighteenth-Century Studies* 11 (Fall 1977): 84-103.
1990. Meyer, P. H. "The French Revolution and the Legacy of the Philosophes." *French Review* 30:6 (May 1957): 429-34.
1991. Peyre, Henri. "The Influence of Eighteenth-Century Ideas on the French Revolution." *Journal of the History of Ideas* 10 (1949): 63-87.
1992. Salmon, J. H. M. "Turgot and Condorcet: Progress, Reform, and Revolution." *History Today* 27 (May 1977): 332-38.

Books

1993. Burlingame, Anne Elizabeth. *Condorcet, the Torch Bearer of the French Revolution.* Boston: Statford, 1930.

1994. Church, William F., ed. *The Influence of the Enlightenment on the French Revolution: Creative, Disastrous or Non-Existent?* Boston: D. C. Heath, 1964.

1995. Crocker, Lester G. *An Age of Crisis: Man and World in Eighteenth Century France.* Baltimore: Johns Hopkins University Press, 1959.

1996. Hazard, Paul. *European Thought in the Eighteenth Century.* New Haven: Yale University Press, 1954.

1997. Martin, Kingsley. *French Liberal Thought in the Eighteenth Century.* New York: Harper and Row, 1963.

1998. Mornet, Daniel. *French Thought in the Eighteenth Century.* Translated by L. M. Levin. Englewood Cliffs, New Jersey: Prentice-Hall, 1929.

1999. Voegelin, Eric. *From Enlightenment to Revolution.* Durham, North Carolina: Duke University Press, 1975.

Class

2000. Kaplow, Jeffry; Gilbert Shapiro; and Elizabeth L. Eisenstein. "Class in the French Revolution: A Discussion." *American Historical Review* 72:2 (January 1967): 497–522.

2001. Lucas, Colin. "Nobles, Bourgeois and the Origins of the French Revolution." *Past and Present,* no. 60 (August 1973): 84–126.

2002. Soboul, Albert. "Classes and Class Struggle during the French Revolution." *Science and Society* 17:3 (Summer 1953): 238–57.

Nobility

Articles

2003. Forster, Robert. "The Survival of the Nobility During the French Revolution." *Past and Present,* no. 37 (July 1967): 71–86.

2004. Goodwin, Albert. "Calonne, the Assembly of French Notables of 1789 and the Origins of the Révolte Nobiliare." *English Historical Review* 61:240 (May 1946): 202–34; 61:241 (September 1946): 329–77.

Books

2005. Ford, Franklin L. *Robe and Sword: The Regrouping of the French Aristocracy After Louis XIV.* New York: Harper and Row, 1965.

2006. Forster, Robert. *The Nobility of Toulouse in the Eighteenth Century: A Social and Economic Study.* Baltimore: Johns Hopkins University Press, 1960.

Bourgeoisie

2007. Barber, Elinor G. *The Bourgeoisie in 18th Century France.* Princeton: Princeton University Press, 1955.
2008. Dawson, Philip. "The *Bourgeoisie de Robe* in 1789." *French Historical Studies* 4:1 (Spring 1965): 1–21.

Sans-Culottes

2009. Soboul, Albert. *The Parisian Sans-Culottes and the French Revolution, 1793–4.* Translated by G. Lewis. Oxford: Clarendon Press, 1964.
2010. _____. *The Sans-Culottes: The Popular Movement and Revolutionary Government, 1793–94.* Translated by R. I. Hall. New York: Anchor Books, 1972.
2011. Williams, Gwyn A. *Artisans and Sans-Culottes: Popular Movements in France and Britain during the French Revolution.* New York: W. W. Norton, 1969.

Peasants

Articles

2012. Davies, Alun. "The Origins of the French Peasant Revolution of 1789." *History* 49:165 (February 1964): 24–41.
2013. Palmer, R. R. "Georges Lefebvre: The Peasants and the French Revolution." *Journal of Modern History* 31:4 (December 1959): 329–42.

Book

2014. Lefebvre, Georges. *Les Paysans du Nord pendant La Révolution Française.* Lille, France: Librairie Papeterie, 1924.

Everyday Life

2015. Lewis, Gwynne. *Life in Revolutionary France.* New York: G. P. Putnam's, 1972.
2016. Robiquet, Jean. *Daily Life in the Time of the French Revolution.* Translated by J. Kirkup. New York: Macmillan, 1965.

Religion

Articles

2017. Connelly, James L. "A Prelate and His Pamphlets: The Defence of the Church during the French Revolution." *Eighteenth Century Life* 5 (Fall 1978): 21–28.

2018. Van Kley, Dale. "Church, State, and the Ideological Origins of the French Revolution: The Debate over the General Assembly of the Gallican Clergy in 1765." *Journal of Modern History* 51:4 (December 1979): 629-66.

Books

2019. Aulard, Alphonse. *Christianity and the French Revolution.* Translated by Lady Frazer. London: E. Benn, 1927.
2020. Jervis, William H. *The Gallican Church and the Revolution.* London: K. Paul, Trench, 1882.

Nationalism

Articles

2021. Palmer, R. R. "The National Idea in France before the Revolution." *Journal of the History of Ideas* 1 (1940).
2022. Shafer, Boyd C. "Bourgeois Nationalism in the Pamphlets on the Eve of the Revolution." *Journal of Modern History* 10:1 (March 1938): 31-50.

Book

2023. Hyslop, Beatrice. *French Nationalism in 1789 According to the General Cahiers.* New York: Octagon Books, 1968.

Paris

Article

2024. Cobb, Richard. "The Beginning of the Revolutionary Crisis in Paris." In *A Second Identity,* by R. Cobb. London: Oxford University Press, 1969.

Books

2025. Censer, Jack Richard. *Prelude to Power: The Parisian Radical Press, 1789-1791.* Baltimore: Johns Hopkins University Press, 1976.
2026. Cobb, Richard. *Paris and Its Provinces, 1792-1802.* New York: Oxford University Press, 1975.
2027. Fischer, John. *Six Summers in Paris, 1789-1794.* New York: Harper and Row, 1966.
2028. Gendron, François. *La Jeunesse Dorée: Episodes de la Révolution française.* Quebec: Presses de l'Université du Quebec, 1979.
2029. Lenotre, C. *Paris in the Revolution.* New York: Brentano's, n.d.
2030. Petersen, Susanne. *Lebensmittelfrage und revolutionäre Politik in Paris, 1792-1793: Studien zum Verhältnis von revolutionärer Bourgeoisie und Volksbewegung bei Herausbildung der Jakobinerdiktatur.* Munich: R. Oldenbourg Verlag, 1979.

2031. Sanborn, Alvan Francis. *Paris and the Social Revolution: A Study of the Revolutionary Elements in the Various Classes of Parisian Society.* Boston: Maynard, 1905.

The Enragés

2032. Cobb, Richard. "The Enragés." In *A Second Identity,* by R. Cobb. London: Oxford University Press, 1969.
2033. Rose, R. B. *The Enragés: Socialists of the French Revolution?* New York: Cambridge University Press, 1965.

Louis XVI and Regicide

Article

2034. Walzer, Michael. "Regicide and Revolution." *Social Research* 40:4 (Winter 1973): 617–42.

Books

2035. Jordon, David P. *The King's Trial: The French Revolution vs. Louis XVI.* Berkeley: University of California Press, 1979.
2036. Padover, Saul K. *The Life and Death of Louis XVI.* New York: Taplinger, 1963.
2037. Walzer, Michael. *Regicide and Revolution.* New York: Cambridge University Press, 1974.

Leaders

Articles

2038. Brace, Richard. "Two Studies in Revolutionary Decision: Robespierre and Lafayette. A Commentary." *Proceedings of the Consortium on Revolutionary Europe* 7 (1977): 51–53.
2039. Idzerda, Stanley. "When and Why Lafayette Became a Revolutionary." *Proceedings of the Consortium on Revolutionary Europe* 7 (1977): 34–50.

Books

2040. Beesly, Augustus Henry. *Life of Danton.* New York: Longmans, Green, 1899.
2041. Gottschalk, Louis. *John Paul Marat: A Study in Radicalism.* Chicago: University of Chicago Press, 1967.
2042. Hampson, Norman. *Danton.* New York: Holmes and Meier, 1978.
2043. Madelin, Louis. *Danton.* New York: Alfred A. Knopf, 1921.

2044. _____. *Figures of the Revolution.* Translated by R. Curtis. New York: Macauley Company, 1929.
2045. Patrick, Alison. *The Men of the First French Republic: Political Alignments in the National Convention of 1792.* Baltimore: Johns Hopkins University Press, 1972.
2046. Thompson, James M. *Leaders of the French Revolution.* New York: Harper and Row, 1962.

Jacobins

Articles

2047. George, Margaret. "The 'World Historical Defeat' of the Républicaines-Révolutionnaires [1793]." *Science and Society* 40:4 (1976-1977): 410-37.
2048. Kennedy, Michael L. "The Foundation of the Jacobin Clubs and the Development of the Jacobin Club Network, 1789-1791." *Journal of Modern History* 51:4 (December 1979): 701-33.
2049. Leśnodorski, Boguslaw. "The State of the Jacobin Dictatorship: Theory and Reality." In *The American and European Revolutions,* edited by J. Pelenski. Iowa City: University of Iowa Press, 1980.
2050. Patrick, Alison. "Political Divisions in the French National Convention, 1792-93." *Journal of Modern History* 41:4 (December 1969): 421-74.
2051. Reisch, Michael. "The Leadership of the Paris Jacobins, 1789-1793." *Proceedings of the Consortium on Revolutionary Europe* 9 (1979): 211-17.

Books

2052. Cobb, Richard. *Terreur et subsistances.* Paris: Librairie Clavreuil, 1965.
2053. Wright, D. G. *Revolution and Terror in France, 1789-1795.* New York: Longman, 1974.

Girondins

2054. Dipadova, Theodore A. "The Girondins and the Question of Revolutionary Government." *French Historical Studies* 9:2 (Spring 1976): 432-50.
2055. Sydenham, M. J. *The Girondins.* London: Athlone Press, 1961.

Directory

Article

2056. Hunt, Lynn A., et al. "The Failure of the Liberal Republic in France, 1795-1799: The Road to Brumaire." *Journal of Modern History* 51:4 (December 1979): 734-59.

Books

2057. Lyons, Martyn. *France Under the Directory.* New York: Cambridge University Press, 1975.
2058. Woloch, Isser. *Jacobin Legacy: The Democratic Movement Under the Directory.* Princeton: Princeton University Press, 1970.

The Revolution and Europe

Article

2059. Schleunes, Karl A. "The French Revolution and the Schooling of European Society: A Model for Explanation." *Proceedings of the Consortium on Revolutionary Europe* 7 (1977): 140–50.

Books

2060. Cobb, Richard. *Reactions to the French Revolution.* New York: Oxford University Press, 1972.
2061. Palmer, R. R. *The World of the French Revolution.* New York: Harper and Row, 1971.
2062. Sloane, William Milligan. *The French War and the Revolution.* New York: Scribners, 1893.

Miscellaneous

Articles

2063. Abray, Jane. "Feminism in the French Revolution." *American Historical Review* 80:1 (February 1975): 43–62.
2064. Cobb, Richard. "The Revolutionary Mentality in France." In *A Second Identity,* by R. Cobb. London: Oxford University Press, 1969.
2065. Furet, François. "Le Catéchisme Révolutionnaire." *Annales: Economies, Sociétés, Civilisations* 26:2 (March-April 1971): 255–89.
2066. Gay, Peter. "Rhetoric and Politics in the French Revolution." *American Historical Review* 66:3 (April 1961): 664–76.
2067. Harris, H. S. "Hegel and the French Revolution." *Clio* 7 (Fall 1977): 5–18.
2068. Higonnet, Patrice L. R. "Babeuf: Communist or Proto-Communist." *Journal of Modern History* 51:4 (December 1979): 773–81.
2069. Hood, James N. "The Continuity of Old Regime Politics in the Early Revolution as a Guarantee of Diversity." *Proceedings of the Consortium on Revolutionary Europe* 9 (1979): 218–28.
2070. _____. "Revival and Mutation of Old Rivalries in Revolutionary France." *Past and Present,* no. 82 (February 1979): 82–115.
2071. Kirkland, John D. "The Revolution in/through the Notion of Civil Society in Rousseau, Kant, and Hegel." *Proceedings of the Consortium on Revolutionary Europe* 9 (1979): 188–94.

2072. Mitchell, Harvey. "Resistance to the Revolution in Western France." *Past and Present*, no. 63 (May 1974): 94–131.
2073. Poster, Mark. "History and Theory: Sartre and Althusser on 1789." *Eighteenth Century: Theory and Interpretation* 20 (Winter 1979): 39–49.
2074. Rose, Steven. "French Revolutionary Infantry Tactics." *Proceedings of the Consortium on Revolutionary Europe* 9 (1979): 149–54.
2075. Soboul, Albert. "Some Problems of the Revolutionary State, 1789–1796." *Past and Present*, no. 65 (November 1974): 52–74.

Books

2076. Bax, Ernest Belfort. *Last Episodes of the French Revolution.* Brooklyn, New York: Haskell House, 1971.
2077. Beik, Paul H. *The French Revolution Seen from the Right.* New York: Howard Fertig, 1971.
2078. Birch, Una. *Secret Societies and the French Revolution.* New York: Gordon Press, 1976.
2079. Bowers, Claude Gernade. *Pierre Vergniaud: Voice of the French Revolution.* New York: Macmillan, 1950.
2080. Buonarroti, Filippo Michele. *Buonarroti's History of Babeuf's Conspiracy for Equality.* London: H. Hetherington, 1836.
2081. Cobb, Richard. *The Police and the People: French Popular Protest, 1789–1820.* London: Oxford University Press, 1970.
2082. Cochin, Augustin. *Les Sociétés de pensée et la démocratie.* Paris: Librairie Plon, 1921.
2083. Dawson, Christopher. *The Gods of Revolution.* New York: New York University Press, 1972.
2084. Dawson, Philip. *Provincial Magistrates and Revolutionary Politics in France, 1789–1795.* Cambridge, Massachusetts: Harvard University Press, 1972.
2085. France, Anatole. *The Gods Are Athirst.* Translated by L. Frey; M. Frey; and R. Zylawy. Norwood, Pennsylvania: Norwood Editions, 1978.
2086. Greer, Donald. *The Incidence of the Emigration During the French Revolution.* Cambridge, Massachusetts: Harvard University Press, 1951.
2087. Henderson, Ernest F. *Symbol and Satire in the French Revolution.* New York: G. P. Putnam's, 1912.
2088. Holtmann, Robert B. *The Napoleonic Revolution.* Philadelphia: Lippincott, 1967.
2089. Hunt, Lynn A. *Revolution and Urban Politics in Provincial France: Troyes and Reims, 1786–1790.* Stanford: Stanford University Press, 1977.
2090. Kim, Kyung-Won. *Revolution and International System.* New York: New York University Press, 1970.
2091. May, Gita. *Madame Roland and the Age of Revolution.* New York: Columbia University Press, 1970.
2092. Palmer, R. R., ed. *The School of the French Revolution.* Princeton: Princeton University Press, 1975.
2093. Popkin, Jeremy D. *The Right-Wing Press in France, 1792–1800.* Chapel Hill: University of North Carolina Press, 1980.
2094. Rose, Steven. *Gracchus Babeuf: The First Revolutionary Communist.* Stanford: Stanford University Press, 1978.

2095. Roustan, Marius. *The Pioneers of the French Revolution.* Translated by F. Whyte. London: Ernest Benn, 1926.
2096. Staël, Madame la Baronne de. *Considérations sur les Principaux Événements de la Révolution Française.* New York: Arno Press, 1979.

Robespierre and the Reign of Terror

During 1793 and 1794 Maximilien de Robespierre personified the French Revolution. He was a Jacobin and a member of the National Convention and its Committee of Public Safety; he was incorruptible and had a fundamental faith in the revolution. He is perhaps one of the least understood of all revolutionists, being seen as either a bloodthirsty fanatic, dictator, and demagogue or an idealist and patriot whose goals were democratic. He was a disciple of Rousseau, believing in the importance of "virtue," and he was determined to create a democratic republic made up of good, honest citizens. The method chosen by Robespierre and his colleagues on the Committee of Public Safety to repress counter-revolutionary forces and promote the revolution was the use of revolutionary courts. The period is known as the "Reign of Terror." Robespierre and the Terror are covered in most of the general works on the French Revolution listed in the previous section. The book edited by Richard Bienvenu (1968) is a good collection of readings. Among the best biographies of Robespierre are those by Norman Hampson (1974), Albert Mathiez (1958), Jean Matrat (1975), George Rudé (1975), and James M. Thompson (1935, 1965). Several articles on Robespierre are also useful, including those by Alfred Cobban (1946, 1948), Joseph I. Shulim (1977), and Albert Soboul (1978). Saint-Just was Robespierre's colleague on the Committee of Public Safety, and he is best portrayed in the biography by Geoffrey Bruun (1966). The most important works on the Terror itself include the article by Richard Cobb (1957) and the books by Crane Brinton (1961), Richard Cobb (1961–1963), Donald Greer (1935), Stanley Loomis (1973), and R. R. Palmer (1941).

Articles

2097. Cobb, Richard. "The Revolutionary Mentality in France, 1793–1794." *History* 52 (1957): 181–96.
2098. Cobban, Alfred. "The Fundamental Ideas of Robespierre." *English Historical Review* 63 (January 1948): 29–51.
2099. _____. "The Political Ideas of Maximilien Robespierre during the Period of the Convention." *English Historical Review* 61 (January 1946): 45–80.
2100. Loubère, L. A. "The Intellectual Origins of French Jacobin Socialism." *International Review of Social History* 4 (1959): 415–31.

2101. Popkin, Jeremy D. "The Royalist Press in the Reign of Terror." *Journal of Modern History* 51:4 (December 1979): 685–700.
2102. Shulim, Joseph I. "The Birth of a Revolutionary: Robespierre in Artois." *Proceedings of the Consortium on Revolutionary Europe* 7 (1977): 22–23.
2103. _____. "The Birth of Robespierre as a Revolutionary: A Horneyan Psycho-Historical Approach." *American Journal of Psychoanalysis* 37 (1977): 343–50.
2104. _____. "Robespierre and the French Revolution (A Review Article)." *American Historical Review* 82:1 (February 1977): 20–38.
2105. Soboul, Albert. "Robespierre and the Contradictions of Jacobinism." *Proceedings of the Annual Meeting of the Western Society of French History* 5 (1978): 87–98.

Books

2106. Belloc, Hilaire. *Robespierre: A Study.* New York: G. P. Putnam's, 1928.
2107. Bienvenu, Richard, ed. *Ninth of Thermidor: The Fall of Robespierre.* Oxford: Oxford University Press, 1968.
2108. Brinton, Crane. *The Jacobins.* New York: Russell and Russell, 1961.
2109. Bruun, Geoffrey. *Saint-Just, Apostle of Terror.* Hamden, Connecticut: Shoe String Press, 1966.
2110. Cobb, Richard. *Les Armées Révolutionnaires: Instrument de la Terreur dans les Départements, Avril 1793-Floréal, An II.* Paris: Mouton, 1961–1963.
2111. Curtis, Eugene. *Saint-Just, Colleague of Robespierre.* New York: Octagon Books, 1973.
2112. Gallo, Max. *Robespierre the Incorruptible, A Psycho-Biography.* Translated by R. Rudorff. New York: Herder and Herder, 1971.
2113. Godfrey, James Logan. *Revolutionary Justice: A Study of the Organization, Personnel and Procedure of the Paris Tribunal, 1793–1795.* Chapel Hill: University of North Carolina Press, 1951.
2114. Greer, Donald. *The Incidence of the Terror during the French Revolution.* Cambridge, Massachusetts: Harvard University Press, 1935.
2115. Hampson, Norman. *The Life and Opinions of Maximilien Robespierre.* London: Duckworth, 1974.
2116. Lewes, George Henry. *The Life of Maximilien Robespierre.* Philadelphia: Carey and Hart, 1849.
2117. Loomis, Stanley. *Paris in the Terror.* New York: Avon Books, 1973.
2118. Lucas, Colin. *The Structure of the Terror: The Example of Javogues and the Loire.* New York: Oxford University Press, 1973.
2119. Markov, Walter M., ed. *Maximilien Robespierre, 1758–1794.* Berlin: Ruetten and Loening, 1958.
2120. Mathiez, Albert. *Etudes sur Robespierre.* Paris: Editions Sociales, 1958.
2121. _____. *Fall of Robespierre and Other Essays.* Fairfield, New Jersey: Augustus Kelley, 1968.
2122. Matrat, Jean. *Robespierre: Or the Tyranny of the Majority.* Translated by A. Kendall and F. Brenner. New York: Scribners, 1975.
2123. Palmer, R. R. *Twelve Who Ruled: The Year of the Terror in the French Revolution.* Princeton: Princeton University Press, 1941.
2124. Rudé, George. *Robespierre: Portrait of a Revolutionary Democratic.* New York: Viking, 1975.

2125. Scott, William. *Terror and Repression in Revolutionary Marseilles.* New York: Barnes and Noble, 1973.
2126. Thompson, James M. *Robespierre.* 2 vols. Oxford: Basil Blackwell, 1935.
2127. _____. *Robespierre and the French Revolution.* New York: Collier Books, 1965.

The Vendée, 1793-1796

The Vendée is a region in western France, and it is also the name given to the archetypical counterrevolution that erupted there in 1793. The revolt was a royalist reaction against popular sovereignty, and a peasant uprising against the religious and conscription policies of the revolutionary government. All the works below are useful, although first and foremost is the book by Charles Tilly (1964).

Articles

2128. Cobb, Richard. "The Comte d'Antraigues and the Counter-Revolutionary Mentality." In *A Second Identity,* by R. Cobb. London: Oxford University Press, 1969.
2129. _____. "The Counter-Revolt." In *A Second Identity,* by R. Cobb. London: Oxford University Press, 1969.
2130. Mitchell, Harvey. "The Vendée and Counterrevolution: A Review Essay." *French Historical Studies* 5:4 (Fall 1968): 405-29.

Books

2131. Crétineau-Joly, J. *Histoire de La Vendée Militaire.* 2 vols. Paris: Plon Frères, 1851.
2132. Faucheux, Marcel. *L'Insurrection Vendéenne de 1793: Aspects Economiques et Sociaux.* Paris: Imprimerie Nationale, 1964.
2133. Godechot, Jacques. *The Counter-Revolution: Doctrine and Reaction, 1789-1804.* Translated by S. Attanasio. New York: Howard Fertig, 1972.
2134. Lewis, Gwynne. *The Second Vendée: The Continuity of Counter-Revolution in the Department of the Gard, 1798-1815.* New York: Oxford University Press, 1978.
2135. Lidove, Marcel. *Les Vendéens de 93.* Paris: Seuil, 1971.
2136. Paret, Peter. *Internal War and Pacification: The Vendée, 1786-96.* Princeton: Center of International Studies, 1961.
2137. Ross, Michael. *Banners of the King: The War of the Vendée, 1793-4.* London: Seeley Service, 1975.
2138. Tilly, Charles. *The Vendée.* Cambridge, Massachusetts: Harvard University Press, 1964.

Edmund Burke and Revolution

Burke was a conservative Englishman who had been sympathetic toward the American Revolution, but in 1790 warned against the excesses of the French Revolution in his *Reflections on the Revolution in France.* He came to believe that the principle of popular sovereignty might be fatal to liberty. That is, whatever a government has the power to do it has the right to do, thus rendering any action legal. From this it followed that even tyranny and aggression were permissible if conducted in the name of the people.

In seeking more information about Burke the articles by Ernest Barker (1945) and Michael Freeman (1978) and the books by Alfred Cobban (1976), Carl B. Cone (1957, 1964), and Isaac Kramnick (1977) are especially useful. The eloquent rejoinder by Thomas Paine (1930) should also be read.

Bibliography

2139. Gandy, Clara I., and Peter J. Stanlis. *Edmund Burke: An Annotated Secondary Bibliography.* New York: Garland, 1981.

Articles

2140. Barker, Ernest. "Burke on the French Revolution." In *Essays on Government,* by E. Barker. Oxford: Clarendon Press, 1945.
2141. Dreyer, Frederick. "Edmund Burke: The Philosopher in Action." *Studies in Burke and His Time* 15:2 (Winter 1973–1974): 121–42.
2142. _____. "Legitimacy and Usurpation in the Thought of Edmund Burke." *Albion* 12:3 (Fall 1980): 257–67.
2143. Freeman, Michael. "Edmund Burke and the Sociology of Revolution." *Political Studies* 25 (December 1977): 459–73.
2144. _____. "Edmund Burke and the Theory of Revolution." *Political Theory* 6 (August 1978): 277–97.
2145. Gurr, Ted Robert. "Burke and the Modern Theory of Revolution. A Reply to Freeman." *Political Theory* 6 (August 1978): 299–311.
2146. Melvin, Peter H. "Burke on Theatricality and Revolution." *Journal of the History of Ideas* 36 (July-September 1975): 447–68.
2147. Paulson, Ronald. "Burke's Sublime and the Representation of Revolution." In *Culture and Politics from Puritanism to the Enlightenment,* edited by P. Zagorin. Berkeley: University of California Press, 1980.

Books

2148. Burke, Edmund. *Reflections on the Revolution in France.* Garden City, New York: Doubleday, 1961.
2149. _____. *The Works of the Right Honorable Edmund Burke.* 7 vols. Boston: Little, Brown, 1866.
2150. Canavan, Francis P. *The Political Reason of Edmund Burke.* Durham, North Carolina: Duke University Press, 1960.
2151. Cobban, Alfred. *Edmund Burke and the Revolt Against the Eighteenth Century.* New York: AMS Press, 1976.
2152. Cone, Carl B. *Burke and the Nature of Politics.* Vol. 1. *The Age of the American Revolution.* Lexington: University of Kentucky Press, 1957.
2153. _____. *Burke and the Nature of Politics.* Vol. 2. *The Age of the French Revolution.* Lexington: University of Kentucky Press, 1964.
2154. Dreyer, Frederick. *Burke's Politics: A Study in Whig Orthodoxy.* Waterloo, Canada: W. Laurier University Press, 1979.
2155. Kramnick, Isaac. *Edmund Burke.* Englewood Cliffs, New Jersey: Prentice-Hall, 1974.
2156. _____. *The Rage of Edmund Burke: Portrait of an Ambivalent Conservative.* New York: Basic Books, 1977.
2157. Langford, Paul, ed. *The Writings and Speeches of Edmund Burke.* Vol. 2. *Party, Parliament and the American Crisis, 1766–1774.* New York: Oxford University Press, 1981.
2158. Macpherson, C. B. *Burke.* New York: Hill and Wang, 1980.
2159. Miller, Alice P. *Edmund Burke and His World.* Greenwich, Connecticut: Devin-Adair, 1978.
2160. Morley, John. *Edmund Burke: A Historical Study.* New York: Arno Press, 1979.
2161. Murray, Robert Henry. *Edmund Burke: A Biography.* London: Oxford University Press, 1931.
2162. O'Gorman, Frank. *Edmund Burke: His Political Philosophy.* Bloomington: Indiana University Press, 1973.
2163. Paine, Thomas. *Rights of Man, Being an Answer to Mr. Burke's Attack on the French Revolution.* London: Dent and Dutton, 1930.
2164. Parkin, C. *The Moral Basis of Burke's Political Thought.* Cambridge: Cambridge University Press, 1956.
2165. Ritcheson, Charles R. *Edmund Burke and the American Revolution.* Atlantic Highlands, New Jersey: Humanities Press, 1976.
2166. Smith, Robert A., ed. *Edmund Burke on Revolution.* New York: Harper and Row, 1968.

Pugachev's Rebellion, 1773–1774

The rebellion led by Emelian Pugachev against the regime of Catherine the Great of Russia was a great peasant insurrection. A Cossack and former soldier, Pugachev, as was an old Russian custom, announced that he was the true tsar, Peter III (Catherine's deceased husband). Catherine had raised peasant hopes that she would provide relief for the deteriorating condition of Russian serfs, but nothing substantial happened. Among other things, Pugachev proclaimed an end to serfdom, and his following among the peasants was large. Even though the rebellion failed it proved to be one of the most formidable peasant insurrections since the Peasants' Revolt of 1525. In addition to the works below, more on the Pugachev Rebellion can be found in histories of Russia in the eighteenth century and biographies of Catherine the Great.

Articles

2167. Longworth, Philip. "Peasant Leadership and the Pugachev Revolt." *Journal of Peasant Studies* 2 (January 1975): 183-205.
2168. Raeff, Marc. "Pugachev's Rebellion." In *Preconditions of Revolution in Early Modern Europe,* edited by R. Forster and J. P. Greene. Baltimore: Johns Hopkins University Press, 1970.

Book

2169. Alexander, John T. *Autocratic Politics in a National Crisis: The Imperial Russian Government and Pugachev's Revolt, 1773-1775.* Bloomington: Indiana University Press, 1969.

4 Modern Europe

"The mark of inhuman treatment of humans is . . . the mark of a beast, whether its insignia is the military or the movement. . . . The revolution will be no better and no more truthful and no more populist and no more attractive than those who brought it into being."
                    Father Daniel Berrigan
                    (1970)

For a people who have usually considered themselves highly civilized and, often, superior to others throughout the world, and for a people—along with Americans—who have looked upon the many coups and revolutions of areas such as Latin America with a bizarre blend of humor and disdain, Europeans have been curiously preoccupied, from the late eighteenth through the twentieth centuries, with revolutions (to say nothing of wars). Wedded to the flaunted glory of European civilization has been the less publicized gory aspects. Still, it might be argued, these revolutions (and wars?) have resulted in the progress of Western civilization. Is such a defense merely after-the-fact justification? This is for each of us to decide.

What is clear is that most of the revolutions and revolutionists covered in this chapter have had a major, if not monumental impact upon their countries and the world. Much of the revolutionary activity of the nineteenth century was, in part at least, an attempt to fulfill the hopes of 1789 and work out the problems arising from industrialization; the articles by Stanley Mellon (1979) and Theodor Schieder (1962) examine some of these issues. In the twentieth century the national revolutions of Europe can be viewed on the basis of their impact on and relation to the rest of the continent and the world; the article by Hugh Seton-Watson (1951) discusses this and other topics. All that is certain is that the European world has changed since 1815, and revolutions have played key roles in the process.

This chapter deals with all of the major and many of the minor European revolutions and revolutionists during the past two centuries. (Marx and Engels, along with works on anarchism, communism, and socialism are located in Chapter 1 since their character is more universal rather than simply European.) The table of contents states which and who these are. Among the titles below are texts and surveys of different blocks of the larger period, such as the volumes in the excellent "Rise of Modern Europe" series which include those by Frederick Artz (1934), William L. Langer (1969), Robert C. Binkley (1935), Carlton J. H. Hayes

(1941), Oron J. Hale (1971), and Raymond Sontag (1971). Other useful such texts and surveys are by J. P. T. Bury (1960), Michael Elliott-Bateman et al (1974), Friedrich Heer (1972), Raymond Postgate (1920), and especially Charles Tilly, Louise Tilly, and Richard Tilly (1975).

There are works which treat both the period of the late eighteenth century and post-1815 era, such as the article by John R. Gillis (1970) and the books by Charles Breunig (1970), David L. Dowd (1967), John Roberts (1976), and especially those first-rate studies by Eric J. Hobsbawm (1962) and George Rudé (1964). There are books which examine revolutions in one region, such as those by F. L. Carsten (1972) for central Europe and Hugh Seton-Watson (1956) for eastern Europe; and there are works which analyze a given subject in more than one revolution, such as the article by Franz Borkenau (1937) on state and revolution in three revolutions. There are works which deal with several revolutions in a single country, such as by Godfrey Elton (1923), John Plamenatz (1965), and Douglas Porch (1974) for France, Theodore S. Hamerow (1958) for Germany, and Edward Crankshaw (1976) and Harrison E. Salisbury (1978) for Russia. There are books which concentrate on some of the minor revolutions of the period, such as those by A. Ezergailis (1974) on the 1917 revolution in Latvia, Victor G. Kiernan (1966) on the 1854 revolution in Spain, and Anatole G. Mazour (1961) and Mikhail Zetlin (1958) on the Russian Decembrist Revolt of 1825. There are memoirs by revolutionists, such as Milovan Djilas (1973) and Vera Figner (1927); and there are biographies of revolutionists or revolutionary theorists not linked to any single revolution, such as by Edward Acton (1979) on Alexander Herzen, Elizabeth L. Eisenstein (1959) on Buonarroti, and Joseph Hamburger (1963) on James Mill. Finally, there are any number of other works which do not fit readily into any of the sections that follow.

Bibliographies

2170. *Bibliographic Guide to Soviet and East European Studies: 1978.* Boston: G. K. Hall, 1979.
2171. Bullock, Alan, and A. J. P. Taylor. *A Select List of Books on European History, 1815-1914.* 2d ed. Oxford: Clarendon Press, 1957.
2172. Medlicott, W. N. *Modern European History, 1789-1945: A Select Bibliography.* London: Routledge and Kegan Paul, 1960.
2173. Ragatz, Lowell J. *A Bibliography for the Study of European History, 1815-1939.* Ann Arbor, Michigan: Edwards Bros., 1942-1956.
2174. Roach, John. *A Bibliography of Modern Europe.* London: Cambridge University Press, 1968.

Historiography

2175. Anderson, E. N. *Nineteenth Century Europe: Crises and Contributions.* Washington, D.C.: American Historical Association Service Center for Teachers of History, 1959.

Documents

2176. Postgate, Raymond, ed. *Revolution from 1789-1906.* London: Grant Richards, 1920.
2177. Zinner, Paul E., ed. *National Communism and Popular Revolt in Eastern Europe: A Selection of Documents on Events in Poland and Hungary, February-November, 1956.* New York: Columbia University Press, 1956.

Reference

2178. Palmer, Alan. *Dictionary of 20th Century History.* New York: Penguin Books, 1979.

Articles

2179. Borkenau, Franz. "State and Revolution in the Paris Commune, the Russian Revolution and the Spanish Civil War." *Sociological Review* 29:1 (1937): 41-75.
2180. Botsford, Keith. "If *les Mao* Won Their Revolution, They Would Immediately Start Another." *The New York Times Magazine* (17 September 1972).
2181. Cobb, Richard. "Revolutionary Situations in France, 1789-1968." In *A Second Identity,* by R. Cobb. London: Oxford University Press, 1969.
2182. Forster, Robert. "The French Revolution and the 'New' Elite, 1800-50." In *The American and European Revolutions,* edited by J. Pelenski. Iowa City: University of Iowa Press, 1980.
2183. Gillis, John R. "Political Decay and the European Revolutions, 1789-1848." *World Politics* 22:3 (April 1970): 344-70.
2184. Golin, Steve. "Stendhal: The Novelist as Revolutionary." *Proceedings of the Consortium on Revolutionary Europe* 8 (1978): 33-43.
2185. Hazlett, J. Stephen. "Education and Revolution during the Nineteenth Century: A Commentary." *Proceedings of the Consortium on Revolutionary Europe* 7 (1977): 162-66.
2186. Isono, Fujiko. "Soviet Russia and the Mongolian Revolution of 1921." *Past and Present,* no. 83 (May 1979): 116-40.
2187. Jones, Larry Eugene. "Inflation, Revolution, and Crisis of Middle-Class Politics: A Study in the Dissolution of the German Party System, 1923-28." *Central European History* 12 (June 1979): 143-68.
2188. Kieniewicz, Stefan. "The Revolutionary Nobleman: An East European Variant of the Liberation Struggle in the Restoration Era." In *The American and European Revolutions,* edited by J. Pelenski. Iowa City: University of Iowa Press, 1980.
2189. McClellan, Woodford. "Revolutionary Exiles: The Russians in the First International and the Paris Commune." *Journal of Modern History* 51:3 (September 1979): abstract.
2190. May, Gita. "Revolution and the Romantic Sensibility." *Proceedings of the Symposium of French-American Studies* (March 1973): 185-200.
2191. Mellon, Stanley. "Nineteenth-Century Perceptions of Revolution." In *Problems in European History,* edited by Harold T. Parker. Durham, North Carolina: Moore Publishing, 1979.

2192. Mitchell, Harvey. "Resistance to Revolution in Western France." *Past and Present*, no. 63 (May 1974): 94–131.
2193. Moon, S. Joan. "The Saint-Simoniennes and the Moral Revolution." *Proceedings of the Consortium on Revolutionary Europe* 6 (1976): 161–75.
2194. Nasaw, David. "From Inquiétude to Revolution." *Journal of Contemporary History* 11:3 (July 1976): 149–72.
2195. Richards, Michael. "Reform, Reaction, Revolution: Russia 1894–1917." In *Problems in European History*. Durham, North Carolina: Moore Publishing, 1979.
2196. Rudé, George. "Ideology and Popular Protest in Revolutionary France, 1789–1871." *Proceedings of the Western Society of French History* 6 (1978): 201–08.
2197. Schieder, Theodor. "The Problem of Revolution in the Nineteenth Century." In *The State and Society in Our Times*, by Theodor Schieder. London: Thomas Nelson, 1962.
2198. Seton-Watson, Hugh. "Twentieth-Century Revolutions." *Political Quarterly* 22:3 (July-September 1951): 251–65.
2199. Sharkey, Stephen R., and Robert S. Dombroski. "Revolution, Myth and Mythical Politics: The Futurist Solution." *Journal of European Studies* 6 (December 1976): 231–47.
2200. Snyder, David, and Charles Tilly. "Hardship and Collective Violence in France, 1830 to 1960." *American Sociological Review* 37:5 (October 1972): 520–32.
2201. Spitzer, Alan B. "The Ambiguous Heritage of the French Restoration: The Distant Consequences of the Revolution and the Daily Realities of the Empire." In *The American and European Revolutions*, edited by J. Pelenski. Iowa City: University of Iowa Press, 1980.
2202. Suny, Ronald. "Populism, Nationalism and Marxism: The Origins of the Revolutionary Parties among the Armenians of the Caucasus." *Armenian Review* 32 (June 1979): 134–51.
2203. Tilly, Charles. "Reflections on the Revolutions of Paris." *Social Problems* 12:1 (1964): 99–121.
2204. Walicki, Andrzej. "The Problem of Revolution in Polish Thought, 1831–48/49." In *The American and European Revolutions*, edited by J. Pelenski. Iowa City: University of Iowa Press, 1980.
2205. Wheeler, Douglas L. "The Portuguese Revolution of 1910." *Journal of Modern History* 44:2 (June 1972): 172–94.

Books

2206. Acton, Edward. *Alexander Herzen and the Role of the Intellectual Revolutionary*. New York: Cambridge University Press, 1979.
2207. Amalrik, Andrei A. *Notebooks of a Revolutionary*. New York: Alfred A. Knopf, 1981.
2208. Artz, Frederick. *Reaction and Revolution, 1814–1832*. New York: Harper and Brothers, 1934.
2209. Binkley, Robert C. *Realism and Nationalism, 1852–1871*. New York: Harper and Brothers, 1935.
2210. Breunig, Charles. *The Age of Revolution and Reaction, 1789–1850*. New York: W. W. Norton, 1970.

140 / Modern Europe

2211. Bury, J. P. T., ed. *The Zenith of European Power, 1830-1870.* Vol. 10 in *The New Cambridge Modern History.* New York: Cambridge University Press, 1960.

2212. Carsten, F. L. *Revolution in Central Europe, 1918-1919.* Berkeley: University of California Press, 1972.

2213. Caute, David. *The Left in Europe, Since 1789.* New York: McGraw-Hill, 1966.

2214. Church, Clive H. *Revolution and Red Tape: The French Ministerial Bureaucracy, 1770-1850.* New York: Oxford University Press, 1981.

2215. Cole, G. D. H. *Socialist Thought: Marxism and Anarchism, 1850-1890.* New York: St. Martin's Press, 1964.

2216. Colton, Ethan T. *Four Patterns of Revolution.* New York: Arno Press, 1935.

2217. Crankshaw, Edward. *The Shadow of the Winter Palace: Russia's Drift to Revolution, 1825-1917.* New York: Viking, 1976.

2218. Dickinson, G. Lowes. *Revolution and Reaction in Modern France.* London: Allen and Unwin, 1927.

2219. Djilas, Milovan. *Memoir of a Revolutionary.* Translated by D. Willen. New York: Harcourt Brace Jovanovich, 1973.

2220. Dowd, David L., ed. *The Age of Revolution, 1770-1870.* Boston: D. C. Heath, 1967.

2221. Dunlop, John B. *The New Russian Revolutionaries.* Belmont, Massachusetts: Nordland, 1975.

2222. Eastman, Max. *Marx, Lenin and the Science of Revolution.* London: Allen and Unwin, 1926.

2223. Eidelberg, Philip Gabriel. *The Great Rumanian Peasant Revolt of 1907: Origins of a Modern Jacquerie.* Leiden: E. J. Brill, 1974.

2224. Eisenstein, Elizabeth L. *The First Professional Revolutionist: Filippo Michele Buonarroti (1761-1837).* Cambridge, Massachusetts: Harvard University Press, 1959.

2225. Elliott-Bateman, Michael, et al. *Revolt to Revolution: Studies in the 19th and 20th Century European Experience.* London: Manchester, 1974.

2226. Elton, Godfrey. *The Revolutionary Idea in France, 1789-1871.* New York: Longmans, Green, 1923.

2227. Engels, Friedrich. *The German Revolutions.* Chicago: University of Chicago Press, 1967.

2228. Ezergailis, A. *The 1917 Revolution in Latvia.* New York: Columbia University Press, 1974.

2229. Figner, Vera. *Memoirs of a Revolutionist.* New York: International Publishers, 1927.

2230. George C. H. *Revolution: European Radicals from Hus to Lenin.* Chicago: Scott, Foresman, 1971.

2231. Hale, Oron J. *The Great Illusion, 1900-1914.* New York: Harper and Row, 1971.

2232. Hall, Walter Phelps. *World Wars and Revolutions: The Course of Europe Since 1900.* New York: Appleton, 1943.

2233. Hamburger, Joseph. *James Mill and the Art of Revolution.* New Haven: Yale University Press, 1963.

2234. Hamerow, Theodore S. *Restoration, Revolution, Reaction: Economics and Politics in Germany, 1815-1871.* Princeton: Princeton University Press, 1958.

2235. Hangen, Welles. *The Muted Revolution: East Germany's Challenge to Russia and the West.* New York: Alfred A. Knopf, 1966.

2236. Hayes, Carlton J. H. *A Generation of Materialism, 1871-1900.* New York: Harper and Brothers, 1941.
2237. Heer, Friedrich. *Europe, Mother of Revolutions.* Translated by C. Kessler and J. Adcock. New York: Praeger, 1972.
2238. Hillquit, Morris. *From Marx to Lenin.* New York: Hanford Press, 1921.
2239. Hobsbawm, Eric J. *The Age of Revolution, 1789-1849.* New York: Mentor Books, 1962.
2240. Horward, Donald D., ed. *The Consortium on Revolutionary Europe, 1750-1850: Proceedings, 1974.* Gainesville: University Presses of Florida, 1978.
2241. Johnston, Robert H. *Tradition Versus Revolution: Russians and the Balkans in 1917.* New York: Columbia University Press, 1977.
2242. Judt, Tony. *Socialism in Provence, 1871-1914: A Study in the Origins of the French Left.* New York: Cambridge University Press, 1979.
2243. Kiernan, Victor G. *The Revolution of 1854 in Spanish History.* Oxford: Clarendon Press, 1966.
2244. Kirkwood, David. *My Life of Revolt.* London: Harrap, 1935.
2245. Kovrig, Bennett. *Communism in Hungary from Kun to Kádár.* Stanford: Hoover Institution, 1979.
2246. Lackner, Bede K., and Kenneth Roy Philp, eds. *Essays on Modern European Revolutionary History.* Austin: University of Texas Press, 1977.
2247. Langer, William L. *Political and Social Upheaval, 1832-1852.* New York: Harper and Row, 1969.
2248. Lindemann, Albert S. *The "Red Years": European Socialism versus Bolshevism, 1919-1921.* Berkeley: University of California Press, 1974.
2249. Lubasz, Heinz, ed. *Revolutions in Modern European History.* New York: Macmillan, 1970.
2250. Margadant, Ted W. *French Peasants in Revolt: The Insurrection of 1851.* Princeton: Princeton University Press, 1979.
2251. Mazour, Anatole G. *The First Russian Revolution, 1825.* Stanford: Stanford University Press, 1961.
2252. Meier, Paul. *William Morris: The Marxist Dreamer.* 2 vols. Translated by F. Grubb. Atlantic Highlands, New Jersey: Humanities Press, 1978.
2253. Mowat, C. L., ed. *The Shifting Balance of World Forces, 1898-1945.* 2d ed. Vol. 12 in *The New Cambridge Modern History.* New York: Cambridge University Press, 1968.
2254. Nalbandian, Louise Z. *The Armenian Revolutionary Movement: The Development of Armenian Political Parties Through the Nineteenth Century.* Berkeley: University of California Press, 1963.
2255. Oren, Nissan. *Bulgarian Communism: The Road to Power, 1934-1944.* New York: Columbia University Press, 1972.
2256. Osborne, John W. *The Silent Revolution: The Industrial Revolution as a Source of Cultural Change.* New York: Scribners, 1970.
2257. Plamenatz, John. *The Revolutionary Movements in France: 1815-1871.* London: Longmans, Green, 1965.
2258. Porch, Douglas. *Army and Revolution: France 1815-1848.* Boston: Routledge and Kegan Paul, 1974.
2259. Postgate, Raymond. *Out of the Past: Some Revolutionary Sketches.* New York: Vanguard, 1926.
2260. Raeff, Marc. *The Decembrist Movement.* Englewood Cliffs, New Jersey: Prentice-Hall, 1966.

2261. Ranke, Leopold von. *History of Servia, and the Servian Revolution.* Translated by A. Kerr. London: H. C. Bohn, 1853.
2262. Reed, Christopher. *Religion, Revolution and the Russian Intelligentsia, 1900-1912.* New York: Barnes and Noble, 1979.
2263. Roberts, John. *Revolution and Improvement: The Western World, 1775-1847.* Berkeley: University of California Press, 1976.
2264. Rosenthal, Bernice G. *D. S. Merezhkovsky and the Silver Age: The Development of a Revolutionary Mentality.* The Hague: Nijhoff, 1975.
2265. Rudé, George. *The Crowd in History: A Study in Popular Disturbances in France and England, 1730-1848.* New York: John Wiley, 1964.
2266. Salisbury, Harrison E. *Black Night, White Snow: Russia's Revolutions, 1905-1917.* Garden City, New York: Doubleday, 1978.
2267. Schulz, Gerhard. *Revolutions and Peace Treaties, 1917-1920.* Translated by M. Jackson. New York: Barnes and Noble, 1972.
2268. Scott, John. *Europe in Revolution.* Boston: Houghton Mifflin, 1945.
2269. Senn, Alfred Erich. *Diplomacy and Revolution: The Soviet Mission to Switzerland, 1918.* Notre Dame, Indiana: University of Notre Dame Press, 1973.
2270. Seton-Watson, Hugh. *The East European Revolution.* New York: Praeger, 1956.
2271. Sewell, William H., Jr. *Work and Revolution in France: The Language of Labor from the Old Regime to 1848.* New York: Cambridge University Press, 1980.
2272. Shipley, Peter. *Revolutionaries in Modern Britain.* Levittown, New York: Transatlantic Arts, 1976.
2273. Shorter, Edward, and Charles Tilly. *Strikes in France, 1830-1968.* New York: Cambridge University Press, 1974.
2274. Smith, Canfield F. *Vladivostok under Red and White Rule: Revolution and Counterrevolution in the Russian Far East, 1920-1922.* Seattle: University of Washington Press, 1975.
2275. Sontag, Raymond. *A Broken World, 1919-1939.* New York: Harper and Row, 1971.
2276. Steenson, Gary P. *Karl Kautsky, 1854-1938: Marxism in the Classical Years.* Pittsburgh: University of Pittsburgh Press, 1978.
2277. Talmon, J. L. *Romanticism and Revolt: Europe, 1815-1848.* New York: Harcourt Brace and World, 1967.
2278. Taylor, A. J. P. *Revolutions and Revolutionaries.* New York: Atheneum, 1980.
2279. Thackeray, Frank W. *Antecedents of Revolution: Alexander I and the Polish Congress Kingdom, 1815-1825.* New York: Columbia University Press, 1980.
2280. Thomis, Malcolm I., and Peter Holt. *Threats of Revolution in Britain, 1789-1848.* Hamden, Connecticut: Archon Books, 1977.
2281. Thompson, Robert. *Revolutionary War in World Strategy, 1945-1969.* New York: Taplinger, 1970.
2282. Tilly, Charles; Louise Tilly; and Richard Tilly. *The Rebellious Century, 1830-1930.* Cambridge, Massachusetts: Harvard University Press, 1975.
2283. Treviranus, G. R. *Revolutions in Russia: Their Lessons For the Western World.* New York: Harper Brothers, 1944.
2284. Ulam, Adam B. *In the Name of the People: Prophets and Conspirators in Prerevolutionary Russia.* New York: Viking, 1977.

2285. _____ . *Russia's Failed Revolutions: From the Decembrists to the Dissidents.* New York: Basic Books, 1980.
2286. Weisser, Michael. *The Peasants of the Montes: The Roots of Rural Rebellion in Spain.* Chicago: University of Chicago Press, 1977.
2287. Woodward, E. L. *French Revolutions.* London: Oxford University Press, 1934.
2288. Zeman, Z. A. B. *The Break-up of the Habsburg Empire, 1914–1918: A Study in National and Social Revolution.* New York: Octagon Books, 1977.
2289. Zetlin, Mikhail. *The Decembrists.* Translated by G. Panin. New York: International Universities Press, 1958.

Tocqueville and Revolution

Born at the time of Napoleon's height, Alexis de Tocqueville was a student of the French Revolution, an observer of the revolutions of 1830 and 1848, and a contemporary of Marx. He believed that revolutions were more likely to occur in free societies than in despotisms because of the degree of communication required. More than anything else, he said, revolution was not the result of conspiracy but was due instead "to the natural emergence of emotions long felt." In his work he analyzed three types of revolutions: political revolutions (which attempted to change the quality of government), social revolutions (which sought to replace one class of leaders with another, or one system of property control with another), and religious revolutions (which aimed to replace one set of principles concerning the destiny and nature of man with another). Any revolution that was all three types at once was likely to be very violent.

Tocqueville, of course, had more to say than this. In addition to the Frenchman's own still readable works, the article by Melvin Richter (1966) and the book by Irving M. Zeitlin (1971) are especially useful for Tocqueville and revolution. The biographies by Hugh Brogan (1973) and J. P. Mayer (1940), and the studies by Jack Lively (1962) and Richard Herr (1962) are also noteworthy.

Articles

2290. DeGiorgio, Fulvio. "Tocqueville: chiesa a rivoluzione." *Studium* 74:4 (1978): 485–97.
2291. Murphy, William J., Jr. "Alex de Tocqueville in New York. The Formulation of the Egalitarian Thesis." *New York Historical Society Quarterly.* 61:1–2 (1977): 69–79.
2292. Richter, Melvin. "Tocqueville's Contributions to the Theory of Revolution." In *Revolution (Nomos VIII),* edited by C. J. Friedrich. New York: Atherton, 1966.

2293. Schleifer, James T. "Images of America after the Revolution: Alex de Tocqueville and Gustave de Beaumont Visit the Early Republic." *Yale University Library Gazette* 51:3 (1977): 125-44.

Books

2294. Brogan, Hugh. *Tocqueville.* Bungay, England: Chaucer Press, 1973.
2295. Drescher, Seymour. *Dilemmas of Democracy: Tocqueville and Modernization.* Pittsburgh: University of Pittsburgh Press, 1968.
2296. Herr, Richard. *Tocqueville and the Old Regime.* Princeton: Princeton University Press, 1962.
2297. Lively, Jack. *The Social and Political Thought of Alexis de Tocqueville.* Oxford: Clarendon Press, 1962.
2298. Mayer, J. P. *Alexis de Tocqueville: A Biographical Essay in Political Science.* New York: Viking, 1940.
2299. _____. *Prophet of the Mass Age: A Study of Alexis de Tocqueville.* London: J. M. Dent, 1939.
2300. Schemann, Ludwig. *Alexis de Tocqueville.* New York: Arno Press, 1979.
2301. Schleifer, James T. *The Making of Tocqueville's "Democracy in America."* Chapel Hill: University of North Carolina Press, 1979.
2302. Tocqueville, Alexis de. *Democracy in America.* Boston: John Allyn, 1876.
2303. _____. *On Democracy, Revolution, and Society: Selected Writings.* Edited by John Stone and Stephen Mennell. Chicago: University of Chicago Press, 1980.
2304. _____. *The Old Regime and the French Revolution.* Translated by S. Gilbert. Garden City, New York: Doubleday, 1955.
2305. _____. *The Recollections of Alexis de Tocqueville.* Edited by J. P. Mayer. London: Harvill Press, 1948.
2306. Zeitlin, Irving M. *Liberty, Equality, and Revolution in Alexis de Tocqueville.* Boston: Little, Brown, 1971.
2307. Zetterbaum, Marvin. *Tocqueville and the Problem of Democracy.* Stanford: Stanford University Press, 1967.

Revolutions of 1830

The forces unleashed by the French Revolution and Napoleon appeared contained by the decade of the 1820s. Reaction, repression, and political stability were the order of the day, or so it seemed. But in 1830 revolution again returned to Europe. Beginning in July in Paris, the fall of the Bourbons from the French throne jeopardized the whole peace settlement of 1815. Revolution spread to Belgium, Poland, Germany, Italy, Switzerland, Spain, and Portugal. Some succeeded, others did not.

No single volume deals with all the revolutions of 1830. Surveys of broader periods which include 1830, such as those by Frederick Artz (1934) and E. J. Hobsbawm (1962) cited in the opening section to this chapter, should be consulted. Most of the material below is on France, the best of which are the articles in the book edited by John M. Merriman (1975) and the book by David H. Pinkney (1972).

Historiography

2308. Church, Clive H. "Forgotten Revolutions: Recent Work on the Revolutions of 1830 in Europe." *European Studies Review* 7 (1977): 95–106.

Articles

2309. Beach, Vincent W. "The Fall of Charles X of France: A Case Study of Revolution." *University of Colorado Studies,* Series in History, No. 2 (November 1961): 21–60.
2310. Bezucha, Robert J. "The Revolution of 1830 and the City of Lyon." In *1830 In France,* edited by J. M. Merriman. New York: New Viewpoints, 1975.
2311. Brown, Mark. "The Comité Franco-Polonais and the French Reaction to the Polish Uprising of November 1830." *English Historical Review* 93 (October 1978): 774–93.
2312. Esler, Anthony. "Youth in Revolt: The French Generation of 1830." In *Modern European Social History,* edited by R. J. Bezucha. Lexington, Massachusetts: D. C. Heath, 1972.
2313. Johnson, Christopher H. "The Revolution of 1830 in French Economic History." In *1830 In France,* edited by J. M. Merriman. New York: New Viewpoints, 1975.
2314. Merriman, John M. "The *Demoiselles* of the Ariège, 1829–1831." In *1830 In France,* edited by J. M. Merriman. New York: New Viewpoints, 1975.
2315. Moss, Bernard H. "Parisian Workers and the Origins of Republican Socialism, 1830–1833." In *1830 In France,* edited by J. M. Merriman. New York: New Viewpoints, 1975.
2316. Newman, Edgar Leon. "*L'Arme du siècle, c'est la plume:* The French Worker Poets of the July Monarchy and the Spirit of Revolution and Reform." *Journal of Modern History* 51:4 (December 1979): abstract.
2317. _____. "The Reaction of the French Worker Poets of the July Monarchy to the French Revolution of 1830." *Proceedings of the Consortium on Revolutionary Europe* 6 (1976): 133–61.
2318. _____. "What the Crowd Wanted in the French Revolution of 1830." In *1830 In France,* edited by J. M. Merriman. New York: New Viewpoints, 1975.
2319. Pilbeam, Pamela. "The Emergence of Opposition to the Orleanist Monarchy, August 1830—April 1831." *English Historical Review* 85 (January 1970): 12–28.
2320. _____. "Popular Violence in Provincial France after the 1830 Revolution." *English Historical Review* 91 (April 1976): 278–97.
2321. Pinkney, David H. "The Crowd in the French Revolution of 1830." *American Historical Review* 70:1 (October 1964): 1–17.
2322. _____. "The Myth of the French Revolution of 1830." In *A Festschrift for Frederick B. Artz,* edited by D. H. Pinkney and T. Ropp. Durham, North Carolina: Duke University Press, 1964.

2323. _____. "Pacification of Paris: The Military Lessons of 1830." In *1830 in France*, edited by J. M. Merriman. New York: New Viewpoints, 1975.
2324. Price, Roger D. "The French Army and the Revolution of 1830." *European Studies Review* 3:3 (July 1973): 243–67.
2325. Richards, Michael. "The Rebellions of 1830 in France and England." *Proceedings of the Consortium on Revolutionary Europe* 8 (1978): 119–36.
2326. Rule, James, and Charles Tilly. "1830 and the Unnatural History of Revolution." *Journal of Social Issues* 28:1 (1972): 49–76.
2327. _____. "Political Process in Revolutionary France, 1830–1832." In *1830 In France*, edited by J. M. Merriman. New York: New Viewpoints, 1975.

Books

2328. Artz, Frederick B. *France Under the Bourbon Restoration, 1814–1830.* Cambridge, Massachusetts: Harvard University Press, 1931.
2329. Hordynski, Jozef. *History of the Late Polish Revolution.* Boston: Printed for Subscribers, 1833.
2330. Leslie, R. F. *Polish Politics and the Revolution of November 1830.* London: University of London, Historical Studies, 1956.
2331. Merriman, John M., ed. *1830 In France.* New York: New Viewpoints, 1975.
2332. Pinkney, David H. *The French Revolution of 1830.* Princeton: Princeton University Press, 1972.
2333. Rader, Daniel L. *The Journalists and the July Revolution in France.* The Hague: Nijhoff, 1973.

Revolutions of 1848

Hovering almost midway between the great revolutions of 1789 and 1917, the revolutions of 1848 stand as a signpost. Never before or since has Europe witnessed a series of upheavals so universal. Where 1789 and 1917 were national revolutions with international repercussions, the 1848 revolutions each erupted as a result of indigenous problems. Revolutionary contagion and even international conspiracy played a role, but mostly the simultaneous disruptions stemmed from other causes, many of which were common to all the countries involved. These revolutions were characterized by little extreme violence, and most of the revolutionists were not seeking to transform society completely. Because of this, or maybe in spite of it, the revolutions of 1848 failed, though their unintended consequences were far reaching. Among other things, the forces of nationalism and Marxism were bolstered tremendously.

There are a number of very good works that treat the revolutions of 1848 as a unit. Among these the books by the following authors stand out: Georges Duveau (1967), George Fasel (1970), Lewis B. Namier (1964), Priscilla Robertson (1960), Jean Sigmann (1973), Peter N. Stearns (1974), and Arnold Whitridge (1949). The literature and historiographical conflict can be sampled in the collections edited by Melvin Kranzberg (1959) and François Fejto (1948). For the views of participants and contemporaries see the books by Alexis de Tocqueville (1948), Alphonse M. Lamartine (n.d.), and the following by Karl Marx which are listed in Chapter 1, in the section "Marx and Marxism": *Revolution and Counter-Revolution* (1896), *The Eighteenth Brumaire of Louis Bonaparte* (1963), *The Revolution of 1848–1849: Articles from the Neue Rheinische Zeitung* (1973), and *The Class Struggles in France, 1848–1850* (1972). Among the better books on the revolutions in the separate countries are those by Jerome Blum (1948) and R. J. Bath (1957) on Austria, Peter H. Amann (1975) and Donald C. McKay (1933) on France, and Theodore S. Hamerow (1966) and Veit Valentin (1940) on Germany.

General

Articles

2334. Gooch, G. P. "The Centenary of 1848 in Germany and Austria." *Contemporary Review* 173 (April 1948): 220–26.
2335. Gottfried, Paul. "Pessimism and the Revolution of 1848." *Review of Politics* 35:2 (April 1973): 193–203.
2336. Hamerow, Theodore S. "1848." In *The Responsibility of Power,* edited by L. Krieger and F. Stern. Garden City, New York: Doubleday, 1967.
2337. Langer, William L. "The Pattern of Urban Revolution in 1848." In *French Society and Culture since the Old Regime,* edited by E. M. Acomb and M. L. Brown. New York: Holt, Rinehart and Winston, 1966.
2338. Large, David. "London in the Year of Revolution, 1848." In *London in the Age of Reform,* edited by J. Stevenson. Oxford: Basil Blackwell, 1977.
2339. Lewis, J. D. "Marxism, Revolution, and Democracy: 1848 and 1948." *Journal of Politics* 11 (1949): 518–65.
2340. Neumann, Sigmund. "The Structure and Strategy of Revolution: 1848 and 1948." *Journal of Politics* 11 (1949): 532–44.
2341. Rothfels, Hans. "1848—One Hundred Years After." *Journal of Modern History* 20:4 (December 1948): 293–313.
2342. Schmitt, Bernadotte E. "1848—as Seen from 1948." *Proceedings of the American Philosophical Society* 93:3 (June 1949): 216–21.

Books

2343. Amann, Peter. *The Revolutions of 1848.* St. Louis: Forum Press, 1976.
2344. De Saint-Armand, Imbert. *The Revolution of Eighteen Forty-Eight.* Norwood, Pennsylvania: Norwood Editions, 1895.
2345. Duveau, Georges. *1848: The Making of a Revolution.* New York: Random House, 1967.
2346. Eastwood, J., and P. Taburi. *'48, The Year of Revolutions.* London: Meridian Books, 1948.

148 / Modern Europe

2347. Eyck, Frank, ed. *The Revolutions of 1848-49.* New York: Harper and Row, 1972.

2348. Fasel, George. *Europe in Upheaval: The Revolutions of 1848.* Chicago: Rand McNally, 1970.

2349. Fejto, François, ed. *The Opening of an Era: 1848.* London: Allan Wingate, 1948.

2350. Hammen, Oscar J. *The Red '48ers: Karl Marx and Friedrich Engels.* New York: Scribners, 1969.

2351. Jennings, Lawrence C. *France and Europe in 1848.* New York: Oxford University Press, 1973.

2352. Kamenka, Eugene, and F. B. Smith, eds. *Intellectuals and Revolution: Socialism and the Experience of 1848.* New York: St. Martin's Press, 1979.

2353. Kranzberg, Melvin, ed. *1848.* Lexington, Massachusetts: D. C. Heath, 1959.

2354. Langer, William L. *Political and Social Upheaval, 1832-1852.* New York: Harper and Row, 1969.

2355. Lougee, Robert W. *Midcentury Revolution, 1848: Society and Revolution in France and Germany.* Lexington, Massachusetts: D. C. Heath, 1972.

2356. Marx, Karl. *The Revolutions of 1848.* Edited by D. Fernbach. New York: Random House, 1973.

2357. Maurice, C. Edmund. *The Revolutionary Movement of 1848-9 in Italy, Austria-Hungary, and Germany.* New York: Haskell House, 1969.

2358. Namier, Lewis B. *1848: The Revolution of the Intellectuals.* Garden City, New York: Doubleday, 1964.

2359. Polišenský, Josef V. *Aristocrats and the Crowd in the Revolutionary Year 1848: A Contribution to the History of Revolution and Counter-Revolution.* Translated by F. Snider. Albany: State University of New York Press, 1980.

2360. Postgate, Raymond. *Story of a Year: 1848.* New York: Oxford University Press, 1956.

2361. Robertson, Priscilla. *Revolutions of 1848: A Social History.* New York: Harper and Row, 1960.

2362. Sigmann, Jean. *1848: The Romantic and Democratic Revolutions in Europe.* New York: Harper and Row, 1973.

2363. Stearns, Peter N. *1848: The Revolutionary Tide in Europe.* New York: W. W. Norton, 1974.

2364. Whitridge, Arnold. *Men in Crisis: The Revolutions of 1848.* New York: Scribners, 1949.

2365. Woodcock, George, ed. *One Hundred Years of Revolution: 1848 and After.* New York: Haskell House, 1974.

Austria

Article

2366. Deak, Istvan. "An Army Divided: The Loyalty Crisis of the Habsburg Officer Corps in 1848-49." *Jahrbuch Institut Deutsche Geschichte* 8 (1979): 207-41.

Books

2367. Bauer, Otto. *Austrian Revolution.* Translated by H. J. Stenning. New York: Burt Franklin, 1970.
2368. Blum, Jerome. *Noble Landowners and Agriculture in Austria, 1815–1848: A Study in the Origins of the Peasant Emancipation of 1848.* Baltimore: Johns Hopkins University Press, 1948.
2369. Rath, R. J. *The Viennese Revolution of 1848.* Austin: University of Texas Press, 1957.
2370. Sked, Alan. *The Survival of the Habsburg Empire: Radetzky, the Imperial Army and the Class War, 1848.* New York: Longman, 1979.
2371. Stiles, William Henry. *Austria in 1848–49.* New York: Harper, 1852.
2372. Walsh, James E. *Eighteen Forty-Eight Austrian Revolutionary Broadsides and Pamphlets: A Catalogue of the Collection at the Houghton Library, Harvard University.* Boston: G. K. Hall, 1976.
2373. Zenker, E. V. *Die Wiener Revolution, 1848.* Vienna: A. Hartleben's Verlag, 1897.

Czechoslovakia

2374. Pech, Stanley Z. *The Czech Revolution of 1848.* Chapel Hill: University of North Carolina Press, 1969.

France

Articles

2375. Applebaum, David A. "The Provisional Government of France in 1848: A Reassessment." *Proceedings of the Consortium on Revolutionary Europe* 8 (1978): 156–65.
2376. Farmer, Paul. "Some Frenchmen Review 1848." *Journal of Modern History* 20:4 (December 1948): 320–25.
2377. Fasel, George. "The Wrong Revolution: French Republicanism in 1848." *French Historical Studies* 8:4 (Fall 1974): 654–77.
2378. Festa-McCormick, Diana. "Literary Impact upon a Revolution: Paris 1848." *American Society for the Legion of Honor Magazine* 49:3 (1978): 153–66.
2379. Hyes, Peter V. "Teachers in Revolutionary France: The *Instituteurs* in 1848." *Proceedings of the Consortium on Revolutionary Europe* 7 (1977): 151–61.
2380. McPhee, Peter. "The Crisis of Radical Republicanism in the French Revolution of 1848." *Historical Studies* 16 (April 1974): 71–88.
2381. Sewell, William H., Jr. "*Corporations Républicains*: The Revolutionary Idiom of Parisian Workers in 1848." *Comparative Studies in Social History* 21 (April 1979): 195–203.

Books

2382. Amann, Peter H. *Revolution and Mass Democracy: The Paris Club Movement of 1848.* Princeton: Princeton University Press, 1975.
2383. Blanc, Louis. *Eighteen Forty-Eight: Historical Revelations.* New York: Howard Fertig, n.d.
2384. De Luna, Frederick A. *French Republic Under Cavaignac, 1848.* Princeton: Princeton University Press, 1969.
2385. Denholm, Anthony. *France in Revolution: 1848.* New York: John Wiley, 1972.
2386. Forstenzer, Thomas R. *French Provincial Police and the Fall of the Second Republic: Social Fear and Counterrevolution.* Princeton: Princeton University Press, 1981.
2387. Gallaher, John G. *The Students of Paris and the Revolution of 1848.* Carbondale: Southern Illinois University Press, 1980.
2388. Lamartine, Alphonse M. *History of the French Revolution of 1848.* New York: AMS Press, n.d.
2389. McKay, Donald C. *The National Workshops: A Study in the French Revolution of 1848.* Cambridge, Massachusetts: Harvard University Press, 1933.
2390. Marriott, J. *The French Revolution of 1848 in Its Economic Aspect.* 2 vols. Oxford: Oxford University Press, 1913.
2391. Merriman, John M. *The Agony of the Republic: The Repression of the Left in Revolutionary France, 1848-1851.* New Haven: Yale University Press, 1978.
2392. Normanby, C. H. Phipps, first Marquis of. *A Year of Revolution, from a Journal Kept in Paris in 1848.* London: Longman, 1857.
2393. Price, Roger, ed. *1848 In France.* Ithaca: Cornell University Press, 1975.
2394. _____. *The French Second Republic: A Social History.* Ithaca: Cornell University Press, 1972.
2395. _____, ed. *Revolution and Reaction: 1848 and the Second French Republic.* New York: Barnes and Noble, 1976.
2396. Story, D., and J. J. Hayes, eds. *The Revolution of 1848 in France.* Lawrence, Massachusetts: University of Queensland Press, 1973.
2397. Tocqueville, Alexis de. *The Recollections of Alexis de Tocqueville.* Edited by J. P. Mayer. London: Harvill Press, 1948.

Germany

Articles

2398. Bazillion, Richard J. "Saxon Liberalism and the German Question in the Wake of the 1848 Revolution." *Canadian Journal of History* 13:1 (April 1978): 61-84.
2399. Bleiber, Helmut. "Volksmassen und Revolution, 1848-49 in Deutschland." *Beitrag Geschichte Arbeiterbewegung* 21:6 (1979): 821-40.
2400. Gilam, Abraham. "German Village Jewry and the Revolution of 1848: The Evidence of *The Scroll of Baisingen.*" *East European Quarterly* 13 (Summer 1979): 129-43.

2401. Hamerow, Theodore S. "History and the German Revolution of 1848." *American Historical Review* 60:1 (October 1954): 27-44.
2402. Hawgood, John A. "The Frankfort Parliament of 1848-1849." *History* 17 (1932): 147-51.
2403. Mattheisen, Donald J. "Liberal Constitutionalism in the Frankfurt Parliament of 1848: An Inquiry Based on Roll-Call Analysis." *Central European History* 12 (June 1979): 124-42.
2404. Meinecke, Friedrich. "The Year 1848 in German History: Reflections on a Centenary." *Review of Politics* 10:4 (October 1948): 475-88.
2405. Obermann, Karl. "Die Auseinandersetzungen zwischen Demokraten und Liberalen im deutschen Vorparlament 1848." *Zeitschrift Geschichtswiss* 27:12 (1979): 1156-72.
2406. Ridley, Hugh. "Intellectual Freedom in Germany's 1848 Revolution: The Trial of Gustav Adolph Schlöffel." *German Life and Letters* 32 (July 1979): 308-17.
2407. With, Christopher B. "Adolph von Menzel and the German Revolution of 1848." *Zeitschrift Kunstgeschichte* 42:2-3 (1979): 195-214.

Books

2408. Best, Heinrich. *Interessenpolitik und nationale Integration, 1848-1849: Handelspolitische Konflikte im frühindustriellen Deutschland.* Göttingen: Vandenhoeck and Ruprecht, 1980.
2409. Eberstein, Alfred, freiherr von. *Ueber die Revolution in Preussen und Deutschland, 1848-1849.* Leipzig: J. Werner, 1899.
2410. Eyck, Frank. *Frankfurt Parliament: Eighteen Forty-Eight to Eighteen Forty-Nine.* New York: St. Martin's Press, 1968.
2411. Faber, Karl-Georg. *Deutsche Geschichte im 19. Jahrhundert: Restauration und Revolution: Von 1815 bis 1851.* Wiesbaden: Akademische Verlagsgesellschaft Athenaion, 1979.
2412. Hamerow, Theodore S. *Restoration, Revolution, Reaction: Economics and Politics in Germany, 1815-1871.* Princeton: Princeton University Press, 1966.
2413. Legge, J. G. *Rhyme and Revolution in Germany: A Study in German History, Life, Literature and Character, 1813-1850.* London: Constable, 1918.
2414. Noyes, Paul. *Organization and Revolution: Working-Class Associations in the German Revolutions of 1848-1849.* Princeton: Princeton University Press, 1966.
2415. Stadelmann, Rudolph. *Social and Political History of the German 1848 Revolution.* Translated by James G. Chastain. Athens: Ohio University Press, 1975.
2416. Stahl, Friedrich J. *What Is the Revolution?* State College, Pennsylvania: Slavia Library, 1977.
2417. Taylor, A. J. P. *The Course of German History.* New York: Coward, McCann, 1946.
2418. Valentin, Veit. *1848: Chapters of German History.* London: Allen and Unwin, 1940.
2419. Zucker, A. E., ed. *The Forty-Eighters: Political Refugees of the German Revolution of 1848.* New York: Russell and Russell, 1967.

Hungary

Articles

2420. Deak, Istvan. "Destruction, Revolution or Reform: Hungary on the Eve of 1848." *Austrian History Yearbook* 12-13 (part 1, 1976-1977): 3-12.
2421. _____. "Reform Triumphant: Hungary's Self-Assertion during the Springtime of the Peoples (March-April 1848)." In *The American and European Revolutions*, edited by J. Pelenski. Iowa City: University of Iowa Press, 1980.
2422. Deme, László. "Moderate Politicians and Government Commissioners in the Hungarian Revolution of 1848." *Eastern European Quarterly* 10:2 (1976): 240-43.
2423. _____. "The Society of Equality in the Hungarian Revolution of 1848." *Slavic Review* 31:1 (March 1972): 71-88.

Books

2424. Deak, Istvan. *The Lawful Revolution: Louis Kossuth and the Hungarians, 1848-1849*. New York: Columbia University Press, 1979.
2425. Sproxton, C. *Palmerston and the Hungarian Revolution*. Cambridge: Cambridge University Press, 1919.

Italy

Article

2426. Ginsborg, Paul. "Peasants and Revolutionaries in Venice and the Veneto, 1848." *Historical Journal* 17:3 (1974): 503-50.

Books

2427. Berkeley, George F. H. *Italy in the Making, 1815-1848*. Vols. 2 and 3. Cambridge: Cambridge University Press, 1969.
2428. Ginsborg, Paul. *Daniele Manin and the Venetian Revolution of 1848-49*. New York: Cambridge University Press, 1979.
2429. Holt, Edgar. *The Making of Italy, 1815-1870*. New York: Atheneum, 1971.
2430. Taylor, A. J. P. *The Italian Problem in European Diplomacy, 1847-1849*. Manchester: University of Manchester Press, 1934.
2431. Trevelyan, G. M. *Garibaldi's Defense of the Roman Republic, 1848-1849*. London: Longmans, Green, 1949.
2432. _____. *Manin and the Venetian Revolution of 1848*. London: Longmans, Green, 1923.
2433. Trollope, Theodosia. *Social Aspects of the Italian Revolution, in a Series of Letters from Florence*. New York: AMS Press, 1975.

Romania

2434. Maciu, Vasile. "Ion Heliade Rădulescu in the Romanian Revolution of 1848." *South Eastern Europe* 6:1 (1979): 46-57.

Spain

2435. Headrick, Daniel R. "Spain and the Revolutions of 1848." *European Studies Review* 6 (April 1976): 197-223.

Paris Commune, 1871

The Paris Commune (which specifically refers to the revolutionary municipal council), or French Revolution of 1871, came in the wake of the German victory over France during the Franco-Prussian War. Following the fall of the government of Napoleon III and a four-month German siege of Paris, the conflict between supporters of republicanism and monarchy became intense. Socialist ideas and aspirations were also present. After the election of a new National Assembly returned some two-thirds monarchist delegates, the republicans of Paris refused to recognize the Assembly's authority. A more than two-month civil war erupted in March between Paris and the rest of the country. The Commune was not communistic. Although there were elements present of anarchism, Marxism, and socialism, most communards identified with aspects of the French revolutionary tradition; more than anything else they were patriotic and republican. The fighting was atrocious beyond previous French experiences. In this century the Commune has been glorified in some quarters as a symbol of modern revolution, the first real proletarian revolution.

The best books on the subject are by Stewart Edwards (1973), Alistair Horne (1965, 1971), Frank Jellinek (1937), Melvin Kranzberg (1950), Edward S. Mason (1967), and Roger L. Williams (1969).

Documents

2436. Edwards, Stewart, ed. *The Communards of Paris, 1871.* Ithaca: Cornell University Press, 1973.

Articles

2437. Busi, Frederick. "The Failure of Revolution." *Massachusetts Review* 12:3 (Summer 1971): 397–408.
2438. Greeman, Richard. "The Permanence of the Commune." *Massachusetts Review* 12:3 (Summer 1971): 388–96.
2439. Johnstone, Monty. "The Paris Commune and Marx's Conception of the Dictatorship of the Proletariat." *Massachusetts Review* 12:3 (Summer 1971): 447–62.
2440. Margadant, Ted W. "The Paris Commune: A Revolution that Failed." *Journal of Interdisciplinary History* 7 (Summer 1976): 91–98.
2441. Peyre, Henri. "The Commune—a Century After." *Massachusetts Review* 12:3 (Summer 1971): 384–87.
2442. Price, Roger. "Conservative Reactions to Social Disorder: The Paris Commune of 1871." *Journal of European Studies* 1 (December 1971): 341–52.
2443. _____. "Ideology and Motivation in the Paris Commune of 1871." *Historical Journal* 15:1 (1972):75–86.
2444. "Revolution and Reaction: The Paris Commune of 1871." *Massachusetts Review* 12:3 (Summer 1971): 382–589.

Books

2445. Antony, Jonquil. *The Siege of Paris and the Commune.* New York: Viking, 1971.
2446. Becker, George J., ed. *Paris Under Siege, 1870–1871.* Ithaca: Cornell University Press, 1972.
2447. Bernstein, Samuel. *Auguste Blanqui and the Art of Insurrection.* London: Lawrence and Wishart, 1971.
2448. Beslay, Charles. *La Verité sur la Commune.* Brussels: Henri Kistemaekers, 1878.
2449. Bourgin, Georges. *Histoire de la Commune.* New York: AMS Press, 1907.
2450. Duveau, Georges. *Le Siege de Paris: Septembre 1870–Janvier 1871.* Paris: Hachette, 1939.
2451. Edwards, Stewart. *The Paris Commune, 1871.* New York: Quadrangle Books, 1973.
2452. Gibson, W. *Paris During the Commune.* New York: Haskell House, 1974.
2453. Harrison, Royden, ed. *English Defense of the Commune: 1871.* Atlantic Highlands, New Jersey: Humanities Press, 1971.
2454. Hicks, John, and Robert Tucker, eds. *Revolution and Reaction: The Paris Commune, 1871.* Amherst: University of Massachusetts Press, 1973.
2455. Horne, Alistair. *The Fall of Paris, the Siege and the Commune, 1870–71.* New York: St. Martin's Press, 1965.

2456. ———. *The Terrible Year: The Paris Commune, 1871.* New York: Viking, 1971.
2457. Jeanneret, Georges. *Paris pendant la Commune Revolutionnaire de 1871.* New York: Clearwater Publishing, 1976.
2458. Jellinek, Frank. *The Paris Commune of 1871.* London: Victor Gollancz, 1937.
2459. Joughin, Jean T. *Paris Commune in French Politics, 1871-1880.* New York: Russell and Russell, 1973.
2460. Kranzberg, Melvin. *The Siege of Paris, 1870-1871.* Ithaca: Cornell University Press, 1950.
2461. Leith, James A., ed. *Images of the Commune.* Montreal: McGill-Queen's University Press, 1978.
2462. Lissagaray, P. O. *History of the Commune of 1871.* New York: Monthly Review Press, 1967.
2463. McClellan, Woodford. *Revolutionary Exiles: The Russians in the First International and the Paris Commune.* London: Frank Cass, 1979.
2464. March, Thomas. *The History of the Paris Commune of 1871.* London: Sonnenschein, 1896.
2465. Marx, Karl, and Frederick Engels. *On the Paris Commune.* Brooklyn Heights, New York: Beekman Publishers, 1971.
2466. Mason, Edward S. *The Paris Commune: An Episode in the History of the Socialist Movement.* New York: Howard Fertig, 1967.
2467. Schulkind, Eugene, ed. *The Paris Commune of 1871: The View from the Left.* New York: Grove Press, 1974.
2468. Trotsky, Leon. *Leon Trotsky on the Paris Commune.* New York: Pathfinder Press, 1971.
2469. Williams, Roger L. *The Commune of Paris, 1871.* New York: John Wiley, 1969.
2470. ———. *The French Revolution, 1870-1871.* New York: W. W. Norton, 1969.
2471. Williams, S. L., ed. *Commune of Paris, Eighteen Seventy-One.* Huntington, New York: Krieger, n.d.

Bulgarian National Revolution, 1876

Bulgaria formed part of the Ottoman Empire, which was considered indivisible by its leaders. In 1876 reform was promised throughout Ottoman lands, but the promise was not kept. Instead, non-Turkish subjects, nationalist zealots among Armenians, Macedonians, Cretans, as well as Bulgars, frequently taunted and defied their Ottoman overlords, even precipitating the massacre of their own people to call world attention to their plight. The Bulgarian National Revolution of 1876 was part of that episode in the history of the Ottoman Empire.

Bibliography

2472. Shashko, Philip. "A Selected Bibliography on the April Uprising of 1876." *South Eastern Europe* 4:2 (1977): 332–46.

Articles

2473. Koser, Konstantin. "The Uprising of April, 1876—The Summit of the Bulgarian National Revolution." *South Eastern Europe* 4:2 (1977): 143–68.
2474. Todorov, Nikolaj. "The Bulgarian National Revolution and the Revolutionary Movement in the Balkans." *Etudes balkaniques* 13:2 (1977): 35–48.
2475. Traikov, Veselin. "The 1876 April Uprising and the Balkan Peoples." *South Eastern Europe* 4:2 (1977): 233–49.

Georges Sorel and Syndicalism

Syndicalism was, at first, a form of trade unionism whose aim was to seize the means of production and distribution; later the state would be overthrown and society controlled. However, controlling society was a means to a greater end: the moral rehabilitation of humankind. Because the class struggle would result in worker solidarity of a high order, syndicalists expected psychological as well as political and economic changes to come about. But the class struggle involved action, creative action from which the new order would spring. Thus, direct action (revolutionary violence) is crucial not only for the end result, but for the psychological effect that such action has.

The classical expression of revolutionary syndicalism can be found in the writing of Georges Sorel, a Frenchman who had earlier in life been a Marxist. Sorel did not create syndicalism, but he did express and expand upon its ideas. For example, he believed that no great mass movement could succeed without a "myth," a belief in some imminent episode that will transform the world; and the myth of the working class is the general strike, out of which the new society will emerge.

Articles

2476. Baker, Anthony S. "Organize for Revolution: The Threat of Syndicalism before the *Belle Epoque.*" *Proceedings of the Western Society of French History* 3 (1975): 453–63.
2477. Crook, W. H. "The Revolutionary Logic of the General Strike." *American Political Science Review* 28:4 (August 1934): 655–63.
2478. Hansen, E., and P. A. Prosper, Jr. "The National Arbeids-Secretariaat. Revolutionary Syndicalism in the Netherlands, 1892–1914." *Societas* 7:2 (1977): 121–44.

2479. Moss, Bernard H. "The Political Origins of Revolutionary Syndicalism." *Proceedings of the Western Society of French History* 2 (1974): 281-87.
2480. Roth, Jack. "Georges Sorel: On Lenin and Mussolini." *Contemporary French Civilization* 2 (Winter 1978): 231-52.
2481. Vernon, Richard. "Commitment and Change: Georges Sorel and the Idea of Revolution." *Journal of Modern History* 51:2 (June 1979): abstract.

Books

2482. Curtis, Michael. *Three Against the Third Republic: Sorel, Barres, and Maurras.* Princeton: Princeton University Press, 1959.
2483. Horowitz, Irving L. *Radicalism and the Revolt Against Reason: The Social Theories of Georges Sorel.* Carbondale: Southern Illinois University Press, 1968.
2484. Humphrey, Richard D. *Georges Sorel—Prophet Without Honor: A Study in Anti-intellectualism.* New York: Octagon, 1971.
2485. Lewis, Arthur. *Syndicalism and the General Strike.* New York: Gordon Press, 1976.
2486. Mazgaj, Paul. *The Action Française and Revolutionary Syndicalism.* Chapel Hill: University of North Carolina Press, 1979.
2487. Ridley, F. F. *Revolutionary Syndicalism in France: The Direct Action of Its Time.* Cambridge: Cambridge University Press, 1970.
2488. Roth, Jack. *The Cult of Violence: Sorel and the Sorelians.* Berkeley: University of California Press, 1980.
2489. Sorel, Georges. *From Georges Sorel: Essay in Socialism and Philosophy.* Edited by J. L. Stanley. New York: Oxford University Press, 1976.
2490. _____. *The Illusion of Progress.* Translated by J. L. Stanley and C. Stanley. Berkeley: University of California Press, 1969.
2491. _____. *Reflections on Violence.* Translated by T. E. Hulme. New York: B. W. Huebsch, 1914.
2492. Stearns, Peter N. *Revolutionary Syndicalism and French Labor.* New Brunswick, New Jersey: Rutgers University Press, 1971.
2493. Vernon, Richard. *Commitment and Change: Georges Sorel and the Idea of Revolution.* Toronto: University of Toronto Press, 1978.

Revolution in Italy

The works below are concerned with revolutionary activity in Italy, from the 1820s to the 1930s. Antonio Gramsci was a communist in the early decades of this century. Giuseppe Ferrari fought for Italian unification in the second half of the nineteenth century, as did Giuseppe Garibaldi. The revolution of 1848 in Italy is treated under the "Revolutions of 1848."

Article

2494. Vivarelli, Roberto. "Revolution and Reaction in Italy 1918–1922." *Journal of Italian History* 1 (Autumn 1978): 235–63.

Books

2495. Adamson, Walter L. *Hegemony and Revolution: Antonio Gramsci's Political and Cultural Theory.* Berkeley: University of California Press, 1980.
2496. Clark, Martin. *Antonio Gramsci and the Revolution that Failed.* New Haven: Yale University Press, 1977.
2497. Davis, John A., ed. *Gramsci and Italy's Passive Revolution.* New York: Barnes and Noble, 1979.
2498. Garibaldi, Giuseppe. *A Toast to Rebellion.* Indianapolis: Bobbs-Merrill, 1935.
2499. Gramsci, Antonio. *Selections From the Prison Notebooks.* Edited and translated by Q. Hoare and G. N. Smith. New York: International Publishers, 1971.
2500. Lovett, Clara M. *Giuseppe Ferrari and the Italian Revolution.* Chapel Hill: University of North Carolina Press, 1979.
2501. Mouffe, Chantal, ed. *Gramsci and Marxist Theory.* Boston: Routledge and Kegan Paul, 1979.
2502. Munro, Ion S. *Through Fascism to World Power: A History of the Revolution in Italy.* New York: Gordon Press, 1976.
2503. Romani, George T. *The Neapolitan Revolution of 1820–1821.* Evanston, Illinois: Northwestern University Studies Social Sciences Series, no. 6, 1950.

Russian Revolution of 1905

In Tsarist Russia the discontent of peasants, workers, and even the bourgeoisie, prevalent from the beginning of the nineteenth century, became acute during its last three decades. Wages were abysmally low, working conditions were wretched, and fundamental rights were limited to a few. The Tsar's power was absolute and he was above the law. Russian intellectuals, first by peaceful means, and then by violence, sought to liberalize social conditions and reform the constitution. The discontent became public during the Russo-Japanese War (1904–1905) as the Russian military gave evidence of its and the government's incompetence. The discontent then evolved into revolution when on January 9, 1905 ("Bloody Sunday") a peaceful demonstration by workers in St. Petersburg was turned into a massacre. Mutinies, uprisings, strikes, and assassinations all followed. The revolution zig-zagged between success and failure all that year until the old order prevailed. Although the revolution failed, token reforms transformed Russia, at least ostensibly, into a parliamentary state. But the discontent remained. Moreover, the revolutionists learned from their mistakes (e.g., they would need the soldiers on their side), so that 1905 was but a prelude to 1917.

To acquire an understanding of the background to the 1905 revolution, a good place to begin is the edited collection by Arthur E. Adams (1965). It would also be wise to examine surveys that stress the prerevolutionary period. Some of these are Michael Karpovich's *Imperial Russia, 1801-1917* (New York, 1957), Hugh Seton-Watson's *The Decline of Imperial Russia, 1855-1914* (New York, 1952), and Donald Treadgold's *Twentieth Century Russia* (New York, 1959). Also very useful are three books cited in the section "Russian Revolution of 1917 and the Bolsheviks" in this chapter; they are by Sergei G. Pushkarev (1963), Franco Venturi (1966), and Avrahm Yarmolinsky (1962). The articles below speak to different aspects of the revolution. The best book on the subject is by Sidney S. Harcave (1964), with those by Lionel Kochan (1967) and Solomon M. Schwarz (1967) also recommended.

Articles

2504. Bird, Thomas E., et al. "Religion and the Revolution of 1905." *Russian History* 4 (part 2, 1977): 101-58.

2505. Hamburg, G. M. "The Russian Nobility on the Eve of the 1905 Revolution." *Russian Review* 38:3 (July 1979): 323-38.

2506. Perrie, Maureen. "The Russian Peasant Movement of 1905-1907: Its Social Composition and Revolutionary Significance." *Past and Present*, no. 57 (November 1972): 123-55.

2507. Strauss, Harlan J. "Revolutionary Types: Russia in 1905." *Journal of Conflict Resolution* 17:2 (June 1973): 297-316.

2508. Vasys, Dalius. "The Lithuanian Social Democratic Party and the Revolution of 1905." *Lituanus* 23:3 (1977): 14-40.

Books

2509. Adams, Arthur E., ed. *Imperial Russia After 1861: Peaceful Modernization or Revolution?* Lexington, Massachusetts: D. C. Heath, 1965.

2510. Fischer, George. *Russian Liberalism.* Cambridge, Massachusetts: Harvard University Press, 1958.

2511. Floyd, David. *Russia in Revolt, 1905.* London: Macdonald, 1969.

2512. Harcave, Sidney S. *First Blood: The Russian Revolution of 1905.* New York: Macmillan, 1964.

2513. Healy, Ann E. *The Russian Autocracy in Crisis, 1905-1907.* Hamden, Connecticut: Archon Books, 1976.

2514. Hough, Richard A. *The Potemkin Mutiny.* Westport, Connecticut: Greenwood, 1975.

2515. Kochan, Lionel. *Russia in Revolution, 1890-1921.* New York: New American Library, 1967.

2516. McNeal, Robert H., ed. *Russia in Transition, 1905-1914: Evolution or Revolution?* Huntington, New York: Krieger, 1976.

160 / Modern Europe

2517. Mehlinger, Howard, and John M. Thompson. *Count Witte and the Tsarist Government in the 1905 Revolution.* Bloomington: Indiana University Press, 1973.
2518. Nevinson, Henry W. *Dawn in Russia or Scenes in the Russian Revolution.* New York: Arno Press, 1971.
2519. Pethybridge, Roger. *Witnesses to the Russian Revolution.* Secaucus, New Jersey: Citadel Press, 1968.
2520. Read, Christopher. *Religion, Revolution, and the Russian Intelligentsia, 1900–1912: The* Vekhi *Debate and Its Intellectual Background.* Totowa, New Jersey: Barnes and Noble, 1980.
2521. Sablinsky, Walter. *The Road to Bloody Sunday: The Role of Father Gapon and the Assembly in the Petersburg Massacre of 1905.* Princeton: Princeton University Press, 1976.
2522. Schwarz, Solomon M. *The Russian Revolution of 1905: The Workers' Movement and the Formation of Bolshevism and Menshevism.* University Park: Pennsylvania State University Press, 1967.
2523. Trotsky, Leon. *1905.* Translated by A. Bostock. New York: Vintage Books, 1972.
2524. Wildman, Allan K. *The Making of a Workers' Revolution: Russian Social Democracy, 1891–1903.* Chicago: University of Chicago Press, 1967.
2525. Zilliacus, Konni. *The Russian Revolutionary Movement.* London: E. P. Dutton, 1905.

Mensheviks and the February (1917) Revolution

Throughout the decade following the Russian Revolution of 1905 the social and economic situation in Russia remained potentially revolutionary. After the outbreak of World War I the miseries of Russians were aggravated by deteriorating conditions, and government ineptitude became pronounced. In February, 1917 the revolution began with striking workers taking to the streets and soldiers going over to their side. It was a popular, largely spontaneous insurrection, with none of the traditional Russian revolutionary parties playing a significant role. A provisional government of middle class and aristocratic officials was formed under the leadership, among others, of Alexander Kerensky, and that government forced the Tsar to abdicate. Also formed was a Soviet (council) of Workers, led mostly by Mensheviks and social revolutionary soldiers, and some Bolsheviks. The Soviet at first supported the Provisional Government, with the Menshevik majority holding that that was their obligation at this bourgeois stage of the revolution. But then a stalemate developed, with the government doing nothing in the fields of economics and war politics, and the Mensheviks refusing to assume power. As the president of the Provisional Government put it, "The Soviet has power without authority; the Government has authority without power." Such a situation was exploited by Lenin, Trotsky, and the Bolsheviks.

The political background to the February Revolution can be viewed profitably in the books by Richard Charques (1958), Michael T. Florinsky (1931), Robert K. Massie (1967), Bernard Pares (1961), and Raymond Pearson (1978). The February Revolution itself has received less attention than that of October, but there are important books to examine. Those by George Buchanan (1923) and Maurice Paléologue (1924–1925) are by Western diplomats. Those by Alexander Kerensky (1927) and Pavel N. Miliukov (1978) are by members of the Provisional Government. Good academic studies are in the articles by Tsuyoshi Hasegawa (1972, 1973, 1977), and the books by Michael M. Boll (1979), Marc Ferro (1972), Leopold H. Haimson (1974)—which also contains documentary material—George Katkov (1967), and Allan K. Wildman (1980).

Bibliography

2526. Bourguina, Anna M. *Russian Social Democracy, the Menshevik Movement: A Bibliography.* Stanford: Hoover Institution, 1968.

Documents

2527. Browder, Robert, and Alexander Kerensky, eds. *The Russian Provisional Government 1917.* 3 vols. Stanford: Hoover Institution, 1961.
2528. Golder, Frank A. *Documents of Russian History, 1914–1917.* New York: Century, 1927.

Articles

2529. Boll, Michael M. "The Emergence of the Petrograd Red Guard (March-June 1917): A Study in the 'Radicalization' of the Petrograd Proletariat." *Journal of Modern History* 51:3 (September 1979): abstract.
2530. Chamberlin, William Henry. "The First Russian Revolution." *Russian Review* 26:1 (January 1967): 4–12.
2531. Getzler, Israel. "The Mensheviks." *Problems of Communism* 16:6 (November-December 1967): 15–29.
2532. Hasegawa, Tsuyoshi. "The Bolsheviks and the Formation of the Petrograd Soviet in the February Revolution." *Soviet Studies* 29:3 (January 1977): 86–107.
2533. _____ . "The Formation of the Militia in the February Revolution: As Aspect of the Origins of Dual Power." *Slavic Review* 32:2 (June 1973): 303–22.
2534. _____ . "The Problem of Power in the February Revolution." *Canadian Slavic Papers* 14 (Winter 1972): 611–32.
2535. Kerensky, Alexander. "The Policy of the Provisional Government of 1917." *Slavonic and East European Review* 11:31 (July 1932): 1–19.

162 / Modern Europe

2536. Schakovskoy, Zinaida. "The February Revolution as Seen by a Child." *Russian Review* 26:1 (January 1967): 68–73.
2537. Wildman, Allan K. "February Revolution in the Russian Army." *Soviet Studies* 22:1 (July 1970): 3–23.

Books

2538. Abramovich, Raphael R. *The Soviet Revolution.* New York: International Universities Press, 1962.
2539. Ascher, Abraham, ed. *The Mensheviks in the Russian Revolution.* Ithaca: Cornell University Press, 1976.
2540. _____. *Pavel Axelrod and the Development of Menshevism.* Cambridge, Massachusetts: Harvard University Press, 1972.
2541. Boll, Michael M. *The Petrograd Armed Workers Movement in the February Revolution: A Study in the Radicalization of the Petrograd Proletariat.* Washington, D.C.: University Press of America, 1979.
2542. Buchanan, George. *My Mission to Russia and Other Diplomatic Memories.* 2 vols. Boston: Little, Brown, 1923.
2543. Cantacuzene, Princess. *Revolutionary Days: Recollections of Romanoffs and Bolsheviki, 1914–1917.* Boston: Small, 1919.
2544. Charques, Richard. *The Twilight of Imperial Russia.* London: Phoenix House, 1958.
2545. Ferro, Marc. *The Russian Revolution of February 1917.* Translated by J. L. Richards. Englewood Cliffs, New Jersey: Prentice-Hall, 1972.
2546. Fitzlyon, Kyril, and Tatiana Browning. *Before the Revolution: A View of Russia Under the Last Tsar.* Woodstock, New York: Overlook Press, 1979.
2547. Florinsky, Michael T. *The End of the Russian Empire.* New Haven: Yale University Press, 1931.
2548. Haimson, Leopold H., ed. *The Mensheviks: From the Revolution of 1917.* Chicago: University of Chicago Press, 1974.
2549. Katkov, George. *Russia 1917: The February Revolution.* New York: Harper and Row, 1967.
2550. Kerensky, Alexander. *The Catastrophe: Kerensky's Own Story of the Russian Revolution.* New York: D. Appleton, 1927.
2551. Massie, Robert K. *Nicholas and Alexandra.* New York: Dell, 1967.
2552. Maynard, John. *Russia in Flux, Before October.* London: Victor Gollancz, 1946.
2553. Miliukov, Pavel N. *The Russian Revolution.* Vol. 1. *The Revolution Divided: Spring, 1917.* Edited by R. Stites. Translated by T. Stites and R. Stites. Gulf Breeze, Florida: Academic International Press, 1978.
2554. Paléologue, Maurice. *An Ambassador's Memoirs.* 3 vols. New York: George H. Doran, 1924–1925.
2555. Pares, Bernard. *The Fall of the Russian Monarchy.* New York: Random House, 1961.
2556. Pearson, Raymond. *The Russian Moderates and the Crisis of Tsarism, 1914–1917.* New York: Barnes and Noble, 1978.
2557. Robinson, Geroid Tanquary. *Rural Russia Under the Old Regime: A History of the Landlord-Peasant World and a Prologue to the Peasant Revolution of 1917.* New York: Macmillan, 1957.

2558. Wildman, Allan K. *The End of the Russian Imperial Army: The Old Army and the Soldiers' Revolt (March-April 1917).* Princeton: Princeton University Press, 1980.

Russian Revolution of 1917 and the Bolsheviks

As much as the French Revolution inaugurated the nineteenth century, the Russian Revolution (along with World War I) did the same for the twentieth. Where the events in France had established the idea of equality and raised doubts about the naturalness of the social order, the revolution of 1917 was the first to establish social justice through economic direction, organized by political action.

After the February Revolution, Lenin, Trotsky, and other Bolshevik leaders returned to Russia from exile and prepared to seize power. This was accomplished in October by armed insurrection undertaken in those cities where power was concentrated. The Bolshevik Revolution occurred during a war which resulted in a national crisis when the government was inept, conditions were confused, and the masses were looking for direction and change. From May until October, by the effective use of propaganda, the cultivation of wide support, and the discrediting and isolation of their rivals, the Bolsheviks prepared for their coup. The actual seizure of power involved a comparatively small, but organized revolutionary force. The Provisional Government had failed to provide land, stability, and peace. The Bolsheviks earned the trust of the workers, and channeled revolutionary feelings to their advantage. Without doubt, the October Revolution achieved a revolutionary change in Russia, however much the caliber of that change is debated.

While it may be obvious, it should nevertheless be stated that the Russian Revolution was a very complex historical process. To gain a feel for this complexity, to become aware of the many relevant questions that have been raised, and to sample the debate and various interpretations of the revolution see the collections edited by Arthur E. Adams (1960) and Daniel R. Brower (1979). The historiographical pieces cited here should also be consulted. For the student interested in eyewitness accounts and memoirs, these are isolated below; Trotsky's history of the revolution is listed under "Trotsky." There are many fine books on the Bolsheviks, including those by Edward H. Carr (1950–1953), Robert V. Daniels (1967), Leopold H. Haimson (1955), Alexander Rabinowitch (1968, 1976), and Adam Ulam (1965). In addition to these, the following on the revolution are also invaluable: Oskar Anweiler (1974), Edward H. Carr (1971, 1979), Isaac Deutscher (1967), Marc Ferro (1980), John L. H.

Keep (1977), Launcelot Owen (1937), Richard Pipes (1968), Edmund Wilson (1953), and Bertram D. Wolfe (1964, 1969). Finally, there are listed many excellent articles on a variety of specialized subjects.

Bibliographies

2559. *American Bibliography of Russian and East European Studies.* Bloomington: Indiana University Press, published annually since 1957.
2560. Grierson, Philip. *Books on Soviet Russia, 1917–1942: A Bibliography and a Guide to Reading.* London: Methuen, 1943.
2561. Horecky, Paul. *Russia and the Soviet Union: A Bibliography Guide.* Chicago: University of Chicago Press, 1965.

Historiographies

2562. Adams, Arthur E. "New Books on the Revolution—Old Wine in New Bottles." *Russian Review* 26:4 (October 1967): 391–98.
2563. Carson, George B., Jr. *Russia Since 1917.* Washington, D.C.: American Historical Association Service Center for Teachers, 1962.
2564. Warth, Robert D. "On the Historiography of the Russian Revolution." *Slavic Review* 26:2 (June 1967): 247–65.

Documents

2565. Bunyan, James, and H. H. Fisher, eds. *The Bolshevik Revolution, 1917–1918.* Stanford: Stanford University Press, 1934.
2566. McCauley, Martin, ed. *The Russian Revolution and the Soviet State, 1917–1921: Documents.* New York: Barnes and Noble, 1975.

Reference

2567. Haupt, Georges, and Jean-Jacques Marie, eds. *Makers of the Russian Revolution: Biographies of Bolshevik Leaders.* Ithaca: Cornell University Press, 1974.
2568. *The Modern Encyclopedia of Russian and Soviet History.* Edited by Joseph L. Wieczynski. Several volumes and dates. Gulf Breeze, Florida: Academic International Press, 1976–.

Eyewitness Accounts and Memoirs

2569. Broido, Eva. *Memoirs of a Revolutionary.* Translated and edited by Vera Broido. London: Oxford University Press, 1967.
2570. Chernov, Victor. *The Great Russian Revolution.* New Haven: Yale University Press, 1936.
2571. Dorr, Rheta Childe. *Inside the Russian Revolution.* New York: Macmillan, 1917.
2572. Goldman, Emma. *My Disillusionment in Russia.* Garden City, New York: Doubleday, Page, 1923.

2573. Heald, Edward T. *Witness to Revolution: Letters from Russia, 1916-1919.* Edited by J. B. Gidney. Kent, Ohio: Kent State University Press, 1972.
2574. Kerensky, Alexander. *The Prelude to Bolshevism: The Kornilov Rebellion.* London: T. Fisher Unwin, 1919.
2575. Lensen, G. A., ed. *War and Revolution: Excerpts from the Letters and Diaries of the Countess Olga Poutiatine.* Tallahassee, Florida: Diplomatic Press, 1972.
2576. Lockhart, Robert H. Bruce. *The Two Revolutions: An Eye-Witness Study of Russia, 1917.* London: Bodley, 1967.
2577. Luxemburg, Rosa. *The Russian Revolution and Leninism or Marxism?* Ann Arbor: University of Michigan Press, 1961.
2578. Melgunov, S. P. *The Bolshevik Seizure of Power.* Translated by J. S. Beaver. Santa Barbara, California: ABC-Clio, 1972.
2579. Mohrenschildt, Dmitri von, ed. *The Russian Revolution of 1917: Contemporary Accounts.* New York: Oxford University Press, 1971.
2580. Olgin, Moissaye J. *The Soul of the Russian Revolution.* New York: Holt, 1917.
2581. Price, Morgan P. *My Reminiscences of the Russian Revolution.* Westport, Connecticut: Hyperion Press, 1980.
2582. Pushkarev, Sergei G. "1917—A Memoir." *Russian Review* 26:1 (January 1967): 54-67.
2583. Reed, John. *Ten Days That Shook the World.* New York: New American Library, 1967.
2584. Schakovskoy, Zinaida. "The October Revolution as Seen by a Child." *Russian Review* 26:4 (October 1967): 376-90.
2585. Serge, Victor. *Memoirs of a Revolutionary.* Translated and edited by P. Sedgwick. London: Oxford University Press, 1967.
2586. Sukhanov, N. N. *The Russian Revolution, 1917.* New York: Oxford University Press, 1955.
2587. Tormay, Cecile. *An Outlaw's Diary: Revolution.* New York: McBride, 1923.
2588. White, D. Fedotoff. *Survival Through War and Revolution in Russia.* Philadelphia: University of Pennsylvania Press, 1939.

Soviet Accounts

2589. Keep, John L. H. "The Great October Revolution." In *Windows on the Russian Past: Essays on Soviet Historiography since Stalin,* edited by S. Baron and N. Heer. Columbus: Ohio State University Press, 1976.
2590. Lyashchenko, Peter I. *History of the National Economy of Russia to the 1917 Revolution.* New York: Macmillan, 1949.
2591. Sobolev, P. N., et al. *The Great October Socialist Revolution.* Translated by D. Skvirsky. Moscow: Progress Publishers, 1977.
2592. Stalin, Joseph. *The October Revolution.* New York: International Publishers, 1934.
2593. Sukanov, N. N. *The Russian Revolution, 1917: A Personal Record.* Edited and translated by J. Carmichael. London: Oxford University Press, 1955.

Bolsheviks and Bolshevism

Articles

2594. Avrich, Paul. "The Bolshevik Revolution and Workers' Control in Russian Industry." *Slavic Review* 22:1 (March 1963): 47–63.
2595. Basil, John D. "Russia and the Bolshevik Revolution." *Russian Review* 27:1 (January 1968): 42–53.
2596. Daniels, Robert V. "The Bolshevik Gamble." *Russian Review* 26:4 (October 1967): 331–40.
2597. Rosenberg, William G. "Bolshevism and the 'Imperatives' of Revolution: Russia, 1917–1921." *Theory and Society* 7:1–2 (January-March 1979): 253–70.
2598. Slusser, Robert M. "On the Question of Stalin's Role in the Bolshevik Revolution." *Canadian Slavonic Papers* 4 (1977): 405–16.

Books

2599. Adams, Arthur E., ed. *The Russian Revolution and Bolshevik Victory.* Lexington, Massachusetts: D. C. Heath, 1960.
2600. Badaev, A. E. *The Bolsheviks in the Tsarist Duma.* New York: International Publications, n.d.
2601. Bettelheim, Charles. *The Bolsheviks and the October Revolution.* New York: Urizen Books, 1976.
2602. Carr, Edward H. *The Bolshevik Revolution: 1917–1923.* 3 vols. London: Macmillan, 1950–1953.
2603. Cohen, Stephen F. *Bukharin and the Bolshevik Revolution.* New York: Alfred A. Knopf, 1973.
2604. Dan, Theodore. *The Origins of Bolshevism.* Translated by J. Carmichael. New York: Schocken, 1970.
2605. Daniels, Robert V. *Red October: The Bolshevik Revolution of 1917.* New York: Scribners, 1967.
2606. Fülöp-Miller, René. *The Mind and Face of Bolshevism.* New York: Harper and Row, 1965.
2607. Gorky, Maxim. *Untimely Thoughts, Essays, on Revolution, Culture and the Bolsheviks, 1917–1918.* New York: Paul S. Eriksson, 1968.
2608. Gurian, Waldemar. *Bolshevism: An Introduction to Soviet Communism.* Notre Dame, Indiana: University of Notre Dame Press, 1963.
2609. _____. *Bolshevism: Theory and Practice.* New York: AMS Press, 1970.
2610. Haimson, Leopold H. *The Russian Marxists and the Origins of Bolshevism.* Boston: Beacon, 1955.
2611. Leites, Nathan. *A Study of Bolshevism.* Glencoe, Illinois: Free Press, 1953.
2612. McNeal, Robert H. *The Bolshevik Tradition: Lenin, Stalin, Khrushchev, Brezhnev.* 2d ed. Englewood Cliffs, New Jersey: Prentice-Hall, 1975.
2613. _____, ed. *The Russian Revolution: Why Did the Bolsheviks Win?* New York: Holt, Rinehart and Winston, 1959.

2614. Miliukov, Pavel N. *Bolshevism: An International Danger. Its Doctrine and Its Practice through War and Revolution*. Westport, Connecticut: Hyperion Press, 1980.
2615. Oppenheim, Samuel A. *The Practical Bolshevik: A. I. Rykov and Russian Communism, 1881-1938*. Stanford: Hoover Institution, 1979.
2616. Rabinowitch, Alexander. *The Bolsheviks Come to Power: The Russian Revolution of 1917 in Petrograd*. New York: W. W. Norton, 1976.
2617. _____. *Prelude to Revolution: The Petrograd Bolsheviks and the July 1917 Uprising*. Bloomington: Indiana University Press, 1968.
2618. Radkey, Oliver Henry. *The Agrarian Foes of Bolshevism: Promise and Default of the Russian Socialist Revolutionaries, February to October 1917*. New York: Columbia University Press, 1958.
2619. Rosenberg, Arthur. *A History of Bolshevism*. New York: Oxford University Press, 1934.
2620. Russell, Bertrand. *The Practice and Theory of Bolshevism*. 2d ed. London: Allen and Unwin, 1949.
2621. Selznick, Philip. *The Organizational Weapon: A Study of Bolshevik Strategy and Tactics*. New York: McGraw-Hill, 1952.
2622. Service, Robert. *The Bolshevik Party in Revolution, 1917-1923: A Study in Organizational Change*. New York: Barnes and Noble, 1979.
2623. Tierney, Brian, et al, eds. *The Bolshevik Revolution: Why Did It Succeed?* New York: Random House, 1977.
2624. Tompkins, Stuart R. *The Triumph of Bolshevism: Revolution or Reaction?* Norman: University of Oklahoma Press, 1974.
2625. Ulam, Adam. *The Bolsheviks: The Intellectual and Political History of the Triumph of Communism in Russia*. New York: Macmillan, 1965.

Russian Revolution

Articles

2626. Anweiler, Oskar. "The Political Ideology of the Leaders of the Petrograd Soviet in the Spring of 1917." In *Revolutionary Russia*, edited by Richard Pipes. Garden City, New York: Doubleday, 1969.
2627. Avrich, Paul. "The Anarchists in the Russian Revolution." *Russian Review* 26:4 (October 1967): 341-50.
2628. Billington, James H. "Six Views of the Russian Revolution." *World Politics* 18:3 (April 1966): 452-73.
2629. Carr, Edward H. "The Russian Revolution and the Peasant." *Proceedings of the British Academy* 49 (1963): 69-93.
2630. Cross, Truman B. "Purposes of Revolution: Victor Chernov and 1917." *Russian Review* 26:4 (October 1967): 351-60.
2631. Daniels, Robert V. "The Kronstadt Revolt of 1921: A Study in the Dynamics of Revolution." *American Slavic and East European Review* 10:4 (December 1951): 241-54.
2632. _____. "The State and Revolution: A Case Study in the Genesis and Transformation of Communist Ideology." *American Slavic and East European Review* 12 (1953): 22-43.

2633. Deutscher, Isaac. "The Russian Revolution." In *The New Cambridge Modern History*, 2d ed., vol. 12. *The Shifting Balance of World Forces, 1898–1945*, edited by C. L. Mowat. Cambridge: Cambridge University Press, 1968.

2634. Elkin, Boris. "The Russian Intelligentsia on the Eve of the Revolution." In *The Russian Intelligentsia*, edited by Richard Pipes. New York: Columbia University Press, 1961.

2635. Ferro, Marc. "The Russian Soldier in 1917: Undisciplined, Patriotic, and Revolutionary." *Slavic Review* 30:3 (September 1971): 483–512.

2636. Getzler, Israel. "Marxist Revolutionaries and the Dilemma of Power." In *Revolution and Politics in Russia*, edited by A. Rabinowitch and J. Rabinowitch. Bloomington: Indiana University Press, 1972.

2637. Hedlin, Myron W. "Zinoviev's Revolutionary Tactics in 1917." *Slavic Review* 34:1 (March 1975): 19–43.

2638. Jones, David R. "The Officers and the October Revolution." *Soviet Studies* 28:4 (April 1976): 207–23.

2639. Keller, Theodore. "To Lead the People: Notes on the Russian Revolutionaries." *Journal of Contemporary Revolutions* 5:3 (Summer 1973): 94–121.

2640. Kingston-Mann, Esther. "Lenin and the Beginnings of Marxist Peasant Revolution: The Burden of Political Opportunity, July-October 1917." *Slavonic and East European Review* 50:121 (October 1972): 570–88.

2641. Kirby, D. G. "A Navy in Revolution: The Russian Baltic Fleet in 1917." *European Studies Review* 4 (October 1974): 345–58.

2642. Owen, Launcelot. "The Russian Agrarian Revolution of 1917." *Slavonic and East European Review* 12:34 (July 1933): 156–66.

2643. Perrie, Maureen. "The Socialist Revolutionaries on 'Permanent Revolution.'" *Soviet Studies* 25:3 (January 1973): 411–13.

2644. Radkey, Oliver Henry. "The Socialist Revolutionaries and the Peasantry after October." In *Russian Thought and Politics*, edited by H. McLean; M. Malia; and G. Fischer. Cambridge, Massachusetts: Harvard University Press, 1957.

2645. Rogger, Hans. "October 1917 and the Tradition of Revolution." *Russian Review* 27:4 (October 1968): 395–413.

2646. "The Russian Revolution: Some Historical Considerations." *Problems of Communism* 16:6 (November-December 1967): 1–91.

2647. Singleton, Seth. "The Tambov Revolt (1920–1921)." *Slavic Review* 25:3 (September 1966): 497–512.

2648. Strakhovsky, Leonid I. "Was there a Kornilov Rebellion?—A Re-appraisal of the Evidence." *Slavonic and East European Review* 33:81 (June 1955): 372–95.

2649. Szamuely, Tibor. "The Birth of Russian Marxism." *Survey* 18:3 (Summer 1972): 56–90.

2650. Theen, Rolf H. W. "The Idea of the Revolutionary State: Tkachev, Trotsky, and Lenin." *Russian Review* 31:4 (October 1972): 383–97.

2651. Timasheff, Nicholas S. "The Russian Revolution: Twenty-Five Years After." *Review of Politics* 5:4 (October 1943): 415–40.

2652. Tucker, Robert C. "Paths of Communist Revolution, 1917–1967." In *The Soviet Union: A Half-Century of Communism*, edited by K. London. Baltimore: Johns Hopkins University Press, 1968.

2653. Turner, Ian. "The Significance of the Russian Revolution." In *A World in Revolution?* edited by E. Kamenka. Canberra: Australian National University, 1970.

2654. Ulam, Adam. "The Historical Role of Marxism and the Soviet System." *World Politics* 8:1 (October 1955): 20–45.

2655. Uldricks, Ted. "The 'Crowd' in the Russian Revolution: Towards Reassessing the Nature of Revolutionary Leadership." *Politics and Society* 4:3 (Spring 1974): 397–413.
2656. Von Laue, Theodore H. "Westernization, Revolution and the Search for a Basis of Authority—Russia in 1917." *Soviet Studies* 19:2 (October 1967): 157–70.
2657. Wittfogel, Karl A. "The Marxist View of Russian Society and Revolution." *World Politics* 12:4 (July 1960): 487–508.
2658. Wolfe, Bertram D. "'War Is the Womb of Revolution': Lenin 'Consults' Hegel." *Antioch Review* 16 (1956): 190–97.
2659. Zelnik, Reginald E. "Russian Workers and the Revolutionary Movement." *Journal of Social History* 6 (Winter 1971–1972): 214–34.

Books

2660. Anweiler, Oskar. *The Soviets: The Russian Workers, Peasants, and Soldiers Councils, 1905–1921.* Translated by R. Hein. New York: Pantheon, 1974.
2661. Avrich, Paul, ed. *The Anarchists in the Russian Revolution.* Ithaca: Cornell University Press, 1973.
2662. ———. *Kronstadt 1921.* New York: W. W. Norton, 1974.
2663. Baron, Samuel H. *Plekhanov: The Father of Russian Marxism.* Stanford University Press, 1963.
2664. Berdyaev, Nicolas. *Russian Revolution.* Ann Arbor: University of Michigan Press, 1961.
2665. Bettelheim, Charles. *Class Struggles in the USSR, First Period: 1917–1923.* Translated by B. Pearce. New York: Monthly Review Press, 1976.
2666. Bradley, John. *Civil War in Russia, 1917–1920.* New York: St. Martin's Press, 1975.
2667. Brower, Daniel R. *Russia and the West: The Origins of the Russian Revolution.* St. Charles, Missouri: Forum Press, 1975.
2668. ———, ed. *The Russian Revolution.* St. Louis: Forum Press, 1979.
2669. Carr, Edward H. *The October Revolution.* New York: Random House, 1971.
2670. ———. *The Russian Revolution: From Lenin to Stalin.* New York: Free Press, 1979.
2671. ———. *Studies in Revolution.* New York: Grosset and Dunlap, 1964.
2672. Cash, Anthony. *Russian Revolution.* New York: Viking, 1968.
2673. Chamberlain, William Henry. *The Russian Revolution, 1917–1921.* 2 vols. New York: Macmillan, 1952.
2674. Cherniavsky, Michael. *Prologue to Revolution: Notes of A. N. Takhontov on the Secret Meetings of the Council of Ministers.* Englewood Cliffs, New Jersey: Prentice-Hall, 1967.
2675. Daniels, Robert V. *The Conscience of Revolution: Communist Opposition in Soviet Russia:* Cambridge, Massachusetts: Harvard University Press, 1960.
2676. ———, ed. *The Russian Revolution.* Englewood Cliffs, New Jersey: Prentice-Hall, 1972.
2677. ———, ed. *The Stalin Revolution.* Lexington, Massachusetts: D. C. Heath, 1965.
2678. Debo, Richard K. *Revolution and Survival: The Foreign Policy of Soviet Russia, 1917–18.* Toronto: University of Toronto Press, 1979.

170 / Modern Europe

2679. Deutscher, Isaac. *The Unfinished Revolution: Russia, 1917-1967.* New York: Oxford University Press, 1967.
2680. Dziewanowski, M. K., ed. *The Russian Revolution: An Anthology.* New York: Thomas Y. Crowell, 1970.
2681. Edelman, Robert. *Gentry Politics on the Eve of the Russian Revolution: The Nationalist Party, 1907-1917.* New Brunswick, New Jersey: Rutgers University Press, 1980.
2682. Elwood, Ralph C., ed. *Reconsiderations on the Russian Revolution.* Columbus, Ohio: Slavica Publications, 1976.
2683. Ferro, Marc. *October 1917: A Social History of the Russian Revolution.* Boston: Routledge and Kegan Paul, 1980.
2684. Fitzpatrick, Shelia, ed. *Cultural Revolution in Russia, 1928-1931.* Bloomington: Indiana University Press, 1978.
2685. Florinsky, Michael T. *Russia, A History and an Interpretation.* New York: Macmillan, 1953.
2686. Footman, David. *Civil War in Russia.* New York: Praeger, 1962.
2687. _____ . *The Russian Revolutions.* London: Faber, 1962.
2688. Gill, Graeme J. *Peasants and Government in the Russian Revolution.* New York: Barnes and Noble, 1979.
2689. Goldston, Robert. *The Russian Revolution.* New York: Fawcett World Library, 1971.
2690. Goodey, Chris. *We, the State: Factory Committees in the Russian Revolution.* New York: Urizen Books, 1977.
2691. Guerman, Mikhail. *Art of the October Revolution.* New York: Harry N. Abrams, 1979.
2692. Johnston, Robert H. *Tradition versus Revolution: Russia and the Balkans in 1917.* New York: Columbia University Press, 1977.
2693. Keep, John L. H. *The Russian Revolution: A Study in Mass Mobilization.* New York: W. W. Norton, 1977.
2694. Kindersley, Richard. *The First Russian Revisionists: A Study of "Legal Marxism" in Russia.* Oxford: Clarendon Press, 1962.
2695. Kochan, Lionel. *Russia in Revolution, 1890-1910.* London: Weidenfeld and Nicolson, 1966.
2696. Koenker, Diane. *Moscow Workers and the 1917 Revolution.* Princeton: Princeton University Press, 1981.
2697. Lampert, Evgeny. *Sons Against Fathers: Studies in Russian Radicalism and Revolution.* Oxford: Clarendon Press, 1965.
2698. _____ . *Studies in Rebellion: A Study of the Origins of Revolutionary Thought in Russia.* Boston: Routledge and Kegan Paul, 1957.
2699. Laqueur, Walter. *The Fate of Revolution: Interpretations of Soviet History.* London: Weidenfeld and Nicolson, 1967.
2700. Lee, Peter, and Graham Bearman. *Russia in Revolution.* Exeter, New Hampshire: Heinemann Educational Books, 1974.
2701. Leggett, George. *The Cheka: Lenin's Political Police.* New York: Oxford University Press, 1981.
2702. Lerner, Warren. *Karl Radek: The Last Internationalist.* Stanford: Stanford University Press, 1970.
2703. Liebman, Marcel. *The Russian Revolution.* New York: Random House, 1972.
2704. Lyons, Eugene. *Assignment in Utopia.* Westport, Connecticut: Greenwood, 1971.

Russian Revolution of 1917 and the Bolsheviks / 171

2705. Mawdsley, Evan. *The Russian Revolution and the Baltic Fleet.* New York: Barnes and Noble, 1979.
2706. Medlin, Virgil. *The Russian Revolution.* Hinsdale, Illinois: Dryden Press, 1973.
2707. Medvedev, Roy. *The October Revolution.* New York: Columbia University Press, 1979.
2708. Moorehead, Alan. *The Russian Revolution.* New York: Harper and Row, 1958.
2709. Owen, Launcelot. *The Russian Peasant Movement, 1906–1917.* London: P. S. King, 1937.
2710. Pethybridge, Roger. *The Spread of the Russian Revolution: Essays on 1917.* New York: St. Martin's Press, 1972.
2711. Pipes, Richard. *The Formation of the Soviet Union: Communism and Nationalism, 1917–1923.* New York: Atheneum, 1968.
2712. _____, ed. *Revolutionary Russia: A Symposium.* Garden City, New York: Doubleday, 1969.
2713. _____. *Russia Under the Old Regime.* New York: Scribners, 1974.
2714. Pomper, Philip. *Peter Lavrov and the Russian Revolutionary Movement.* Chicago: University of Chicago Press, 1972.
2715. _____. *The Russian Revolutionary Intelligentsia.* New York: Thomas Y. Crowell, 1970.
2716. Pushkarev, Sergei G. *The Emergence of Modern Russia, 1801–1917.* Translated by R. H. McNeal and T. Yedlin. New York: Holt, Rinehart and Winston, 1963.
2717. Rabinowitch, Alexander, and Janet Rabinowitch, eds. *Revolution and Politics in Russia.* Bloomington: Indiana University Press, 1972.
2718. Radkey, Oliver Henry. *The Election to the Russian Constituent Assembly of 1917.* Cambridge, Massachusetts: Harvard University Press, 1950.
2719. _____. *The Sickle Under the Hammer: The Russian Socialist Revolutionaries in the Early Months of Soviet Rule.* New York: Columbia University Press, 1963.
2720. Rauch, Georg von. *A History of Soviet Russia.* Translated by P. Jacobsohn and A. Jacobsohn. New York: Praeger, 1972.
2721. Rosenberg, William G. *Liberals in the Russian Revolution: The Constitutional Democratic Party, 1917–1921.* Princeton: Princeton University Press, 1974.
2722. Salisbury, Harrison E. *Russia in Revolution.* New York: Holt, Rinehart and Winston, 1978.
2723. Seton-Watson, Hugh. *The Russian Empire, 1801–1917.* New York: Oxford University Press, 1967.
2724. Shanin, Teodor. *The Awkward Class: Political Sociology of Peasantry in a Developing Society: Russia 1910–1925.* New York: Oxford University Press, 1972.
2725. Smith, Canfield F. *Vladiovostok Under Red and White Rule: Revolution and Counterrevolution in the Russian Far East, 1920–1922.* Seattle: University of Washington Press, 1976.
2726. Smith, Clarence Jay. *The Russian Struggle for Power, 1914–1917.* New York: Philosophical Library, 1956.
2727. Smith, Edward Ellis. *The Young Stalin: The Early Years of an Elusive Revolutionary.* New York: Farrar, 1967.
2728. Steinberg, I. N. *In the Workshop of the Revolution.* New York: Holt, Rinehart and Winston, 1953.

172 / Modern Europe

2729. Sternberg, Fritz. *The End of a Revolution: Soviet Russia, From Revolution to Reaction.* New York: Day, 1953.
2730. Suny, Roger G. *Baku Commune, 1917–1918: Class and Nationality in the Russian Revolution.* Princeton: Princeton University Press, 1972.
2731. Tompkins, Stuart R. *The Russian Intelligentsia: Makers of the Revolutionary State.* Norman: University of Oklahoma Press, 1957.
2732. Treviranus, G. R. *Revolutions in Russia: Their Lessons for the Western World.* New York: Harper and Brothers, 1944.
2733. Tucker, Robert C. *Stalin as Revolutionary, 1879–1929: A Study in History and Personality.* New York: W. W. Norton, 1973.
2734. Venturi, Franco. *Roots of Revolution.* New York: Grosset and Dunlap, 1966.
2735. Voline (V. M. Eichenbaum). *The Unknown Revolution.* New York: Free Life Editions, 1975.
2736. Von Laue, Theodore H. *Why Lenin? Why Stalin? A Reappraisal of the Russian Revolution, 1900–1930.* 2d ed. Philadelphia: Lippincott, 1971.
2737. Wallace, Donald Mackenzie. *Russia on the Eve of War and Revolution.* New York: Vintage, 1961.
2738. Williams, Albert Rhys. *Journey into Revolution: Petrograd, 1917–1918.* Edited by L. Williams. Chicago: Quadrangle Books, 1969.
2739. _____. *Through the Russian Revolution.* New York: Boni and Liveright, 1921.
2740. Wilson, Edmund. *To the Finland Station.* Garden City, New York: Doubleday, 1953.
2741. Wolfe, Bertram D. *An Ideology in Power: Reflections on the Russian Revolution.* New York: Stein and Day, 1969.
2742. _____. *Revolution and Reality: Essays on the Origin and Fate of the Soviet System.* Chapel Hill: University of North Carolina Press, 1981.
2743. _____. *Three Who Made a Revolution:* New York: Dell, 1964.
2744. Yarmolinsky, Avrahm. *Road to Revolution: A Century of Russian Radicalism.* New York: Collier Books, 1962.

Lenin and Leninism

Lenin was the central figure in the Russian Revolution. He was both a thinker and a man of action, a revolutionary theorist and a revolutionist. He gave new life and meaning to Marxism, and he became the leader of Russia. He combined the revolutionary theory of Marx with the revolutionary tradition of Russia, and then brought them both to life in the Russia of his day. He transformed Marxism, an ideology suitable for advanced capitalist nations, into Marxism-Leninism, a theory for revolution and progress in backward countries. Lenin was also concerned with revolutionary strategy, and he stressed organization as the means by which the revolutionary elite or party would direct the masses.

Probably the best place to learn about Lenin is his writings. Selections from his works are brought together in the edited collections listed under the document heading below, while his major works appear under his name. The better biographies of Lenin are by Angelica Balabanova (1964), Robert Conquest (1972), Nina Gourfinkle (1972), Christopher Hill (1971), Nadezhda Krupskaya (1942; she was his wife), Stanley W. Page (1972), Stefan T. Possony (1964), David Shub (1966), Donald W. Treadgold (1955), and Bertram Wolfe (1978). To sample the leading views on Lenin see the collection edited by Stanley W. Page (1970). The best studies of Leninism are by Neil Harding (1978), Georg Lukács (1971), and Alfred G. Meyer (1962). The articles by Rodney Barfield (1971), Francis Bennett Becker (1937), Robert V. Daniels (1957), and Stanley W. Page (1950, 1952) are also helpful.

Historiography

2745. Warth, Robert D. "Lenin: The Western Image Forty Years After." *Antioch Review* 24:4 (Winter 1964-1965): 530-37.

Documents

2746. Christman, Henry M., ed. *Essential Works of Lenin.* New York: Bantam Books, 1966.
2747. Connor, James E., ed. *Lenin on Politics and Revolution.* New York: Pegasus, 1968.
2748. Possony, Stefan T., ed. *Lenin Reader.* South Bend, Indiana: Henry Regnery, 1966.
2749. Tucker, Robert C., ed. *The Lenin Anthology.* New York: W. W. Norton, 1975.

Articles

2750. Barfield, Rodney. "Lenin's Utopianism: *State and Revolution.*" *Slavic Review* 30:1 (March 1971): 45-56.
2751. Becker, Francis Bennett. "Lenin's Application of Marx's Theory of Revolutionary Tactics." *American Sociological Review* 2:3 (June 1937): 353-64.
2752. Daniels, Robert V. "Lenin and the Russian Revolutionary Tradition." *Harvard Slavic Studies* 4 (1957).
2753. Heller, Michael. "Lenin and the Cheka: The Real Lenin." *Survey* 24:2 (Spring 1979): 175-92.
2754. Kingston-Mann, Esther. "Lenin and the Beginnings of Marxist Peasant Revolution: The Burden of Political Opportunity, July-October 1917." *Slavonic and East European Review* 50:121 (October 1972): 570-88.
2755. Korotkov, I. "The Military-Theoretical Legacy of Lenin." *Soviet Military Review* (April 1968): 2-6.
2756. Menashe, Louis. "Vladimir Illyich Bakunin: An Essay on Lenin." *Socialist Revolution* 18 (November-December 1973): 9-54.

2757. Page, Stanley W. "Lenin: Prophet of World Revolution from the East." *Russian Review* 11:2 (April 1952): 67–77.
2758. _____. "Lenin and Self-Determination." *Slavonic and East European Review* 28:71 (April 1950): 342–58.

Books

2759. Andics, Hellmut. *Rule of Terror: Russia Under Lenin and Stalin.* New York: Holt, Rinehart and Winston, 1969.
2760. Balabanova, Angelica. *Impressions of Lenin.* Translated by I. Cesari. Ann Arbor: University of Michigan Press, 1964.
2761. Bukharin, Nikolai. *Lenin as a Marxist.* London: Communist Party of Great Britain, 1925.
2762. Cash, Anthony. *Lenin.* New York: Viking, 1972.
2763. Claudin-Urondo, Carmen. *Lenin and the Cultural Revolution.* Translated by B. Pearce. Atlantic Highlands, New Jersey: Humanities Press, 1977.
2764. Cliff, Tony. *Lenin.* 2 vols. London: Pluto Press, 1975–1976.
2765. Conquest, Robert. *V. I. Lenin.* New York: Viking, 1972.
2766. Dutt, R. Palme. *Life and Teachings of V. I. Lenin.* New York: International Publishers, 1934.
2767. Fischer, Louis. *The Life of Lenin.* New York: Harper and Row, 1964.
2768. Gorky, Maxim. *Days With Lenin.* New York: International Publishers, 1932.
2769. Gourfinkle, Nina. *Portrait of Lenin.* New York: McGraw-Hill, 1972.
2770. Hammond, Thomas T. *Lenin on Trade Unions and Revolution, 1893–1917.* New York: Columbia University Press, 1957.
2771. Harding, Neil. *Lenin's Political Thought: Theory and Practice in the Democratic Revolution.* New York: St. Martin's Press, 1979.
2772. Hill, Christopher. *Lenin and the Russian Revolution.* Middlesex, England: Penguin Books, 1971.
2773. Katkov, George, and Harold Shukman. *Lenin's Path to Power: Bolshevism and the Destiny of Russia.* London: Macdonald, 1971.
2774. Kiernan, T., ed. *Selected Essays on Lenin.* New York: Philosophical Library, 1971.
2775. Krupskaya, Nadezhda. *Memories of Lenin.* London: Lawrence and Wishart, 1942.
2776. Lenin, V. I. *Collected Works.* 45 vols. Moscow: Foreign Languages Publishing House, 1960–1970.
2777. _____. *Imperialism: The Highest Stage of Capitalism.* New York: International Publishers, 1939.
2778. _____. *Marx, Engels, Marxism.* Moscow: Foreign Languages Publishing House, 1947.
2779. _____. *The Proletarian Revolution in Russia.* New York: Communist Press, 1918.
2780. _____. *The State and Revolution.* London: Martin Lawrence, 1932.
2781. _____. *Two Tactics of Social-Democracy in the Democratic Revolution.* New York: International Publishers, 1935.
2782. _____. *What Is To Be Done?* Moscow: Progress Publishers, 1969.

2783. Lewin, Moshe. *Lenin's Last Struggle.* New York: Random House, 1968.
2784. Lukács, Georg. *Lenin: A Study on the Unity of His Thought.* Translated by N. Jacobs. Cambridge, Massachusetts: M.I.T. Press, 1971.
2785. McNeal, Robert H. *Bride of the Revolution: Krupskaya and Lenin.* Ann Arbor: University of Michigan Press, 1972.
2786. Marcu, Valeriu. *Lenin.* New York: Macmillan, 1928.
2787. Maxton, James. *Lenin.* New York: D. Appleton, 1932.
2788. Meyer, Alfred G. *Leninism.* New York: Praeger, 1962.
2789. Morgan, Michael. *Lenin.* New York: Free Press, 1973.
2790. Page, Stanley W., ed. *Lenin: Dedicated Marxist or Revolutionary Pragmatist?* Lexington, Massachusetts: D. C. Heath, 1970.
2791. _____. *Lenin and World Revolution.* New York: McGraw-Hill, 1972.
2792. Payne, Robert. *The Life and Death of Lenin.* New York: Avon Books, 1967.
2793. Pospelov, P. M., et al. *Lenin: A Biography.* Moscow: Progress Publishers, 1965.
2794. Possony, Stefan T. *Lenin, the Compulsive Revolutionary.* Chicago: Henry Regnery, 1964.
2795. Schapiro, Leonard, and Peter Reddaway, eds. *Lenin: The Man, the Theorist, the Leader: A Reappraisal.* New York: Praeger, 1967.
2796. Shub, David. *Lenin: A Biography.* Baltimore: Penguin Books, 1966.
2797. Shukman, Harold. *Lenin and the Russian Revolution.* New York: Putnam, 1967.
2798. Silverman, Saul. *Lenin.* Englewood Cliffs, New Jersey: Prentice-Hall, 1972.
2799. Solzhenitsyn, Alexander. *Lenin in Zurich.* New York: Farrar, Straus and Giroux, 1976.
2800. Stalin, Joseph. *Leninism.* 2 vols. New York: International Publishers, 1933.
2801. _____. *Problems of Leninism.* Moscow: Foreign Languages Publishing House, 1953.
2802. Theen, Rolf H. W. *Lenin: Genesis and Development of a Revolutionary.* Philadelphia: Lippincott, 1973.
2803. Treadgold, Donald. W. *Lenin and His Rivals.* New York: Praeger, 1955.
2804. Trotsky, Leon. *Lenin.* New York: Minton, Balch, 1925.
2805. Valentinov, Nikolay. *Encounters with Lenin.* London: Oxford University Press, 1968.
2806. Vernadsky, George. *Lenin, Red Dictator.* New Haven: Yale University Press, 1931.
2807. Volskii, N. V. *The Early Years of Lenin.* Translated and edited by R. H. W. Theen. Ann Arbor: University of Michigan Press, 1969.
2808. Warth, Robert D. *Lenin.* New York: Twayne, 1973.
2809. Williams, Albert Rhys. *Lenin: The Man and His Work.* New York: Scott and Seltzer, 1919.
2810. Wolfe, Bertram. *The Bridge and the Abyss: The Troubled Friendship of Maxim Gorky and V. I. Lenin.* New York: Praeger, 1967.
2811. _____. *Lenin.* New York: Stein and Day, 1978.
2812. Zetkin, Klara. *Reminiscences of Lenin.* New York: International Publishers, 1934.

Trotsky

After Lenin, Leon Trotsky was probably the greatest and most important figure of the Russian Revolution. He was Lenin's close associate and a prime organizer of the Red Army. Although they had not always agreed on key points, the two men merged their ideas in 1917. Trotsky accepted Lenin's party to lead the revolution and represent the workers. Lenin accepted Trotsky's position that the power necessary for a socialist revolution could be gained immediately. Lenin also accepted Trotsky's idea of a single-party dictatorship, which melded perfectly with his idea of a minority dictatorship in the party. Trotsky also developed a theory of permanent revolution; that is, the Russian Revolution was the first step in a world revolution that would continue permanently until all the world had reached socialism.

Trotsky was a prolific writer; his many books are represented below in the titles under his name. To sample this massive output see the anthology edited by Isaac Deutscher (1964). The articles provide insight into particular aspects of Trotsky's life and thought. The standard biography is the three-volume work by Isaac Deutscher (1954, 1959, 1963). Good shorter studies are by Joel Carmichael (1975), Irving Howe, (1978), Baruch Knei-paz (1978), Ronald Segal (1979), and Robert D. Warth (1977).

Bibliography

2813. Sinclair, Louis. *Leon Trotsky: A Bibliography.* Stanford: Hoover Institution, 1972.

Documents

2814. Deutscher, Isaac, ed. *The Age of Permanent Revolution: A Trotsky Anthology.* New York: Dell, 1964.

Articles

2815. Eastman, Max. "Great in Time of Storm: The Character and Fate of Leon Trotsky." In *Heroes I Have Known,* by M. Eastman. New York: Simon and Schuster, 1942.

2816. Gottschalk, Louis. "Leon Trotsky and the Natural History of Revolutions." *American Journal of Sociology* 44:3 (November 1938): 339–54.

2817. Heyman, Neil M. "Leon Trotsky: Propagandist to the Red Army." *Studies in Comparative Communism,* no. 1–2 (1977): 24–43.

2818. Rowney, Don Karl. "Development of Trotsky's Theory of Revolution, 1898–1907." *Studies in Comparative Communism,* no. 1–2 (1977): 18–33.

Books

2819. Archer, Jules. *Trotsky, World Revolutionary.* New York: Messner, 1973.
2820. Carmichael, Joel. *Trotsky: An Appreciation of His Life.* New York: St. Martin's Press, 1975.
2821. Day, Richard B. *Leon Trotsky and the Politics of Economic Isolation.* Cambridge: Cambridge University Press, 1973.
2822. Deutscher, Isaac. *The Prophet Armed: Trotsky, 1879–1921.* New York: Oxford University Press, 1954.
2823. _____. *The Prophet Outcast: Trotsky, 1929–1940.* New York: Oxford University Press, 1963.
2824. _____. *The Prophet Unarmed: Trotsky, 1921–1929.* New York: Oxford University Press, 1959.
2825. Eastman, Max. *Leon Trotsky: The Portrait of a Youth.* London: Faber and Gwyer, 1926.
2826. Hansen, Joseph, et al. *Leon Trotsky: The Man and His Works.* New York: Pathfinder Press, 1969.
2827. Howe, Irving. *Leon Trotsky.* New York: Viking, 1978.
2828. Knei-paz, Baruch. *The Social and Political Thought of Leon Trotsky.* New York: Oxford University Press, 1978.
2829. Olgin, Moissaye J. *Trotskyism: Counter-Revolution in Disguise.* San Francisco: Proletarian Publishers, 1975.
2830. Payne, Robert. *The Life and Death of Trotsky.* New York: McGraw-Hill, 1977.
2831. Segal, Ronald. *Leon Trotsky.* New York: Pantheon Books, 1979.
2832. Serge, Victor, and Natalya Sedova Trotsky. *The Life and Death of Leon Trotsky.* Translated by A. J. Pomerans. New York: Basic Books, 1975.
2833. Smith, Irving H. *Trotsky.* Englewood Cliffs, New Jersey: Prentice-Hall, 1973.
2834. Trotsky, Leon. *Between Red and White. A Study of Some Fundamental Questions of Revolution.* Great Britain: Communist Party of Great Britain, 1922.
2835. _____. *The History of the Russian Revolution.* Translated by M. Eastman. 3 vols. New York: Simon and Schuster, 1932.
2836. _____. *In Defense of Marxism.* New York: Pathfinder Press, 1973.
2837. _____. *Marxism in Our Time.* New York: Pathfinder Press, 1972.
2838. _____. *My Life.* New York: Grosset and Dunlap, 1960.
2839. _____. *Our Revolution: Essays on Working-Class and International Revolution, 1904–1917.* New York: H. Holt, 1918.
2840. _____. *Permanent Revolution and Results and Prospects.* Translated by J. G. Wright. New York: Pathfinder Press, 1969.
2841. _____. *The Revolution Betrayed.* New York: Pathfinder Press, 1965.
2842. _____. *The Russian Revolution.* Edited by F. W. Dupee. Garden City, New York: Doubleday, 1959.
2843. _____. *The Transitional Program for Socialist Revolution.* New York: Pathfinder Press, 1974.
2844. _____. *Trotsky's Diary in Exile, 1935.* Translated by E. Zarudnaya. Cambridge, Massachusetts: Harvard University Press, 1976.
2845. _____. *Writings of Leon Trotsky.* 15 vols. New York: Pathfinder Press, 1972–1980.

2846. Van Heijenoort, Jean. *With Trotsky in Exile: From Prinkipo to Coyoacán.* Cambridge, Massachusetts: Harvard University Press, 1978.
2847. Warth, Robert D. *Leon Trotsky.* Boston: Twayne, 1977.
2848. Wistrich, Robert. *Fate of a Revolutionary: The Legacy of Leon Trotsky.* Totowa, New Jersey: Rowman and Littlefield, 1979.
2849. Wyndham, Francis, and David King. *Trotsky.* New York: Praeger, 1972.

Revolution in Greece

The works below are concerned with revolutionary activity in Greece, particularly with the Revolution of 1821 and what is questionably referred to as a revolution that occurred in the 1960s. Greek communism and its relationship to revolution is also examined.

Articles

2850. Frazee, Charles A. "The Greek Catholic Islanders and the Revolution of 1821." *East European Quarterly* 13:3 (1979): 315–26.
2851. Ladis, Fondas. "Democratic or Socialist Revolution in Greece?" *Monthly Review* (December 1972): 38–53.
2852. Papandreou, Andreas. "Greece: Neocolonialism and Revolution." *Monthly Review* (December 1972): 13–22.
2853. Reinerman, Alan J. "Metternich, the Papacy, and the Greek Revolution." *East European Quarterly* 12:2 (1978): 177–88.

Books

2854. Blaquiere, Edward. *The Greek Revolution: Its Origins and Progress.* London: G. and W. B. Whittaker, 1824.
2855. Finlay, George. *History of the Greek Revolution and the Reign of King Otho.* Atlantic Highlands, New Jersey: Humanities Press, 1971.
2856. Howe, Samuel Bridley. *An Historical Sketch of the Greek Revolution.* Rev. ed. Austin, Texas: Center for Neo-Hellenic Studies, 1966.
2857. Kousoulas, D. George. *Revolution and Defeat: The Story of the Greek Communist Party.* New York: Oxford University Press, 1965.
2858. Stockton, Bayard. *Phoenix with a Bayonet: A Journalist's Interim Report on the Greek Revolution.* Ann Arbor, Michigan: Georgetown, 1971.

Finnish Revolution, 1917–1918

Finnish nationalism began to develop soon after the country was conquered by Russia in 1809. In the early 1900s Russia tried to Russianize Finland, but this met with growing opposition. Further crisis was averted as Russia became engulfed first in World War I and then in her own revolution. Finland declared her independence in December 1917; but in preparing for this move the Finns had become divided into two groups—socialists (Red Guard) and nonsocialists (White Guard), with each demanding independence, but with the socialists also wanting revolutionary social changes. A civil war broke out in early 1918, ending after about five months in a victory for the White Guard. The struggle for independence and the civil war comprised the revolution.

Articles

2859. Hamalainen, Pekka K. "Revolution, Civil War, and Ethnic Relations: The Case of Finland." *Journal of Baltic Studies* 5:2 (1974): 117–25.
2860. Jussila, Osmo. "Nationalism and Revolution: Political Dividing Lines in the Grand Duchy of Finland during the Last Years of Russian Rule." *Scandinavian Journal of History* 2:4 (1977): 289–309.

Books

2861. Hamalainen, Pekka K. *In Time of Storm: Revolution, Civil War, and the Ethnolinguistic Issue in Finland.* Albany: State University of New York Press, 1979.
2862. Upton, Anthony F. *The Finnish Revolution, 1917–1918.* Minneapolis: University of Minnesota Press, 1981.

Ukrainian Revolution, 1917–1921

From the eighteenth century, the Ukraine had been under Russian rule, but with the Russian Revolution the people of the Ukraine tried to form an independent state. Lenin's government, in an initial rush of enthusiasm, issued a decree granting any nationality within the Russian empire the right to withdraw from it if they chose. The Ukrainians took advantage of this to proclaim autonomy and then independence, as Finland had already done. But with World War I and the civil war in Russia still raging,

Soviet policy changed. In 1922 the Ukraine became one of the four original republics of the Union of Soviet Socialist Republics. The revolution had failed to maintain Ukrainian independence.

Article

2863. Guthier, Steven L. "The Popular Base of Ukrainian Nationalism in 1917." *Slavic Review* 38:1 (March 1979): 30–47.

Books

2864. Fedyshyn, O. S. *Germany's Drive to the East and the Ukrainian Revolution, 1917–1918.* New Brunswick, New Jersey: Rutgers University Press, 1971.
2865. Hunczak, Taras, ed. *The Ukraine, 1917–1921: A Study in Revolution.* Cambridge, Massachusetts: Harvard University Press, 1977.
2866. Motyl, Alexander J. *The Turn to the Right: The Ideological Origins and Development of Ukrainian Nationalism, 1919–1929.* New York: Columbia University Press, 1980.
2867. Palij, Michael. *The Anarchism of Nestor Makhno, 1918–1921: An Aspect of the Ukrainian Revolution.* Seattle: University of Washington Press, 1977.
2868. Reshetar, John S., Jr. *The Ukrainian Revolution, 1917–1920: A Study in Nationalism.* Princeton: Princeton University Press, 1952.

Hungarian Revolution, 1918–1919

The disintegration of the Austro-Hungarian Empire in World War I saw a communist attempt to revolutionize Hungary. The country had become an independent republic in 1918, but the next year, under the direction of Béla Kun, a soviet regime was set up and maintained. This led the opposition forces, domestic and foreign, to merge and then to defeat Kun and the communists.

Bibliographies

2869. Bako, Elemer. *Guide to Hungarian Studies.* 2 vols. Stanford: Hoover Institution, 1973.
2870. Völgyes, Ivan. *The Hungarian Soviet Republic, 1919: An Evaluation and a Bibliography.* Stanford: Hoover Institution, 1970.

Articles

2871. Deak, Istvan. "Budapest and the Hungarian Revolutions of 1918–1919." *Slavonic and East European Review* 46:106 (January 1968): 129–40.
2872. Nezhinsky, L. N. "The Revolution of 1919 in Hungary." *Voprosy Istorii* 3 (1979): 56–69.
2873. Pastor, Peter. "The Hungarian Revolution's Road from Wilsonianism to Leninism, 1918–19." *East Central Europe* 3:2 (1976): 210–19.

Books

2874. Janos, Andrew C., and William B. Slottman, eds. *Revolution in Perspective: Essays on the Hungarian Soviet Republic.* Berkeley: University of California Press, 1971.
2875. Jaszi, Oscar. *Revolution and Counter-Revolution in Hungary.* New York: Howard Fertig, 1969.
2876. Pastor, Peter. *Hungary between Wilson and Lenin: The Hungarian Revolution of 1918–1919 and the Big Three.* New York: Columbia University Press, 1976.
2877. Szilassy, Sander. *Revolutionary Hungary: 1918–1921.* Astor, Florida: Danubian Press, 1971.
2878. Tokes, Rudolf L. *Béla Kun and the Hungarian Soviet Republic: The Origins and Role of the Revolutions of 1918–1919.* Stanford: Hoover Institution, 1967.
2879. Völgyes, Ivan, ed. *Hungary in Revolution, 1918–19: Nine Essays.* Lincoln: University of Nebraska Press, 1972.

German Revolution, 1918–1919, and Rosa Luxemburg

Following Germany's defeat in World War I, liberals and socialists of many shades sought to establish new regimes. One such group, led by Rosa Luxemburg and Karl Liebknecht, was the Spartacists. They were Leninist in belief and tried to bring about a proletarian revolution in Germany, like that in Russia. Although successful at first with Bolshevik aid, the Spartacists' uprising was crushed, and Luxemburg and Liebknecht were murdered while in police custody. Luxemburg was a brilliant and passionate revolutionist. Had she lived she might have been able to transform the Spartacist, or Communist Party of Germany into one that would have provided leadership of the world revolutionary movement. Had that happened, the fate of Hitler, Stalin, and of course the world would have been different.

On the revolution, see the books by Werner T. Angress (1963),

Rudolf Coper (1955), Ralph H. Lutz (1934, 1968), A. J. Ryder (1967), and Richard M. Watt (1968). The best biography of Rosa Luxemburg is by J. P. Nettl (1974).

Article

2880. Ritterberger, V. "Revolution and Pseudo-Democratization: The Formation of the Weimar Republic." In *Crisis, Choice, and Change,* edited by G. A. Almond et al. Boston: Little, Brown, 1973.

Books

2881. Angress, Werner T. *Stillborn Revolution:The Communist Bid for Power in Germany, 1919-23.* Princeton: Princeton University Press, 1963.
2882. Basso, Lelio. *Rosa Luxemburg: A Reappraisal.* New York: Praeger, 1975.
2883. Bithell, Jethro, ed. *Germany: A Companion to German Studies.* 5th ed. London: Methuen, 1955.
2884. Burdick, Charles B., and Ralph H. Lutz, eds. *The Political Institutions of the German Revolution, 1918-1919.* Stanford: Hoover Institution, 1966.
2885. Calkins, Kenneth R. *Hugo Haase: Democrat and Revolutionary.* Durham, North Carolina: Carolina Academic Press, 1979.
2886. Coper, Rudolf. *Failure of a Revolution.* Cambridge: Cambridge University Press, 1955.
2887. Ettinger, Elzbieta, ed. *Comrade and Lover: Rosa Luxemburg's Letters to Leo Jogiches.* Cambridge, Massachusetts: M.I.T. Press, 1979.
2888. Frölich, Paul. *Rosa Luxemburg.* New York: Howard Fertig, 1970.
2889. Geras, Norman. *The Legacy of Rosa Luxemburg.* New York: Schocken, 1976.
2890. Haffner, Sebastian. *Failure of a Revolution: Germany, 1918-1919.* Translated by G. Rapp. La Salle, Illinois: Library Press, 1973.
2891. Halperin, Samuel William. *Germany Tried Democracy: A Political History of the Reich from 1918-1933.* Hamden, Connecticut: Archon Books, 1963.
2892. Lutz, Ralph H., ed. *The Causes of the German Collapse.* Hamden, Connecticut: Shoe String Press, 1934.
2893. _____. *Fall of the German Empire, 1914-1918.* 2 vols. New York: Octagon Books, 1969.
2894. _____. *The German Revolution, 1918-1919.* New York: AMS Press, 1968.
2895. Luxemburg, Rosa. *The Accumulation of Capital.* New York: Monthly Review Press, 1964.
2896. _____. *The National Question: Selected Writings.* Edited by H. B. Davis. New York: Monthly Review Press, 1981.
2897. _____. *Reform or Revolution.* New York: Pathfinder Press, 1973.
2898. _____. *Rosa Luxemburg Speaks.* Edited by M. Waters. New York: Pathfinder Press, 1970.
2899. _____. *Selected Political Writings of Rosa Luxemburg.* Edited by D. Howard. New York: Monthly Review Press, 1971.

2900. Mitchell, Allan. *Revolution in Bavaria, 1918-1919*. Princeton: Princeton University Press, 1965.
2901. Morgan, David W. *The Socialist Left and the German Revolution: A History of the German Independent Social Democratic Party, 1917-1922*. Ithaca: Cornell University Press, 1975.
2902. Nettl, J. P. *Rosa Luxemburg*. Mexico: Ediciones Era, 1974.
2903. Peck, Abraham. *Radicals and Reactionaries: The Crisis of Conservatism in Wilhelmine Germany*. Washington, D.C.: University Press of America, 1978.
2904. Ryder, A. J. *The German Revolution of 1918: A Study of German Socialism in War and Revolt*. Cambridge: Cambridge University Press, 1967.
2905. Watt, Richard M. *The Kings Depart: The Tragedy of Germany: Versailles and the German Revolution*. New York: Simon and Schuster, 1968.

Irish Revolution, 1916-1922

After being subjected to English control for hundreds of years, Ireland gained her independence in 1922. Although the revolution per se dates from the Easter Rebellion of 1916, in reality it has roots deep in Anglo-Irish history. Irish nationalism had developed during the nineteenth century as the rallying point for solutions to the people's problems. Then, as the English continued to do very little that was constructive, demands for home rule evolved into a struggle for independence. By the start of this century nationalism had become a revolutionary force. While the English were fighting on the Continent (in World War I), the various Irish revolutionary groups launched the revolution on Easter Monday, 1916. Although the masses had not joined the fight, the ferocity of the English response rallied the people to the cause of independence. Ireland (minus Ulster) was the first country in the twentieth century to liberate itself from foreign domination through her own efforts. And while there are important differences, the Irish Revolution nonetheless set a pattern for other revolutionary movements in the underdeveloped world.

The best general surveys of the revolution and its historical background are by George Dangerfield (1976), Edgar Holt (1960), Lawrence J. McCaffrey (1968, 1979), Oliver MacDonagh (1964), Nicholas Mansergh (1966), Patrick O'Farrell (1971, 1975), Alan J. Ward (1980), and Desmond Williams (1966). Other, more specialized studies that are useful are by J. Bowyer Bell (1972), D. G. Boyce (1972), Mary C. Bromage (1956), R. B. McDowell (1964), Francis X. Martin (1967), David Miller (1973), Leon Ó Broin (1971, 1976), and Eric Strauss (1951). The books by Michael Collins (1922) and Eamonn De Valera (1977) are by two of the most important leaders of the revolution.

184 / Modern Europe

Bibliographies

2906. Elton, G., ed. *Annual Bibliography of British and Irish History 1976.* Atlantic Highlands, New Jersey: Humanities Press, 1977.
2907. Mulvey, Helen F. "Modern Irish History Since 1940: A Bibliographical Survey (1600—1922)." *The Historian* 27 (August 1965): 516-59.

Documents

2908. Connolly, James. *Selected Writings.* Edited by P. B. Elwis. New York: Monthly Review Press, 1973.
2909. Hepburn, A. C. *The Conflict of Nationality in Modern Ireland.* New York: St. Martin's Press, 1980.
2910. Macardle, Dorothy. *The Irish Republic: A Documented Chronicle of the Anglo-Irish Conflict and the Partitioning of Ireland, With a Detailed Account of the Period 1916-1923.* London: Victor Gollancz, 1938.

Articles

2911. Boyle, John. "Irish Labour and the Rising." *Éire-Ireland* 2:3 (Autumn 1967): 122-31.
2912. Bromage, Mary C. "Ireland's Unfinished Revolution." *South Atlantic Quarterly* 71:1 (Winter 1972): 16-29.
2913. Costigan, Giovanni. "The Anglo-Irish Conflict, 1919-1922: A War of Independence or Systematized Murder?" *University Review* 5 (Spring 1968).
2914. Davenport, Gary T. "Sean O'Faolain's Troubles: Revolution and Provincialism in Modern Ireland." *South Atlantic Quarterly* 75:3 (Summer 1976): 312-22.
2915. Davis, Richard. "Arthur Griffiths, 1872-1922: Architect of Modern Ireland, Part I: To the Easter Rising." *History Today* 29 (March 1979): 139-46; "Arthur Griffiths, Architect of Modern Ireland, Part II: 1916-1922." *History Today* 29 (April 1979): 248-56.
2916. Ó Broin, Leon. "Revolutionary Nationalism in Ireland: The I.R.B., 1858-1924." In *Nationality and the Pursuit of National Independence,* edited by T. W. Moody. Belfast: Appletree Press, 1978.
2917. Quinn, Peter A. "Yeats and Revolutionary Nationalism: The Centenary of '98." *Éire-Ireland* 15:3 (Fall 1980): 47-64.
2918. Townshend, Charles. "The Irish Republican Army and the Development of Guerrilla Warfare, 1916-1921." *English Historical Review* 94 (April 1979): 318-45.
2919. Van Der Wusten, H. "The United Kingdom and Its Irish Contenders (1800-1922)." *Netherlands Journal of Sociology* 16:2 (October 1980): 171-84.

Books

2920. Akenson, Donald H. *The Church of Ireland: Ecclesiastical Reform and Revolution, 1800-1885.* New Haven: Yale University Press, 1971.
2921. Barry, Tom. *Guerrilla Days in Ireland.* New York: Devin-Adair, 1956.

2922. Beaslai, P. *Michael Collins, Soldier and Statesman.* Dublin: Talbot Press, 1937.
2923. Beckett, J. C. *The Making of Modern Ireland, 1603-1923.* New York: Alfred A. Knopf, 1966.
2924. Bell, J. Bowyer. *The Secret Army: A History of the IRA, 1916-1970.* London: Sphere Books, 1972.
2925. Bennett, Richard. *The Black and Tans.* Boston: Houghton Mifflin, 1959.
2926. Boyce, D. G. *Englishmen and Irish Troubles: British Public Opinion and the Making of Irish Policy, 1918-1922.* Cambridge, Massachusetts: M.I.T. Press, 1972.
2927. Bromage, Mary C. *De Valera and the March of a Nation.* New York: Noonday Press, 1956.
2928. Caulfield, Max. *The Easter Rebellion.* Westport, Connecticut: Greenwood, 1975.
2929. Coffey, Thomas M. *Agony at Easter: The Nineteen Sixteen Irish Uprising.* New York: Macmillan, 1969.
2930. Collins, M. E. *Ireland, 1800-1970.* New York: Longman, 1976.
2931. Collins, Michael. *The Path to Freedom.* Dublin: Talbot Press, 1922.
2932. Comerford, Anthony. *Easter Rising: Dublin 1916.* New York: Viking, 1969.
2933. Costigan, Giovanni. *A History of Modern Ireland.* New York: Pegasus, 1969.
2934. Curran, Joseph M. *The Birth of the Irish Free State, 1921-1923.* University: University of Alabama Press, 1980.
2935. Dangerfield, George. *The Damnable Question: A Study of Anglo-Irish Relations.* Boston: Atlantic-Little, Brown, 1976.
2936. Darby, John. *Conflict in Northern Ireland: The Development of a Polarized Community.* New York: Barnes and Noble, 1976.
2937. De Valera, Eamonn. *Peace and War.* Saint Clair Shores, Michigan: Scholarly Press, 1977.
2938. Edwards, Ruth Dudley. *Patrick Pearse: The Triumph of Failure.* New York: Taplinger, 1978.
2939. Figgis, Darrell. *Recollections of the Irish War.* London: E. Benn, 1927.
2940. Fitzpatrick, David. *Politics and Irish Life, 1913-1921: Provincial Experience of War and Revolution.* Dublin: Gill and Macmillan, 1977.
2941. Gibbon, Peter. *The Origins of Ulster Unionism: The Formation of Popular Protestant Politics and Ideology in Nineteenth-Century Ireland.* Manchester: Manchester University Press, 1975.
2942. Greaves, C. Desmond. *Liam Mellows and the Irish Revolution.* Brooklyn Heights, New York: Beekman Publishers, 1970.
2943. Gwynn, Denis Rolleston. *Daniel O'Connell, the Irish Liberator.* London: Hutchinson, 1929.
2944. _____. *The Life of John Redmond.* London: Harrap, 1932.
2945. Hay, Edward. *History of the Irish Insurrection.* Brooklyn, New York: Revisionist Press, 1973.
2946. Holt, Edgar. *Protest in Arms: The Irish Troubles, 1916-1923.* London: McClelland, 1960.
2947. Jackson, T. A. *Ireland Her Own: An Outline History of the Irish Struggle for National Freedom and Independence.* New York: International Publishers, 1970.

186 / Modern Europe

2948. Jones, Francis P. *History of the Sinn Fein Movement and the Irish Rebellion of 1916.* New York: P. J. Kenedy, 1921.

2949. Lyons, F. S. L. *Ireland Since the Famine.* New York: Scribners, 1971.

2950. McCaffrey, Lawrence J. *Ireland: From Colony to Nation State.* Englewood Cliffs, New Jersey: Prentice-Hall, 1979.

2951. _____. *The Irish Question, 1800-1922.* Lexington: University of Kentucky Press, 1968.

2952. MacDonagh, Michael. *The Life of William O'Brien, the Irish Nationalist: A Biographical Study of Irish Nationalism, Constitutional and Revolutionary.* London: Ernest Benn, 1928.

2953. MacDonagh, Oliver. *Ireland: The Union and Its Aftermath.* Edison, New Jersey: Allen and Unwin, 1977.

2954. _____. *The Irish Question, 1840-1920.* Rev. ed. Toronto: University of Toronto Press, 1964.

2955. McDowell, R. B. *The Irish Administration, 1801-1914.* Toronto: University of Toronto Press, 1964.

2956. Mc Hugh, Roger, ed. *Dublin, 1916.* London: Arlington Books, 1966.

2957. Mac Lysaght, Edward. *Changing Times: Ireland Since 1898.* Atlantic Highlands, New Jersey: Humanities Press, 1979.

2958. Mansergh, Nicholas. *The Irish Question, 1840-1920.* Rev. ed. Toronto: University of Toronto Press, 1966.

2959. Martin, Francis X., ed. *Leaders and Men of the Easter Rising, 1916.* Ithaca: Cornell University Press, 1967.

2960. _____, and F. J. Byrne, eds. *The Scholar Revolutionary: Eoin Mac Neill.* New York: Harper and Row, 1973.

2961. Miller, David. *Church, State, and Nation in Ireland, 1898-1921.* Pittsburgh: University of Pittsburgh Press, 1973.

2962. _____. *Queen's Rebels: Ulster Loyalism in Historical Perspective.* New York: Barnes and Noble, 1978.

2963. Moody, T. W., and Francis X. Martin. *The Course of Irish History.* New York: Keybright and Talley, 1967.

2964. Neeson, Eoin. *Civil War in Ireland.* Elmsford, New York: British Book Centre, 1971.

2965. Nowlan, Kevin B., ed. *The Making of 1916.* Dublin: Stationery Office, 1969.

2966. O'Brien, Conor Cruise, ed. *The Shaping of Modern Ireland.* Toronto: University of Toronto Press, 1960.

2967. O'Brien, Joseph V. *William O'Brien and the Course of Irish Politics, 1881-1918.* Berkeley: University of California Press, 1976.

2968. Ó Broin, Leon. *Dublin Castle and the 1916 Rising.* New York: New York University Press, 1971.

2969. _____. *Revolutionary Underground: The Story of the Irish Republican Brotherhood 1858-1924.* Totowa, New Jersey: Rowman and Littlefield, 1976.

2970. O'Conner, Frank. *The Big Fellow: Michael Collins and the Irish Revolution.* Dublin: Clonmore and Reynolds, 1965.

2971. O'Connor, Ulick, ed. *Irish Liberation.* New York: Random House, 1975.

2972. O'Faolain, Sean. *DeValera.* Middlesex, England: Penguin Books, 1939.

2973. O'Farrell, Patrick. *England and Ireland Since 1800.* London: Oxford University Press, 1975.

2974. _____. *Ireland's English Question: Anglo-Irish Relations, 1534-1970.* New York: Schocken, 1971.

2975. O'Hegarty, Patrick S. *A History of Ireland under the Union, 1801 to 1922.* London: Methuen, 1952.
2976. O'Neill, Brian. *Easter Week.* New York: International Publishers, 1939.
2977. Pakenham, Frank, and Thomas P. O'Neill. *Eamon DeValera.* Boston: Houghton Mifflin, 1971.
2978. Rumpf, E., and A. C. Hepburn. *Nationalism and Socialism in Twentieth-Century Ireland.* New York: Barnes and Noble, 1977.
2979. Skeffington, F. Sheehy. *Michael Davitt: Revolutionary Agitator and Labour Leader.* London: Mac Gibbon and Kee, 1967.
2980. Stephens, James. *The Insurrection in Dublin.* Atlantic Highlands, New Jersey: Humanities Press, 1972.
2981. Strauss, Eric. *Irish Nationalism and British Democracy.* New York: Columbia University Press, 1951.
2982. Thompson, William Irwin. *The Imagination of an Insurrection: Dublin, Easter 1916.* New York: Harper and Row, 1967.
2983. Ward, Alan J. *The Easter Rising: Revolution and Irish Nationalism.* Arlington Heights, Illinois: AHM Publishing, 1980.
2984. Williams, Desmond, ed. *The Irish Struggle, 1916–1926.* Toronto: University of Toronto Press, 1966.

Nazi Revolution, 1933

The Nazi Revolution brought Hitler to power. (The word "Nazi" was originally a derisory contraction of the name National Sozialist, Hitler's political party.) It was a conservative movement to make Germany safe for small business, small farmers, and those in small towns; ironically though, during the time in which the Nazis were successful big business prospered the most. The Nazi Revolution was built around a racial ideology of Aryan superiority, and it capitalized on the treatment Germany had received after World War I. It sought to establish a new faith and a new way of life, but became instead reactionary, regressive, and racist.

The purpose of this section is to give the reader material with which to study the 1933 revolution and Hitler's rise to power. (Many of the books below contain thorough bibliographies for anyone interested in learning more about Nazi Germany.) The book edited by John L. Snell (1973) is a good place to start to grasp the variety of historical opinions on the nature of the Nazi Revolution. Several good histories that cover this period are by Martin Broszat (1966), Richard Hanser (1971), Hajo Holborn (1973), Hermann Rauschning (1939, 1941), James M. Rhodes (1980), David Schoenbaum (1966), William L. Shirer (1960), A. J. P. Taylor (1946), and Eliot B. Wheaton (1968). Among the best biographies of Hitler are those by Alan Bullock (1962), Joachim C. Fest (1975), and John Toland (1976). For the student interested in survey histories of the period the following are recommended: Hajo Holborn, *A History of Modern Germany, 1840–*

1945 (New York, 1969); Herman Mau and Helmut Krausnick, *German History, 1933-1945* (London, 1959); Hannah Voight, *The Burden of Guilt: A Short History of Germany, 1914-1945* (New York, 1964); and David Childs, *Germany Since 1918* (New York, 1971).

Bibliography

2985. Laqueur, Walter, ed. *Fascism: A Reader's Guide: Analyses, Interpretations, Bibliography.* Berkeley: University of California Press, 1977.

Documents

2986. Noakes, Jeremy, and Geoffrey Pridham, eds. *Documents on Nazism.* New York: Viking, 1975.

Article

2987. Lerner, Daniel. "The Nazi Elite." In *World Revolutionary Elites: Studies in Coercive Ideology Movements,* edited by H. D. Lasswell and D. Lerner. Cambridge, Massachusetts: M.I.T. Press, 1965.

Books

2988. Allen, William Sheridan. *The Nazi Seizure of Power.* 2d ed. New York: Quadrangle Books, 1965.
2989. Baumont, Maurice, et al, eds. *The Third Reich.* New York: Praeger, 1955.
2990. Bithell, Jethro, ed. *Germany: A Companion to German Studies.* 5th ed. London: Methuen, 1955.
2991. Broszat, Martin. *German National Socialism, 1919-1945.* Santa Barbara, California: ABC-Clio, 1966.
2992. Bullock, Alan. *Hitler: A Study in Tyranny.* Rev. ed. New York: Harper and Row, 1962.
2993. Fest, Joachim C. *Hitler.* New York: Random House, 1975.
2994. Forman, James D. *Fascism: The Meaning and Experience of Reactionary Revolution.* New York: New Viewpoints, 1974.
2995. Hanser, Richard. *Putsch! How Hitler Made Revolution.* New York: Peter H. Wyden, 1971.
2996. Heiden, Konrad. *Der Fuehrer: Hitler's Rise to Power.* Boston: Houghton, 1944.
2997. Herberle, Rudolf. *From Democracy to Nazism.* Baton Rouge: Louisiana State University Press, 1945.
2998. Holborn, Hajo, ed. *Republic to Reich: The Making of the Nazi Revolution.* New York: Random House, 1973.
2999. Hoover, Calvin B. *Germany Enters the Third Reich.* New York: Macmillan, 1933.
3000. Kohn, Hans, ed. *German History: Some New German Views.* Boston: Beacon Press, 1954.

3001. Kornhauser, William. *The Politics of Mass Society.* Glencoe, Illinois: Free Press, 1959.
3002. Mayer, Milton. *They Thought They Were Free: The Germans, 1933-1945.* Chicago: University of Chicago Press, 1955.
3003. Mosse, George L. *The Crisis of German Ideology: Intellectual Origins of the Third Reich.* New York: Grosset and Dunlap, 1964.
3004. Neumann, Franz. *Behemoth: The Structure and Practice of National Socialism.* London: Oxford University Press, 1942.
3005. Nolte, Ernst. *Three Faces of Fascism.* Translated by L. Vennewitz. New York: Holt, Rinehart and Winston, 1965.
3006. Pridham, Geoffrey. *Hitler's Rise to Power: The Nazi Movement in Bavaria, 1928-1933.* London: Hart-Davis MacGibbon, 1973.
3007. Rauschning, Hermann. *The Conservative Revolution.* New York: Putnam, 1941.
3008. _____. *The Revolution of Nihilism.* New York: Alliance, 1939.
3009. Rhodes, James M. *The Hitler Movement: A Modern Millenarian Revolution.* Stanford: Hoover Institution, 1980.
3010. Schoenbaum, David. *Hitler's Social Revolution.* Garden City, New York: Doubleday, 1966.
3011. Shirer, William L. *The Rise and Fall of the Third Reich.* New York: Simon and Schuster, 1960.
3012. Snell, John L., ed. *The Nazi Revolution.* Rev. ed. Lexington, Massachusetts: D. C. Heath, 1973.
3013. Taylor, A. J. P. *The Course of German History.* New York: Coward, McCann, 1946.
3014. Toland, John. *Adolf Hitler.* Garden City, New York: Doubleday, 1976.
3015. Van Paassan, Pierre, ed. *Nazism: An Assault on Civilization.* New York: Harrison Smith and Robert Haas, 1934.
3016. Vermeil, Edmond. *Germany in the Twentieth Century.* New York: Praeger, 1956.
3017. Wheaton, Eliot B. *The Nazi Revolution.* Garden City, New York: Doubleday, 1968.

Spanish Civil War, 1936-1939

Following half a century of struggle by various left-wing and revolutionary groups, the ruling dictatorship in Spain was overthrown, the monarchy ended, and a republic established. A provisional government of republicans and socialists ruled the country until a general election in 1936 gave the parties of the left a large majority. A reform program was begun, which by this time caused alarm to already suspicious groups of army officers, large landowners, industrialists, and higher clergy. Soldiers supported by these groups invaded Spain from Morocco in order to overthrow the government and install a fascist dictatorship; the leader of the insurgents was General Francisco Franco. Receiving help from Mussolini and Hitler, Franco waged a successful civil war for almost three years. Until they were replaced in the 1940s and 1950s by Mao Tse-tung, Fidel Castro, and Che Guevara, the Spanish Civil War and the International Brigade (i.e., an organization of communist, socialist, and liberal volunteers from many countries) remained the symbols of socialist revolution against fascism.

For an introduction to the complex perspectives and viewpoints involved in the Spanish Civil War see the collection and bibliography edited by Gabriel Jackson (1967). The best general histories of the Civil War are by Burnett Bolloten (1961, 1979), Pierre Broué and Emile Témime (1970), Robert G. Colodny (1958), Ronald Fraser (1979), Gabriel Jackson (1965, 1974), Stanley G. Payne (1970), Paul Preston (1978), and Hugh Thomas (1961). The books by Herbert L. Matthews (1938, 1946) are by a perceptive war correspondent for *The New York Times*. Specialized studies may be gleaned from the titles.

Bibliography

3018. Wilgus, A. Curtis. *Latin America, Spain and Portugal: A Selected and Annotated Bibliographical Guide to Books Published, 1954–1974*. Metuchen, New Jersey: Scarecrow Press, 1977.

Articles

3019. Blinkhorn, Martin, ed. "Modern Spain." *European Studies Review* 9 (January 1979), special issue.
3020. Preston, Paul. "The Struggle against Fascism in Spain: *Leviatán* and the Contradictions of the Socialist Left, 1934–1936." *European Studies Review* 9 (January 1979): 81–104.
3021. Southworth, H. R. "La propaganda católica y la guerra civil española." *Historia 16* 4 (November 1979): 70–83.
3022. Stone, Glyn. "Britain, Non-Intervention and the Spanish Civil War." *European Studies Review* 9 (January 1979): 129–49.
3023. Thomas, Hugh. "¿Por qué estalló la guerra civil en 1936?" *Nueva Histórico* 3 (February 1979): 16–21.
3024. Viñas, Angel. "Gold, the Soviet Union and the Spanish Civil War." *European Studies Review* 9 (January 1979): 105–28.

Books

3025. Barea, Arturo. *The Forging of a Rebel*. New York: Reynal and Hitchcock, 1946.
3026. Benson, Frederick R. *Writers in Arms: The Literary Impact of the Spanish Civil War*. New York: New York University Press, 1967.
3027. Blinkhorn, Martin. *Carlism and Crisis in Spain, 1931–1939*. New York: Cambridge University Press, 1975.
3028. Bolloten, Burnett. *The Grand Camouflage: The Spanish Civil War and Revolution, 1936–1939*. New York: Praeger, 1961.

3029. _____. *The Spanish Revolution: The Left and the Struggle for Power during the Civil War.* Chapel Hill: University of North Carolina Press, 1979.
3030. Borkenau, Franz. *The Spanish Cockpit.* Ann Arbor: University of Michigan Press, 1937.
3031. Brenan, Gerald. *The Spanish Labyrinth: An Account of the Social and Political Background of the Spanish Civil War.* Cambridge: Cambridge University Press, 1962.
3032. Broué, Pierre, and Emile Témime. *The Revolution and the Civil War in Spain.* Translated by T. White. Cambridge, Massachusetts: M.I.T. Press, 1970.
3033. Cardozo, Harold G. *March of a Nation: My Year of Spain's Civil War.* London: Eyre and Spottiswoode, 1937.
3034. Carr, Raymond, ed. *The Republic and the Civil War in Spain.* New York: St. Martin's Press, 1971.
3035. _____. *The Spanish Tragedy: The Civil War in Perspective.* London: Weidenfeld and Nicolson, 1977.
3036. _____, and Juan Pablo Fusi. *Spain: Dictatorship to Democracy.* Winchester, Massachusetts: Allen and Unwin, 1979.
3037. Cattell, David T. *Communism and the Spanish Civil War.* New York: Russell and Russell, 1965.
3038. Colodny, Robert G. *Spain: The Glory and the Tragedy.* Atlantic Highlands, New Jersey: Humanities Press, 1970.
3039. _____. *The Struggle for Madrid: The Central Epic of the Spanish Conflict, 1936–37.* New York: Paine-Whitman, 1958.
3040. Conze, Edward. *Spain Today: Revolution and Counter-Revolution.* New York: Greenberg, 1936.
3041. Coverdale, John F. *Italian Intervention in the Spanish Civil War.* Princeton: Princeton University Press, 1976.
3042. Dolgoff, Samuel. *The Anarchist Collectives: Workers' Self-Management in the Spanish Revolution.* New York: Free Life Editions, 1974.
3043. Edwards, Jill. *The British Government and the Spanish Civil War, 1936–1939.* London: Macmillan, 1979.
3044. Esch, P. A. M. van Der. *Prelude to War: The International Repercussion of the Spanish Civil War.* New York: Gordon Press, 1976.
3045. Fernsworth, Lawrence. *Spain's Struggle for Freedom.* Boston: Beacon, 1957.
3046. Fraser, Ronald. *Blood of Spain: An Oral History of the Spanish Civil War.* New York: Pantheon, 1979.
3047. Gibbs, Jack. *The Spanish Civil War.* Totowa, New Jersey: Rowman and Littlefield, 1973.
3048. Goldston, Robert. *The Civil War in Spain.* Greenwich, Connecticut: Fawcett Publications, 1966.
3049. Guttman, Allen, ed. *American Neutrality and the Spanish Civil War.* Boston: D. C. Heath, 1963.
3050. Jackson, Gabriel. *A Concise History of the Spanish Civil War.* Scranton, Pennsylvania: John Day, 1974.
3051. _____. *The Spanish Republic and the Civil War.* Princeton: Princeton University Press, 1965.
3052. _____, ed. *The Spanish Civil War.* Chicago: Quadrangle Books, 1972.
3053. _____, ed. *The Spanish Civil War: Domestic Crisis or International Conspiracy?* Lexington, Massachusetts: D. C. Heath, 1967.

3054. Jellinek, Frank. *The Civil War in Spain.* New York: Howard Fertig, 1969.

3055. Landis, Arthur H., *Spain: The Unfinished Revolution.* New York: International Publishers, 1975.

3056. Low, Mary, and Juan Brea. *Red Spanish Notebook: The First Six Months of the Revolution and Civil War.* London: M. Secker and Warburg, 1937.

3057. Lunn, Arnold. *Spanish Rehearsal for World War: An Eye Witness Account of the Spanish Civil War.* Old Greenwich, Connecticut: Devin-Adair, 1975.

3058. Malefakis, Edward E. *Agrarian Reform and Peasant Revolution in Spain: Origins of the Civil War.* New Haven: Yale University Press, 1971.

3059. Manuel, Frank E. *The Politics of Modern Spain.* New York: McGraw-Hill, 1938.

3060. Matthews, Herbert L. *The Education of a Correspondent.* New York: Harcourt, Brace, 1946.

3061. _____ . *Half of Spain Died: A Reappraisal of the Spanish Civil War.* New York: Scribners, 1973.

3062. _____ . *Two Wars and More to Come.* New York: Carrick and Evans, 1938.

3063. Meaker, Gerald H. *The Revolutionary Left in Spain, 1914-1923.* Stanford: Stanford University Press, 1974.

3064. Mendizabal Villalba, Alfredo. *The Martyrdom of Spain: Origins of a Civil War.* London: G. Bles, 1938.

3065. Morrow, Felix. *Revolution and Counter-Revolution in Spain.* New York: Pathfinder Press, 1974.

3066. Ortega y Gasset, José. *Invertebrate Spain.* Translated by M. Adams. New York: W. W. Norton, 1937.

3067.. Orwell, George. *Homage to Catalonia.* New York: Harcourt, Brace and World, 1952.

3068. Payne, Robert. *The Civil War in Spain, 1936-1939.* New York: Putnam, 1962.

3069. Payne, Stanley G. *Falange: A History of Spanish Fascism.* Stanford: Stanford University Press, 1961.

3070. _____ . *The Spanish Revolution.* New York: W. W. Norton, 1970.

3071. Peers, Edgar A. *The Spanish Tragedy, 1930-1936.* New York: Oxford University Press, 1936.

3072. Preston, Paul. *The Coming of the Spanish Civil War: Reform, Reaction and Revolution in the Second Republic, 1931-1936.* New York: Barnes and Noble, 1978.

3073. Purcell, Hugh. *The Spanish Civil War.* New York: Putnam, 1973.

3074. Puzzo, Dante E. *Spain and the Great Powers, 1936-1941.* New York: New York University Press, 1962.

3075. _____ . *Spanish Civil War.* Florence, Kentucky: Van Nostrand Reinhold, 1969.

3076. Richards, Vernon. *Lessons of the Spanish Revolution.* New York: Chip's Bookshop, 1972.

3077. Robinson, Richard A. H. *The Origins of Franco's Spain: The Right, the Republic and Revolution, 1931-1936.* Pittsburgh: University of Pittsburgh Press, 1971.

3078. Rosenstone, Robert A. *Crusade of the Left: The Lincoln Battalion in the Spanish Civil War.* Washington, D.C.: University Press of America, 1980.

3079. Sanchez, Jose M. *Reform and Reaction: The Politico-Religious Background of the Spanish Civil War.* Chapel Hill: University of North Carolina Press, 1963.
3080. Sender, Ramon. *Counter-Attack in Spain.* Boston: Houghton, 1937.
3081. Snellgrove, Laurence Ernest. *Franco and the Spanish Civil War.* New York: McGraw-Hill, 1965.
3082. Sommerfield, John. *Volunteer in Spain.* London: Lawrence and Wishart, 1937.
3083. Sperber, Murray A., ed. *And I Remember Spain: A Spanish Civil War Anthology.* New York: Collier Books, 1974.
3084. Taylor, F. Jay. *The United States and the Spanish Civil War.* New York: Twayne, 1956.
3085. Thomas, Hugh. *The Spanish Civil War.* New York: Harper and Row, 1961.
3086. Tisa, John, ed. *The Palette and the Flame: Posters of the Spanish Civil War.* New York: International Publishers, 1980.
3087. Toynbee, Philip, ed. *The Distant Drum: Reflections on the Spanish Civil War.* New York: David McKay, 1977.
3088. Trotsky, Leon. *The Spanish Revolution (1931-39).* New York: Pathfinder Press, 1973.
3089. Turnbull, Patrick. *Spanish Civil War.* New York: Hippocrene Books, 1978.
3090. Weintraub, Stanley. *The Last Great Cause: The Intellectuals and the Spanish Civil War.* New York: Weybright and Talley, 1968.
3091. Werstein, Irving. *Cruel Years: The Story of the Spanish Civil War.* New York: Messner, 1969.

Revolution in Yugoslavia, 1941-1945

In June, 1941 Hitler's army seized control over the government of Yugoslavia. Two resistance groups fought the Nazis: the Chetniks, led by an army colonel, and the Partisans, led by the communist Tito. They also fought each other until, with the Allied victory and support, Tito emerged triumphant. Yugoslavia became a republic in November, 1945.

Article

3092. Denitch, Bogdan Denis. "Violence and Social Change in the Yugoslav Revolution." *Comparative Politics* 8:3 (April 1976): 465-78.

Books

3093. Avakumovich, Ivan. *History of the Communist Party of Yugoslavia.* 2 vols. Aberdeen, Scotland: Aberdeen University Press, 1964.
3094. Denitch, Bogdan Denis. *The Legitimation of a Revolution: The Yugoslav Case.* New Haven: Yale University Press, 1976.

194 / Modern Europe

3095. Djilas, Milovan. *Tito: The Story From Inside.* Translated by V. Kojic and R. Hayes. New York: Harcourt Brace Jovanovich, 1980.
3096. Hoffman, George W., and Fred W. Neal. *Yugoslavia and the New Communism.* New York: Twentieth Century Fund, 1962.
3097. Johnson, Ross. *Transformation of Communist Ideology: The Yugoslav Case, 1943-1953.* Cambridge, Massachusetts: M.I.T. Press, 1972.
3098. Milazzo, Matteo J. *The Chetnik Movement and the Yugoslav Resistance.* Baltimore: Johns Hopkins University Press, 1975.
3099. Ristic, Dragisa N. *Yugoslavia's Revolution of 1941.* University Park: Pennsylvania State University Press, 1966.
3100. Tomasevich, Jozo. *The Chetniks: War and Revolution in Yugoslavia, 1941-1945.* Stanford: Stanford University Press, 1975.
3101. Vucinich, Wayne S., ed. *Contemporary Yugoslavia.* Berkeley: University of California Press, 1969.
3102. Zaninovich, M. George. *The Development of Socialist Yugoslavia.* Baltimore: Johns Hopkins University Press, 1968.

Revolution in Poland, 1956

Despite resistance, Poland became communist by 1948. In 1952, the government adopted a constitution patterned after that of Russia. But many Poles were unhappy with their government's policies and Russian domination. Discontent turned revolutionary in 1956, and resulted in some positive changes.

3103. Gibney, Frank. *The Frozen Revolution: Poland, A Study in Communist Decay.* New York: Farrar, Straus and Giroux, 1959.
3104. Syrop, Konrad. *Spring in October: The Polish Revolution of 1956.* London: Weidenfeld, 1957.
3105. Weydenthal, Jan B. de. *The Communism of Poland.* Stanford: Hoover Institution, 1979.

Hungarian Revolution, 1956

As a satellite state of the USSR, Hungary's government exercised little independence. Since reform could only come from within the established communist party, those who sought reform from without could not help but be frustrated. In the 1950s the government of Hungary undertook a modest program of liberalization. This in turn encouraged some Hungarians to demand more freedom. Revolutionary ferment resulted in an insurrection by the people of Budapest in 1956, which had to be suppressed by Russian troops. Although the revolution failed, life in Hungary did improve as a result of some economic decentralization and greater social freedom.

Bibliographies

3106. Bako, Elemer. *Guide to Hungarian Studies.* 2 vols. Stanford: Hoover Institution, 1973.
3107. Halasz de Beky, I. L. "A Bibliography of the Hungarian Revolution." *Canadian-American Review of Hungarian Studies* 3:2 (1976): 195-202.

Articles

3108. Arendt, Hannah. "Totalitarian Imperialism: Reflections on the Hungarian Revolution." *Journal of Politics* 20 (1958): 5-43.
3109. Gosztony, Peter. "The Hungarian Revolution of 1956 Viewed from Two Decades' Distance." *Canadian-American Review of Hungarian Studies* 3:2 (1976): 139-53.

Books

3110. Aczél, Tamás, ed. *Ten Years After: The Hungarian Revolution in the Perspective of History.* New York: Holt Rinehart and Winston, 1966.
3111. Anderson, Andy. *Hungary '56.* Detroit: Black and Red, 1976.
3112. Barber, Noel. *Seven Days to Freedom: The Hungarian Uprising, 1956.* New York: Stein and Day, 1974.
3113. Fejto, François. *Behind the Rape of Hungary.* New York: David McKay, 1957.
3114. Kecskemeti, Paul. *The Unexpected Revolution: Social Forces in the Hungarian Uprising.* Stanford: Stanford University Press, 1961.
3115. Király, Béla K., and Paul Jónás, eds. *The Hungarian Revolution of 1956 in Retrospect.* New York: Columbia University Press, 1978.
3116. Lasky, Melvin J., ed. *The Hungarian Revolution.* New York: Praeger, 1957.
3117. Lomax, Bill. *Hungary, 1956.* New York: St. Martin's Press, 1977.
3118. McCarger, J. *Hungarian Revolution.* New York: Holt, Rinehart and Winston, 1973.
3119. Marton, Endre. *The Forbidden Sky: Inside the Hungarian Revolution.* Boston: Little, Brown, 1971.
3120. Mikes, Georges. *The Hungarian Revolution.* London: Andre Deutsch, 1957.
3121. Radvanyi, James. *Hungary and the Superpowers: The 1956 Revolution and Realpolitik.* Stanford: Hoover Institution, 1976.
3122. Vali, Ferenc A. *Rift and Revolt in Hungary: Nationalism versus Communism.* Cambridge, Massachusetts: Harvard University Press, 1961.
3123. Wagner, Francis S., ed. *The Hungarian Revolution in Perspective.* Washington, D.C.: F. F. Memorial Foundation, 1967.
3124. Zinner, Paul E. *Revolution in Hungary.* New York: Columbia University Press, 1962.

French Revolution, 1968

Behind this revolution were anti-capitalist, anti-imperialist, and anti-Vietnam War feelings. In March, 1968 several students were arrested for bombing a number of American establishments in Paris. Protests resulted in the formation of the "22 March Movement" of student revolutionists led by Daniel Cohn-Bendit (see his two books below); other political and revolutionary groups lent their support. At first the protests concentrated on university conditions, but they were transformed into a rebellion against society when the police were called in. The fighting was escalated by actions of both the government and the students, and it soon spread from Paris to the provinces. By mid-May the rebellion had hardened into a New Left revolution attempting to overthrow the government of Charles De Gaulle and the capitalist system. Workers from factories also joined the revolt. By late May some nine million workers were on strike. At this point De Gaulle began to capitalize upon the differences between the students and workers, and the revolution lost its steam. Although the revolution failed, it is significant as the first attempted revolution in a Western industrialized society after World War II.

Most of the works in this section offer helpful analyses of the 1968 revolution. The articles are all concise and very useful. Among the books those by Raymond Aron (1969), Henri Lefebvre (1969), Allan Priaulx and Sanford J. Ungar (1969), J. J. Servan-Schreiber (1969), Daniel Singer (1971), and Alain Touraine (1971) stand out.

Bibliography

3125. Wylie, Laurence; Franklin D. Chu; and Mary Terrall. *France: The Events of May-June 1968, A Critical Bibliography.* Cambridge, Massachusetts: Council for European Studies, Harvard University, 1973.

Articles

3126. Ambler, John S. "The Politics of French University Reform; Ten Years after May." *Contemporary French Civilization* 3 (Fall 1978): 11-29.

3127. Aron, Raymond. "Student Rebellion: Vision of the Future or Echo from the Past." *Political Science Quarterly* 84:2 (June 1969): 289-310.

3128. Aubéry, Pierre. "Après mai 1968: La France va-t-elle passer de la révolte à la révolution?" *Contemporary French Civilization* 2 (Winter 1978): 191-204.

3129. _____. "A quoi ça sert de se révolter (1968)." *Contemporary French Civilization* 1 (Fall 1976): 59-82.

3130. Decker, Jane Elizabeth. "Direct Democracy and Revolutionary Organization in the 1968 French Student-Worker Revolt." *Proceedings of the Western Society of French History* 6 (1978): 406-14.

3131. Duff, Peggy. "The French Revolution: 1968." *Our Generation* (May 1968): 66-94.
3132. Ehrmann, Henry. "The Explosion of 1968: Revolution or Psychodrama." *Proceedings of the Symposium of French-American Studies* (March 1973): 201-12.
3133. Ellul, Jacques. "The Psychology of a Rebellion: May-June 1968." In *Struggles in the State: Sources and Patterns of World Revolution*, edited by G. A. Kelly and C. W. Brown, Jr. New York: John Wiley, 1970.
3134. Katsiaficas, George. "The Meaning of May 1968." *Monthly Review* (January 1978): 13-30.
3135. Lichtheim, George. "What Happened in France." *Commentary* (September 1968): 39-49.
3136. Mendel, Arthur P. "Why the French Communists Stopped the Revolution." *Review of Politics* 31:1 (January 1969): 3-27.
3137. Taylor, Edmond. "Revolution and Reaction in France." *Foreign Affairs* 47 (October 1968): 99-109.

Books

3138. Ardagh, John. *The New French Revolution.* New York: Harper and Row, 1969.
3139. Aron, Raymond. *The Elusive Revolution.* New York: Praeger, 1969.
3140. Bourges, Hervé. *The French Student Revolt: The Activists Speak.* Translated by B. R. Brewster, New York: Hill and Wang, 1968.
3141. Brown, Bernard E. *The French Revolt: May 1968.* New York: McCaleb-Seiler, 1970.
3142. _____ . *Protest in Paris: Anatomy of a Revolt.* Morristown, New Jersey: General Learning, 1974.
3143. Cohn-Bendit, Daniel, and Gabriel Cohn-Bendit. *Obsolete Communism: The Left-Wing Alternative.* New York: McGraw-Hill, 1968.
3144. Cohn-Bendit, Daniel, et al. *The French Student Revolt: The Leaders Speak.* New York: Hill and Wang, 1968.
3145. Gregoire, R., and F. Perlman. *Worker-Student Action Committees: France, May 1968.* Detroit: Black and Red, 1969.
3146. Hauss, Charles. *The New Left in France: The Unified Socialist Party.* Westport, Connecticut: Greenwood, 1978.
3147. Johnson, Richard. *The French Communist Party versus the Student: Revolutionary Politics in May-June 1968.* New Haven: Yale University Press, 1972.
3148. Lefebvre, Henri. *The Explosion: Marxism and the French Upheaval.* New York: Monthly Review Press, 1969.
3149. Posner, Charles, ed. *Reflections on the Revolution in France, 1968.* Baltimore: Penguin Books, 1970.
3150. Poster, Mark. *Existential Marxism in Post War France: From Sartre to Althusser.* Princeton: Princeton University Press, 1976.
3151. Priaulx, Allan, and Sanford J. Ungar. *Almost Revolution.* New York: Dell, 1969.
3152. Quattrocchi, Angelo, and Tom Nairn. *The Beginning of the End: France, May 1968.* London: Panther Books, 1968.

3153. Schnapp, Alain, and Pierre Vidal-Naquet. *The French Student Uprising, November 1967-June 1968: An Analytical Report.* Translated by M. Jolas. Boston: Beacon, 1972.
3154. Seale, Patrick, and Maureen McConville. *Red Flag Black Flag: French Revolution, 1968.* New York: Putnam, 1968.
3155. Servan-Schrieber, J. J. *The Spirit of May.* New York: McGraw-Hill, 1969.
3156. Singer, Daniel. *Prelude to Revolution: France in May 1968.* New York: Hill and Wang, 1971.
3157. Touraine, Alain. *The May Movement: Revolt and Reform.* Translated by L. Mayhew. New York: Random House, 1971.
3158. *Writing on the Wall: France, May 1968.* Edited by Vladimir Fišera. New York: St. Martin's Press, 1979.

Czechoslovakian Revolution, 1968

During the 1960s Czechoslovakia's agricultural and industrial production dropped, with shortages of food and other goods resulting. The government was criticized, even by the Communist Party. At the same time, intellectuals called for greater freedom of expression and the recognition of Slovak rights. In 1968, a new government under Alexander Dubcek introduced a program of liberal reforms. But the "Prague Spring" was short-lived. Russia, fearing that this new program would weaken Communist control in Czechoslovakia, and possibly result in similar demands in other communist countries, gathered troops from several Eastern bloc powers and invaded Czechoslovakia. The reforms were rescinded and the country forced to submit. The revolution was over.

Bibliography

3159. Hejzlar, Zdenek, and Vladimir V. Kusin. *Czechoslovakia 1968–1969: Annotation, Bibliography, Chronology.* New York: Garland, 1974.

Documents

3160. Remington, Robin A., ed. *Winter in Prague: Documents on Czechoslovak Communism in Crisis.* Cambridge, Massachusetts: M.I.T. Press, 1969.

Articles

3161. Barnard, F. M. "The Prague Spring and Masaryk's Humanism." *East Central Europe* 5:2 (1978): 215–31.
3162. Bridge, S. "Why Czechoslovakia? And Why 1968?" *Studies in Comparative Communism* 8:4 (1975): 413–29.

3163. Pravda, Vitezslav. "The Czechoslovak Revolution: Background, Forces and Objectives." *New Politics* 7:1 (Winter 1968): 24-41.
3164. Skilling, H. Gordon. "The Prague Spring Reassessed." *Slavic Review* 38:4 (December 1979): 663-66.

Books

3165. Evans, Les, ed. *Invasion of Czechoslovakia*. New York: Pathfinder Press, n.d.
3166. Golan, Galia. *The Czechoslovakian Reform Movement: Communism in Crisis, 1962-1968*. Cambridge: Cambridge University Press, 1971.
3167. Kaplan, Frank L. *Winter into Spring: The Czechoslovak Press and the Reform Movement, 1963-1968*. New York: Columbia University Press, 1977.
3168. Kusin, Vladimir V. *Intellectual Origins of the Prague Spring: The Development of Reformist Ideas in Czechoslovakia, 1958-1967*. New York: Cambridge University Press, 1971.
3169. Littell, Robert, ed. *The Czech Black Book*. New York: Avon Books, 1969.
3170. Mezerik, Avrahm G., ed. *Czechoslovakia Invasion*. New York: International Review Service, 1968.
3171. Mlynar, Zdenek. *Nightfrost in Prague: The End of Humane Socialism*. Translated by P. Wilson. New York: Karz, 1980.
3172. Page, Benjamin B. *The Czechoslovak Reform Movement, 1963-1968: A Study in the Theory of Socialism*. Atlantic Highlands, New Jersey: Humanities Press, 1973.
3173. Paul, David W. *The Cultural Limits of Revolutionary Politics: Change and Continuity in Socialist Czechoslovakia*. New York: Columbia University Press, 1979.
3174. Schwartz, Harry. *Prague's 200 Days: The Struggle for Democracy in Czechoslovakia*. New York: Praeger, 1969.
3175. Skilling, H. Gordon. *Czechoslovakia's Interrupted Revolution*. Princeton: Princeton University Press, 1977.
3176. Valenta, Jiri. *Soviet Invasion of Czechoslovakia, 1968: Anatomy of a Decision*. Baltimore: Johns Hopkins University Press, 1979.
3177. Windsor, Philip, and Adam Roberts. *Czechoslovakia Nineteen Sixty-Eight: Reform, Repression and Resistance*. New York: Columbia University Press, 1969.
3178. Zartman, I. William. *Czechoslovakia: Intervention and Impact*. New York: New York University Press, 1970.
3179. Zeman, Z. A. B. *Prague Spring*. New York: Hill and Wang, 1969.

Portuguese Revolution, 1974

After being the dictator of Portugal since 1932, Prime Minister Salazar suffered a stroke in 1968; he died two years later. During the 1960s anti-colonial revolutions had erupted in Angola, Mozambique, and

Guinea-Bissau, Portugal's colonies in Africa. Fighting between Portuguese troops, financed in part by NATO, and African guerrillas continued into the 1970s. With Salazar's dictatorial leadership gone and the African revolutions becoming a greater drain on her resources, Portugal became less and less stable. In 1974, in a revolution led by the army, the government was overthrown. Portugal became increasingly democratic and soon acknowledged the independence of her African colonies.

Bibliography

3180. Lomax, William. *Revolution in Portugal: 1974-1976. A Bibliography.* Portuguese Studies, essay no. 2. Durham, New Hampshire: International Conference Group on Modern Portugal, 1978.

Articles

3181. "A Revolution Tamed: A Survey of Portugal." *The Economist* (28 May 1977).
3182. Cook, Don. "Portugal's Moderate Revolution." *Los Angeles Times* (6 October 1974).
3183. Cunhal, Alvaro. "Results and Prospects of the Portuguese Revolution." *World Marxist Review* 20 (January 1977): 18-31.
3184. Davies, John Paton. "Revolution of the Red Carnations." *The New York Times Magazine* (13 July 1975).
3185. Fauvet, Paul. "Four Years On: The Portuguese Revolution." *Marxism Today* (April 1978): 101-10.
3186. Gervasio, Antonio. "The Fight for Land: Part of the Revolution." *World Marxist Review* 19 (May 1976): 39-48.
3187. Maxwell, Kenneth. "The Thorns of the Portuguese Revolution." *Foreign Affairs* 54 (January 1976): 250-70.
3188. Mittelman, James. "Portugal's Counter-Revolution." *Journal of South African Affairs* 3 (April 1978): 153-58.
3189. Nunes, Albano. "The Portuguese Communists in the Struggle for Peace." *World Marxist Review* 21 (January 1978): 44-52.
3190. Paiva, Vasco, and Agostinho Lopes. "A Force Committed to the Revolutionary Process. Experience of Peasant Organization and Struggle in Portugal." *World Marxist Review* 22 (June 1979): 23-27.
3191. Pimlott, Ben. "Parties and Voters in the Portuguese Revolution: The Elections of 1975-1976." *Parliamentary Affairs* 30 (Winter 1977): 35-58.
3192. _____. "Were the Soldiers Revolutionary? The Armed Forces Movement in Portugal 1973-1976." *Journal of Iberian Studies* 7:1 (1978): 13-21.
3193. Pittman, John. "A Glimpse of Portugal's Future." *World Marxist Review* 21 (January 1978): 125-29.
3194. Rutledge, Ian. "Land Reform and the Portuguese Revolution." *Journal of Peasant Studies* 5:1 (1977): 79-98.
3195. Szulc, Tad. "Behind Portugal's Revolution." *Foreign Policy* (Winter 1975-1976): 3-62.

3196. Wiarda, Howard J. "The Portuguese Revolution: Towards Explaining the Political Behavior of the Armed Forces Movement." *Iberian Studies* 4:1 (1975): 53-61.

Books

3197. Braganca-Cunha, Vincente. *Revolutionary Portugal.* New York: Gordon Press, 1976.
3198. Cunhal, Alvaro. *Portugal—The Democratic and National Revolution.* New York: International Publishers, 1975.
3199. Fields, Rona M. *The Portuguese Revolution and the Armed Forces Movement.* New York: Praeger, 1976.
3200. Graham, Lawrence S., and Harry M. Makler, eds. *Contemporary Portugal: The Revolution and Its Antecedents.* Austin: University of Texas Press, 1979.
3201. Green, Gil. *Portugal's Revolution.* New York: International Publishers, 1976.
3202. Harsgor, M. *Portugal in Revolution.* Beverly Hills, California: Sage, 1976.
3203. Mailer, Phil. *Portugal: The Impossible Revolution?* New York: Free Life Editions, 1977.
3204. Porch, Douglas. *The Portuguese Armed Forces and the Revolution.* Stanford: Hoover Institution, 1978.
3205. Robinson, Richard A. H. *Contemporary Portugal: A History.* Winchester, Massachusetts: Allen and Unwin, 1979.

5 North America

"Those who won our independence by revolution were not cowards. They did not fear political change. They did not exalt order at the cost of liberty."
Louis Brandeis
Supreme Court Justice
(1927)

When compared with Europe, Asia, Africa, and Latin America, English-speaking North America has been remarkably free from major revolutions since the United States gained its independence. Any number of reasons can be offered by way of explanation, not the least of which is the fact that the region consists of only two nations, not ten or twenty or more. In addition, both the United States and Canada had their beginnings on essentially virgin new found land, both had few obstacles to growth and expansion (with all due respect to American Indians for what was done to them), both profited from the progress and mistakes of European civilization and from the labor of those who emigrated or were transported forcibly to their shores, and both usually had new frontiers into which restless energy and rebellious creativity could be channeled. Other, less flattering explanations can also be suggested, including the economic and physical exploitation both of some Americans and parts of the underdeveloped world, subtle forms of repression of dissidents, and the maintenance of an essentially middle class society which has meant that the majority have had more to lose than gain from revolution.

If then, there have been no great North American revolutions since 1776, there has been significant revolutionary activity, most of it following World War II. That activity has been concentrated in two, sometimes overlapping spheres: among mostly young and privileged Americans with socialist-leaning ideas (i.e., New Left) for the purpose of ridding the country of its inconsistencies and least flattering characteristics; and among black Americans to gain the levels of freedom and equality guaranteed by law.

Below are a number of works dealing with still other kinds of revolutionary activity. In addition to some general works there are selections on the Dorr Rebellion of 1842 by Marvin E. Gettleman (1973) and A. M. Mowry (1901), on slave revolts by Herbert Aptheker (1939, 1966) and Charles L. Wagandt (1964), on Chicano rebels by Jose A. Gutierrez (n.d.), and on Puerto Rican rebels by Frank Browning (1970) and the Young Lords Party and Michael Abramson (1971). There are also two fine articles by William O. Douglas (1961) and Edward Pessen (1973) which look at the course and spirit of revolution in the United States.

Reference

3206. Rossen, Johnny (Appleseed), ed. *The Little Red, White and Blue Book, 1776-1968: Revolutionary Quotations by Great Americans.* New York: Grove Press, 1969.

Articles

3207. Alperovitz, Gar. "The United States, Revolution, and the Cold War: Perspective and Prospect." In *Cold War Essays,* edited by G. Alperovitz. Garden City, New York: Doubleday, 1970.
3208. Browning, Frank. "From Rumble to Revolution: The Young Lords." *Ramparts* (October 1970): 19-25.
3209. Douglas, William O. "The U.S. and the Revolutionary Spirit." *Saturday Review* (10 June 1961).
3210. Hoffer, Eric. "Whose Country Is America?" *The New York Times Magazine* (22 November 1970).
3211. Pessen, Edward. "Why the United States Has Never Had a Revolution—Only 'Revolutions.'" *South Atlantic Quarterly* 72:1 (Winter 1973): 29-42.

Books

3212. American Enterprise Institute for Public Policy Research, ed. *America's Continuing Revolution.* Garden City, New York: Doubleday, 1975.
3213. Aptheker, Herbert. *Nat Turner's Slave Rebellion.* New York: Grove Press, 1966.
3214. _____. *Negro Slave Revolts in the United States.* New York: International Publishers, 1939.
3215. Ash, Roberta. *Social Movements in America.* Chicago: Markham, 1972.
3216. Brzezinski, Zbigniew. *Between Two Ages: America's Role in the Technetronic Era.* New York: Viking, 1970.
3217. Gettleman, Marvin E. *The Dorr Rebellion.* New York: Random House, 1973.
3218. Gutierrez, Jose A. *La Raza and Revolution.* Palo Alto, California: R. and E. Research Assoc., n.d.
3219. Mowry, A. M. *The Dorr War.* Providence, Rhode Island: Preston and Rounds, 1901.
3220. Novack, George, ed. *America's Revolutionary Heritage: Marxist Essays.* New York: Pathfinder Press, 1976.
3221. O'Conner, Harvey. *Revolution in Seattle.* New York: Monthly Review Press, 1964.
3222. Rockefeller, John D., III. *The Second American Revolution: Some Personal Observations.* New York: Harper and Row, 1974.
3223. Sisson, Dan. *The American Revolution of 1800.* New York: Alfred A. Knopf, 1974.
3224. Wagandt, Charles L. *The Mighty Revolution: Negro Emancipation in Maryland, 1862-1864.* Baltimore: Johns Hopkins University Press, 1964.
3225. Young Lords Party, and Michael Abramson. *Palante.* New York: McGraw-Hill, 1971.

American Revolution, 1776-1783

The American Revolution was the single most important episode in the history of the colonies and states of America. Progressing from protest, to riot, to rebellion, and finally to revolution Americans cast off Britain's tutelage, rejected the ideas of monarchy, made citizens out of subjects and states out of colonies, and established a central government based upon principles of popular rule, republicanism, and nationalism. But were these changes really revolutionary or were they only a cover for an aristocratic struggle between ruling elites? Did the new nation differ that significantly from her colonial past in terms of her laws, institutions, and traditions? Was the society of independent America radically restructured? With regard to the relationship between individuals and their government, their society, and one another, did the attitudes and ideas of America change? These and similar questions confront anyone who attempts to come to grips with America's past.

Several other factors and questions should be kept in mind. Unlike the French and Russian Revolutions, the American Revolution did not attempt to establish new foundations for society; the foundations of America had developed as the colonial experience modified English and European ideas, institutions, and habits. Therefore, the revolution was not so much aimed at disrupting a social or political order as it was to fulfill a destiny. And from its combined English and colonial heritage it chose and discarded until it produced something new and different. The revolution also propelled into the world of ideas and action the notion that the social and political hierarchy, in existence for a millennium, was not part of the natural order of the universe and did not have to be that way. With this in mind, what then is America's place in the history of revolutions? How much did the American Revolution influence the coming of the French Revolution of 1789 and colonial revolutions in Latin America, Asia, and Africa?

All this and more should be kept in mind in studying the American Revolution. An appreciation for the historical conflict can be gained from any of the historiographical selections below. A good place to begin is with general works that survey the whole period; among the best are those by John Alden (1954, 1969), Merrill Jensen (1968), Dan Lacy (1966), Page Smith (1976), and Gordon S. Wood (1969). Excellent collections of articles and excerpts from books are found in the books edited by George Athan Billias (1980), Jack P. Greene (1968), John R. Howe, Jr. (1970), Stephen G. Kurtz and James H. Hutson (1973), John C. Wahlke (1973), and Alfred F. Young (1976). Most of the above mentioned works also have bibliographic guides or essays that can be of assistance. The rest of what lies below is divided topically and in such a way as to be of maximum value in selecting the necessary kinds of material.

Bibliographies

3226. Freidel, Frank, and Richard K. Showman, eds. *Harvard Guide to American History.* 2 vols. Rev. ed. Cambridge, Massachusetts: Harvard University Press, 1974.
3227. Phillips, Leona. *Colonial Days and the Revolutionary War: An Annotated Bibliography.* New York: Gordon Press, 1976.
3228. Shy, John, ed. *The American Revolution.* Arlington Heights, Virginia: AHM Publishing, 1973.
3229. Smith, Dwight L., ed. *Era of the American Revolution: A Bicentennial Bibliography.* Santa Barbara, California: ABC-Clio, 1975.
3230. White, J. Todd, and Charles H. Lesser, eds. *Fighters for Independence: A Guide to Sources of Biographical Information on Soldiers and Sailors of the American Revolution.* Chicago: University of Chicago Press, 1977.

Historiographies

3231. Beloff, Max. *The Debate on the American Revolution, 1761–1783.* New York: Barnes and Noble, 1960.
3232. Billias, George Athan. "The Revolutionary Era: Reinterpretations and Revisions." In *American History: Retrospect and Prospect,* edited by G. A. Billias and G. N. Grob. New York: Free Press, 1971.
3233. Christie, I. R. "The Historians' Quest for the American Revolution." In *Statesmen, Scholars and Merchants,* edited by Anne Whiteman et al. New York: Oxford University Press, 1973.
3234. Craven, Wesley F. "The Revolutionary Era." In *The Reconstruction of American History,* edited by John Higham. New York: Humanities Press, 1962.
3235. Greene, Jack P. "The Plunge of Lemmings: A Consideration of Recent Writings on British Politics and the American Revolution." *South Atlantic Quarterly* 67:1 (Winter 1968): 141–75.
3236. _____. *The Reappraisal of the American Revolution in Recent Historical Literature.* Washington, D.C.: American Historical Association Service Center for Teachers of History, 1967.
3237. Jensen, Merrill. "Historians and the Nature of the American Revolution." In *The Reinterpretation of Early American History,* edited by Ray A. Billington. San Marino, California: Huntington Library, 1966.
3238. Morgan, Edmund S., ed. *The American Revolution: Two Centuries of Interpretation.* Englewood Cliffs, New Jersey: Prentice-Hall, 1965.
3239. Stuart, Reginald C. "The Origins of American Nationalism to 1783: An Historiographical Survey." *Canadian Review of Studies in Nationalism* 6 (Fall 1979): 139–51.

Documents

3240. Bailyn, Bernard. *Pamphlets of the American Revolution, 1750–1776.* Cambridge, Massachusetts: Harvard University Press, 1965.
3241. Barkan, Elliott R., ed. *Edmund Burke on the American Revolution.* Gloucester, Massachusetts: Peter Smith, 1972.

3242. Cohen, Lester H. *The Revolutionary Histories: Contemporary Narratives of the American Revolution.* Ithaca: Cornell University Press, 1980.
3243. Dann, John C., ed. *The Revolution Remembered: Eyewitness Accounts of the War of Independence.* Chicago: University of Chicago Press, 1980.
3244. Davies, K. G., ed. *Documents of the American Revolution.* Totowa, New Jersey: Biblio Distribution Centre. Several volumes and dates.
3245. Greene, Jack P., ed. *Colonies to Nation, 1763-1789: A Documentary History of the American Revolution.* New York: W. W. Norton, 1975.
3246. Idzerda, Stanley J., ed. *Lafayette in the Age of the American Revolution: Selected Letters and Papers, 1776-1790.* Ithaca: Cornell University Press. Several volumes and dates.
3247. Jacobs, Wilbur R. *Great Documents of the American Revolution.* Santa Barbara, California: ABC-Clio, 1975.
3248. Jensen, Merrill, ed. *Tracts of the American Revolution, 1763-1776.* Indianapolis, Indiana: Bobbs-Merrill, 1967.
3249. Morison, Samuel E., ed. *Sources and Documents Illustrating the American Revolution, 1764-1788.* 2d ed. New York: Oxford University Press, 1965.
3250. Pole, J. R., ed. *The Revolution in America, 1754-1788: Documents and Commentaries.* Stanford: Stanford University Press, 1970.
3251. Wheeler, Richard. *Voices of 1776: The Story of the American Revolution in the Words of Those Who Were There.* New York: Thomas Y. Crowell, 1972.

Reference

3252. Boatner, Mark M., III. *Encyclopedia of the American Revolution.* Rev. exp. ed. New York: David McKay, 1974.
3253. Cappon, Lester J. *Atlas of Early American History.* Vol. 2. *The Revolutionary Era.* Princeton: Princeton University Press, 1976.

Overviews, Surveys, Interpretations

Articles

3254. Andrews, Charles M. "The American Revolution: An Interpretation." *American Historical Review* 31:2 (January 1926): 218-32.
3255. Bailyn, Bernard. "The Central Themes of the American Revolution: An Interpretation." In *Essays on the American Revolution,* edited by S. G. Kurtz and J. H. Hutson. Chapel Hill: University of North Carolina Press, 1973.
3256. Morgan, Edmund S. "The American Revolution: Revisions in Need of Revising." *William and Mary Quarterly,* 3d ser. 14:1 (January 1957): 3-15.
3257. _____. "Conflict and Consensus in the American Revolution." In *Essays on the American Revolution,* edited by S. G. Kurtz and J. H. Hutson. Chapel Hill: University of North Carolina Press, 1973.
3258. Morris, Richard B. "'We the People of the United States': The Bicentennial of a People's Revolution." *American Historical Review* 82:1 (February 1977): 1-19.
3259. Robson, Eric. "The American Revolution Reconsidered." *History Today* 2 (February 1952): 126-32.

3260. Schlesinger, Arthur M. "The American Revolution Reconsidered." *Political Science Quarterly* 34:1 (March 1919): 63–75.
3261. Smelser, Marshall. "An Understanding of the American Revolution." *Review of Politics* 38:3 (July 1976): 297–312.

Books

3262. Alden, John. *The American Revolution 1775–1783.* New York: Harper and Row, 1954.
3263. _____. *A History of the American Revolution.* New York: Alfred A. Knopf, 1969.
3264. Aptheker, Herbert. *American Revolution, 1763–1783.* New York: International Publishers, 1960.
3265. Berkhofer, Robert F., Jr., ed. *The American Revolution: The Critical Issues.* Boston: Little, Brown, 1971.
3266. Billias, George Athan, ed. *The American Revolution: How Revolutionary Was It?* 3d ed. New York: Holt, Rinehart and Winston, 1980.
3267. Birch, R. C. *1776—The American Challenge.* New York: Longman, 1976.
3268. Bradford, M. E. *A Better Guide Than Reason: Studies in the American Revolution.* La Salle, Illinois: Sherwood Sugden, 1979.
3269. Brown, Richard Maxwell, and Don E. Fehrenbacher, eds. *Tradition, Conflict, and Modernization: Perspectives on the American Revolution.* New York: Academic Press, 1977.
3270. Calhoon, Robert McCluer. *Revolutionary America: An Interpretive Overview.* New York: Harcourt Brace Jovanovich, 1976.
3271. Catton, Bruce, and William B. Catton. *The Bold and Magnificent Dream: America's Founding Years, 1492–1815.* Garden City, New York: Doubleday, 1978.
3272. Chalmers, George. *An Introduction to the History of the Revolt of the American Colonies.* Saint Clair Shores, Michigan: Scholarly Press, 1977.
3273. Dimock, Martha McHutchison. *A Chronicle of the American Revolution, 1763–1783.* New York: Harper and Row, 1976.
3274. Dupuy, R. Ernest, and Trevor N. Dupuy. *An Outline History of the American Revolution.* New York: Harper and Row, 1975.
3275. Ferguson, E. James. *The American Revolution: A General History, 1763–1790.* Rev. ed. Homewood, Illinois: Dorsey Press, 1979.
3276. Fleming, Thomas. *1776: Year of Illusions.* New York: W. W. Norton, 1975.
3277. Fowler, William M., Jr., and Wallace Coyle, eds. *The American Revolution: Changing Perspectives.* Boston: Northeastern University Press, 1979.
3278. Greene, Jack P., ed. *The Ambiguity of the American Revolution.* New York: Harper and Row, 1968.
3279. _____, ed. *The Reinterpretation of the American Revolution, 1763–1789.* New York: Harper and Row, 1968.
3280. Hardy, Jack. *The First American Revolution.* New York: International Publishers, 1937.
3281. Hooker, Richard J., ed. *The American Revolution.* New York: John Wiley, 1970.
3282. Jensen, Merrill. *Founding of a Nation.* New York: Oxford University Press, 1968.

3283. Kurtz, Stephen G., and James H. Hutson, eds. *Essays on the American Revolution.* Chapel Hill: University of North Carolina Press, 1973.
3284. Labaree, Benjamin W. *America's Nation-Time: 1607–1789.* New York: W. W. Norton, 1976.
3285. Lacy, Dan. *The Meaning of the American Revolution.* New York: New American Library, 1966.
3286. Leder, Lawrence H. *America, 1603–1789: Prelude to a Nation.* 2d ed. Minneapolis, Minnesota: Burgess, 1978.
3287. _____, ed. *the Meaning of the American Revolution.* Chicago: Quadrangle Books, 1969.
3288. Main, Jackson T. *The Sovereign States, 1775–1783.* New York: New Viewpoints, 1973.
3289. Martin, James Kirby. *In the Course of Human Events: An Interpretive Exploration of the American Revolution.* Arlington Heights, Illinois: AHM Publishing, 1979.
3290. _____, and K. R. Stubaus. *American Revolution: Whose Revolution?* Huntington, New York: Robert E. Krieger, 1978.
3291. Meaney, Neville, ed. *Studies on the American Revolution.* South Melbourne: Macmillan Company of Australia, 1976.
3292. Miller, John C. *Triumph of Freedom, 1775–1783.* Boston: Little, Brown, 1948.
3293. Mitchell, Broadus. *The Price of Independence: A Realistic View of the American Revolution.* New York: Oxford University Press, 1974.
3294. Morgan, Edward S. *The Birth of the Republic, 1763–1789.* Rev. ed. Chicago: University of Chicago Press, 1977.
3295. _____. *The Challenge of the American Revolution.* New York: W. W. Norton, 1976.
3296. Morris, Richard B. *The American Revolution.* New York: Robert E. Krieger, 1979.
3297. _____. *The American Revolution Reconsidered.* New York: Harper and Row, 1967.
3298. Pole, J. R. *The Decision for American Independence.* Philadelphia: Lippincott, 1975.
3299. _____. *The Foundations of American Independence, 1763–1815.* Indianapolis, Indiana: Bobbs-Merrill, 1972.
3300. Rankin, Hugh F. *The American Revolution.* New York: Capricorn Books, 1965.
3301. Roger, Alan, and Alan Lawson, eds. *From Revolution to Republic.* Cambridge, Massachusetts: Schenkman, 1976.
3302. Simmons, R. C. *The American Colonies: From Settlement to Independence.* New York: David McKay, 1976.
3303. Smith, Page. *A New Age Now Begins: A People's History of the American Revolution.* 2 vols. New York: McGraw-Hill, 1976.
3304. Stage, John L., and Dan Lacy. *The Birth of America.* New York: Grosset and Dunlap, 1976.
3305. Suggs, George G., Jr., ed. *Perspectives on the American Revolution: A Bicentennial Contribution.* Carbondale: Southern Illinois University Press, 1977.
3306. Trevelyan, George Otto. *The American Revolution.* 4 vols. New York: Longmans, Green, 1899–1907.

3307. Van Tyne, Claude H. *The American Revolution, 1776–1783.* New York: AMS Press, 1972.

3308. Wood, Gordon S. *The Creation of the American Republic, 1776–1787.* Chapel Hill: University of North Carolina Press, 1969.

3309. Wood, Sidney, and John Thwaites. *The American Revolution.* Exeter, New Hampshire: Heinemann Educational Books, 1980.

3310. Young, Alfred F., ed. *The American Revolution: Explorations in the History of American Radicalism.* De Kalb: Northern Illinois University Press, 1976.

Contemporary Accounts by Patriots

3311. Ramsay, David. *The History of the American Revolution.* 2 vols. New York: Russell and Russell, 1968. First published in 1793.

3312. Warren, Mercy Otis. *History of the Rise, Progress, and Termination of the American Revolution.* 3 vols. New York: AMS Press, 1970. First published in 1805.

Contemporary Accounts by Loyalists

3313. Hutchinson, Thomas. *The History of the Colony and Province of Massachusetts-Bay.* 3 vols. Edited by L. S. Mayo. Cambridge, Massachusetts: Harvard University Press, 1936. First published in 1781.

3314. Oliver, Peter. *Origin and Progress of the American Rebellion.* Edited by D. Adair and J. A. Schultz. Stanford: Stanford University Press, 1961. Written prior to Oliver's death in 1791.

Coming of the Revolution

Articles

3315. Dormon, James H. "Collective Behaviour in the American Popular Resistance, 1765–1775: A Theoretical Prospectus." *Historian* 42 (November 1979): 1–17.

3316. Greene, Jack P. "'A Posture of Hostility': A Reconsideration of Some Aspects of the Origins of the American Revolution." *Proceedings of the American Antiquarian Society* 87 (April 1977): 27–68.

3317. ———. "The Seven Years' War and the American Revolution: The Causal Relationship Reconsidered." *Journal of Imperial Commonwealth History* 8 (January 1980): 85–105.

3318. ———. "An Uneasy Connection: An Analysis of the Preconditions of the American Revolution." In *Essays on the American Revolution,* edited by S. G. Kurtz and J. H. Hutson. Chapel Hill: University of North Carolina Press, 1973.

3319. Hacker, Louis M. "The First American Revolution." In *The Causes of the American Revolution,* edited by John C. Wahlke. Boston: D. C. Heath, 1950.

3320. Jezierski, John V. "*Imperii in Imperio:* The 1754 Albany Plan of Union and the Origins of the American Revolution." *North Dakota Quarterly* 42 (Summer 1974): 18–35.

3321. Merritt, Richard L., and Robert T. Chapel. "Symbolic Division of North America, 1752–1775." *Canadian Review of Studies in Nationalism* 6 (Fall 1979): 193–217.

3322. Morris, James. "From the Denial of a Dream to a Revolution." *Journal of Historical Studies* 3 (Fall 1977): 33–40.

3323. Van Alstyne, Richard W. "Revolution and Patriotism in America, 1763–1775." *Canadian Review of Studies in Nationalism* 6 (Fall 1979): 152–74.

Books

3324. Ammerman, David. *In the Common Cause: American Response to the Coercive Acts of 1775.* New York: W. W. Norton, 1975.

3325. Andrews, Charles M. *Colonial Background of the American Revolution.* New Haven: Yale University Press, 1961.

3326. Becker, Carl. *The Eve of the Revolution.* New Haven: Yale University Press, 1918.

3327. Boorstin, Daniel. *The Americans: The Colonial Experience.* New York: Random House, 1958.

3328. Booth, Sally S. *Seeds of Anger: Revolts in America, 1670–1771.* New York: Hastings House, 1977.

3329. Bridenbaugh, Carl. *The Spirit of '76: The Growth of American Patriotism before Independence.* New York: Oxford University Press, 1977.

3330. Currey, Cecil B. *Road to Revolution: Benjamin Franklin in England, 1765–1775.* Garden City, New York: Doubleday, 1968.

3331. Dickerson, O. M. *The Navigation Acts and the American Revolution.* New York: Octagon Books, 1974.

3332. Gipson, Lawrence H. *The British Empire before the American Revolution.* 15 vols. New York: Alfred A. Knopf, 1958–1970.

3333. _____ . *The Coming of the Revolution, 1763–1775.* New York: Harper and Row, 1954.

3334. Greene, Jack P., et al. *Society, Freedom and Conscience: The Coming of the Revolution in Virginia, Massachusetts, and New York.* New York: W. W. Norton, 1977.

3335. Jones, Alice Hanson. *Wealth of a Nation To Be: The American Colonies on the Eve of the Revolution.* New York: Columbia University Press, 1980.

3336. Knollenberg, Bernhard. *The Growth of the American Revolution, 1766–1775.* New York: Free Press, 1974.

3337. _____ . *Origin of the American Revolution, 1759–1766.* New York: Macmillan, 1960.

3338. Labaree, Benjamin W. *The Boston Tea Party.* Boston: Northeastern University Press, 1980.

3339. Launitz-Schurer, Leopold S., Jr. *Loyal Whigs and Revolutionaries: The Making of the Revolution in New York, 1765–1776.* New York: New York University Press, 1981.

3340. Lucas, Stephen E. *Portents of Rebellion: Rhetoric and Revolution in Philadelphia, 1765–76.* Philadelphia: Temple University Press, 1976.

3341. Maier, Pauline. *From Resistance to Revolution: Colonials, Radicals and the Development of American Opposition to Britain, 1765–1776.* New York: Alfred A. Knopf, 1972.

3342. Miller, John C. *Origins of the American Revolution.* Boston: Little, Brown, 1943.
3343. Miller, Lillian. *In the Minds and Hearts of the People: Prologue to the American Revolution, 1760-1774.* Greenwich, Connecticut: New York Graphic Society, 1974.
3344. Morgan, Edmund S. *Stamp Act Crisis: Prologue to Revolution.* Rev. ed. New York: Macmillan, 1963.
3345. Nash, Gary B. *The Urban Crucible: Social Change, Political Consciousness, and the Origins of the American Revolution.* Cambridge, Massachusetts: Harvard University Press, 1979.
3346. Reid, John Phillip. *In Defiance of the Law: The Standing-Army Controversy, the Two Constitutions, and the Coming of the American Revolution.* Chapel Hill: University of North Carolina Press, 1981.
3347. _____. *In a Rebellious Spirit: The Argument of Facts, the Liberty Riot, and the Coming of the American Revolution.* University Park: Pennsylvania State University Press, 1979.
3348. Rossiter, Clinton. *The First American Revolution: The American Colonies on the Eve of Independence.* New York: Harcourt, Brace and World, 1956.
3349. Ryerson, Richard Alan. *"The Revolution Is Now Begun": The Radical Committees of Philadelphia, 1765-1776.* Philadelphia: University of Pennsylvania Press, 1977.
3350. Savelle, Max. *Seeds of Liberty.* New York: Alfred A. Knopf, 1948.
3351. Schlesinger, Arthur M. *The Colonial Merchants and the American Revolution.* New York: Atheneum, 1968.
3352. _____. *Prelude to Independence: The Newspaper War on Britain, 1764-1776.* New York: Alfred A. Knopf, 1958.
3353. Shaw, Peter. *American Patriots and the Rituals of Revolution.* Cambridge, Massachusetts: Harvard University Press, 1980.
3354. Weslager, C. A. *The Stamp Act Congress.* Newark: University of Delaware Press, 1980.

Causes of the Revolution

3355. Egerton, H. E. *The Causes and Character of the American Revolution.* Oxford: Clarendon Press, 1923.
3356. Van Tyne, Claude H. *The Causes of the War of Independence.* New York: Houghton Mifflin, 1922.
3357. Wahlke, John C., ed. *The Causes of the American Revolution.* 3d ed. Lexington, Massachusetts: D. C. Heath, 1973.
3358. Wright, Esmond, ed. *Causes and Consequences of the American Revolution.* Chicago: Quadrangle Books, 1966.

Ideology and Philosophy

Articles

3359. Appleby, Joyce. "The Social Origins of American Revolutionary Ideology." *Journal of American History* 64 (1978): 935–58.
3360. Bailyn, Bernard. "Political Experience and Enlightenment Ideas in Eighteenth-Century America." *American Historical Review* 67:2 (January 1962): 339–51.
3361. Cohen, Lester H. "Explaining the Revolution: Ideology and Ethics in Mercy Otis Warren's Historical Theory." *William and Mary Quarterly* 37 (April 1980): 200–18.
3362. Colbourn, H. Trevor. "The Debate on the American Revolution as an Intellectual Movement." *North Dakota Quarterly* 42 (Summer 1974): 7–17.
3363. Diamond, Martin. "The American Idea of Equality: The View from the Founding." *Review of Politics* 38:3 (July 1976): 313–31.
3364. Gay, Peter. "Enlightenment Thought and the American Revolution." In *The Role of Ideology in the American Revolution,* edited by J. R. Howe, Jr. New York: Holt, Rinehart and Winston, 1970.
3365. Grimes, Alan P. "Conservative Revolution and Liberal Rhetoric: The Declaration of Independence." *Journal of Politics* 38 (August 1976): 1–19.
3366. Handlin, Oscar, and Mary Handlin. "James Burgh and American Revolutionary Theory." *Proceedings of the Massachusetts Historical Society* 73 (January-December 1961): 38–57.
3367. Morgan, Edmund S. "The American Revolution Considered as an Intellectual Movement." In *Paths of American Thought,* edited by A. M. Schlesinger, Jr. and M. M. White. Boston: Houghton Mifflin, 1963.
3368. Mullett, Charles F. "Classical Influences on the American Revolution." *Classical Journal* 35 (1939): 92–104.
3369. Phillips, W. Alison. "The Declaration of Independence." *Edinburgh Review* 244 (July 1926): 1–17.
3370. Tate, Thad W. "The Social Contract in America, 1774–1787: Revolutionary Theory as a Conservative Instrument." *William and Mary Quarterly,* 3d ser. 22:3 (July 1965): 375–91.
3371. Wood, Gordon S. "Republicanism as a Revolutionary Ideology." In *The Role of Ideology in the American Revolution,* edited by J. R. Howe, Jr. New York: Holt, Rinehart and Winston, 1970.

Books

3372. Bailyn, Bernard. *The Ideological Origins of the American Revolution.* Cambridge, Massachusetts: Harvard University Press, Belknap Press, 1967.
3373. Becker, Carl. *Declaration of Independence: A Study in the History of Political Ideas.* New York: Random House, 1942.
3374. Buel, Richard, Jr. *Securing the Revolution: Ideology in American Politics, 1789–1815.* Ithaca: Cornell University Press, 1972.
3375. Colbourn, H. Trevor. *The Lamp of Experience: Whig History and the Intellectual Origins of the American Revolution.* New York: W. W. Norton, 1974.
3376. Howe, John R., Jr., ed. *The Role of Ideology in the American Revolution.* New York: Holt, Rinehart and Winston, 1970.

3377. Koch, Adrienne. *Power, Morals and the Founding Fathers: Essays in the Interpretation of the American Enlightenment.* Ithaca: Cornell University Press, 1961.
3378. Tassi, Aldo. *The Political Philosophy of the American Revolution.* Washington, D.C.: University Press of America, 1978.
3379. White, Morton. *The Philosophy of the American Revolution.* New York: Oxford University Press, 1978.

Politics and Political Thought

Articles

3380. Buel, Richard, Jr. "Democracy and the American Revolution: A Frame of Reference." *William and Mary Quarterly,* 3d ser. 21:2 (April 1964): 165–90.
3381. Countryman, Edward. "Consolidating Power in Revolutionary America: The Case of New York, 1775–1783." *Journal of Interdisciplinary History* 6 (Spring 1976): 645–77.
3382. Ernst, Joseph. "Political Economy and Reality: Problems in the Interpretation of the American Revolution." *Canadian Review of American Studies* 7 (Fall 1976): 109–18.
3383. Hartz, Louis. "American Political Thought and the Revolution." *American Political Science Review* 46:2 (June 1952): 321–42.
3384. Jensen, Merrill. "Democracy and the American Revolution." *Huntington Library Quarterly* 20 (August 1957): 321–41.
3385. Kenyon, Cecelia M. "Republicanism and Radicalism in the American Revolution: An Old-Fashioned Interpretation." *William and Mary Quarterly,* 3d ser. 19:2 (April 1962): 153–82.
3386. Langford, Paul. "Old Whigs, Old Tories, and the American Revolution." *Journal of Imperial Commonwealth History* 8 (January 1980): 106–30.
3387. McColley, Robert. "Radical Political Thought in the American Revolution." *Journal of Illinois State Historical Society* 69 (May 1976): 91–99.

Books

3388. Adams, Randolph G. *The Political Ideas of the American Revolution.* 3d ed. New York: Barnes and Noble, 1958.
3389. Boorstin, Daniel. *The Genius of American Politics.* Chicago: University of Chicago Press, 1953.
3390. Brown, Richard. *Revolutionary Politics in Massachusetts: The Boston Committee of Correspondence and the Towns, 1772–1774.* Cambridge, Massachusetts: Harvard University Press, 1970.
3391. Brown, Robert E. *Middle-Class Democracy and the Revolution in Massachusetts, 1691–1780.* Ithaca: Cornell University Press, 1955.
3392. Hawke, David. *In the Midst of a Revolution: The Politics of Confrontation in Colonial America.* Philadelphia: University of Pennsylvania Press, 1974.
3393. Lockridge, Kenneth A. *Settlement and Unsettlement in Early America: The Crisis of Political Legitimacy before the Revolution.* New York: Cambridge University Press, 1981.

3394. Rossie, Jonathan G. *The Politics of Command in the American Revolution.* Syracuse, New York: Syracuse University Press, 1977.
3395. Rossiter, Clinton. *The Political Thought of the American Revolution.* New York: Harcourt, Brace and World, 1963.

Society and Social Interpretations

Articles

3396. Berthoff, Rowland, and John M. Murrin. "Feudalism, Communalism, and the Yeoman Freeholder: The American Revolution Considered as a Social Accident." In *Essays on the American Revolution,* edited by S. G. Kurtz and J. H. Hutson. Chapel Hill: University of North Carolina Press, 1973.
3397. Greene, Jack P. "The Social Origins of the American Revolution: An Evaluation and an Interpretation." *Political Science Quarterly* 88:1 (March 1973): 1-22.
3398. _____. "Values and Society in Revolutionary America." *Annals of the American Academy of Political and Social Sciences* 426 (1976): 53-69.
3399. Hoerder, Dirk. "'Mobs, a Sort of Them at Least, Are Constitutional': The American Revolution, Popular Participation, and Social Change." *Amerikastudien* 21:2 (1976): 289-306.
3400. Lemisch, Jesse. "The American Revolution Seen from the Bottom Up." In *Towards a New Past,* edited by B. J. Bernstein. New York: Pantheon Books, 1968.
3401. _____. "Jack Tar in the Streets: Merchant Seamen in the Politics of Revolutionary America." *William and Mary Quarterly,* 3d ser. 25:3 (July 1968): 371-407.
3402. Lockridge, Kenneth A. "Social Change and the Meaning of the American Revolution." *Journal of Social History* 6 (Summer 1973): 403-39.
3403. Marina, William. "Revolution and Social Change: The American Revolution as a People's War." *Literature of Liberty* 1 (April-June 1978): 5-39.
3404. Morgan, Edmund S. "The American Revolution: Was There 'A People'?" *New York Review of Books* (15 July 1976).
3405. Nisbet, Robert. "The Social Impact of the Revolution." *Wilson Quarterly* 1 (Autumn 1976): 93-107.
3406. Tolles, Frederick B. "The American Revolution Considered as a Social Movement: A Re-Evaluation." *American Historical Review* 60:1 (October 1954): 1-12.
3407. Weir, Robert M. "Who Shall Rule at Home: The American Revolution as a Crisis of Legitimacy for the Colonial Elite." *Journal of Interdisciplinary History* 6:4 (Spring 1976): 679-700.

Books

3408. Greene, Evarts Boutell. *The Revolutionary Generation, 1763-1790.* New York: Macmillan, 1943.
3409. Hoerder, Dirk. *Crowd Action in Revolutionary Massachusetts, 1765-1780.* New York: Academic Press, 1977.

3410. Jameson, J. Franklin. *The American Revolution Considered as a Social Movement.* Princeton: Princeton University Press, 1926.
3411. MacLeod, Duncan J. *Slavery, Race and the American Revolution.* New York: Cambridge University Press, 1975.
3412. Nash, Gary B. *The Urban Crucible: Social Change, Political Consciousness, and the Origins of the American Revolution.* Cambridge, Massachusetts: Harvard University Press, 1979.
3413. Risjord, Norman. *Representative Americans: The Revolutionary Generation.* Lexington, Massachusetts: D. C. Heath, 1980.

Economic Interpretations

3414. Egnal, Marc, and Joseph A. Ernst. "An Economic Interpretation of the American Revolution." *William and Mary Quarterly,* 3d ser. 29:1 (January 1972): 3-32.
3415. Hacker, Louis M. "The American Revolution: Economic Aspects." *Marxist Quarterly* 1 (1937): 46-67.
3416. Ver Steeg, Clarence L. "The American Revolution Considered as an Economic Movement." *Huntington Library Quarterly* 20 (August 1957): 361-72.

Legal and Constitutional Aspects

Articles

3417. Humphreys, Robert A. "The Rule of Law and the American Revolution." *Law Quarterly Review* 53 (1937): 80-98.
3418. Main, Jackson T. "Government by the People: The American Revolution and the Democratization of the Legislatures." *William and Mary Quarterly,* 3d ser. 23:3 (July 1966): 391-407.
3419. Mullett, Charles F. "Coke and the American Revolution." *Economica* 12 (1932): 457-71.
3420. Royster, Charles. "'The Nature of Treason': Revolutionary Virtue and American Reactions to Benedict Arnold." *William and Mary Quarterly* 35 (April 1979): 163-93.

Books

3421. Jensen, Merrill. *The Articles of Confederation: An Interpretation of the Social-Constitutional History of the American Revolution, 1774-1781.* Madison: University of Wisconsin Press, 1940.
3422. McIlwain, Charles H. *The American Revolution: A Constitutional Interpretation.* New York: Macmillan, 1923.
3423. Mullett, Charles F. *Fundamental Law and the American Revolution, 1760-1776.* New York: Columbia University Press, 1933.

Leaders and Leadership

Articles

3424. Colbourn, H. Trevor. "John Dickinson, Historical Revolutionary." *Pennsylvania Magazine of History and Biography* 83 (July 1959): 283–86.

3425. Depauw, Linda Grant. "Politicizing the Politically Inert: The Problem of Leadership in the American Revolution." In *The American Revolution: Changing Perspectives*, edited by W. M Fowler, Jr. and W. Coyle. Boston: Northeastern University Press, 1979.

3426. Elkins, Stanley, and Eric McKitrick. "The Founding Fathers: Young Men of the Revolution." *Political Science Quarterly* 76:2 (June 1961): 181–216.

Books

3427. Bowen, Catherine D. *John Adams and the American Revolution.* New York: Grosset and Dunlap, 1957.

3428. Dabney, Virginius, ed. *The Patriots: The American Revolution, Generation of Genius.* New York: Atheneum, 1975.

3429. Davis, Burke. *George Washington and the American Revolution.* New York: Random House, 1975.

3430. Douglass, Elisha P. *Rebels and Democrats.* Chicago: Quadrangle Books, 1965.

3431. Elkins, Stanley, and Eric McKitrick. *The Founding Fathers: Young Men of the Revolution.* Washington, D.C.: American Historical Association Service Center for Teachers of History, 1962.

3432. Flexner, James T. *The Face of Liberty: Founders of the United States.* New York: Clarkson N. Potter, 1976.

3433. Fritz, Jean. *Cast for a Revolution: Some American Friends and Enemies, 1728–1814.* Boston: Houghton Mifflin, 1972.

3434. Hutson, James H. *John Adams and the Diplomacy of the American Revolution.* Lexington: University Press of Kentucky, 1979.

3435. Maier, Pauline. *The Old Revolutionaries: Political Lives in the Age of Samuel Adams.* New York: Alfred A. Knopf, 1980.

3436. Martin, James Kirby. *Men in Rebellion: Governmental Leaders and the Coming of the American Revolution.* New Brunswick: Rutgers University Press, 1973.

3437. Morgan, Edmund S. *The Meaning of Independence: John Adams, George Washington, and Thomas Jefferson.* New York: W. W. Norton, 1978.

3438. Morris, Richard B., et al, eds. *John Jay: The Making of a Revolutionary.* New York: Harper and Row, 1975.

3439. _____. *Seven Who Shaped Our Destiny: The Founding Fathers as Revolutionaries.* New York: Harper and Row, 1973.

3440. Nettels, Curtis P. *George Washington and American Independence.* Westport, Connecticut: Greenwood, 1977.

3441. Sydnor, Charles S. *American Revolutionaries in the Making.* New York: Free Press, 1965.

3442. Watterson, John S. *Thomas Burke: Restless Revolutionary.* Washington, D.C.: University Press of America, 1980.

Revolutionary War

Articles

3443. Shy, John. "The American Revolution: The Military Conflict Considered as a Revolutionary War." In *Essays on the American Revolution*, edited by S. G. Kurtz and J. H. Hutson. Chapel Hill: University of North Carolina Press, 1973.
3444. York, Neil L. "Clandestine Aid [Mostly French] and the American Revolutionary War Effort: A Re-Examination." *Military Affairs* 43 (February 1979): 26-30.

Books

3445. Augur, Helen. *The Secret War of Independence.* Westport, Connecticut: Greenwood, 1976.
3446. Barnes, Eric W. *Free Men Must Stand: The American War of Independence.* New York: McGraw-Hill, 1962.
3447. Belcher, Henry. *The First American Civil War: First Period, 1775-1778.* Saint Clair Shores, Michigan: Scholarly Press, 1976.
3448. Bray, Robert, and Paul Bushnell, eds. *The Diary of a Common Soldier in the American Revolution, 1775-1783: An Annotated Edition of the Diary of Jeremiah Greenman.* De Kalb: Northern Illinois University Press, 1976.
3449. Dupuy, R. Ernest, et al. *The American Revolution: A Global War.* New York: David McKay, 1977.
3450. Evans, R. E. *The War of American Independence.* New York: Cambridge University Press, 1976.
3451. Fisher, Sydney George. *The Struggle for American Independence.* 2 vols. Philadelphia: Lippincott, 1908.
3452. Goldston, Robert. *American War of National Liberation: 1763-1783.* New York: E. P. Dutton, 1976.
3453. Higginbotham, Don. *The War of American Independence: Military Attitudes, Policies and Practice, 1763-1789.* Bloomington: Indiana University Press, 1977.
3454. _____ , ed. *Reconsiderations on the Revolutionary War: Selected Essays.* Westport, Connecticut: Greenwood, 1978.
3455. Higgins, W. Robert, ed. *The Revolutionary War in the South: Power, Conflict, and Leadership.* Durham, North Carolina: Duke University Press, 1979.
3456. Mackesy, Piers. *The War for America, 1775-1783.* Cambridge, Massachusetts: Harvard University Press, 1964.
3457. Pearson, Michael. *The Revolutionary War: An Unbiased Account.* New York: Capricorn Books, 1973.
3458. Peckham, Howard H., ed. *The Toll of Independence: Engagements and Battle Casualties of the American Revolution.* Chicago: University of Chicago Press, 1974.
3459. Robson, Eric. *The American Revolution in Its Political and Military Aspects, 1763-1783.* New York: W. W. Norton, 1966.
3460. Royster, Charles. *A Revolutionary People at War: The Continental Army and American Character, 1775-1783.* Chapel Hill: University of North Carolina Press, 1980.

3461. Shy, John, ed. *A People Numerous and Armed: Reflections on the Military Struggle for American Independence.* New York: Oxford University Press, 1976.
3462. Stout, Neil R. *The Perfect Crisis: The Beginning of the Revolutionary War.* New York: New York University Press, 1976.

America and Britain

Articles

3463. Adams, Thomas R. "The British Pamphlet Press and the American Controversy, 1764–1783." *Proceedings of the American Antiquarian Society* 89 (part 1, 1979): 33–88.
3464. Adu-Shumays, Mary D. "British Views of America and the American Revolution." *Southern Quarterly* 14 (July 1976): 307–31.
3465. Christie, Ian R. "British Politics and the American Revolution." *Albion* 9:3 (Fall, 1977): 204–26.
3466. Ketchum, Richard M. "England's Vietnam: The American Revolution." *American Heritage* (June 1971): 6.
3467. Labaree, Benjamin W. "The Idea of American Independence: The British View, 1774–1776." *Massachusetts Historical Society Proceedings* 82 (1970): 3–20.
3468. Langford, Paul. "London and the American Revolution." In *London in the Age of Reform,* edited by J. Stevenson. Oxford: Basil Blackwell, 1977.
3469. Ritcheson, Charles R. "Imperial Thought and the American Revolution." *Amerikastudien* 21:2 (1976): 281–88.
3470. Sheps, Arthur. "The American Revolution and the Transformation of English Republicanism." *Historical Reflections* 2 (Summer 1975): 3–28.

Books

3471. Barrow, Thomas C. *Trade and Empire: The British Customs Service in Colonial America, 1660–1775.* Cambridge, Massachusetts: Harvard University Press, 1967.
3472. Becker, Robert A. *Revolution, Reform, and the Politics of American Taxation, 1763–1783.* Baton Rouge: Louisiana State University Press, 1980.
3473. Bonwick, Colin. *English Radicals and the American Revolution.* Chapel Hill: University of North Carolina Press, 1977.
3474. Christie, Ian R. *Crisis of Empire: Great Britain and the American Colonies, 1754–1783.* New York: W. W. Norton, 1966.
3475. _____ , and Benjamin W. Labaree. *Empire or Independence, 1760–1776: A British-American Dialogue on the Coming of the American Revolution.* New York: W. W. Norton, 1977.
3476. Coupland, Reginald. *America Revolution and the British Empire.* New York: Russell and Russell, 1965.
3477. Derry, John. *English Politics and the American Revolution.* New York: St. Martin's Press, 1977.
3478. Gutteridge, George H. *English Whiggism and the American Revolution.* Berkeley: University of California Press, 1942.

3479. Henretta, James A. *"Salutary Neglect": Colonial Administration under the Duke of Newcastle.* Princeton: Princeton University Press, 1972.
3480. Kammen, Michael G. *A Rope of Sand: The Colonial Agents, British Politics and the American Revolution.* New York: Random House, 1974.
3481. Katz, Stanley Nider. *Newcastle's New York: Anglo-American Politics, 1732-1753.* Cambridge, Massachusetts: Harvard University Press, Belknap Press, 1968.
3482. Kavich, Martin, and Andrew Meleish, eds. *The American Revolution through British Eyes.* Evanston, Illinois: Row, Peterson, 1962.
3483. Lutnick, Solomon. *The American Revolution and the British Press, 1775-1783.* Columbia: University of Missouri Press, 1967.
3484. Namier, Lewis. *England in the Age of the American Revolution.* London: Macmillan, 1963.
3485. Olson, Alison Gilbert. *Anglo-American Politics, 1660-1775: The Relationship Between Parties in England and Colonial America.* New York: Oxford University Press, 1973.
3486. Ritcheson, Charles R. *British Politics and the American Revolution.* Norman: University of Oklahoma Press, 1954.
3487. Smith, Paul H. *Loyalists and Redcoats: A Study in British Revolutionary Policy.* Chapel Hill: University of North Carolina Press, 1964.
3488. Sosin, Jack M. *Agents and Merchants: British Colonial Policy and the Origins of the American Revolution, 1763-1775.* Lincoln: University of Nebraska Press, 1965.
3489. Toohey, Robert E. *Liberty and Empire: British Radical Solutions to the American Problem, 1774-1776.* Lexington: University Press of Kentucky, 1978.
3490. Ubbelohde, Carl. *Vice-Admiralty Courts and the American Revolution.* Chapel Hill: University of North Carolina Press, 1960.
3491. Van Tyne, Claude H. *England and America: Rivals in the American Revolution.* New York: Russell and Russell, 1969.
3492. Wickwire, Franklin B. *British Subministers and Colonial America, 1763-1783.* Princeton: Princeton University Press, 1966.
3493. Wright, Esmond, ed. *Red, White and True Blue: The Loyalists in the Revolution.* New York: AMS Press, 1976.

Religious Considerations

Articles

3494. Ahlstrom, Sydney E. "Religion, Revolution and the Rise of Modern Nationalism: Reflections on the American Experience." *Church History* 44 (December 1975): 492-504.
3495. Elliott, Emory. "The Dove and Serpent: The Clergy in the American Revolution." *American Quarterly* 31 (Summer 1979): 186-203.
3496. James, Sydney V. "Religion and the American Revolution: The Development of the Federal Style in the Relations between Religion and Civil Authority." In *The American and European Revolutions,* edited by J. Pelenski. Iowa City: University of Iowa Press, 1980.

3497. McLoughlin, William G. "'Enthusiasm for Liberty': The Great Awakening as the Key to the Revolution." *Proceedings of the American Antiquarian Society* 87 (April 1977): 69–95.

3498. _____. "The Role of Religion in the Revolution: Liberty of Conscience and Cultural Cohesion in the New Nation." In *Essays on the American Revolution,* edited by S. G. Kurtz and J. H. Hutson. Chapel Hill: University of North Carolina Press, 1973.

3499. Morgan, Edmund S. "The Puritan Ethic and the American Revolution." *William and Mary Quarterly,* 3d ser. 24:1 (January 1967): 3–43.

3500. Stout, Harry S. "Religion, Communications, and the Ideological Origins of the American Revolution." *William and Mary Quarterly* 34 (October 1977): 519–41.

Books

3501. Baldwin, Alice. *The New England Clergy and the American Revolution.* Durham, North Carolina: Duke University Press, 1928.

3502. Brauer, Jerald C., ed. *Religion and the American Revolution.* Philadelphia: Fortress Press, 1976.

3503. Greene, Jack P., and William G. McLoughlin. *Preachers and Politicians: Two Essays on the Origins of the American Revolution.* Charlottesville: University Press of Virginia, 1977.

3504. Hanley, Thomas. *The American Revolution and Religion.* Washington, D.C.: Catholic University of America Press, 1972.

3505. Heimert, Alan. *Religion and the American Mind, From the Great Awakening to the Revolution.* Cambridge, Massachusetts: Harvard University Press, 1966.

3506. McKeel, Arthur J. *The Relation of the Quakers to the American Revolution.* Washington, D.C.: University Press of America, 1979.

Women and the Revolution

Articles

3507. Berkin, Carol Ruth. "Remembering the Ladies: Historians and the Women of the American Revolution." In *The American Revolution: Changing Perspectives,* edited by W. M. Fowler, Jr. and W. Coyle. Boston: Northeastern University Press, 1979.

3508. Cometti, Elizabeth. "Women in the American Revolution." *New England Quarterly* 20 (1947): 329–46.

3509. Kerber, Linda K. "The Limits of Politicization: American Women and the American Revolution." In *The American and European Revolutions,* edited by J. Pelenski. Iowa City: University of Iowa Press, 1980.

Books

3510. Engle, Paul. *Women in the American Revolution.* Chicago: Follett, 1976.
3511. Evans, Elizabeth. *Weathering the Storm: Women of the American Revolution.* New York: Scribners, 1975.
3512. Meyer, Edith P. *Petticoat Patriots of the Revolution.* New York: Vanguard Press, 1978.

The Revolution in World History

Articles

3513. Barrow, Thomas C. "The American Revolution as a Colonial War for Independence." *William and Mary Quarterly,* 3d ser. 25:3 (July 1968): 452–64.
3514. Bestor, Arthur R. "The American Revolution as World Experiment: European and American Roots." *Archives Rechts- und Sozialphilosophy*; Beiheft 10 (1977): 31–59.
3515. Kim, Sung Bok. "The American Revolution and the Modern World." In *Legacies of the American Revolution,* edited by L. Gerlach et al. Logan: Utah State University Press, 1978.
3516. Nelson, William H. "The Revolutionary Character of the American Revolution." *American Historical Review* 70:4 (July 1965): 998–1014.
3517. Rainbolt, John C. "Americans' Initial View of Their Revolution's Significance for Other Peoples, 1776–1788." *Historian* 35 (May 1973): 418–33.

Books

3518. Kaplan, Lawrence S., ed. *The American Revolution and "A Candid World."* Kent, Ohio: Kent State University Press, 1977.
3519. Morris, Richard B. *The Emerging Nations and the American Revolution.* New York: Harper and Row, 1970.
3520. *La révolution américaine et L'Europe.* Paris: Editions du Centre National de la Recherche Scientifique, 1979.
3521. Van Alstyne, Richard. *Empire and Independence: International History of the American Revolution.* New York: John Wiley, 1965.

Miscellaneous

Articles

3522. Brown, Richard. "Violence and the American Revolution." In *Essays on the American Revolution,* edited by S. G. Kurtz and J. H. Hutson. Chapel Hill: University of North Carolina Press, 1973.
3523. Bumsted, J. M. "Loyalists and Nationalists: An Essay on the Problem of Definitions." *Canadian Review of Studies on Nationalism* 6 (Fall 1979): 218–32.

3524. Chaffin, Robert J. "Was the American Revolution Really Revolutionary?" *Midwest Quarterly* 19 (Autumn 1977): 7-23.

3525. Dziewanowski, M. K. "Tadeusz Kościuszko, Kazimierz Pulaski, and the American War of Independence: A Study in National Symbolism and Mythology." In *The American and European Revolutions,* edited by J. Pelenski. Iowa City: University of Iowa Press, 1980.

3526. Grampp, William D. "Adam Smith and the American Revolutionists." *History of Politics and Economics* 11 (Summer 1979): 179-91.

3527. Jehlen, Myra J. "Hector St. John Crèvecoeur: A Monarcho-Anarchist in Revolutionary America." *American Quarterly* 31 (Summer 1979): 204-22.

3528. Klein, Randolph Shipley. "Prismatic Patriotism during the Era of the American Revolution." *Canadian Review of Studies in Nationalism* 6 (Fall 1979): 175-92.

3529. McCants, David A. "The Authenticity of William Wirt's Version of Patrick Henry's 'Liberty or Death' Speech." *Virginia Magazine of History and Biography* 87 (October 1979): 387-402.

3530. Okoye, F. Nwabueze. "Chattel Slavery as the Nightmare of the American Revolution." *William and Mary Quarterly* 38 (January 1980): 3-28.

3531. Savelle, Max. "Nationalism and Other Loyalties in the American Revolution." *American Historical Review* 67:4 (July 1962): 901-23.

3532. Wood, Gordon S. "Rhetoric and Reality in the American Revolution." *William and Mary Quarterly,* 3d ser. 23:1 (January 1966): 3-32.

3533. Zuckerman, Michael. "The Irrelevant Revolution: 1776 and Since." *American Quarterly* 30 (Summer 1978): 224-42.

Books

3534. Alden, John. *The South in the Revolution, 1763-1789.* Baton Rouge: Louisiana State University Press, 1957.

3535. Crow, Jeffrey J., and Larry E. Tise, eds. *The Southern Experience in the American Revolution.* Chapel Hill: University of North Carolina Press, 1978.

3536. Cumming, William F., and Hugh Rankin. *The Fate of a Nation: The American Revolution through Contemporary Eyes.* New York: Praeger, 1975.

3537. Davidson, Philip. *Propaganda and the American Revolution, 1763-1783.* Chapel Hill: University of North Carolina Press, 1941.

3538. Ellis, Joseph J. *After the Revolution: Profiles of Early American Culture.* New York: W. W. Norton, 1979.

3539. Fitzpatrick, John C. *Spirit of the Revolution.* Port Washington, New York: Kennikat Press, 1970.

3540. Gerlach, Larry, et al, eds. *Legacies of the American Revolution.* Logan: Utah State University Press, 1980.

3541. Greene, Jack P., and Pauline Maier, eds. *Interdisciplinary Studies of the American Revolution.* Beverly Hills, California: Sage, 1976.

3542. Holzer, Hans. *The Spirits of Seventy-Six: A Psychic Inquiry into the American Revolution.* Indianapolis, Indiana: Bobbs-Merrill, 1976.

3543. Jensen, Merrill. *The American Revolution Within America.* New York: New York University Press, 1974.

3544. Jones, Howard Mumford. *O Strange New World.* New York: Viking, 1964.

3545. Kammen, Michael. *A Season of Youth: The American Revolution and the Historical Imagination.* New York: Alfred A. Knopf, 1978.

3546. Lesser, Charles H. *The Sinews of Independence.* Chicago: University of Chicago Press, 1976.
3547. Lynn, Kenneth S. *A Divided People.* Westport, Connecticut: Greenwood, 1977.
3548. Niles, Hezekiah. *Principles and Acts of the Revolution in America.* New York: Burt Franklin, 1971.
3549. Silverman, Kenneth. *A Cultural History of the American Revolution.* New York: Thomas Y. Crowell, 1976.

Samuel Adams

Samuel Adams was perhaps the leading spokesman for American independence. His speeches and writings went far to stir the discontent among the colonists before the revolutionary war. His words helped bring on the Boston Massacre (1770), and he played a leading role in the establishment of the Committees of Correspondence (1772). As head of Boston's patriots, Adams played a central role in the Boston Tea Party (1773), which in turn encouraged Britain to abandon policies of compromise. He was one of America's first revolutionists. All the articles below are quite good. The standard biography is by John C. Miller (1936). Adams is also featured in many of the works in the previous section.

Articles

3550. Akers, Charles W. "Sam Adams—And Much More." *New England Quarterly* 47 (1974): 120–31.
3551. Maier, Pauline. "Coming to Terms with Samuel Adams." *American Historical Review* 81:1 (February 1976): 12–37.
3552. Parrington, Vernon. "Samuel Adams, the Mind of the American Democrat." In *The Colonial Mind, 1620–1800.* New York: Harcourt, Brace and World, 1927.
3553. Williams, William Appleman. "Samuel Adams: Calvinist, Mercantilist, Revolutionary." *Studies on the Left* 1:2 (Winter 1960): 47.

Books

3554. Adams, Samuel. *Writings.* 4 vols. Edited by Harry A. Cushing. New York: Octagon, 1968.
3555. Beach, Stewart. *Samuel Adams: The Fateful Years, 1764–1776.* New York: Dodd, Mead, 1965.
3556. Canfield, Cass. *Samuel Adam's Revolution (1765–1776).* New York: Harper and Row, 1976.
3557. Frankel, Harry. *Sam Adams and the American Revolution.* New York: Pathfinder Press, n.d.

3558. Harlow, Ralph V. *Samuel Adams, Promoter of the American Revolution.* New York: Octagon, 1972.
3559. Hosmer, James K. *Samuel Adams.* New York: AMS Press, 1898.
3560. Lewis, Paul. *The Grand Incendiary: A Biography of Samuel Adams.* New York: Dial Press, 1973.
3561. Miller, John C. *Sam Adams: Pioneer in Propaganda.* Stanford: Stanford University Press, 1936.
3562. Wells, William V. *Life and Public Services of Samuel Adams.* New York: Arno Press, 1888.

Thomas Jefferson

Like his contemporary Benjamin Franklin, Jefferson lays claim to being a Renaissance man—interested and talented in a great variety of enterprises. He was the author of the Declaration of Independence and was largely responsible for the Bill of Rights. He fought against tyranny and established what is still referred to as Jeffersonian Democracy (i.e., a nation of landowning farmers living under as little government as possible).

Many of the works below contribute to our understanding of Jefferson as revolutionist. Among the better ones are those by Vernon Parrington (1927), Fawn Brodie (1974), Henry S. Commager (1975), Adrienne Koch (1964), Dumas Malone (1951, 1969), Page Smith (1976), and Otto Vossler (1980). Naturally, Jefferson appears in many of the works in the section "American Revolution, 1776–1783" in this chapter.

Articles

3563. Parrington, Vernon. "Thomas Jefferson: Agrarian Democrat." In *The Colonial Mind, 1620–1800.* New York: Harcourt, Brace and World, 1927.
3564. Tauber, Gisela. "Reconstruction in Psychoanalytic Biography: Understanding Thomas Jefferson." *Journal of Psychohistory* 7 (Fall 1979): 189–207.

Books

3565. Bowers, Claude G. *The Young Jefferson, 1743–1789.* New York: AMS Press, 1977.
3566. Brodie, Fawn. *Thomas Jefferson: An Intimate History.* New York: W. W. Norton, 1974.
3567. Commager, Henry S. *Jefferson, Nationalism, and the Enlightenment.* New York: George Braziller, 1975.
3568. Jefferson, Thomas. *Autobiography of Thomas Jefferson.* New York: G. P. Putnam's, 1959.

3569. _____ . *Jeffersonian Cyclopedia: A Comprehensive Collection of the Views of Thomas Jefferson.* 2 vols. Edited by John P. Foley. New York: Russell and Russell, 1967.
3570. Kimball, Marie. *Jefferson, the Road to Glory, 1743-1776.* Westport, Connecticut: Greenwood, 1977.
3571. Koch, Adrienne. *The Philosophy of Thomas Jefferson.* New York: Times Books, 1964.
3572. Malone, Dumas. *Jefferson and the Ordeal of Liberty.* Boston: Little, Brown, 1969.
3573. _____ . *Jefferson and the Rights of Man.* Boston: Little, Brown, 1951.
3574. Peterson, Merrill D. *Adams and Jefferson: A Revolutionary Dialogue.* Athens: University of Georgia Press, 1976.
3575. _____ , ed. *The Portable Thomas Jefferson.* New York: Penguin Books, 1977.
3576. Smith, Page. *Jefferson: A Revealing Biography.* New York: McGraw-Hill, 1976.
3577. Vossler, Otto. *Jefferson and the American Revolutionary Ideal.* Translated by C. Philippon and B. Wishy. Washington, D.C.: University Press of America, 1980.
3578. Wills, Garry. *Inventing America: Jefferson's Declaration of Independence.* Garden City, New York: Doubleday, 1978.

Thomas Paine

A pamphleteer and agitator, Paine's writings (especially his *Common Sense* and *The Crisis* series) greatly influenced the political thinking of the leaders of the American Revolution. It has been said that he was an "Englishman by birth, French citizen by decree, and American by adoption." During the French Revolution he wrote the *Rights of Man* in response to Edmund Burke's attack on that revolution. The articles by Jack P. Greene (1978) and Vernon Parrington (1927) are useful. The best books are by Eric Foner (1976) and David Freeman Hawke (1974).

Articles

3579. Greene, Jack P. "Paine, America, and the 'Modernization' of Political Consciousness." *Political Science Quarterly* 93:1 (Spring 1978): 73-92.
3580. Parrington, Vernon. "Tom Paine: Republican Pamphleteer." In *The Colonial Mind, 1620-1800.* New York: Harcourt, Brace and World, 1927.

Books

3581. Aldridge, A. O. *Man of Reason: The Life of Thomas Paine.* Philadelphia: Lippincott, 1959.
3582. Best, Mary A. *Thomas Paine, Prophet and Martyr of Democracy.* New York: Gordon Press, n.d.
3583. Blanchard, Calvin. *The Life of Thomas Paine.* Saint Clair Shores, Michigan: Scholarly Press, 1976.
3584. Buchanan, John G. *Thomas Paine, American Revolutionary Writer.* Charlotteville, New York: Samttar Press, 1976.
3585. Chalmers, George. *The Life of Thomas Paine.* Saint Clair Shores, Michigan: Scholarly Press, 1977.
3586. Conway, Moncure D. *The Life of Thomas Paine.* Folcroft, Pennsylvania: Folcroft Library Editions, 1973.
3587. Foner, Eric. *Tom Paine and the American Revolution.* New York: Oxford University Press, 1976.
3588. Hawke, David Freeman. *Paine.* New York: Harper and Row, 1974.
3589. Paine, Thomas. *Common Sense and Other Political Writings.* Edited by Nelson F. Adkins. Indianapolis, Indiana: Bobbs-Merrill, 1953.
3590. Pearson, Hesketh. *Tom Paine.* Philadelphia: Richard West, 1937.
3591. Sedwick, Ellery. *Thomas Paine.* Folcroft, Pennsylvania: Folcroft Library Editions, 1978.
3592. Williamson, Audrey. *Thomas Paine: His Life, Work and Times.* New York: St. Martin's Press, 1973.
3593. Wilson, Jerome D., and William F. Ricketson. *Thomas Paine.* Boston: Twayne, 1978.
3594. Woodward, William. *Tom Paine.* Westport, Connecticut: Greenwood, 1973.

New Left, c. 1962–?1972

The New Left was a non-structured movement for radical and revolutionary societal change. Although it was composed of many different groups, using diverse revolutionary methods, and proclaiming goals and purposes which differed in detail, all had certain fundamental ideas and purposes more or less in common. That is, the movement sought to destroy both imperialist-capitalist power and Stalinist state capitalism; in other words, the New Left opposed American capitalism *and* Russian communism. The New Left had its roots in the contradictions of the post-World War II West and the failure of the "Old" Left (i.e., western communist, socialist, and other left-wing groups) to resolve those contradictions. Its philosophical basis was rooted in Marxism-Leninism, with strains of anarchism. In the United States, the New Left emerged from the student movements of the early 1960s, and then was inspired by the triumph of the Cuban Revolution and the struggles of the Vietnamese and other Third World peoples. It had many heroes, especially Mao Tse-tung, Che Guevara, and Ho Chi Minh, but no formal leaders. In brief, the New Left was a revolutionary movement without a revolution of its own.

The thoughts and ideas of New Left activists can be sampled from among those articles and books noted below. Some of the better articles which have sought to explain the New Left from without are by David Horowitz (1971), Christopher Jencks (1967), Staughton Lynd (1969), Armand L. Mauss (1971), John Rossen (1971), and Kirkpatrick Sale (1971, 1973). Among the more useful books are those by Roderick Aya and Norman Miller (1971), Edward J. Bacciocco, Jr. (1974), Maurice Cranston (1971), John P. Diggins (1973), Stephen Goode (1974), Kenneth Keniston (1968, 1971), Lawrence Lader (1980), Arthur Lothstein (1971), Charles Reich (1970), Theodore Roszak (1968), Irwin Unger (1974), and Milton Viorst (1979). Additional attention should be paid to the section on Student Rebellions (in Chapter 1) which in some cases overlaps this one, and those sections dealing with the French Revolution of 1968 (in Chapter 4), Herbert Marcuse (in Chapter 5), and the Black Revolution (in Chapter 5), all of which were, to some extent, part of the New Left.

Bibliography

3595. Spahn, Theodore J., and Janet P. Spahn. *From Radical Left to Extreme Right: A Bibliography.* 2d ed. Metuchen, New Jersey: Scarecrow Press, 1976.

Documents

3596. Teodori, Massimo, ed. *The New Left: A Documentary History.* New York: Bobbs-Merrill, 1969.

Reference

3597. Kehde, Ned, ed. *The American Left, 1955–1970: A National Union Catalog of Pamphlets Published in the United States and Canada.* Westport, Connecticut: Greenwood, 1976.

3598. Mueller, R. H. *From Radical Left to Extreme Right: Current Publications of Protest, Controversy, and Dissent with Passionate Summaries.* 2 vols. 2d ed. Ann Arbor, Michigan: Campus Publications, 1970.

Activists' Accounts/Articles

3599. Berrigan, Daniel. "Father Berrigan's Letter to the Weathermen." *Village Voice* (21 January 1971).

3600. _____, and Robert Coles. "A Dialogue Underground." *New York Review of Books* (18 March 1971).

3601. Dohrn, Bernardine. "Fierce Against the Man." *New Morning—Changing Weather: Weather Underground Communique* (December 1970).

3602. Hayden, Tom. "The Trial." *Ramparts* (July 1970): 10–62.
3603. Oglesby, Carl. "The Idea of the New Left." *Evergreen Review* (February 1969): 51.
3604. _____. "Revolution: Violence or Nonviolence." *Liberation* 13:3 (July-August 1968): 36–38.
3605. Rubin, Jerry. "Yippie Manifesto." *Evergreen Review* (May 1969): 41.

Activists' Accounts/Books

3606. Berrigan, Philip. *Prison Journals of a Priest Revolutionary.* New York: Holt, Rinehart and Winston, 1970.
3607. Cowan, Paul. *The Making of an Un-American.* New York: Viking, 1970.
3608. Harris, David. *Goliath.* New York: Richard W. Baron, 1970.
3609. Hayden, Tom. *Rebellion and Repression.* New York: World, 1970.
3610. Hoffman, Abbie. *Revolution for the Hell of It.* New York: Dial Press, 1968.
3611. _____. *Soon To Be a Major Motion Picture.* New York: G. P. Putnam's, 1980.
3612. _____. *Woodstock Nation.* New York: Random House, 1969.
3613. Mungo, Raymond. *Famous Long Ago: My Life and Hard Times with the Liberation News Service.* Boston: Beacon, 1970.
3614. Myerson, Michael. *These Are the Good Old Days: Coming of Age as a Radical in America's Late, Late Years.* New York: Grossman Publishers, 1970.
3615. Powell, W. *The Anarchist Cookbook.* New York: Lyle Stuart, 1970.
3616. Richmond, Al. *A Long View from the Left: Memoirs of an American Revolutionary.* Boston: Houghton Mifflin, 1973.
3617. Rubin, Jerry. *Do It! Scenarios of the Revolution.* New York: Simon and Schuster, 1970.

Articles

3618. Apter, David E. "An Epitaph for Two Revolutions that Failed." *Daedalus* 103:4 (Fall 1974): 85–103.
3619. "Are We in the Middle of the 'Second American Revolution'?" *The New York Times Magazine* (17 May 1970).
3620. Ciardi, John. "The New Left: Why Violence?" *Saturday Review* (23 January 1971): 12.
3621. Clecak, Peter. "The Revolution Delayed: The Political and Cultural Revolutionaries in America." *Massachusetts Review* 12:3 (Summer 1971): 590–619.
3622. Dalrymple, Willard. "The Youth Revolution." *Intellectual Digest* 2:11 (July 1972): 80–81.
3623. "Guerrilla War in the USA." *Scanlan's* (January 1971).
3624. Hentoff, Nat. "Beyond the Ballot: Survival and Revolution." *Evergreen Review* (April 1971): 53–55.
3625. _____. "Dangerous Games: Play acting at Violent Revolution." *Evergreen Review* (May 1971): 21.
3626. Horowitz, David. "Revolutionary Karma vs. Revolutionary Politics." *Ramparts* (May 1971): 27–33.
3627. Jencks, Christopher. "Limits of the New Left." *New Republic* (21 October 1967): 19–21.

3628. Kopkind, Andrew. "The New Left: Chicago and After." *New York Review of Books* (28 September 1967).
3629. _____ . "The New (Left) Conservatism." *Village Voice* (21 January 1980).
3630. Lynd, Staughton. "The New Left." *Annals of the American Academy of Political and Social Science* 382 (March 1969): 64–72.
3631. McReynolds, David. "The Revolution Is Over. Now the Struggle Begins." *Village Voice* (23 July 1970).
3632. Mauss, Armand L. "On Being Strangled by the Stars and Stripes: The New Left, the Old Left and the Natural History of American Radical Movements." *Journal of Social Issues* 27:1 (1971): 1–20.
3633. Moore, Barrington, Jr. "Revolution in America?" *New York Review of Books* (30 January 1969).
3634. O'Brien, James P. "The Development of the New Left." *Annals of the American Academy of Political and Social Science* 395 (May 1971): 15–25.
3635. Reich, Charles. "The Greening of America." *The New Yorker* (26 September 1970): 42–111.
3636. Revel, Jean-François. "Without Marx or Jesus: The New American Revolution Has Begun." *Saturday Review* (24 July 1971): 14–31.
3637. Rossen, John. "Revolutionary Nationalism and the American Left." *Evergreen Review* (July 1971): 18.
3638. Sale, Kirkpatrick. "Political Violence: Awakening from the American Dream." *Evergreen Review* (May 1971): 19.
3639. _____ . "The Radicals Were Right All Along: The Government Was Out to Do Them In." *Los Angeles Times* (30 July 1973).

Books

3640. Ali, Tariq, ed. *New Revolutionaries: A Handbook of the International Radical Left.* New York: Morrow, 1969.
3641. Andreski, Stanislav. *Prospects of a Revolution in the U.S.A.* New York: Harper and Row, 1974.
3642. Aya, Roderick, and Norman Miller, eds. *The New American Revolution.* New York: Free Press, 1971.
3643. Bacciocco, Edward J., Jr. *The New Left in America: Reform to Revolution, 1956–1970.* Stanford: Hoover Institution, 1974.
3644. Barber, Benjamin R. *Superman & Common Men: Freedom, Anarchy and the Revolution.* New York: Praeger, 1971.
3645. Baritz, L. *The American Left: Radical Political Thought in the Twentieth Century.* New York: Basic Books, 1971.
3646. Barnes, Jack, et al. *Towards an American Socialist Revolution: A Strategy for the 1970's.* New York: Pathfinder Press, 1970.
3647. Bone, Christopher. *The Disinherited Children: A Study of the New Left and the Generation Gap.* New York: Halsted Press, 1977.
3648. Boskin, Joseph, and Robert A. Rosenstone, eds. *Seasons of Rebellion: Protest and Radicalism in Recent America.* New York: Holt, Rinehart and Winston, 1972.
3649. Camejo, Peter. *How to Make a Revolution in the U.S.* New York: Pathfinder Press, 1969.

3650. Clecak, Peter. *Radical Paradoxes: Dilemmas of the American Left, 1945-1970.* New York: Harper and Row, 1973.
3651. Coyne, John R. *The Kumquat Statement: Anarchy in the Groves of Academe.* New York: Cowles, 1970.
3652. Cranston, Maurice, ed. *The New Left: Six Critical Essays.* New York: Library Press, 1971.
3653. _____ , ed. *Prophetic Politics: Critical Interpretations of the Revolutionary Impulse.* New York: Simon and Schuster, 1972.
3654. Diggins, John P. *The American Left in the Twentieth Century.* New York: Harcourt Brace Jovanovich, 1973.
3655. Epstein, Jason. *The Great Conspiracy Trial: An Essay on Law, Liberty and the Constitution.* New York: Random House, 1970.
3656. Esler, Anthony, ed. *The Youth Revolution: The Conflict of Generations in Modern History.* Lexington, Massachusetts: D. C. Heath, 1974.
3657. Feigelson, Naomi. *The Underground Revolution: Hippies, Yippies and Others.* New York: Funk and Wagnalls, 1970.
3658. Gerberding, William P., and Duane E. Smith, eds. *The Radical Left: The Abuse of Discontent.* Boston: Houghton Mifflin, 1970.
3659. Gitlin, Todd. *The Whole World is Watching: Mass Media in the Making and Unmaking of the New Left.* Berkeley: University of California Press, 1980.
3660. Goode, Stephen. *Affluent Revolutionaries: A Portrait of the New Left.* New York: New Viewpoints, 1974.
3661. Goodman, Mitchell. *Movement Toward a New America: The Beginnings of a Long Revolution.* Philadelphia: Pilgrim Press, 1970.
3662. Hope, Marjorie. *The New Revolutionaries.* Boston: Little, Brown, 1970.
3663. Horowitz, David, et al. *Counter Culture and Revolution.* Philadelphia: Philadelphia Books Co., 1972.
3664. Howe, Irving, ed. *Beyond the New Left.* New York: McCall, 1970.
3665. _____ , ed. *The Radical Papers.* Garden City, New York: Doubleday, 1965.
3666. Iglitzin, Lynn B. *Violent Conflict in American Society.* San Francisco: Chandler, 1972.
3667. Jacobs, Harold, ed. *Weatherman.* Berkeley: Ramparts Press, 1970.
3668. Jacobs, Paul, and Saul Landau. *The New Radicals.* New York: Random House, 1966.
3669. Keniston, Kenneth. *Young Radicals: Notes on Committed Youth.* New York: Harcourt, Brace and World, 1968.
3670. _____ . *Youth and Dissent: The Rise of a New Opposition.* New York: Harcourt Brace Jovanovich, 1971.
3671. King, Richard. *The Party of Eros: Radical Social Thought and the Realm of Freedom.* Chapel Hill: University of North Carolina Press, 1972.
3672. Lader, Lawrence. *Power on the Left: American Radical Movements Since 1946.* New York: W. W. Norton, 1980.
3673. Lasch, Christopher. *The Agony of the American Left.* New York: Random House, 1969.
3674. Leamer, Laurence. *The Paper Revolutionaries: The Rise of the Underground Press.* New York: Simon and Schuster, 1972.
3675. Lerner, Michael P. *The New Socialist Revolution: An Introduction to Its Theory and Strategy.* New York: Delacorte Press, 1973.

3676. Lewis, Anthony, and *The New York Times. Portrait of a Decade: The Second American Revolution.* New York: Bantam Books, 1971.
3677. Long, Priscilla, ed. *The New Left.* Boston: Porter Sargent, 1969.
3678. Lothstein, Arthur, ed. *"All We Are Saying . . .": The Philosophy of the New Left.* New York: Capricorn Books, 1971.
3679. Luce, Phillip Abbott. *The New Left.* New York: David McKay, 1966.
3680. Lukas, J. Anthony. *The Barnyard Epithet and Other Obscenities: Notes on the Chicago Conspiracy Trial.* New York: Harper and Row, 1970.
3681. McReynolds, David. *We Have Been Invaded by the Twenty-First Century.* New York: Praeger, 1970.
3682. Nobile, Philip, ed. *The Con III Controversy: The Critics Look at* The Greening of America. New York: Pocket Books, 1971.
3683. O'Brien, J. *A History of the New Left.* Boston: New England Free Press, 1968.
3684. Oglesby, Carl, ed. *The New Left Reader.* New York: Grove Press, 1969.
3685. Powers, Thomas. *Diana: The Making of a Terrorist.* Boston: Houghton Mifflin, 1971.
3686. Rand, Ayn. *The New Left: The Anti-Industrial Revolution.* New York: New American Library, 1971.
3687. Reich, Charles A. *The Greening of America.* New York: Random House, 1970.
3688. Revel, Jean-François. *Without Marx or Jesus: The New American Revolution Has Begun.* Garden City, New York: Doubleday, 1971.
3689. Rosen, Milton K. *Revolution Today: U.S.A.* Jericho, New York: Exposition Press, 1970.
3690. Rositzke, Harry. *Left On! The Glorious Bourgeois Cultural Revolution.* New York: Quadrangle Books, 1973.
3691. Roszak, Theodore. *The Making of a Counter Culture.* Garden City, New York: Doubleday, 1968.
3692. Rubenstein, Richard E. *Left Turn: Origins of the Next American Revolution.* Boston: Little, Brown, 1973.
3693. _____. *Rebels in Eden: Mass Political Violence in the United States.* Boston: Little, Brown, 1970.
3694. Sale, Kirkpatrick. *SDS.* New York: Random House, 1973.
3695. Sargent, Lyman T. *New Left Thought: An Introduction.* Homewood, Illinois: Dorsey Press, 1972.
3696. Skolnick, Jerome H. *The Politics of Protest.* New York: Ballantine Books, 1969.
3697. Slater, Philip. *The Pursuit of Loneliness: American Culture at the Breaking Point.* Boston: Beacon, 1970.
3698. Stein, David Lewis. *Living the Revolution: The Yippies in Chicago.* Indianapolis: Bobbs-Merrill, 1970.
3699. Toplin, Robert Brent. *Unchallenged Violence, an American Ordeal.* Westport, Connecticut: Greenwood, 1975.
3700. Unger, Irwin. *The Movement: A History of the American New Left, 1959–1972.* New York: Dodd, Mead, 1974.
3701. Vickers, George R. *The Formation of the New Left.* Lexington, Massachusetts: Lexington Books, 1975.

232 / North America

3702. Viorst, Milton. *Fire in the Streets: America in the 1960's.* New York: Simon and Schuster, 1979.
3703. Weinstein, James. *Ambiguous Legacy: The Left in American Politics.* New York: New Viewpoints, 1975.
3704. Wolfe, Alan, ed. *Why the New Left Died.* New York: Lieber-Atherton, 1979.
3705. Young, Nigel. *An Infantile Disorder? The Crisis and Decline of the New Left.* Boulder, Colorado: Westview Press, 1978.
3706. Zorza, Richard. *The Right to Say "We."* New York: Praeger, 1970.

Herbert Marcuse

Marcuse was the spiritual father of the New Left. He wrote in the classical language of dialectics and gave the New Left a personal and philosophical connection to the tradition of revolutionary thought. Marcuse modified the ideas of Marx in the light of new world-wide contradictions existing in advanced capitalism. For example, the working class in capitalist societies he saw not as a true proletariat, but as an aristocracy of labor which is passive, conservative, and counterrevolutionary. For a Marxian revolution to become a reality, the unemployed, unemployable, and minorities, acting in concert with students and intellectuals in the West, would have to synchronize their actions with the exploited masses of the Third World. Marcuse's articles tend to be easier to digest than his books, but these should not be ignored. Of the books which try to explain Marcuse, those by Alasdair MacIntyre (1970) and Robert W. Marks (1969) are among the best.

Articles

3707. Gómez Cafarenel, José. "Meditación sobre Marcuse (con ocasión de su muerta, 29 de julio de 1978)." *Razón y Fe* (September 1979): 216–24.
3708. Marcuse, Herbert. "Marcuse Defines His New Left Line." *The New York Times Magazine* (27 October 1968).
3709. _____. "The Question of Revolution." *New Left Review,* no. 45 (September-October 1967): 3–7.
3710. _____. "Re-Examination of the Concept of Revolution." *New Left Review,* no. 56 (July-August 1969): 27–34.
3711. "Revolution or Reform: Herbert Marcuse and Karl Popper." *University Review* 21 (November 1971): 11.

Books

3712. Breines, P., ed. *Critical Interruptions: New Left Perspective on Herbert Marcuse.* New York: Herder and Herder, 1970.
3713. Fry, John. *Marcuse—Dilemma and Liberation: A Critical Analysis.* Atlantic Highlands, New Jersey: Humanities Press, 1974.

3714. Lipshires, Sidney. *Herbert Marcuse: From Marx to Freud and Beyond.* Cambridge, Massachusetts: Schenkman, 1974.
3715. MacIntyre, Alasdair. *Herbert Marcuse: An Exposition and a Polemic.* New York: Viking, 1970.
3716. Marcuse, Herbert. *Counterrevolution and Revolt.* Boston: Beacon, 1972.
3717. _____. *An Essay on Liberation.* Boston: Beacon, 1969.
3718. _____. *One-Dimensional Man: Studies in the Ideology of Advanced Industrial Society.* Boston: Beacon, 1964.
3719. _____. *Reason and Revolution.* Boston: Beacon, 1960.
3720. _____. *Soviet Marxism, A Critical Analysis.* New York: Columbia University Press, 1958.
3721. Marks, Robert W. *The Meaning of Marcuse.* New York: Ballantine Books, 1969.
3722. Steuernagel, Gertrude A. *Political Philosophy as Therapy: Marcuse Reconsidered.* Westport, Connecticut: Greenwood, 1979.
3723. Vivas, Eliseo. *Contra Marcuse.* New York: Dell, 1972.

Black Revolution, c. 1954–

If the Black Revolution has not been a true revolution on all its fronts, it at least has been revolutionary in its anger, protest, and potential. Rooted in the oppression and discrimination during the 100 years following the American Civil War, fanned by years of unfulfilled hopes and promises, and finally sparked by the frustrations of the civil rights movements of the 1950s, in some quarters the black movement took on revolutionary proportions seeking to overthrow the whole system. "Black Power" became both a slogan and a state of mind. Many blacks, led by Stokely Carmichael, Angela Y. Davis, Huey P. Newton, Bobby Seale, and Malcolm X, among others, argued that American blacks were in a position analogous to black Africans under the domination of colonial powers and, therefore, should respond accordingly. The Black Revolution has had a history checkered with periods of violence and peaceful protest. While the potential for escalated violence remains, in recent years American blacks have sought economic gains (green power) to improve their lot.

The position and attitude of black revolutionists is articulated in the books below by the activists. The articles and books by the following are also especially helpful: Kenneth B. Clark (1965), Harold Cruse (1964, 1968), Lewis M. Killian (1968, 1972), John H. Bracy, Jr., August Meier, and Elliot Rudwick (1970), Theodore Draper (1970), James A. Geschwender (1971), and Benjamin Muse (1968).

Activists' Accounts

3724. Boggs, James. *The American Revolution: Pages from a Negro Worker's Notebook.* New York: Monthly Review Press, 1963.
3725. Carmichael, Stokely, and Charles V. Hamilton. *Black Power.* New York: Random House, 1967.
3726. Cleaver, Eldridge. *Post-Prison Writings and Speeches.* New York: Random House, 1969.
3727. _____. *Soul on Ice.* New York: Dell, 1968.
3728. Davis, Angela Y., and Other Political Prisoners. *If They Come in the Morning: Voices of Resistance.* New York: Third Press, 1971.
3729. Edwards, Harry. *Black Students.* New York: Free Press, 1970.
3730. Foner, Philip S., ed. *The Black Panthers Speak.* Philadelphia: Lippincott, 1970.
3731. Foreman, James. *The Making of Black Revolutionaries: A Personal Account.* New York: Macmillan, 1972.
3732. Heath, G. Louis, ed. *The Black Panthers Leaders Speak.* Metuchen, New Jersey: Scarecrow Press, 1976.
3733. Jackson, George L. *Blood in My Eye.* New York: Random House, 1972.
3734. King, Martin Luther, Jr. *Conscience for Change.* Toronto: Canadian Broadcasting Corporation, 1967.
3735. Lester, Jules. *Revolutionary Notes.* New York: Richard W. Baron, 1969.
3736. Malcolm X. *The Autobiography of Malcolm X.* New York: Grove Press, 1966.
3737. Newton, Huey P. *Revolutionary Suicide.* New York: Harcourt Brace Jovanovich, 1973.
3738. Seale, Bobby. *Seize the Time.* New York: Random House, 1970.
3739. *Soledad Brother: The Prison Letters of George Jackson.* New York: Coward, McCann, 1970.

Articles

3740. Blake, J. Herman. "Black Nationalism." *Annals of the American Academy of Political and Social Science* 382 (March 1969): 15–25.
3741. Boskin, Joseph. "The Revolt of the Urban Ghettos, 1964–1967." *Annals of the American Academy of Political and Social Science* 382 (March 1969): 1–14.
3742. Caplan, Nathan S., and Jeffrey M. Paige. "A Study of Ghetto Rioters." *Scientific American* 219:2 (August 1968): 15–21.
3743. Clark, Kenneth B. "The Wonder Is There Have Been So Few Riots." *The New York Times Magazine* (5 September 1965).
3744. Cruse, Harold. "Roots of Revolutionary Nationalism." *Black America* (Fall 1964).
3745. Gramont, Sanche de. "Our Other Man in Algiers." *The New York Times Magazine* (1 November 1970).
3746. Herod, Charles C. "Black Nationalism in America." *Canadian Review of Studies in Nationalism* 6 (1979): 196–217.
3747. Killian, Lewis M. "The Significance of Extremism in the Black Revolution." *Social Problems* 20:1 (1972): 41–48.

3748. Long, Durward. "Black Protest." In *Protest! Student Activism in America,* edited by J. Foster and D. Long. New York: Morrow, 1970.

3749. Ricks, Timothy. "Black Revolution: A Matter of Definition." *American Behavioral Scientist* 12:4 (March-April 1969): 21–26.

3750. Szulc. Tad. "George Jackson Radicalizes the Brothers in Soledad and San Quentin." *The New York Times Magazine* (1 August 1971).

3751. Turner, John B., and Whitney M. Young, Jr. "Who Has the Revolution or Thoughts on the Second Reconstruction." *Daedalus* 94:4 (Fall 1965): 1148–63.

3752. Woodward, C. Vann. "After Watts—Where Is the Negro Revolution Headed?" *The New York Times Magazine* (29 August 1965).

Books

3753. Barbour, Floyd B., ed. *The Black Power Revolt.* Boston: Porter Sargent, 1968.

3754. Bracy, John H., Jr., et al. *Conflict and Competition: Studies in the Black Protest Movement.* Belmont, California: Wadsworth, 1971.

3755. Bracey, John H., Jr.; August Meier; and Elliot Rudwick, eds. *Black Nationalism in America.* Indianapolis, Indiana: Bobbs-Merrill, 1970.

3756. Brink, William, and Louis Harris. *The Negro Revolution in America.* New York: Simon and Schuster, 1964.

3757. Brisbane, Robert H. *Black Activism: Racial Revolution in the United States, 1954–1970.* Valley Forge, Pennsylvania: Judson Press, 1974.

3758. _____ . *The Black Vanguard: Origins of the Black Social Revolution, 1900–1960.* Valley Forge, Pennsylvania: Judson Press, 1970.

3759. Bunge, William. *Fitzgerald: The Geography of a Revolution.* Cambridge, Massachusetts: Schenkman, 1972.

3760. Button, James W. *Black Violence: Political Impact of the 1960s Riots.* Princeton: Princeton University Press, 1978.

3761. Cruse, Harold. *Rebellion or Revolution?* New York: Morrow, 1968.

3762. Draper, Theodore. *The Rediscovery of Black Nationalism.* New York: Viking, 1970.

3763. Durden-Smith, Jo. *Who Killed George Jackson? Fantasies, Paranoia and the Revolution.* New York: Alfred A. Knopf, 1976.

3764. Editors of *Ebony* et al. *Black Revolution.* Chicago: Johnson, 1970.

3765. Fogelson, Robert M. *Violence as Protest: A Study of Riots in the Ghetto.* Garden City, New York: Doubleday, 1971.

3766. Geschwender, James A., ed. *The Black Revolt: The Civil Rights Movement, Ghetto Uprisings and Separatism.* Englewood Cliffs, New Jersey: Prentice-Hall, 1971.

3767. Goldman, Peter. *The Death and Life of Malcolm X.* Urbana: University of Illinois Press, 1980.

3768. Goldston, Robert. *The Negro Revolution.* New York: New American Library, 1969.

3769. Heath, G. Louis. *Off the Pigs! The History and Literature of the Black Panther Party.* Metuchen, New Jersey: Scarecrow Press, 1976.

3770. Hercules, Frank. *American Society and Black Revolution.* New York: Harcourt Brace Jovanovich, 1972.

3771. Hooker, James R. *Black Revolutionary: George Padmore's Path from Communism to Pan-Africanism.* New York: Praeger, 1967.

3772. Killian, Lewis M. *The Impossible Revolution: Black Power and the American Dream.* New York: Random House, 1968.

3773. Lockwood, Lee. *Conversations with Eldridge Cleaver (Algiers).* New York: McGraw-Hill, 1970.

3774. Lomax, Louis E. *The Negro Revolt.* New York: Signet Books, 1963.

3775. Major, Reginald. *A Panther is a Black Cat.* New York: Morrow, 1972.

3776. Mann, Eric. *Comrade George: An Investigation into the Life, Political Thought, and Assassination of George Jackson.* New York: Harper and Row, 1974.

3777. Marine, Gene. *Black Panthers.* New York: New American Library, 1969.

3778. Muse, Benjamin. *The American Negro Revolution: From Nonviolence to Black Power, 1963–1967.* Bloomington: Indiana University Press, 1968.

3779. Nadelson, Regina. *Who Is Angela Davis? The Biography of a Revolutionary.* New York: Peter H. Wyden, 1972.

3780. Nelson, Truman. *The Right of Revolution.* Boston: Beacon, 1968.

3781. Ross, James R., ed. *War Within: Violence or Nonviolence in the Black Revolution.* New York: Sheed and Ward, 1971.

3782. Thomas, Tony. *A Strategy for Black Liberation.* New York: Pathfinder Press, n.d.

3783. Wolfenstein, Eugene Victor. *The Victims of Democracy: Malcolm X and the Black Revolution.* Berkeley: University of California Press, 1981.

Quebec Revolutionary Nationalism

Beginning in the 1960s the French-speaking Canadian province of Quebec began to exercise varying degrees of independence and self-direction. Some among the population clamored for Quebec to secede from the Canadian confederation to form a separate nation. These revolutionary nationalists, especially the *Front de Libération du Québec,* engaged in a variety of terrorist activities to achieve their goal. But such tactics frightened many Quebecers, and the movement for secession did not improve its position significantly. Nevertheless, elements of revolutionary nationalism have survived as a part of the Quebec political scene.

Articles

3784. Bourgeault, Guy. "Le nationalisme Québécois et l'Eglise." *Canadian Review of Studies in Nationalism* 5 (Fall 1978): 189–207.

3785. Dion, Leon, and Micheline De Seve. "Québec ou l'emergence d'une formule politique alternative." *Canadian Review of Studies in Nationalism* 5 (Fall 1978): 258–83.

3786. Moore, Marie-France. "Nationalisme et contre-culture au Québec." *Canadian Review of Studies in Nationalism* 5 (Fall 1978): 284–306.
3787. Roback, Leo, and Louis-Marie Tremblay. "Le nationalisme au sein des syndicats Québécois." *Canadian Review of Studies in Nationalism* 5 (Fall 1978): 237–57.

Books

3788. Jacobs, Jane. *The Question of Separatism: Quebec and the Struggle over Sovereignty.* New York: Random House, 1980.
3789. Linteau, Paul-André, et al. *Histoire du Québec contemporain: De la Confédération à la crise, 1867–1929.* Quebec: Boréal Express, 1979. A second, forthcoming volume will carry the account to the present.
3790. Reid, Malcolm. *The Shouting Signpainters: A Literary and Political Account of Quebec Revolutionary Nationalism.* Toronto: McClelland and Stewart, 1972.
3791. Vallières, Pierre. *White Niggers of America: The Precocious Autobiography of a Quebec "Terrorist."* New York: Monthly Review Press, 1971.

Latin America

"The expression 'law and order' is used by those in power, not by us, as a false slogan to justify their abuses. We are not interested in their law or their order, but only with justice."
Simón Bolívar

Throughout the history of Latin America, revolutions and coups d'etat have played key roles in bringing about changes in the control and exercise of power, and sometimes improvements for the people. Revolution, usually accompanied by violence, has been of three types: (1) revolutionary wars for independence (i.e., these took place during the last decade of the eighteenth century and the first three decades of the nineteenth); (2) coups d'etat, or struggles for political power primarily involving the army or aristocracy, or both (i.e., most Latin American revolutions during the nineteenth and twentieth centuries have been of this variety; Bolivia, for example, has had 189 coups/revolutions as of August, 1980 during its 155 year history, with about a dozen occurring since the major social revolution of 1952); (3) the "great" revolutions (i.e., revolutions which have been popularly based and involved not only changes in the political structure, but in the social, economic, and cultural areas as well; only Mexico in 1910, Bolivia in 1952, Cuba in 1959, and possibly Nicaragua in 1978–1979 are in this category).

The revolutionary wars of independence did little more than establish most Latin American countries as independent states. Little was done to alter the basic political and social structures. Essentially what happened was that an indigenous elite replaced a foreign elite. It is perhaps because of this incompleteness that successive revolutions became necessary. But since the coups have involved and benefitted only a small privileged minority in each country, and since the general living conditions of the masses have been poor, Latin America has been a breeding ground for revolutionary activity, particularly in those countries which have not profited from major social revolutions. Complicating matters further has been the influence of such factors as industrialization, urbanization, modernization, raised expectations and levels of awareness, and the long arm of neocolonialism. Latin America has been and is a continent of conflict and contrast between tradition and innovation, rich and poor, and power brokers and the disenfranchised. It has been a land of endemic revolution and revolutionary activity.

The focus of this chapter is the major and many of the minor Latin American revolutions and revolutionists. The table of contents states and the section introductions explain which and who these are. Among the titles immediately following these paragraphs there are several other kinds of works. There are a variety of survey histories and general items, including those that are especially useful by Victor Alba (1969), Douglas A. Chalmers (1975), Simon Collier (1974), Alexander T. Edelmann (1969), J. Halcro Ferguson (1963), Robert A. Humphreys (1946, 1969), and Benjamin Keen and Mark Wasserman (1980). There are works on lesser known revolts and revolutions, such as those by Harold Blakemore (1965) and Maurice H. Hervey (1976) on the revolution in Chile in 1891, John Nikol and Francis X. Hulbrook (1977) on the revolution in Panama in 1903, C. E. Haring (1933) on the revolution in Chile in 1931, Louis A. Pérez, Jr. (1974) and Luis E. Aguilar (1972) on the Cuban revolution of 1933, Harris Gaylord Warren (1950) on the revolution in Paraguay in 1936–1940, and John Patrick Bell (1972) on the Costa Rican revolution of 1948.

Further, there are selections on Marxism and communism in Latin America, such as those by Luis E. Aguilar (1970, 1978), Robert J. Alexander (1957, 1973), and Karl M. Schmitt (1965). There are works on guerrilla warfare by Malcolm Deas (1968), Richard Gott (1971), James Kohl and John Litt (1974), and Jean Lartéguy (1970). There are books on leadership and elites by Robert J. Alexander (1962) and Seymour M. Lipset and Aldo Solari (1967). There are works on the Latin American military by John J. Johnson (1964), H. E. Landsberger (1970), Edwin Lieuwen (1961), and Abraham F. Lowenthal (1976). There are works on nationalism by Robert N. Burr (1961) and Kalman H. Silvert (1961). And there are works on religion and the Catholic Church by François Houtart (1965), J. L. Mecham (1966), and David E. Mutchler (1971).

In addition, there are titles dealing with Latin America's relationship with foreign powers, such as those by Penny Lernoux (1980) and Martin C. Needler (1977). There are works on peasants and peasant movements by Leon G. Campbell (1979), Harry E. Vanden (1978), Gerrit Huizer (1973), and H. E. Landsberger (1969). There are books on social and political structures and change by Richard N. Adams et al (1961), Robert F. Adie and Guy E. Poitras (1974), June Nash et al (1977), and Paul E. Sigmund (1970). And there are comparative analyses (most of which examine the great revolution in Mexico along with those in either Cuba or Bolivia, or both) by Cole Blaiser (1967), Susan Eckstein (1975, 1976), Frank Tannenbaum (1960), and Daniel Cosío Villegas (1961). Finally, there are a number of other works which do not fit naturally into any of the sections that follow.

Bibliographies

3792. Bayitch, S. A. *Latin America and the Caribbean: A Bibliographical Guide to Works in English*. Coral Gables, Florida: University of Miami Press, 1967.
3793. Chilcote, Ronald H. *Revolution and Structural Change in Latin America: A Bibliography*. 2 vols. Stanford: Hoover Institution, 1970.

3794. Griffin, Charles C., ed. *Latin America: A Guide to Historical Literature.* Austin: University of Texas Press, 1971.
3795. Humphreys, Robert A. *Latin American History: A Guide to the Literature in English.* New York: Oxford University Press, 1958.
3796. Lauerhass, Ludwig. *Library Resources on Latin America: Research Guide and Bibliographic Introduction.* Los Angeles: UCLA Latin American Center, 1978.
3797. Wilgus, A. Curtis. *Latin America, Spain and Portugal: A Selected and Annotated Bibliographical Guide to Books Published, 1954–1974.* Metuchen, New Jersey: Scarecrow Press, 1977.

Historiographies

3798. Esquenazi-Mayo, Roberto, and M. C. Meyer, eds. *Latin American Scholarship since World War II: Trends in History, Political Science, Literature, Geography, and Economics.* Lincoln: University of Nebraska Press, 1971.
3799. Whitaker, Arthur P. *Latin American History Since 1825.* Washington, D.C.: American Historical Association Service Center for Teachers of History, 1961.

Documents

3800. Keen, Benjamin, ed. *Latin American Civilization.* 2 vols. Boston: Houghton Mifflin, 1974.

Articles

3801. Aguilar, Luis E. "Fragmentation of the Marxist Left." *Problems of Communism* 19:4 (July-August 1970): 1–12.
3802. AlRoy, Gil Carl. "Revolutionary Conditions in Latin America." *Review of Politics* 29:3 (July 1967): 417–22.
3803. Arnade, Kurt Conrad. "The Technique of *Coup d'Etat* in Latin America." *United Nations World* 4 (1950): 21–25.
3804. Berle, Adolph A. "Latin America: The Hidden Revolution." *Reporter* (28 May 1959).
3805. Blaiser, Cole. "Studies of Social Revolution: Origins in Mexico, Bolivia, and Cuba." *Latin American Research Review* 2:3 (Summer 1967): 28–64.
3806. Blakemore, Harold. "The Chilean Revolution of 1891 and Its Historiography." *Hispanic American Historical Review* 45:3 (August 1965): 393–421.
3807. Blanksten, G. "Revolutions." In *Government and Politics in Latin America,* edited by H. E. Davis. New York: Ronald Press, 1958.
3808. Bridges, Thomas. "Haya de la Torre: Reflections of a Revolutionary." *Américas* 32 (April 1980): 4–8.
3809. Britton, John A. "Carleton Beals on the Ambiguities of Revolutionary Change in Mexico and Peru." *Studies in Social Science* 17 (June 1978): 89–98.
3810. Burr, Robert N., ed. "Latin America's Nationalistic Revolutions." *Annals of the American Academy of Political and Social Science* 334 (March 1961): 1–206.
3811. Campbell, Leon G. "Recent Research on Andean Peasant Revolts, 1750–1820." *Latin American Research Review* 14:1 (Winter 1979): 3–49.

3812. Deas, Malcolm. "Guerrillas in Latin America: A Perspective." *World Today* 24:2 (February 1968): 72-78.
3813. Denton, Charles F. "Costa Rica: A Democratic Revolution." In *Latin American Politics and Development*, edited by H. J. Wiarda and H. F. Kline. Boston: Houghton Mifflin, 1979.
3814. Eckstein, Susan. "How Economically Consequential Are Revolutions? A Comparison of Mexico and Bolivia." *Studies in Comparative International Development* 10:3 (Fall 1975): 48-62.
3815. Fitzgibbon, Russell H. "Revolution in Latin America: A Tentative Prognosis." *Virginia Quarterly Review* 39:2 (Spring 1963): 206-26.
3816. _____. "Revolutions: Western Hemisphere." *South Atlantic Quarterly* 55:3 (July 1956): 263-79.
3817. Fortuny, José Manuel. "Has the Revolution Become More Difficult in Latin America?" *Peace, Freedom and Socialism* (August 1965): 26-32.
3818. Gerassi, John. "Latin America: The Left on the Move." *Ramparts* (September 1971): 22-25.
3819. Gott, Richard. "Defeat of the Revolution?" *Evergreen Review* (February 1971): 29.
3820. Grayson, George W., Jr. "Latin Revolts Shift to Cities: Peasants, Radicals Don't Mix." *Los Angeles Times* (17 January 1971).
3821. Handal, Schafik. "Reflections on Continental Strategy for Latin American Revolutionaries." *World Marxist Review* 11: 4 (April 1968): 50-59.
3822. Haring, C. E. "The Chilean Revolution of 1931." *Hispanic American Historical Review* 13:2 (May 1933): 197-203.
3823. Herrick, Paul B., Jr., and Robert S. Robins. "Varieties of Latin American Revolutions and Rebellions." *Journal of Developing Areas* 10 (April 1976): 317-36.
3824. Huberman, Leo, and Paul Sweezy. "The Latin American Revolution: A New Phase." *Monthly Review* (February 1967): 1-20.
3825. Kinnaird, Lawrence. "The Western Fringe of Revolution." *Western Historical Quarterly* 7 (July 1976): 253-70.
3826. Midlarsky, Manus, and Raymond Tanter. "Toward a Theory of Political Instability in Latin America." *Journal of Peace Research* 3 (1967): 209-26.
3827. Montalva, Eduardo Frei. "The Second Latin American Revolution." *Foreign Affairs* 50 (October 1971): 83-96.
3828. Nikol, John, and Francis X. Hulbrook. "Naval Operations in the Panama Revolution of 1903." *American Neptune* 37 (October 1977): 253-61.
3829. Nunn, Frederick M. "Military Rule in Chile: The Revolutions of September 5, 1924, and January 23, 1925." *Hispanic American Historical Review* 47:1 (February 1967): 1-21.
3830. Pérez, Louis A., Jr. "The Military and Political Aspects of the 1933 Cuban Revolution: The Fall of Machado." *The Americas* 31 (October 1974): 172-84.
3831. Quinana, Segundo V. Linares. "The Etiology of Revolution in Latin America." *Western Political Quarterly* 4:2 (June 1951): 254-67.
3832. Riding, Alan. "Guatemala: State of Siege." *The New York Times Magazine* (24 August 1980).
3833. Savelle, Max. "Reflections on Revolution in America." *The Americas* 33 (October 1976): 185-204.
3834. Silvert, Kalman H. "Nationalism in Latin America." *Annals of the American Academy of Political and Social Science* 334 (March 1961): 1-9.

3835. Sutton, Horace. "The Palm Tree Revolt." *Saturday Review* (27 February 1971): 15.
3836. Szulc, Tad. "Radical Winds in the Caribbean." *The New York Times Magazine* (25 May 1980).
3837. Tannenbaum, Frank. "The Mexican and Cuban Revolutions." In *The Latin Americas: The Couchiching Conference,* edited by D. L. B. Hamlin. Toronto: The Canadian Institute on Public Affairs, University of Toronto Press, 1960.
3838. Vanden, Harry E. "The Peasants as a Revolutionary Class: An Early Latin American View." *Journal of Interamerican Studies and World Affairs* 20 (May 1978): 191–210.
3839. Warren, Harris Gaylord. "The Paraguayan Revolution of 1904." *The Americas* 36 (January 1980): 365–84.
3840. _____. "Political Aspects of the Paraguayan Revolution, 1936–1940." *Hispanic American Historical Review* 30:1 (February 1950): 2–25.
3841. Wiarda, Howard J. "The Dominican Republic: The Politics of a Frustrated Revolution." In *Latin American Politics and Development,* edited by H. J. Wiarda and H. F. Kline. Boston: Houghton Mifflin, 1979.
3842. _____, and Harvey F. Kline. "Latin America and Its Alternative Futures." In *Latin American Politics and Development,* edited by H. J. Wiarda and H. F. Kline. Boston: Houghton Mifflin, 1979.

Books

3843. Adams, Richard N., et al. *Social Change in Latin America Today.* New York: Vintage, 1961.
3844. Adie, Robert F., and Guy E. Poitras. *Latin America: The Politics of Immobility.* Englewood Cliffs, New Jersey: Prentice-Hall, 1974.
3845. Aguilar, Luis E. *Cuba 1933—Prologue to Revolution.* Ithaca: Cornell University Press, 1972.
3846. _____. *Marxism in Latin America.* 2d ed. Philadelphia: Temple University Press, 1978.
3847. Alba, Victor. *The Latin Americans.* New York: Praeger, 1969.
3848. Alexander, Robert J. *Communism in Latin America.* New Brunswick, New Jersey: Rutgers University Press, 1957.
3849. _____. *Prophets of Revolution: Profiles of Latin American Leaders.* New York: Macmillan, 1962.
3850. _____. *Trotskyism in Latin America.* Stanford: Hoover Institution, 1973.
3851. _____, et al. *The Communist Tide in Latin America: A Selected Treatment.* Austin: University of Texas, Humanities Research Center, 1973.
3852. Anderson, Thomas P. *Matanza: El Salvador's Communist Revolt of 1932.* Lincoln: University of Nebraska Press, 1971.
3853. Beals, Carleton. *Latin America: World in Revolution.* New York: Abelard-Schuman, 1963.
3854. Bell, John Patrick. *Crisis in Costa Rica: The 1948 Revolution.* Austin: University of Texas Press, 1972.
3855. Bell, Wendell, ed. *The Democratic Revolution in the West Indies.* Cambridge, Massachusetts: Schenkman, 1967.
3856. Bernstein, Harry. *Modern and Contemporary Latin America.* Philadelphia: Lippincott, 1952.

3857. Blackman, Morris J., and Ronald G. Hellman, eds. *Terms of Conflict: Ideology in Latin American Politics.* Philadelphia: Institute for the Study of Human Issues, 1977.
3858. Burnett, Ben G., and Kenneth F. Johnson, eds. *Political Forces in Latin America.* Belmont, California: Wadsworth, 1970.
3859. Chalmers, Douglas A. *Revolution and Social Change in Latin America.* New York: Macmillan, 1975.
3860. Clissold, Stephen. *Latin America: New World, Third World* New York: Praeger, 1972.
3861. Cockcroft, James D., et al. *Dependence and Underdevelopment: Latin America's Political Economy.* Garden City, New York: Doubleday, 1972.
3862. Collier, Simon. *From Cortés to Castro: An Introduction to the History of Latin America, 1492–1973.* New York: Macmillan, 1974.
3863. Conde, Roberto Cortes. *The First Stages of Modernization in Spanish America.* New York: Harper and Row, 1974.
3864. Dandler, Jorge, ed. *Contradictions in the Andes: Bolivia, Chile and Peru.* Garden City, New York: Doubleday, 1975.
3865. Davis, Harold E. *Makers of Democracy in Latin America.* New York: H. W. Wilson, 1945.
3866. _____. *Revolutionaries, Traditionalists and Dictators in Latin America.* New York: Cooper Square Publishers, 1972.
3867. Duff, Ernest A., and John F. McCamant. *Violence and Repression in Latin America: A Quantitative and Historical Analysis.* New York: Free Press, 1976.
3868. Duncan, W. Raymond, and James N. Goodsell. *The Quest for Change in Latin America.* New York: Oxford University Press, 1970.
3869. Eckstein, Susan. *The Impact of Revolution: A Comparative Analysis of Mexico and Bolivia.* Beverly Hills, California: Sage, 1976.
3870. Edelmann, Alexander T. *Latin American Government and Politics: The Dynamics of a Revolutionary Society.* Homewood, Illinois: Dorsey Press, 1969.
3871. Fagg, John Edwin. *Cuba, Haiti, and the Dominican Republic.* Englewood Cliffs, New Jersey: Prentice-Hall, 1965.
3872. Ferguson, J. Halcro. *The Revolutions of Latin America.* London: Thames and Hudson, 1963.
3873. Frank, Andre Gunder. *Latin America: Underdevelopment or Revolution.* New York: Monthly Review Press, 1969.
3874. Furtado, Celso. *Economic Development of Latin America: A Survey from Colonial Times to the Cuban Revolution.* 2d ed. New York: Cambridge University Press, 1977.
3875. Gott, Richard. *Guerrilla Movements in Latin America.* Garden City, New York: Doubleday, 1971.
3876. Halperin-Donghi, Tulio. *The Aftermath of Revolution in Latin America.* Translated by J. de Bunsen. New York: Harper and Row, 1973.
3877. Hansen, Joseph. *The Leninist Strategy of Party Building: The Debate on Guerrilla Warfare in Latin America.* New York: Pathfinder Press, 1980.
3878. Harris, Louis K., and Victor Alba. *The Political Culture and Behavior of Latin America.* Kent, Ohio: Kent State University Press, 1974.
3879. Hervey, Maurice H. *Dark Days in Chile: The Revolution of 1891.* New York: Gordon Press, 1976.
3880. Hodges, Donald C. *The Latin American Revolution: Politics & Strategy from Apro-Marxism to Guevarism.* New York: Morrow, 1974.

244 / Latin America

3881. _____, ed. *Philosophy of the Urban Guerrilla: The Revolutionary Writings of Abraham Guillén.* New York: Morrow, 1973.
3882. Horowitz, Irving Louis, ed. *Masses in Latin America.* New York: Oxford University Press, 1970.
3883. _____ ; Josue de Castro; and John Gerassi, eds. *Latin American Radicalism.* New York: Random House, 1969.
3884. Houtart, François. *The Church and the Latin American Revolution.* New York: Sheed and Ward, 1965.
3885. Huizer, Gerrit. *Peasant Rebellion in Latin America.* Harmondsworth, England: Penguin Books, 1973.
3886. Humphreys, Robert A. *The Evolution of Modern Latin America.* New York: Oxford University Press, 1946.
3887. _____. *Tradition and Revolt in Latin America.* New York: Columbia University Press, 1969.
3888. Jackson, D. Bruce. *Castro, the Kremlin, and Communism in Latin America.* Baltimore: Johns Hopkins University Press, 1969.
3889. Johnson, John J. *The Military and Society in Latin America.* Stanford: Stanford University Press, 1964.
3890. Johnson, Richard A. *The Mexican Revolution of Ayutla, 1854–1855.* Rock Island, Illinois: Augustana College Library, 1939.
3891. Keen, Benjamin, and Mark Wasserman. *A Short History of Latin America.* Boston: Houghton Mifflin, 1980.
3892. Kohl, James, and John Litt. *Urban Guerrilla Warfare in Latin America.* Cambridge, Massachusetts: M.I.T. Press, 1974.
3893.. Landsberger, H. E., ed. *The Church and Social Change in Latin America.* Notre Dame, Indiana: University of Notre Dame Press, 1970.
3894. _____. *Latin American Peasant Movements.* Ithaca: Cornell University Press, 1969.
3895. Lartéguy, Jean. *The Guerrillas: New Patterns in Revolution in Latin America.* Translated by S. Hochman. New York: New American Library, 1970.
3896. *Latin America: World in Revolution.* Westport, Connecticut: Greenwood, 1974.
3897. Lazar, Arpad von, and Robert R. Kaufman, eds. *Reform and Revolution: Readings in Latin American Politics.* Boston: Allyn and Bacon, 1969.
3898. Lernoux, Penny. *Cry of the People: United States Involvement in the Rise of Fascism, Torture, and Murder and the Persecution of the Catholic Church in Latin America.* New York: Doubleday, 1980.
3899. Lewis, Gordon K. *Notes on the Puerto Rican Revolution: An Essay on American Dominance and Caribbean Resistance.* New York: Monthly Review Press, 1975.
3900. Lieuwen, Edwin. *Arms and Politics in Latin America.* New York: Praeger, 1961.
3901. Lipset, Seymour M., and Aldo Solari, eds. *Elites in Latin America.* New York: Oxford University Press, 1967.
3902. López, Adalberto. *The Revolt of the Comuñeros, 1721–1735: A Study in the Colonial History of Paraguay.* Cambridge, Massachusetts: Schenkman, 1976.
3903. Lowenthal, Abraham F., ed. *Armies and Politics in Latin America.* New York: Holmes and Meier, 1976.

3904. Mac Eoin, Gary. *Revolution Next Door.* New York: Holt, Rinehart and Winston, 1971.
3905. Mander, John. *The Unrevolutionary Society: The Power of Latin Conservatism in a Changing World.* New York: Alfred A. Knopf, 1969.
3906. Marti, Jose. *Our America: Writings on Latin America and the Cuban Struggle for Independence.* Edited by P. Foner. New York: Monthly Review Press, 1978.
3907. Martz, John, ed. *The Dynamics of Change in Latin American Politics.* Englewood Cliffs, New Jersey: Prentice-Hall, 1971.
3908. Mecham, J. L. *Church and State in Latin America: A History of Politico-Ecclesiastical Relations.* Rev. ed. Chapel Hill: University of North Carolina Press, 1966.
3909. Mercier Vega, Luis. *Roads to Power in Latin America.* New York: Praeger, 1969.
3910. Moreno, Francisco J., and Barbara Mitrani, eds. *Conflict and Violence in Latin American Politics.* New York: Thomas Y. Crowell, 1971.
3911. Mutchler, David E. *The Church as a Political Force in Latin America.* New York: Praeger, 1971.
3912. Nash, June, et al, eds. *Ideology and Social Change in Latin America.* New York: Gordon and Breach, 1977.
3913. Needler, Martin C. *The United States and the Latin American Revolution.* Rev. ed. Los Angeles: UCLA Latin American Center, 1977.
3914. Nun, Jose. *Latin America: The Hegemonic Crisis and the Military Coup.* Berkeley: University of California, Institute of International Studies, 1969.
3915. Pearse, Andrew. *The Latin American Peasant.* London: Frank Cass, 1975.
3916. Pérez, Louis A., Jr. *Intervention, Revolution, and Politics in Cuba, 1913–1921.* Pittsburgh: University of Pittsburgh Press, 1978.
3917. Petras, James F. *Politics and Social Structure in Latin America.* New York: Monthly Review Press, 1970.
3918. _____ , and Robert LaPorte, Jr. *Cultivating Revolution: The United States and Agrarian Reform in Latin America.* New York: Random House, 1971.
3919. _____ , and Maurice Zeitlin, eds. *Latin America: Reform or Revolution?* Greenwich, Connecticut: Fawcett World Library, 1968.
3920. Pierson, William W., and Federico G. Gil. *Governments of Latin America.* New York: McGraw-Hill, 1967.
3921. Pollock, David H., and Archibald R. M. Ritter, eds. *Latin American Prospects for the 1970's: What Kinds of Revolutions?* New York, Praeger, 1973.
3922. Powelson, John P. *Latin America: Today's Economic and Social Revolution.* New York: McGraw-Hill, 1964.
3923. Puhle, H. J., ed. *Revolution und Reformen in Lateinamerika: Geschichte und Gesellschaft.* Göttingen: Vandenhoeck and Ruprecht, 1976.
3924. Ratliff, William. *Castroism and Communism in Latin America, 1959–1976: The Varieties of Marxist-Leninist Experience.* Washington, D. C.: American Enterprise Institute, 1976.
3925. Remmer, Karen L., and Gilbert W. Merkx, eds. *New Perspectives on Latin America: Political Conflict and Social Change.* New York: Arno Press, 1976.
3926. Robe, Stanley L. *Revolution in the West: The Writings of los De Abajo.* Berkeley: University of California Press, 1978.

3927. Schmitt, Karl M. *Communism in Mexico.* Austin: University of Texas Press, 1965.
3928. Selser, Gregorio. *Sandino.* Translated by C. Belfrage. New York: Monthly Review Press, 1981.
3929. Sigmund, Paul E. *Models of Political Change in Latin America.* New York: Praeger, 1970.
3930. Silvert, Kalman H. *Conflict Society: Reaction and Revolution in Latin America.* Rev. ed. New York: Harper and Row, 1968.
3931. Stavenhagen, Rodolfo, ed. *Agrarian Problems and Peasant Movements in Latin America.* Garden City, New York: Doubleday, 1970.
3932. Szulc, Tad. *The Winds of Revolution: Latin America Today and Tomorrow.* New York: Praeger, 1963.
3933. Tannenbaum, Frank. *The Future of Democracy in Latin America.* New York: Alfred A. Knopf, 1975.
3934. Vallier, Ivan. *Catholicism, Social Control, and Modernization in Latin America.* Englewood Cliffs, New Jersey: Prentice-Hall, 1970.
3935. Veliz, Claudio, ed. *Obstacles to Change in Latin America.* New York: Oxford University Press, 1969.
3936. _____ , ed. *The Politics of Conformity in Latin America.* New York: Oxford University Press, 1967.
3937. Villegas, Daniel Cosío. *Change in Latin America: The Mexican and Cuban Revolutions.* Lincoln: University of Nebraska Press, 1961.
3938. White, Richard Alan. *Paraguay's Autonomous Revolution, 1810–1840.* Albuquerque: University of New Mexico Press, 1978.
3939. Wiarda, Howard J., ed. *Politics and Social Change in Latin America.* Amherst: University of Massachusetts Press, 1974.
3940. _____ , and Harvey F. Kline, eds. *Latin American Politics & Development.* Boston: Houghton Mifflin, 1979.
3941. Williams, Edward J., and Freeman J. Wright. *Latin American Politics: A Developmental Approach.* Palo Alto, California: Mayfield, 1975.
3942. Wynia, Gary W. *The Politics of Latin American Development.* Cambridge: Cambridge University Press, 1978.

Latin American Independence Revolutions

Toward the end of the eighteenth century, the sharpest division existing within the white ruling class of Spanish America was between the Spaniards born in the colonies (called Creoles) and the European-born Spaniards (called Peninsulars). This conflict was intensified by Enlightenment ideas from Europe and the success of the American and French Revolutions. The most important result attributable directly to the French Revolution was the slave revolt in Haiti under the leadership, among others, of Toussaint L'Ouverture and Henri Christophe; Haiti became independent in 1804. But more than anything else for Spanish

America, the decline of Spain after 1808 transformed the idea of independence into a realistic goal. Creoles took over control, but Spain did not give up without a fight. Only after more than a decade of war did most of Latin America achieve its political independence. However, the existing economic and social structures were left intact.

The best overview and synthesis of these revolutions is by John Lynch (1973); his book also contains a comprehensive annotated bibliography. Other general surveys are by Jay Kinsbruner (1973) and Richard Graham (1972). The collection edited by Robert A. Humphreys and John Lynch (1965) brings together conflicting interpretations of the causes of the upheavals. For the revolution in Haiti see the books by Thomas O. Ott (1973) and the biographies by Ralph Korngold (1965) and Hubert Cole (1967). For Simon Bolívar see the biographies by John J. Johnson and D. M. Ladd (1968) and Gerhard Masur (1969). The independence movements in the other countries can be found by checking the actual titles. The books by Charles C. Griffin (1941), W. W. Kaufmann (1951), and Arthur P. Whitaker (1941) are on the attitudes of foreign powers toward Latin American independence.

Historiographies

3943. Gibson, Charles. *The Colonial Period in Latin American History.* Washington, D. C.: American Historical Association Service Center for Teachers of History, 1958.
3944. Humphreys, Robert A. "The Historiography of the Spanish American Revolutions." *Hispanic American Historical Review* 36:1 (February 1956): 81–93.

Articles

3945. Griffin, Charles C. "Economic and Social Aspects of the Era of Spanish-American Independence." *Hispanic American Historical Review* 29:1 (February 1949): 170–87.
3946. Lacerte, Robert K. "The Evolution of Land and Labor in the Haitian Revolution, 1791–1820." *The Americas* 34 (April 1978): 449–59.
3947. Matthewson, Timothy. "George Washington's Policy toward the Haitian Revolution." *Diplomatic History* 3 (Summer 1979): 321–36.

Books

3948. Belaunde, Victor A. *Bolivar and the Political Thought of the Spanish-American Revolution.* New York: Octagon Books, 1967.
3949. Cole, Hubert. *Christophe, King of Haiti.* New York: Viking, 1967.
3950. Collier, Simon. *Ideas and Politics of Chilean Independence, 1808–1833.* New York: Cambridge University Press, 1969.
3951. Domínguez, Jorge I. *Insurrection or Loyalty: The Breakdown of the Spanish American Empire.* Cambridge, Massachusetts: Harvard University Press, 1980.

3952. Fisher, L. E. *The Background of the Revolution for Mexican Independence.* New York: Gordon Press, 1976.

3953. Flores Caballero, Romeo. *Counterrevolution: The Role of the Spaniards in the Independence of Mexico, 1804–1838.* Translated by J. E. Rodríquez. Lincoln: University of Nebraska Press, 1974.

3954. Genovese, Eugene D. *From Rebellion to Revolution.* New York: Vintage, 1980.

3955. Graham, Richard. *Independence in Latin America.* New York: Alfred A. Knopf, 1972.

3956. Griffin, Charles C. *The United States and the Disruption of the Spanish Empire, 1800–1822.* New York: Octagon Books, 1941.

3957. Hamill, H. M., Jr. *The Hidalgo Revolt: Prelude to Mexican Independence.* Gainesville: University of Florida Press, 1966.

3958. Heinl, Robert D., Jr., and Nancy G. Heinl. *Written in Blood: The Story of the Haitian People, 1492–1971.* Boston: Houghton Mifflin, 1978.

3959. Humphreys, Robert A., and John Lynch, eds. *The Origins of the Latin American Revolutions, 1808–1826.* New York: Alfred A. Knopf, 1965.

3960. James, C. L. R. *Black Jacobin: Toussaint L'Ouverture and the San Domingo Revolution.* New York: Random House, 1963.

3961. Johnson, John J., and D. M. Ladd. *Simon Bolivar and Spanish American Independence, 1783–1830.* New York: D. Van Nostrand, 1968.

3962. Kaufmann, W. W. *British Policy and the Independence of Latin America, 1802–1828.* New Haven: Yale University Press, 1951.

3963. Kinsbruner, Jay. *Bernardo O'Higgins.* Boston: Twayne, 1968.

3964. _____ . *The Spanish-American Independence Movement.* Hinsdale, Illinois: Dryden Press, 1973.

3965. Korngold, Ralph. *Citizen Toussaint.* New York: Hill and Wang, 1965.

3966. L'Ouverture, Toussaint. *Toussaint L'Ouverture: A Biography and Autobiography.* New York: Arno Press, 1863.

3967. Lynch, John. *The Spanish American Revolutions, 1808–1826.* New York: W. W. Norton, 1973.

3968. Masur, Gerhard. *Simon Bolivar.* 2d ed. Albuquerque: University of New Mexico Press, 1969.

3969. Metford, J. C. J. *San Martín, the Liberator.* London: Longmans, Green, 1950.

3970. Moses, Bernard. *Spain's Declining Power in South America, 1730–1806.* Berkeley: University of California Press, 1919.

3971. _____ . *The Spanish Dependencies in South America.* 2 vols. New York: Harper and Brothers, 1914.

3972. O'Leary, Daniel Florencio, *Bolivar and the War of Independence.* Austin: University of Texas Press, 1970.

3973. Ott, Thomas O. *The Haitian Revolution, 1789–1804.* Knoxville: University of Tennessee Press, 1973.

3974. Paxson, Frederic L. *The Independence of the South-American Republics: A Study in Recognition and Foreign Policy.* Philadelphia: Ferris and Leach, 1903.

3975. Robertson, William S. *Rise of the Spanish-American Republics: As Told in the Lives of Their Liberators.* New York: Free Press, 1965.

3976. Russell-Wood, A. J. R., ed. *From Colony to Nation: Essays on the Independence of Brazil.* Baltimore: Johns Hopkins University Press, 1975.

3977. Steward, Theophilus G. *Haitian Revolution, 1791 to 1804.* New York: Russell and Russell, 1971.
3978. Street, John. *Artigas and the Emancipation of Uruguay.* London: Cambridge University Press, 1959.
3979. Trend, J. B. *Bolivar and the Independence of Spanish America.* New York: Macmillan, 1948.
3980. Whitaker, Arthur P. *The United States and the Independence of Latin America, 1800-1830.* Baltimore: Johns Hopkins University Press, 1941.
3981. Worcester, Donald E. *Bolivar.* Boston: Little, Brown, 1977.
3982. Ybarra, T. R. *Bolivar, the Passionate Warrior.* New York: I. Washburn, 1929.

Mexican Revolution, 1910

Until the time of Castro and the Cuban Revolution, the Mexican Revolution was the most important and influential of Latin American upheavals. It was a nationalist revolution aimed at identifying the people with their nation, its past and its culture. It sought to lend a cohesiveness to a people who had always been divided by race, class, language, and culture. In short, the revolution was intended to create a true Mexican nation.

Initially the revolution took the form of a political conflict, with the revolutionists seeking to eliminate the dictatorial regime of Porfirio Díaz and establish a more democratic system. But in its first decade (1910-1920) it developed into a social and economic revolution aimed at radically altering the roles played by the military, the Catholic Church, and foreign capitalists. The revolution also attempted to make changes in the social structure, abolish the system of large estates, initiate agrarian reform, and improve education.

The meaning and significance of the Mexican Revolution has been subject to a wealth of interpretations by Mexicans and non-Mexicans alike. This has been due in large measure to the absence of a revolutionary philosophy and to a variety of contending concepts. The collections edited by Charles C. Cumberland (1967) and Stanley R. Ross (1966) bring together many of these conflicting views. Among the best surveys of the revolution are those by Jan Bazant (1977), Howard F. Cline (1963), Charles C. Cumberland (1952, 1968, 1972), Robert E. Quirk (1970), Frank Tannenbaum (1950, 1966), and James W. Wilkie and Albert L. Michaels (1969). Among the more noteworthy specialized studies are those by Robert E. Quirk (1973) on the Catholic Church, Frank R. Brandenburg (1964) on the economy, Ramón Eduardo Ruiz (1976) on labor, Carlton Beals (1932) on Porfirio Díaz, Stanley R. Ross (1955) on Madero, and Robert P. Millon (1969) and John Womack, Jr. (1968) on Zapata.

Bibliography

3983. Ramos, Roberto. *Bibliografia de la Revolucion Mexicana.* 3 vols. New York: Gordon Press, 1976.

Historiography

3984. Bailey, David C. "Revisionism and the Recent Historiography of the Mexican Revolution." *Hispanic American Historical Review* 58:1 (February 1978): 62–79.

Documents

3985. Hanrahan, Gene Z., ed. *Documents on the Mexican Revolution.* 3 vols. Salisbury, North Carolina: Documentary Publications, 1976–1978.

Overviews, Surveys, and Interpretations

Articles

3986. Cabrera, Luis. "The Mexican Revolution—Its Causes, Purposes and Results." *Annals of the American Academy of Political and Social Science* 69 (January 1917) supplement: 1–17.
3987. Calvert, Peter. "The Institutionalization of the Mexican Revolution." *Journal of Inter-American Studies* 11:4 (October 1969): 503–17.
3988. Camp, Roderic A. "The Elitelore of Mexico's Revolutionary Family." *Journal of Latin American Lore* 4 (Winter 1978): 149–82.
3989. Carr, Barry. "Recent Regional Studies of the Mexican Revolution." *Latin American Research Review* 15:1 (Winter 1980): 3–14.
3990. Cline. Howard F. "Mexico: A Matured Latin-American Revolution, 1910–1960." *Annals of the American Academy of Political and Social Science* 334 (March 1961): 84–94.
3991. Falcón, Romana. "Los orígenes populares de la revolución de 1910—el caso de San Luis Potosí." *Histórico mexicano* 29 (October-December 1979): 197–240.
3992. Goldfrank, Walter L. "Theories of Revolution and Revolution without Theory: The Case of Mexico." *Theory and Society* 7:1–2 (January-March 1979): 135–65.
3993. Hall, Linda B. "The Mexican Revolution and the Crisis in Naco: 1914–1915." *Journal of the West* 16 (October 1977): 27–35.
3994. Hansis, Randall. "The Political Strategy of Military Reform: Alvaro Obregón and Revolutionary Mexico, 1920–1924." *The Americas* 36 (October 1979): 197–232.
3995. Herzog, Jesús Silva. "Rise and Fall of Mexico's Revolution." *Nation* (22 October 1949): 395–96.
3996. Joseph, Gilbert M. "The Fragile Revolution: Cacique Politics and Revolutionary Process in Yucatán." *Latin American Research Review* 15:1 (Winter 1980): 41–64.

3997. Levine, Robert M. "The Mexican Revolution: A Retrospective View." *Current History* (May 1974): 195.
3998. Maciás, Anna. "The Mexican Revolution Was No Revolution for Women." In *Latin America: A Historical Reader*, edited by L. Hanke. Boston: Little, Brown, 1974.
3999. Navarro, Moisés Gonzáles. "The Lopsided Revolution." In *Obstacles to Change in Latin America*, edited by C. Véliz. New York: Oxford University Press, 1965.
4000. Ross, Stanley R. "Mexico: Golden Anniversary of the Revolution." *Current History* (March 1960): 150.
4001. _____. "Mexico: The Preferred Revolution." In *Politics of Change in Latin America*, edited by J. Maier and R. W. Weatherhead. New York: Praeger, 1964.
4002. Stevens, Evelyn P. "Mexico's One-Party State: Revolutionary Myth and Authoritarian Reality." In *Latin American Politics and Development*, edited by H. J. Wiarda and H. F. Kline. Boston: Houghton Mifflin, 1979.
4003. Tannenbaum, Frank. "Reflections on the Mexican Revolution." *Journal of International Affairs* 9:1 (1955): 37-46.
4004. Wasserman, Mark. "The Social Origins of the 1910 Revolution in Chihuahua." *Latin American Research Review* 15:1 (Winter 1980): 15-40.
4005. Whitaker, Arthur P., ed. "Mexico Today." *Annals of the American Academy of Political and Social Science* 208 (1940): 1-186.
4006. Yoder, Dale. "The Mexican Revolution." *Sociology and Social Research* 11 (1927): 351-64.

Books

4007. Alba, Victor. *The Mexicans: The Making of a Nation.* New York: Praeger, 1967.
4008. Atkins, Ronald. *Revolution! Mexico Nineteen Ten to Twenty.* New York: John Day, 1970.
4009. Baerlein, Henry. *Mexico, the Land of Unrest: Being Chiefly an Account of What Produced the Outbreak of 1910.* London: Herbert and Daniel, 1913.
4010. Bazant, Jan. *A Concise History of Mexico from Hidalgo to Cardenas, 1805-1940.* New York: Cambridge University Press, 1977.
4011. Brenner, Anita. *Wind That Swept Mexico: The History of the Mexican Revolution, 1910-1942.* New York: Harper and Brothers, 1943.
4012. Call, Tomme Clark. *The Mexican Venture: From Political to Industrial Revolution in Mexico.* New York: Oxford University Press, 1953.
4013. Cameron, Charlotte. *Mexico in Revolution.* New York: Gordon Press, 1976.
4014. Cline, Howard F. *Mexico: Revolution to Evolution, 1940-1960.* New York: Oxford University Press, 1963.
4015. Cockcroft, James. *Intellectual Precursors of the Mexican Revolution, 1900-1913.* Austin: University of Texas Press, 1968.
4016. Cumberland, Charles C. *Mexican Revolution: The Constitutionalist Years.* Austin: University of Texas Press, 1972.
4017. _____. *Mexican Revolution: Genesis Under Madero.* Austin: University of Texas Press, 1952.

4018. _____. *Mexico: The Struggle for Modernity.* New York: Oxford University Press, 1968.
4019. _____, ed. *The Meaning of the Mexican Revolution.* Boston: D. C. Heath, 1967.
4020. Dillon, E. J. *President Obregón, A World Reformer.* London: Hutchinson, 1923.
4021. Dulles, John W. F. *Yesterday in Mexico: A Chronicle of Revolution, 1919–1936.* Austin: University of Texas Press, 1961.
4022. Gruening, Ernest. *Mexico and Its Heritage.* New York: Century, 1928.
4023. Hellman, Judith A. *Mexico in Crisis.* New York: Holmes and Meier, 1978.
4024. Hodges, Donald, and Ross Gandy. *Mexico 1910–1976: Reform or Revolution?* London: Zed Press, 1980.
4025. Ibanez, V. Blasco. *Mexico in Revolution.* New York: E. P. Dutton, 1920.
4026. Johnson, William Weber. *Heroic Mexico: The Violent Emergence of a Modern Nation.* Garden City, New York: Doubleday, 1968.
4027. Lieuwen, Edwin. *Mexican Militarism, The Political Rise and Fall of the Revolutionary Army, 1910–1940.* Albuquerque: University of New Mexico Press, 1968.
4028. McCreary, Guy Weddington. *From Glory to Oblivion: The Real Truth about the Mexican Revolution.* New York: Vantage Press, 1976.
4029. McCullagh, Francis. *Red Mexico: A Reign of Terror in America.* New York: L. Carrier, 1926.
4030. McLeish, John L. *Highlights of the Mexican Revolution.* New York: Gordon Press, 1976.
4031. Magon, Ricardo F. *Land and Liberty: Anarchist Influences in the Mexican Revolution.* Boston: Carrier Pigeon, 1978.
4032. Meyer, Jean A. *The Cristero Rebellion.* New York: Cambridge University Press, 1976.
4033. _____. *La Revolución Mejicana, 1910–1940.* Barcelona, Spain: DOPESA, 1973.
4034. Meyer, Michael C. *Mexican Rebel: Pascual Orozco and the Mexican Revolution, 1910–1915.* Lincoln: University of Nebraska Press, 1967.
4035. Niemeyer, E. V., Jr. *Revolution at Querétaro: The Mexican Constitutional Convention of 1916–1917.* Austin: University of Texas Press, 1974.
4036. Quirk, Robert E. *The Mexican Revolution: 1914–1915.* New York: W. W. Norton, 1970.
4037. _____. *Mexico.* Englewood Cliffs, New Jersey: Prentice-Hall, 1971.
4038. Reed, John. *Insurgent Mexico.* New York: Simon and Schuster, 1969.
4039. Ross, Stanley R., ed. *Is the Mexican Revolution Dead?* New York: Alfred A. Knopf, 1966.
4040. Ruiz, Ramón Eduardo. *The Great Rebellion: Mexico, 1905–1924.* New York: W. W. Norton, 1980.
4041. Rutherford, John. *Mexican Society during the Revolution: A Literary Approach.* New York: Oxford University Press, 1971.
4042. Sanchez, George I. *Mexico: A Revolution by Education.* New York: Viking, 1936.
4043. Scott, Robert E. *Mexican Revolution in Transition.* Rev. ed. Urbana: University of Illinois Press, 1964.
4044. Tannenbaum, Frank. *Mexico: Struggle for Peace and Bread.* New York: Alfred A. Knopf, 1950.

4045. _____. *Peace by Revolution: Mexico after 1910.* New York: Columbia University Press, 1966.
4046. Wilkie, James W. and Albert L. Michaels, eds. *Revolution in Mexico: Years of Upheaval, 1910-1940.* New York: Random House, 1969.
4047. Wolfskill, George, and Douglas W. Richmond, eds. *Essays on the Mexican Revolution: Revisionist Views of the Leaders.* Austin: University of Texas Press, 1979.

The Church

4048. Bazant, Jan, and M. P. Costeloe, eds. *Alienation of Church Wealth in Mexico: Social and Economic Aspects of the Liberal Revolution, 1856-1875.* New York: Cambridge University Press, 1971.
4049. Quirk, Robert E. *The Mexican Revolution and the Catholic Church, 1910-1929.* Bloomington: Indiana University Press, 1973.

The Economy

4050. Brandenburg, Frank R. *The Making of Modern Mexico.* Englewood Cliffs, New Jersey: Prentice-Hall, 1964.
4051. Kemmerer, Edwin Walter. *Inflation and Revolution: Mexico's Experience, 1912-1917.* Princeton: Princeton University Press, 1940.
4052. Mosk, Sanford A. *Industrial Revolution in Mexico.* Berkeley: University of California Press, 1950.
4053. Tannenbaum, Frank. *The Mexican Agrarian Revolution.* New York: Macmillan, 1929.
4054. Wilkie, James W. *The Mexican Revolution: Federal Expenditure and Social Change Since 1910.* 2d ed. Berkeley: University of California Press, 1970.

Labor

4055. Anderson, Rodney D. "Mexican Workers and the Politics of Revolution, 1906-1911." *Hispanic American Historical Review* 54:1 (February 1974): 94-113.
4056. Ashby, Joe C. *Organized Labor and the Mexican Revolution Under Lázaro Cárdenas.* Chapel Hill: University of North Carolina Press, 1967.
4057. Eckstein, Susan. *The Poverty of Revolution: The State and the Urban Poor in Mexico.* Princeton: Princeton University Press, 1977.
4058. Hart, John M. "Nineteenth-Century Urban Labor Precursors of the Mexican Revolution: The Development of an Ideology." *The Americas* 30 (January 1974): 297-318.
4059. _____. "The Urban Working Class and the Mexican Revolution: The Case of the Casa del Obrero Mundial." *Hispanic American Historical Review* 58:1 (February 1978): 1-20.
4060. Ruiz, Ramón Eduardo. *Labor and the Ambivalent Revolutionaries: Mexico, 1911-1923.* Baltimore: Johns Hopkins University Press, 1976.

Peasantry

4061. Brading, D. A., ed. *Caudillo and Peasant in the Mexican Revolution.* New York: Cambridge University Press, 1980.
4062. Buve, Raymond Th. J. "Peasant Movements, Caudillos and Land Reform during the Revolution (1910-1917) in Tlaxcala, Mexico." *Boletin de Estúdios Latinoamericanos y del Caribe* 18 (June 1975): 112-52.
4063. Waterbury, Ronald. "Non-revolutionary Peasants: Oaxaca Compared to Morelos in the Mexican Revolution." *Comparative Studies in Society and History* 17 (1975): 10-42.

Diplomacy

4064. Calvert, Peter. *The Mexican Revolution, 1910-1914: The Diplomacy of Anglo-American Conflict.* Cambridge: At the University Press, 1968.
4065. Cline, Howard F. *The United States and Mexico.* Cambridge, Massachusetts: Harvard University Press, 1961.
4066. Hill, Larry D. *Emissaries to a Revolution: Woodrow Wilson's Executive Agents in Mexico.* Baton Rouge: Louisiana State University Press, 1973.
4067. Smith, Robert F. *The United States and Revolutionary Nationalism in Mexico, 1916-1932.* Chicago: University of Chicago Press, 1972.

Lázaro Cárdenas

4068. Brown, Lyle C. "Cárdenas: Creating a *Campesino* Power Base for Presidential Policy." In *Essays on the Mexican Revolution,* edited by G. Wolfskill and D. W. Richmond. Austin: University of Texas Press, 1979.
4069. Townsend, William Cameron. *Lázaro Cárdenas: Mexican Democrat.* Ann Arbor, Michigan: G. Wahr, 1952.
4070. Weyl, Nathaniel, and Sylvia Weyl. *The Reconquest of Mexico: The Years of Lázaro Cárdenas.* London: Oxford University Press, 1939.

Venustiano Carranza

4071. Beezley, William H. "Governor Carranza and the Revolution in Coahuila." *The Americas* 33 (July 1976): 50-61.
4072. Estañol, Jorge Vera. *Carranza and His Bolshevik Regime.* Los Angeles: Wayside Press, 1920.
4073. Richmond, Douglas W. "Carranza: The Authoritarian Populist as Nationalist President." In *Essays on the Mexican Revolution,* edited by G. Wolfskill and D. W. Richmond. Austin: University of Texas Press, 1979.

Porfirio Díaz

4074. Beals, Carleton. *Porfirio Díaz*. Philadelphia: Lippincott, 1932.
4075. Creelman, James. *Diaz, Master of Mexico*. New York: D. Appleton, 1911.
4076. Godoy, Jose F. *Porfirio Diaz*. New York: Gordon Press, 1976.

Francisco I. Madero

4077. Beezley, William H. "Madero: The 'Unknown' President and His Political Failure to Organize Rural Mexico." In *Essays on the Mexican Revolution,* edited by G. Wolfskill and D. W. Richmond. Austin: University of Texas Press, 1979.
4078. Knudson, Jerry W. "Document: When Did Francisco I. Madero Decide on Revolution?" *The Americas* 30 (April 1974): 529–34.
4079. Ross, Stanley R. *Francisco I. Madero: Apostle of Mexican Democracy.* New York: Columbia University Press, 1955.

Pancho Villa

4080. Arnold, Oren. *Pancho Villa: The Mexican Centaur.* Tuscaloosa, Alabama: Portals Press, 1978.
4081. Braddy, Haldeen. *The Paradox of Pancho Villa.* El Paso: Texas Western Press, 1978.
4082. Katz, Friedrich. "Pancho Villa, Peasant Movements and Agrarian Reform in Northern Mexico." In *Caudillo and Peasant in the Mexican Revolution,* edited by D. A. Brading. New York: Cambridge University Press, 1980.
4083. ———. "Villa: Reform Governor of Chihuahua." In *Essays on the Mexican Revolution,* edited by G. Wolfskill and D. W. Richmond. Austin: University of Texas Press, 1979.
4084. Peterson, Jessie, and Thelma Cox Knoles, eds. *Pancho Villa: Intimate Recollections by People Who Knew Him.* New York: Hastings House, 1977.

Emiliano Zapata

4085. Dunn, H. H. *The Crimson Jester: Zapata of Mexico.* New York: Gordon Press, 1976.
4086. Fuentes, Carlos. "Zapata's Revolution." *New York Review of Books* (13 March 1969).
4087. Millon, Robert P. *Zapata: The Ideology of a Peasant Revolutionary.* New York: International Publishers, 1969.
4088. Parkinson, Roger. *Zapata: A Biography.* New York: Stein and Day, 1975.
4089. Pinchon, Edgcumb. *Zapata the Unconquerable.* New York: Doubleday, Doran, 1941.

4090. White, Robert A. "Mexico: The Zapata Movement and the Revolution." In *Latin American Peasant Movements,* edited by H. A. Landsberger. Ithaca: Cornell University Press, 1969.

4091. Womack, John, Jr. *Zapata and the Mexican Revolution.* New York: Random House, 1968.

Guatemalan Revolution, 1944

For more than 100 years prior to the revolution of 1944 Guatemala was ruled directly by a landowning elite and indirectly by such American corporations as the United Fruit Company. The revolution, led by progressive intellectuals and officers, launched an agrarian reform program directed especially against the United Fruit Company. But the United States was displeased and worked to undermine the new government. Further, financial and military assistance was given to an invasion force of right-wing dissidents and mercenaries who overthrew the revolutionary government in a 1954 CIA-supported coup. The revolution had gone some distance toward improving the life of the working classes. The fact that it was not given a chance to succeed may have squashed faith in reform and constitutional politics as a means for peaceful change. Since 1954 Guatemala has been the scene of left-wing guerrilla insurrections and governmental terror and counterinsurgency.

Articles

4092. Grieb, Kenneth J. "The Guatemalan Military and the Revolution of 1944." *The Americas* 32 (April 1976): 524–43.

4093. Pearson, Neale J. "Guatemala: The Peasant Union Movement, 1944–1954." In *Latin American Peasant Movements,* edited by H. E. Landsberger. Ithaca: Cornell University Press, 1969.

4094. Wasserstrom, Robert. "Revolution in Guatemala: Peasants and Politics under the Arbenz Government." *Comparative Studies in Society and History* 17:4 (October 1975): 443–78.

4095. Weaver, Jerry L. "Guatemala: The Politics of a Frustrated Revolution." In *Latin American Politics and Development,* edited by H. J. Wiarda and H. F. Kline. Boston: Houghton Mifflin, 1979.

4096. Weiner, Peter H. "Guatemala: The Aborted Revolution." *Harvard Review* 4:1 (Summer–Fall 1966): 35–48.

Books

4097. Adams, Richard N. *Crucifixion by Power: Essays on Guatemalan National Social Structure, 1944-1966.* Austin: University of Texas Press, 1970.
4098. Inman, Samuel Guy. *A New Day in Guatemala: A Study of the Present Social Revolution.* Wilton, Connecticut: Worldover Press, 1951.
4099. Schneider, Ronald M. *Communism in Guatemala.* New York: Praeger, 1959.

Revolution in Bolivia, 1952

Bolivia, as with Peru and Ecuador, the other Andean republics, had a social and economic structure which was among the most archaic in all of Latin America. Movements for change sought modernization and greater social justice for the masses. In 1952 the National Revolutionary Movement (MNR), a middle class group, overthrew the rule of the great landlords and tin barons with support of Indian miners and peasants. (The Indians comprised about seventy percent of the population.) The revolution brought real benefits to the masses, especially in terms of agrarian reform. Although the old order was destroyed, the MNR proved incapable of achieving a lasting new one. The government became increasingly conservative until it was overthrown by right-wing generals in 1964. Since then the military has dominated Bolivia's political life, and coups have been frequent. In this political sense the Bolivian national revolution has yet to be completed.

The best books on the revolution are by Robert J. Alexander (1958), Dwight B. Heath, Charles J. Erasmus, and Hans C. Buechler (1969), Herbert S. Klein (1969), and James M. Malloy (1971). For the revolution since 1952 see the books by James M. Malloy and Richard S. Thorn (1971), Christopher Mitchell (1978), and Cornelius H. Zondag (1966). The articles treat more specialized subjects.

Articles

4100. Alexander, Robert J. "Organized Labor and the Bolivian National Revolution." In *National Labor Movements in the Postwar World,* edited by E. M. Kasslow. Evanston, Illinois: Northwestern University Press, 1963.
4101. Goodrich, Carter. "An Eyewitness Account of the 1952 Revolution in Bolivia." In *Latin America: A Historical Reader,* edited by L. Hanke. Boston: Little, Brown, 1974.
4102. Hauberg, C. A. "Challenge in Bolivia." *Current History* (March 1960): 155-64.

4103. Heath, Dwight B. "The Revolution Didn't Change Everything for the Bolivian Indians." In *Latin America: A Historical Reader,* edited by L. Hanke. Boston: Little, Brown, 1974.
4104. Klein, Herbert S. "The Crisis of Legitimacy and the Origins of Social Revolution: The Bolivian Experience." *Journal of Inter-American Studies* 10:1 (January 1968): 102-16.
4105. Knudson, Jerry W. "The Press and the Bolivian National Revolution." *Journalism Monographs* 31 (November 1973): 1-48.
4106. Kohl, James V. "Peasant and Revolution in Bolivia, April 9, 1952-August 2, 1953." *Hispanic American Historical Review* 58:2 (May 1978): 208-23.
4107. Malloy, James M. "Bolivia: An Incomplete Revolution." In *Latin American Politics and Development,* edited by H. J. Wiarda and H. F. Kline. Boston: Houghton Mifflin, 1979.
4108. Patch, Richard W. "Bolivia: The Restrained Revolution." *Annals of the American Academy of Political and Social Science* 334 (March 1961): 123-32.
4109. _____. "Bolivia: U.S. Assistance in a Revolutionary Setting." In *Social Change in Latin America Today,* by Richard Adams et al. New York: Harper and Row, 1963.
4110. Pearse, Andrew. "Peasants and Revolution: The Case of Bolivia." *Economy and Society* 1 (1972): 255.

Books

4111. Alexander, Robert J. *The Bolivian National Revolution.* New Brunswick, New Jersey: Rutgers University Press, 1958.
4112. Andrade, Victor. *My Missions for Revolutionary Bolivia, 1944-1962.* Pittsburgh: University of Pittsburgh Press, 1976.
4113. Arnade, Charles W. *The Emergence of the Republic of Bolivia.* New York: Russell and Russell, 1970.
4114. Gutierrez, Alberto Ostra. *The Tragedy of Bolivia.* New York: Devin-Adair, 1958.
4115. Heath, Dwight B.; Charles J. Erasmus; and Hans C. Buechler. *Land Reform and Social Revolution in Bolivia.* New York: Praeger, 1969.
4116. Kelley, Jonathan, and Herbert S. Klein. *Revolution and the Rebirth of Inequality: A Theory Applied to the Bolivian National Revolution.* Berkeley: University of California Press, 1980.
4117. Klein, Herbert S. *Parties and Political Change in Bolivia, 1880-1952.* Cambridge: Cambridge University Press, 1969.
4118. Malloy, James M. *Bolivia: The Uncompleted Revolution.* Pittsburgh: University of Pittsburgh Press, 1971.
4119. _____, and Richard S. Thorn, eds. *Beyond the Revolution: Bolivia Since 1952.* Pittsburgh: University of Pittsburgh Press, 1971.
4120. Mitchell, Christopher. *The Legacy of Populism in Bolivia: From the MNR to Military Rule.* New York: Praeger, 1978.
4121. Zondag, Cornelius H. *The Bolivian Economy, 1952-1965: The Revolution and Its Aftermath.* New York: Praeger, 1966.

Cuban Revolution, 1959

Cuba in the first half of the twentieth century suffered from chronic political instability and economic exploitation. A dictatorship ran the country in the 1950s. Then, in 1959, the country became the scene of the most successful social and socialist revolution in Latin America. The Cuban masses had experienced enough to know that their poverty was not inevitable, and the middle class saw its economic future as bleak. Cuban nationalism was also a potent force. Fidel Castro and his followers took advantage of this and brought about a revolution that was really the climax of a long historical struggle. Under the banner of Marxism and with the active assistance of the Soviet Union, the Cuban government has made great progress—the flight of thousands of Cubans to the United States in 1980 notwithstanding—toward improving the well-being of most of the people.

The character of the Cuban Revolution has been a cause for dispute from the beginning. Most of that dispute revolves around the extent to which the events of 1959 comprised a peasant revolution, a workers' revolution, or a middle class revolution. The best surveys are by Leo Huberman and Paul M. Sweezy (1960), K. S. Karol (1970), Ramón Eduardo Ruiz (1968), and Hugh Thomas (1971, 1977). On the background to the revolution see the books by C. R. Barent (1962) and Robert Freeman Smith (1966). On economic history see the book edited by E. Dudley Seers (1964). On the military see Louis A. Pérez, Jr.'s book (1976). The books by Oscar Lewis et al (1975, 1977, 1978) explain the revolution through the lives of ordinary Cubans. Herbert Matthews' books (1964, 1975) are by a fine journalist. Carlos Franqui's diary (1980) is by Castro's former propaganda minister who broke with the Cuban leader in 1968. Among the best post-revolution assessments are those by Rolando E. Bonachea and Nelson P. Valdés (1972) and Carmelo Mesa-Lago (1971, 1978).

Bibliographies

4122. Fort, Gilberto V. *The Cuban Revolution of Fidel Castro Viewed From Abroad: An Annotated Bibliography.* Lawrence: University of Kansas Libraries, 1960.

4123. Peraza, Fermin, ed. *Revolutionary Cuba: A Bibliographical Guide.* Coral Gables, Florida: University of Miami Press, 1970.

4124. Pérez, Louis A., Jr. *The Cuban Revolutionary War, 1953–1958: A Bibliography.* Metuchen, New Jersey: Scarecrow Press, 1976.

4125. Valdés, Nelson P., and Edwin Lieuwen. *The Cuban Revolution, 1959–1969: A Research-Study Guide.* Albuquerque: University of New Mexico Press, 1971.

Overviews, Surveys, and Interpretations

Articles

4126. Azicri, Max. "Women's Development Through Revolutionary Mobilization: A Study of the Federation of Cuban Women." *International Journal of Women's Studies* 2 (January-February 1979): 27-50.

4127. Baran, Paul A. "Reflections on the Cuban Revolution." *Monthly Review* (January 1961): 459-70; (February 1961): 518-29.

4128. Corbitt, Duvon C. "Cuban Revisionist Interpretations of Cuba's Struggle for Independence." *Hispanic American Historical Review* 43:3 (August 1963): 395-403.

4129. Draper, Theodore. "Runaway Revolution." *Reporter* (12 May 1960): 14-60.

4130. Fitzgibbon, Russell H. "The Revolution Next Door: Cuba." *Annals of the American Academy of Political and Social Science* 334 (March 1961): 113-22.

4131. Goldenberg, Boris. "The Cuban Revolution: An Analysis." *Problems of Communism* 12:5 (September-October 1963): 1-8.

4132. Kline, Harvey F. "Cuba: The Politics of Socialist Revolution." In *Latin American Politics and Development*, edited by H. J. Wiarda and H. F. Kline. Boston: Houghton Mifflin, 1979.

4133. Kling, Merle. "Cuba: A Case Study of a Successful Attempt to Seize Political Power by the Application of Unconventional Warfare." *Annals of the American Academy of Political and Social Science* 341 (May 1962): 42-52.

4134. Lavine, Harold. "Social Revolution in Cuba." *Commentary* (October 1959): 324-28.

4135. Murkland, H. B. "Cuba: The Evolution of Revolution." *Current History* (March 1960): 129-33.

4136. Padula, Alfred. "Financing Castro's Revolution 1956-58." *Review Interamerica* 8 (Summer 1979): 234-46.

4137. Smith, Robert Freeman. "Castro's Revolution, Domestic Sources and Consequences." In *Cuba and the United States: Long-Range Perspectives*, edited by J. N. Plank. Washington, D.C.: Brookings Institution, 1967.

4138. Suárez, Andrés. "The Cuban Revolution: The Road to Power." *Latin American Research Review* 7:3 (Fall 1972): 5-29.

4139. Thomas, Hugh. "Middle-Class Politics and the Cuban Revolution." In *The Politics of Conformity in Latin America*, edited by C. Véliz. London: Oxford University Press, 1967.

4140. _____. "The Origins of the Cuban Revolution." *World Today* 19:10 (October 1963): 448-60.

4141. Zeitlin, Maurice. "Cuba: Revolution Without a Blueprint." *Trans-action* (April 1969): 38-42.

Books

4142. Barkin, David P., and Nita R. Manitzas, eds. *Cuba: The Logic of the Revolution*. Edison, New Jersey: Mss Information, 1974.

4143. Bonachea, Ramon L., and Marta S. Martin. *The Cuban Insurrection, 1952-1959*. Edison, New Jersey: Transaction Books, 1974.

4144. Domínguez, Jorge I. *Cuba: Order and Revolution.* Cambridge, Massachusetts: Harvard University Press, Belknap Press. 1978.
4145. Dorschner, John, and Roberto Fabricio. *The Winds of December.* New York: Coward, McCann and Geoghegan, 1980.
4146. Dumont, René. *Cuba: Socialism and Development.* New York: Grove Press, 1970.
4147. Enos, John L. *An Analytic Model of Political Allegiance and Its Application to the Cuban Revolution.* Santa Monica, California: Rand, P-3197, August 1965.
4148. Green, Gil. *Revolution, Cuban Style.* New York: International Publishers, 1970.
4149. Hansen, Joseph. *Dynamics of the Cuban Revolution.* New York: Pathfinder Press, 1978.
4150. Horowitz, Irving Louis. *Cuban Communism.* New York: Aldine, 1970.
4151. Huberman, Leo, and Paul M. Sweezy, *Cuba: Anatomy of a Revolution.* New York: Monthly Review Press, 1960.
4152. Karol, K. S. *Guerrillas in Power: The Course of the Cuban Revolution.* Translated by Arnold Pomerans. New York: Hill and Wang, 1970.
4153. Mills, C. Wright. *Listen Yankee: The Revolution in Cuba.* New York: Ballantine Books, 1960.
4154. Morray, J. P. *The Second Cuban Revolution.* New York: Monthly Review Press, 1962.
4155. Nelson, Lowry. *Cuba: The Measure of a Revolution.* Minneapolis: University of Minnesota Press, 1972.
4156. Phillips, Ruby Hart. *Cuba: Island of Paradox.* New York: McGraw-Hill, 1960.
4157. Ruiz, Ramón Eduardo. *Cuba: The Making of a Revolution.* Amherst: University of Massachusetts Press, 1968.
4158. Sartre, Jean-Paul. *Sartre on Cuba.* New York: Ballantine Books, 1961.
4159. Seers, E. Dudley, ed. *Cuba: The Economic and Social Revolution.* Chapel Hill: University of North Carolina Press, 1964.
4160. Suchlicki, Jaime. *University Students and Revolution in Cuba.* Coral Gables, Florida: University of Miami Press, 1969.
4161. _____ , ed. *Cuba, Castro, and Revolution.* Coral Gables, Florida: University of Miami Press, 1972.
4162. Taber, Robert. *M-26: Biography of a Revolution.* New York: Lyle Stuart, 1961.
4163. Thomas, Hugh. *Cuba: The Pursuit of Freedom.* New York: Harper and Row, 1971.
4164. _____ . *The Cuban Revolution.* New York: Harper and Row, 1977.
4165. Weyl, Nathaniel. *Red Star Over Cuba.* New York: Devin-Adair, 1962.
4166. Zeitlin, Maurice. *Revolutionary Politics and the Cuban Working Class.* Princeton: Princeton University Press, 1967.

Background

Articles

4167. Blackburn, Robin. "Prologue to the Cuban Revolution." *New Left Review,* no. 21 (October 1963): 52–91.
4168. Gil, Federico G. "Antecedents of the Cuban Revolution." *Centennial Review of Arts and Science* 6:3 (Summer 1962): 376–82.
4169. Hennessy, C. A. M. "The Roots of Cuban Nationalism." *International Affairs* 39 (July 1963): 346–58.
4170. O'Connor, James. "The Foundations of Cuban Socialism." *Studies on the Left* 4:4 (Fall 1964): 97–117.
4171. Wood, Dennis B. "The Long Revolution: Class Relations and Political Conflict in Cuba, 1868–1968." *Science and Society* 34:1 (Spring 1970): 1–41.

Books

4172. Barent, C. R. *Twentieth Century Cuba: The Background of the Castro Revolution.* Garden City, New York: Doubleday, 1962.
4173. Farber, Samuel. *Revolution and Reaction in Cuba, 1933–1960: A Political Sociology from Machado to Castro.* Middletown, Connecticut: Wesleyan University Press, 1976.
4174. Mac Gaffey, Wyatt, and Clifford Barnett. *Twentieth-Century Cuba: The Background of the Castro Revolution.* Garden City, New York: Doubleday, 1965.
4175. O'Connor, James. *The Origins of Socialism in Cuba.* Ithaca: Cornell University Press, 1969.
4176. Pérez, Louis A., Jr. *Army Politics in Cuba, 1898–1958.* Pittsburgh: University of Pittsburgh Press, 1976.
4177. Smith, Robert Freeman, ed. *Background to Revolution: The Development of Modern Cuba.* New York: Alfred A. Knopf, 1966.
4178. Suchlicki, Jaime. *Cuba: From Columbus to Castro.* New York: Scribners, 1974.

Participant and Eyewitness Accounts

4179. Franqui, Carlos. *Diary of the Cuban Revolution.* Translated by E. Kerrigan; P. Freeman; and H. St. Martin. New York: Penguin Books, 1980.
4180. Gilly, Adolfo. *Inside the Cuban Revolution.* Translated by F. Gutierrez. Westport, Connecticut: Greenwood, 1964.
4181. Lewis, Oscar, et al. *Four Men—Living the Revolution: An Oral History of Contemporary Cuba.* Urbana: University of Illinois Press, 1975.
4182. _____, et al. *Four Women—Living the Revolution: An Oral History of the Cuban Revolution.* Urbana: University of Illinois Press, 1977.
4183. _____, et al. *Neighbors: Living the Revolution, An Oral History of Contemporary Cuba.* Urbana: University of Illinois Press, 1978.
4184. Matthews, Herbert. *Cuba.* New York: Macmillan, 1964.
4185. _____. *Revolution in Cuba: An Essay in Understanding.* New York: Scribners, 1975.
4186. Smith, Earl E. T. *The Fourth Floor: An Account of the Castro Communist Revolution.* New York: Random House, 1962.

Religion

4187. Crahan, Margaret E. "Salvation through Christ or Marx: Religion in Revolutionary Cuba." In *Churches and Politics in Latin America*, edited by D. H. Levine. Beverly Hills, California: Sage, 1980.
4188. Dewart, Leslie. *Christianity and Revolution: The Lesson of Cuba.* New York: Herder and Herder, 1963.

Peasants

4189. AlRoy, Gil Carl. "The Meaning of 'Peasant Revolution': The Cuban Case." *International Review of History and Political Science* 2:2 (1965).
4190. _____. "The Meaning of 'Peasant Revolution': What Next?" *International Review of History and Political Science* 2:3 (1965).
4191. _____. "The Peasantry in the Cuban Revolution." *Review of Politics* 29:1 (January 1967): 87-99.

Cuban Revolution and the Outside World

4192. Domínguez, Jorge I. "Castro's Revolution Is Secure, With Help from a Friendly Russian Bear." *Los Angeles Times* (7 January 1979).
4193. Ferguson, J. Halcro. "The Cuban Revolution and Latin America." *International Affairs* 37 (July 1961): 285-92.
4194. Goldenberg, Boris. *The Cuban Revolution and Latin America.* New York: Praeger, 1965.
4195. Levesque, Jacques. *The USSR and the Cuban Revolution: Soviet Ideological and Strategical Perspectives, 1959-77.* New York: Praeger, 1978.
4196. Smith, Robert Freeman. *The United States and Cuba: Business and Diplomacy, 1917-1960.* New Haven: College and University Press, 1960.
4197. Weinstein, Martin, ed. *Revolutionary Cuba in the World Arena.* Philadelphia: ISHI Publications, 1979.

Post-Revolution Assessments

Articles

4198. Karol, K. S. "In Cuba, Fidel Castro's Revolutionary Dreams Go Up in Smoke." *Los Angeles Times* (13 April 1980).
4199. LeoGrande, William M. "Party Development in Revolutionary Cuba." *Journal of Interamerican Studies and World Affairs* 21 (November 1979): 457-80.
4200. Morgan, Ted. "Cuba." *The New York Times Magazine* (1 December 1974).
4201. Ritter, Archibald R. M. "The Cuban Revolution: A New Orientation." *Current History* 74 (February 1978): 53.
4202. Volsky, George. "Cuba Twenty Years Later." *Current History* 76 (February 1979): 54.

Books

4203. Bonachea, Rolando E., and Nelson P. Valdés, eds. *Cuba in Revolution.* Garden City, New York: Doubleday, 1972.
4204. Mesa-Lago, Carmelo. *Cuba in the 1970s.* Rev. ed. Albuquerque: University of New Mexico Press, 1978.
4205. _____, ed. *Revolutionary Change in Cuba.* Pittsburgh: University of Pittsburgh Press, 1971.
4206. Nicholson, Joe, Jr. *Inside Cuba.* New York: Sheed and Ward, 1974.
4207. Ritter, Archibald R. M. *The Economic Development of Revolutionary Cuba: Strategy and Performance.* New York: Praeger, 1974.
4208. Sutherland, Elizabeth. *The Youngest Revolution: A Personal Report on Cuba.* New York: Dial Press, 1969.
4209. Yglesias, J. *In the Fist of the Revolution: Life in a Cuban Country Town.* New York: Pantheon Books, 1968.

Castro and Castroism

Fidel Castro is one of the few figures in the history of revolutions who has been successful during the several stages through which his revolution has passed. During the actual revolution he was both agitator and prophet. Since coming to power he has been both statesman and administrator. He has been a revolutionist who was able to rise above class differences and establish a relationship with the Cuban people based more upon his personal charisma than his ideas. In fact, Castro's ideas on revolution and society were vague and general until after 1959. For Cuba, Castroism has been a policy for stimulating the consciences of the people and satisfying their material needs. For Latin America, it has stood for a revolutionary new beginning, with only a dedicated guerrilla band needed to launch the struggle.

As a controversial figure Castro has had his supporters and critics. Among the more favorable views of Castro are the books by Lee Lockwood (1967) and Herbert Matthews (1969). More critical are those by Theodore Draper (1962, 1965) and Edward Gonzalez (1974). Other noteworthy studies are by Harvey F. Kline (1978), Maurice Halperin (1973), Frank Mankiewicz and Kirby Jones (1976), and Andrés Suárez (1967).

Articles

4210. Chapelle, Dickey. "How Castro Won." In *Modern Guerrilla Warfare: Fighting Communist Guerrilla Movements, 1941–1961,* edited by F. M. Osanka. New York: Free Press, 1962.

4211. Devlin, Kevin. "The Permanent Revolution of Fidel Castro." *Problems of Communism* 17:1 (January-February 1968): 1-11.
4212. Goytisolo, Juan. "20 Years of Castro's Revolution." *The New York Review of Books* (22 March 1979).
4213. Kline, Harvey F. "Fidel Castro and the Cuban Revolution." In *Government and Leaders,* edited by E. Feit. Boston: Houghton Mifflin, 1978.
4214. Nordheimer, Jon. "20 Years With Fidel." *The New York Times Magazine* (31 December 1978).

Books

4215. Brennan, Ray. *Castro, Cuba and Justice.* Garden City, New York: Doubleday, 1959.
4216. Castro, Fidel. *History Will Absolve Me.* New York: Liberal Press, 1959.
4217. _____. *Selected Works of Fidel Castro.* Vol. 1, *Revolutionary Struggle, 1947-1958.* Edited by R. E. Bonachea and N. P. Valdés. Cambridge, Massachusetts: M.I.T. Press, 1971.
4218. Casuso, Teresa. *Cuba and Castro.* New York: Random House, 1961.
4219. Draper, Theodore. *Castroism: Theory and Practice.* New York: Praeger, 1965.
4220. _____. *Castro's Revolution: Myths and Realities.* New York: Praeger, 1962.
4221. Dubois, Jules. *Fidel Castro.* Indianapolis: Bobbs-Merrill, 1959.
4222. Gonzalez, Edward. *Cuba Under Castro: The Limits of Charisma.* Boston: Houghton Mifflin, 1974.
4223. Goodsell, James Nelson, ed. *Fidel Castro's Personal Revolution in Cuba: 1959-1973.* New York: Alfred A. Knopf, 1974.
4224. Halperin, Maurice. *The Rise and Decline of Fidel Castro: An Essay in Contemporary History.* Berkeley: University of California Press, 1973.
4225. _____. *The Taming of Fidel Castro.* Berkeley: University of California Press, 1981.
4226. Llerena, Mario. *The Unsuspected Revolution: The Birth and Rise of Castroism.* Ithaca: Cornell University Press, 1978.
4227. Lockwood, Lee. *Castro's Cuba, Cuba's Fidel.* New York: Macmillan, 1967.
4228. Mankiewicz, Frank, and Kirby Jones, eds. *With Fidel: A Portrait of Castro and Cuba.* New York: Ballantine Books, 1976.
4229. Martin, Lionel. *The Early Fidel.* New York: Lyle Stuart, 1978.
4230. Matthews, Herbert. *Fidel Castro.* New York: Simon and Schuster, 1969.
4231. Meneses, Enrique. *Fidel Castro.* Translated by J. Halcro Ferguson. New York: Taplinger, 1968.
4232. Suárez, Andrés. *Cuba: Castroism and Communism, 1959-1966.* Cambridge, Massachusetts: M.I.T. Press, 1967.
4233. Urrutia Lleo, Manuel. *Fidel Castro and Company, Inc.* New York: Praeger, 1964.
4234. Wilkerson, Loree. *Fidel Castro's Political Program from Reformism to Marxism-Leninism.* Gainesville: University of Florida Press, 1965.

Che Guevara

Che Guevara, revolutionist, was a unique blend of dedicated, perpetual fighter, righteous idealist, and theoretical pragmatist. He was a charismatic leader who set an example of self-sacrifice; most of his adult life was spent either in making or preparing for revolution. The revolutions he participated in and prepared for were for the betterment of humankind; his ideals were pure. Although he became a communist, his ideas on revolution came more from practical experience than from any party line. Such is the stuff that creates myth and legend. Che's ideas on revolution and guerrilla warfare were an attempt to adapt established Marxist theory to Latin American conditions. There was no nationalism in his ideas on revolution, and this along with his failure to follow his own guidelines, led to his capture and death in Bolivia in 1967.

The biography by Richard Harris (1970) is the most objective and analytical; those by Daniel James (1970) and Andrew Sinclair (1970) are also good.

Documents

4235. Hodges, Donald C. *The Legacy of Che Guevara: A Documentary Study.* London: Thames and Hudson, 1977.
4236. Mallin, Jay, ed. *"Che" Guevara on Revolution: A Documentary Overview.* Coral Gables, Florida: University of Miami Press, 1970.

Articles

4237. Gall, Norman. "The Legacy of Che Guevara." *Commentary* (December 1967): 31-44.
4238. Gittings, John. "Roads to Revolution: A Guerrilla's Diary." *Far Eastern Economic Review* (15 August 1968): 313-16.
4239. Guevara, Che. "Tactics and Strategy of the Latin-American Revolution." *Tricontinental Bimonthly* (July-October 1970): 5-13.
4240. Lamberg, Robert F. "Che in Bolivia: The 'Revolution' That Failed." *Problems of Communism* 19:4 (July-August 1970): 25-37.
4241. Moreno, José A. "Che Guevara on Guerrilla Warfare: Doctrine, Practice and Evaluation." *Comparative Studies in Society and History* 12:2 (April 1970): 114-33.

Books

4242. Debray, Regis. *Che's Guerrilla War.* New York: Penguin Books, 1976.
4243. *The Diary of Che Guevara: Bolivia: November 7, 1966-October 7, 1967.* Edited by R. Scheer. New York: Bantam Books, 1968.

4244. Ebon, Martin. *Che: The Making of a Legend.* New York: Signet Books, 1969.
4245. Gerassi, John. *Venceremos! Speeches and Writings of Che Guevara.* New York: Simon and Schuster, 1968.
4246. González, Luis J., and Gustavo A. Sánchez Salazar. *The Great Rebel: Che Guevara in Bolivia.* New York: Grove Press, 1969.
4247. Guevara, Che. *Che Guevara Speaks: Selected Speeches and Writings.* New York: Pathfinder Press, 1980.
4248. _____. *Guerrilla Warfare.* Translated by J. P. Morray. New York: Random House, 1969.
4249. _____. *On Vietnam and World Revolution.* New York: Pathfinder Press, 1967.
4250. _____. *Reminiscences of the Cuban Revolutionary War.* Translated by V. Ortiz. New York: Grove Press, 1968.
4251. _____. *Socialism and Man.* New York: Pathfinder Press, n.d.
4252. Harris, Richard. *Death of a Revolutionary: Che Guevara's Last Mission.* New York: W. W. Norton, 1970.
4253. James, Daniel. *Che Guevara.* New York: Stein and Day, 1970.
4254. _____, ed. *Complete Bolivian Diaries of Che Guevara.* New York: Stein and Day, 1968.
4255. Lowy, Michael. *The Marxism of Che Guevara: Philosophy, Economics, and Revolutionary Warfare.* New York: Monthly Review Press, 1974.
4256. Rojo, Ricardo. *My Friend Ché.* New York: Grove Press, 1968.
4257. Sauvage, Leo. *Che Guevara: The Failure of a Revolutionary.* Englewood Cliffs, New Jersey: Prentice-Hall, 1974.
4258. Sinclair, Andrew. *Che Guevara.* New York: Viking, 1970.

Regis Debray

Regis Debray is a French Marxist philosopher and journalist who wrote about the Cuban Revolution after a couple of visits to that country. His writing, however, was not intended to be descriptive or analytical only, but to show how a Cuban-style revolution could be launched all over Latin America. His ideas on revolution parallel those of Che Guevara, and involve the peasantry playing the leading class role, and a guerrilla band (*foco*) providing direction. Debray was in Bolivia when Che was captured. The books by Leo Huberman and Paul M. Sweezy (1968) and Hartmut Ramm (1978) are the best on Debray, after Debray himself of course.

Articles

4259. Blackburn, Robin, and Perry Anderson. "The Marxism of Regis Debray." *New Left Review*, no. 45 (September-October 1967): 8–12.
4260. Fallaci, Oriana, and Nicole Bonnett. "Two 'Last' Interviews with Regis Debray." *Evergreen Review* (April 1971): 39.
4261. Lewis, Gordon. "Theory and Practice of Insurrection." *Caribbean Studies* (July 1968): 83–85.
4262. Petras, James. "Guerrilla Movements in Latin America—II." *New Politics* 6:2 (Spring 1967): 58–72.
4263. Quartem, Joao. "Regis Debray and the Brazilian Revolution." *New Left Review*, no. 59 (January-February 1970).
4264. Torres, Simon, and Julio Aronde. "Debray and the Cuban Experience." *Monthly Review* (July-August 1968): 44–68.

Books

4265. Debray, Regis. *La Critique des Armes*. Paris: Seuil, 1975.
4266. _____ . *Les Epreuves du Feu*. Paris: Seuil, 1975.
4267. _____ . *Revolution in the Revolution?* New York: Grove Press, 1967.
4268. _____ . *Strategy for Revolution: Essays on Latin America*. New York: Monthly Review Press, 1970.
4269. Huberman, Leo, and Paul M. Sweezy, eds. *Regis Debray and the Latin American Revolution*. New York: Monthly Review Press, 1968.
4270. Ramm, Hartmut. *The Marxism of Regis Debray: Between Lenin and Guevara*. Lawrence: Regents Press of Kansas, 1978.
4271. Slovo, Joe. *The Theories of Regis Debray.* London: African Communist Pamphlet, 1968.

Chilean Revolution and Salvador Allende, 1970–1973

The Chilean road to socialism, a "revolution by the ballot," was traversed for three years. The Socialist government of Salvador Allende attempted an untried form of transition to socialism, one that would come about without violence or disruption of democratic procedures. This unusual revolution can only be explained through an understanding of Chile's history, particularly the high regard Chileans held for their constitution and the non-political nature of the army. But the going was difficult, and the revolution was undermined from the start both at home and abroad. The experiment came to a violent and bloody end with a military coup in September, 1973. Even in defeat, Chile's unique example of peaceful socialization has had a profound impact upon the history of revolutions. Is a similar revolution possible? Would Allende have succeeded with greater cooperation by the middle class and the military, and less U.S.-sponsored sabotage? Or is peaceful revolution a contradiction in terms? Such questions are important not only for theoretical debates, but also for countries such as France, Italy, Portugal, and Spain which have large Marxist parties. Allende's government was succeeded by a military one which has been brutal and repressive.

The best available overview of Chilean history and society is by Federico Gil (1966), but it was published before the Allende years. The best books on the revolution itself are by Stefan De Vylder (1976) and Paul E. Sigmund (1977). Also helpful are the volumes by Robert J. Alexander (1978), Edward Boorstein (1977; he is an American economist who was employed by Allende's government), Regis Debray (1971), Dale L. Johnson (1973), Frederick M. Nunn (1976), and Ian Roxborough et al (1977). For U.S. complicity see the books by James Petras and Morris Morley (1975) and Paul M. Sweezy and Harry Magdoff (1974).

Documents

4272. Hahm, Ben, ed. *Documents of the Chilean Road to Socialism.* 7 vols. Philadelphia: Institute for the Study of Human Issues, 1977–1981.

Articles

4273. Ascherson, Neal. "The Real Tragedy of the Downfall of Allende." *Los Angeles Times* (23 September 1973).
4274. Belnap, David F. "Chile's Allende: The Roots of Disaster." *Los Angeles Times* (7 October 1973).
4275. Blackey, Robert. "Lost in Chile: A Dream and an Alternative." *The New York Times* (20 September 1973).
4276. "The Bloody End of a Marxist Dream." *Time* (24 September 1973).
4277. "Chile: The Brutal Death of an Idea." *Newsweek* (24 September 1973).
4278. Collier, Bernard, and Jonathan Kendell. "Chile: A Devastating End for a Unique, Troubled Venture." *The New York Times* (16 September 1973).
4279. Davidson, Sara. "Living Through the Allende Revolution." *The New York Times Magazine* (17 October 1971).
4280. Fagen, Richard R. "The Intrigues before Allende Fell." *Los Angeles Times* (6 October 1974).
4281. Falcoff, Mark. "Why Allende Fell: A New Perspective." *Los Angeles Times* (19 September 1976).
4282. Faúndez, Julio. "The Chilean Road to Socialism." *Political Quarterly* 46:2 (July-August 1975): 310–25.
4283. Gall, Norman. "The Chileans Have Elected a Revolution." *The New York Times Magazine* (1 November 1970).
4284. García Márquez, Gabriel. "The Death of Salvador Allende." *Harper's Magazine* (March 1974): 46–53.
4285. Hudson, Rexford A. "The Role of the Constitutional Conflict over Nationalization in the Downfall of Salvador Allende." *Inter-American Ecclesiastical Affairs* 31 (Spring 1978): 63–80.

4286. Llanos, M. A., and Barbara A. Shaver. "Allende: The Communist Strategy in Chile." *North Dakota Quarterly* 45 (Spring 1977): 6-24.

4287. Nogee, Joseph L., and John W. Sloan. "Allende's Chile and the Soviet Union: A Policy Lesson for Latin American Nations Seeking Autonomy." *Journal of Interamerican Studies and World Affairs* 21 (August 1979): 339-68.

4288. Portes, Alejandro. "Leftist Radicalism in Chile." *Comparative Politics* 2:2 (January 1970): 251-74.

4289. Rosenstein-Redan, Paul N. "Allende's Big Failing: Incompetence." *The New York Times* (16 June 1974).

4290. Suchlicki, Jaime, and Leon Gouré. "The Allende Regime: Actions and Reactions." *Problems of Communism* 20:3 (May-June 1971): 49-61.

4291. Valenzuela, J. Samuel, and Arturo Valenzuela. "Chile and the Breakdown of Democracy." In *Latin American Politics and Development*, edited by H. J. Wiarda and H. F. Kline. Boston: Houghton Mifflin, 1979.

4292. Zeitlin, Maurice. "Chilean Revolution: The Bullet or the Ballot." *Ramparts* (April 1971): 20-28.

Books

4293. Alexander, Robert J. *The Tragedy of Chile.* Westport, Connecticut: Greenwood, 1978.

4294. Allende, Salvador. *Chile's Road to Socialism.* Edited by Joan E. Garces. Translated by J. Darling. Baltimore: Penguin Books, 1973.

4295. Boorstein, Edward. *Allende's Chile: An Inside View.* New York: International Publishers, 1977.

4296. Castro, Fidel. *Fidel in Chile.* New York: International Publishers, 1972.

4297. Cusack, David. *Revolution and Reaction: The Internal Dynamics of Conflict and Confrontation in Chile.* Denver, Colorado: University of Denver Graduate School of International Studies, 1977.

4298. Debray, Regis. *The Chilean Revolution: Conversations with Allende.* New York: Pantheon Books, 1971.

4299. Dinges, John, and Saul Landau. *Assassination on Embassy Row.* New York: Pantheon Books, 1980.

4300. Evans, Les, ed. *Disaster in Chile: Allende's Strategy and Why It Failed.* New York: Pathfinder Press, 1974.

4301. Feinberg, Richard E. *The Triumph of Allende: Chile's Legal Revolution.* New York: New American Library, 1972.

4302. Gil, Federico. *The Political System of Chile.* Boston: Houghton Mifflin, 1966.

4303. _____ , et al. *Chile at the Turning Point: Lessons of the Socialist Years, 1970-1973.* Philadelphia: Institute for the Study of Human Issues, 1979.

4304. Horne, Alistair. *Small Earthquake in Chile: Allende's South America.* New York: Viking, 1972.

4305. Johnson, Dale L., ed. *The Chilean Road to Socialism.* Garden City, New York: Doubleday, 1973.

4306. Kinsbruner, Jay. *Chile: A Historical Interpretation.* New York: Harper and Row, 1973.

4307. Loveman, Brian. *Struggle in the Countryside: Politics and Rural Labor in Chile, 1919-1973.* Bloomington: Indiana University Press, 1976.

4308. Medhurst, Kenneth, ed. *Allende's Chile.* New York: St. Martin's Press, 1973.
4309. Morris, David J. *We Must Make Haste—Slowly: The Process of Revolution in Chile.* New York: Random House, 1973.
4310. Moss, Robert. *Chile's Marxist Experiment.* New York: Halsted Press, 1974.
4311. North American Congress on Latin America. *New Chile.* Berkeley: NACLA, 1973.
4312. Nunn, Frederick M. *The Military in Chilean History.* Albuquerque: University of New Mexico Press, 1976.
4313. O'Brien, Philip, ed. *Allende's Chile.* New York: Praeger, 1976.
4314. Palacios, Jorge. *Chile: An Attempt at "Historic Compromise": The Real Story of the Allende Years.* Chicago: Banner Press, 1979.
4315. Petras, James, and Hugo Zemelman Merino. *Peasants in Revolt: A Chilean Case Study, 1965-1971.* Translated by T. Flory. Austin: University of Texas Press, 1973.
4316. Raptis, Michel. *Revolution and Counter-Revolution in Chile: A Dossier on Workers' Participation in the Revolutionary Process.* Translated by J. Simmonds. New York: St. Martin's Press, 1975.
4317. Roxborough, Ian, et al. *Chile: The State and Revolution.* New York: Holmes and Meier, 1977.
4318. Sandford, Robinson Rojas. *The Murder of Allende and the End of the Chilean Way to Socialism.* Translated by A. Conrad. New York: Harper and Row, 1975.
4319. Sigmund, Paul E. *The Overthrow of Allende and the Politics of Chile, 1964-1976.* Pittsburgh: University of Pittsburgh Press, 1977.
4320. Smirnow, Gabriel. *The Revolution Disarmed: Chile 1970-1973.* New York: Monthly Review Press, 1981.
4321. Sobel, Lester A., ed. *Chile and Allende.* New York: Facts On File, 1975.
4322. Stickter, Jim. *Allende and the Saga of Chile.* 2d ed. Corpus Christi, Texas: Hemisphere House, 1978.
4323. Sweezy, Paul M., and Harry Magdoff, eds. *Revolution and Counter-Revolution in Chile.* New York: Monthly Review Press, 1974.
4324. Vargas, Florencia, and José Manuel Vergara. *Coup! Allende's Last Day.* New York: Stein and Day, 1975.
4325. White, Judy, ed. *Chile's Days of Terror: Eyewitness Accounts of the Military Coup.* New York: Pathfinder Press, 1974.
4326. Zammit, J. Ann, ed. *The Chilean Road to Socialism.* Austin: University of Texas Press, 1973.

Economy and Agrarian Reform

4327. De Vylder, Stefan. *Allende's Chile: The Political Economy of the Rise and Fall of the Unidad Popular.* New York: Cambridge University Press, 1976.
4328. Mamalakis, M. J. *The Growth and Structure of the Chilean Economy from Independence to Allende.* New Haven: Yale University Press, 1976.
4329. Stallings, Barbara. *Class Conflict and Economic Development in Chile, 1958-1973.* Stanford: Stanford University Press, 1978.

4330. Steenland, Kyle. *Agrarian Reform under Allende: Peasant Revolt in the South.* Albuquerque: University of New Mexico Press, 1978.
4331. Winn, Peter, and Cristobal Kay. "Agrarian Reform and Rural Revolution in Allende's Chile." *Journal of Latin American Studies* 6 (May 1974): 135-59.

U.S. Involvement

4332. Birns, Laurence R. "Allende's Fall, Washington's Push." *The New York Times* (15 September 1974).
4333. *Covert Action in Chile, 1963-1973: Staff Report of the Select Committee to Study Governmental Operations with Respect to Intelligence Activities, United States Senate.* Washington, D.C.: U.S. Government Printing Office, 1976.
4334. Petras, James, and Morris Morley. *The United States and Chile: Imperialism and the Overthrow of the Allende Government.* New York: Monthly Review Press, 1975.
4335. Uribe, Armando. *The Black Book of American Intervention in Chile.* Translated by J. Casart. Boston: Beacon Press, 1975.

Revolution in Uruguay and the Tupamaros

Uruguay was once considered, by Latin Americans and outsiders, to be the most democratic and progressive nation in the entire region. By 1970, however, the country was on its way toward becoming an authoritarian, military, and fascist state. This metamorphosis was long in the making, and occurred for a variety of reasons; the article by Philip B. Taylor, Jr. (1979) provides a detailed summary of Uruguayan history as well as an analysis of more recent events. In response to this change a group of urban guerrillas emerged, called the Tupamaros (after Túpac Amaru, the last royal Inca to revolt against the Spaniards in 1780; see the book by L. E. Fisher [1966] and the articles and book by Leon G. Campbell [1978] in the section "Revolution in Peru" below). Coming from and even being supported by some among the wealthy upper bourgeoisie families, the Tupamaros engaged in terrorist acts (e.g., kidnappings, bombings) for the joint purpose of discrediting the elite oligarchy and creating the conditions for revolution. But the country at large remained unconvinced, and the military pursued the Tupamaros relentlessly until the guerrillas were all but eliminated by the mid-1970s.

Articles

4336. Nuñez, Carlos. "The Tupamaros: Armed Vanguard in Uruguay." *Red Sky/Blue Sky* (April 1970).
4337. Taylor, Philip B., Jr. "Uruguay: The Costs of Inept Political Corporatism." In *Latin American Politics and Development,* edited by H. J. Wiarda and H. F. Kline. Boston: Houghton Mifflin, 1979.

Books

4338. Gilio, Maria Esther. *The Tupamaro Guerrillas.* Translated by A. Edmondson. New York: Saturday Review Press, 1972.
4339. Jackson, Sir Geoffrey. *Surviving the Long Night: An Autobiographical Account of a Political Kidnapping.* New York: Vanguard, 1974.
4340. Porzecanski, Arturo C. *Uruguay's Tupamaros: The Urban Guerrilla.* New York: Irvington Publishers, 1973.
4341. Wilson, Carlos. *The Tupamaros: The Unmentionables.* Boston: Branden Press, 1974.

Nicaraguan Revolution, 1978-1979

From 1936 to 1979 Nicaragua was ruled by the Somoza family; until the 1970s that rule was comparatively restrained and moderate, and thus the family had the support of most of the country. But with the rule of Anastasio Somoza (from 1964) the situation changed; press censorship and human rights violations became more and more widespread, and Somoza's greed and corruption became known. In 1974 a guerrilla organization, formed in 1962 and called the Sandinist Front of National Liberation (after Augusto Sandino, a revolutionary leader of a prolonged guerrilla struggle against U.S. interventionist forces who was murdered in 1934 by the founder of the Somoza dynasty), escalated its challenge to the government. In response Somoza, who had American backing, imposed martial law and, in his efforts to liquidate the Sandinists, overreacted—much like Batista had done in Cuba—and alienated increasing numbers of the population. The revolution had begun. Strikes, popular uprisings, and bloody civil war ravaged the country until the Sandinists defeated and drove Somoza from the country in July, 1979. Since then the new Sandinist government has been trying to heal and rebuild the nation. How successful they will be awaits future developments.

For background on the Nicaraguan Revolution see the article by Thomas W. Walker (1979) and the book by Eduardo Crawley (1979). For more on Augusto Sandino see the book by Neill Macaulay (1967). For the revolution itself all the articles and the book edited by Pedro Camejo and Fred Murphy (1980) will have to suffice until more work is done.

Articles

4342. LeoGrande, William M. "The Revolution in Nicaragua." *Foreign Affairs* 58 (Fall 1979): 28-50.
4343. Meisler, Stanley. "Nicaragua 1979 and Cuba 1959: Their Similarities Are Scant." *Los Angeles Times* (29 July 1979).
4344. Millett, Richard. "Nicaragua: It Has Been Neither the Best, Nor Worst of Times." *Los Angeles Times* (13 July 1980).
4345. Pearson, Neale J. "Nicaragua in Crisis." *Current History* 76 (February 1979): 78.
4346. Ridenour, Ron. "Nicaragua: Running with the Revolution." *Oui* (June 1979).
4347. Riding, Alan. "Nicaragua: A Delicate Balance." *The New York Times Magazine* (2 December 1979).
4348. _____. "Reality Transforms Nicaragua's Revolutionists Into Pragmatists." *The New York Times* (20 July 1980).
4349. Walker, Thomas W. "Nicaragua: The Somoza Family Regime." In *Latin American Politics and Development*, edited by H. J. Wiarda and H. F. Kline. Boston: Houghton Mifflin, 1979.
4350. _____. "The Sandinist Victory in Nicaragua." *Current History* 78 (January 1980): 57.

Books

4351. Bell, Belden, ed. *Nicaragua: An Ally Under Siege*. Washington, D.C.: Council on American Affairs, 1978.
4352. Camejo, Pedro, and Fred Murphy, eds. *A Portrait of the Nicaraguan Revolution*. New York: Pathfinder Press, 1980.
4353. Crawley, Eduardo. *Dictators Never Die: Nicaragua and the Somoza Dynasty*. New York: St. Martin's Press, 1979.
4354. Macaulay, Neill. *The Sandino Affair*. Chicago: Quadrangle Books, 1967.
4355. Millett, Richard. *Guardians of the Dynasty: A History of the U.S. Created Guardia Nacional de Nicaragua and the Somoza Family*. Maryknoll, New York: Orbis Books, 1977.

Revolutions in Argentina

Although Argentina is a highly developed nation in terms of its economic and social features, politically it has been quite unstable. Military coups, disorder, and severe repression have afflicted the nation. For example,

Revolutions in Argentina / 275

the revolution of 1930 established the country's first military government. The military returned the reins of government to civilians in 1932, but in 1943 a coup took it back again. Then Juan Perón came to power. He was deposed in 1955, as were successive civilian and military administrations. Thus, revolutionary coups and, from the early 1960s, guerrilla movements have characterized Argentina's political history. The works below offer a sample of this activity.

Article

4356. Hasbrouck, Alfred. "The Argentine Revolution of 1930." *Hispanic American Historical Review* 18:3 (August 1938): 285–321.

Books

4357. Ciria, Alberto. *Parties and Power in Modern Argentina (1930–1946).* Albany: State University of New York Press, 1974.
4358. Ferns, H. S. *The Argentine Republic, 1516–1971.* New York: Barnes and Noble, 1971.
4359. Gallo, Ezequiel. *Farmers in Revolt: The Revolutions of 1893 in the Province of Sante Fe, Argentina.* London: Athlone Press, 1976.
4360. Goldwert, Martin. *Democracy, Militarism, and Nationalism in Argentina, 1930–1966.* Austin: University of Texas Press, 1972.
4361. Greenup, Ruth, and Leonard Greenup. *Revolution Before Breakfast: Argentina, 1941–1946.* Chapel Hill: University of North Carolina Press, 1947.
4362. Halperin-Donghi, Tulio. *Politics, Economics and Society in Argentina in the Revolutionary Period.* New York: Cambridge University Press, 1975.
4363. Hodges, Donald C. *Argentina, 1943–1976: The National Revolution and Resistance.* Albuquerque: University of New Mexico Press, 1976.
4364. Keen, Benjamin. *David Curtis De Forest and the Revolution of Buenos Aires.* Westport, Connecticut: Greenwood, 1947.
4365. Potash, Robert A. *The Army and Politics in Argentina, 1928–1945.* Stanford: Stanford University Press, 1969.
4366. Rock, David. *Politics in Argentina, 1890–1930: The Rise and Fall of Radicalism.* New York: Cambridge University Press, 1975.
4367. Scobie, James R. *Argentina: A City and a Nation.* 2d ed. New York: Oxford University Press, 1971.
4368. _____. *Revolution on the Pampas: A Social History of Argentine Wheat.* Austin: University of Texas Press, 1964.
4369. Smith, Peter H. *Argentina and the Failure of Democracy: Conflict Among the Political Elites, 1904–1955.* Madison: University of Wisconsin Press, 1974.
4370. Snow, Peter G. *Political Forces in Argentina.* New York: Praeger, 1979.

Revolutions in Brazil

The Brazilian Revolution of 1930 (preceded by military revolts such as the Prestes Column in 1924) was a civil-military movement that overthrew the old republic and replaced it with the authoritarian regime of Getúlio Vargas, who ruled as president and dictator until 1945. There was a coup in that year, and others in 1954, 1964, and 1968, with each resulting in authoritarian regimes. Repressive tactics by the government from 1968 swelled the ranks of the Brazilian left and saw increased guerrilla activities. All of this is chronicled in the works below.

Bibliography

4371. Harmon, Ronald, and Bobby Chamberlain. *Brazil: A Working Bibliography.* Tempe: Arizona State University, Center for Latin American Studies, 1975.

Articles

4372. Conniff, Michael L. "The Tenentes in Power: A New Perspective on the Brazilian Revolution of 1930." *Journal of Latin American Studies* 10 (May 1978): 61–82.
4373. Gramont, Sanche de. "How One Pleasant, Scholarly Young Man from Brazil Became a Kidnapping, Gun-Toting, Bombing Revolutionary." *The New York Times Magazine* (15 November 1970).
4374. Nachman, Robert G. "Positivism and Revolution in Brazil's First Republic: The 1904 Revolt." *The Americas* 34 (July 1977): 20–39.
4375. Trusker, Andy. "The Politics of Violence: The Urban Guerrilla in Brazil." *Ramparts* (October 1970): 30.
4376. Wirth, John D. "Tenentismo in the Brazilian Revolution of 1930." *Hispanic American Historical Review* 44:2 (May 1964): 161–79.
4377. Young, Jordon M. "Military Aspects of the 1930 Brazilian Revolution." *Hispanic American Historical Review* 44:2 (May 1964): 180–96.

Books

4378. Alves, Marcio Moreira. *A Grain of Mustard Seed: The Awakening of the Brazilian Revolution.* Garden City, New York: Doubleday, 1973.
4379. Câmara, Dom Hélder. *Revolution Through Peace.* New York: Harper and Row, 1971.
4380. Cunha, Euclides da. *Rebellion in the Backlands.* Translated by S. Putnam. Chicago: University of Chicago Press, 1957.
4381. de Castro, Josue. *Death in the Northeast: Poverty and Revolution in the Northeast of Brazil.* New York: Random House, 1969.
4382. Dulles, John W. F. *Anarchists and Communists in Brazil, 1900–1935.* Austin: University of Texas Press, 1974.

4383. Fernandes, Florestan. *Reflections on the Brazilian Counter-revolution.* Armonk, New York: M. E. Sharpe, 1981.
4384. Flynn, Peter. *Brazil: A Political Analysis.* London: Ernest Benn, 1978.
4385. Horowitz, Irving Louis. *Revolution in Brazil: Politics and Society in a Developing Nation.* New York: E. P. Dutton, 1964.
4386. Macaulay, Neill. *The Prestes Column: A Revolution in Brazil.* New York: Franklin Watts, 1974.
4387. Melo, Father Antônio. *The Coming Revolution in Brazil.* Translated by R. Menzel. New York: Exposition Press, 1970.
4388. Schneider, Ronald M. *The Political System of Brazil: Emergence of a Modernizing Authoritarian Regime, 1864–1970.* New York: Columbia University Press, 1971.
4389. Skidmore, T. L. *Politics in Brazil, 1930–1964: An Experiment in Democracy.* New York: Oxford University Press, 1967.
4390. Stepan, Alfred. *The Military in Politics: Changing Patterns in Brazil.* Princeton: Princeton University Press, 1971.
4391. Wirth, John D. *The Politics of Brazilian Development, 1930–1954.* Stanford: Stanford University Press, 1970.
4392. Young, Jordon M. *The Brazilian Revolution of 1930 and the Aftermath.* New Brunswick, New Jersey: Rutgers University Press, 1967.

Revolutions in Colombia and Camilo Torres

The first revolution in Colombia was the revolt of the Comuneros in 1781 when that land formed part of what was then known as New Granada; the book by John Leddy Phelan (1978) assesses the revolt. Between 1886 and 1930 there were periods of civil war, which the article by Helen Delpar (1976) discusses. The period of social reform/revolution, 1930–1956, is detailed in the book by Vernon Lee Fluharty (1957). Guerrilla activity began in the 1950s and continued sporadically thereafter. One such guerrilla was Camilo Torres, a priest and sociologist from an upper middle class background who concluded that to be a Christian in Colombia was to be a revolutionist. He joined the communist-led guerrilla National Liberation Army because he supported their proposals to combat poverty, hunger, illiteracy, and ineffective public services. Torres was killed in a clash with government forces in 1966. In death he became a source of inspiration for many Latin Americans. Most of the remaining titles deal with Torres and Colombia's guerrilla movements.

Articles

4393. Delpar, Helen. "Road to Revolution. The Labor Party of Colombia, 1886–1899." *The Americas* 32 (January 1976): 48–70.
4394. Hobsbawm, E. J. "The Revolutionary Situation in Colombia." *World Today* 19:6 (June 1963): 248–58.
4395. Hope, Marjorie. "Revolution in Colombia?" *Liberation* 11:6 (September 1966): 18–22.
4396. _____. "Revolution or Reform in Colombia." *Progressive* (July 1966): 25–26.

Books

4397. Broderick, Walter J. *Camilo Torres: A Biography of the Priest-Guerrillero.* Garden City, New York: Doubleday, 1975.
4398. Dix, Robert H. *Colombia: The Political Dimensions of Change.* New Haven: Yale University Press, 1967.
4399. Fluharty, Vernon Lee. *Dance of the Millions: Military Rule and the Social Revolution in Colombia, 1930–1956.* Pittsburgh: University of Pittsburgh Press, 1957.
4400. Gerassi, John, ed. *Revolutionary Priest: The Complete Writings and Messages of Camilo Torres.* New York: Random House, 1971.
4401. Guzman, German. *Camilo Torres.* New York: Sheed and Ward, 1969.
4402. Martz, John D. *Colombia: A Contemporary Political Survey.* Chapel Hill: University of North Carolina Press, 1962.
4403. Maullin, Richard. *Soldiers, Guerrillas and Politics in Colombia.* Lexington, Massachusetts: Lexington Books, 1973.
4404. Payne, James. *Patterns of Conflict in Colombia.* New Haven: Yale University Press, 1968.
4405. Phelan, John Leddy. *The People and the King: The Comunero Revolution in Colombia, 1781.* Madison: University of Wisconsin Press, 1978.
4406. Torres, Camilo R. *Camilo Torres: His Life and His Message.* Translated by V. M. O'Grady. Springfield, Illinois: Templegate, 1968.

Revolution in Peru

Revolution in Peru dates from the late eighteenth century and the Túpac Amaru Revolt; see the articles and books by Leon G. Campbell (1978) and L. E. Fisher (1966). Other upheavals, mostly Indian revolts, occurred in the nineteenth and early twentieth centuries; these are noted in Jeffrey L. Klaiber's book (1977). In the area of revolutionary ideology José Mariátegui attempted to merge Indian traditions with Marxism; see the article and book by John M. Baines (1970, 1972). The revolutionary

Aprista movement from the 1930s on is the subject of the books by Grant Hilliker (1971), Harry Kantor (1966), and P. F. Klaren (1973). The book by Héctor Béjar (1970) is by a communist guerrilla leader. Finally, 1968 saw the beginning of Peru's "ambiguous revolution" in which a military junta, taking control following a coup, nationalized key industries and natural resources; since 1975 that revolution has halted its advance. Most of the remaining works below deal with the 1968 revolution.

Articles

4407. Baines, John M. "José Mariátegui and the Ideology of Revolution in Peru." *Rocky Mountain Social Science Journal* (October 1970): 109-16.
4408. Campbell, Leon G. "The Army of Peru and the Túpac Amaru Revolt, 1780-1784." In *Historia, Problema y Promesa,* edited by F. M. Quesada et al. Lima, Peru: Catholic University, 1978.
4409. _____. "Church and State in Colonial Peru: The Bishop of Cuzco and the Túpac Amaru Rebellion of 1780." *Journal of Church and State* 22:2 (Spring 1980): 251-70.
4410. _____. "Rebel or Royalist? Bishop Juan Manuel de Moscoso y Peralta and the Túpac Amaru Revolt in Peru, 1780-1784." *Revista de Historia de America* 86 (July-December 1978): 135-67.
4411. Chaplin, David. "Peru's Postponed Revolution." *World Politics* 20:3 (April 1968): 393-420.
4412. Conine, Ernest. "Is Peru's Military Revolution a Key to the Future?" *Los Angeles Times* (22 April 1973).
4413. Goodsell, Charles T. "That Confounding Revolution in Peru." *Current History* 68 (January 1975): 20-23.
4414. Klaiber, Jeffrey L. "Religion and Revolution in Peru: 1920-1945." *The Americas* 31 (January 1975): 289-312.
4415. Lowenthal, Abraham F. "Peru's Ambiguous Revolution." *Foreign Affairs* 52 (July 1974): 799-817.
4416. Maitan, Livio. "The Revolt of the Peruvian Campesinos." *International Socialist Review* 26 (Spring 1965): 38-41.
4417. Niedergang, Marcel. "Revolutionary Nationalism in Peru." *Foreign Affairs* 49 (April 1971): 454-63.
4418. Palmer, David Scott. "Peru: Authoritarianism and Reform." In *Latin American Politics and Development,* edited by H. J. Wiarda and H. F. Kline. Boston: Houghton Mifflin, 1979.
4419. "Peru: Bourgeois Revolution and Class Struggle." *Latin American Perspectives* 4:3 (Summer 1977): 2-159.
4420. Werlich, David P. "Peru: The Lame Duck 'Revolution.'" *Current History* 76 (February 1979): 62.
4421. _____. "The Peruvian Revolution in Crisis." *Current History* 72 (February 1977): 61.

Books

4422. Baines, John M. *Revolution in Peru: Mariátegui and the Myth.* Birmingham: University of Alabama Press, 1972.
4423. Béjar, Héctor. *Peru 1965: Notes on a Guerrilla Experience.* New York: Monthly Review Press, 1970.
4424. Campbell, Leon G. *The Military and Society in Colonial Peru, 1750-1810.* Philadelphia: American Philosophical Society, 1978.
4425. Chaplin, David, ed. *Peruvian Nationalism: A Corporatist Revolution.* New Brunswick, New Jersey: Transaction Books, 1976.
4426. Fisher, L. E. *The Last Inca Revolt, 1780-1783.* Norman: University of Oklahoma Press, 1966.
4427. Fitzgerald, E. V. K. *The State and Economic Development: Peru Since 1968.* Cambridge: Cambridge University Press, 1976.
4428. Handelman, Howard. *Struggle in the Andes: Peasant Political Participation in Peru.* Austin: University of Texas Press, 1974.
4429. Hilliker, Grant. *The Politics of Reform in Peru: The Aprista and Other Mass Parties of Latin America.* Baltimore: Johns Hopkins University Press, 1971.
4430. Kantor, Harry. *The Ideology and Program of the Peruvian Aprista Movement.* New York: Octagon Books, 1966.
4431. Klaiber, Jeffrey L. *Religion and Revolution in Peru, 1824-1976.* Notre Dame, Indiana: University of Notre Dame Press, 1977.
4432. Klaren, P. F. *Modernization, Dislocation, and Aprismo: Origins of the Peruvian Aprista Party.* Austin: University of Texas Press, 1973.
4433. Lowenthal, Abraham F., ed. *The Peruvian Experiment: Continuity and Change under Military Rule.* Princeton: Princeton University Press, 1975.
4434. Palmer, David Scott. *Revolution from Above: Military, Government, and Population Participation in Peru, 1968-1972.* Ithaca: Cornell University Press, 1973.
4435. Philip, G. D. *The Rise and Fall of the Peruvian Military Radicals, 1968-1976.* Atlantic Highlands, New Jersey: Humanities Press, 1978.
4436. Pike, Frederick B. *The Modern History of Peru.* New York: Praeger, 1967.
4437. Tullis, F. L. *Lord and Peasant in Peru: A Paradigm of Political and Social Change.* Cambridge, Massachusetts: Harvard University Press, 1970.

Revolutions in Venezuela

The foundations for revolutionary change in Venezuela were laid with the students' rebellion of 1928. Beginning in the late 1930s, dissident political parties were given greater latitude, and when the election of 1945 seemed to presage more difficult times, a revolution brought about change. This revolution is most thoroughly examined in the book by Robert J. Alexander (1964). Communist and guerrilla activities have been in evidence sporadically since the late 1950s.

Articles

4438. Burggraaff, Winfield J. "The Military Origins of Venezuela's 1945 Revolution." *Caribbean Studies* (October 1971): 35–54.

4439. Slote, Walter H. "Case Analysis of a Revolutionary." In *A Strategy for Research on Social Policy*, edited by F. Bonilla and J. S. Michelena. Cambridge, Massachusetts: M.I.T. Press, 1967.

Books

4440. Alexander, Robert J. *The Communist Party of Venezuela*. Stanford: Hoover Institution, 1969.

4441. _____ . *The Venezuelan Democratic Revolution: Profile of the Regime of Romulo Betancourt*. New Brunswick, New Jersey: Rutgers University Press, 1964.

4442. Bonilla, Frank, and Jose A. Michelena. *The Politics of Change in Venezuela*. 3 vols. Cambridge, Massachusetts: M.I.T. Press, 1967–1971.

4443. Levine, Daniel H. *Conflict and Political Change in Venezuela*. Princeton: Princeton University Press, 1973.

4444. Powell, John D. *Political Mobilization of the Venezuelan Peasant*. Cambridge, Massachusetts: Harvard University Press, 1971.

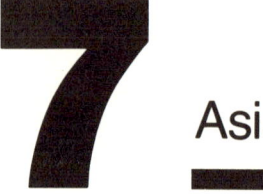

Asia

"If revolution seeks to correct social injustice, its first act, when power is seized, should be to guarantee a certain freedom in the midst of its efforts to establish a new justice—otherwise the creation of a new and equally intolerable tyranny becomes inevitable."
Albert Camus

Where the history of Europe and the Americas has been generally characterized by change, both revolutionary and evolutionary, the history of Asia—at least prior to the twentieth century—is best described by stasis. Buddhism, Hinduism, Taoism, and Confucianism all espouse philosophies and attitudes toward life markedly different from Judeo-Christian traditions. From the late fifteenth century the West confronted the East, extending its influence and control, and reenforcing its sense of cultural superiority. By the nineteenth century the peoples of Asia had become increasingly dissatisfied with their position vis-à-vis Europe. Imperialism was a system whereby Asian affairs were conducted, Asian resources exploited, and Asian people employed (and discriminated against) all for the benefit of foreigners, mostly Europeans. In brief, Asian revolutions burst forth in large measure as a reaction to economic, political, social, and cultural-psychological humiliation.

But Asian revolutions were not simply attempts to cast off everything foreign. On the contrary, those who revolted actually sought to imitate and profit from Western science, industry, and power, but in order that they might preserve their own identity and independence.

Other factors influenced the coming of revolutions in Asia. Among them were (1) the Russo-Japanese War (1905) in which an Asian people defeated a great European power for the first time; (2) World War I in which Asian economics were stimulated, Asian minds were moved by Woodrow Wilson's Fourteen Points, and from which concessions followed; and (3) the Russian Revolution in which not only capitalism, but imperialism as well was denounced. For Asians, nationalism became as potent a force in revolutionary activity as any other.

This chapter concentrates on the major and many of the minor Asian revolutions and revolutionists. Those of China dominate these pages, but significant entries are also for revolutionary upheavals in India, Vietnam, and many of the other Asian countries; the table of contents lists and the section introductions explain which these are. The titles immediately below are divided into several parts. After the various bibliographies and historiographies, there are subsections on China and India, and miscellaneous subsections on the rest of the continent; the titles

among them are different from those in the rest of the sections in this chapter.
For China there are books on the pre-1911 period by John K. Fairbank and Liu Kwang-Ching (1979), Albert Feuerwerker (1975), and Philip A. Kuhn (1970), on the post-1911 period by Jean Chesneaux (1979), Jürgen Domes (1973), and Wang Gungwu (1977), and on the general history of China and her revolutions by, among others, Lucien Bianco (1971), Jean Chesneaux et al (1976, 1977), O. Edmund Chubb (1964), Wolfgang Franke (1971), John Robottom (1969), David N. Rowe (1959), and Franz Schurmann and Orville Schell (1967). In addition, there are works on other Chinese uprisings such as those on the May Fourth Movement by Chow Tse-tung (1960) and Lin Yu-Sheng (1978), and on peasant revolts by Jean Chesneaux (1973). There are works on leadership in China, such as the article by Robert E. Bedeski (1978), and the books by Chün-tu Hsüeh (1971) and Jane L. Price (1975). There are books on ideas and ideology by James C. Hsuing (1970), Franz Schurmann (1968), Benjamin Schwartz (1968), and Chester C. Tan (1971). There are works on Marxist influences on China, such as the articles by Arif Dirlik (1974), Albert Feuerwerker (1961), and Karl A. Wittfogel (1962), and the book by Maurice Meisner (1967). And there are books on foreign relations by John K. Fairbank (1958), Joseph R. Levenson (1971), Michael Lindsay (1955), and Peter Van Ness (1970). Many of these would be helpful in studying any one specific Chinese revolution.

The works in the subsection on India either are not concerned with the Sepoy Mutiny and Gandhi and the Indian Revolution, or they cover a broader spectrum of Indian history.

Among the works in the miscellaneous subsections are several comparative studies, such as the articles by Robert E. Bedeski (1977), King C. Chen (1975), Richard Gaulton and Hiroshi Itoh (1976), and Robert S. Newman (1979), regional studies, such as the books by W. M. Ball (1952), Geoffrey Fairbairn (1968), Milton Osborne (1971), and Victor Purcell (1962), works on communism in Asia, such as those by A. Doak Barnett (1976) and Robert A. Scalapino (1965), works on nationalism, such as those by R. S. Chavran (1973), Michael Leifer (1970), and J. Romein and J. E. Romein (1962), and works on Asia and the West, such as those by Wilfred Burchett (1963) and Robert J. Lifton (1973). There are also works on revolutionary activity in Pakistan by Tariq Ali (1971) and Herbert Feldman (1967), in Burma by U Ba Maw (1968) and E. Sarkisyanz (1965), in Japan by Stephen S. Large (1977) and Paul Akamatsu (1972), in Bangladesh by Lawrence Lifschultz (1979), in Mongolia by Fujiko Isono (1976), and in Tibet by Dawa Norbu (1979).

Bibliographies/General

4445. *Bibliography of Asian Studies,* an annual publication of the *Journal of Asian Studies.* Ann Arbor, Michigan: Association for Asian Studies.
4446. Birnbaum, Eleazar. *Books on Asia from the Near East to the Far East.* Toronto: University of Toronto Press, 1971.

4447. Nunn, G. Raymond. *Asia: A Selected and Annotated Guide to Reference Works.* Cambridge, Massachusetts: M.I.T. Press, 1971.

Bibliographies/China

4448. Berton, Peter, and Eugene Wu. *Contemporary China: A Research Guide.* Stanford: Hoover Institution, 1967.
4449. *China Old and New: A Comprehensive Bibliography.* Edited by Howard Spriggle. Norwood, Pennsylvania: Norwood Editions, 1973.
4450. Harris, Richard. *Modern China.* Reader's Guides, 4th ser., no. 5. Cambridge: Cambridge University Press, 1961.
4451. Hucker, Charles O. *China: A Critical Bibliography.* Tucson: University of Arizona Press, 1962.
4452. _____. *Chinese History, A Bibliographic Review.* Washington, D.C.: American Historical Association Service Center for Teachers of History, 1958.
4453. Kirby, E. Stuart, ed. *Contemporary China: Economic and Social Studies, Documents, Bibliography, Chronology.* 4 vols. Hong Kong: University of Hong Kong, 1955-1960.
4454. Phillips, Leona, and Jill Phillips. *Chinese History: An Annotated Bibliography.* New York: Gordon Press, 1978.
4455. Sorich, Richard, ed. *Contemporary China: A Bibliography of Reports on China Published by the United States Joint Publications Research Service.* New York: Readex Microprint Corp., 1961.
4456. Tsien, Tsuen-Hsuin, and James K. Chen, eds. *China: An Annotated Bibliography of Bibliographies.* Boston: G. K. Hall, 1978.
4457. Wu, Eugene. *Leaders of Twentieth-Century China: An Annotated Bibliography.* Stanford: Hoover Institution, 1956.
4458. Yuan Tung-li. *China in Western Literature.* New Haven: Far Eastern Publications, Yale University, 1958.

Bibliographies/South Asia

4459. Case, Margaret H. *South Asia History, 1750-1950: A Guide to Periodicals, Dissertations, and Newspapers.* Princeton: Princeton University Press, 1968.
4460. Pearson, J. D. *South Asian Bibliography: A Handbook and Guide.* Atlantic Highlands, New Jersey: Humanities Press, 1979.
4461. Wilson, Patrick. *Government and Politics of India and Pakistan, 1885-1955: A Bibliography of Works in Western Languages.* Berkeley: University of California Press, 1956.
4462. _____. *South Asia: A Selected Bibliography on India, Pakistan, Ceylon.* New York: American Institute of Pacific Relations, 1957.

Bibliographies/Southeast Asia

4463. Hobbs, Cecil C. *Southeast Asia: An Annotated Bibliography.* Washington, D.C.: Library of Congress, 1952.
4464. Tregonning, Kennedy G. *Southeast Asia: A Critical Bibliography.* Tucson: University of Arizona Press, 1969.

Bibliography/Northeast Asia

4465. Kerner, Robert J. *Northeastern Asia: A Selected Bibliography.* 2 vols. Berkeley: University of California Press, 1939.

Historiographies

4466. Crane, Robert I. *The History of India: Its Study and Interpretation.* Washington, D.C.: American Historical Association Service Center for Teachers of History, 1958.
4467. _____ . *A History of South Asia.* Washington, D.C.: American Historical Association Pamphlets, 1973.
4468. Fairbank, John K. *New Views of China's Tradition and Modernization.* Washington, D.C.: American Historical Association Service Center for Teachers of History, 1968.
4469. Quan, Lau-king. *Introduction to Asia: A Selective Guide to Background Reading.* Washington, D.C.: Library of Congress, 1955.

China/General

Articles

4470. Armentrout, L. Eve. "The Canton Rising of 1902-1903: Reformers, Revolutionaries and the Second Taiping." *Modern Asian Studies* 10 (February 1976): 83-105.
4471. Bedeski, Robert E. "State and Revolution in China after Mao: Leadership, Sovereignty, and the 'Three Worlds.'" *Pacific Affairs* 51 (Spring 1978): 67-83.
4472. Chan, F. Gilbert, and Ka-Chef Yip. "Nationalism in China: Chinese and Japanese Sources." *Canadian Review of Studies in Nationalism* 6 (1979): 80-98.
4473. Chen, Yu-Shih. "Mao Tun and the Wild Roses: A Study of the Psychology of Revolutionary Commitment." *China Quarterly* 78 (June 1979): 296-323.
4474. Dirlik, Arif. "Mirror to Revolution: Early Marxist Images of Chinese History." *Journal of Asian Studies* 33:2 (February 1974): 193-223.
4475. _____ . "National Development and Social Revolution in Early Chinese Marxist Thought." *China Quarterly* 58 (April-May 1974): 286-309.
4476. Feuerwerker, Albert. "China's History in Marxian Dress." *American Historical Review* 66:2 (January 1961): 323-53.
4477. Gillin, Donald G. "'Peasant Nationalism' in the History of Chinese Communism." *Journal of Asian Studies* 23:2 (February 1964): 269-89.
4478. Johnson, Chalmers. "The Two Chinese Revolutions." *China Quarterly* 39 (July-September 1969): 12-29.
4479. Rawlinson, Frank. "A Study of the Rebellions in China." *Chinese Recorder* 36 (March 1905).
4480. Scalapino, Robert A., and H. Shiffren. "Early Socialist Currents in the Chinese Revolutionary Movement." *Journal of Asian Studies* 18:3 (May 1959): 321-42.

286 / Asia

4481. Thaxton, Ralph. "Peasants, Capitalism, and Revolution: On Capitalism as a Force for Liberation in Revolutionary China." *Comparative Political Studies* 12 (October 1979): 289-334.
4482. Wakeman, Frederic, Jr. "Rebellion and Revolution: The Study of Popular Movements in Chinese History." *Journal of Asian Studies* 36:4 (August 1977): 201-38.
4483. Wittfogel, Karl A. "The Marxist View of China." *China Quarterly* 11 (July-September 1962): 1-20.

Books

4484. Bianco, Lucien. *Origins of the Chinese Revolution, 1915-1949.* Translated by M. Bell. Stanford: Stanford University Press, 1971.
4485. Bown, Colin, and Tony Edwards. *Revolution in China, 1911-1949.* Exeter, New Hampshire: Heinemann Educational Books, 1974.
4486. Chai, Winberg, ed. *The Search for a New China: A Capsule History, Ideology, Leadership of the Chinese Communist Party.* New York: G. P. Putnam's, 1975.
4487. Ch'en, Jerome. *China and the West: Society and Culture, 1815-1937.* Bloomington: Indiana University Press, 1979.
4488. Ch'en, Kung-Po. *Communist Movement in China.* New York: Octagon Books, 1966.
4489. Chesneaux, Jean. *China: The People's Republic, 1949-1976.* Translated by P. Auster and L. Davis. New York: Pantheon, 1979.
4490. _____. *Peasant Revolts in China, 1840-1949.* Translated by C. A. Curwen. New York: W. W. Norton, 1973.
4491. Chesneaux, Jean; Françoise Le Barbier; and Marie-Claire Bergère. *China: From the 1911 Revolution to Liberation.* Translated by P. Auster and L. Davis. New York: Pantheon, 1977.
4492. Chesneaux, Jean; Marianne Bastid; and Marie-Claire Bergère. *China: From the Opium Wars to the 1911 Revolution.* Translated by A. Destenay. New York: Pantheon, 1976.
4493. Chow Tse-tung. *The May Fourth Movement.* Cambridge, Massachusetts: Harvard University Press, 1960.
4494. Chubb, O. Edmund. *Twentieth Century China.* New York: Columbia University Press, 1964.
4495. Crook, David, and Isabel Crook. *Revolution in a Chinese Village: Ten Mile Inn.* London: Routledge and Kegan Paul, 1959.
4496. Davis, Fei-Ling. *Primitive Revolutionaries of China.* Exeter, New Hampshire: Heinemann, 1979.
4497. Domes, Jürgen. *The Internal Politics of China, 1949-1972.* Translated by R. Machetzki. New York: Praeger, 1973.
4498. Elvin, Mark. *The Pattern of Chinese Past.* Stanford: Stanford University Press, 1973.
4499. Fairbank, John K. *The United States and China.* Cambridge, Massachusetts: Harvard University Press, 1958.
4500. _____, and Liu Kwang-Ching, eds. *The Cambridge History of China.* Vol 2. *Late Ch'ing 1800-1911.* New York: Cambridge University Press, 1979.
4501. Feuerwerker, Albert. *Rebellion in Nineteenth-Century China.* Michigan Papers in Chinese Studies, no. 21. Ann Arbor: Center for Chinese Studies, University of Michigan, 1975.

4502. Franke, Wolfgang. *A Century of Chinese Revolution, 1851-1949.* New York: Harper and Row, 1971.
4503. Grieder, Jerome B. *Hu Shih and the Chinese Renaissance: Liberalism in the Chinese Revolution, 1917-1937.* Cambridge, Massachusetts: Harvard University Press, 1970.
4504. Gungwu, Wang. *China and the World since 1949: The Impact of Independence, Modernity and Revolution.* New York: St. Martin's Press, 1977.
4505. Holcombe. Arthur N. *The Spirit of the Chinese Revolution.* New York: Alfred A. Knopf, 1930.
4506. Hsüeh Chün-tu. *Huang Hsing and the Chinese Revolution.* Stanford: Stanford University Press, 1961.
4507. _____ , ed. *Revolutionary Leaders of Modern China.* New York: Oxford University Press, 1971.
4508. Hsuing, James C. *Ideology and Practice: The Evolution of Chinese Communism.* New York: Praeger, 1970.
4509. Hu Chang-tu, et al. *China: Its People, Its Society, Its Culture.* New Haven: Human Relations Area Files, 1960.
4510. Jordan, Donald A. *The Northern Expedition: China's National Revolution of 1926-1928.* Honolulu: University Press of Hawaii, 1976.
4511. Kuhn, Philip A. *Rebellion and Its Enemies in Late Imperial China: Militarization and Social Structure, 1796-1864.* Cambridge, Massachusetts: Harvard University Press, 1970.
4512. Lattimore, Owen. *History and Revolution in China.* Atlantic Highlands, New Jersey: Humanities Press, 1970.
4513. Levenson, Joseph R. *Liang Ch'i-ch'ao and the Mind of Modern China.* Cambridge, Massachusetts: Harvard University Press, 1959.
4514. _____ . *Revolution and Cosmopolitanism: The Western Stage and the Chinese Stages.* Berkeley: University of California Press, 1971.
4515. Lewis, Charlton M. *Prologue to the Chinese Revolution: The Transformation of Ideas and Institutions in Hunan Province, 1891-1907.* Cambridge, Massachusetts: East Asian Research Center, Harvard University, 1976.
4516. Li Chien-nung. *The Political History of China, 1840-1928.* Princeton: Princeton University Press, 1956.
4517. Lindsay, Michael. *China and the Cold War, A Study in International Politics.* New York: Cambridge University Press, 1955.
4518. Mackerras, Colin, ed. *China: The Impact of Revolution.* New York: Longman, 1976.
4519. Maitan, Livio. *Party, Army and Masses in China.* New York: Schocken, 1976.
4520. Meadows, Thomas Taylor. *The Chinese and Their Rebellions.* Stanford: Academic Reprints, 1953.
4521. Meisner, Maurice. *Li Ta-chao and the Origins of Chinese Marxism.* Cambridge, Massachusetts: Harvard University Press, 1967.
4522. Mende, Tibor. *The Chinese Revolution.* London: Thames and Hudson, 1961.
4523. Nee, Victor, and James Peck, eds. *China's Uninterrupted Revolution: From 1840 to the Present.* New York: Pantheon, 1976.
4524. P'eng Shu-tse. *The Chinese Communist Party in Power.* New York: Monad Press, 1980.
4525. Perry, Elizabeth J. *Rebels and Revolutionaries in North China, 1845-1945.* Stanford: Stanford University Press, 1980.

4526. Price, Jane L. *Cadres, Commanders, and Commissars: The Training of the Chinese Communist Leadership.* Boulder, Colorado: Westview Press, 1975.
4527. Robottom, John. *China in Revolution.* New York: McGraw-Hill, 1969.
4528. Ronning, Chester. *A Memoir of China in Revolution: From the Boxer Rebellion to the People's Republic.* New York: Pantheon Books, 1974.
4529. Rowe, David N. *Modern China: A Brief History.* Princeton: D. Van Nostrand, 1959. Contains documents as well.
4530. Roy, M. N. *Revolution and Counterrevolution in China.* Calcutta: Renaissance Publishing Company, 1948.
4531. Scalapino, Robert A., ed. *Elites in the People's Republic of China.* Seattle: University of Washington Press, 1972.
4532. Schurmann, Franz. *Ideology and Organization in Communist China.* 2d ed. Berkeley: University of California Press, 1968.
4533. _____ , and Orville Schell, eds. *The China Reader II: Republican China: Nationalism, War, and the Rise of Communism, 1911–1949.* New York: Random House, 1967.
4534. _____ , eds. *The China Reader III: Communist China: Revolutionary Reconstruction and International Confrontation, 1949 to the Present.* New York: Random House, 1967.
4535. Schwartz, Benjamin. *Communism and China: Ideology in Flux.* Cambridge, Massachusetts: Harvard University Press, 1968.
4536. Sheridan, James E. *China in Disintegration: The Republican Era in Chinese History, 1912–1949.* Riverside, New Jersey: Free Press, 1975.
4537. Simone, Vera, ed. *China in Revolution.* Greenwich, Connecticut: Fawcett World Library, 1968.
4538. Solomon, Richard H. *A Revolution Is Not a Dinner Party: A Feast of Images of the Maoist Transformation of China.* Garden City, New York: Doubleday, 1975.
4539. Suttmeier, Richard P. *Science, Technology and China's Drive for Modernization.* Stanford: Hoover Institution. 1980.
4540. Tan, Chester C. *Chinese Political Thought in the Twentieth Century.* Garden City, New York: Doubleday, 1971.
4541. Thornton, Richard C. *China: A Political History, 1917–1980.* Boulder, Colorado: Westview Press, 1981.
4542. _____ . *China: The Struggle for Power, 1917–1972.* Bloomington: Indiana University Press, 1974.
4543. Topping, Seymour. *Journey Between Two Chinas.* New York: Harper and Row, 1972.
4544. Trager, Frank N., and William Henderson, eds. *Communist China, 1949– 1969.* New York: New York University Press, 1970.
4545. Trotsky, Leon. *Problems of the Chinese Revolution.* 2d ed. Translated by M. Shachtman. New York: Paragon Book Gallery, 1962.
4546. Van Ness, Peter. *Revolution and Chinese Foreign Policy: Peking's Support for Wars of National Liberation.* Berkeley: University of California Press, 1970.
4547. Vohra, Ranbir, ed. *The Chinese Revolution, 1900–1950.* Boston: Houghton Mifflin, 1974.
4548. Waller, Derek J. *The Government and Politics of Communist China.* Garden City, New York: Doubleday, 1971.

4549. Waung, W. S. *Revolution and Liberation: A Short History of Modern China from 1900-1970.* Atlantic Highlands, New Jersey: Humanities Press, 1971.
4550. Wilson, Dick. *Anatomy of China.* New York: Weybright and Talley, 1967.
4551. Yang, C. K. *Religion in Chinese Society.* Berkeley: University of California Press, 1961.
4552. Yu-Sheng, Lin. *Crisis of Chinese Consciousness: Radical Antiradicalism in the May Fourth Era.* Madison: University of Wisconsin Press, 1978.

India/General

Articles

4553. Gordon, Leonard A. "Portrait of a Bengal Revolutionary." *Journal of Asian Studies* 27:2 (February 1968): 197-216.
4554. Moraes, Dom. "Indian Revolutionaries With a Chinese Accent." *The New York Times Magazine* (8 November 1970).
4555. Sankaran, Nair V. "An Episode of Terrorism in South India." *Journal of Kerala Studies* 5 (December 1978): 513-28.

Books

4556. Edwardes, Michael. *British India, 1772-1947.* New York: Taplinger, 1968.
4557. _____. *The History of India.* New York: Grosset and Dunlap, 1970.
4558. Majumdar, Ramesh Chandra, et al. *An Advanced History of India.* 2d ed. New York: St. Martin's Press, 1959.
4559. Misra, B. B. *The Administrative History of India, 1834-1947.* Bombay: Oxford University Press, 1970.
4560. Narayan, Jayaprakash. *Prison Diary.* Seattle: University of Washington Press, 1978.
4561. _____. *Towards Total Revolution.* 4 vols. Seattle: University of Washington Press, 1979.
4562. Seal, Anil. *The Emergence of Indian Nationalism.* London: Cambridge University Press, 1968.
4563. Wallbank, Thomas W. *India: A Survey of the Heritage and Growth of Indian Nationalism.* New York: H. Holt, 1948.

Miscellaneous

Articles

4564. Ali, Tariq. "Rebellion in Pakistan: Prelude to the Indian Revolution?" *Ramparts* (June 1971): 16-19.
4565. Bedeski, Robert E. "The Concept of the State: Sun Yat-sen and Mao Tse-tung." *China Quarterly* 70 (June 1977): 338-54.

4566. Chen, King C. "Some Comparisons between the Chinese and Vietnamese Revolutions." *Asian Profile* 3 (June 1975): 227–42.
4567. Fatimi, S. "The Kemalist Revolution and the Pakistan Freedom Movement: A Study in Historical Parallelism." *Journal of the Regional Cultural Institute* 7:1 (1974): 15–29.
4568. Gaulton, Richard, and Hiroshi Itoh. "Comparative Revolutions: The 1911 Revolution in China and the Meiji Restoration in Japan." *Asian Thought and Society* 1 (September 1976): 145–62.
4569. Heder, Stephen. "Kampuchea's Armed Struggle: The Origins of an Independent Revolution." *Bulletin of Concerned Asian Scholars* 11 (January-March 1979): 2–23.
4570. Isono, Fujiko. "The Mongolian Revolution of 1921." *Modern Asian Studies* 10 (July 1976): 375–94.
4571. Large, Stephen S. "The Romance of Revolution in Japanese Anarchism and Communism during the Taishō Period." *Modern Asian Studies* 11 (July 1977): 441–68.
4572. McColl, Robert W. "A Political Geography of Revolution: China, Vietnam, and Thailand." *Journal of Conflict Resolution* 11:2 (June 1967): 153–67.
4573. Mast, Herman, III, and William G. Saywell. "Revolution out of Tradition: The Political Ideology of Tai Chi-t'ao." *Journal of Asian Studies* 34:1 (November 1974): 73–98.
4574. Newman, Robert S. "Brahmin and Mandarin: A Comparison of the Cambodian and Vietnamese Revolutions (Part I). *Asian Quarterly* 2 (1979): 149–64.
4575. _____. "Brahmin and Mandarin: A Comparison of the Cambodian and Vietnamese Revolutions (Part II)." *Asian Quarterly* 3 (1979): 203–13.
4576. Norbu, Dawa. "The 1959 Tibetan Rebellion: An Interpretation." *China Quarterly* 77 (March 1979): 74–93.
4577. Recto, Manuelito M. "Prologue to a Revolution." *Bulletin of American History Collections* 7 (January-March 1979): 50–74.
4578. Thompson, Robert. "Revolutionary War in Southeast Asia." *Orbis* 19 (Fall 1975): 958–70.
4579. Yoke, Kitazawa. "Vietnam, Cambodia and China: The Political Roots of Revolution and War." *Ampo* 11: 1 (1979): 10–12.

Books

4580. Akamatsu, Paul. *Meiji 1868: Revolution and Counter-Revolution in Japan.* Translated by M. Kochan. New York: Harper and Row, 1972.
4581. Ball, W. M. *Nationalism and Communism in East Asia.* Melbourne: Melbourne University Press, 1952.
4582. Ba Maw, U. *Breakthrough in Burma: Memoirs of a Revolution, 1939–46.* New Haven: Yale University Press, 1968.
4583. Barnett, A. Doak. *Communist China and Asia.* New York: Harper and Row, 1960.
4584. _____ , ed. *Communist Strategies in Asia.* Westport, Connecticut: Greenwood, 1976.
4585. Burchett, Wilfred. *The Furtive War: The United States in Vietnam and Laos.* New York: International Publishers, 1963.

4586. Chavran, R. S. *Nationalism in Asia.* Columbia, Missouri: South Asia Books, 1973.
4587. Fairbairn, Geoffrey. *Revolutionary Warfare and Communist Strategy: The Threat to South East Asia.* London: Faber and Faber, 1968.
4588. Feldman, Herbert. *Revolution in Pakistan: A Study of the Martial Law Administration.* New York: Oxford University Press, 1967.
4589. Girling, John L. S. *People's War: Conditions and Consequences in China and South East Asia.* New York: Praeger, 1969.
4590. Gough, Kathleen, and Hari P. Sharma, eds. *Imperialism and Revolution in South Asia.* New York: Monthly Review Press, 1973.
4591. Hudson, G. F., ed. *Reform and Revolution in Asia.* New York: St. Martin's Press, 1973.
4592. Lattimore, Owen. *Nationalism and Revolution in Mongolia.* New York: Oxford University Press, 1955.
4593. Leifer, Michael. *Nationalism, Revolution and Evolution in South-East Asia.* New York: International Publications Service, 1970.
4594. Lewis, John Wilson, ed. *Peasant Rebellion and Communist Revolution in Asia.* Stanford: Stanford University Press, 1974.
4595. Lifschultz, Lawrence. *Bangladesh: The Unfinished Revolution.* London: Zed Press, 1979.
4596. Lifton, Robert J. *America and the Asian Revolutions.* Edison, New Jersey: Transaction Books, 1973.
4597. McVey, Ruth T. *The Calcutta Conference and the Southeast Asian Uprising.* New York: Cornell University, Southeast Asia Program, 1958.
4598. Osborne, Milton. *Region of Revolt: Focus on Southeast Asia.* Baltimore: Penguin Books, 1971.
4599. Purcell, Victor. *The Revolution in Southeast Asia.* London: Thames and Hudson, 1962.
4600. Romein, J., and J. E. Romein. *The Asian Century: A History of Modern Nationalism in Asia.* Translated by R. T. Clark. Berkeley: University of California Press, 1962.
4601. Sarkisyanz, Emanuel. *Buddhist Backgrounds of the Burmese Revolution.* The Hague: Martinus Nijhoff, 1965.
4602. Scalapino, Robert A., ed. *The Communist Revolution in Asia: Tactics, Goals and Achievements.* Englewood Cliffs, New Jersey: Prentice-Hall, 1965.
4603. _____ , and Bernard B. Fall, eds. *The Communist Revolution in Asia: The Pathet Lao: A Liberation Movement.* Englewood Cliffs, New Jersey: Prentice-Hall, 1965.
4604. Scott, James C. *The Moral Economy of the Peasant: Subsistence and Rebellion in Southeast Asia.* New Haven: Yale University Press, 1976.
4605. Shaplen, Robert. *Time Out of Hand: Revolution and Reaction in Southeast Asia.* New York: Harper and Row, 1969.
4606. _____ . *A Turning Wheel: Three Decades of the Asian Revolution.* New York: Random House, 1979.
4607. Trager, Frank N., ed. *Marxism in Southeast Asia: A Study of Four Countries.* Stanford: Stanford University Press, 1959.
4608. Zasloff, Joseph J., and MacAlister Brown, eds. *Communism in Indochina: New Perspectives.* Lexington, Massachusetts: Lexington Books, 1975.

Taiping Rebellion, 1850–1864

T'ai-p'ing means "great peace." Ironically, in this monumental popular upheaval some twenty million people are thought to have died. Economic pressures, including inflation and rising taxes, as well as resentment against foreign intervention and the ruling Manchu dynasty led to the Taiping Rebellion. The protracted nature of the struggle, the chief aim of which was the establishment of a popular government, saw China sink into chronic banditry and disorder. After fourteen years the Manchus, with some European assistance, suppressed the rebellion. Among the best works on the subject are the article by Philip A. Kuhn (1977) and the books by Albert Feuerwerker (1975), Jen Yu-Wen (1973), Robert H. T. Lin (1979), Franz Michael (1966), Vincent Y. C. Shih (1967), and Ssu-yü Teng (1950, 1977).

Historiography

4609. Ssu-yü Teng. *Historiography of the Taiping Rebellion.* Cambridge, Massachusetts: Harvard University Press, 1962.

Documents

4610. Cheng, J. C. *Chinese Sources for the Taiping Rebellion, 1850–1864.* New York: Paragon, 1963.
4611. Davids, Jules, ed. *The Treaty System and the Taiping Rebellion, 1842–1860.* 21 vols. Wilmington, Delaware: Scholarly Resources, 1979.

Articles

4612. Kuhn, Philip A. "Origins of the Taiping Vision: Cross Cultural Dimensions of a Chinese Rebellion." *Comparative Studies in Social History* 19:3 (July 1977): 350–66.
4613. Laffey, Ella S. "In the Wake of the Taipings: Some Patterns of Local Revolt in Kwangsi Province, 1850–1875." *Modern Asian Studies* 10 (February 1976): 65–81.
4614. Taylor, George E. "The Taiping Rebellion." *Chinese Social and Political Science Review* 16:4 (1932–1933): 545–614.

Books

4615. Anderson, Lady Flavia G. *The Rebel Emperor.* Garden City, New York: Doubleday, 1959.
4616. Boardman, Eugene Powers. *Christian Influence upon the Ideology of the Taiping Rebellion, 1851–1864.* Madison: University of Wisconsin Press, 1952.

4617. Brine, Lindeasy. *Taeping Rebellion in China: A Narrative of Its Rise and Progress, Based upon Original Documents and Information Obtained in China.* London: J. Murray, 1862.
4618. Cahill, Holgel. *A Yankee Adventure: The Story of Ward and the Taiping Rebellion.* New York: Macaulay, 1930.
4619. Callery, Joseph M. *History of the Insurrection in China.* Translated by J. Oxenford. New York: Harper and Brothers, 1853.
4620. Curwen, C. A. *Taiping Rebel: The Deposition of Li Hsiu-Che'eng.* New York: Cambridge University Press, 1977.
4621. Feuerwerker, Albert. *Rebellion in Nineteenth-Century China.* Ann Arbor: University of Michigan Papers in Chinese Studies, no. 21, 1975.
4622. Gregory, James S. *Great Britain and the Taipings.* New York: Praeger, 1969.
4623. Hail, William J. *Tseng Kuo-Fan and the Taiping Rebellion.* New York: Paragon, 1964.
4624. Jen Yu-Wen. *The Taiping Revolutionary Movement.* New Haven: Yale University Press, 1973.
4625. Lin, Robert H. T. *The Taiping Revolution: A Failure of Two Missions.* Washington, D.C.: University Press of America, 1979.
4626. Lindley, Augustus F. *Ti-Ping Tien-Kwoh: The History of the Ti-Ping Revolution.* London: Day and Son, 1866.
4627. MacFarlane, Charles. *The Chinese Revolution.* London: G. Routledge, 1853.
4628. Marx, Karl. *Marx on China, 1853–1860: Articles from the* New York Daily Tribune. Introduction and notes by D. Torr. London: Lawrence and Wishart, 1951.
4629. Michael, Franz. *The Taiping Rebellion.* 3 vols. Seattle: University of Washington Press, 1966.
4630. Shih, Vincent Y. C. *The Taiping Ideology: Its Sources, Interpretations and Influences.* Seattle: University of Washington Press, 1967.
4631. Ssu-yü Teng. *New Light on the History of the Taiping Rebellion.* Cambridge, Massachusetts: Harvard University Press, 1950.
4632. _____. *The Taiping Rebellion and the Western Powers: A Comprehensive Survey.* 2d ed. Taipei: Yee Wen Publishing, 1977.

Boxer Rebellion, 1900

Climaxing a movement in the late 1800s against the spread of Western and Japanese influences in China, the Boxer Rebellion was a bloody uprising directed against foreigners and Chinese Christians. The movement was started by a secret Chinese society called *I-ho-ch'uan,* meaning "Righteous and Harmonious Fists," and dubbed "Boxers" by Westerners. The rebellion had to be put down by a rescue force from eight nations. Although not a revolution per se, the rebellion, along with the earlier Taiping Rebellion, had revolutionary overtones, and the revolutionary movement in China, aiming at expelling the ruling Manchu dynasty along with foreigners, spread rapidly throughout the country. The books by Victor W. Purcell (1963) and Chester C. Tan (1966) are among the best on the subject.

4633. *Boxer Rising: A History of the Boxer Trouble in China.* New York: Paragon, 1967.
4634. Clements, Paul H. *The Boxer Rebellion.* New York: AMS Press, 1915.
4635. Duiker, William J. *Cultures in Collision: The Boxer Rebellion.* San Rafael, California: Presidio Press, 1978.
4636. Fleming, Peter. *The Siege of Peking.* New York: Alfred A. Knopf, 1959.
4637. Hirschfeld, Burt. *Fifty-Five Days of Terror: The Story of the Boxer Rebellion.* New York: Messner, 1964.
4638. Martin, William A. *Siege in Peking: China Against the World.* New York: Barnes and Noble, 1972.
4639. Purcell, Victor W. *The Boxer Uprising: A Background Study.* Hamden, Connecticut: Shoe String Press, 1963.
4640. Steiger, George N. *China and the Occident: The Origin and Development of the Boxer Movement.* New York: Russell and Russell, 1966.
4641. Tan, Chester C. *The Boxer Catastrophe.* New York: Octagon Books, 1966.

Chinese National Revolution and Sun Yat-sen, 1911–1927

With the National Revolution of 1911, China took her first major step toward merging her history with Western influences. Although the country had been ruled since the seventeenth century by the Manchus, that dynasty was always considered foreign, and an anti-Manchu posture was part of Chinese nationalism—and had been an ingredient of the recent rebellions. By 1900 several revolutionary groups and a variety of revolutionary ideas had gained adherents. One such group was the *Kuomintang* (KMT), or National Party, whose leader was Sun Yat-sen. The revolution began in October, 1911, with its goals summed up in the words "democracy" and "modernization." The Manchus were overthrown and a republic established.

The ideals of the Chinese Republic were embodied in Dr. Sun's "Three Principles of the People": nationalism, democracy, people's livelihood. But they were more theoretical than practical, and the initial success of the revolution was followed by considerable internal conflict. Although the old order was dead, the fate of the republic was unclear. New revolutionary leaders appeared, including communists. Moreover, a pattern was being established: each of China's revolutionary steps toward modernization was being supported by earlier movements whose successes inadequately met rising expectations and frustrations.

Among the best books on the 1911 Revolution are those by Michael Gasster (1969), C. T. Liang (1962), and Harley F. MacNair (1931). For Sun Yat-sen see the books by Harold Z. Schiffrin (1968), Lyon Sharman (1934), and C. Martin Wilbur (1976). The reader should also examine some of the books under the subsection on China which follows the introduction to this chapter; for example, see those by Lucien Bianco (1971), Jean Chesneaux, Françoise Le Barbier, and Marie-Claire Bergère (1977), John K. Fairbank (1958), Wolfgang Franke (1971), John Robottom (1969), and Franz Schurmann and Orville Schell (1967).

Historiography

4642. Hsieh, Winston. *Chinese Historiography on the Revolution of 1911: A Critical Survey and a Selected Bibliography.* Stanford: Hoover Institution, 1975.

Documents

4643. Eudin, S. J., and Robert C. North, eds. *Soviet Russia and the East, 1920-1927: A Documentary Survey.* Stanford: Stanford University Press, 1957.
4644. Wilbur, C. Martin, and Julie How, eds. *Documents on Communism, Nationalism, and Soviet Advisers in China, 1918-1927.* New York: Columbia University Press, 1956.

Articles

4645. Dingle, E. J. "China's Revolution, 1911-1912." *Spectator* (7 September 1912): 337-38.
4646. Ewing, Thomas E. "Revolution on the Chinese Frontier: Outer Mongolia in 1911." *Journal of Asian History* 12:2 (1978): 101-19.
4647. Farjenel, F. "Through the Chinese Revolution." *Spectator* (13 November 1915): 665-67.
4648. Fincher, John. "Political Provincialism and the National Revolution." In *China in Revolution,* edited by Mary C. Wright. New Haven: Yale University Press, 1968.
4649. Fung, Edmund S. K. "Military Subversion in the Chinese Revolution of 1911." *Modern Asian Studies* 9 (February 1975): 103-23.
4650. George, Brian T. "The State Department and Sun Yat-sen: American Policy and the Revolutionary Disintegration of China, 1920-1924." *Pacific Historical Review* 46 (August 1977): 387-408.
4651. Gregor, A. James, and Maria Hsia Chang. "Nazionalfascismo and the Revolutionary Nationalism of Sun Yat-sen." *Journal of Asian Studies* 39:1 (November 1979): 21-38.
4652. Metallo, Michael V. "American Missionaries, Sun Yat-sen, and the Chinese Revolution." *Pacific Historical Review* 47 (May 1978): 261-82.
4653. Olenik, J. Kenneth. "Teng Yen-ta and the Theory of Mass Revolution in Kuomintang Ideology." *Asian Thought and Society* 8 (September 1978): 178-92.
4654. Wong, Young-tsu. "Popular Unrest and the 1911 Revolution in Jiangsu." *Modern China* 3:3 (July 1977): 321-44.

4655. Wright, Mary C. "From Revolution to Restoration: The Transformation of Kuomintang Ideology." *Far Eastern Quarterly* 14:4 (August 1955): 515–32.
4656. Young, Ernest P. "Leadership and Constituencies in the 1911 Revolution." *Modern China* 2:2 (April 1976): 221–26.
4657. _____ . "Nationalism, Reform, and Republican Revolution: China in the Early Twentieth Century." In *Modern East Asia: Essays in Interpretation.* New York: Harcourt Brace and World, 1970.
4658. Zhang, Kaiyuan. "A General Review of the Study of the Revolution of 1911 in the People's Republic of China." *Journal of Asian Studies* 39:3 (May 1980): 525–31.

The Revolution

Books

4659. Brown, Arthur. *The Chinese Revolution.* New York: Student Volunteer Movement, 1912.
4660. Des Forges, Roger V. *Hsi-liang and the Chinese National Revolution.* New Haven: Yale University Press, 1973.
4661. Dingle, E. J. *China's Revolution, 1911 1912: A Historical and Political Record of the Civil War.* San Francisco: Chinese Materials, 1972.
4662. Esherick, Joseph W. *Reform and Revolution in China: The 1911 Revolution in Hunan and Hubei.* Berkeley: University of California Press, 1976.
4663. Gasster, Michael. *Chinese Intellectuals and the Revolution of 1911: The Birth of Modern Chinese Radicalism.* Seattle: University of Washington Press, 1969.
4664. Kent, Percy Horace. *Passing of the Manchus.* New York: Longmans, Green, 1912.
4665. Lee, Ta-Ling. *Foundations of the Chinese Revolution, 1905–1912 (An Historical Record of the T'ung-meng Hui).* New York: St. John's University Press, 1970.
4666. Liang, C. T. *The Chinese Revolution of 1911.* New York: St. John's University Press, 1962.
4667. Liew, K. S. *Struggle for Democracy: Sung Chiao-jen and the 1911 Chinese Revolution.* Berkeley: University of California Press, 1971.
4668. MacNair, Harley F. *China in Revolution: An Analysis of Politics and Militarism Under the Republic.* Chicago: University of Chicago Press, 1931.
4669. Price, Don C. *Russia and the Roots of the Chinese Revolution, 1896–1911.* Cambridge, Massachusetts: Harvard University Press, 1974.
4670. Rankin, Mary B. *Early Chinese Revolutionaries: Radical Intellectuals in Shanghai and Chekiang, 1902–1911.* Cambridge, Massachusetts: Harvard University Press, 1971.
4671. Reid, John G. *The Manchu Abdication and the Powers, 1908–1912.* Westport, Connecticut: Greenwood, 1973.
4672. Rhoads, Edward. *China's Republican Revolution: The Case of Kwangtung, 1895–1913.* Cambridge, Massachusetts: Harvard University Press, 1975.
4673. Whiting, Allen S. *Soviet Policies in China, 1917–24.* New York: Columbia University Press, 1954.

4674. Woo, T. C. *The Kuomintang and the Future of the Chinese Revolution.* London: Allen and Unwin, 1928.
4675. Yen Ching Hwang. *The Overseas Chinese and the 1911 Revolution.* New York: Oxford University Press, 1977.

Sun Yat-sen

Books

4676. Cantlie, James, and C. Jones. *Sun Yat Sen.* Norwood, Pennsylvania: Norwood Editions, 1912.
4677. Hensman, Charles R. *Sun Yat-Sen.* Naperville, Illinois: Alec R. Allenson, 1971.
4678. Leng, Shao-chuan, and Norman Palmer. *Sun Yat-sen and Communism.* London: Thames and Hudson, 1961.
4679. Linebarger, Paul M. *The Political Doctrines of Sun Yat-Sen.* Westport, Connecticut: Hyperion Press, 1973.
4680. _____. *Sun Yat-Sen and the Chinese Republic.* New York: AMS Press, 1969.
4681. Martin, Bernard. *Strange Vigour: The Biography of Sun Yat-Sen.* Port Washington, New York: Kennikat Press, 1970.
4682. Restarick, Henry B. *Sun Yat Sen, Liberator of China.* Westport, Connecticut: Hyperion Press, 1980.
4683. Schiffrin, Harold Z. *Sun Yat-Sen and the Origins of the Chinese Revolution.* Berkeley: University of California Press, 1968.
4684. Sharman, Lyon. *Sun Yat-sen: His Life and Its Meaning.* Stanford: Stanford University Press, 1934.
4685. Sun Yat-sen. *Memories of a Chinese Revolutionary.* New York: AMS Press, 1927.
4686. _____. *Sun Yat-Sen: His Political and Social Ideals.* Translated by L. S. Hsu. Los Angeles: University of Southern California Press, 1933.
4687. Wilbur, C. Martin. *Sun Yat-Sen: Frustrated Patriot.* New York: Columbia University Press, 1976.
4688. Williams, Maurice. *Sun Yat-Sen Versus Communism.* Westport, Connecticut: Hyperion Press, 1975.

Chinese Communist Revolution, 1927–1949

The Chinese Communist Revolution grew out of social, and especially rural problems and crises, and was molded by nationalist efforts and the ideology of Marxism-Leninism. Moreover, those problems and crises were aggravated by ineffective leadership, foreign interference, war lord abuses, oppression by the landowning classes, and a rapid rise in the population. Only further revolution and revolutionary changes would resolve China's problems, or so it seemed to the Chinese Communist Party (CCP), established in 1921.

The ruling KMT party turned against the CCP in 1927, and the new revolution was underway. The KMT proved to be inefficient and corrupt. While the CCP failed to form a proletarian base, other Chinese Communists, including Mao Tse-tung, began to organize the peasants; it was this organization which was the key to the success of the revolution. The formation of a well organized army followed. Civil war between the KMT and the CCP, and later, war with Japan (World War II) as well, carried the revolution into the late 1940s, until the CCP gained power in 1949.

The Chinese Communist Revolution succeeded because of two broadly complex reasons, one internal, the other external. First, the military struggle was made inseparable from the political, while both were shifted from urban to rural areas; moreover, patience was exercised and it was agreed to engage in a protracted armed struggle rather than depend upon a decisive sudden confrontation. Second, the revolutionists fought against both the imperialist West and aggressive Japan, thus fostering nationalism, while promising that socialism would enable China to catch up with and later surpass the capitalist countries.

The revolution was not a socialist revolution. Victory in 1949 was over a feudal past and the evils of imperialism. It was only in the 1950s that private property was eliminated and the socialization of the economy begun. However, it was in the course of socializing China that further problems arose and another revolution became necessary.

There are many excellent studies of the Chinese Communist Revolution. The few being singled out here are among the broader examinations: A. Doak Barnett (1963), Lionel Max Chassin (1965), Robert S. Elegant (1971), C. P. Fitzgerald (1952, 1964, 1971), Maurice Meisner (1978), and Suzanne Pepper (1978). Also valuable are some of the books under the subsection on China which follows the introduction to this chapter, such as those by Lucien Bianco (1971), Jean Chesneaux, Françoise Le Barbier, and Marie-Claire Bergère (1977), Wolfgang Franke (1971), and Franz Schurmann and Orville Schell (1967). Also especially noteworthy are the books by Edgar Snow (1957, 1968, 1972), an astute journalist who spent much time in China. On the CCP see the books by Edward Friedman (1976), Jacques Guillermaz (1973), and James P. Harrison (1972). On the Chinese army see John Gittings' book (1967). For the Long March see the book by Dick Wilson (1972). For Chinese Communism see the book by Benjamin Schwartz (1958).

Bibliographies

4689. Henderson, Martha T. *A Selected Bibliography of Communist China in Western Languages.* Cambridge, Massachusetts: Center for International Studies, M.I.T., 1954.

Chinese Communist Revolution, 1927-1949 / 299

4690. Hsüeh, Chün-tu. *The Chinese Communist Movement, 1921-1937: An Annotated Bibliography.* Stanford: Hoover Institution, 1960.
4691. _____. *The Chinese Communist Movement, 1937-1949: An Annotated Bibliography.* Stanford: Hoover Institution, 1962.
4692. Israel, John. *The Chinese Student Movement, 1927-1937: A Bibliographical Essay Based on the Resources of the Hoover Institution.* Stanford: Hoover Institution, 1959.
4693. Rhoads, Edward. *Chinese Red Army, 1927-1963: An Annotated Bibliography.* Cambridge, Massachusetts: Harvard University Press, 1964.

Historiography

4694. Cole, Allan Burnett. *Forty Years of Chinese Communism: Selected Readings With Commentary.* Washington, D.C.: American Historical Association Service Center for Teachers of History, 1962.

Reference

4695. Klein, Donald W., and Ann B. Clark. *A Biographic Dictionary of Chinese Communism, 1921-1965.* 2 vols. Cambridge, Massachusetts: Harvard University Press, 1971.
4696. Wilbur, Clarence M. *Chinese Sources on the History of the Chinese Communist Movement.* New York: East Asian Institute of Columbia University, 1950.

Documents

4697. Brandt, Conrad; Benjamin Schwartz; and John K. Fairbank. *A Documentary History of Chinese Communism.* Cambridge, Massachusetts: Harvard University Press, 1952.
4698. Chai, Winberg, ed. *Essential Works of Chinese Communism.* Rev. ed. New York: Bantam Books, 1972.
4699. Cole, Allan Burnett. *Forty Years of Chinese Communism: Selected Readings with Commentary.* New York: Macmillan, 1962.
4700. Compton, Boyd. *Mao's China: Party Reform Documents, 1942-44.* Seattle: University of Washington Press, 1952.
4701. Jacobs, Dan N., and H. Baerwald, eds. *Chinese Communism: Selected Documents.* New York: Harper and Row, 1963.
4702. Rea, Kenneth W., ed. *Canton in Revolution: The Collected Papers of Earl Swisher, 1925-1928.* Boulder, Colorado: Westview Press, 1977.
4703. Selden, Mark, ed. *People's Republic of China: A Documentary History of Revolutionary Change.* New York: Monthly Review Press, 1979.

Overviews, Surveys, Interpretations

Articles

4704. Goldstein, Steven M. "The Chinese Revolution and the Colonial Areas: The View from Yenan, 1937-41." *China Quarterly* 75 (September 1978): 594-622.
4705. Levy, Richard. "Analyzing China's Socialist Revolution: Review Essay." *Bulletin of Concerned Asian Scholars* 9 (October-December 1977): 38-49.
4706. Nee, Victor. "Towards a Social Anthropology of the Chinese Revolution." *Bulletin of Concerned Asian Scholars* 11 (1979): 40-50.
4707. Schwartz, Benjamin. "Totalitarian Consolidation and the Chinese Model." *China Quarterly* 2 (April-June 1960): 16-42.
4708. Wittfogel, Karl A. "Social Revolution in China." In *A World in Revolution?* edited by E. Kamenka. Canberra: Australian National University, 1970.
4709. Ying-Mao Kau. "Urban and Rural Strategies in the Chinese Communist Revolution." In *Peasant Rebellion and Communist Revolution in Asia*, edited by J. W. Lewis. Stanford: Stanford University Press, 1974.

Books

4710. Barnett, A. Doak. *China on the Eve of Communist Takeover.* New York: Praeger, 1963.
4711. _____ . *Communist China in Perspective.* New York: Praeger, 1962.
4712. Belden, Jack. *China Shakes the World.* New York: Monthly Review Press, 1970.
4713. Cell, Charles P. *Revolution at Work: Mobilization Campaigns in China.* New York: Academic Press, 1977.
4714. Chapman, H. *The Chinese Revolution, 1926-27.* London: Constable, 1928.
4715. Chassin, Lionel Max. *The Communist Conquest of China: A History of the Civil War, 1945-1949.* Cambridge, Massachusetts: Harvard University Press, 1965.
4716. Ch'en Pōta. *Stalin on the Chinese Revolution.* Peking: Foreign Languages Press, 1953.
4717. Chesneaux, Jean. *The Chinese Labor Movement, 1919-1927.* Translated by H. M. Wright. Stanford: Stanford University Press, 1968.
4718. Collier, John, and Elsie Collier. *China's Socialist Revolution.* New York: Monthly Review Press, 1973.
4719. Davin, Delia. *Woman-Work: Women and the Party in Revolutionary China.* New York: Oxford University Press, 1976.
4720. Dirlik, Arif. *Revolution and History: Origins of Marxist Historiography in China, 1919-1937.* Berkeley: University of California Press, 1978.
4721. Eastman, Lloyd E. *The Abortive Revolution: China Under Nationalist Rule, 1927-1937.* Cambridge, Massachusetts: Harvard University Press, 1974.
4722. Elegant, Robert S. *Mao's Great Revolution.* New York: World, 1971.
4723. Epstein, Israel. *The Unfinished Revolution in China.* Boston: Little, Brown, 1947.
4724. Fitzgerald, C. P. *The Birth of Communist China.* Baltimore: Penguin Books, 1964.

4725. _____. *Communism Takes China: How the Revolution Went Red.* New York: American Heritage Press, 1971.
4726. _____. *Revolution in China.* New York: Praeger, 1952.
4727. Gelder, Stuart, ed. *The Chinese Communists.* London: Victor Gollancz, 1946.
4728. Goldston, Robert. *The Rise of Red China.* New York: Fawcett World Library, 1972.
4729. Griffin, Patrick E. *Chinese Communist Treatment of Counterrevolutionaries, 1924-1949.* Princeton: Princeton University Press, 1976.
4730. Hart, Thomas G. *The Dynamics of Revolution.* Stockholm: Statsvetenskapliga Institutionen, 1971.
4731. Ho Kan-Chih *A History of the Modern Chinese Revolution.* Peking: Foreign Languages Press, 1969.
4732. Hsiao Tso-liang. *The Land Revolution in China, 1930-34: A Study of Documents.* Seattle: University of Washington Press, 1969.
4733. Isaacs, Harold R. *The Tragedy of the Chinese Revolution.* New York: Atheneum, 1966.
4734. Kataoka, Tetsuya. *Resistance and Revolution in China: The Communists and the Second United Front.* Berkeley: University of California Press, 1974.
4735. Lapwood, Ralph, and Nancy Lapwood. *Through the Chinese Revolution.* Westport, Connecticut: Hyperion Press, 1973.
4736. Lieberthal, Kenneth G. *Revolution and Tradition in Tientsin, 1949-1952.* Stanford: Stanford University Press, 1980.
4737. Malraux, André. *Man's Fate.* New York: Vintage, 1969.
4738. Meisner, Maurice. *Mao's China: A History of the People's Republic.* New York: Free Press, 1978.
4739. Misselwitz, Henry F. *The Dragon Stirs: An Intimate Sketch-book of China's Kuomintang Revolution, 1927-29.* New York: Harbinger House, 1941.
4740. Pepper, Suzanne. *Civil War in China: The Political Struggle, 1945-1949.* Berkeley: University of California Press, 1978.
4741. Pratt, Helen Gay. *China and Her Unfinished Revolution.* New York: American Council, Institute of Pacific Relations, 1937.
4742. Schell, Orville, and Joseph Esherick. *Modern China: The Story of a Revolution.* New York: Alfred A. Knopf, 1972.
4743. Selden, Mark. *The Yenan Way in Revolutionary China.* Cambridge, Massachusetts: Harvard University Press, 1971.
4744. Smedley, Agnes. *Battle Hymn of China.* New York: Alfred A. Knopf, 1945.
4745. Solomon, Richard H. *Mao's Revolution and the Chinese Political Culture.* Berkeley: University of California Press, 1971.
4746. Strong, Anna Louise. *China's Millions: The Revolutionary Struggles from 1927-1935.* London: Victor Gollancz, 1936.
4747. _____. *The Chinese Conquer China.* Garden City, New York: Doubleday, 1949.
4748. Swarup, Shanti. *A Study of the Chinese Communist Movement, 1927-1934.* London: Oxford University Press, 1966.
4749. T'ang Leang-li. *China in Revolt.* London: Noel Douglas, 1927.
4750. _____. *Inner History of the Chinese Revolution.* London: Routledge and Kegan Paul, 1930.
4751. Townsend, Peter. *China Phoenix: The Revolution in China.* Westport, Connecticut: Hyperion Press, 1975.

302 / Asia

4752. Van Slyke, Lyman P., ed. *The Chinese Communist Movement: A Report of the United States War Department, July 1945.* Stanford: Stanford University Press, 1968.
4753. Wint, Guy. *Communist China's Crusade: Mao's Road to Power and the New Campaign for World Revolution.* New York: Praeger, 1965.
4754. _____ . *Dragon and Sickle: How Communist Revolution Happened in China.* New York: Praeger, 1959.

Eyewitness Accounts

4755. Abend, Hallett Edward. *My Life in China, 1926-1941.* New York: Harcourt, Brace, 1943.
4756. Band, Claire, and William Band. *Two Years with the Chinese Communists.* New Haven: Yale University Press, 1948.
4757. Bodde, Derk. *Peking Diary 1948-9: A Year of Revolution.* Greenwich, Connecticut: Fawcett World Library, 1967.
4758. Chen, Percy. *China Called Me: My Life Inside the Chinese Revolution.* Boston: Little Brown, 1979.
4759. Ch'en Pōta. *Notes on Ten Years of Civil War, 1927-1936.* Westport, Connecticut: Hyperion Press, 1975.
4760. Snow, Edgar. *The Long Revolution.* New York: Random House, 1972.
4761. _____ . *Random Notes on Red China, 1936-1945.* Cambridge, Massachusetts: Harvard University Press, 1957.
4762. _____ . *Red Star Over China.* Rev. ed. New York: Grove Press, 1968.
4763. T'ang, Leang-li. *Inner History of the Chinese Revolution.* New York: Gordon Press, 1976.
4764. Wang Fan-Hsi. *Chinese Revolutionary: Memories, 1919-1949.* Translated by G. Benton. New York: Oxford University Press, 1980.

Chinese Communist Party

4765. Chang Kuo-T'ao. *The Rise of the Chinese Communist Party, 1921-1927.* Lawrence: University Press of Kansas, 1971.
4766. Friedman, Edward. *Backward Toward Revolution: The Chinese Revolutionary Party.* Berkeley: University of California Press, 1976.
4767. Guillermaz, Jacques. *A History of the Chinese Communist Party, 1921-1949.* Translated by A. Destenay. New York: Random House, 1973.
4768. Harrison, James P. *The Long March to Power: A History of the Chinese Communist Party, 1921-72.* New York: Praeger, 1972.
4769. Hu Chiao-mu. *Thirty Years of the Communist Party of China.* Peking: Foreign Languages Press, 1952.
4770. Wang, Shih. *A Brief History of the Chinese Communist Party.* Washington, D.C.: Joint Publications Research Service, 1961.

Leadership

Article

4771. Lee, Ming T. "The Founders of the Chinese Communist Party: A Study in Revolutionaries." *Civilisations* 18:1 (1968):113-27.

Books

4772. Elegant, Robert S. *China's Red Masters: Political Biographies of Chinese Communist Leaders.* New York: Twayne, 1951.
4773. Hsiao Tso-liang. *Power Relations Within the Chinese Communist Movement, 1930-34.* Seattle: University of Washington Press, 1962.
4774. Lewis, John Wilson, ed. *Party Leadership and Revolutionary Power in China.* New York: Cambridge University Press, 1970.
4775. _____. *Leadership in Communist China.* Ithaca: Cornell University Press, 1963.
4776. Lindbeck, John M. H., ed. *China: Management of a Revolutionary Society.* Seattle: University of Washington Press, 1971.

Military

4777. Epstein, Israel. *The People's War.* London: Victor Gollancz, 1939.
4778. Gittings, John. *The Role of the Chinese Army.* London: Oxford University Press, 1967.
4779. Griffith, Samuel B., II. *The Chinese People's Liberation Army.* New York: McGraw-Hill, 1967.
4780. Lin Piao. *Long Live the Victory of People's War.* Peking: Foreign Languages Press, 1965.
4781. Liu, Frederick Fu. *A Military History of Modern China: 1924-1949.* Princeton: Princeton University Press, 1956.
4782. O'Ballance, Edgar. *The Red Army of China.* London: Faber and Faber, 1962.

Long March

4783. Chen Ch'ang-feng. *On the Long March with Chairman Mao.* Peking: Foreign Languages Press, 1959.
4784. Wilson, Dick. *The Long March, 1935: The Epic of Chinese Communism's Survival.* New York: Viking, 1972.

Communism, Marxism, Leninism

Articles

4785. Meisner, Maurice. "Leninism and Maoism: Some Populist Perspectives on Marxism-Leninism in China." *China Quarterly* 45 (January-March 1971): 2-36.
4786. _____. "Yenan Communism and the Rise of the Chinese People's Republic." In *Modern East Asia: Essays in Interpretation,* edited by J.B. Crowley. New York: Harcourt, Brace and World, 1970.
4787. Walder, Andrew G. "Marxism, Maoism and Social Change." *Modern China* 3:1 (January 1977): 101-18.

Books

4788. Chan, F. Gilbert, ed. *China at the Crossroads, 1928-1949: Republicanism versus Communism.* New York: New Viewpoints, 1978.
4789. Ch'en Kung-Po. *The Communist Movement in China.* Edited by C.M. Wilbur. New York: East Asian Institute, Columbia University, 1960.
4790. Garvey, J.E. *Marxist-Leninist China: Military and Social Doctrine.* New York: Exposition Press, 1960.
4791. Harris, Nigel. *The Mandate of Heaven: Marx and Mao in Modern China.* New York: Horizon Press, 1979.
4792. Houn, Franklin W. *Short History of Chinese Communism.* Englewood Cliffs, New Jersey: Prentice-Hall, 1973.
4793. Lotveit, Trygve. *Chinese Communism, 1931-1934.* Atlantic Highlands, New Jersey: Humanities Press, 1975.
4794. Schwartz, Benjamin. *Chinese Communism and the Rise of Mao.* 3d ed. Cambridge, Massachusetts: Harvard University Press, 1958.

Class, Peasants, Bourgeoisie

Articles

4795. Bergère, Marie-Claire. "The Role of the Bourgeoisie." In *China in Revolution,* edited by Mary C. Wright. New Haven: Yale University Press, 1968.
4796. Bianco, Lucien. "Les Paysans et la Révolution Chine, 1919-1949." *Politique Etrangère* 2 (1968): 117-41.
4797. _____. "Peasants and Revolution: The Case of China." *Journal of Peasant Studies* 2 (April 1975): 313-35.
4798. McDonald, Angus W., Jr. "The Hunan Peasant Movement: Its Urban Origins." *Modern China* 1:2 (April 1975): 180-203.
4799. Marks, Robert B. "The World Can Change! Guangdong Peasants in Revolution." *Modern China* 3:1 (January 1977): 65-100.
4800. Thaxton, Ralph. "On Peasant Revolution and National Resistance: Toward a Theory of Peasant Mobilization and Revolutionary War with Special Reference to Modern China." *World Politics* 30:1 (October 1977): 24-57.
4801. Yokoyama, Suguru. "The Peasant Movement in Hunan." *Modern China* 1:2 (April 1975): 204-38.

Books

4802. Harrison, James P. *The Communists and the Chinese Peasant Rebellion.* New York: Atheneum, 1968.
4803. Hofheinz, Roy, Jr. *The Broken Wave: The Chinese Communist Peasant Movement, 1922-1928.* Cambridge, Massachusetts: Harvard University Press, 1977.
4804. McDonald, Angus W., Jr. *The Urban Origins of Rural Revolution: Elites and the Masses in Hunan Province, China, 1911-1927.* Berkeley: University of California Press, 1978.

Nationalism

4805. Chan, F. Gilbert, and Thomas H. Etzold, eds. *China in the 1920s: Nationalism and Revolution.* New York: New Viewpoints, 1976.
4806. Israel, John. *Student Nationalism in China, 1927-1937.* Stanford: Stanford University Press, 1966.
4807. Johnson, Chalmers A. *Peasant Nationalism and Communist Power: The Emergence of Revolutionary China, 1937-1945.* Stanford: Stanford University Press, 1962.

Everyday Life

Articles

4808. Hinton, William. "Hinton Re-Examines 'Fanshen.'" *Progressive Labor* (February 1969): 107.
4809. Pepper, Suzanne. "Education and Revolution: The 'Chinese Model' Revisited." *Asian Survey* 18:9 (September 1978): 847-90.
4810. Thaxton, Ralph. "Tenants in Revolution: The Tenacity of Traditional Morality." *Modern China* 1:3 (July 1975): 323-58.

Books

4811. Frolic, B. Michael. *Mao's People: Sixteen Portraits of Life in Revolutionary China.* Cambridge, Massachusetts: Harvard University Press, 1980.
4812. Hinton, William. *Fanshen: A Documentary of Revolution in a Chinese Village.* New York: Monthly Review Press, 1966.

Foreign Relations

4813. Borg, Dorothy. *American Policy and the Chinese Revolution, 1925-1928.* New York: Macmillan, 1947.
4814. Feis, Herbert. *The China Tangle: The American Effort in China from Pearl Harbor to the Marshall Mission.* Princeton: Princeton University Press, 1953.

306 / Asia

4815. McLane, Charles B. *Soviet Policy and the Chinese Communists, 1931–1946.* New York: Columbia University Press, 1958.
4816. Moore, Harriet L. *Soviet Far Eastern Policy, 1931–1945.* Princeton: Princeton University Press, 1945.
4817. North, Robert C. *Moscow and Chinese Communists.* Rev. ed. Stanford: Stanford University Press, 1963.

Mao Tse-tung and Maoism

Mao Tse-tung was the great leader (from 1931) of the Chinese Communist Revolution, and for more than a quarter of a century afterwards as well—though he may have ultimately outlived his usefulness to China. His success lay in adapting and adjusting Marxism-Leninism to the conditions of China as an underdeveloped country; he Sinified Marxism-Leninism to make it applicable to Chinese history, reality, and peculiarities. For Mao revolution meant a peasant army, led by an elite Communist Party, operating from the countryside, struggling to achieve political power.

There has been considerable scholarly dispute over the question of Mao's originality as a theorist, but there is little disagreement concerning the originality in his application of that theory. His contributions (e.g., shifting the focus of the revolution from urban centers to rural areas; emphasizing class alliances and united front tactics; developing a party based on the peasantry, not the proletariat; concentrating on a prolonged military conflict based on rural guerrilla warfare) lay less in his writings than in his deeds. The greatest value of his thought stems from its practical basis, as it was a reflection and extension of China's problems. However, his lack of firsthand experience with the world outside China gave him a simplistic view of global affairs.

The many fine articles below examine specialized aspects of Mao and Maoism. Among the best studies of Mao are those by Jerome Ch'en (1965, 1969), Arthur A. Cohen (1964), Han Suyin (1972), Stanley Karnow (1972), Stuart Schram (1966, 1969), Ross Terrill (1980), and Dick Wilson (1980). An examination of Mao's own writings would also be instructive.

Bibliographies

4818. Ch'en, Jerome. *Mao Papers: Anthology and Bibliography.* New York: Oxford University Press, 1970.
4819. Starr, John Bryan, and Nancy A. Dyer. *Post-Liberation Works of Mao Zedong: A Bibliography and Index.* Berkeley: Center for Chinese Studies, University of California, 1976.

Articles

4820. Adie, I. W. A. C. "Mao's Idea of a World Order." *Asian Thought and Society* 2 (September 1977): 164–84.
4821. Bianco, Lucien. "Essai de definition du Maoïsme." *Annales: Economique, societatis, civilisation* 34 (September-October 1979): 1094–1108.
4822. Cheng, Peter P., et al. "Mao's Legacy: A Symposium." *Asian Survey* 17:11 (November 1977): 1001–59.
4823. D'Hoop, Jean-Marie. "Mao Tsé-Toung et la conduite de la guerre populaire." *Revue histoire deuxième guerre mondiale* 115 (1979): 95–110.
4824. Dittmer, Lowell. "Power and Personality in China: Mao Tse-tung, Liu Shao-ch'i, and the Politics of Charismatic Succession." *Studies in Comparative Communism* 7:1–2 (Spring-Summer 1974): 21–49.
4825. Esherick, Joseph W. "On the 'Restoration of Capitalism': Mao and Marxist Theory." *Modern China* 5:1 (January 1979): 41–78.
4826. Fairbank, John K. "On the Death of Mao." *New York Review of Books* (14 October 1976).
4827. Feuerwerker, Albert. "Mao vs. Modernism." *Intellectual Digest* 2:12 (August 1972): 38–40.
4828. Gray, Jack. "The Economics of Maoism." *Bulletin of the Atomic Scientists* 25:2 (February 1969): 42–51.
4829. Halperin, Morton H. "Mao Tse-tung's Revolutionary Strategy and Peking's International Behavior." *American Political Science Review* 59:1 (March 1965): 80–99.
4830. I-Kua Chou. "The Mind of a Revolutionary." *Problems of Communism* 16:2 (March-April 1967): 91–99.
4831. Johnson, Chalmers. "Pregnant with 'Meaning'—Mao and the Revolutionary Ascetic." *Journal of Interdisciplinary History* 7:3 (Winter 1977): 499–508.
4832. Katzanbach, Edward L., and Gene Z. Hanrahan. "The Revolutionary Strategy of Mao Tse-tung." *Political Science Quarterly* 70:3 (September 1955): 321–40.
4833. Kitagawa, Joseph M. "One of the Many Faces of China: Maoism as a Quasi-Religion." *Japanese Journal of Religious Studies* 1 (June-September 1974): 125–42.
4834. Lew, Roland. "Maoism and the Chinese Revolution." In *The Socialist Register, 1975*. London: Merlin Press, 1975.
4835. Lowenthal, Richard. "Mao's Revolution: The Chinese Handwriting on the Wall." *Encounter* (April 1967): 3–9.
4836. Meisner, Maurice. "Utopian Socialist Themes in Maoism." In *Peasant Rebellion and Communist Rebellion in Asia*, edited by J.W. Lewis. Stanford: Stanford University Press, 1974.
4837. Nucleus Group of the First Ministry of Machine Building. "Raise High Chairman Mao's Banner of Continuing Revolution and Accelerate the Realization of Agricultural Mechanization." *Chinese Economics Studies* 12 (Fall-Winter 1978–1979): 11–20.
4838. Rejai, M. "Redefinition of 'Maoism'" *Journal of Asian and African Studies* 2:3–4 (July-October 1967): 186–91.
4839. Rossanda, Rossana. "Mao's Marxism." In *The Socialist Register, 1971*. London: Merlin Press, 1971.

4840. Schram, Stuart. "Chinese and Leninist Components in the Thought of Mao Tse-tung." *Asian Survey* 3:6 (June 1963): 259-73.
4841. _____. "Mao Tse-tung and the Theory of the Permanent Revolution."*China Quarterly* 46 (April-June 1971): 221-44.
4842. Schwartz, Benjamin. "On the 'Originality' of Mao Tse-tung." *Foreign Affairs* 34 (October 1955): 67-76.
4843. Starr, John Bryan. "Conceptual Foundations of Mao Tse-tung's Theory of Continuous Revolution." *Asian Survey* 11:6 (June 1971): 610-28.
4844. Sudama, Trevor. "Analysis of Classes by Mao Tse-tung, 1923-1939." *Journal of Contemporary Asia* 8:3 (1978): 355-73.
4845. Tang, Peter S.H. "Mao Tsetung Thought since the Cultural Revolution." *Studies in Soviet Thought* 13 (September-December 1973): 265-78.
4846. Taurer, Bernard. "Mao Tse-tung and His Permanent Cultural Revolution." *World Affairs* 140 (Fall 1977): 152-65.
4847. Van Ness, Peter. "Mao Tse-tung and Revolutionary 'Self-Reliance.'" *Problems of Communism* 20: 1-2 (January-April 1971): 68-74.
4848. Walder, Andrew G. "Marxism, Maoism and Social Change: A Reexamination of the 'Voluntarism' in Mao's Strategy and Thought." *Modern China* 3:2 (April 1977): 125-60.
4849. "What is Maoism? A Symposium." *Problems of Communism* 15:5 (September-October 1966): 1-30.
4850. Whyte, Martin King. "Bureaucracy and Modernization in China: The Maoist Critique." *American Sociological Review* 38:2 (April 1973): 149-63.
4851. Wittfogel, Karl A. "The Legend of 'Maoism.'" *China Quarterly* 1 (January-March 1960): 72-86; 2 (April-June 1960): 16-30.
4852. Wright, Tennant C., S.J. "Mao: Behind the Marxist Mask, a Loving Altruism." *Los Angeles Times* (16 October 1977).
4853. Wylie, Raymond F. "Mao Tse-tung, Ch'en Po-ta and the 'Sinification of Marxism,' 1936-38." *China Quarterly* 79 (September 1979): 447-80.

Books

4854. Archer, Jules. *Mao Tse-tung.* New York: Washington Square Press, 1973.
4855. Avakian, Bob. *The Immortal Contributions of Mao Tsetung.* Chicago: Liberation Books, 1979.
4856. _____. *The Loss in China and the Revolutionary Legacy of Mao Tsetung.* Chicago: Liberation Books, 1978.
4857. Boorman, Scott A. *The Protracted Game: A Wei-Ch'i Interpretation of Maoist Revolutionary Strategy.* New York: Oxford University Press, 1969.
4858. Bouc, Alain. *Mao Tse-tung: A Guide to His Thought.* Translated by P. Auster and L. Davis. New York: St. Martin's Press, 1977.
4859. Carter, Peter. *Mao.* New York: Oxford University Press, 1977.
4860. Ch'en, Jerome. *Mao.* Englewood Cliffs, New Jersey: Prentice-Hall, 1969.
4861. _____. *Mao and the Chinese Revolution.* London: Oxford University Press, 1965.
4862. Ch'en Pōta. *Mao Tse-tung on the Chinese Revolution.* Peking: Foreign Languages Press, 1953.

4863. Cohen, Arthur A. *The Communism of Mao Tse-tung.* Chicago: University of Chicago Press, 1964.
4864. DeFrancis, John. *Annotated Quotations from Chairman Mao.* New Haven: Yale University Press, 1975.
4865. Delyusin, Lev. *The Socio-Political Essence of Maoism.* Mystic, Connecticut: Lawrence Verry, 1977.
4866. Devillers, Philippe. *What Mao Really Said.* Translated by T. White. New York: Schocken, 1969.
4867. Fitzgerald, C.P. *Mao Tse-tung and China.* New York: Holmes and Meier, 1976.
4868. Gray, Jack. *Mao Tse-tung.* Valley Forge, Pennsylvania: Judson Press, 1974.
4869. Han Suyin. *The Morning Deluge: Mao Tse-tung and the Chinese Revolution, 1893-1954.* Boston: Little, Brown, 1972.
4870. _____ . *Wind in the Tower: Mao Tsetung and the Chinese Revolution, 1949-1975.* Boston: Little, Brown, 1976.
4871. Howard, Roger. *Mao Tse Tung and the Chinese People.* New York: Monthly Review Press, 1977.
4872. Hsiung, James C., ed. *The Logic of Maoism.* New York: Praeger, 1974.
4873. Karnow, Stanley. *Mao and China: From Revolution to Revolution.* New York: Viking, 1972.
4874. Kerry, Tom. *The Mao Myth: The Legacy of Stalinism in China.* New York: Pathfinder Press, 1977.
4875. Li Jui. *The Early Revolutionary Activities of Comrade Mao Tse-tung.* Edited by J.C. Hsiung. Translated by A.W. Sariti. White Plains, New York: M. E. Sharpe, 1977.
4876. MacGregor-Hastie, Roy. *The Red Barbarians: The Life and Times of Mao Tse-tung.* Philadelphia: Chilton, 1961.
4877. Mao Tse-tung. *Analysis of the Classes in Chinese Society.* Peking: Foreign Languages Press, 1956.
4878. _____ . *The Chinese Revolution and the Chinese Communist Party.* Peking: Foreign Languages Press, 1959.
4879. _____ . *On Guerrilla Warfare.* New York: Praeger, 1961.
4880. _____ . *Mao Tse-tung: An Anthology of His Writings.* Edited by A. Freemantle. New York: Mentor Books, 1962.
4881. _____ . *Quotations From Chairman Mao Tse-tung.* New York: Bantam Books, 1967.
4882. _____ . *Selected Works.* 4 vols. New York: International Publishers, 1956.
4883. _____ , and Lin Piao. *Post-Revolutionary Writings.* Edited by K. Fan. Garden City, New York: Doubleday, 1972.
4884. Michael, Franz. *Mao and the Perpetual Revolution.* Woodbury, New York: Barron's, 1977.
4885. Mohanty, Manoranjan. *The Political Philosophy of Mao Tsetung.* Columbia, Missouri: South Asia Books, 1978.
4886. Onate, Andres D. *Chairman Mao and the Chinese Communist Party.* Chicago: Nelson-Hall, 1979.
4887. Paloczi-Horvath, G. *Mao Tse-tung, Emperor of the Blue Ants.* London: Secker and Warburg, 1962.

4888. Payne, Robert. *Mao Tse-tung, Ruler of Red China.* London: Secker and Warburg, 1950.

4889. _____. *Portrait of a Revolutionary: Mao Tse-tung.* London: Abelard-Schuman, 1961.

4890. Purcell, Hugh. *Mao Tse-tung.* New York: St. Martin's Press, 1977.

4891. Pye, Lucian W. *Mao Tse-tung: The Man in the Leader.* New York: Basic Books, 1976.

4892. Rejai, M., ed. *Mao Tse-tung on Revolution and War.* Garden City, New York: Doubleday, 1969.

4893. Rue, John E. *Mao Tse-tung in Opposition, 1927–35.* Stanford: Stanford University Press, 1966.

4894. Schram, Stuart. *Mao Tse-tung.* Baltimore: Penguin Books, 1966.

4895. _____. *The Political Thought of Mao Tse-tung.* Rev. ed. New York: Praeger, 1969.

4896. Siao-Yu. *Mao Tse-tung and I Were Beggars.* New York: Macmillan, 1973.

4897. Starr, John Bryan. *Continuing the Revolution: The Political Thought of Mao.* Princeton: Princeton University Press, 1979.

4898. Tarling, Nicholas. *Mao and the Transformation of China, 1921–49.* Exeter, New Hampshire: Heinemann, 1977.

4899. Terrill, Ross. *Mao: A Biography.* New York: Harper and Row, 1980.

4900. Uhalley, Stephen, Jr. *Mao Tse-tung: A Critical Biography.* New York: New Viewpoints, 1975.

4901. Wakeman, Frederic, Jr. *History and Will: Philosophical Perspectives of Mao Tse-tung's Thought.* Berkeley: University of California Press, 1976.

4902. Wilson, Dick. *The People's Emperor: Mao. A Biography of Mao Tse-tung.* Garden City, New York: Doubleday, 1980.

4903. _____, ed. *Mao Tse-tung in the Scales of History.* Cambridge: Cambridge University Press, 1977.

4904. Wylie, Raymond F. *The Emergence of Maoism: Mao Tse-tung, Ch'en Po-ta, and the Search for Chinese Theory, 1935–1945.* Stanford: Stanford University Press, 1980.

4905. Yeh Ching. *Inside Mao Tse-tung Thought: An Analytical Blueprint of His Actions.* Translated by S. C. Pan et al. Hicksville, New York: Exposition Press, 1975.

4906. Yen Chang-Lin. *In His Mind a Million Bold Warriors: Reminiscences of the Life of Chairman Mao.* San Francisco: China Books, 1972.

Chinese Cultural Revolution, 1966–1969

By the mid-1960s Mao Tse-tung, it appeared, came to believe that the Chinese Revolution had become institutionalized. The CCP was more concerned with its own self-preservation and prestige than with advancing socialism; it was bureaucratic and had lost contact with the masses. The "four olds"—old ideas, old cultures, old customs, and old habits—

still had to be eliminated. To put China back on track the Cultural Revolution was launched. Put simply, it was presented as a nationwide struggle over how best to carry out the commonly accepted ideals of Chinese Communism, and it revealed the importance Mao attached to the cultural and ideological development of the minds of his people.

The Cultural Revolution can be examined in light of twentieth century Chinese history in that it was an extension of China's earlier revolutions. Mao hoped to preserve the revolutionary character of China and to prevent the long-range goals from being abridged. The class struggle had to be continued even after the party was in power so as to prevent the country from returning to capitalism—which, ironically, it is showing signs of doing as the 1980s begin.

The Cultural Revolution was cast as a revolution of revitalization. It was a revolution against history, against the typical course of successful revolutions (e.g., Russian) in the sense that it was an effort to perpetuate the goals of the earlier upheaval rather than lose sight of them. It was seen as Mao's attempt to preserve the principles of egalitarian socialism under siege from "creeping" capitalism.

New information has come to light, however, suggesting that the Cultural Revolution as an ideological movement was almost a complete fraud. The revolution was not simply a good idea gone astray. Testimony and evidence introduced at the trial of the Gang of Four in late 1980 portrayed the upheaval as a power struggle by Mao and his supporters to enlarge their power. Mao's regime executed thousands of political opponents and jailed tens of thousands more on false charges. It used secret arrests, torture, illegal searches, wiretapping and electronic bugging, and sex traps, all for the purpose of purging enemies and dictating the lives of the people.

Thus, the full story of the Cultural Revolution is not yet available. Although the notion of the revolution as an ideological movement is a myth, the problems cited by Mao in 1966 are still present. Clearly, much work remains to be done.

Among the many fine books on the revolution are those by Richard Baum (1971, 1975), Jean Esmein (1973), Jack Gray and Patrick Cavendish (1968), William Hinton (1972), K. S. Karol (1968), Simon Leys (1978), Robert Jay Lifton (1968), Roderick Mac Farquhar (1974), David Milton, Nancy Milton, and Franz Schurmann (1974), and Thomas W. Robinson (1971). The titles of the articles should be examined for more specialized approaches. The reader should also be on the lookout for new studies that will incorporate the latest revelations.

Bibliography

4907. Wang, James C. *The Cultural Revolution in China: An Annotated Bibliography.* New York: Garland Publishing, 1975.

Documents

4908. *CCP Documents of the Great Proletarian Cultural Revolution, 1966-1967.* Hong Kong: Union Research Institute, 1968.
4909. Far, K. H., ed. *The Chinese Cultural Revolution: Selected Documents.* New York: Grove Press, 1968.
4910. Hinton, Harold C., ed. *The People's Republic of China, 1949-1979: A Documentary Survey.* 5 vols. Wilmington, Delaware: Scholarly Resources, 1980.

Origins

Articles

4911. Bridgham, Philip. "Mao's 'Cultural Revolution': Origin and Development." *China Quarterly* 29 (January-March 1967): 1-35.
4912. Chan, Sylvia. "Political Assessment of Intellectuals before the Cultural Revolution." *Asian Survey* 18:9 (September 1978): 891-911.
4913. Dittmer, Lowell. "'Line Struggle' in Theory and Practice: The Origins of the Cultural Revolution Reconsidered." *China Quarterly* 72 (December 1977): 675-712.
4914. Neuhauser, Charles. "The Chinese Communist Party in the 1960s: Prelude to the Cultural Revolution." *China Quarterly* 32 (October-December 1967): 3-36.

Books

4915. Baum, Richard. *Prelude to Revolution: Mao, the Party, and the Peasant Question, 1962-1966.* New York: Columbia University Press, 1975.
4916. Kwong, Julia. *Chinese Education in Transition: Prelude to the Cultural Revolution.* Montreal: McGill-Queen's University Press, 1979.
4917. MacFarquhar, Roderick. *The Origins of the Cultural Revolution.* New York: Columbia University Press, 1974.

The Revolution

Articles

4918. Ahmad, S. H. "China's 'Cultural Revolution.'" *International Studies* 9 (July 1967): 13-54.
4919. Ahn, Byung-joon. "The Cultural Revolution and China's Search for Political Order." *China Quarterly* 58 (April-May 1974): 249-85.
4920. Baum, Richard. "The New Revolution: III: Ideology, Redivivus." *Problems of Communism* 16:3 (May-June 1967): 1-11.
4921. ———. "Revolution and Reaction in the Chinese Countryside: The Socialist Education Movement in Cultural Revolutionary Perspective." *China Quarterly* 38 (April-June 1969): 92-119.

4922. Blecher, Marc J., and Gordon White. "Micropolitics in Contemporary China: A Technical Unit During and After the Cultural Revolution." *International Journal of Politics* 8 (Summer 1979): 1–133.
4923. Bonavia, David. "The Fate of the 'New Born Things' of China's Cultural Revolution." *Pacific Affairs* 51 (Summer 1978): 177–94.
4924. Bridgham, Philip. "Mao's Cultural Revolution in 1967: The Struggle to Seize Power." *China Quarterly* 34 (April-June 1968): 6–37.
4925. _____. "Mao's Cultural Revolution: The Struggle to Seize Power." *China Quarterly* 41 (January-March 1970): 1–25.
4926. Dittmer, Lowell. "Thought Reform and Cultural Revolution: An Analysis of Symbolism of Chinese Polemics." *American Political Science Review* 71:1 (March 1977): 67–85.
4927. Dorrill, William F. "Transfer of Legitimacy in the Chinese Communist Party: Origins of the Maoist Myth." *China Quarterly* 36 (October-December 1968): 45–60.
4928. Elegant, Robert S. "China's Next Phase." *Foreign Affairs* 46 (October 1967): 137–50.
4929. Frolic, B. Michael. "What the Cultural Revolution Was All About." *The New York Times Magazine* (24 October 1971).
4930. Goldman, Merle. "China's Ideological Controversies against the Background of the Cultural Revolution." *Asian Thought and Society* 2 (September 1977): 239–52.
4931. Hsiao, Gene T. "The Background and Development of 'The Proletarian Cultural Revolution.'" *Asian Survey* 7:6 (June 1967): 389–404.
4932. Hsüeh, Chün-tu. "The Cultural Revolution and Leadership Crisis in Communist China." *Political Science Quarterly* 82:2 (June 1967): 1–20.
4933. Ito, Kikuzo, and Minoru Shibata. "The Dilemma of Mao Tse-tung." *China Quarterly* 35 (July-September 1968): 58–77.
4934. Joffe, Ellis. "China in Mid-1966: Cultural Revolution or Struggle for Power?" *China Quarterly* 27 (July-September 1966): 123–48.
4935. Johnson, Chalmers. "China: The Cultural Revolution in Structural Perspective." *Asian Survey* 8:1 (January 1968): 1–15.
4936. La Dany, L. "Mao's China: The Decline of a Dynasty." *Foreign Affairs* 45 (July 1967): 616–23.
4937. Lee, Hong Yung. "Mao's Strategy for Revolutionary Change: A Case Study of the Cultural Revolution." *China Quarterly* 77 (March 1979): 50–73.
4938. Lewis, John Wilson. "Revolutionary Struggle and the Second Generation in Communist China." *China Quarterly* 21 (January-March 1965): 126–47.
4939. Mac Farquhar, Roderick. "Mao's Last Revolution." *Foreign Affairs* 45 (October 1966): 112–24.
4940. Oksenberg, Michel. "The Institutionalization of the Chinese Communist Revolution: The Ladder of Success on the Eve of the Cultural Revolution." *China Quarterly* 36 (October-December 1968): 61–92.
4941. Perkins, Dwight H. "Economic Growth in China and the Cultural Revolution (1960-April 1967)." *China Quarterly* 30 (April-June 1967): 33–48.
4942. Pfeffer, Richard M. "The Pursuit of Purity: Mao's Cultural Revolution." *Problems of Communism* 18:6 (November-December 1969): 12–25.
4943. _____. "Serving the People and Continuing the Revolution." *China Quarterly* 52 (October-December 1972): 620–53.
4944. Pollard, D. E. "The Short Story in the Cultural Revolution." *China Quarterly* 73 (March 1978): 99–121.

4945. Raddock, David M. "Between Generations: Activist Chinese Youths in Pursuit of a Political Role in the San-Fan and in the Cultural Revolution." *China Quarterly* 79 (September 1979): 511–28.
4946. Schurmann, Franz. "The Attack of the Cultural Revolution on Ideology and Organization." In *China in Crisis,* edited by Ping-ti Ho and Tang Tsou. Vol. 1, book 2. Chicago: University of Chicago Press, 1968.
4947. Schwarcz, Vera. "How Literary Rebels Became Cultural Revolutionaries." *Journal of Asian Studies* 37:4 (August 1978): 725–29.
4948. Schwartz, Benjamin. "The Reign of Virtue: Some Broad Perspectives on Leader and Party in the Cultural Revolution." *China Quarterly* 35 (July-September 1968): 1–17.
4949. Tang Tsou. "The Cultural Revolution and the Chinese Political System." *China Quarterly* 38 (April-June 1969): 63–91.
4950. _____. "The Cultural Revolution, Then and Now." *The New York Times* (1 September 1974).
4951. Teiwes, Frederick C. "Before and After the Cultural Revolution." *China Quarterly* 58 (April-May 1974): 332–48.
4952. Terrill, Ross. "The New Revolution: II: The Siege Mentality." *Problems of Communism* 16:2 (March-April 1967): 1–10.
4953. United Kingdom, Foreign Office. "Mao's Cultural Revolution" (December 1967).
4954. Vogel, Ezra F. "From Revolutionary to Semi-Bureaucrat: The 'Regularization' of Cadres." *China Quarterly* 29 (January-March 1967): 36–60.
4955. Wang, Gungwu. "May 4th and the GPCR: The Cultural Revolution Remedy." *Pacific Affairs* 52 (Winter 1979–1980): 674–90.
4956. Wylie, Ray. "Revolution Within a Revolution." *Bulletin of the Atomic Scientists* 25:2 (February 1969): 29–32.
4957. Yuan-Li Wu. "Economics, Ideology, and the Cultural Revolution." *Asian Survey* 8:3 (March 1968): 223–35.

Books

4958. Ahn, Byung-joon. *Chinese Politics and the Cultural Revolution: Dynamics of Policy Processes.* Seattle: University of Washington Press, 1976.
4959. An, Tai Sung. *Mao Tse-tung's Cultural Revolution.* Indianapolis, Indiana: Pegasus, 1972.
4960. Barcata, Louis. *China in the Throes of the Cultural Revolution.* New York: Hart, 1968.
4961. Baum, Richard, ed. *China in Ferment: Perspectives on the Cultural Revolution.* Englewood Cliffs, New Jersey: Prentice-Hall, 1971.
4962. Bettelheim, Charles. *Cultural Revolution and Industrial Organization in China: Changes in Management and the Division of Labor.* New York: Monthly Review Press, 1975.
4963. Brugger, Bill, ed. *China: The Impact of the Cultural Revolution.* New York: Barnes and Noble, 1978.
4964. Chen, Jack. *Inside the Cultural Revolution.* New York: Macmillan, 1975.
4965. Chiou, C. L. *Maoism in Action: A Cultural Revolution.* New York: Crane-Russak, 1974.

4966. Chuang, H. C. *The Great Proletarian Cultural Revolution.* Studies in Chinese Communist Terminology, no. 12. Berkeley: Center for Chinese Studies, University of California, 1967.
4967. Cullman, L. *Cultural Revolution in the Provinces.* Cambridge, Massachusetts: Harvard University Press, 1971.
4968. Daubier, Jean. *A History of the Chinese Cultural Revolution.* Translated by R. Seaver. New York: Random House, 1974.
4969. Dittmer, Lowell. *Liu Shao-ch'i and the Chinese Cultural Revolution: The Politics of Mass Criticism.* Berkeley: University of California Press, 1975.
4970. Dorrill, William F. *Power, Policy and Ideology in the Making of China's "Cultural Revolution."* Santa Monica, California: Rand Corporation, 1971.
4971. Dutt, Gargi, and V. P. Dutt. *China's Cultural Revolution.* New York: Asia Publishing House, 1970.
4972. Esmein, Jean. *The Chinese Cultural Revolution.* Garden City, New York: Doubleday, 1973.
4973. Gray, Jack, and Patrick Cavendish. *Chinese Communism in Crisis: Maoism and the Cultural Revolution.* New York: Praeger, 1968.
4974. Hiniker, Paul J. *Revolutionary Ideology and Chinese Reality: Dissonance Under Mao.* Beverly Hills, California: Sage, 1977.
4975. Hinton, William. *Hundred Day War: The Cultural Revolution at Tsinghua University.* New York: Monthly Review Press, 1972.
4976. _____ . *Turning Point in China: An Essay on the Cultural Revolution.* New York: Monthly Review Press, 1972.
4977. Hsia, Adrian. *The Chinese Cultural Revolution.* Translated by G. Onn. Somers, Connecticut: Seabury Press, 1972.
4978. Karol, K. S. *China: The Other Communism.* 2d. ed. Translated by T. Baistow. New York: Hill and Wang, 1968.
4979. Keesing's Research Report. *The Cultural Revolution in China.* New York: Scribners, 1967.
4980. Lee, Hong Yung. *The Politics of the Chinese Cultural Revolution: A Case Study.* Berkeley: University of California Press, 1978.
4981. Leys, Simon. *The Chairman's New Clothes: Mao and the Cultural Revolution.* New York: St. Martin's Press, 1978.
4982. Lifton, Robert Jay. *Revolutionary Immortality: Mao Tse-tung and the Chinese Cultural Revolution.* New York: Random House, 1968.
4983. Liu, Alan P. *Political Culture and Group Conflict in Communist China.* Santa Barbara, California: ABC-Clio, 1976.
4984. Lo, Ruth Earnshaw, and Katharine S. Kinderman. *In the Eye of the Typhoon.* New York: Harcourt Brace Jovanovich, 1980.
4985. Lotta, Raymond. *And Mao Makes 5: Mao Tsetung's Last Great Battle.* Chicago: Banner Press, 1978.
4986. Milton, David; Nancy Milton; and Franz Schurmann, eds. *The China Reader IV: People's China: Social Experimentation, Politics, Entry onto the World Scene, 1966 through 1972.* New York: Random House, 1974.
4987. Myrdal, Jan, and Gun Kessle. *China: The Revolution Continued.* Translated by P. B. Austin. New York: Random House, 1972.
4988. Nee, Victor, and James Peck, eds. *Essays on the Chinese Cultural Revolution.* New York: Pantheon Books, 1974.

4989. Oksenberg, Michael, et al. *The Cultural Revolution in Review.* Michigan Papers in Chinese Studies, no. 2. Ann Arbor: Center for Chinese Studies, University of Michigan, 1968.

4990. Pye, Lucian W., et al. *China: Management of a Revolutionary Society.* Edited by J. M. H. Lindbeck. Seattle: University of Washington Press, 1971.

4991. Rice, Edward E. *Mao's Way.* Berkeley: University of California Press, 1972.

4992. Robinson, Joan. *The Cultural Revolution in China.* Baltimore: Penguin Books, 1969.

4993. Robinson, Thomas W., ed. *The Cultural Revolution in China.* Berkeley: University of California Press, 1971.

4994. Salisbury, Harrison. *To Peking and Beyond: A Report on the New Asia.* New York: Quadrangle Books, 1973.

4995. Schram, Stuart, ed. *Authority, Participation and Cultural Change in China.* New York: Cambridge University Press, 1974.

4996. Wheelwright, E. L., and Bruce McFarlane. *The Chinese Road to Socialism: Economics of the Cultural Revolution.* New York: Monthly Review Press, 1970.

Everyday Life

4997. Hunter, Neale. *Shanghai Journal: An Eyewitness Account of the Cultural Revolution.* New York: Praeger, 1969.

4998. Macciocchi, Maria Antonietta. *Daily Life in Revolutionary China.* New York: Monthly Review Press, 1972.

4999. Milton, David, and Nancy Milton. *The Wind Will Not Subside: Years in Revolutionary China—1964-1969.* New York: Pantheon Books, 1976.

Military, Red Guards, Youth

Articles

5000. Domes, Jürgen. "The Cultural Revolution and the Army." *Asian Survey* 8:5 (May 1968): 349-63.

5001. Israel, John. "The Red Guards in Historical Perspective: Continuity and Change in the Chinese Youth Movement." *China Quarterly* 30 (April-June 1967): 1-32.

5002. Leader, Shelah Gilbert. "The Communist Youth League and the Cultural Revolution." *Asian Survey* 14:8 (August 1974): 700-15.

5003. Lee, Hong Yung. "The Radical Students in Kwangtung during the Cultural Revolution." *China Quarterly* 64 (December 1975): 645-83.

5004. London, Miriam, and Ivan D. London. "China's Lost Generation: The Fate of the Red Guards Since 1968." *Saturday Review/World* (30 November 1974): 12.

5005. Nelsen, Harvey. "Military Forces in the Cultural Revolution." *China Quarterly* 51 (July-September 1972): 444-76.

Books

5006. Granqvist, Hans. *The Red Guard: A Report on Mao's Revolution.* Translated by E. J. Friis. New York: Praeger, 1967.
5007. Pan, Stephen, and Raymond J. de Jaegher. *Peking's Red Guard: The Great Proletarian Cultural Revolution.* New York: Twin Circle, 1968.
5008. Rosen, Stanley. *Red Guard Factionalism in China's Cultural Revolution: A Social Analysis.* Boulder, Colorado: Westview Press, 1981.
5009. Singer, Martin. *Educated Youth and the Cultural Revolution in China.* Ann Arbor: University of Michigan Center for Chinese Studies, 1971.

Aftermath

5010. Bulletin of the Atomic Scientists. *China After the Cultural Revolution.* New York: Random House, 1969.
5011. Chang, Y. C. *Factional and Coalition Politics in China: The Cultural Revolution and Its Aftermath.* New York: Praeger, 1976.
5012. Domes, Jürgen. *China after the Cultural Revolution: Politics between Two Party Congresses.* Translated by A. Berg and D. Goodman. Berkeley: University of California Press, 1977.
5013. Gudoshnikov, L. M., et al. *China: Cultural Revolution and After.* Mystic, Connecticut: Lawrence Verry, 1979.

Vietnamese Revolution, 1945-1973

The Vietnamese Revolution was waged first against the French (who had controlled the country from the mid-nineteenth century), then the United States, and always against other Vietnamese. Two key underlying elements in the revolution were the struggle for national independence and xenophobia. Although Vietnamese Communists provided the leadership, the revolution was not specifically to install communists in power; instead it was an anti-colonial struggle to establish independence, and the communists were in the forefront of that struggle.

The French were defeated because their military superiority was inadequate in what was fundamentally a political conflict; the Vietnamese fought for survival, the French did not. The Americans were defeated because they engaged in a limited war against a Vietnamese opponent for whom the war was total. The revolution was also a civil war between two rival groups, one centered in the North (Communist oriented) and one in the South (Western oriented).

Among the best books on the subject are those by Chester A. Bain (1967), Dennis J. Duncanson (1968), Bernard B. Fall (1956, 1963, 1967),

John T. McAlister, Jr. (1969), John T. McAlister, Jr. and Paul Mus (1971), Douglas Pike (1966, 1970, 1978), and Jeffrey Race (1972). The books by Le Duan (1965, 1971), Vo Nguyen Giap (1962, 1976), and Xuan Khu Dang (1963) are by Vietnamese revolutionary leaders.

Bibliographies

5014. Cotter, Michael, ed. *Vietnam.* Boston: G. K. Hall, 1977.
5015. Jumper, Roy. *Vietnam: An Annotated Bibliography.* Salisbury, North Carolina: Documentary Publications, 1980.
5016. Leitenberg, Milton, and Richard Dean Burns. *The Vietnam Conflict: Its Geographical Dimensions, Political Traumas, and Military Developments.* Santa Barbara, California: ABC-Clio, 1973.
5017. Phan Thien Chau. *Vietnamese Communism: A Research Bibliography.* Westport, Connecticut: Greenwood, 1975.

Documents

5018. Cameron, Allan W., ed. *Viet-Nam Crisis: A Documentary History.* Ithaca: Cornell University Press, 1971.
5019. *Documents of the August 1945 Revolution in Vietnam.* Canberra: Department of International Relations, Australian National University, 1963.
5020. Viet Nam, Democratic Republic of. *Breaking Our Chains: Documents of the Vietnamese Revolution of August 1945.* Hanoi: Foreign Languages Publishing House, 1960.
5021. _____ . *A Heroic People: Memoirs from the Revolution.* Hanoi: Foreign Languages Publishing House, 1960.

Articles

5022. Carver, George. "The Real Revolution in South Viet Nam." *Foreign Affairs* 43 (April 1965): 387–408.
5023. Doan Van Toai. "A Lament for Vietnam." *The New York Times Magazine* (29 March 1981).
5024. Glazunov, Y. "Vietnam's Road to Socialism." *International Affairs* 9 (September 1978): 23–30.
5025. Lansdale, Edward G. "Viet Nam: Do We Understand Revolution?" *Foreign Affairs* 43 (October 1964): 75–86.
5026. Le Duan. "Vietnamese Revolution at a New Stage." *Political Affairs* 56 (July-August 1977): 45–52.
5027. McAlister, John T., Jr. "Vietnam's 'Mandate of Heaven' May Mandate More Fighting." *Los Angeles Times* (28 January 1973).
5028. Marr, David G. "Nationalism and Revolution in Vietnam: A Review Article." *Pacific Affairs* 50 (Spring 1977): 86–90.
5029. Osborne, Milton. "Continuity and Motivation in the Vietnamese Revolution: New Light from the 1930s." *Pacific Affairs* 47 (Spring 1974): 37–55.
5030. Petros, James. "Vietnam: The Future of Revolution in the Third World." *Liberation* 17:9 (May 1973): 17–20.

Vietnamese Revolution, 1945-1973 / 319

5031. Roberts, Dick. "The Vietnamese Revolution and World Politics." *International Socialist Review* 33 (December 1972): 12.
5032. Rousset, Pierre. "The Vietnamese Revolution and the Role of the Party." *International Socialist Review* 35 (April 1974): 4-25.
5033. Sacks, I. Milton. "Marxism in Viet Nam." In *Marxism in Southeast Asia*, edited by F. N. Trager. Stanford: Stanford University Press, 1959.
5034. Smith, Robert B. "Rebellion and Repression and the Vietnam War." *Annals of the American Academy of Political and Social Science* 391 (September 1970): 156-67.
5035. Turnbull, Patrick. "The Battle of Dien Bien Phu, 1954." *History Today* 29 (April 1979): 230-39.
5036. Vien, Nguyen Khac. "Vietnam Since Liberation: A Dialogue." *Marxism Today* 23 (February 1979): 49-54.
5037. _____. "The Vietnamese Experience and the Third World." *Bulletin of Concerned Asian Scholars* 6 (September-October 1974): 7-11.
5038. White, Christine Pelzer. "The Peasants and the Party in the Vietnamese Revolution." In *Peasants and Politics: Grass Roots Reactions to Change in Asia*. Melbourne: Edward Arnold, forthcoming.
5039. _____. "The Vietnamese Revolutionary Alliance: Intellectuals, Workers and Peasants." In *Peasant Rebellion and Communist Revolution in Asia*, edited by J. W. Lewis. Stanford: Stanford University Press, 1974.
5040. Young, Stephen B. "Vietnamese Marxism: Transition in Elite Ideology." *Asian Survey* 19:8 (August 1979): 770-79.

Books

5041. Andrews, William R. *The Village War: Vietnamese Communist Revolutionary Activities in Dinh Tuong Province, 1960-1964*. St. Louis: University of Missouri Press, 1973.
5042. Bain, Chester A. *Vietnam: The Roots of Conflict*. Englewood Cliffs, New Jersey: Prentice-Hall, 1967.
5043. Berman, Paul. *Revolutionary Organization*. Lexington, Massachusetts: Lexington Books, 1974.
5044. Buell, Hal. *Vietnam: Land of Many Dragons*. New York: Dodd, Mead, 1968.
5045. Burchett, Wilfred. *Grasshoppers and Elephants: Why Viet Nam Fell*. New York: Urizen Books, 1977.
5046. _____. *Vietnam: Inside Story of the Guerrilla War*. New York: International Publishers, 1965.
5047. _____. *Vietnam Will Win!* New York: Monthly Review Press, 1969.
5048. Buttinger, Joseph. *A Dragon Defiant: A Short History of Vietnam*. New York: Praeger, 1972.
5049. _____. *Vietnam: A Political History*. New York: Praeger, 1968.
5050. _____. *Vietnam: The Unforgettable Tragedy*. New York: Horizon Press, 1976.
5051. Cannon, Terry. *Vietnam: A Thousand Years of Struggle*. San Francisco: People's Press, 1969.
5052. Chandler, Robert W. *War of Ideas: The U.S. Propaganda Campaign in Vietnam*. Boulder, Colorado: Westview Press, 1981.

5053. Cooper, Bert, et al. *Case Studies in Insurgency and Revolutionary Warfare: Vietnam, 1941-1954.* Washington, D.C.: Special Operations Research Office, American University, 1964.
5054. Duiker, William J. *The Communist Road to Power in Vietnam.* Boulder, Colorado: Westview Press, 1981.
5055. _____. *The Rise of Nationalism in Vietnam, 1900-1941.* Ithaca: Cornell University Press, 1976.
5056. _____. *Vietnam.* Boulder, Colorado: Westview Press, 1982.
5057. Duncanson, Dennis J. *Government and Revolution in Vietnam.* London: Oxford University Press, 1968.
5058. Dung, Van Tien. *Our Great Spring Victory: An Account of the Liberation of South Vietnam.* Translated by J. Spragens, Jr. New York: Monthly Review Press, 1978.
5059. Fall, Bernard B. *Hell in a Very Small Place: The Siege of Dien Bien Phu.* New York: Lippincott, 1967.
5060. _____. *The Two Viet-Nams.* New York: Praeger, 1963.
5061. _____. *The Viet-Minh Regime.* New York: Institute of Pacific Relations, 1956.
5062. Fitz Gerald, Frances. *Fire in the Lake: The Vietnamese and the Americans in Vietnam.* Boston: Little, Brown, 1972.
5063. Gettleman, Marvin, ed. *Vietnam.* New York: Fawcett World Library, 1965.
5064. _____; Susan Gettleman; Lawrence Kaplan; and Carol Kaplan, eds. *Conflict in Indo-China.* New York: Random House, 1970.
5065. Goldston, Robert. *The Vietnamese Revolution.* New York: Dell, 1973.
5066. Henderson, William Darryl. *Why the Viet Cong Fought: A Study of Motivation and Control in a Modern Army in Combat.* Westport, Connecticut: Greenwood, 1979.
5067. Hoang Van Chi. *From Colonialism to Communism: A Case History of North Vietnam.* New York: Praeger, 1964.
5068. Hodgkin, Thomas. *Vietnam: The Revolutionary Path.* New York: St. Martin's Press, 1980.
5069. Le Duan. *On the Socialist Revolution in Vietnam.* Hanoi: Government Publications, 1965.
5070. _____. *The Vietnamese Revolution: Fundamental Problems and Essential Tasks.* New York: International Publishers, 1971.
5071. McAlister, John T., Jr. *Vietnam: The Origins of Revolution.* Garden City, New York: Doubleday, 1969.
5072. _____, and Paul Mus. *The Vietnamese and Their Revolution.* New York: Harper and Row, 1971.
5073. Mallin, Jay. *Terror in Vietnam.* Princeton: D. Van Nostrand, 1966.
5074. Marr, David G. *Vietnamese Anticolonialism.* Berkeley: University of California Press, 1971.
5075. _____, and Jayne Werner, eds. *Tradition and Revolution in Vietnam.* Washington, D.C.: Indochina Resource Center, 1974.
5076. Millett, Allan R., ed. *A Short History of the Vietnam War.* Bloomington: Indiana University Press, 1978.
5077. O'Ballance, Edgar. *The Indo-China War, 1945-1954: A Study in Guerrilla Warfare.* London: Faber and Faber, 1964.
5078. O'Neill, Robert J. *General Giap, Politician and Strategist.* New York: Praeger, 1969.

5079. Patti, Archimedes L. A. *Why Viet Nam? Prelude to America's Albatross.* Berkeley: University of California Press, 1980.
5080. Pike, Douglas. *History of Vietnamese Communism, 1925–1976.* Stanford: Hoover Institution, 1978.
5081. _____. *Viet Cong.* Cambridge, Massachusetts: M.I.T. Press, 1966.
5082. _____. *War, Peace, and the Viet Cong.* Cambridge, Massachusetts: M.I.T. Press, 1970.
5083. Race, Jeffrey. *War Comes to Long An: Revolutionary Conflict in a Vietnamese Province.* Berkeley: University of California Press, 1972.
5084. Shaplen, Robert. *The Lost Revolution: The U.S. in Vietnam, 1946–1966.* Rev. ed. New York: Harper and Row, 1966.
5085. Shibata, Shingo. *Lessons of the Vietnam War: Philosophical Considerations on the Vietnam Revolution.* Atlantic Highlands, New Jersey: Humanities Press, 1973.
5086. Tanham, George K. *Communist Revolutionary Warfare: From the Vietminh to the Viet Cong.* Rev. ed. New York: Praeger, 1967.
5087. Trullinger, James Walker, Jr. *Village at War: An Account of Revolution in Vietnam.* New York: Longman, 1980.
5088. Turley, William S. *Vietnamese Communism in Comparative Perspective.* Boulder, Colorado: Westview Press, 1980.
5089. Turner, Robert F. *Vietnamese Communism: Its Origins and Development.* Stanford: Hoover Institution, 1975.
5090. Vien, Nguyen Khac. *Tradition and Revolution in Vietnam.* Berkeley, California: Indochina Resource Center, 1975.
5091. Vo Nguyen Giap. *How We Won the War.* Philadelphia: Recon Publications, 1976.
5092. _____. *People's War, People's Army.* New York: Praeger, 1962.
5093. Woodside, Alexander B. *Community and Revolution in Vietnam.* Boston: Houghton Mifflin, 1976.
5094. Xuan Khu Dang ("Truong Chinh"). *Primer for Revolt: The Communist Takeover in Viet-Nam.* New York: Praeger, 1963.

Ho Chi Minh

Ho Chi Minh was the founder of the League for the Independence of Viet Nam (the Viet Minh), a nationalist/communist organization that led the way in the Vietnamese Revolution. Ho, a father figure to his people, was a man of action. It was his concern for his people in the face of French exploitation that drove him to communism, but the most important ideological component of his leadership was nationalism. The best biographies of Ho are by David Halberstam (1971), N. Khac Huyen (1971), and Jean Lacouture (1968). The collections edited by Bernard B. Fall (1968) and Jack Woodis (1970) should also be consulted.

Articles

5095. Chen, King C. "Ho Chi Minh: The Man and His Ideas." *Asian Thought and Society* 1 (April 1976): 24–32.
5096. Schurmann, Franz. "Eulogy to Ho Chi Minh." *Ramparts* (November 1969): 52–60.
5097. Sethna, D. P. "Ho Chi Minh—The Disillusioned Leader." *Tempo* 5 (April-May 1975): 5–6.
5098. Shaplen, Robert. "The Enigma of Ho Chi Minh." *Reporter* (27 January 1955): 11–19.

Books

5099. Fall, Bernard B., ed. *Ho Chi Minh on Revolution*. New York: Signet Books, 1968.
5100. Fenn, Charles. *Ho Chi Minh: A Biographical Introduction*. New York: Scribners, 1973.
5101. Halberstam, David. *Ho*. New York: Random House, 1971.
5102. Ho Chi Minh. *Prison Diary*. Translated by A. Palmer. Hanoi: Foreign Languages Publishing House, 1965.
5103. ———. *Selected Works*. 3 vols. Hanoi: Foreign Languages Publishing House, 1960–1961.
5104. Huyen, N. Khac. *Vision Accomplished? The Enigma of Ho Chi Minh*. New York: Macmillan, 1971.
5105. Lacouture, Jean. *Ho Chi Minh*. New York: Random House, 1968.
5106. Neumann-Hoditz, R. *Portrait of Ho Chi Minh*. Translated by J. Hargreaves. New York: Herder and Herder, 1972.
5107. Woodis, Jack, ed. *Ho Chi Minh: Selected Articles and Speeches, 1920–1967*. New York: International Publishers, 1970.

Revolution in Laos

Articles

5108. Jonas, A., and G. Tanham. "Laos: A Phase in Cyclic Regional Revolution." *Orbis* 5 (Spring 1961): 64–73.
5109. Pin, A. "Laos: The Progress of the Revolution." *New Times* 49 (December 1977): 23–26.
5110. Stuart-Fox, Martin. "The Lao Revolution: Errors and Achievements." *World Review* 16 (July 1977): 3–15.
5111. ———. "The Lao Revolution: Leadership and Policy Differences." *Australian Outlook* 31 (August 1977): 279–88.

Books

5112. Adams, Nina S., and Alfred W. McCoy, eds. *Laos: War and Revolution.* New York: Harper and Row, 1970.
5113. Langer, Paul F., and Joseph J. Zasloff. *North Vietnam and the Pathet Lao: Partners in the Struggle for Laos.* Cambridge, Massachusetts: Harvard University Press, 1970.
5114. Toye, Hugh. *Laos: Buffer State or Battleground.* New York: Oxford University Press, 1968.
5115. Zasloff, Joseph J. *The Pathet Lao.* Lexington, Massachusetts: Lexington Books, 1973.

Revolution in Cambodia

Articles

5116. Kamm, Henry. "Life in 'Liberated' Cambodia." *The New York Times Magazine* (18 May 1980).
5117. Ky Son. "Khmerization and Revolution." *Vietnamese Studies* 39 (1974): 159–98.
5118. Rousset, Pierre. "Cambodia: Background to the Revolution." *Journal of Contemporary Asia* 7 (1977): 513–28.

Books

5119. Hildebrand, George C., and Gareth Porter. *Cambodia: Starvation and Revolution.* New York: Monthly Review Press, 1978.
5120. Simon, Sheldon W. *War and Politics in Cambodia: A Communications Analysis.* Durham, North Carolina: Duke University Press, 1974.

Revolution in Thailand

Articles

5121. Morell, David, and Chairanan Samudavanija. "Thailand's Revolutionary Insurgency: Changes in Leadership Potential." *Asian Survey* 19:4 (April 1979): 315–32.
5122. Tarling, Nicholas. "King Prajadhipok and the Apple Cart: British Attitudes towards the 1932 Revolution." *Journal of Siam Society* 66 (January 1976): 1–38.
5123. Turton, Andrew. "The Peasantry of Thailand: Scientific and Social Revolution." *Comparative Studies in Social History* 20:4 (October 1978): 621–25.
5124. Watson, Andrew. "Revolution in Sian." *Far Eastern Economic Review* (20 April 1967): 123–26.

Books

5125. Keyes, Charles F. *Thailand.* Boulder, Colorado: Westview Press, 1982.
5126. Landon, Kenneth P. *Siam in Transition: A Brief Survey of Cultural Trends in the Five Years since the Revolution of 1932.* Shanghai: Kelly and Walsh, 1939.

Revolution in Indonesia

Most of the titles below are concerned with the Indonesian Revolution of 1945–1947, a successful anti-colonial revolution for independence from the Dutch. That revolution was led by Achmed Sukarno and his Nationalist Party. The Indonesian Communist Party (PKI) supported Sukarno, but were faced with attempts to eliminate them following independence in 1947. A coup d'etat in 1965 overthrew Sukarno. The best books on the revolution are by George McT. Kahin (1952), Anthony Reid (1974), and Donald E. Weatherbee (1966). For Indonesian Communists see Donald Hindley's book (1964). The book by D. M. Aidit (1964) is by the man who led the PKI, from its formation in 1920 to his death in 1965.

Articles

5127. Kahin, Audrey. "Some Preliminary Observations on West Sumatra during the Revolution." *Indonesia* 18 (October 1974): 77–118.
5128. Soejatno. "Revolution and Social Tensions in Surakarta, 1945–1950." *Indonesia* 17 (April 1974): 99–112.

Books

5129. Aidit, D. M. *The Indonesian Revolution and the Immediate Tasks of the Communist Party of Indonesia.* Peking: Foreign Languages Press, 1964.
5130. Anderson, Benedict R. *Java in a Time of Revolution.* Ithaca: Cornell University Press, 1972.
5131. Coast, John. *Recruit to Revolution: Adventure and Politics in Indonesia.* New York: AMS Press, 1952.
5132. Fryer, D. W., and James C. Jackson. *Indonesia.* Boulder, Colorado: Westview Press, 1977.
5133. Hindley, Donald. *The Communist Party of Indonesia, 1951–1963.* Berkeley: University of California Press, 1964.
5134. Jackson, Karl D. *Traditional Authority, Islam, and Rebellion: A Study of Indonesian Political Behavior.* Berkeley: University of California Press, 1980.

5135. Kahin, George McT. *Nationalism and Revolution in Indonesia.* Ithaca: Cornell University Press, 1952.
5136. Njoto. *Strive for the Victory of the Indonesian Revolution with the Weapons of Dialectical and Historical Materialism.* Peking: Foreign Languages Press, 1964.
5137. Palmier, Leslie. *Communists in Indonesia: Power Pursued in Vain.* Garden City, New York: Doubleday, 1973.
5138. Reid, Anthony. *The Indonesian National Revolution, 1945-1950.* New York: Longman, 1974.
5139. Sloan, Stephen. *A Study in Political Violence: The Indonesian Experience.* Chicago: Rand McNally, 1971.
5140. Smail, John R. W. *Bandung in the Early Revolution, 1945-1946: A Study in the Social History of the Indonesian Revolution.* Ithaca: Southeast Asia Program, Cornell University, 1964.
5141. Weatherbee, Donald E. *Ideology in Indonesia: Sukarno's Indonesian Revolution.* New Haven: Yale University Press, 1966.
5142. Wilson, Greta O. *Regents, Reformers, and Revolutionaries: Indonesian Voices of Colonial Days. Selected Historical Readings, 1899-1949.* Honolulu: University Press of Hawaii, 1978.

Revolution in Malaya

Articles

5143. Han, Sin Fong. "A Constitutional Coup d'Etat: An Analysis of the Birth and Victory of the Berjaya Party in Sabah, Malaysia." *Asian Survey* 19 (April 1979): 379-89.
5144. Stenson, Michael. "The Ethnic and Urban Bases of Communist Revolt in Malaya." In *Peasant Rebellion and Communist Revolution in Asia,* edited by J. W. Lewis. Stanford: Stanford University Press, 1974.

Books

5145. King, Frank H. H. *The New Malayan Nation: A Study of Communalism and Nationalism.* New York: Institute of Pacific Relations, 1957.
5146. Pye, Lucian W. *Guerrilla Communism in Malaya, Its Social and Political Meaning.* Princeton: Princeton University Press, 1956.
5147. Short, Anthony. *The Communist Insurrection in Malaya, 1948-1960.* New York: Crane-Russak, 1974.
5148. Stenson, Michael. *Repression and Revolt: The Origins of the 1948 Communist Insurrection in Malaya and Singapore.* Athens: Ohio University, Center for International Studies, 1965.

Revolution in Korea

Article

5149. Noumoff, S. J. "The Struggle for Revolutionary Authenticity: The Experience of the DPRK (Korea)." *Journal of Contemporary Asia* 9:1 (1979): 27-52.

Books

5150. Kim Byong Sik. *Modern Korea: The Socialist North, Revolutionary Perspectives in the South, and Unification.* New York: International Publishers, 1970.
5151. Kim Il Sung. *Revolution and Socialist Construction in Korea: Selected Writings of Kim Il Sung.* New York: International Publishers, 1971.
5152. Se-Jim Kim. *The Politics of Military Revolution in Korea.* Chapel Hill: University of North Carolina Press, 1972.

Sepoy Mutiny, 1857

In May, 1857, the Sepoys (Indian soldiers) revolted against their British officers. Before the Mutiny was finally suppressed in 1859 it had spread to large parts of India, and it resulted in the end of the rule of the British East India Company. The rebellion was more than a mere army revolt and less than a nationalistic uprising. From its inception until today, the extent and significance of the Mutiny has been a subject for historical debate. Certainly the Mutiny involved more than soldiers, contained elements of civil rebellion, and reflected general dissatisfaction with British rule. But equally certain is that there was no organized national conspiracy, little coordination, and no plans for the future if success had followed. At the very least, the conflict did have revolutionary overtones to the extent that it stimulated Indian nationalism and drove a deeper wedge between the British and the Indians.

The Mutiny and its historical ramifications are examined in the collection edited by Ainslee T. Embree (1963). Among the best books are those by George Dangerfield (1933), Christopher Hibbert (1978), Ramesh Chandra Majumdar (1957), George B. Mallison (1968), Thomas R. Metcalf (1964), F. W. Rawding (1977), and Surendra Nath Sen (1957).

Articles

5153. Brereton, J. M. "The White Mutiny [British forces in India 1857–1861]." *History Today* 29 (April 1979): 257–64.
5154. Nutt, Katharine F. "The Sepoy Mutiny of 1857: The New Look." *Midwest Quarterly* 21 (Autumn 1979): 81–96.

Books

5155. Bahadurke, Syed Ahmed Khan. *The Causes of the Indian Revolt.* Benares: Medical Hill Press, 1873.
5156. Chattopadhyaya, Haraprasad. *The Sepoy Mutiny, 1857: A Social Study and Analysis.* New York: Bookland, 1957.
5157. Chaudhuri, Sashi Bhusan. *Civil Rebellion in the Indian Mutiny, 1857– 1859.* Calcutta: World Press Private, 1957.
5158. _____. *English Historical Writings on the Indian Mutiny, 1857–1859.* Calcutta: World Press Private, 1979.
5159. Dangerfield, George. *Bengal Mutiny: The Story of the Sepoy Rebellion.* New York: Harcourt, Brace, 1933.
5160. Edwardes, Michael. *Battles of the Indian Mutiny.* London: Pan Books, 1970.
5161. _____. *A Season in Hell.* New York: Taplinger, 1973.
5162. Embree, Ainslee T., ed. *1857 in India: Mutiny or War of Independence?* Boston: D. C. Heath, 1963.
5163. Fariqi, Khwaja A. *Dastanbury: A Diary of the Indian Revolt of 1857 by Mirza Asadullah Ghalib.* New York: Asia Publishing House, 1971.
5164. Hibbert, Christopher. *The Great Mutiny: India in 1857.* New York: Viking, 1978.
5165. Hilton, Major-General Richard. *The Indian Mutiny.* London: Hollis and Carter, 1957.
5166. Holmes, T. Rice. *A History of the Indian Mutiny.* Folcroft, Pennsylvania: Folcroft Library Editions, 1978.
5167. Hutchinson, David, and N. A. Chick, eds. *Annals of the Indian Rebellion, 1857–58.* Totowa, New Jersey: Rowman and Littlefield, 1974.
5168. Ladendorf, Janice M. *Revolt in India: 1857–58.* New York: International Publications Service, 1966.
5169. McLane, John R., ed. *The Political Awakening of India.* Englewood Cliffs, New Jersey: Prentice-Hall, 1970.
5170. Majumdar, Ramesh Chandra. *The Sepoy Mutiny and the Revolt of 1857.* Calcutta: K. L. Mukhopadhyay, 1957.
5171. Mallison, George B., ed. *Kaye's and Mallison's History of the Indian Mutiny of 1857–1858.* Westport, Connecticut: Greenwood, 1968.
5172. Metcalf, Thomas R. *The Aftermath of Revolt: India, 1857–1870.* Princeton: Princeton University Press, 1964.
5173. Palmer, J. A. B. *The Mutiny Outbreak at Meerut in 1857.* New York: Cambridge University Press, 1966.
5174. Rawding, F. W. *The Rebellion in India, 1857.* New York: Cambridge University Press, 1977.

328 / Asia

5175. Russell, William H. *My Indian Mutiny Diary.* London: Cassell, 1957.
5176. Sen, Surendra Nath. *Eighteen Fifty-Seven.* New York: Luzak, 1957.
5177. Thompson, Edward J. *The Other Side of the Medal.* New York: Harcourt, Brace, 1926.
5178. _____, and G. T. Garratt. *Rise and Fulfillment of British Rule in India.* London: Macmillan, 1934.
5179. Vibart, Cononel E. *The Sepoy Mutiny.* Norwood, Pennsylvania: Norwood Editions, n.d.
5180. Wilkinson-Latham, Christopher. *Indian Mutiny.* New York: Hippocrene Books, 1977.

Indian Revolution and Gandhi, 1920–1949

By the end of World War I Indians were on the verge of revolution against British rule. Nationalist groups had existed for some time, but the most serious obstacle was the absence of genuine political unity. Adding to the problem were linguistic and religious differences, plus a caste system which prevented effective organization of the masses. But the forces of nationalism proved irresistible, and Mohandas K. Gandhi rose to prominence to show Indians how they could free themselves from the British yoke.

Gandhi launched a revolution unique in the method it provided to achieve Indian independence. That method, known as *satyagraha* ("truth force"), employed mass civil disobedience, nonviolence, passive resistance, and boycotts. Gandhi was able to release the power hidden within the Indian people, and he turned weaknesses into strengths; for example, he accepted his people's fatalism and passivity, and from it constructed a movement of non-cooperation in which passivity and endurance were turned into sources of energy and strength. By identifying himself with common Indians he reestablished unity and made the revolution possible.

The Indian Revolution travelled a long and hard road. Independence was not won until after World War II, but with it came the partition of the Indian subcontinent into two new nations, (predominantly) Hindu India and (predominantly) Moslem Pakistan. Such a division Gandhi had struggled to avoid right up until his assassination in 1948 by an anti-Moslem Hindu fanatic.

For the revolution per se, see the books by Abul Kalam Azad (1960), Subhas Chandra Bose (1935, 1952), and V. P. Menon (1957). The books by Jawaharlal Nehru (1950, 1956) are by Gandhi's chief disciple who later was the leader of independent India. For Gandhi, a good place to begin is the collection edited by Martin Deming Lewis (1965). Among the better biographies are those by Geoffrey Ashe (1968), Louis Fischer (1950, 1954), Ved Mehta (1977), B. R. Nanda (1958), F. W. Rawding (1980),

William L. Shirer (1980), and George Woodcock (1971). Other important studies of Gandhi are by Joan V. Bondurant (1965), Judith M. Brown (1972, 1977), Erik H. Erikson (1969), Francis G. Hutchins (1973), and Gene Sharp (n.d.). And, of course, Gandhi's own writings should be consulted. Finally, there are important works of related interest in Chapter 1 in the section "Nonviolence."

Bibliographies

5181. Diwakar, Ranganath R., et al. *Mohandas Karamchand Gandhi: A Bibliography.* Columbia, Missouri: South Asia Books, 1974.
5182. Mahar, J. Michael. *India: A Critical Bibliography.* Tucson: University of Arizona Press, 1964.
5183. *Mohandas Karamchand Gandhi: A Bibliography.* New Delhi: Orient Longmans, 1976.
5184. Satyaprakash. *Gandhiana, 1962-76: A Bibliography.* Columbia, Missouri: South Asia Books, 1977.
5185. Sharma, Jagdish. *Mahatma Gandhi, Bibliography.* 2d ed. Mystic, Connecticut: Lawrence Verry, 1968.

Documents

5186. Pandey, B. N., ed. *The Indian Nationalist Movement, 1885-1947: Select Documents.* New York: St. Martin's Press, 1979.
5187. Philips, Cyril H., ed. *The Evolution of India and Pakistan, 1858 to 1947: Selected Documents.* New York: Oxford University Press, 1962.

The Revolution

Articles

5188. Bhattacharyya, Jhanabrata. "An Examination of Leadership Entry in Bengal Peasant Revolts, 1937-1947." *Journal of Asian Studies* 37:4 (August 1978): 611-35.
5189. Ebert, Theodor. "Non Violent Insurrection or Revolutionary Warfare?" *Fellowship* (September 1968): 17-21.
5190. Gupta, Maya. "A Review of Revolutionary Terrorism in India, 1927-29." *Journal of Indian History* 55 (December 1977): 189-204.
5191. Raikov, A. V. "Indian National-Revolutionary Organizations in the 1920s." *Narod: Azii Afrikaanse* 20:1 (1974): 71-82.
5192. Raman, A. S. "Revolution in India." *Contemporary Review* 233 (September 1978): 149-54.
5193. Timberg, Thomas A. "Revolution and Growth: Two Case Studies from India." *Political Science Quarterly* 88:1 (March 1973): 86-93.

Books

5194. Alexander, Horace. *India Since Cripps.* Harmondsworth, England: Penguin Books, 1944.
5195. Amery, Leopold. *India and Freedom.* London: Oxford University Press, 1942.
5196. Andrews, Charles F. *India and Britain: A Moral Challenge.* London: Student Christian Movement Press, 1935.
5197. Azad, Abul Kalam. *India Wins Freedom.* New York: Longmans, Green, 1960.
5198. Berg, Lasse, and Lisa Berg. *Face to Face: Fascism and Revolution in India.* Berkeley: Ramparts Press, 1971.
5199. Bhuyan, Arun. *The Quit India Movement.* Columbia, Missouri: South Asia Books, 1975.
5200. Bose, Arun Coomer. *Indian Revolutionaries Abroad, 1905-1922: In the Background of International Development.* Patna, India: Bharati Bhawan, 1971.
5201. Bose, Subhas Chandra. *The Indian Struggle, 1920-1934.* London: Wishart and Company, 1935.
5202. _____. *The Indian Struggle, 1935-42.* Calcutta: Chuckerbertty, Chatterjee, 1952.
5203. Chopra, P. N. *Quit India Movement.* Columbia, Missouri: South Asia Books, 1976.
5204. Coatman, John. *India: The Road to Self-Government.* London: George Allen and Unwin, 1942.
5205. Desai, A. R. *Social Background of Indian Nationalism.* Rev. ed. Bombay: Popular Book Depot, 1954.
5206. Duffett, W. E. *India Today, the Background of the Indian Nationalist Movement.* Toronto: University of Toronto Press, 1941.
5207. Edwardes, Michael. *The Last Years of British India.* London: New English Library, 1967.
5208. Fuller, J. F. C. *India In Revolt.* London: Eyre and Spottiswoode, 1931.
5209. Guha, Arun C. *First Spark of Revolution: The Early Phase of India's Struggle for Independence, 1900-1920.* Port Washington, New York: Kennikat, 1971.
5210. _____. *The Story of the Indian Revolution.* New York: Paragon, 1972.
5211. Haithcox, John P. *Communism and Nationalism in India: M. N. Roy and the Comintern Policy, 1920-1939.* Princeton: Princeton University Press, 1971.
5212. Hinshaw, Cecil E. *Nonviolent Resistance: A Nation's Way to Peace.* Wallingford, Pennsylvania: Pendle Hill, 1956.
5213. Lajpat Rai, Lala. *Young India: An Interpretation and a History of the Nationalist Movement from Within.* New York: B. W. Huebsch, 1916.
5214. Ligt, Bart de. *The Conquest of Violence.* New York: E. P. Dutton, 1938.
5215. Menon, V. P. *Transfer of Power in India.* Princeton: Princeton University Press, 1957.
5216. Nehru, Jawaharlal. *Independence and After.* New York: Day, 1950.
5217. _____. *Towards a New Revolution.* New Delhi: Indian National Congress, 1956.
5218. Sandhu, Swaram S. *Nonviolence in Indian Religious Thought and Political Action.* Ardmore, Pennsylvania: Dorrance, 1977.

5219. Sen, Mohit. *Revolution in India: Path and Problems.* Columbia, Missouri: South Asia Books, 1977.
5220. Shridharani, Krishnalal. *War Without Violence.* Bombay: Bharatiya Vidya Bhavan, 1962.
5221. Smith, W. R. *Nationalism and Reform in India.* New Haven: Yale University Press, 1938.
5222. Wolpert, Stanley A. *Tilak and Gokhale: Revolution and Reform in the Making of Modern India.* Berkeley: University of California Press, 1977.
5223. Zaidi, A. Moin, ed. *The Way Out to Freedom: An Enquiry in the Quit India Movement.* Columbia, Missouri: South Asia Books, 1973.

Gandhi

Articles

5224. Chauhan, D. S. "Mohandas Karamchand Gandhi: Reconstruction, Revolutionary Thought, and Action Strategy." *Asian Quarterly* 1 (1974): 65–79.
5225. Kabir, Humayun. "The Revolutionary Significance of Gandhi." In *Gandhi: Maker of Modern India?* edited by M. D. Lewis. Boston: D. C. Heath, 1965.
5226. Mandelbaum, David G. "The Study of Life History: Gandhi." *Current Anthropology* 14:3 (June 1973):177–206.
5227. Rattan, Ram. "The Anatomy of Gandhi's Satyagraha." *Gandhi Margins* 17 (January 1973): 84–106.
5228. Subrahmanian, N. "Gandhi: An Intellectual Assessment." *Quest* 98 (November-December 1975): 47–52.
5229. Watson, I. Bruce. "Satyagraha: The Gandhian Synthesis." *Journal of Indian History* 55 (April-August 1977): 325–35.

Books

5230. Alexander, Horace. *Gandhi Remembered.* Wallingford, Pennsylvania: Pendle Hill, 1969.
5231. Andrews, C. F. *Mahatma Gandhi—His Own Story.* 2 vols. New York: Macmillan, 1930–1931.
5232. Ashe, Geoffrey. *Gandhi.* New York: Stein and Day, 1968.
5233. Birla, G. D. *In the Shadow of the Mahatma.* Bombay: Orient Longmans, 1953.
5234. Biswas, S. C., ed. *Gandhi: Theory and Practice, Social Impact and Contemporary Relevance.* Simla: Indian Institute of Advanced Study, 1969.
5235. Bolton, Glorney. *The Tragedy of Gandhi.* London: George Allen and Unwin, 1934.
5236. Bondurant, Joan V. *Conquest of Violence: The Gandhian Philosophy of Conflict.* Rev. ed. Berkeley: University of California Press, 1965.
5237. Bose, Nirmal Kumar. *Gandhiji: The Man and His Mission.* Bombay: Bharatiya Vidya Bhavan, 1966.

5238. _____. *My Days With Gandhi.* Columbia, Missouri: South Asia Books, 1974.
5239. _____. *Selections from Gandhi.* Ahmedabad: Navajivan Publishing House, 1948.
5240. _____. *Studies in Gandhism.* Calcutta: Indian Associated Publishing Co., 1947.
5241. Brown, Judith M. *Gandhi and Civil Disobedience: The Mahatma in Indian Politics, 1928–1934.* New York: Cambridge University Press, 1977.
5242. _____. *Gandhi's Rise to Power: Indian Politics, 1915–1922.* Cambridge: Cambridge University Press, 1972.
5243. Chaudury, P. C. Ray. *Gandhiji's First Struggle in India.* Ahmedabad: Navajivan Publishing House, 1955.
5244. Datta, Dhirendra Mohan. *The Philosophy of Mahatma Gandhi.* Madison: University of Wisconsin Press, 1953.
5245. Devanesen, Chandran D. S. *The Making of the Mahatma.* New York: International Publications Service, 1973.
5246. Dhawan, Gopinath. *The Political Philosophy of Mahatma Gandhi.* Ahmedabad: Navajivan Publishing House, 1957.
5247. Diwakar, Ranganath R. *Satyagraha: Its Technique and History.* Bombay: Hind Kitabs, 1946.
5248. Easwaran, Eknath. *Gandhi the Man.* Petaluma, California: Nilgiri Press, 1978.
5249. Eaton, Jeanette. *Gandhi: Fighter Without a Sword.* New York: Macmillan, 1962.
5250. Erikson, Erik H. *Gandhi's Truth: On the Origins of Militant Nonviolence.* New York: W. W. Norton, 1969.
5251. Fischer, Louis. *Gandhi: His Life and Message for the World.* New York: New American Library, 1954.
5252. _____. *The Life of Mahatma Gandhi.* New York: Harper and Row, 1950.
5253. Gandhi, Mohandas K. *An Autobiography, or the Story of My Experiments with Truth.* Ahmedabad: Navajivan Publishing House, 1956.
5254. _____. *The Collected Works of Mahatma Gandhi.* 9 vols. New Delhi: Publishing Division, Ministry of Information and Broadcasting, Government of India, 1958–1963.
5255. _____. *Gandhi's Letters to A Disciple.* New York: Harper, 1950.
5256. _____. *Hind Swaraj, or Indian Home Rule.* Ahmedabad: Navajivan Publishing House, 1958.
5257. _____. *Non-Violence in Peace and War.* 2 vols. Ahmedabad: Navajivan Publishing House, 1948–1949.
5258. _____. *Non-Violent Resistance.* New York: Schocken, 1961.
5259. _____. *Swaraj in One Year.* Madras: Ganesh, 1921.
5260. Ghosh, P. C. *Mahatma Gandhi As I Saw Him.* Mystic, Connecticut: Lawrence Verry, 1968.
5261. Goldston, Robert C. *The Death of Gandhi.* New York: Franklin Watts, 1973.
5262. Green, Martin. *The Challenge of the Mahatmas.* New York: Basic Books, 1978.

5263. Gregg, Richard B. *Psychology and Strategy of Gandhi's Nonviolent Resistance.* New York: Garland Publishing, n.d.
5264. Horsburgh, H. J. N. *Gandhi.* Valley Forge, Pennsylvania: Judson Press, 1972.
5265. Hunt, James D. *Gandhi in London.* New Delhi: Promilla, 1978.
5266. Hutchins, Francis G. *India's Revolution: Gandhi and the Quit India Movement.* Cambridge, Massachusetts: Harvard University Press, 1973.
5267. Iyer, Raghavan. *The Moral and Political Thought of Mahatma Gandhi.* New York: Oxford University Press, 1973.
5268. Jack, H. A., ed. *The Gandhi Reader.* Bloomington: Indiana University Press, 1956.
5269. Karunakaran, K. P. *New Perspectives on Gandhi.* New York: International Publications Service, 1969.
5270. Keer, Dhananjay. *Mahatma Gandhi: Political Saint and Unarmed Prophet.* New York: International Publications Service, 1974.
5271. Kripalani, Krishna, ed. *All Men Are Brothers: Life and Thoughts of Mahatma Gandhi as Told in His Own Words.* Ahmedabad: Navajivan Publishing House, 1960.
5272. Lahiry, Ashutosh. *Gandhi in Indian Politics: A Critical View.* Columbia, Missouri: South Asia Books, 1976.
5273. Lewis, Martin Deming, ed. *Gandhi: Maker of Modern India?* Boston: D. C. Heath, 1965.
5274. Mahadevan, T. K. *Gandhi My Refrain: Controversial Essays, 1950-1972.* New York: International Publications Service, 1974.
5275. _____ , ed. *The Relevance of Mahatma Gandhi to the World of Thought.* New York: International Publications Service, 1973.
5276. _____ , ed. *Truth and Nonviolence: A UNESCO Symposium on Gandhi.* Port Washington, New York: Kennikat, 1970.
5277. Mehta, Ved. *Mahatma Gandhi and His Apostles,* New York: Viking, 1977.
5278. Misra, D. K. *Gandhi and Social Order.* New York: International Publications Service, 1974.
5279. Nanda, B. R. *Mahatma Gandhi: A Biography.* Boston: Beacon, 1958.
5280. Nehru, Jawaharlal. *Mahatma Gandhi.* New York: Asia Publishing House, 1976.
5281. Panter-Brick, Simone. *Gandhi Against Machiavellism: Non-Violence in Politics.* New York: Asia Publishing House, 1967.
5282. Polak, H. S. L.; H. N. Brailsford; and Lord Pethick-Lawrence. *Mahatma Gandhi.* Bombay: Jaico Publishing House, 1962.
5283. Powers, Paul, ed. *The Meanings of Gandhi.* Honolulu: University of Hawaii Press, 1971.
5284. Radhakrishnan, S., ed. *Mahatma Gandhi: Essays and Reflections on His Life and Work.* Bombay: Jaico Publishing House, 1956.
5285. Rawding, F. W. *Gandhi.* New York: Cambridge University Press, 1980.
5286. Rothermund, Indira. *The Philosophy of Restraint: Gandhi's Strategy and Indian Politics.* Bombay: Popular Prakashan, 1963.
5287. Sharp, Gene. *Gandhi Wields the Weapon of Moral Power.* Mystic, Connecticut: Lawrence Verry, n. d.

5288. Sheehan, Vincent. *Mahatma Gandhi: A Great Life in Brief.* New York: Alfred A. Knopf, 1955.
5289. Shirer, William L. *Gandhi: A Memoir.* New York: Simon and Schuster, 1980.
5290. Woodcock, George. *Mohandas Gandhi.* New York: Viking, 1971.

Revolution in Afghanistan

The articles below refer to the coup d'etat of 1978 which installed a USSR backed government, and to the rebellion that began in 1979, following the Soviet invasion of Afghanistan, and is still underway as this is being written.

5291. Hyman, Anthony. "Afghanistan's Unpopular Revolution: Reforming Zeal Fails to Enthuse the People," *Round Table* 275 (July 1979): 222–26.
5292. Khan, M. Afzal. "With the Afghan Rebels." *The New York Times Magazine* (13 January 1980).
5293. Negaran, Hannah. "The Afghan Coup of April 1978: Revolution and International Security." *Orbis* 23 (Spring 1979): 93–113.
5294. Newell, Richard S. "Revolution and Revolt in Afghanistan." *World Today* 34:11 (November 1979): 432–42.

Revolution in Turkey

There are three Turkish revolutions covered by the titles below: (1) the Turkish Revolution of 1908, led by a reform party called the Young Turks which revolted against the sultan and sought to restore the greatness of the Ottoman Empire; (2) the National Revolution of 1919–1923, led by Mustafa Kemal, which resulted in the founding of the Republic of Turkey; and (3) the revolutionary coup d'etat of 1960 which led to the establishment of the Second Republic of Turkey.

Articles

5295. Karpat, Kemal H. "The Military and Politics in Turkey, 1960–1964: A Socio-Cultural Analysis of a Revolution." *American Historical Review* 75:6 (October 1970): 1654–83.
5296. Mardin, S. "Ideology and Religion in the Turkish Revolution." *International Journal of Middle East Studies* 2:3 (1971): 197–211.
5297. Quataert, Donald. "The Economic Climate of the 'Young Turk Revolution' in 1908" *Journal of Modern History* 51:3 (September 1979): abstract.

Books

5298. Allen, Henry E. *The Turkish Transformation: A Study in Social and Religious Development.* Chicago: University of Chicago Press, 1935.
5299. Davison, Roderic H. *Turkey.* Englewood Cliffs, New Jersey: Prentice-Hall, 1968.
5300. Emin, Ahmed. *Turkey in the World War.* New Haven: Yale University Press, 1930.
5301. Harris, George S. *The Origins of Communism in Turkey.* Stanford: Hoover Institution, 1967.
5302. Howard, Harry N. *The Partition of Turkey, 1913-1923.* Norman: University of Oklahoma Press, 1931.
5303. Kinross, Lord. *Ataturk: A Biography of Mustafa Kemal.* New York: Morrow, 1965.
5304. Lewis, Bernard. *The Emergence of Modern Turkey, 1913-1923.* 2d ed. New York: Oxford University Press, 1968.
5305. Lewis, Geoffrey. *Turkey.* New York: Praeger, 1955.
5306. Ramsaur, Ernest Edmondson, Jr. *The Young Turks: Prelude to the Revolution of 1908.* Princeton: Princeton University Press, 1957.
5307. Webster, Donald E. *The Turkey of Atatürk: Social Progress in the Turkish Reformation.* Philadelphia: American Academy of Political and Social Science, 1939.
5308. Weiker, Walter F. *The Turkish Revolution, 1960-1961: Aspects of Military Politics.* Washington, D.C.: Brookings Institution, 1963.

Revolution in the Philippines

There are several revolutionary upheavals covered by the works below, beginning with nineteenth century rebellions against Spanish rule. After independence (1946), a group of communist-led rebels, known as Huks, tried to seize power in efforts that lasted until 1954. The Democratic Revolution of 1972 refers to the declaration of martial law and, the following year, the establishment of a new constitution under the dictatorial presidency of Ferdinand Marcos.

Articles

5309. Agpalo, R. E. "Revolution and the Philippine Political System." *Solidarity* 4 (July 1969): 64-77.
5310. Ancheta, Celedonio A. "Democratic Revolution: A Turning Point on Land Reform and Foreign Relations." *Philippine Historical Association: Historical Bulletin* 12 (January-December 1968): 275-84.
5311. Capino, Diosdado G. "Revolutionary Trends in the Democratic Revolution." *Philippine Historical Association: Historical Bulletin* 19 (January-December 1975): 134-44.

5312. _____. "Revolutionary Trends in the New Society." *Philippine Historical Association: Historical Bulletin* 18 (January-December 1974): 78-88.
5313. Doeppers, Daniel F. "The Philippine Revolution and the Geography of Schism." *Geography Review* 66 (April 1976): 158-77.
5314. Foronda, Marceline A., Jr. "The Humanist Dimension of the Democratic Revolution." *Philippine Historical Association: Historical Bulletin* 19 (January-December 1975): 155-59.
5315. Lent, John A. "The Philippine Press during the Revolution and the Filipino-American War." *Asian Thought and Society* 3 (December 1978): 308-21.
5316. Peralta, Cresencio. "The Spirituo-Moral Revolution in Our Time." *Philippine Historical Association: Historical Bulletin* 18 (January-December 1974): 101-07.
5317. Resurreccion, Celedonio O. "The Democratic Revolution: The Turning Point." *Philippine Historical Association: Historical Bulletin* 19 (January-December 1975): 113-19.
5318. _____. "Syndromes of an Economic Revolution." *Philippine Historical Association: Historical Bulletin* 18 (January-December 1974): 53-63.
5319. Salamanca, Bonifacio S. "The Democratic Revolution: Turning Point in Philippine Political History." *Philippine Historical Association: Historical Bulletin* 19 (January-December 1975): 127-33.
5320. Santos, Gloria M. "The Historical Background of the Philippine Democratic Revolution of 1972." *Philippine Historical Association: Historical Bulletin* 19 (January-December 1975): 120-26.
5321. Stanley, Peter W. "America and the Conservative Revolution in the Philippines." *Harvard Magazine* 78 (May 1976): 38-49.
5322. Tongko, Primo L. "The Political Revolution in Our Time." *Philippine Historical Association: Historical Bulletin* 18 (January-December 1974): 108-13.

Books

5323. Constantino, Renato. *The History of the Philippines: From the Spanish Colonization to the Second World War.* New York: Monthly Review Press, 1981.
5324. Kerkvliet, Benedict J. *The Huk Rebellion: A Study of Peasant Revolt in the Philippines.* Berkeley: University of California Press, 1977.
5325. Majul, Cesar Adib. *The Political and Constitutional Ideas of the Philippine Revolution of 1896.* Rev. ed. New York: Oriole Editions, 1974.
5326. Marcos, Ferdinand E. *The Democratic Revolution in the Philippines.* Englewood Cliffs, New Jersey: Prentice-Hall International, 1974.
5327. Stanley, Peter W. *A Nation in the Making: The Philippines and the United States, 1899-1921.* Cambridge, Massachusetts: Harvard University Press, 1974.
5328. Steinberg, David J. *Philippines.* Boulder, Colorado: Westview Press, 1981.
5329. Sturtevant, David R. *Popular Uprisings in the Philippines, 1840-1940.* Ithaca: Cornell University Press, 1976.

8 Africa

"Nothing is so loved by tyrants as obedient subjects. Nothing so soon destroys freedom as cowardly and servile acquiescence. Men will never have any more liberty than they demand and are ready to fight to take and preserve."
    Clarence Darrow
    (1932)

Most African revolutions have been either anti-colonial (i.e., wars of national liberation) or struggles against some form of neocolonialism. Their purpose has been to terminate oppression and exploitation, and achieve self-determination. These revolutions have also been both nationalist and social in that each, in its own distinct way, has sought to transform a colony into an independent, modern, and progressive welfare state, and its people, hitherto subjects, into citizens.

Aside from overcoming the expected opposition of mother countries, the goal of African anti-colonial revolutions has often involved the actual creation of a nation and the bringing of a people into the modern world. African revolutionists have had to instill a sense of nationality that is often in conflict with more traditional loyalty to a tribe or local community. This has not been an easy task, frequently accounting for post-revolution difficulties. Another problem has been the existence, at best, of only a small native middle class and very little usable capital.

African revolutions have been more socialistic than capitalistic, but this has been so more for economic and moral reasons than political. The general view has been that a revolution along socialist lines would best establish a society based on justice, planning, and comprehensive national growth. The new nations of Africa have been more interested in establishing their own identity, and not being swallowed by East-West rivalries. Their socialism has been neither completely communistic nor anti-capitalistic. It has been instead, theoretically at least, a kind of humanist socialism, lacking the rhetoric of the class struggle, containing elements of private enterprise, and adapting itself to African conditions. Self-government is but the first step toward full independence, which will only be achieved when African economies are freed from excessive dependence on the developed countries, and when African societies have reestablished their spiritual and cultural values.

The African revolutions (and revolutionists) which form the framework for this chapter almost all occurred or climaxed following World War II—though their roots, to be sure, reach further into the past—with most of them taking place during the 1960s and 1970s. The table of contents indicates which (and, for the revolutionists, who) these are. Among the titles immediately below, following the bibliographies and books of documents, are a variety of works. There are surveys on African history by Philip Curtin et al (1978), Basil Davidson (1968, 1978), J. D. Fage (1978), John Hatch (1965), and Roland Oliver and J. D. Fage (1962). There are broad examinations of Africa's revolutionary situation, including articles by Colin Legum (1972), and Bernard A. Nkemdirim (1977), and books by Fenner Brockway (1974), James Cameron (1961), Richard Gibson (1972), Russell Warren Howe (1969), Robert I. Rotberg (1971), and Immanuel Wallerstein (1961, 1967). There are a number of regional studies, including those by Wilfred Burchett (1978), John S. Saul (1979), and J. B. Webster and A. A. Boahen (1967). There are also studies on revolutionary activities in the Congo, Nigeria, Ghana, the Sudan, Rwanda, Uganda, Tanzania, and Kenya.

On a more specialized level there are the following: (1) on Pan-Africanism see the articles by Opoku Agyeman (1978) and W. Alphaeus Hunton (1978), and the books by Adekunle Ajala (1974) and C. L. R. James (1971); (2) on nationalism see the articles by Giovanni Arrighhi and John S. Saul (1969) and B. S. Sharma (1973), and the book by Henry S. Wilson (1969); (3) on socialism see the books by William H. Friedland and Carl G. Rosberg, Jr. (1964) and Bismarck U. Mwansasu and Cranford Pratt (1979); (4) on colonialism see the study by Peter Duignan and Lewis Gann (1970); (5) for ideology and intellectual revolutionary origins see the article by James A. McCain (1975), and the book by Lilyan Kesteloot (1972); (6) for religion see the article by Adrian Hastings (1975), and the books by John K. Cooley (1965) and Ian Linden (1977); and (7) for the peasantry see the articles by Basil Davidson (1974) and John S. Saul (1975), and the book by Martin A. Klein (1980).

Bibliographies

5330. African Bibliographic Center. *Current Themes in African Historical Studies: A Selected Bibliographical Guide to Research in African History.* Westport, Connecticut: Negro Universities Press, 1970.
5331. Berman, Sanford. "African Liberation Movements: A Preliminary Bibliography." *Ufahamu* 3:1 (Spring 1972): 107-28.
5332. Duignan, Peter, ed. *Guide to Research and Reference Works on Sub-Saharan Africa.* Stanford: Hoover Institution, 1972.
5333. _____, and Lewis Gann, eds. *Colonialism in Africa.* Vol. 5. *A Bibliographical Guide to Colonialism in Sub-Saharan Africa.* New York: Cambridge University Press, 1973.
5334. Easterbrook, David L. "Bibliography of Africana Bibliographies, 1976-77." *African Journal* 9:4 (1978): 293-306.
5335. Glazier, Kenneth M. *Africa South of the Sahara: A Select and Annotated Bibliography, 1958-1963.* Stanford: Hoover Institution, 1964.

5336. _____. *Africa South of the Sahara: A Select and Annotated Bibliography, 1964-1968.* Stanford: Hoover Institution, 1969.
5337. Martello, William E., and Jeffrey E. Butler, eds. *The History of Sub-Saharan Africa: A Select Bibliography of Books and Reviews, 1945-1975.* Boston: G. K. Hall, 1978.
5338. Paden, John N., and Edward W. Soja, eds. *The African Experience.* Vol. 3A. *Bibliography.* Evanston, Illinois: Northwestern University Press, 1970.
5339. Panofsky, Hans E. *A Bibliography of Africana.* Westport, Connecticut: Greenwood, 1975.
5340. Scheven, Yvette. *Bibliographies for African Studies, 1970-1975.* Waltham, Massachusetts: African Studies Association, Brandeis University, 1977.
5341. Shaw, Robert, and Richard Sklar, eds. *A Bibliography for the Study of African Politics.* Vol. 1. Waltham, Massachusetts: African Studies Association, Brandeis University, 1978.
5342. Solomon, Alan C., ed. *A Bibliography for the Study of African Politics.* Vol. 2. Waltham, Massachusetts: African Studies Association, Brandeis University, 1978.

Documents

5343. Brownlie, Ian. *Basic Documents on African Affairs.* Oxford: Clarendon Press, 1971.
5344. Langley, J. Ayo. *Ideologies of Liberation in Black Africa, 1856-1970: Documents on Modern African Political Thought from Colonial Times to the Present.* Totowa, New Jersey: Rowman and Littlefield, 1979.

Articles

5345. Agyeman, Opoku. "The Super Marxists and Pan-Africanism." *Journal of Black Studies* 8 (June 1978): 489-510.
5346. Arrighhi, Giovanni, and John S. Saul. "Nationalism and Revolution in Sub-Saharan Africa." *The Socialist Register* 6 (1969): 137-88.
5347. Buijtenhuijs, Rob. "The Revolutionary Potential of Black Africa: Dissident Elites." *African Perspectives,* no. 2 (1978): 135-46.
5348. Davidson, Basil. "African Peasants and Revolution." *Journal of Peasant Studies* 1 (April 1974): 269-90.
5349. Depelchin, Jacques. "Pan-African Marxism or the Reduction of Marxism to a Reactionary Ideology: A Reply to Agyeman's 'Pan-Africanism and the Supermarxists.'" *Utafiti* 3:1 (1978): 65-90.
5350. Esedebe, P. Olisanwuche. "Some Recent Studies on Pan-Africanism." *Journal of the Historical Society of Sierra Leone* 1 (July 1979): 72-79.
5351. Gerhart, John D. "Africa's New Revolutionaries: Three Profiles." *Harvard Review* 4:1 (Summer-Fall 1966): 25-34.
5352. Hastings, Adrian. "Christianity and Revolution." *African Affairs* 74 (July 1975): 347-61.
5353. Hunton, W. Alphaeus. "The Roots of Pan-Africanism." *Freedomways* 18:3 (1978): 153-63.

5354. Kaniki, Martin H. Y. "The Idara Rebellion of 1931: A Reappraisal." *Journal of the Historical Society of Sierra Leone* 1 (July 1979): 57–64.
5355. Legum, Colin. "Africa's Contending Revolutionaries." *Problems of Communism* 21:2 (March-April 1972): 2–15.
5356. McCain, James A. "Ideology in Africa: Some Perceptual Types." *African Studies Review* 18 (April 1975): 61–87.
5357. Mazrui, Ali A. "The Different Concepts of Revolution in East Africa." *African Review* 2:1 (April 1972): 28–51.
5358. Mbengo, F. "Marxist Theories of Class and Class Struggle." *Utafiti* 3:1 (1978): 9–44.
5359. Mpakati, Attati. "Problems and Nature of Anti-Colonial Struggle in Africa." *Pan-African Journal* 6 (Spring 1973): 239–52.
5360. Nkemdirim, Bernard A. "Reflections on Political Conflict, Rebellion, and Revolution in Africa." *Journal of Modern African Studies* 15:1 (March 1977): 75–90.
5361. Ntalaja, Nzongola. "Peasants and Nationalism: An African Overview." *Pan-African Journal* 7 (Fall 1974): 263–68.
5362. Nzongola, Georges N. "The Bourgeoisie and Revolution in the Congo." *Journal of Modern African Studies* 8:4 (December 1970): 511–30.
5363. Obinani, F. Chuckwuma. "The Roots and Direction of the Nigerian Revolution." *Harvard Review* 4:1 (Summer-Fall 1966) 12–24.
5364. Obinyan, Tom Uwa. "Reflections on Why Men Rebel." *Nigerian Journal of Sociology and Anthropology* 3 (September 1977): 115–40.
5365. Ojwok, Omwony. "Who Is to Lead the Popular Anti-imperialist Revolution in Africa?: In Refutation of Issa G. Shivji's Petty-Bourgeois Neo-Marxist Line." *Utafiti* 3:1 (1978): 105–40.
5366. Ross, Robert. "African Resistance to the Imposition of Colonialism: A Historlographical Review." *Itinerario* 3:2 (1979):89–96.
5367. Saul, John S. "African Peasants and Revolution." *Review of African Political Economy*, no. 1 (1975): 41–68.
5368. Segal, Ronald. "How U.S. Could Get Burned in Africa." *Los Angeles Times* (28 January 1973).
5369. Sekyi, H. V. H. "The Year of Revolution in Ghana." *African Affairs* 72 (April 1973): 197–201.
5370. Sharma, B. S. "African Nationalism: An Unfinished Revolution." *Africa Quarterly* 13:1 (April-June 1973): 66–79.
5371. Wai, Dunstan M. "Revolution, Rhetoric, and Reality in the Sudan." *Journal of Modern African Studies* 17:1 (March 1979): 71–94.
5372. Weinstein, Warren, and Thomas Turner. "Introduction to Peasant Rebellion and Ethnic Conflict in Africa." *Pan-African Journal* 7 (Fall 1974): 185–92.

Books

5373. Ajala, Adekunle. *Pan-Africanism: Evolution, Progress, and Prospects.* New York: St. Martin's Press, 1974.
5374. Ake, Claude. *Revolutionary Pressure in Africa.* Belfast, Maine: Bern Porter, 1979.
5375. Akintoye, S. A. *Emergent African States: Topics in Twentieth Century African History.* New York: Longman, 1977.

Africa / 341

5376. _____ . *Revolution and Power Politics in Yorubaland, 1840-1893: Ibadan Expansion and the Rise of Ekitiparapo.* New York: Humanities Press, 1971.

5377. Beshir, Mohamed Omer. *Revolution and Nationalism in the Sudan.* New York: Barnes and Noble, 1974.

5378. Brace, Richard M. *Morocco, Algeria, Tunisia.* Englewood Cliffs, New Jersey: Prentice-Hall, 1964.

5379. Brockway, Fenner. *The Colonial Revolution.* New York: St. Martin's Press, 1974.

5380. Burchett, Wilfred. *Southern Africa Arises: Angola, Mozambique, Rhodesia, Namibia and South Africa.* New York: Urizen Books, 1978.

5381. Cameron, James. *The African Revolution.* New York: Random House, 1961.

5382. Carter, G. M. *Independence for Africa.* New York: Praeger, 1960.

5383. Césaire, Aimé. *Discourse on Colonialism.* Translated by J. Pinkham. New York: Monthly Review Press, 1972.

5384. Cooley, John K. *Baal, Christ and Mohammed: Religion and Revolution in North Africa.* New York: Holt, Rinehart and Winston, 1965.

5385. Curtin, Philip, et al. *African History.* Boston: Little, Brown, 1978.

5386. Davidson, Basil. *Africa in History.* London: Weidenfeld and Nicolson, 1968.

5387. _____ . *Let Freedom Come: Africa in Modern History.* Boston: Little, Brown, 1978.

5388. Decalo, S. *Coups and Army Rule in Africa: Studies in Military Style.* New Haven: Yale University Press, 1977.

5389. Duignan, Peter, and Lewis Gann, eds. *Colonialism in Africa.* Vol. 2. *The History and Politics of Colonialism, 1914-1960.* New York: Cambridge University Press, 1970.

5390. Fage, J. D. *A History of Africa.* New York: Alfred A. Knopf, 1978.

5391. Feinstein, Alan. *African Revolutionary: The Life and Times of Nigeria's Aminu Kano.* New York: Quadrangle Books, 1973.

5392. Friedland, William H., and Carl G. Rosberg, Jr., eds. *African Socialism.* Stanford: Stanford University Press, 1964.

5393. Gibson, Richard. *African Liberation Movements.* New York: Oxford University Press, 1972.

5394. Grundy, Kenneth W. *Guerrilla Struggle in Africa: An Analysis and Preview.* New York: Grossman Publishers, 1971.

5395. Hatch, John. *A History of Postwar Africa.* New York: Praeger, 1965.

5396. Howe, Russell Warren. *The African Revolution.* New York: Harper and Row, 1969.

5397. Isichei, Elizabeth. *History of West Africa Since 1800.* New York: Africana Publishing Company, 1977.

5398. James, C. L. R. *History of Pan-African Revolt.* 2d ed. Washington, D.C.: Drum and Spear Press, 1971.

5399. Kanza, Thomas. *Evolution and Revolution in Africa.* Cambridge, Massachusetts: Schenkman, 1974.

5400. Kesteloot, Lilyan. *Intellectual Origins of the African Revolution.* Edison, New Jersey: Inscape Corp., 1972.

5401. Klein, Martin A. *Peasants in Africa: Historical and Comparative Perspectives.* Beverly Hills, California: Sage, 1980.

5402. Linden, Ian. *Church and Revolution in Rwanda.* New York: Africana Publishing Company, 1977.
5403. Miller, Norman. *Military Coup in Uganda.* Hanover, New Hampshire: American Universities Field Staff, East Africa Series, 10:3, 1971.
5404. Mwansasu, Bismarck U., and Cranford Pratt, eds. *Towards Socialism in Tanzania.* Buffalo: University of Toronto Press, 1979.
5405. Nkoana, Mathew. *Crisis in the Revolution.* London: Mafube Publications, 1969.
5406. Oliver, Roland, and J. D. Fage. *A Short History of Africa.* Baltimore: Penguin Books, 1962.
5407. Padmore, George. *Gold Coast Revolution.* London: Dennis Dobson, 1953.
5408. Panikkar, K. Madhu. *Revolution in Africa.* Bombay: Asia Publishing House, 1961.
5409. Potholm, Christian P. *Theory and Practice of African Politics.* Englewood Cliffs, New Jersey: Prentice-Hall, 1979.
5410. Rosberg, Carl G., and John Nottingham. *The Myth of Mau Mau: Nationalism in Kenya.* New York: Praeger, 1966.
5411. Rotberg, Robert I., ed. *Rebellion in Black Africa.* London: Oxford University Press, 1971.
5412. _____ , and Ali A. Mazrui, eds. *Protest and Power in Black Africa.* New York: Oxford University Press, 1970.
5413. Sagay, J. O., and D. A. Wilson. *Africa: A Modern History, 1800-1975.* New York: Holmes and Meier, 1980.
5414. Saul, John S. *The State and Revolution in East Africa.* New York: Monthly Review Press, 1979.
5415. von Albertini, Rudolf. *Decolonization: The Administration and Future of the Colonies, 1919-1960.* New York: Holmes and Meier, 1981.
5416. Wallerstein, Immanuel. *Africa: The Politics of Independence.* New York: Random House, 1961.
5417. _____ . *Africa: The Politics of Unity.* New York: Random House, 1967.
5418. Webster, J. B., and A. A. Boahen. *History of West Africa: The Revolutionary Years—1815 to Independence.* New York: Praeger, 1967.
5419. Wilson, Henry S. *Origins of West African Nationalism.* London: Macmillan, 1969.

Kwame Nkrumah

The Gold Coast, later Ghana, in West Africa, was the first British African colony to achieve independence, and Kwame Nkrumah was the nationalist leader of the independence movement. Nkrumah was a revolutionary theorist and Pan-Africanist who advocated a system he called "consciencism," an effort to enable African society to utilize its Euro-Christian and Islamic heritage to fit the African personality, to forge progress out of the conflict within the African conscience, and to institute socialism in order to restore African humanist and egalitarian principles. Nkrumah became president of Ghana and ruled as a dictator. He was overthrown after a military coup d'etat in 1966.

The articles below approach Nkrumah from specialized avenues. Among the biographies, Basil Davidson's (1973) is the best. Nkrumah wrote extensively, and his works are readily available.

Bibliography

5420. Clarke, R. E. "Kwame Nkrumah: A Selected Bibliography." *Sierra Leone Library Journal* 2 (January 1975): 143-59.

Articles

5421. Apter, David E. "Nkrumah, Charisma, and the Coup." *Daedalus* 97:3 (Summer 1968): 757-92.
5422. Asante, S. K. B. "Kwame Nkrumah and Pan-Africanism: The Early Phase, 1945-1961." *Universitas* 3 (October 1973): 36-49.
5423. Carmichael, Stokely: "Marxism-Leninism and Nkrumahism." *Black Scholar* 4:5 (February 1973): 41-43.
5424. "A Marxist-Leninist Analysis of Nkrumahism." *African Red Family* 1:2 (1973): 21-31.
5425. M'Bou-Yembi, Léon. "Les contributions théoriques de Nkrumah."*Annales Ecole National Administration* 3 (1979): 27-44.
5426. Ninsin, Kwame A. "Nkrumah's Socialism: A Reappraisal." *Ufahamu* 9:1 (Spring 1979): 82-110.
5427. Okadigbo, Miriam. "Consciencism as the Key to Nkrumah." *Umoja* 2 (Spring 1978): 41-52.
5428. Onoge, Omafume F. "Class Struggle and Bourgeois Ideology in Africa: A Review of Kwame Nkrumah's *Class Struggle in Africa.*" *Utafiti* 3:1 (1978): 91-104.
5429. Von Laue, Theodore H. "Reflections on Kwame Nkrumah." *Yale Review* 64 (March 1975): 321-33.

Books

5430. Davidson, Basil. *Black Star.* New York: Praeger, 1973.
5431. Editors of "The Spark." *Some Essential Features of Nkrumahism.* New York: International Publishers, 1964.
5432. Howell, Thomas A., and Jeffrey Rajasooria, eds. *Ghana and Nkrumah.* New York: Facts On File, 1974.
5433. Nkrumah, Kwame. *Africa Must Unite.* London: William Heinemann, 1963.
5434. _____. *Class Struggle in Africa.* New York: International Publishers, 1970.
5435. _____. *Consciencism.* New York: Monthly Review Press, 1964.
5436. _____. *Ghana: The Autobiography of Kwame Nkrumah.* London: Thomas Nelson, 1957.

5437. _____. *Handbook of Revolutionary Warfare.* New York: International Publishers, 1969.
5438. _____. *I Speak of Freedom: A Statement of African Ideology.* New York: Praeger, 1961.
5439. _____. *Neo-Colonialism: The Last Stage of Imperialism.* New York: International Publishers, 1965.
5440. _____. *Revolutionary Path.* New York: International Publishers, 1973.
5441. _____. *Towards Colonial Freedom.* London: William Heinemann, 1960.
5442. Omari, T. Peter. *Kwame Nkrumah: The Anatomy of an African Dictatorship.* New York: Holmes and Meier, 1970.
5443. Phillips, J. F. V. *Kwame Nkrumah and the Future of Africa.* New York: Praeger, 1961.
5444. Timothy, Bankole. *Kwame Nkrumah: His Rise to Power.* Evanston, Illinois: Northwestern University Press, 1963.

Algerian Revolution, 1954-1962

Algeria was unique among colonies, French or other, in that France did not consider Algeria a colony at all. It was an integral part of France, even having representation in the French National Assembly—though such representation was heavily weighted in favor of the European, or *colon*, settlers in Algeria. Since the *colons* controlled the economy and owned most of the land, they strongly opposed any moves toward independence for fear the Algerian Moslem majority would seek revenge.

In 1954, coming on the heels of France's defeat in Indochina, the Algerian Revolution began. It was an intense, violent, and costly struggle. Algerian nationalism, dormant and even non-existent prior to the revolution, emerged as a powerful force. The Algerian Revolution became a movement by Algerians to enter the modern world and blend it with Islamic values.

Revolution was the only choice Algerians had since the *colons* and France refused to grant reforms. The National Liberation Front (FLN) was the revolutionary organization which led the way. Although it was successful, the FLN failed to provide a program for the future, which resulted in many problems after independence.

Algeria was not the first African country to gain its independence. But it was the first to begin a total revolutionary war of national liberation, and to create an international issue out of what France tried in vain to contain as a domestic squabble. As such, the Algerian Revolution was a point of reference, a standard of revolution for African people.

There are many fine works on the revolution, including those by Pierre Bourdieu (1962), Michael K. Clark (1960), Joan Gillespie (1961), David C. Gordon (1966), Paul Henissart (1970), Alistair Horne (1977),

Arslan Humbaraci (1966), Martha C. Hutchinson (1978), and David Ottaway and Marina Ottaway (1970). On the FLN and post-revolutionary developments see the books by Henry F. Jackson (1977) and W. B. Quandt (1969).

Bibliographies

5445. Heggoy, Alf Andrew. "Books on the Algerian Revolution in English: Translations and Anglo-American Contributions." *African Historical Studies* 3:1 (1970) 163-68.
5446. Lawless, Richard I. *Algerian Bibliography: English Language Publications, 1830-1973.* New York: Unipub-Xerox, 1976.

Articles

5447. Ali, Bashir Hadj. "Lessons of the Algerian Liberation Struggle." In *Guerrilla Warfare and Marxism,* edited by W. J. Pomeroy. New York: International Publishers, 1968.
5448. De Bonis, J. "Introduction à une réflexion sur la révolution algérienne." *Cahiers Communisme* (October 1978): 74-79.
5449. Klein, Jean. "Un épisode de la décolonisation: la guerre d'Algérie (1954-1962)." *Francia* 6 (1978): 640-45.
5450. Mortimer, Robert A. "The Algerian Revolution in Search of the African Revolution." *Journal of Modern African Studies* 8:3 (October 1970): 363-87.
5451. Murray, Roger, and Tom Weingraf. "The Algerian Revolution." *New Left Review,* no. 22 (December l963): 14-65.
5452. Revere, Robert B. "Revolutionary Ideology in Algeria." *Polity* 5 (Summer 1973): 477-88.
5453. Rohdie, S. "Liberation and Violence in Algeria." *Studies on the Left* 6:3 (May-June 1966): 83-89.
5454. Talbott, John. "Terrorism and the Liberal Dilemma: The Case of the 'Battle of Algiers.'" *Contemporary French Civilization* 2 (Winter 1978): 177-90.
5455. Van Dyke, Stuart, Jr. "Response to Rebellion: The Algerian French and the February 6, 1956 Crisis." *French Colonial Studies* 2 (1978): 97-114.
5456. Wall, Irwin M. "The French Communists and the Algerian War." *Journal of Contemporary History* 12:3 (July 1977): 521-44.

Books

5457. Andrews, William G. *French Politics and Algeria: The Process of Policy Formation, 1954-1962.* New York: Irvington Publishers, 1962.
5458. Behr, Edward. *The Algerian Problem.* Westport, Connecticut: Greenwood, 1976.
5459. Bourdieu, Pierre. *Algeria 1960.* New York: Cambridge University Press, 1979.
5460. _____. *The Algerians.* Translated by A. C. M. Ross. Boston: Beacon, 1962.
5461. Brace, Richard, and Joan Brace. *Ordeal in Algeria.* New York: Van Nostrand, 1960.

5462. Clark, Michael K. *Algeria in Turmoil: The Rebellion: Its Causes, Its Effects, Its Future.* New York: Grosset and Dunlap, 1960.
5463. Courrière, Yves. *La guerre d'Algérie.* 4 vols. Paris: Fayard, 1968-1971.
5464. Danziger, Raphael. *Abd al-Qadir and the Algerians: Resistance to the French and Internal Consolidation.* New York: Holmes and Meier, 1977.
5465. Gillespie, Joan. *Algeria: Rebellion and Revolution.* New York: Praeger, 1961.
5466. Gordon, David C. *The Passing of French Algeria.* London: Oxford University Press, 1966.
5467. Heggoy, Alf Andrew. *Insurgency and Counterinsurgency in Algeria.* Bloomington: Indiana University Press, 1972.
5468. Henissart, Paul. *Wolves in the City: The Death of French Algeria.* New York: Simon and Schuster, 1970.
5469. Horne, Alistair. *A Savage War of Peace: Algeria, 1954-1962.* New York: Viking, 1977.
5470. Humbaraci, Arslan. *Algeria: A Revolution That Failed.* New York: Praeger, 1966.
5471. Hutchinson, Martha C. *Revolutionary Terrorism: The FLN in Algeria, 1954-1962.* Stanford: Hoover Institution, 1978.
5472. Jackson, Henry F. *The FLN in Algeria: Party Development in a Revolutionary Society.* Westport, Connecticut: Greenwood, 1977.
5473. Kraft, Joseph. *The Struggle for Algeria.* Garden City, New York: Doubleday, 1961.
5474. Matthews, Tanya. *War in Algeria: Background for Crisis.* Bronx, New York: Fordham University Press, 1962.
5475. Mezerik, Avrahm G., ed. *The Algerian-French Conflict.* New York: International Review Service, 1958.
5476. O'Ballance, Edgar. *The Algerian Insurrection.* Hamden, Connecticut: Archon Books, 1967.
5477. Ottaway, David, and Marina Ottaway. *Algeria: The Politics of a Socialist Revolution.* Berkeley: University of California Press, 1970.
5478. Pickles, Dorothy M. *Algeria and France.* Westport, Connecticut: Greenwood, 1976.
5479. Quandt, W. B. *Revolution and Political Leadership: Algeria 1954-1968.* Cambridge, Massachusetts: M.I.T. Press, 1969.
5480. Roy, Jules. *The War in Algeria.* New York: Grove Press, 1960.
5481. Smith, Tony. *The French Stake in Algeria, 1945-1962.* Ithaca: Cornell University Press, 1978.
5482. Talbott, John. *The War without a Name: France in Algeria, 1954-1962.* New York: Alfred A. Knopf, 1980.
5483. Tillion, Germaine. *Algeria: The Realities.* Translated by R. Matthews. New York: Alfred A. Knopf, 1958.
5484. _____. *France and Algeria: Complementary Enemies.* Translated by R. Howard. New York: Alfred A. Knopf, 1961.

Frantz Fanon

Frantz Fanon, a black psychiatrist from Martinique, was educated in France and worked in an Algerian hospital (from 1952) where he soon found himself supporting the cause of the revolutionists. As a result of what he saw and from treating patients he became increasingly vocal against the evils of colonialism. He eventually became the editor and a contributor to the official FLN newspaper, *El Moujahid*. He developed a Pan-African frame of reference. His ideas on revolution are contained in his writings, the most important of which is *The Wretched of the Earth*, completed just before he died from leukemia in 1961.

Revolution to Fanon was more than a struggle for political independence; it was part of the process of the regeneration of man and society, of self-liberation and rebirth. Through revolution a suppressed people could undo the negative effects of colonization. Fanon analyzed many subjects subsumed under revolution, including violence, imperialism, Arab and Black Africa, socialism, religion, class consciousness, the peasantry, the bourgeoisie, and revolutionary parties. Through his writings Fanon became an important and influential revolutionary theorist.

The best studies of Fanon are by Irene L. Gendzier (1972) and Emmanuel Hansen (1977). The book by Jack Woddis (1972) compares Fanon's theories with several other revolutionary theorists. There are many fine articles on Fanon, including those by Paul A. Beckett (1972, 1973), Robert Blackey (1974), Irene L. Gendzier (1966, 1976), G. K. Grohs (1968), Emmanuel Hansen (1976, 1977), B. Marie Perinbam (1973, 1978), and Martin Staniland (1969). Fanon's own books should also be consulted.

Bibliography

5485. Hansen, Emmanuel. "Frantz Fanon: A Bibliographical Essay." *Pan-African Journal* 5 (Winter 1972): 387–406.

Articles

5486. Beckett, Paul A. "Algeria vs. Fanon: The Theory of Revolutionary Decolonization, and the Algerian Experience." *Western Political Quarterly* 26:1 (March 1973): 5–27.
5487. _____. "Frantz Fanon and Sub-Saharan Africa: Notes on the Contemporary Significance of His Thought." *Africa Today* 19 (Spring 1972): 59–72.
5488. Blackey, Robert. "Fanon and Cabral: A Contrast in Theories of Revolution for Africa." *Journal of Modern African Studies* 12:2 (June 1974): 191–209.
5489. Bourgi, A. C., and J.-C. Williams. "La pensée politique de Frantz Fanon." *Présence Africaine*, no. 88 (1973): 139–62.

5490. Bulhan, Hussein Abdilahi. "Frantz Fanon: The Revolutionary Psychiatrist." *Race and Class* 21 (Winter 1980): 251-72.
5491. Burke, Edmund, III. "Frantz Fanon's *The Wretched of the Earth.*" *Daedalus* 105:1 (Winter 1976): 127-35.
5492. Forsythe, Dennis. "Frantz Fanon—the Marx of the Third World." *Phylon* 34 (June 1973): 160-70.
5493. Geismar, Peter, and Peter Worsley. "Frantz Fanon: Evolution of a Revolutionary." *Monthly Review* (May 1969): 23-30.
5494. Gendzier, Irene L. "Frantz Fanon: In Search of Justice." *Middle East Journal* 20:4 (Autumn 1966): 534-44.
5495. _____ . "Psychology and Colonialism: Some Observations." *Middle East Journal* 30:4 (Autumn 1976): 501-15.
5496. Gottheil, F. M. "Fanon and the Economics of Colonialism." *Quarterly Review of Economics and Business* 7:3 (Autumn 1967): 73-82.
5497. Grohs, G. K. "Frantz Fanon and the African Revolution." *Journal of Modern African Studies* 6:4 (December 1968): 543-56.
5498. Hansen, Emmanuel. "Freedom and Revolution in Frantz Fanon." *Universitas* 5 (May-November 1976): 19-40.
5499. _____ . "Freedom and Revolution in the Thought of Frantz Fanon." *African Development* 9:2 (February 1977): 17-42.
5500. Jackson, Henry. "Political and Social Ideas of Frantz Fanon: Relevance to Black Americans." *Pan-African Journal* 5 (Winter 1972): 473-92.
5501. Jinadu, L. Adele. "Some Aspects of the Political Philosophy of Frantz Fanon." *African Studies Review* 16:2 (September 1973): 255-89.
5502. _____ . "Some Aspects of the Political Philosophy of Frantz Fanon." *Pan-African Journal* 5 (Winter 1972): 493-522.
5503. _____ . "Some Comments on Frantz Fanon and the Historiography of African Politics." *Journal of Devastated Areas* 7 (January 1973): 287-97.
5504. Martin, Guy. "Fanon on Violence and the Revolutionary Process." *African Insight* 2 (1974): 14-19.
5505. _____ . "Fanon's Relevance to Contemporary African Political Thought." *Ufahamu* 4:3 (Winter 1974): 11-34.
5506. Masilela, Ntongela. "Theory, Praxis and History: Frantz Fanon and José Carlos Mariategui." *Ufahamu* 8:2 (Fall 1978): 66-87.
5507. Nguyen Nghe. "Frantz Fanon et les problèmes de l'indépendance." *La Pensée* 107 (February 1963): 22-36.
5508. Obiechina, Emmanuel. "Frantz Fanon." *Ufahamu* 3:2 (Fall 1972): 97-116.
5509. Perinbam, B. Marie. "Fanon and the Revolutionary Peasantry—the Algerian Case." *Journal of Modern African Studies* 11:3 (September 1973): 427-45.
5510. _____ . "Violence, Morality and History in the Colonial Syndrome: Frantz Fanon's Perspectives." *Journal of South African Affairs* 3 (January 1978): 7-34.
5511. Quellel, Charif. "Frantz Fanon and the Colonized Man." *Africa Today* 17 (January-February 1970): 8-11.
5512. Ralston, Richard David. "Fanon and His Critics: The New Battle of Algiers." *Cultural Development* 8:3 (1976): 463-92.
5513. Smith, Robert C. "Fanon and the Concept of Colonial Violence." *Black World* 22 (May 1973): 23-33.
5514. Staniland, Martin. "Frantz Fanon and the African Political Class." *African Affairs* 68 (January 1969): 4-25.

5515. Sutton, Horace. "Fanon: The Revolutionary as Prophet." *Saturday Review* (17 July 1971): 16.
5516. Wandibba, Simiyu. "Fanon and the Colonized." *Joliso* 2:2 (1974): 119-21.
5517. Zolberg, Aristide. "Frantz Fanon: A Gospel for the Damned." *Encounter* (November 1966): 56-63.

Books

5518. Bouvier, Pierre. *Fanon.* Paris: Editions Universitaires, 1971.
5519. Caute, David. *Frantz Fanon.* New York: Viking, 1970.
5520. Fanon, Frantz. *Black Skin, White Masks.* Translated by C. L. Markmann. New York: Grove Press, 1967.
5521. _____. *Studies in a Dying Colonialism.* Translated by H. Chevalier. New York: Monthly Review Press, 1965.
5522. _____. *Toward the African Revolution.* Translated by H. Chevalier. New York: Grove Press, 1967.
5523. _____. *The Wretched of the Earth.* Translated by C. Farrington. New York: Grove Press, 1966.
5524. *Frantz Fanon.* Elmsford, New York: British Book Centre, 1976.
5525. Geismar, Peter. *Fanon: The Revolutionary as Prophet.* New York: Grove Press, 1971.
5526. Gendzier, Irene L. *Frantz Fanon: A Critical Study.* New York: Pantheon Books, 1972.
5527. Hansen, Emmanuel. *Frantz Fanon: Social and Political Thought.* Columbus: Ohio State University Press, 1977.
5528. Lucas, Philippe. *Sociologie de Frantz Fanon.* Algiers: SNED, 1971.
5529. Woddis, Jack. *New Theories of Revolution.* New York: International Publishers, 1972.
5530. Zahar, Renate. *Frantz Fanon: Colonialism and Alienation. Concerning Frantz Fanon's Political Theory.* Translated by W. F. Feuser. New York: Monthly Review Press, 1974.
5531. _____. *L'Oeuvre de Frantz Fanon.* Paris: Maspero, 1970.

Revolution in Zanzibar, 1964

The East African country of Tanganyika became a United Nations trust territory under British rule in 1946. Under the guidance of Julius Nyerere and his Tanganyika African National Union Party, independence was achieved smoothly in 1961; Nyerere became the first president. In 1963 nearby Zanzibar was granted independence, with Sheik Muhammed Shamte Hamadi as prime minister. However, early in 1964, there was a violent revolution in Zanzibar. The Afro-Shirazi Party, representing the African majority, ousted the sheik's Arab minority government. A new African people's republic came into existence and quickly aligned itself with the communist world. At about the same time there was a mutiny in the Tanganyikan army which was defeated with British help. Nyerere survived this blow and gained control of the extremism in Zanzibar by bringing about a union of the island of Zanzibar with his own republic, which was then renamed Tanzania.

Articles

5532. Lemarchand, René. "Revolutionary Phenomena in Stratified Societies: Rwanda and Zanzibar." *Civilisations* 18:1 (1968): 16–51.
5533. Rey, Lucien. "The Revolution in Zanzibar." *New Left Review*, no. 25 (May-June 1964): 29–32.

Books

5534. Lofchie, Michael F. *Zanzibar: Background to Revolution.* Princeton: Princeton University Press, 1965.
5535. Martin, Esmond B. *Zanzibar: Tradition and Revolution.* Pomfret, Vermont: David and Charles, 1979.
5536. Okello, John. *Revolution in Zanzibar.* Nairobi: East African Publishing House, 1967.

Nyerere, Senghor, Touré

Julius Nyerere is an African nationalist and socialist, and has been president of Tanzania since 1964. In his own country he has introduced government controls to allow for more centralized economic planning. Although not a revolutionist per se, his thinking and state of mind, as well as that of Senghor and Touré, has been revolutionary.

Léopold-Sédar Senghor, a leading African thinker and socialist, was elected president of Senegal in 1960. Earlier, in 1948, he had founded the party that governs the country. Before Senegal gained independence in 1960, Senghor represented the colony in the French National Assembly, and he was the first African to hold a seat in the French Cabinet.

Sékou Touré, militant African nationalist and socialist, became the first president of Guinea in 1958. His government has followed a policy of nationalization and state control of industry and commerce. Calling his system "communocracy," he has stressed the sovereignty and solidarity of Africans over individualism and liberalism. By emphasizing the participation of all people in politics Touré arrived at a theory of "popular dictatorship"; the party which heads the dictatorship must be in the vanguard of the masses as well as in their midst. However, as different from communist parties, the African party is supposed to be a mass, not an elite organization.

Julius Nyerere

5537. Landor, Alfred. "Close-up of Julius Nyerere." *Contemporary Review* 235 (December 1979): 281–84.
5538. Nyerere, Julius. *Freedom and Socialism: A Selection from Writings and Speeches, 1965–1967.* New York: Oxford University Press, 1970.
5539. _____. *Freedom and Unity: A Selection from Writings and Speeches, 1952–1965.* New York: Oxford University Press, 1967.
5540. _____. *Nyerere on Socialism.* New York: Oxford University Press, 1969.
5541. _____. *Ujamaa: Essays on Socialism.* New York: Oxford University Press, 1971.

Léopold-Sédar Senghor

5542. Senghor, Léopold-Sédar. *Nationhood and the African Road to Socialism.* New York: Panther House, 1971.
5543. _____. *On African Socialism.* New York: Praeger, 1964.

Sékou Touré

5544. Adamolekun, 'Ladipo. *Sékou Touré's Guinea: An Experiment in Nation Building.* London: Methuen, 1976.
5545. Touré, Sékou. *The Permanent Struggle: Selected Writings by Sékou Touré.* New York: Ramparts Press, 1974.

Revolutions in Portuguese Africa

Portugal's hold on her African colonies dated back to the "age of exploration" of the fifteenth and sixteenth centuries. Angola, Mozambique, and Guinea-Bissau (also known as Portuguese Guinea or Guiné) were classified as mere provinces or extensions of Portugal, and the Africans were treated as a labor force with few rights. Portugal's "civilizing mission" was a euphemism for exploitation. The European country had been losing control of Guinea-Bissau earlier than the other two, and were it not for the impact on morale in Angola and Mozambique, and on Portugal itself, the mother country might have given up the colony long ago since it was costing more than it was yielding. But Portugal needed the oil, coffee, and diamonds she extracted from Angola, and the sugar and cotton grown in Mozambique. Besides, giving up her colonies would surely have revealed Portugal as the poor, backward state she was. Thus, the struggles

352 / Africa

in Portugal's colonies were anti-colonial revolutions; and Portugal, supported by NATO, fought three wars simultaneously for more than a decade. The revolutions involved full-scale guerrilla warfare, and the revolutionists were supported by neighboring independent states.

There are separate sections immediately following this one dealing with the revolutions in Angola, Mozambique, and Guinea-Bissau. This section confronts works that focus on Portugal and two or three of the anti-colonial conflicts together.

Bibliography/Documents

5546. Chilcote, Ronald H., ed. *Emerging Nationalism in Portuguese Africa: A Bibliography of Documentary Ephemera Through 1965.* Stanford: Hoover Institution, 1969.

Articles

5547. Blackey, Robert. "Free At Last: Portuguese Colonies after Independence." *ASA Review of Books '79* (African Studies Association) 5 (1979): 174–76.
5548. Davidson, Basil. "The Liberation Struggle in Angola and Portuguese Guinea." *Africa Quarterly* 10:1 (April-June 1970): 25–31.
5549. Henriksen, Thomas H. "Angola and Mozambique: Intervention and Revolution." *Current History* 71 (November 1976): 153.
5550. _____. "End of an Empire: Portugal's Collapse in Africa" *Current History* 68 (May 1975): 211.
5551. _____. "People's War in Angola, Mozambique, and Guinea-Bissau." *Journal of Modern African Studies* 14:3 (September 1976): 377–400.
5552. _____. "Portugal in Africa: Comparative Notes on Counterinsurgency." *Orbis* 21 (Summer 1977): 395–412.
5553. _____. "Some Notes on the National Liberation Wars in Angola, Mozambique, and Guinea-Bissau." *Military Affairs* 41 (February 1977): 30–36.
5554. Miller, Joseph C. "The Politics of Decolonization in Portuguese Africa." *African Affairs* 74 (April 1975): 135–47.
5555. Mohr, Charles. "It's Nearly Over for Portugal." *The New York Times* (27 April 1975).
5556. Nevins, Lawrence. "Revolution/Counterrevolution in Portuguese Africa." *Worldview* 17:1 (1974): 5–11.
5557. O'Brien, Jay. "Portugal and Africa: A Dying Imperialism." *Monthly Review* (May 1974): 19–37.
5558. Udokang, Okon. "Portuguese African Policy—A Critical Re-Appraisal." *African Review* 6:3 (July 1976): 289–312.
5559. Whitaker, Paul M. "The Revolutions of 'Portuguese' Africa." *Journal of Modern African Studies* 8:1 (April 1970): 15–35.

Books

5560. Chilcote, Ronald H. *Portuguese Africa.* Englewood Cliffs, New Jersey: Prentice-Hall, 1967.
5561. Humbaraci, Arslan, and N. Muchnik. *Portugal's African Wars: Angola, Guinea Bissao, Mozambique.* New York: Third Press, 1974.
5562. Minter, William. *Portuguese Africa and the West.* New York: Monthly Review Press, 1974.

Angolan Revolution, 1961-1975

The revolution in Angola (once also known as Portuguese West Africa) was one of three contemporaneous anti-colonial revolutions waged against Portuguese sovereignty (see the section "Revolutions in Portuguese Africa" in this chapter). Portuguese rule was harsh, and resulted in fighting, initiated in 1960 by the Bantus, who comprised most of the population. By 1961 the struggle escalated to bloody guerrilla war and revolution.

The Angolans, although united against the Portuguese, were not united amongst themselves. Three rival parties dominated the rebel forces: the National Front for the Liberation of Angola (FNLA), the National Union for the Total Independence of Angola (UNITA), and the Popular Movement for the Liberation of Angola (MPLA). Although Portugal, following its own revolution in 1974 (see the section "Portuguese Revolution, 1974" in Chapter 4), acknowledged the independence of Angola in 1975, the civil war among the three parties continued into the following year. Matters were complicated by the fact of foreign support from the United States, France, and other countries to an FNLA-UNITA coalition, and from Cuba, Russia, and other communist countries for MPLA. The forces of the latter were ultimately triumphant.

Among the best books on the Angolan Revolution are those by Gerald J. Bender (1978), Basil Davidson (1972), and John Marcum (1969, 1978). The book by Ole Gjerstad (1976) is an eyewitness examination of life in Angola after the revolution.

Articles

5563. Agyeman, Opoku. "Pan-Africanism and the Angolan Crisis." *Studies Affricain* 1 (Fall 1979): 234-54.
5564. Boyd, Herbert. "Angola: Background and Analysis." *Black World* 25 (March 1976): 16-23.
5565. Breytenbach, W. J. "Angola: Fragmented Resistance and the Civil War." *Africa Institute Bulletin* 14:1-2 (1976): 3-12.

5566. Clarence-Smith, W. G. "The Myth of Uneconomic Imperialism: The Portuguese in Angola, 1836-1926." *Journal of South African Studies* 5 (April 1979): 165-80.
5567. Davidson, Basil. "Angola: A Success that Changes History." *Race and Class* 18 (Summer 1976): 23-38.
5568. _____. "Toward a New Angola." *People's Power* (July-September 1977): 5-12.
5569. Ebinger, Charles K. "External Intervention in Internal War: The Politics and Diplomacy of the Angolan Civil War." *Orbis* 20 (Fall 1976): 669-99.
5570. Hodges, Tony. "The Struggle for Angola." *Round Table* (April 1976): 173-84.
5571. Lanne, Bernard. "L'Angola de 1975 à 1979." *Afrique contemporaine* 18 (November-December 1979): 5-7.
5572. Marcum, John A. "Angola: Background to the Conflict." *Mawazo* 4:4 (1976): 3-25.
5573. _____. "Lessons of Angola." *Foreign Affairs* 54 (April 1976): 407-25.
5574. Minter, William. "Imperial Network and External Dependency: Implications for the Angola Liberation Struggle." *Africa Today* 21 (Winter 1974): 25-40.
5575. Nwafor, Azinna. "The Liberation of Angola." *Monthly Review* (January 1976): 1-12.
5576. Penvenne, Jeanne. "Angola Under the Portuguese." *International Journal of African Historical Studies* 12:11 (1979): 96-105.

Books

5577. Barnett, Charles, and Albert Harvey. *Revolution in Angola*. Indianapolis, Indiana: Bobbs-Merrill, 1971.
5578. Bender, Gerald J. *Angola under the Portuguese: The Myth and the Reality.* Berkeley: University of California Press, 1978.
5579. Chilcote, Ronald H., ed. *Protest and Resistance in Angola and Brazil.* Berkeley: University of California Press, 1972.
5580. Dash, Leon. *Get off My Mountain: The Roots of Revolution in Angola.* Washington, D.C.: Howard University Press, 1977.
5581. Davidson, Basil. *In the Eye of the Storm: Angola's People.* Garden City, New York: Doubleday, 1972.
5582. Gjerstad, Ole. *The People in Power: An Account from Angola's Second War of National Liberation.* Oakland, California: LSM Information Center, 1976.
5583. Henderson, Lawrence W. *Angola: Five Centuries of Conflict.* Ithaca: Cornell University Press, 1979.
5584. Marcum, John. *The Angolan Revolution.* Vol. 1. *The Anatomy of an Explosion.* Cambridge, Massachusetts: M.I.T. Press, 1969.
5585. _____. *The Angolan Revolution.* Vol. 2. *Exile Politics and Guerrilla Warfare, 1962-1976.* Cambridge, Massachusetts: M.I.T. Press, 1978.
5586. Okuma, Thomas Masaji. *Angola in Ferment: The Background and Prospects of Angolan Nationalism.* Boston: Beacon, 1962.
5587. Panikkar, K. Madhu. *Angola in Flames.* New York: Asia Publishing House, 1962.
5588. Pélissier, René. *La colonie du minotaure: Nationalismes et révoltes en Angola (1926-1961).* Orgeval, France: René Pélissier, 1978.

5589. _____ . *Les guerres grises: Résistance et révoltes en Angola (1845–1941).* Orgeval, France: René Pélissier, 1977.
5590. Steenkamp, Willem. *Adeus Angola.* Capetown, South Africa: Howard Timmins, 1976.
5591. Wheeler, Douglas L., and René Pélissier. *Angola.* New York: Praeger, 1971.

Revolution in Mozambique, 1964–1975

The revolution in Mozambique (once also known as Portuguese East Africa) was one of the trio of anti-colonial revolutions directed against Portuguese dominance (see the section "Revolutions in Portuguese Africa" in this chapter). During the 1950s, Portugal had begun a series of six-year plans to improve economic development in Mozambique. But the Africans rebelled and called for self-government. By the early 1960s Mozambique nationalists based in nearby foreign countries established several liberation parties, the most important of which was (and is) the Marxist oriented Front for the Liberation of Mozambique (Frelimo). Fighting between these parties, now trained in guerrilla warfare, and Portuguese troops began in 1964. Following the Portuguese Revolution of 1974 (see the section "Portuguese Revolution, 1974" in Chapter 4), the new Lisbon government terminated the fighting, and independence was conceded in 1975, with Frelimo surviving as the only legal political party.

The articles by Adrian Hastings (1974), Thomas H. Henriksen (1973, 1978), and John S. Saul (1973, 1974) are the most helpful on the subject. The book by Thomas H. Henriksen (1978) covers a greater chronology but should also be consulted. The articles by Basil Davidson (1979) and John S. Saul (1979) cover post-revolutionary Mozambique. The book by Eduardo Mondlane (1969) is by the founder and president of Frelimo (until he was assassinated in 1969).

Bibliography

5592. Opello, Walter C. "Mozambican Nationalism." *Canadian Review of Studies in Nationalism* 5 (1979): 101–26.

Articles

5593. Davidson, Basil. "The Revolution of People's Power: Notes on Mozambique 1979." *Race and Class* 21 (Autumn 1979): 127–44.
5594. Dunn, D. Elwood. "The OAU and the Mozambique Revolution." *Issue* 3 (Spring 1973): 29–32.

356 / Africa

5595. Friedland, Elaine A. "Mozambican Nationalists Resistance 1920-1949." *Afrika Zamani* (December 1978): 156-72.
5596. Hastings, Adrian. "Some Reflections upon the War in Mozambique." *African Affairs* 73 (July 1974): 263-76.
5597. Henriksen, Thomas H. "Marxism and Mozambique." *African Affairs* 77 (October 1978): 441-62.
5598. _____. "The Revolutionary Thought of Eduardo Mondlane." *Genève-Afrique* 12:1 (1973): 37-52.
5599. Isaacman, Allen F. "The Tradition of Resistance in Mozambique." *Africa Today* 22 (July-September 1975): 21-36.
5600. Mugomba, Agrippah T. "Education in Mozambique: From Underdevelopment to Revolution." *Journal of South African Affairs* 3 (October 1978): 421-32.
5601. Panguene, Armando. "The National Liberation Struggle in Mozambique: A Process of Transformation." *Freedomways* 3 (1972): 183-88.
5602. Saul, John S. "Frelimo and the Mozambique Revolution." *Monthly Review* (March 1973): 22-52.
5603. _____. "Mozambique—the New Phase." *Monthly Review* (March 1979): 1-19.
5604. _____. "Portugal and the Mozambican Revolution." *Monthly Review* (September 1974): 45-64.
5605. Seegers, A. "Strategy in National Revolutions: Some Aspects of FRELIMO's Revolutionary Strategy." *Politikon: South African Journal of Political Science* 4 (June 1977): 64-76.
5606. Shore, Herb. "Mondlane, Machel and Mozambique: From Rebellion to Revolution." *Africa Today* 21 (Winter 1974): 3-14.

Books

5607. Henriksen, Thomas H. *Mozambique: A History.* London: Rex Collings, 1978.
5608. Isaacman, Allen F. *The Tradition of Resistance in Mozambique: The Zambesi Valley.* Berkeley: University of California Press, 1977.
5609. Mondlane, Eduardo. *Struggle in Mozambique.* Baltimore: Penguin Books, 1969.

Revolution in Guinea-Bissau, 1963-1974

Guinea-Bissau is the smallest and least known of Portugal's former colonies in Africa. The revolution there also attracted the least worldwide attention, though it was no less important, especially because of the brilliance of its leader, Amilcar Cabral (see the section "Amilcar Cabral" in this chapter). In the 1950s Portuguese Guineans sought reforms for their country from an unresponsive Portugal. In 1956 Cabral helped found the Party for the Independence of Guinea and Cape Verde (PAIGC; the Cape Verde Islands are some 600 miles off the coast of Guinea-Bissau and are considered part of that country). The party built up its organization carefully and secretly, and the goal of independence became widely accepted. Cabral also created a guerrilla force. After peaceful means to achieve independence failed, the revolution began in 1963. In the absence of suitable guerrilla terrain (e.g., jungles, mountains), PAIGC forces conducted an educational campaign and were thereby able to depend upon local people to shield them from Portuguese troops. By 1969 Portugal was virtually defeated, although she held on to the little she had left until the independence of Guinea-Bissau was recognized in 1974.

The articles and books by Gérard Chailiand (1969, 1973), Ronald H. Chilcote (1974, 1977), Basil Davidson (1968, 1969, 1970, 1973, 1974), and Lars Rudebeck (1972, 1974, 1979) are the best on the revolution. Several of the articles and the book by Chantal Sarrazin and Ole Gjerstad (1978) concentrate on Guinea-Bissau after independence.

Bibliography

5610. McCarthy, Joseph M. *Guinea-Bissau and Cape Verde: A Comprehensive Bibliography.* New York: Garland, 1977.

Documents

5611. Gjerstad, Ole, ed. *Guinea-Bissau: Toward Final Victory: Selected Speeches and Documents from PAIGC.* Richmond, British Columbia, Canada: LSM Press, 1974.

Articles

5612. Cabral, Luis. "'Portuguese' Guinea: United Front against Imperialism." *Tricontinental Magazine* (November-December 1969): 141-46.
5613. Chailiand, Gérard. "The PAIGC without Cabral: An Assessment." *Ufahamu* 3:3 (Winter 1973): 87-95.
5614. Chilcote, Ronald H. "Guinea-Bissau's Struggle: Past and Present." *Africa Today* 24 (January-March 1977): 31-40.
5615. _____. "Struggle in Guinea-Bissau." *Africa Today* 21 (Winter 1974): 57-62.
5616. Davidson, Basil. "Guinea-Bissau Builds for Independence." *New World Review* 41:2 (1973): 36-42.
5617. _____. "The Liberation Struggle in Angola and Portuguese Guinea." *Africa Quarterly* 10:1 (April-June 1970): 25-31.
5618. _____. "Notes on a Liberation Struggle." *Transition* 9:45 (1974): 18-21.
5619. _____. "The Prospect for Guinea-Bissau." *Third World* (April 1973): 3-6.
5620. _____. "Revolt of 'Portuguese' Guinea." *Tricontinental Magazine* (September-October 1968): 88-91.

5621. _____. "Victory and Reconciliation in Guinea-Bissau." *Africa Today* 21 (Fall 1974): 5–22.
5622. Glantz, Michael H. "The War of the Maps: Portugal vs. PAIGC." *Pan-African Journal* 6 (Autumn 1973): 285–96.
5623. Hodges, Tony. "Guinea-Bissau: Five Years of Independence." *Africa Report* 24:1–2 (January-February 1979): 4–9.
5624. Lobban, Richard. "Guinea-Bissau: 24 September 1973 and Beyond." *Africa Today* 21 (Winter 1974): 15–24.
5625. Matteos, Salahudin. "The Cape Verdeans and the PAIGC Struggle for National Liberation." *Ufahamu* 3:3 (Winter 1973): 43–48.
5626. Minter, William. "Learning from Guinea-Bissau." *Bulletin of the Southern Association of Africa* 7 (February 1979): 10–11.
5627. Moolman, J. H. "Portuguese Guinea: The Untenable War." *Africa Institute Bulletin* 12:6 (1974): 243–60.
5628. Obichere, Boniface L. "Reconstruction in Guinea-Bissau: From Revolutionaries and Guerrillas to Bureaucrats and Politicians." *Current Bibliography of African Affairs* 8:3 (1975): 204–19.
5629. O'Brien, Jay. "Tribe, Class, and Nation: Revolution and the Weapon of Theory in Guinea-Bissau." *Race and Class* 19 (Summer 1977): 1–18.
5630. Pattee, Richard. "Portuguese Guinea: A Crucial Struggle." *South African International* 4 (January 1974): 132–48.
5631. Pinto, Cruz. "Guinea-Bissau's Liberation Struggle Against Portuguese Colonialism." *Freedomways* 3 (1972): 189–95.
5632. Rudebeck, Lars. "Development and Class Struggle in Guinea-Bissau." *Monthly Review* (January 1979): 14–23.
5633. _____. "Political Mobilisation in Guinea-Bissau." *Journal of Modern African Studies* 10:1 (May 1972): 1–18.
5634. Urdang, Stephanie. "Fighting Two Colonialisms: The Women's Struggle in Guinea-Bissau." *African Studies Review* 18 (December 1975): 29–34.
5635. Venter, Al J., Jr. "Portugal's War in Guiné-Bissau." *Munger Africana Library Notes* (April 1973): 1–202.
5636. Zartman, I. William. "Africa's Quiet War: Portuguese Guinea." *Africa Report* 9:2 (February 1964): 8–12.
5637. _____. "Guinea: The Quiet War Goes On." *Africa Report* 12:8 (November 1967): 67–72.

Books

5638. Chailiand, Gérard. *Armed Struggle in Africa: With the Guerrillas in "Portuguese" Guinea*. Translated by D. Rattray and R. Leonhardt. New York: Monthly Review Press, 1969.
5639. CIDAC. *Guine-Bissau: 3 annos de independencia*. Lisbon: CIDAC, 1976.
5640. Davidson, Basil. *The Liberation of Guiné: Aspects of an African Revolution*. Baltimore: Penguin Books, 1969.
5641. Rudebeck, Lars. *Guinea-Bissau: A Study of Political Mobilization*. Uppsala, Sweden: Scandinavian Institute of African Studies, 1974.
5642. Sarrazin, Chantal, and Ole Gjerstad. *Sowing the First Harvest: Reconstruction in Guinea-Bissau*. Oakland, California: LSM Information Center, 1978.
5643. Venter, Al J., Jr. *Report on Portugal's War in Guinea-Bissau*. Pasadena, California: Munger Africana Library, 1973.

Amilcar Cabral

Cabral, a Lisbon trained agronomist, was the leader and personification of the Revolution in Guinea-Bissau. Although he is not widely known outside of Africa and limited intellectual circles, Cabral was a revolutionist and revolutionary theorist of major proportions, even though an assassin terminated his life in 1973 before his work was completed. Cabral's thought blends theoretical analysis with application of theory to the mundane problems of winning a revolution and building a new order. Thus, he insisted that the revolution look beyond the liberation struggle to the future evolution of society. Cabral had a great deal to say about such factors as neocolonialism, social classes and structure, party organization and responsibility, Marxism, and political and military leadership. He was a practical, sensible, and farsighted revolutionist. His ideas are as valuable, perhaps, as those of any other twentieth century revolutionist.

Along with a thorough reading of Cabral's own writings, his thought is best analyzed in the articles by David A. Andelman (1970), Henry Bienen (1977), Gérard Chailiand (1973, 1977–1978), Ronald H. Chilcote (1968), Charles McCollester (1973), and Bernard Magubane (1971). The article by Robert Blackey (1974) compares the ideas of Cabral and Frantz Fanon. The books in the previous section by Gérard Chailiand (1969) and Basil Davidson (1969) should also be consulted. Cabral still awaits a biographer.

Bibliography

5644. Chilcote, Ronald H. "Amilcar Cabral: A Bio-Bibliography of His Life and Thought. 1925–1973." *African Journal* 5 (Winter 1974–1975): 289–307.

Articles

5645. Andelman, David A. "Profile: Amilcar Cabral." *Africa Report* 15:5 (May 1970): 18–19.
5646. Andrade, Mario de. "Amilcar Cabral: Profil d'un révolutionnaire africain." *Présence Africaine*, no. 86 (1973): 3–19.
5647. Bienen, Henry. "State and Revolution: The Work of Amilcar Cabral." *Journal of Modern African Studies* 15:4 (December 1977): 555–75.
5648. Blackey, Robert. "Fanon and Cabral: A Contrast in Theories of Revolution for Africa." *Journal of Modern African Studies* 12:2 (June 1974): 191–209.
5649. Cabral, Amilcar. "A Brief Report on the Situation of the Struggle (January-August 1971)." *Ufahamu* 2:3 (Winter 1972): 5–28.
5650. _____. "Culture and Nationalism." *Transition* 9:45 (1974): 12–17.
5651. _____. "Determined to Resist." *Tricontinental Magazine* (September-October 1968): 114–26.

5652. _____. "Identity and Dignity in the Context of the National Liberation." *Pan-African Journal* 6 (Autumn 1973): 369–78.
5653. _____. "Identity and Dignity in the National Liberation Struggle." *Africa Today* 19 (Fall 1972): 39–47.
5654. _____. "National Liberation and the Social Structure." In *Guerrilla Warfare and Marxism*, edited by W. J. Pomeroy. New York: International Publishers, 1968.
5655. _____. "Original Writings." *Ufahamu* 3:3 (Winter 1973): 31–42.
5656. _____. "PAIGC: Optimistic and Fighter." *Tricontinental Magazine* (July-October 1970): 167–74.
5657. _____. "A Report to Our Friends." *Africa Today* 19 (Winter 1972): 7–13.
5658. _____. "Report on Portuguese Guinea and the Liberation Movement." *Ufahamu* 1:2 (Fall 1970): 69–103.
5659. _____. "Role of Culture in the Battle for Independence." *UNESCO Courier* 26 (November 1973): 12–16.
5660. _____. "The Role of Culture in the Struggle for Independence." *International Journal of Politics* 7 (Winter 1977–1978): 18–43.
5661. _____. "The Struggle Has Taken Root." *Black Scholar* 4:10 (July-August 1973): 28–32.
5662. Chailiand, Gérard. "Amilcar Cabral." *International Journal of Politics* 7 (Winter 1977–1978): 3–17.
5663. _____. "The Legacy of Amilcar Cabral." *Ramparts* (April 1973): 17–20.
5664. Chilcote, Ronald H. "The Political Thought of Amilcar Cabral." *Journal of Modern African Studies* 6:3 (October 1968): 373–88.
5665. Ferreira, Eduardo. "Theory of Revolution and Background to His Assassination." *Ufahamu* 3:3 (Winter 1973): 49–68.
5666. Hauser, George, and Lawrence W. Henderson. "In Memory of Amilcar Cabral: Two Statements." *Africa Today* 20 (Winter 1973): 3–6.
5667. Hubbard, Maryinez L. "Culture and History in a Revolutionary Context: Approaches to Amilcar Cabral." *Ufahamu* 3:3 (Winter 1973): 69–86.
5668. McCollester, Charles. "The Political Thought of Amilcar Cabral." *Monthly Review* (March 1973): 10–21.
5669. Magubane, Bernard. "Amilcar Cabral: Evolution of Revolutionary Thought." *Ufahamu* 2:2 (Fall 1971): 71–87.
5670. Mmbaga, J. K. "Amilcar Cabral: The Anatomy of an African Revolutionary." *Kale* (1974): 11–24.
5671. Morgado, Michael S. "Amilcar Cabral's Theory of Cultural Revolution." *Black Images* 3:2 (1974): 3–16.
5672. Nyang, Sulayman Sheih. "The Political Thought of Amilcar Cabral: A Synthesis." *Odu* (January 1976): 3–20.
5673. Opoku, K. "Cabral and the African Revolution." *Présence Africaine* 1–2 (1978): 45–60.

Books

5674. Cabral, Amilcar. *Our People Are Our Mountains.* London: Committee for Freedom in Mozambique, Angola and Guinea, 1971.
5675. _____. *Return to the Source: Selected Speeches.* Edited by Africa Information Service. New York: Monthly Review Press, 1976.
5676. _____. *Revolution in Guinea.* New York: Monthly Review Press, 1969.

Libyan Revolution, 1969-1970

Italy gained control of Libya after this north African country had been part of the Ottoman Empire for several hundred years. After World War II Italy lost Libya, and the United Nations declared it independent in 1951. The country became a monarchy. In what is called the Libyan Revolution, military officers overthrew the monarchy in 1969. Colonel Mu'ammar El Qaddafi, leader of the group, became prime minister in 1970. Qaddafi, virtually a dictator, is a self-proclaimed revolutionist and Arab nationalist.

Articles

5677. Deeb, Marius K. "Islam and Arab Nationalism in al-Qaddhafi's Ideology." *Journal of South Asian and Middle East Studies* 2 (Winter 1978): 12-26.
5678. Lenczowski, George. "Popular Revolution in Libya." *Current History* (February 1974): 57.
5679. Sanger, Richard H. "Libya: Conclusions on an Unfinished Revolution." *Middle East Journal* 29:4 (Autumn 1975): 409-17.
5680. Sheehan, Edward R. F. "Colonel Qaddhafi—Libya's Mystical Revolutionary." *The New York Times Magazine* (6 February 1972).

Books

5681. Ansell, Meredith O., and Ibrahim Massaud Al-Afif. *The Libyan Revolution: A Sourcebook of Legend and Historical Documents.* Vol. I. *1 September 1969-30 August 1970.* Stoughton, Wisconsin: Oleander Press, 1972.
5682. First, Ruth. *Libya: The Elusive Revolution.* New York: Holmes and Meier, 1975.

Ethiopian Revolution, 1974–1977

Haile Selassie had been emperor of Ethiopia since 1930. He had created military and educational systems to convert his weak feudal inheritance into an authoritarian state. But the products of these systems at times resisted his rule. In 1960, Haile Selassie had to crush a revolt led by officers of his bodyguard unit. In the 1970s a severe drought led to demonstrations and unrest. The emperor was arrested and replaced by a military government in 1974. By 1975 the revolution had extended its reach to include a far reaching process of social transformation. Socialism was proclaimed, Russian influence increased, a war was fought against neighboring Somalia, a separatist movement in Eritrea was combated, and a bloody effort at power consolidation was begun that resulted in the loss of many skilled people.

The historiographical article by John M. Cohen (1979) provides excellent direction for beginning an examination of the Ethiopian Revolution. Complementing the many articles are several good books, most of which include material based on first hand experiences as well as more traditional scholarship. These include the books by Colin Legum (1975), John Markakis and Nega Ayele (1978), Marina Ottaway and David Ottaway (1978), and Brian Thompson (1975). Excellent background to the revolution is provided in the books by John M. Cohen and Dov Weintraub (1975) and Patrick Gilkes (1975). Raúl Valdés Vivó's book (1978) is by a Cuban Communist official.

Historiography

5683. Cohen, John M. "Revolution and Publication: Ethiopia since 1974." *ASA Review of Books '79* (African Studies Association) 5 (1979): 154–62.

Articles

5684. Archer, George D., and Milkias Paulos. "The Second Scramble for Africa." *Horn Africa* 2 (July-September 1979): 55–66.
5685. Beshah, Teferra-Worq, and John W. Harbeson. "Afar Pastoralists in Transition and the Ethiopian Revolution." *Journal of African Studies* 5 (Fall 1978): 249–67.
5686. Brietzke, Paul. "Law, Revolution, and the Ethiopian Peasant." *Rural African* (Fall 1975): 7–38.
5687. Chege, Michael. "The Revolution Betrayed: Ethiopia, 1974–79." *Journal of Modern African Studies* 17:3 (September 1979): 359–80.
5688. Cohen, John M., et al. "Rural Development Issues Following Ethiopian Land Reform." *Africa Today* 23:2 (1976): 7–28.

5689. Fessehatzion, Tekie. "The Eritrean Struggle for Independence and National Liberation." *Horn Africa* 1 (April-June 1978): 29-34.
5690. Gilkes, Patrick. "The Coming Struggle for Ethiopia." *Africa Report* 19:3 (March 1974): 33-35, 43.
5691. _____. "Ethiopia: More Decentralization as Land Reform Progresses." *African Development* 10:7 (July 1976): 661-65.
5692. _____. "Ethiopia—A Real Revolution?" *World Today* 31:1 (January 1975): 15-23.
5693. Gupta, Vijay. "The Ethiopian Revolution: Causes and Results." *India Quarterly* 34 (April-June 1978): 158-74.
5694. Hamilton, David. "Ethiopia's Embattled Revolutionaries." *Conflict Studies* (April 1977): 1-20.
5695. Harbeson, John W. "Ethiopia: Whither the Revolution?" *Africa Report* 21:7-8 (July-August 1976): 48-50.
5696. _____. "Perspectives on the Ethiopian Revolution." *Ethiopianist Notes* 1 (Spring 1977): 1-8.
5697. _____. "Revolution and Rural Development in Ethiopia." *Rural African* (Fall 1975): 1-6.
5698. _____. "Socialism, Traditions, and Revolutionary Politics in Contemporary Ethiopia." *Review Canada Etudes Africa* 11:2 (1977): 217-34.
5699. Heiden, Linda. "The Eritrean Struggle for Independence." *Monthly Review* (June 1978): 13-28.
5700. Jones, W. "Problems of the Ethiopian Revolution." *African Communist* (1977): 84-93.
5701. Katz, Donald R. "Children's Revolution: A Bloodbath in Ethiopia." *Horn Africa* 1 (July-September 1978): 3-12.
5702. _____. "Ethiopia after the Revolution: Vultures Return to the Land of Sheba." *Rolling Stone* (21 September 1978).
5703. Koehn, Peter. "Ethiopian Politics: Military Intervention and Prospects for Further Change." *Africa Today* 22:2 (Summer 1975): 7-21.
5704. Kraft, Joseph. "Letter from Addis Ababa." *The New Yorker* (31 July 1978).
5705. Lebel, Phillip. "Economic and Social Predictors of the Ethiopian Revolution." *Horn Africa* 1 (April-June 1978): 53-60.
5706. Legum, Colin. "Realities of the Ethiopian Revolution." *World Today* 33:8 (August 1977): 305-12.
5707. Love, Robert S. "Economic Change in Pre-revolutionary Ethiopia." *African Affairs* 78 (July 1979): 339-56.
5708. Markakis, John, and Nega Ayele. "Class and Revolution in Ethiopia." *Review of African Politics and Economics* (January-April 1977): 99-108.
5709. Monteiro, Anthony. "The Bright Future of the Ethiopian Revolution." *Freedomways* 18:3 (1978): 136-50.
5710. Ottaway, Marina. "Democracy and New Democracy: The Ideological Debate in the Ethiopian Revolution." *African Studies Review* 21:1 (1978): 19-31.
5711. "Revolution in Ethiopia." *Monthly Review* 29:3 (July-August 1977): 46-60.
5712. Skurnik, W. A. E. "Revolution and Change in Ethiopia." *Current History* 68 (May 1975): 206.
5713. Valdelin, Jan. "Ethiopia 1974-7: From Anti-Feudal Revolution to Consolidation of the Bourgeois State." *Race and Class* 19 (Spring 1978): 379-98.
5714. Warr, Michael. "There's a Revolution in Ethiopia." *Horn Africa* 2 (July-September 1979): 4-9.

364 / Africa

Books

5715. Cohen, John M., and Dov Weintraub. *Land and Peasants in Imperial Ethiopia: The Social Background to a Revolution.* Atlantic Highlands, New Jersey: Humanities Press, 1975.
5716. Gilkes, Patrick. *The Dying Lion: Feudalism and Modernization in Ethiopia.* New York: St. Martin's Press 1975.
5717. Hiwer, Addis. *Ethiopia: From Autocracy to Revolution.* London: Review of African Political Economy, Occasional Paper No. 1, 1975.
5718. Legum, Colin. *Ethiopia: The Fall of Haile Selassie's Empire.* New York: Holmes and Meier, 1975.
5719. Markakis, John, and Nega Ayele. *Class and Revolution in Ethiopia.* London: Spokesman, 1978.
5720. Ottaway, Marina, and David Ottaway. *Ethiopia: Empire in Revolution.* New York: Holmes and Meier, 1978.
5721. Potholm, Christian P. *Liberation and Exploitation: The Struggle for Ethiopia.* Washington, D.C.: University Press of America, 1977.
5722. Scholler, Heinrich, and Paul Brietzke. *Ethiopia: Revolution, Law and Politics.* Munich: Weltforum Verlag, 1976.
5723. Selassie, Bereket Habte. *Conflict and Intervention in the Horn of Africa.* New York: Monthly Review Press, 1980.
5724. Thompson, Brian. *Ethiopia: The Country That Cut Off Its Head: A Diary of the Revolution.* London: Robson Books, 1975.
5725. Vivó, Raúl Valdés. *Ethiopia's Revolution.* New York: International Publishers, 1978.

Revolution in Southern Africa

The items in this section deal primarily with the liberation struggles by the majority of black Africans against the minority of whites in Southern Africa. After years of guerrilla warfare, Zimbabwe (formerly Rhodesia) began to be ruled by a black majority government in 1979. The conflict in the Union of South Africa is still in progress.

Bibliographies

5726. Ansari, S. *Liberation Struggle in Southern Africa: A Bibliography.* Columbia, Missouri: South Asia Books, 1972.
5727. Pollak, Karen, and Oliver B. Pollak. *Rhodesia/Zimbabwe: An International Bibliography.* Boston: G. K. Hall, 1978.

Documents

5728. Liberation Support Movement, eds. *Zimbabwe: The Final Advance: Documents on the Zimbabwe Liberation Movement.* Oakland, California: LSM Information Center, 1978.
5729. Nyangoni, C. K., and G. M. K. Nyandoro, eds. *Zimbabwe Independence Movements: Select Documents.* New York: Barnes and Noble, 1979.

Articles

5730. Bomani, Paul. "The Prognosis for the Liberation of Zimbabwe." *Journal of Southern African Affairs* 3 (July 1978): 343-52.
5731. Bratton, Michael. "Settler State, Guerrilla War, and Rural Underdevelopment in Rhodesia." *Issue* 9 (Spring-Summer 1979): 56-62.
5732. Bruton, James K. "Counter-Insurgency in Rhodesia." *Military Review* 59 (March 1979): 26-39.
5733. Davidson, Basil. "Zimbabwe's Robert Mugabe Comes Out of the Shadows at Last." *Los Angeles Times* (9 March 1980).
5734. Duly, Leslie Clement, and Joan Krueger Wadlow. "A Review of the Study of Nationalism in Southern Africa, 1974-1979." *Canadian Review of Studies in Nationalism* 6 (1979): 173-94.
5735. Hull, Richard W. "The Continuing Crisis in Rhodesia." *Current History* 78 (March 1980): 107.
5736. _____. "Rhodesia in Crisis." *Current History* 76 (May 1979): 105.
5737. Jordan, K. "Trade Unionism v. Revolution in South Africa." *Race Today* 6 (March 1974): 76-80; (May 1974): 147-48.
5738. Kileff, Clive, and Leland W. Robinson. "From Rhodesia to Zimbabwe: Contemporary Black Nationalist Organizations." *International Review of History and Political Science* 15 (February 1978): 39-54.
5739. Mubako, Simbi V. "Aspects of the Zimbabwe Liberation Movement 1966-1976." *Mohlomi* 2 (1978): 38-65.
5740. Ntalaja, Nzongola. "Imperialism and the Liberation Struggle in Southern Africa." *Issue* 9 (Spring-Summer 1979): 14-16.

Books

5741. Bunting, Brian. *Moses Kotane: South African Revolutionary.* Chicago: Inkululeko, 1975.
5742. Carter, Gwendolen M., and Patrick O'Meara. *Southern Africa: The Continuing Crisis.* Bloomington: Indiana University Press, 1979.
5743. Center for Black Education. *African Liberation: An Analytical Report on Southern Africa.* Washington, D.C.: Drum and Spear Press, 1972.
5744. Gann, Lewis, and Peter Duignan. *South Africa: War, Revolution, or Peace?* Stanford: Hoover Institution, 1978.
5745. Gerhart, Gail. *Black Power in South Africa: The Evolution of an Ideology.* Berkeley: University of California Press, 1978.
5746. Good, Robert C. *U.D.I.: The International Politics of the Rhodesian Rebellion.* Princeton: Princeton University Press, 1973.

5747. Liberation Support Movement. *Namibia: SWAPO Fight for Freedom.* Oakland, California: LSM Information Center, 1978.
5748. Magubane, Bernard M. *The Political Economy of Race and Class in South Africa.* New York: Monthly Review Press, 1979.
5749. Maxey, Kees. *The Fight for Zimbabwe: The Armed Conflict in Southern Rhodesia since UDI.* New York: Africana Publishing Company, 1975.
5750. Nyangoni, Wellington W. *African Nationalism in Zimbabwe.* Washington, D.C.: University Press of America, 1977.
5751. Raeburn, Michael. *We Are Everywhere: Narrative Accounts of Rhodesian Guerrillas.* New York: Random House, 1979.
5752. Sithole, Ndabaningi. *Roots of a Revolution: Scenes from Zimbabwe's Struggle.* New York: Oxford University Press, 1977.
5753. Sizwe, No. *One Azania, One Nation: The National Question in South Africa.* London: Zed Press, 1979.
5754. Utete, C. Munhamu Botsio. *The Road to Zimbabwe. The Political Economy of Settler Colonialism, National Liberation and Foreign Intervention.* Washington, D.C.: University Press of America, 1978.

Other Third World Countries and the Middle East

> "Do you know of any revolution, even a scientific one, that has taken place without bloodshed? No despot is ever going to give up his throne because you ask him to give it up, or because you beg him to go away. The final word is always an act of war."
>
> Mehdi Bazargan
> Prime Minister of Iran
> (September 17, 1979)

The Third World generally refers to the underdeveloped areas of the world, and often to non-white peoples as well. Therefore, most of the revolutions highlighted in the previous chapters on Latin America, Asia, and Africa fall under this rubric. They have been revolutions against imperialism and some form of colonialism or neocolonialism. They have also been social and economic revolutions, often brought about or led by a Western-educated elite who have aimed at making their countries more modern and industrial. Thus, collectively, they are often referred to as "revolutions of modernization." What has been said by way of generalization in the introductions to Chapters 6, 7, and 8 can apply equally to any of them, as well as here, and therefore will not be repeated.

The works immediately below actually comprise a kind of miscellaneous section to the three previous chapters in that they treat the Third World in general or a characteristic or portion of it not confined to any single continent. Some of the better books taking an overview of the Third World are those by Fred Carrier (1976), Gérard Chailiand (1977), David C. Gordon (1971), Richard Harris (1962), Joel S. Migdal (1974), Norman Miller and Roderick Aya (1971), and Peter Worsley (1970). For strategies of national liberation see the books by J. Bowyer Bell (1976) and Donald C. Hodges and Robert E. A. Shanab (1972). On leadership see the volume by Jean Lacouture (1970). For nationalism see the works by John H. Kautsky (1962) and Elie Kedourie (1970). For ideology see the book edited by Paul E. Sigmund, Jr. (1963). And for relations between the Third World and the United States and the Soviet Union see the books by Richard J. Barnet (1972) and Alexandre A. Bennigsen and S. Enders Wimbush (1979).

Articles

5755. Barka, Mehdi Ben. "National Revolution in Africa and Asia" *Revolution* 1:3 (1963): 17-21.

5756. Franda, Marcus W. "Revolution and Tradition in the Middle East, Africa, and South Asia." *National Security Affairs Forum* (Spring-Summer 1976): 23-32.

5757. Selden, Mark. "Revolutions and Third World Development." In *National Liberation,* edited by N. Miller and R. Aya. New York: Free Press, 1971.

Books

5758. Ahmad, Eqbal. *Revolution and Reaction in the Third World.* New York: Pantheon Books, 1972.

5759. Barnet, Richard J. *Intervention and Revolution: The United States in the Third World.* Rev. ed. New York: New American Library, 1972.

5760. Bell, J. Bowyer. *On Revolt: Strategies of National Liberation.* Cambridge, Massachusetts: Harvard University Press, 1976.

5761. Bennigsen, Alexandre A., and S. Enders Wimbush. *Muslim National Communism in the Soviet Union: A Revolutionary Strategy for the Colonial World.* Chicago: University of Chicago Press, 1979.

5762. Brown, Emily C. *Har Dayal: Hindu Revolutionary and Rationalist.* Tucson: University of Arizona Press, 1975.

5763. Carrier, Fred. *The Third World Revolution.* Atlantic Highlands, New Jersey: Humanities Press, 1976.

5764. Chailiand, Gérard. *Revolution in the Third World: Myths and Prospects.* New York: Viking, 1977.

5765. Emerson, Rupert. *From Empire to Nation: The Rise to Self-Assertion of Asian and African People.* Cambridge, Massachusetts: Harvard University Press, 1960.

5766. Gordon, David C. *Self-Determination and History in the Third World.* Princeton: Princeton University Press, 1971.

5767. Harris, Richard. *Independence and After: Revolution in Underdeveloped Countries.* London: Oxford University Press, 1962.

5768. Hodges, Donald C., and Robert E. A. Shaneb, eds. *NLF: National Liberation Fronts, 1960-1970.* New York: Morrow, 1972.

5769. Kautsky, John H., ed. *Political Change in Underdeveloped Countries: Nationalism and Communism.* New York: John Wiley, 1962.

5770. Kedourie, Elie. *Nationalism in Asia and Africa.* New York: World, 1970.

5771. Lacouture, Jean. *The Demigods: Charismatic Leadership in the Third World.* Translated by P. Wolf. New York: Alfred A. Knopf, 1970.

5772. Melotti, Umberto. *Marx and the Third World.* Translated by P. Ransford. Atlantic Highlands, New Jersey: Humanities Press, 1977.

5773. Migdal, Joel S. *Peasants, Politics, and Revolution: Pressures toward Political and Social Change in the Third World.* Princeton: Princeton University Press, 1974.

5774. Miller, Norman, and Roderick Aya, eds. *National Liberation: Revolution in the Third World.* New York: Free Press, 1971.

5775. Mountjoy, Alan B., ed. *The Third World: Problems and Perspectives.* New York: St. Martin's Press, 1979.

5776. Paige, Jeffrey M. *Agrarian Revolution: Social Movements and Export Agriculture in the Underdeveloped World.* New York: Free Press, 1975.
5777. Schmitt, D. *Dynamics of the Third World: Political and Social Change.* Englewood Cliffs, New Jersey: Winthrop Publishing, 1974.
5778. Sigmund, Paul E., Jr., ed. *The Ideologies of the Developing Nations.* New York: Praeger, 1963.
5779. Silber, Irwin. *Voices of National Liberation.* New York: Clark Boardman Company, 1970.
5780. *A Socialist Oriented State: Instrument of Revolutionary Change.* Chicago: Progress Publishers, 1978.
5781. *The Third World: Premises of U.S. Policy.* San Francisco: Institute for Contemporary Studies, 1978.
5782. Worsley, Peter. *The Third World.* 2d ed. Chicago: University of Chicago Press, 1970.

Middle East Revolutions

The Middle East is treated in this separate section because it includes countries that are either African (e.g., Egypt) or Asian (e.g., Iran). The revolutions in these countries are not placed in the chapters covering these continents because the Middle East is a commonly and historically recognized region, and because there are the items below that examine the area as a unit.

Much of what has been said about neocolonialism and nationalism, and about social, political, and economic developments in the Third World also applies to the Middle East. But what has not been said or implied, except for the revolutions in Algeria and Libya, is that Islamic revolutionists have developed varying kinds of Islamic socialism which are viewed, theoretically at least, as being neither an evolution from capitalism nor a step toward communism, but a form of social justice based upon Islam.

The titles below include several general examinations of the Middle East by Eugene M. Fisher and M. Cherif Bassiouni (1972), Sydney N. Fisher (1969), George M. Haddad (1969–1973), G. E. Kirk (1960), Humphrey Trevelyan (1971), and P. J. Vatikiotis (1972). In addition, there are works on Arab socialism by Sami A. Hanna and George H. Gardner (1969) and A. M. Said (1972). For revolutionary Islam see the works by Thomas Hodgkin (1980) and G. H. Jansen (1980). For ideology see Leonard Binder's book (1964). On nationalism consult the books by George Antonius (1965), Walid W. Kazziha (1975), and Hisham B. Sharabi (1966). For Palestinian revolutionists see the books by Mehmood Hussain (1975), Glenn M. Jubran (n.d.), and Rosemary Sayigh (1979). This section also includes works on revolutionary activity in Egypt (prior to 1952), Iran (prior to 1978), Iraq, Lebanon, Saudi Arabia, and Israel.

Bibliographies

5783. Atiyeh, George N. *The Contemporary Middle East, 1948-1973: An Annotated and Selective Bibliography.* Boston: G. K. Hall, 1975.
5784. Clements, Frank. *The Emergence of Arab Nationalism.* Wilmington, Delaware: Scholarly Resources, 1977. Bibliography.
5785. Ettinghausen, Richard, ed. *A Selected and Annotated Bibliography of Books and Periodicals in Western Languages Dealing with the Near and Middle East.* Washington, D.C.: Middle East Institute, 1952.
5786. Grimwood-Jones, Diana, et al, eds. *Arab-Islamic Bibliography.* Atlantic Highlands, New Jersey: Humanities Press, 1977.
5787. Rossi, Peter M., and Wayne E. White, eds. *Articles on the Middle East, 1947-1971: A Cumulation of Bibliographies from the Middle East Journal.* Ann Arbor, Michigan: Pierian Press, 1978.

Historiography

5788. Davison, Roderic H. *The Near and Middle East: An Introduction to History and Bibliography.* Washington, D.C.: American Historical Association Service Center for Teachers of History, 1959.

Reference

5789. Simon, Reeva S. *The Modern Middle East: A Guide to Research Tools in the Social Sciences.* Boulder, Colorado: Westview Press, 1978.

Documents

5790. Hanna, Sami A., and George H. Gardner. *Arab Socialism: A Documentary Survey.* Salt Lake City: University of Utah Press, 1969.

Articles

5791. Braun, Frank H. "Anatomy of a Palace Revolution that Failed." *International Journal of Middle East Studies* 9 (February 1978): 63-72.
5792. Devereux, Robert. "Suleyman Pasha's 'The Feeling of the Revolution.'" *Middle East Studies* 15 (January 1979): 1-35.
5793. Farsoun, Samih K., and Walter F. Caroll. "State Capitalism and Counterrevolution in the Middle East: A Thesis." In *Social Change in the Capitalist World,* edited by B. H. Kaplan. Beverly Hills, California: Sage 1978.
5794. Hodgkin, Thomas. "The Revolutionary Tradition in Islam." *Race and Class* 21 (Winter 1980): 221-38.
5795. Hollingworth, Clare. "The Ba'athist Revolution in Iraq." *World Today* 19:5 (May 1963): 225-30.
5796. Hottinger, Arnold. "Does Saudi Arabia Face Revolution?" *The New York Review of Books* (28 June 1979).
5797. Kelly, J. B. "Hadramaut, Oman, Dhufar: The Experience of Revolution." *Middle East Studies* 12 (May 1976): 213-30.
5798. Marr, Phebe Ann. "The Iraqi Revolution: A Case Study of Army Rule." *Orbis* 14 (Fall 1970): 714-39.

5799. Oberling, Pierre. "The Role of Religious Minorities in the Persian Revolution, 1906-1912." *Journal of Asian History* 12:1 (1978): 1-29.
5800. Omar, F., "The Nature of the Iranian Revolts in the Early Abbasid Period." *Islamic Culture* 1 (1974): 1-9.
5801. Philipp, Mangol Bayat. "The Concepts of Religion and Government in the Thought of Mîrzâ Aqâ Khân Kirmânî, a Nineteenth-Century Persian Revolutionary." *International Journal of Middle East Studies* 4 (September 1974): 381-400.
5802. Stanwood, Frederick. "Revolution and the 'Old Reactionary Policy': Britain in Persia, 1917." *Journal of Imperial Commonwealth History* 6 (January 1978): 144-65.
5803. Suleiman, Michael W. "Crisis and Revolution in Lebanon." *Middle East Journal* 26:1 (Winter 1972): 11-24.
5804. Tignor, Robert L. "The Egyptian Revolution of 1919: New Directions in the Egyptian Economy." *Middle East Studies* 3 (October 1976): 41-68.

Books

5805. Antonius, George. *The Arab Awakening: The Story of the Arab National Movement.* New York: Capricorn Books, 1965.
5806. Batatu, Hanna. *The Old Social Classes and the Revolutionary Movements of Iraq.* Princeton: Princeton University Press, 1978.
5807. Begin, Menachem. *The Revolt.* New York: Nash Publishing, 1977.
5808. Binder, Leonard. *The Ideological Revolution in the Middle East.* New York: John Wiley, 1964.
5809. Browne, Edward G. *The Persian Revolution of 1905-1909.* Cambridge: Cambridge University Press, 1910.
5810. Fisch, Harold. *The Zionist Revolution: A New Perspective.* New York: St. Martin's Press, 1978.
5811. Fisher, Eugene M., and M. Cherif Bassiouni. *Storm over the Arab World: A People in Revolution.* Chicago: Follett, 1972.
5812. Fisher, Sydney N. *The Middle East: A History.* 2d ed. New York: Alfred A. Knopf, 1969.
5813. Haddad, George M. *Revolutions and Military Rule in the Middle East.* 3 vols. New York: Robert Speller, 1969-1973.
5814. Halpern, Manfred. *The Politics of Social Change in the Middle East and North Africa.* Princeton: Princeton University Press, 1963.
5815. Hussain, Mehmood. *The Palestine Liberation Organization: A Study in Ideology, Strategy, and Tactics.* New York: International Publications Service, 1975.
5816. Jansen, G. H. *Militant Islam.* New York: Harper and Row, 1980.
5817. Jubran, Glenn M. *Our Struggle: The Palestine Revolution, 1968-70.* New York: Vantage, n.d.
5818. Kazziha, Walid W. *Revolutionary Transformation in the Arab World: Habash and His Comrades from Nationalism to Marxism.* New York: St. Martin's Press, 1975.
5819. Khadduri, Majid. *Republican Iraq: A Study in Iraqi Politics since the Revolution of 1958.* New York: Oxford University Press, 1969.
5820. Khaled, Leila. *My People Shall Live: The Autobiography of a Revolutionary.* London: Hodder and Stoughton, 1973.

5821. Kirk, G. E. *A Short History of the Middle East.* Rev. 6th ed. New York: Praeger, 1960.
5822. Koury, Enver M. *Patterns of Mass Movements in Arab Revolutionary Progressive States.* Hawthorne, New York: Mouton Publishers, 1970.
5823. Laffin, John. *Fedayeen.* New York: Free Press, 1973.
5824. McDaniel, Robert. *The Shuster Mission and the Persian Constitutional Revolution.* Minneapolis: Bibliotheca Islamica, 1974.
5825. O'Ballance, Edgar. *Arab Guerilla Power.* Hamden, Connecticut: Shoe String Press, 1973.
5826. Porath, Y. *The Palestinian Arab National Movement: From Riots to Rebellion.* Vol. 2. 1929-1939. Totowa, New Jersey: Frank Cass, 1978.
5827. Said, A. M. *Arab Socialism.* London: Blanford Press, 1972.
5828. Sayigh, Rosemary. *Palestinians: From Peasants to Revolutionaries.* London: Zed Press, 1979.
5829. Shaban, M. A. *The Abbasid Revolution.* New York: Cambridge University Press, 1971.
5830. Sharabi, Hisham B. *Nationalism and Revolution in the Arab World.* Princeton: Van Nostrand, 1966.
5831. _____ , ed. *Palestine Guerrillas: Their Credibility and Effectiveness.* Washington, D.C.: Middle East Institute, 1970.
5832. Simson, H. J. *British Rule in Palestine and the Arab Rebellion of 1936-1937.* Salisbury, North Carolina: Documentary Publications, 1977.
5833. Trevelyan, Humphrey. *The Middle East in Revolution.* Boston: Gambit, 1971.
5834. Vatikiotis, P. J., ed. *Revolution in the Middle East, and Other Case Studies.* Totowa, New Jersey: Rowman and Littlefield, 1972.

Revolution in Egypt, 1952

When Britain granted her independence in 1922, Egypt became a kingdom. After World War II Egypt and other members of the Arab League fought unsuccessfully against the new nation of Israel. Although an armistice was arranged in 1949, Egypt did not sign it. Within the country discontent increased. There were riots in 1951 and 1952 caused as a result of the government's failure to crush Israel, widespread corruption in the royal government, and Britain's continued occupation of the Suez Canal Zone. The Egyptian Revolution began in July, 1952 when an army group called the Free Officers seized control of the government and forced King Farouk to abdicate in favor of his infant son. Reform programs were begun. In 1953 reform extended to ending the monarchy and declaring Egypt a republic. A power struggle followed between the new president, Mohammed Naguib, and the deputy prime minister, Gamal Abdel Nasser, with Nasser emerging with complete control by 1954.

Revolution in Egypt, 1952 / 373

Among the best books on the Egyptian Revolution are those by Dan Hofstadter (1973), Charles P. Issawi (1963), and P. J. Vatikiotis (1968, 1978).

Articles

5835. Dekemejian, R. Hrair. "Marx, Weber and the Egyptian Revolution." *Middle East Journal* 30:2 (Spring 1976): 158-72.
5836. Peretz, Don. "Democracy and the Revolution in Egypt." *Middle East Journal* 13:1 (Winter 1959): 26-40.
5837. Vatikiotis, P. J. "Egypt 1966: The Assessment of a Revolution: An Interpretive Essay." *World Today* 22:6 (June 1966): 242-51.

Books

5838. Baker, Raymond William. *Egypt's Uncertain Revolution under Nasser and Sadat.* Cambridge, Massachusetts: Harvard University Press, 1978.
5839. Berque, Jacques. *Egypt: Imperialism and Revolution.* Translated by J. Stewart. New York: Praeger, 1972.
5840. Harris, Christina P. *Nationalism and Revolution in Egypt.* The Hague: Mouton, 1964.
5841. Hofstadter, Dan, ed. *Egypt and Nasser.* Vol. 1. *1952-56: A Revolution Finds Its Leader.* New York: Facts On File, 1973.
5842. _____, ed. *Egypt and Nasser.* Vol. 2. *1957-66: Trials of an Expanding Revolution.* New York: Facts On File, 1973.
5843. _____, ed. *Egypt and Nasser.* Vol. 3. *Military Defeat, Death and Aftermath.* New York: Facts On File, 1973.
5844. Issawi, Charles P. *Egypt in Revolution.* London: Oxford University Press, 1963.
5845. Jankowski, James P. *Egypt's Young Rebels: "Young Egypt," 1933-1952.* Stanford: Hoover Institution, 1975.
5846. Joesten, Joachim. *Nasser, the Rise to Power.* Westport, Connecticut: Greenwood, 1974.
5847. Little, Tom. *Egypt.* New York: Praeger, 1959.
5848. Nasser, G. A. *Philosophy of the Revolution.* Washington, D.C.: Public Affairs Press, 1955.
5849. O'Brien, Patrick. *Revolution in Egypt's Economic System: From Private Enterprise to Socialism, 1952-1965.* New York: Oxford University Press, 1966.
5850. Qayyum, Shah A. *Egypt Reborn: A Study of Egypt's Freedom Movement, 1945-52.* New York: International Publications Service, 1973.
5851. Richmond, John. *Egypt in Modern Times.* New York: Columbia University Press, 1977.
5852. Sadat, Anwar El. *Revolt on the Nile.* New York: John Day, 1957.
5853. Vatikiotis, P.J. *Nasser and His Generation.* New York: St. Martin's Press, 1978.
5854. _____, ed. *Egypt since the Revolution.* London: George Allen and Unwin, 1968.

Iranian Revolution, 1978–1979

In 1941 Britain and Russia occupied Iran, banished the reigning shah (who had founded the Pahlavi dynasty in the 1920s), and replaced him with his twenty-one year old son Mohammed Reza. From the start the new Shah of Iran was perceived as the tool of foreign powers. The British had put him on the throne and, later, the Americans restored him to it in 1953 after he was chased from the country by nationalists. The Shah's survival depended on American military and economic aid. In the 1960s, with American encouragement, the Shah undertook a program of reform and modernization in order to broaden the domestic base of his support. But he tolerated no opposition or dissent. In the meantime, American involvement became more complicated. By the 1970s the Shah's reform program waned, and the opposition to his harsh rule—from several Islamic and separatist groups—intensified. Iran's political system had no safety valves, and it finally exploded in revolution. Thus, the Shah undermined his own throne, and the United States defeated its own purposes by the manner in which it lent support.

The articles by R. W. Apple, Jr. (1979) and Nicholas Gage (1978) are analytical looks at Iran by two skilled journalists. Among the best books on the revolution are those by Richard W. Cottam (1979), Michael M. J. Fischer (1980), Fred Halliday (1979), Nikki R. Keddie (1979), and Amin Saikal (1980). Fereydoun Hoveyda's book (1980) is by the brother of one of the Shah's prime ministers. The book by Ashraf Pahlavi (1980) is by the Shah's sister. Good examinations of post-revolutionary Iran are in the articles by Richard W. Cottam (1980), Youssef M. Ibrahim (1979), John Kifner (1980), and Doyle McManus (1980). Not to be overlooked are the in-depth interviews conducted by Oriana Fallaci (1979).

Documents

5855. Alexander, Yonah, and Allan Nanes, eds. *The United States and Iran: A Documentary History.* Frederick, Maryland: University Publications of America, 1980.

Articles

5856. Ahmad, Eqbal, ed. "The Iranian Revolution" *Race and Class* 21:1 (Summer 1979), special issue.
5857. Apple, R. W., Jr. "Iran: Heart of the Matter." *The New York Times Magazine* (11 March 1979).

5858. Baraheni, Reza. "Terror in Iran." *The New York Review of Books* (28 October 1976).
5859. Bill, J. "Iran and the Crisis of '78." *Foreign Affairs* 57:2 (1978–1979): 323–42.
5860. Cottam, Richard W. "Revolutionary Iran." *Current History* 78 (January 1980): 12.
5861. Fallaci, Oriana. "'Everybody Wants to be Boss': An Interview with Mehdi Bazargan, Prime Minister of Iran." *The New York Times Magazine* (28 October 1979).
5862. _____. "An Interview with Khomeini." *The New York Times Magazine,* (7 October 1979).
5863. Fathi, Asghar. "The Role of the 'Rebels' in the Constitutional Movement in Iran." *International Journal of Middle East Studies* 10 (February 1979): 55–66.
5864. Gage, Nicholas. "Iran: Making of a Revolution." *The New York Times Magazine* (17 December 1978).
5865. Gregory, Dick, and Barbara Reynolds. "Inside Khomeini's Iran." *Playboy* (December 1980): 158.
5866. Halliday, Fred. "Can Iran's Revolution Survive the Release of the American Hostages?" *Los Angeles Times* (25 January, 1981).
5867. _____. "Why Is This Man Doing These Awful Things? Khomeini Is Driven by Dogmatism and Political Necessity." *Los Angeles Times* (25 November 1979).
5868. Ibrahim, Youssef M. "Inside Iran's Cultural Revolution." *The New York Times Magazine* (14 October 1979).
5869. "Iranian Islamic Movement Speaks [an interview with Ayatollah Khomeini]." *Los Angeles Times* (17 September 1979).
5870. "Iran's Kurds: Autonomy or Else." *The Economist* (28 April 1979).
5871. "Iran's Savonarola?" *The Economist* (10 February 1979).
5872. Jaynes, Gregory. "Iranian Women: Looking Beyond the Chador." *The New York Times Magazine* (22 April 1979).
5873. Keddie, Nikki R. "Khomeini's Fundamentalism Is as Revolutionary as His Politics." *Los Angeles Times* (13 January 1980).
5874. "The Khomeini Era Begins." *Time* (12 February 1979).
5875. Kifner, John. "A Year Without the Shah: Outlook in Iran's Revolution." *The New York Times* (20 January 1980).
5876. McManus, Doyle. "Iran: The Children Devour Their Revolution." *Los Angeles Times* (6 April 1980).
5877. "Militant Islam: The Soldiers of Allah Advance." *The Economist* (27 January 1979).
5878. Morgenthaler, Eric. "Iran's Volatile Left Wing." *Wall Street Journal* (23 March 1979).
5879. Petrossian, Vahe. "Dilemmas of the Iranian Revolution." *World Today* 36:1 (January 1980): 19–25.
5880. Schanche, Don A. "Islam Rebirth—Diversity in Revolution." *Los Angeles Times* (24 May 1979).
5881. "The Unknown Ayatullah Khomeini: A Portrait of the Islamic Mystic at the Center of the Revolution." *Time* (16 July 1979).
5882. Whetten, Lawrence L. "The Lessons of Iran." *World Today* 35:10 (October 1979): 391–99.

Books

5883. Akhavi, Shahragh. *Religion and Politics in Contemporary Iran: Clergy-State Relations During the Pahlavi Period.* Albany: State University of New York Press, 1980.
5884. Balta, Paul, and Claudine Rulleau. *L'Iran Insurge.* Paris: Editions Sinbad, 1979.
5885. Baraheni, Reza. *The Crowned Cannibals: Writings on Repression in Iran.* New York: Random House, 1977.
5886. Cottam, Richard W. *Nationalism in Iran.* Pittsburgh: University of Pittsburgh Press, 1979.
5887. Fischer, Michael M. J. *Iran: From Religious Dispute to Revolution.* Cambridge, Massachusetts: Harvard University Press, 1980.
5888. Forbis, William H. *Fall of the Peacock Throne: The Story of Iran.* New York: Harper and Row, 1980.
5889. Graham, Robert. *Iran: The Illusion of Power.* New York: St. Martin's Press, 1978.
5890. Halliday, Fred. *Iran: Dictatorship and Development.* New York: Penguin Books, 1979.
5891. Helms, Cynthia. *An Ambassador's Wife in Iran.* New York: Dodd, Mead, 1981.
5892. Hoveyda, Fereydoun. *The Fall of the Shah.* New York: Wyndham Books, 1980.
5893. Inlow, E. Burke. *Shahanshah: A Study of Monarchy in Iran.* India: Motilal Banarsidass, 1979.
5894. Jazani, Bizhan. *Capitalism and Revolution in Iran: Selected Writings.* Westport, Connecticut: Lawrence Hill, 1980.
5895. Johnson, Gail. *High Level Manpower in Iran: From Hidden Conflict to Crisis.* New York: Praeger, 1979.
5896. Karanjia, R. K. *The Mind of a Monarch.* Winchester, Massachusetts: Allen and Unwin, 1977.
5897. Keddie, Nikki R. *Iran: Religion, Politics and Society.* Totowa, New Jersey: Frank Cass, 1980.
5898. Kedourie, Elie, and Sylvia G. Haim. *Iran: Towards Modernity—Studies in Thought, Politics, and Society.* Totowa, New Jersey: Biblio Distribution Centre, 1979.
5899. Khomeini, Ayato'llah Rehu'llah. *Islamic Government.* Translated by H. Algar. Berkeley, California: Mizan Press, 1979.
5900. Ledeen, Michael, and William Lewis. *Debacle: The American Failure in Iran.* New York: Alfred A. Knopf, 1981.
5901. Lenczowski, George, ed. *Iran Under the Pahlavis.* Stanford: hoover Institution, 1978.
5902. Nickbin, Saber. *Iran: The Unfolding Revolution.* London: Relgocrest Ltd., 1979.
5903. Nobari, Ali-Reza, ed. *Iran Erupts: Independence, News and Analysis of the Iranian National Movement.* Stanford: Iran-America Documentation Group, 1978.
5904. Nussbaumer, Heinz. *Khomeini, Revolutionär in Allahs Namen: Biografie.* Berlin: Herbig, 1979.

5905. O'Donnell, Terence. *Garden of the Brave in War.* New Haven, Connecticut: Ticknor and Fields, 1980.
5906. Pahlavi, Ashraf. *Faces in a Mirror: Memoirs from Exile.* Englewood Cliffs, New Jersey: Prentice-Hall, 1980.
5907. Pahlavi, Mohammad Reza. *Answer to History.* New York: Stein and Day, 1980.
5908. Rizvi, Saiyid Athar Abbas. *Iran, Royalty, Religion and Revolution.* Canberra: Ma'rifat Publishing House, 1980.
5909. Roosevelt, Kermit: *Countercoup: The Bloody Struggle for the Control of Iran.* New York: McGraw-Hill, 1979.
5910. Rubin, Barry. *Paved With Good Intentions: The American Experience and Iran.* New York: Oxford University Press, 1980.
5911. Saibel, Bob. *Iran: A People in Revolution.* Chicago: Banner Press, 1980.
5912. Saikal, Amin. *The Rise and Fall of the Shah.* Princeton: Princeton University Press, 1980.
5913. Sharma, Nasira, ed. *Echoes of Iranian Revolution: Poems of Revolt and Liberation.* New York: Advent Books, 1979.
5914. Zabih, Sepher. *Iran's Revolutionary Upheaval: An Interpretive Essay.* Corte Madera, California: Alchemy Books, 1979.

Addendum

The following titles were added too late to be included within the main body of the text. They are, however, arranged (and identified) in the same order as the text, by chapter and section. Further, they have been incorporated into the indexes.

Chapter 1

Psychology of Revolution

5915. Pois, Robert A. "Psychohistory and the National Socialist Revolution in Symbolism: A Historiographical Problem." *Journal of Psychohistory* 7 (Winter 1979–1980): 307–21.

Economics and Revolution

5916. Selucky, Radoslav. *Marxism, Socialism, Freedom: Towards a General Theory of Labor-Managed Systems.* New York: St. Martin's Press, 1979.

Ideology

5917. Gombin, Richard. *The Radical Tradition: A Study in Modern Revolutionary Thought.* Translated by R. Sawyer. New York: St. Martin's Press, 1979.
5918. Rudé, George. *Ideology and Popular Protest.* New York: Pantheon Books, 1980.

Millennial Movements

5919. Hopkins, James K. *A Woman to Deliver Her People: Joanna Southcott and English Millenarianism in an Era of Revolution.* Austin: University of Texas Press, 1981.
5920. Schwartz, Hillel. *The French Prophets: The History of a Millenarian Group in Eighteenth-Century England.* Berkeley: University of California Press, 1980.
5921. Williams, Ann, ed. *Prophecy and Millenarianism.* New York: Longman, 1980.

War, the Military, and Guerrillas

5922. Scott, Samuel F. "The Soldiers of Rochambeau's Expeditionary Corps: From the American Revolution to the French Revolution." In *La révolution américaine et l'Europe.* Paris: Editions du Centre National de la Recherche Scientifique, 1979.

Terrorism

5923. Beres, Louis René. *Terrorism and Global Security: The Nuclear Threat.* Boulder, Colorado: Westview Press, 1979.
5924. Herman, Valentine, and Rob Van der Laan Bouma. "Nationalists without a Nation: South Moluccan Terrorism in The Netherlands." *Terrorism* 4:1–4 (1980): 223–57.
5925. Lodge, Juliet, ed. *Terrorism: A Challenge to the State.* New York: St. Martin's Press, 1981.
5926. Mauny, Michel de. "Terrorisme et pouvoir jacobin." *Ecrits Paris* 384 (1978): 65–76.
5927. Mickolus, Edward F. *Transnational Terrorism: A Chronology of Events, 1968–1979.* Westport, Connecticut: Greenwood, 1980.
5928. Miller, Abraham H. *Terrorism and Hostage Negotiations.* Boulder, Colorado: Westview Press, 1980.
5929. O'Neill, Bard E., et al., eds. *Insurgency in the Modern World.* Boulder, Colorado: Westview Press, 1980.
5930. Staar, Richard F., and Brian Jenkins. "Worldwide Terrorism: the Soviet Union Is at the Bottom of It ... But Finger-Pointing Won't Solve Problem." *Los Angeles Times* (1 May 1981).
5931. Trautmann, Frederic. *The Voice of Terror: A Biography of Johann Most.* Westport, Connecticut: Greenwood, 1980.

Student Rebellions

5932. Lichter, S. Robert. "Young Rebels: A Psychopolitical Study of West German Male Radical Students." *Comparative Politics* 12 (October 1979): 27–48.

Radicalism

5933. Calhoun, Craig. *The Question of Class Struggle: Social Foundations of Popular Radicalism during the Industrial Revolution.* Chicago: University of Chicago Press, 1981.

Anarchism

5934. Kaplan, Temma. *Anarchists of Andalusia, 1868–1903.* Princeton: Princeton University Press, 1977.
5935. ———. "Other Scenarios: Women and Spanish Anarchism." In *Becoming Visible: Women in European History,* edited by Renate Bridenthal and Claudia Koonz. Boston: Houghton Mifflin, 1977.
5936. Lida, Clara. *Anarquismo y revolución en la España del XIX.* Madrid: Siglo Veintiuno, 1972.
5937. Ritter, Alan. *Anarchism: A Theoretical Analysis.* New York: Cambridge University Press, 1981.

Marx and Marxism

5938. Cummins, Ian. *Marx, Engels and National Movements.* New York: St. Martin's Press, 1980.

5939. Hobsbawm, Eric J., ed. *The History of Marxism.* Vol. 1, *Marxism in Marx's Day.* Bloomington: Indiana University Press, 1981. The first of four projected volumes.
5940. Kiernan, Victor G. *Marxism and Imperialism.* New York: St. Martin's Press, 1975.
5941. Kossok, Manfred. "Karl Marx und die Grundlegung wissenschaftlicher Revolutionsauffassung." *Zeitschrift Geschichtswiss* 28:2 (1980): 99–118.
5942. McBride, William Leon. *The Philosophy of Marx.* New York: St. Martin's Press, 1977.
5943. MacIntyre, Stuart. *A Proletarian Science: Marxism in Britain, 1917–1933.* New York: Cambridge University Press, 1980.
5944. Narkiewicz, Olga A. *Marxism and the Reality of Power, 1919–1980.* New York: St. Martin's Press, 1981.
5945. Russell, James. *Marx-Engels Dictionary.* Westport, Connecticut: Greenwood, 1981.

Friedrich Engels

5946. Berger, Martin. "The Revolutionary Heritage: Engels and the Theory of the Vanishing Army." *Red River Valley Historical Journal of World History* 4 (Winter 1979): 122–32.

Socialism

5947. Bukharin, Nikolai. *Selected Writings on the State and the Transition to Socialism.* Armonk, New York: M. E. Sharpe, 1981.
5948. Horvat, Branko. *The Political Economy of Socialism: A Marxist Social Theory.* Armonk, New York: M. E. Sharpe, 1981.

Nationalism and Revolution

5949. Kamenka, Eugene, ed. *Nationalism: The Nature and Evolution of an Idea.* New York: St. Martin's Press, 1976.
5950. Palumbo, Michael, and William O. Shanahan, eds. *Nationalism: Essays in Honor of Louis L. Snyder.* Westport, Connecticut: Greenwood, 1981.

Women and Revolution

5951. Bell, Susan Groag, ed. *Women: From the Greeks to the French Revolution.* Stanford: Stanford University Press, 1980.
5952. Bobroff, Anne. "The Bolsheviks and the Working Woman, 1905–1920." *Soviet Studies* 27:2 (October 1974): 540–67.
5953. Engel, Barbara. "Women as Revolutionaries: The Case of the Russian Populists." In *Becoming Visible: Women in European History,* edited by Renate Bridenthal and Claudia Koonz. Boston: Houghton Mifflin, 1977.
5954. Luke, Louise E. "Marxian Women: Soviet Variants." In *Through the Looking Glass of Soviet Literature.* New York: Columbia University Press, 1953.
5955. McNeal, Robert H. "Women in the Russian Radical Movement." *Journal of Social History* 6 (Winter 1971–1972): 143–63.

5956. Slaughter, Jane, and Robert Kern, eds. *European Women on the Left: Socialism, Feminism, and the Problems Faced by Political Women, 1880 to the Present.* Westport, Connecticut: Greenwood, 1981.
5957. Trimberger, Ellen Kay. "Women in the Old and New Left: The Evolution of a Politics of Personal Life." *Feminist Studies* 5 (Fall 1979): 433–61.

Modernization and Revolution

5958. Bonazzi, Tiziano. "Some Problems Relating to the American Revolution and the Early Process of Modernization in Western Societies." In *La révolution américaine et l'Europe.* Paris: Editions du Centre National de la Recherche Scientifique, 1979.
5959. Israeli, Raphael. "Sadat's Egypt and Teng's China: Revolution versus Modernization." *Political Science Quarterly* 95:3 (Fall 1980): 361–72.

Comparative Studies

5960. Dippel, Horst. "Franklin et Condorcet, révolution et ordre social. Quelques remarques sur leurs théories sociales." In *La révolution américaine et l'Europe.* Paris: Editions du Centre National de la Recherche Scientifique, 1979.
5961. Lerner, Warren. *A History of Socialism and Communism in Modern Times: Theorists, Activists, and Humanists.* Englewood Cliffs, New Jersey: Prentice-Hall, 1982.
5962. Nora, Pierre, and Alain Clement. "L'Amérique et la France: Deux révolutions et deux mondes." In *La révolution américaine et l'Europe.* Paris: Editions du Centre National de la Recherche Scientifique, 1979.
5963. Rosenberg, William G., and Marilyn B. Young. *Transforming Russia and China: Revolutionary Struggle in the Twentieth Century.* New York: Oxford University Press, 1982.
5964. Stourzh, Gerald. "The Declaration of Rights: Popular Sovereignty and the Supremacy of the Constitution. Divergences between the American and French Revolutions." In *La révolution américaine et l'Europe.* Paris: Editions du Centre National de la Recherche Scientifique, 1979.

Miscellaneous

5965. Evans, David P. "A Foreign Troop . . ." [the American Revolution and the Viet Nam War]. *United States Naval Institute Proceedings* 106 (June 1980): 32–37.
5966. Gutting, Gary, ed. *Paradigms and Revolutions: Appraisals and Applications of Thomas Kuhn's Philosophy of Science.* Notre Dame, Indiana: University of Notre Dame Press, 1980.
5967. Libiszowska, Zofia. "L'influence de la révolution méricaine en Pologne." In *La révolution américaine et l'Europe.* Paris: Editions de Centre National de la Recherche Scientifique, 1979.
5968. Powell, T. G. *Mexico and the Spanish Civil War.* Albuquerque: University of New Mexico Press, 1981.
5969. Wallot, Jean-Pierre. "La révolution américaine et le Québec." In *La révolution américaine et l'Europe.* Paris: Editions du Centre National de la Recherche Scientifique, 1979.
5970. Wriston, Harry M. "The Age of Revolution." *Foreign Affairs* 39 (July 1961): 533–48.

Chapter 2

Greece

5971. Mendels, Doron. "Messene 215 B.C.—An Enigmatic Revolution" *Historia* 29:2 (1980): 246-50.

Rome

5972. Hackl, Ursula. "Der Revolutionsbegriff und die ausgehende römische Republik." *Review storia antichità* 9 (1979): 95-103.

Medieval

5973. Jones, Thomas M. *War of the Generations: The Revolt of 1173-4.* Ann Arbor, Michigan: University Microfilms International for the Medieval Text Association, 1980.

Chapter 3

5974. Haas, Arthur. "The Impact of the French Revolution on Central and Southeastern Europe: Some Thoughts, Comments and Comparisons." *Proceedings of the Consortium on Revolutionary Europe* 1 (1980): 286-91.
5975. Sédillot, René. "Les socialistes utopistes français avant Marx: 1. Au temps du curé Meslier et de Jean-Jacques." *Historia* 402 (May 1980): 80-98.
5976. ———, "Les socialistes utopistes français avant Marx: 2. Les enragés, Babeuf, et les autres." *Historia* 403 (June 1980): 108-17.
5977. Skowronek, Jerzy. "The Model of Revolution in East-Central European Political Thought during the Napoleonic Era." *Acta Poloniae Historica* 41 (1980): 123-46.
5978. Zacek, Joseph F. "The French Revolution, Napoleon, and the Czechs." *Proceedings of the Consortium on Revolutionary Europe* 1 (1980): 254-63.

Peasants' Revolt, 1524-1525

5979. Blickle, Peter, ed. *Aufruhr und Empörung? Studien zum bäuerlichen Widerstand im Alten Reich.* Munich: Verlag C. H. Beck, 1980.
5980. ———. *The Revolution of 1525: The German Peasants' War from a New Perspective.* Translated by H. C. E. Midelfort and T. A. Brady, Jr. Baltimore: Johns Hopkins University Press, 1981.
5981. Crossley, Robert N. *Luther and the Peasants' War.* New York: Exposition Press, 1974.
5982. Reimer, A. James. "Bloch's Interpretation of Muenzer: History, Theology, and Social Change." *Clio* 9 (Winter 1980): 253-67.
5983. Scott, Tom. "The Peasants' War: A Historiographical Review (pt. 1)." *Historical Journal* 22 (September 1979): 693-720.
5984. ———. "Reformation and Peasants' War in Waldshut and Environs: A Structural Analysis (pt. 2)." *Archiven Reformationsgeschichte* 70 (1979): 140-69.

5985. Sessions, Kyle. *Faces in the Peasant Revolt.* St. Louis: Forum Press, 1977.

Revolt of the Netherlands, 1566-1609

5986. Grayson, J. C. "The Civic Militia in the County of Holland, 1560-81: Politics and Public Order in the Dutch Revolt." *BMGN* 95:1 (1980): 35-63.

The Fronde, 1648-1653

5987. Golden, Richard M. *The Godly Rebellion: Parisian "Curés" and the Religious Fronde, 1652-1662.* Chapel Hill: University of North Carolina Press, 1981.
5988. Goubert, Pierre. "Le temps de la Fronde (1648-1652)." *Histoire* 12 (1979): 32-40.

The Puritan Revolution, 1640-1660

5989. Blackwood, B.G. "The Lancashire Gentry and the Great Rebellion, 1640-60." *Remains Lancashire and Cheshire* 25 (1978): v-xiii, 1-184.
5990. Gentles, Ian. "The Sale of Bishops' Lands in the English Revolution, 1646-1660." *English Historical Review* 95 (July 1980): 573-96.
5991. Morrill, J. S. "The Northern Gentry and the Great Rebellion." *Northern History* 15 (1979): 66-87.

Glorious Revolution, 1688-1689

5992. Schwoerer, Lois G. *The Declaration of Rights, 1689.* Baltimore: Johns Hopkins University Press, 1981.

Rousseau and Revolution

5993. Ball, Terence. "On Re-reading Rousseau and His Critics." *Midwest Quarterly* 21 (Spring 1980): 333-46.
5994. Mukherjee, Subrata. "Man and Society in Rousseau." *Political Science Review* 17 (July-December 1978): 25-38.

Age of the Democratic Revolution, 1760-1815

5995. Brancourt, Jean-Pierre. "L'explosion révolutionnaire et l'Europe." *Revue universelle* 52 (1979): 51-58.
5996. Godechot, Jacques. *Regards sur l'époque révolutionnaire.* Toulouse: Privat, 1980.

French Revolution, 1789-1799

5997. Ado, Anatolii V. "Les paysans et la Révolution française." *Cahiers histoire Institute Maurice Thorez* 12:27 (1978): 39-65.
5998. Baskiewicz, Jan. "La Révolution française aux yeux des révolutionnaires." *Acta Poloniae Historica* 37 (1978): 71-93.

Addendum / 385

5999. Beauvois, Daniel. "L'Affaire Danton." *Annales Historiques de la Révolution Française* 52 (April 1980): 294–305.
6000. Bernet, Jacques. "Rousseau, Voltaire, et la Révolution française à Compiègne." *Annales histoire compiègnoises* 3–4 (1978): 8–24.
6001. Bertaud, Jean-Paul. "L'armée de la Révolution (1789–An VI). Etude sociale." *Annales Historiques de la Révolution Française* 51 (October 1979): (abstract) 661–70.
6002. Brunel, François. "Résistance jacobine et luttes politiques en l'an II." *Cahiers histoire Institute Maurice Thorez* 13:32–33 (1979): 113–28.
6003. Censer, Jack R. "The Political Engravings of the *Révolutions de France et de Brabant, 1789–1791.*" *Eighteenth-Century Life* 5 (Summer 1979): 105–24.
6004. Cerati, Marie. *Le club des citoyennes républicaines révolutionnaires.* Paris: Editions Sociales, 1966.
6005. Cholvy, Gérard. "Résistance populaire et clandestinité sous la Révolution française: la bordure orientale et méridionale du Massif central face à la persécution religieuse." *Revue Vivarais* (special no., 1979): 175–90.
6006. Cochin, Augustin. *L'esprit du jacobinisme: Une interprétation sociologique de la Révolution française.* Paris: Universitaires de France, 1979.
6007. _____. *La révolution et la libre-pensée: La socialisation de la personne, 1789–1792; La socialisation des biens, 1793–1794.* Paris: Copernic, 1979.
6008. Cousin, Bernard. "La Révolution française et l'ex-voto peint." *Annales Historiques de la Révolution Française* 52 (April 1980): 280–93.
6009. Deschuytter, Joseph. "Paris, août 1789: un témoignage anglais." *Annales Historiques de la Révolution Française* 52 (January 1980): (abstract) 126–28.
6010. Dominique, Michel. "La Révolution française, vie de Blond en Haute-Vienne." *Ethnology* 6–7 (1978): 124–30.
6011. Duhet, Paule-Marie. *Les femmes et la Révolution, 1789–1794.* Paris: Collection Archives Julliard, 1971.
6012. Forrest, Alan. *The French Revolution and the Poor.* New York: St. Martin's Press, 1981.
6013. Furet, François. *Penser la Révolution française.* Paris: Gallimard, 1978.
6014. Gauthier, Florence. "Égalitarisme agraire dans la Révolution française: le mouvement des masses paysannes picardes." *Lendemains* 3:12 (1978): 27–45.
6015. Godechot, Jacques. "L'influence de la tactique et de la stratégie de la guerre d'indépendance américaine sur la tactique et la stratégie française de l'armée de terre." *Revue internationale histoire militaire* 41 (1979): 141–48.
6016. Gough, Hugh. "Politics and Power: The Triumph of Jacobinism in Strasbourg, 1791–1793." *Historical Journal* 23 (June 1980): 327–52.
6017. Graham, Ruth. "Loaves and Liberty: Women in the French Revolution." In *Becoming Visible: Women in European History,* edited by Renate Bridenthal and Claudia Koonz. Boston: Houghton Mifflin, 1977.
6018. Granier, Jean. "Hegel et la Révolution française." *Annales Historiques de la Révolution Française* 52 (January 1980): 1–28.
6019. Harris, Jean-Pierre. "Fouché en Nivernais: une révolution dans la Révolution (29 juillet–13 novembre 1793)." *Pays lorrain* 60:2 (1979): 10–18.
6020. Higonnet, Patrice L. R. *Class, Ideology, and the Rights of Nobles during the French Revolution.* New York: Oxford University Press, 1981.
6021. _____. "The Politics of Linguistic Terrorism and Grammatical Hegemony during the French Revolution." *Social History* 5 (January 1980): 41–70.

6022. Holzapfel, Kurt. "Lazare Carnot—Politik und Kriegsführung in der Französischen Revolution (1792-1794)." *Militärgeschichte* 18:2 (1979): 172-81.
6023. Hufton, Owen. "Women in Revolution, 1789-1796." *Past and Present,* no. 53 (1971).
6024. Kaiser, Thomas E. "Politics and Political Economy in the Thought of the Ideologues." *History of Politics and Economics* 12 (Summer 1980): 141-60.
6025. Kennedy, Emmet. "A Philosophe in the Age of Revolution: Destutt de Tracy and the Origins of 'Ideology.'" *Journal of Modern History* 52:2 (June 1980): abstract.
6026. Kennedy, Michael L. "Les clubs des Jacobins et la presse sous l'Assemblée nationale, 1789-1791." *Revue histoire* (Paris) 535 (July 1980): 49-64.
6027. _____. *The Jacobin Clubs in the French Revolution: The First Years.* Princeton: Princeton University Press, 1981.
6028. Laurent, Marcel. "Le partage des communaux à Ennezat à l'époque révolutionnaire." *Revue Auvergne* 92:3 (1978): 167-95.
6029. Lefort, Claude. "Penser la révolution dans la Révolution française." *Annales-Economies, Sociétés, Civilizations* 35 (March 1980): 334-52.
6030. Luraghi, Raimondo. "De la Guerre de Sept Ans à la Guerre d'Indépendance: Les antécédents de la guerre révolutionnaire." In *La révolution américaine et l'Europe.* Paris: Editions du Centre National de la Recherche Scientifique, 1979.
6031. Manceron, Claude. *The French Revolution.* Vol. 3, *Their Gracious Pleasure.* New York: Alfred A. Knopf, 1981.
6032. Möller, Horst. "Lorenz von Steins Interpretation der Französischen Revolution von 1789." *Staat* 18:4 (1979): 521-48.
6033. Neher-Bernheim, Renée. "La Révolution française: tentation messianique, la curieuse histoire des frères Frey." *Yod* 3:5 (1978): 13-21.
6034. Oury, Raymond. "Geispolsheim entre dans la Révolution" *Alsace histoire* 16 (1978): 204-06.
6035. Popkin, Jeremy D. "The French Revolutionary Press: New Findings and New Perspectives." *Eighteenth-Century Life* 5 (Summer 1979): 90-104.
6036. Racz, Elizabeth. "The Women's Rights Movement in the French Revolution." *Science and Society* 16:2 (Spring 1952): 151-74.
6037. Rice, G. W. "Debating the Causes of the French Revolution." *History News* (New Zealand) 38 (1979): 12-16.
6038. Rose, R. B. "The Paris Districts and Direct Democracy, 1789-1790." *Bulletin of the John Rylands Library* 61:2 (1979): 422-43.
6039. Stephens, Winifred. *Women of the French Revolution.* London: Chapman and Hall, 1922.
6040. Vovelle, Michel. "Religion et révolution. La déchristianisation de l'an II." *ournal of Modern History* 52:2 (June 1980): abstract.
6041. Wick, Daniel L. "The Court Nobility and the French Revolution: The Example of the Society of Thirty." *Eighteenth-Century Studies* 13 (Spring 1980): 263-84.

Robespierre and the Reign of Terror

6042. Coiffard, Aimé. "Les comités de surveillance du district de Grasse: contribution à l'étude de la Terreur." *Annales Société, Science, Littérature Cannes* 27 (1979): 91-113.

6043. Deschuytter, Joseph. "Un inédit de Robespierre." *Annales Historiques de la Révolution Française* 52 (January 1980): 130-31.
6044. Hérissay, Jacques. "Danton vaincu par Robespierre." *Historia* 402 (May 1980): 122-32.
6045. Kelly, George Armstrong. "Conceptual Sources of the Terror." *Eighteenth-Century Studies* 14 (Fall 1980): 18-36.

The Vendée, 1793-1796

6046. Bertin, P. "Un Comtois en Vendée: Jean-Pierre Travot." *Jura français* 163 (1979): 49-52.
6047. Boizard, René. "René Forest, un des chefs de l'armée vendéenne en 1793." *Savoir* 9 (1979): 14-21.
6048. Girault de Coursac, Pierrette. "La Vendée avant la Vendée." *Découverte* 26 (1979): 35-48.
6049. Petitfrère, Claude. "Les causes de la Vendée et de la chouannerie." *Savoir* 10 (1979): 4-13.

Edmund Burke and Revolution

6050. Freeman, Michael. *Edmund Burke and the Critique of Political Radicalism.* Chicago: University of Chicago Press, 1980.

Chapter 4

6051. Adler, Douglas D. "Friedrich Adler: Evolution of a Revolutionary." *German Studies Review* 1 (October 1978): 260-84.
6052. Bloomfield, Jon. *Passive Revolution: Politics and the Czechoslovak Working Class, 1945-8.* New York: St. Martin's Press, 1979.
6053. Djordjevic, Dimitrije. "The 1833 Peasant Uprising in Serbia." *Balkan Studies* 20:2 (1979): 235-55.
6054. _____, and Stephen Fischer-Galati. *The Balkan Revolutionary Tradition.* New York: Columbia University Press, 1981.
6055. Fišera, Vladimir, ed. *Writing on the Wall, May 1968: A Documentary Anthology.* New York: St. Martin's Press, 1979.
6056. Hutton, Patrick H. *The Cult of the Revolutionary Tradition: The Blanquists in French Politics, 1864-1893.* Berkeley: University of California Press, 1981.
6057. Lowry, Bullitt, and Elizabeth Ellington Gunter, eds. *The Red Virgin: Memoirs of Louise Michel.* University: University of Alabama Press, 1981.
6058. Rogel, Carole. "The Slovenes and the Revolutionary Period." *Proceedings of the Consortium on Revolutionary Europe* 1 (1980): 264-74.
6059. Suda, Zdeněk L. *Zealots and Rebels: A History of the Communist Party of Czechoslovakia.* Stanford: Hoover Institution, 1980.
6060. Wills, Antoinette. *Crime and Punishment in Revolutionary Paris.* Westport, Connecticut: Greenwood, 1981.

Tocqueville and Revolution

6061. Segal, Howard P. "Tocqueville and the Problem of Social Change: A Reconsideration." *South Atlantic Quarterly* 77:4 (Fall 1978): 492-503.

Revolutions of 1830

6062. Demier, Francis. "Les modèles révolutionnaires du 'Parti national' en 1830." *Romantisme* 28-29 (Summer 1980): 47-68.
6063. Fizaine, Jean-Claude. "Les Romantismes et la révolution de juillet." *Romantisme* 28-29 (Summer 1980): 29-46.
6064. Knibiehler, Yvonne. "Une révolution 'nécessaire': Thiers, Mignet, et l'école fataliste." *Romantisme* 28-29 (Summer 1980): 279-88.
6065. Péron-Lecouturier, S. "La révolution de 1830 vue par des Falaisiens." *Annales de Normandie* 30 (October 1980): 276-82.
6066. Trenard, Louis. "A l'écoute de la presse du Nord: la Révolution belge (août 1830-février 1831)." *Franse Nederlanden* (1980): 117-38.

Revolutions of 1848

6067. Blumberg, Arnold. "Revolution at Second Hand: A Prussian Consul Views the Political World 1848." *Australian Journal of Politics and History* 25 (August 1979): 250-53.
6068. Christofferson, Thomas R. "The French National Workshops of 1848: The View from the Provinces." *French Historical Studies* 11 (Fall 1980): 505-20.
6069. Sewell, William H., Jr. "*Corporations républicaines:* The Revolutionary Idiom of Parisian Workers in 1848." *Comparative Studies in Social History* 21 (April 1979): 195-203.

Paris Commune, 1871

6070. Bernstein, Samuel. "The Paris Commune." *Science and Society* 5:2 (Spring 1941): 117-47.
6071. Haupt, Heinz-Gerhard. "Comment adapter les moyens révolutionnaires aux buts de la révolution? Réflexions à porter de l' expérience à la Commune de Paris (1871)." *Mouvement social* 111 (April 1980): 119-26.
6072. Koberdova, I. "La Commune de Paris et les débuts du mouvement ouvrier polonais." *Mouvement social* 111 (April 1980): abstract.
6073. Weinberg, Henry H. "Zola and the Paris Commune: The *La Cloche* Chronicles." *Nineteenth-Century French Studies* 8:1-2 (1979-1980): 79-86.

Georges Sorel and Syndicalism

6074. Stanley, John L. *The Sociology of Virtue: The Political and Social Theories of Georges Sorel.* Berkeley: University of California Press, 1981.

Mensheviks and the February (1917) Revolution

6075. Hasegawa, Tsuyoshi. *The February Revolution: Petrograd, 1917.* Seattle: University of Washington Press, 1981.

6076. Katkov, George. *The Kornilov Affair, Russia 1917: Kerensky and the Breakup of the Russian Army.* New York: Longman, 1980.

Russian Revolution of 1917 and the Bolsheviks

6077. Breshkovsky, Catherine. *Hidden Springs of the Russian Revolution.* London: Oxford University Press, 1931.
6078. Dukes, Paul. *October and the World: Perspectives on the Russian Revolution.* New York: St. Martin's Press, 1979.
6079. McClelland, James C. "Utopianism versus Revolutionary Heroism in Bolshevik Policy: The Proletarian Culture Debate." *Slavic Review* 39 (September 1980); 403–25.
6080. Meijer, J. M. *Knowledge and Revolution.* Assen: Van Gorcum, 1955.
6081. Nilsson, Nils Åke, ed. *Art, Society, Revolution: Russia, 1917–1921.* Stockholm: Almqvist and Wiksell International, 1979.
6082. Rosenthal, Bernice Glatzer. "Love on the Tractor: Women in the Russian Revolution and After." In *Becoming Visible: Women in European History,* edited by Renate Bridenthal and Claudia Koonz. Boston: Houghton Mifflin, 1977.
6083. Thompson, John M. *Revolutionary Russia, 1917.* New York: Scribners, 1981.

Lenin and Leninism

6084. Filatov, V. P., et al. *Lenin the Revolutionary.* Moscow: Progress Publishers, 1981.

Hungarian Revolution, 1918–1919

6085. Congdon, Lee. "Hungary in Crisis: Communism and the Intellectual—1918." *East European Quarterly* 14:2 (1980): 155–69.

German Revolution, 1918–1919, and Rosa Luxemburg

6086. Borowsky, Peter. "Die 'bolschewistische Gefar' und die Ostpolitik der Volksbeauftragten in der Revolution 1918/19." *Schriftenreihe Forschungsinstitute Friedrich-Ebert-Stiftung* 137 (1978): 389–403.
6087. Keller, Elke. "Rosa Luxemburg." *Beitrag Geschichte Arbeiterbewegung* 22:2 (1980): 253–63.
6088. Klein, Fritz. "Krieg—Revolution—Frieden 1914 bis 1920." *Zeitschrift Geschichtswiss* 28:6 (1980): 544–54.

Irish Revolution, 1916–1922

6089. Moody, T. W. *Davitt and Irish Revolution, 1846–1882.* New York: Oxford University Press, 1981.
6090. Townshend, Charles. "The Irish Railway Strike of 1920: Industrial Action and Civil Resistance in the Struggle for Independence." *Irish Historical Studies* 21 (March 1979): 265–82.

Spanish Civil War, 1936-1939

6091. Borrás Llop, José María. "La Bolsa de París y la guerra civil española (1936-1939)." *Moneda y Crédito* 152 (March 1980): 105-36.
6092. Caudet, Francisco. "La poesía burlesca de la guerra civil Española: 1936-1939." *Cuaderno americana* 234:6 (1980): 137-44.
6093. Davis, Daniel S. *Spain's Civil War: The Last Great Cause.* New York: E. P. Dutton, 1974.
6094. García Basauri, Mercedes. "La sección femenina en la guerra civil española." *Historia* 16:5 (June 1980): 45-56.
6095. Torbado, Jesús, and Manuel Leguineche. *The Forgotten Men.* Translated by N. Festinger. New York: Holt, Rinehart and Winston, 1981.

Portuguese Revolution, 1974

6096. Graham, Lawrence S. "Is the Portuguese Revolution Dead?" *Luso-Brazilian Review* 16:2 (1979): 147-59.
6097. Harvey, Robert. *Portugal: Birth of a Democracy.* New York: St. Martin's Press, 1978.
6098. Krugman, Paul, and J. Braga de Macedo. "The Economic Consequences of the April 25th Revolution." *Economia* (Portugal) 3:3 (1979): 487-507.

Chapter 5

6099. Johnpoll, Bernard K. *The Impossible Dream: The Rise and Demise of the American Left.* Westport, Connecticut: Greenwood, 1981.

American Revolution, 1776-1783

6100. Adams, Thomas R. *The American Controversy: A Bibliographical Study of the British Pamphlets about the American Disputes, 1764-1783.* 2 vols. Providence, Rhode Island: Brown University Press, 1980.
6101. Allen, Harry C. "The American Revolution and British Imperialism." In *La révolution américaine et l'Europe.* Paris: Editions du Centre National de la Recherche Scientifique, 1979.
6102. Archdeacon, Thomas J. "American Historians and the American Revolution: A Bicentennial Overview." *Wisconsin Magazine of History* 63 (Summer 1980): 278-98.
6103. Ascoli, Peter. "American Propaganda in the French Language Press during the American Revolution." In *La Révolution américaine et l'Europe.* Paris: Editions du Centre National de la Recherche Scientifique, 1979.
6104. Atwood, Rodney. *The Hessians: Mercenaries from Hessen-Kassel in the American Revolution.* New York: Cambridge University Press, 1980.
6105. Bonomi, Patricia U., ed. *Party & Political Opposition in Revolutionary America.* Tarrytown, New York: Sleepy Hollow Press, 1981.
6106. Countryman, Edward. *A People in Revolution: The American Revolution and Political Society in New York, 1760-1790.* Baltimore: Johns Hopkins University Press, 1981.

6107. Edwards, Owen Dudley, and George Shepperson, eds. *Scotland, Europe and the American Revolution.* New York: St. Martin's Press, 1977.
6108. Ernst, Joseph. "English Canada and the American Revolution." In *La révolution américaine et l'Europe.* Paris: Editions du Centre National de la Recherche Scientifique, 1979.
6109. Fulton, Richard M., ed. *The Revolution That Wasn't: A Contemporary Assessment of 1776.* Port Washington, New York: Kennikat Press, 1981.
6110. Gough, Robert. "Charles H. Lincoln, Carl Becker, and the Origins of the Dual-Revolution Thesis." *William and Mary Quarterly* 38 (January 1981): 97–109.
6111. Greene, Jack P. "Social Context and the Causal Pattern of the American Revolution: A Preliminary Consideration of New York, Virginia, and Massachusetts." In *La révolution américaine et l'Europe.* Paris: Editions du Centre National de la Recherche Scientifique, 1979.
6112. Hartog, Hendrik, ed. *Law in the American Revolution and the Revolution in the Law.* New York: New York University Press, 1981.
6113. Hoerder, Dirk. "Some Aspects of Crowd Action during the American Revolution: A Comparative View." In *La révolution américaine et l'Europe.* Paris: Editions du Centre National de la Recherche Scientifique, 1979.
6114. Kennett, Lee. "The American Revolution Considered as a Model of Revolutionary War." In *La révolution américaine et l'Europe.* Paris: Editions du Centre National de la Recherche Scientifique, 1979.
6115. Leonard, Thomas C. "News for a Revolution: The Exposé in America, 1768–1773." *Journal of American History* 67 (June 1980): 26–40.
6116. Lumpkin, Henry. *From Savannah to Yorktown: The American Revolution in the South.* Columbia: University of South Carolina Press, 1981.
6117. Mekeel, Arthur J. *The Relation of the Quakers to the American Revolution.* Washington, D. C.: University Press of America, 1979.
6118. Meyer, Jean. "La guerre d'indépendance américaine et les problèmes naval européens. Rapports de force et influence sur le conflict." In *La révolution américaine et l'Europe.* Paris: Editions du Centre National de la Recherche Scientifique, 1979.
6119. Potter, Jim. "The American Revolution and British Imperial Trade." In *La révolution américaine et l'Europe.* Paris: Editions du Centre National de la Recherche Scientifique, 1979.
6120. Reid, John Phillip, ed. *The Briefs of the American Revolution.* New York: New York University Press, 1981.
6121. Royster, Charles. *Light-Horse Harry Lee and the Legacy of the American Revolution.* New York: Alfred A. Knopf, 1981.
6122. Ryan, Dennis P., ed. *A Salute to Courage: The American Revolution as Seen through the Wartime Writings of Officers in the Continental Army and Navy.* New York: Columbia University Press, 1979.
6123. Wendel, Jacques M. "Turgot and the American Revolution." *Modern Age* 23:3 (1979): 282–89.

New Left, c. 1962–?1972

6124. Alpert, Jane. *Growing Up Underground.* New York: William Morrow, 1981.
6125. Berman, Paul. "A Change in the Weather." *Village Voice* (October 28–November 3, 1981).

6126. Betsworth, Roger G. *The Radical Movement of the 1960's.* Metuchen, New Jersey: Scarecrow Press, 1980.

Herbert Marcuse

6127. Berciamo, Modesto. "Herbert Marcuse, El primer marxista heideggeriano." *Pensamiento* 36 (April 1980): 131-64.

Black Revolution, c. 1954

6128. Carson, Clayborne. *In Struggle: SNCC and the Black Awakening of the 1960s.* Cambridge, Massachusetts: Harvard University Press, 1981.
6129. Herod, Charles C. "Black Nationalism in America." *Canadian Review of Studies in Nationalism* 7 (1980): 27-69.

Quebec Revolutionary Nationalism

6130. Lambert, Robert D. "Contemporary Quebec Nationalism, 1978-1979." *Canadian Review of Studies in Nationalism* 7 (1980): 90-109.

Chapter 6

6131. Arriola, Jorge Luis. "Evolución y revolución en el movimiento liberal de 1871." *Anales de la Sociedad de Geografía e Historia de Guatemala* 49 (January-December 1976): 99-121.
6132. Cáceres Prendes, Jorge Rafael. "Consideraciones sobre el discurso politico de la Revolutión de 1948 en El Salvador." *Annales estúdios Centroamerico* 5 (1979): 33-52.

Latin American Independence Revolutions

6133. Albornoz, Oswaldo. "La iglesia en las guerras de independencia." *Annales* (U. Central Quito) 353 (1975): 98-111.
6134. Hamnett, Brian R. "Mexico's Royalist Coalition: The Response to Revolution, 1808-1821." *Journal of Latin American Studies* 1 (May 1980): 55-86.

Mexican Revolution, 1910

6135. Benjamin, Thomas. "Revolución interrumpida—Chiapas y el interinato presidencial—1911." *Histórico mexico* 1 (July-September 1980): 79-98.
6136. Falcón, Romana. "Los Orígenes populares de la Revolución de 1910? El caso de San Luis Potosí." *Histórico mexico* 2 (October-December 1979): 197-240.
6137. Hall, Linda B. *Alvaro Obregón: Power and Revolution in Mexico, 1911-1920.* College Station: Texas A and M University Press, 1981.
6138. ———. "Álvaro Obregón y el partido único mexicano." *Histórico mexico* 4 (April-June 1980): 602-22.

6139. Henderson, Peter V. N. *Félix Díaz, the Porfirians and the Mexican Revolution.* Lincoln: University of Nebraska Press, 1981.
6140. Katz, Friedrich. *The Secret War in Mexico: Europe, the United States, and the Mexican Revolution.* Chicago: University of Chicago Press, 1981.
6141. Knox, A. J. Graham. "Henequen Haciendas Maya Peones and the Mexican Revolutionary Promises of 1910: Reform and Reaction in Yucatan, 1910–1940." *Caribbean Studies* 1–2 (April–July 1977): 55–82.
6142. LaFrance, David G. "Madero, Serdán y los albores del movimiento revolucionario en Puebla." *Histórico mexico* 3 (January–March 1980): 472–512.
6143. Maciás, Anna. "Women and the Mexican Revolution, 1910–1920." *The Americas* 37 (July 1980): 53–82.

Cuban Revolution, 1959

6144. MacEwan, Arthur. *Revolution and Economic Development in Cuba.* New York: St. Martin's Press, 1981.

Chilean Revolution and Salvador Allende, 1970–1973

6145. Faúndez, Julio. "The Defeat of Politics: Chile under Allende." *Boletin Estúdios Latin-america Caribe* (Amsterdam) 28 (June 1980): 59–76.
6146. Whelan, James. *Allende: Death of a Marxist Dream.* New Rochelle, New York: Arlington House, 1981.

Nicaraguan Revolution, 1978–1979

6147. Diederich, Bernard. *Somoza: American-Made Dictator.* New York: E. P. Dutton, 1981.
6148. Meiselas, Susan. *Nicaragua: June 1978–July 1979.* New York: Pantheon Books, 1981.

Revolution in Argentina

6149. Rock, David. "Repression and Revolt in Argentina." *New Scholar* 1–2 (1981): 105–20.

Revolution in Brazil

6150. Amado, Janaína. *Conflito social no Brazil: A revolta dos "Mucker," Rio Grande do Sul, 1868–1898.* São Paulo: Edições Símbolo, 1978.

Revolution in Peru

6151. Stein, William W. "Rebellion in Huaraz: The Newspaper Account of an 'Obscure' Revolt in Peru." *Dialectical Anthropology* 2 (July 1980): 127–54.

Chapter 7

6152. Brugger, Bill. *China: Liberation and Transformation, 1942–1962.* 2nd ed. Totowa, New Jersey: Barnes and Noble, 1981.
6153. Ghosh, Prodyot Kumar. "Organizational Structure of a Revolutionary Secret Society: Anushilan Samiti, 1901–1918." *Bengal Past and Present* 47 (July–December 1978): 139–48.
6154. Hall, D. G. E. *A History of South-East Asia.* 4th ed. New York: St. Martin's Press, 1981.
6155. Henningham, Stephen. "The Contribution of 'Limited Violence' to the Bihar Civil Disobedience Movement." *South Asia* 2 (March–September 1979): 60–77.
6156. Hinton, Harold C., ed. *The People's Republic of China, 1949–1979: A Documentary Survey.* 5 vols. Wilmington, Delaware: Scholarly Resources, 1980.
6157. Huang Sung Kang. *Lu Hsun and the New Culture Movement of Modern China.* Amsterdam: Djambatan, 1957.
6158. Huber, Thomas M. *The Revolutionary Origins of Modern Japan.* Stanford: Stanford University Press, 1981.
6159. Linebarger, Paul. *The China of Chiang Kai-shek.* Boston: World Peace Foundation, 1941.
6160. Lu Hsun. *The Selected Works of Lu Hsun.* 3 vols. Peking: Foreign Language Press, 1956.
6161. Perry, Elizabeth J., ed. *Chinese Perspectives on the Nien Rebellion.* Armonk, New York: M. E. Sharpe, 1981.
6162. _____. "When Peasants Speak: Sources for the Study of Chinese Rebellions." *Modern China* 6:1 (January 1980): 72–85.
6163. Spence, Jonathan D. *The Gate of Heavenly Peace: The Chinese and Their Revolution, 1895–1980.* New York: Viking, 1981.
6164. Wolpert, Stanley. *A New History of India.* 2nd ed. New York: Oxford University Press, 1982.

Chinese National Revolution and Sun Yat-sen, 1911–1927

6165. Chan, F. Gilbert. "Revolutionary Leadership in Transition: Sun Yat-sen and His Comrades, 1905–1925." *Asian Profile* 8 (February 1980): 11–24.
6166. Zhang, Lei. "On Sun Yat-sen's Principle of Democracy." *Lishi Yanjiu* 1 (1980): 55–84.

Chinese Communist Revolution, 1927–1949

6167. Wheeler, Lois. *Edgar Snow's China.* New York: Random House, 1981.

Mao Tse-tung and Maoism

6168. Earnshaw, Graham. "China's Leaders Unveil New Portrait of Mao: The Great Helmsman Plotted a Course Filled With Errors." *Los Angeles Times* (5 July 1981).

Chinese Cultural Revolution, 1966-1969

6169. Munro, Robin. "Settling Accounts with the Cultural Revolution at Beijing University, 1977-1978." *China Quarterly* 82 (June 1980): 308-33.

Vietnamese Revolution, 1945-1973

6170. Doyle, Edward, et al. *The Vietnam Experience: Setting the Stage.* Boston: Boston Publishing Company, 1981. Volume 1 of 14 projected volumes.
6171. Harrison, James Pinckney. *The Endless War: Fifty Years of Struggle in Vietnam.* Riverside, New Jersey: Free Press, 1981.

Indian Revolution and Gandhi, 1920-1949

6172. Brown, Judith M. "Makers of the Twentieth Century: M. K. Gandhi." *History Today* 30 (May 1980): 16-21.
6173. Nair, Pyarelal. *Mahatma Gandhi.* Vol. 2, *The Discovery of Satyagraha— On the Threshold.* Bombay: Sevak Prakashan, 1980.

Revolution in Turkey

6174. Alkan, M. Turker. "Turkey: Rise and Decline of Political Legitimacy in a Revolutionary Regime." *Journal of South Asian and Middle East Studies* 4 (Winter 1980): 37-48.

Chapter 8

6175. Ajala, Adekunle. "The Rising Tide of Pan-Africanism, 1924-1963." *Tarikh* 6:3 (1980): 35-46.
6176. Basu, A. R. "Interaction between Elites and Nationalist Movements: Studies of Colonial Situations in Morocco, Algeria and Tunisia." *Indian Political Science Review* 12 (July 1978): 217-26.
6177. Baynham, Simon. "Equatorial Guinea: The Terror and the Coup." *World Today* 36:2 (February 1980): 65-71.
6178. Bridgman, Jon M. *The Revolt of the Hereros.* Berkeley: University of California Press, 1981.
6179. Esedebe, P. Olisanwuche. "The Growth of the Pan African Movement, 1893-1927." *Tarikh* 6:3 (1980): 18-34.
6180. _____. "'Pan-Africanism': Origins and Meaning." *Tarikh* 6:3 (1980): 3-17.
6181. Evans, Peter. "Tanzania: The Revolution as Reconstruction." *Harvard Review* 4:1 (Summer-Fall 1966): 1-11.
6182. Fieldhouse, D. K. *Colonialism, 1870-1945: An Introduction.* New York: St. Martin's Press, 1981.
6183. Jinadu, L. Adele. "A Review Essay of Revolutionary Pressures in Africa." *Nigerian Journal of Economics and Social Studies* 19 (July 1977): 7-24.

6184. Milene, Charles. *The Soviet Union and Africa: The History of the Involvement.* Translated by J. Fisher. Lanham, Maryland: University Press of America, 1980.
6185. Ola, Opeyemi. "Pan-Africanism: An Ideology of Development." *Présence Africain* 4 (1979): 66–95.
6186. Oliver, Roland, and Anthony Atmore. *Africa Since 1800.* 3rd ed. New York: Cambridge University Press, 1981.
6187. Smith, Earl. "Pan-Africanism—A Political, Economic and Social Philosophy." *Freedomways* 20:1 (1980): 27–37.
6188. Von Albertini, Rudolph. "Colonialism and Underdevelopment: Critical Remarks on the Theory of Dependency." *Itinerario* 4:1 (1980): 42–52.

Algerian Revolution, 1954–1962

6189. Naylor, Phillip Chivique. "Algeria and France: The Post-Colonial Relationship, 1962–1975." *Proceedings of the French Colonial History Society* 5 (1979): 58–69.

Frantz Fanon

6190. Nursey-Bray, Paul. "Race and Nation: Ideology in the Thought of Frantz Fanon." *Journal of Modern African Studies* 18:1 (March 1980): 135–42.

Angolan Revolution, 1961–1975

6191. Dingeman, Jim. "Angola: Portugal in Africa." *Strategy and Tactics* (May–June 1976): 22–29.

Revolution in Mozambique, 1964–1975

6192. Davidson, Basil. "The Revolution of People's Power." *Monthly Review* (July–August, 1980): 75–89.
6193. Morosini, Giuseppe. "Tradizione e rivoluzione culturale in Mozambico." *Africa* 35 (March 1980): 43–84.

Revolution in Guinea-Bissau, 1963–1974

6194. Foy, Colm. "Unidade E Luta: The Struggle for Unity between Guinea-Bissau and Cape Verde." *People's Power* (Winter 1979): 10–27.

Ethiopian Revolution, 1974–1977

6195. "Women and Revolution in Eritrea." *Liberation* 6 (March–June 1977): 14–23.

Revolution in Southern Africa

6196. Willers, David. "The Politics of Violence in South Africa." *South Africa International* 11 (July 1980): 29–41.

Chapter 9

6197. Ayoob, Mohammed, ed. *Conflict and Intervention in the Third World.* New York: St. Martin's Press, 1980.
6198. Tibi, Bassam. *Arab Nationalism: A Critical Inquiry.* Translated by M. F. Sluglett and P. Sluglett. New York: St. Martin's Press, 1981.

Iranian Revolution, 1978-1979

6199. Abidi, A. "The Iranian Revolution: Its Origins and Dimensions." *International Studies* (New Delhi) 18 (April 1979): 129-62.
6200. Benard, Cheryl. "Islam and Women: Some Reflections on the Experience of Iran." *Journal of South Asian and Middle East Studies* 4 (Winter 1980): 10-26.
6201. Bordewich, F. "Fascism Without Swastikas: Misreading the Iranian Revolution." *Harper's* 261 (July 1980): 65-71.
6202. Cottam, Richard W. "Revolutionary Iran and the War with Iraq." *Current History* 80 (January 1981): 5-10.
6203. Homan, Roger. "The Origins of the Iranian Revolution." *International Affairs* (London) 56 (Autumn 1980): 673-77.
6204. Keddie, Nikki R. "Will Iran's Bloody Factional Fighting Escalate Into Civil War?" *Los Angeles Times* (5 July 1981).
6205. _____ , with a section by Yann Richard. *Roots of Revolution: An Interpretative History of Modern Iran.* New Haven: Yale University Press, 1981.
6206. Ramazani, Nesta. "Behind the Veil: Status of Women in Revolutionary Iran." *Journal of South Asian and Middle East Studies* 4 (Winter 1980): 27-36.
6207. Ramazani, R. K. "Iran's Revolutions: Patterns, Problems and Prospects." *International Affairs* 56 (Summer 1980): 443-57.
6208. Steinbach, Udo. "Iran—Half Time in the Islamic Revolution." *Aussenpolitische* 31:1 (1980): 52-68.
6209. Stempel, John D. *Inside the Iranian Revolution.* Bloomington: Indiana University Press, 1981.

Quotations on Revolution

"It is an observation of one of the profoundest inquiries into human affairs that a revolution of government is the strongest proof that can be given by a people, of their virtue and good sense."
          John Adams

"In the abstract theory of our government the obedience of the citizen is not due to an unconstitutional law: he may lawfully resist its execution."
          John Quincy Adams

"The firebrand revolutionary freedom fighter is the first to destroy the rights and even the lives of the next generation of rebels."
          Saul Alinsky
          Playboy "Interview" (March, 1972)

"History is like a relay race of revolutions; the torch of idealism is carried by one group of revolutionaries until it too becomes an establishment, and then the torch is snatched up and carried on the next leg of the race by a new generation of revolutionaries. The cycle goes on and on, and along the way the values of humanism and social justice the rebels champion take shape and change and are slowly implemented in the minds of all men even as their advocates falter and succumb to the materialistic decadence of the prevailing status quo."
          Saul Alinsky
          Playboy "Interview" (March, 1972)

"During revolutions green plants don't get enough water."
          Anonymous
          Chilean gardener (1973)

"A revolution is not a spectacle! There are no spectators! Everyone participates whether they know it or not."
          Anonymous
          Late 1960s, New Left

"History shows that freedom is born in pain. A price must be set on tyranny and the tyrants must pay the price."
          Anonymous. From the Greek
          Underground (1971)

"Revolution that, like Saturn, devours its own children has deviated from its proper path."
          Anonymous

"Revolutionaries should all be shot before they shoot the unrevolutionaries."
          Anonymous student

"Revolutionary activity without serious study, planning and thought has a tendency to become counterrevolutionary."
          Anonymous

"We do not know what kind of society we would replace this one with, but this one must be destroyed. To find out what kind of society will come out of this destruction, we must go through the experience of the revolution. Perhaps we will discover that we must remain in a constant state of revolution."
          Anonymous

"When you have a revolution cooking on the stove make sure you have a revolutionist for a chef."
Anonymous

"If we do not soon bestir ourselves for a bloody revolution, we cannot leave anything to our children but poverty and slavery."
Die Arbeiter Zeitung (1886)
Chicago Labor Party

"Inferiors revolt in order that they may be equal, and equals that they may be superior."
Aristotle

"Revolutions are not about trifles, but they spring from trifles."
Aristotle

"Revolution to me would mean people recognizing the sanctity of human life, and that's the revolution that has never happened. There have been lots of revolutions—people throwing over the government and taking other people's property. But all the good that comes out of a violent revolution comes in spite of the violence."
Joan Baez
"Thoughts on a Sunday Afternoon"
Evergreen Review (June 1971)

"Revolutions are not made either by individuals or by secret societies. They come automatically, in a measure; the power of things, the current of events and facts, produces them. They are long preparing in the depth of the obscure consciousness of the masses—then they break out suddenly, not seldom on apparently slight occasion."
Mikhail Bakunin

"Do you know of any revolution, even a scientific one, that has taken place without bloodshed? No despot is ever going to give up his throne because you ask him to give it up, or because you beg him to go away. The final word is always an act of war."
Mehdi Bazargan
Prime Minister of Iran
September 17, 1979

"Revolutions aren't wedding invitations, you know, and they're not suited for impatient people."
Mehdi Bazargan
Prime Minister of Iran
September 17, 1979

"In the kind of disintegrated atmosphere that arises after a revolution, any idea can materialize and any excess can happen. That doesn't mean, however, that these things must also become crystallized and permanent."
Mehdi Bazargan
Prime Minister of Iran
September 17, 1979

"You say you want a revolution,/Well you know,/We all want to change the world."
Beatles (1968)

"It is an illusion to think you can have a revolution without prisons."
Ahmed Ben Bella
Algerian President (1963)

"Boredom has more to do with modern political revolution than justice has. In 1917, that boring Lenin who wrote so many boring pamphlets and letters on organizational questions was, briefly, all passion, all radiant interest. The Russian revolution promised mankind a permanently interesting life. When Trotsky spoke of permanent revolution he really meant permanent interest. In the early days the revolution was a work of inspiration. Workers,

peasants, soldiers were in a state of excitement and poetry. When this short brilliant phase ended, what came next? The most boring society in history."
Saul Bellow
Humboldt's Gift (1976)

"The mark of inhuman treatment of humans is . . . the mark of a beast, whether its insignia is the military or the movement. . . . The revolution will be no better and no more truthful and no more populist and no more attractive than those who brought it into being."
Father Daniel Berrigan
August, 1970

"The right of revolt belongs to any people who can save its soul in no other way. Once the hope of reform perishes in the heart of any brave people, the desperate condition of revolution sets in."
Bluntschli

"The expression 'law and order' is used by those in power, not by us, as a false slogan to justify their abuses. We are not interested in their law or their order, but only with justice."
Simón Bolívar

"Every great revolution has destroyed the State apparatus which it found. After much vacillation and experimentation, every revolution has set another apparatus in its place, in most cases of quite a different character from the one destroyed; for the changes in the state order which a revolution produces are no less important than the changes in the social order."
Franz Borkenau

"Those who won our independence by revolution were not cowards. They did not fear political change. They did not exalt order at the cost of liberty."
Supreme Court Justice
Louis Brandeis (1927)

"I consider myself neither legally nor morally bound to obey laws made by a body in which I have no representation. Do not deceive yourselves into believing that penalties will deter men from the course they believe is right."
H. Rap Brown (1967)

"The only politics relevant to black people is the politics of revolution. The politics of culture is not in itself revolution. . . . People can get so hooked up in their culture and their egos, so inflated about being black that they have no desire to fight."
H. Rap Brown

"Women as a class have never subjugated another group; we have never marched off to wars of conquest in the name of the fatherland. We have never been involved in a decision to annex the territory of a neighboring country, or to fight for foreign markets on distant shores. Those are the games men play, not us. *We* see it differently. We want to be neither oppressors nor oppressed. The women's revolution is the final revolution of them all."
Susan Brownmiller
"Sisterhood Is Powerful"
The New York Times Magazine
(March 15, 1970)

"A revolution is justified only when it rises unconsciously from the soil rather than being conjured up."
Jacob Burckhardt

"The Americans have made a discovery, or think they have made one, that we mean to oppress them. We have made a discovery, or think we have made one, that they intend to rise in rebellion against us . . . we know not how to advance; they know not how to retreat . . . some party must give way."
Edmund Burke (1769)

"All the great heralds of revolution have incited men, not to destroy the old, but to establish the new."
  C. D. Burns
  The Principles of Revolution

"A revolution is dead when it has no friends in the outside world."
  Amilcar Cabral (1966)

"A revolution is not always a source of evil and tears, just as fire does not always produce devastation."
  Luis Cabrera (1917)

"A revolution means the use of force to destroy an unsatisfactory system and the employment of force and intelligence to built the new system."
  Luis Cabrera (1916)

"When a system of work is right, but we fail to obtain results from our efforts for lack of efficiency, the task of the reformer consists in improving that system. But when a system is radically wrong, we must abandon that system and find a better one."
  Luis Cabrera (1916)

"All modern revolutions have ended in a reinforcement of state power."
  Albert Camus

"Every revolutionary ends by becoming either an oppressor or a heretic."
  Albert Camus

"Freedom . . . is the motivating principle of all revolutions."
  Albert Camus
  The Rebel (1962)

"If revolution seeks to correct social injustice, its first act, when power is seized, should be to guarantee a certain freedom in the midst of its efforts to establish a new justice—otherwise the creation of a new and equally intolerable tyranny becomes inevitable."
  Albert Camus

"A revolution is . . . a struggling, working beehive of men who, though filled with good intentions, lack experience, lack knowledge, lack training. And suddenly, there is thrust on the shoulders of these men the task of making the nation move forward, administering everything."
  Fidel Castro (1966)

"A 'revolution' is an ambiguous entity. In any single 'revolution' there may in fact be one, two, or several, each treading on the heels of the one before and kicking viciously at the one behind."
  David Caute

"No man has ever seen a revolution. Mobs pouring through the palaces, blood pouring down the gutters, the guillotine lifted higher than the throne, a prison in ruins, a people in arms—these things are not revolution, but the results of revolution. . . . You cannot see a revolution; you can only see that there is a revolution. And there never has been in the history of the world a real revolution, brutally active and decisive, which was not preceded by unrest and new dogmas in the region of invisible things. All revolutions began by being abstract. Most revolutions began by being quite pedantically abstract."
  G. K. Chesterton
  Selected Essays

"An oppressed people are authorized, whenever they can, to rise and break their fetters."
  Henry Clay (1818)

"The influence of the Enlightenment cannot be disregarded in any history of the French Revolution; but the revolutionaries did not set their course by its light in the beginning, nor did they steer the ship of state into the haven of the Enlightenment in the end."
Alfred Cobban

"The Revolution was, in the words of Albert Schweitzer, 'a fall of snow on blossoming trees.'"
Alfred Cobban

"The word *revolutionary* can be applied only to revolutions which have liberty as their object."
Marquis de Condorcet
Sur Le Sens Du Mot Révolutionnaire (1793)

"However good the outcome, any revolution is a serious crisis, disturbing men's consciences, shattering inward security, and jeopardizing every commitment made by the state."
Friedrich Dahlmann (c. 1848)

"Nothing is so loved by tyrants as obedient subjects. Nothing so soon destroys freedom as cowardly and servile acquiescence. Men will never have any more liberty than they demand and are ready to fight to take and preserve."
Clarence Darrow (1932)

"For a revolutionary, failure is a springboard. As a source of theory it is richer than victory: it accumulates experience and knowledge."
Regis Debray
Revolution in the Revolution? (1967)

"Full opportunity for full development is the unalienable right of all. He who denies it is a tyrant, he who does not demand it is a coward; he who is indifferent to it is a slave; he who does not desire it is dead. The earth for all the people! That is the demand."
Eugene V. Debs (1904)

"The most heroic word in all languages is—REVOLUTION!
Eugene V. Debs (1907)

"That whenever any Form of Government becomes destructive to these ends [i.e., life, liberty and the pursuit of happiness], it is the Right of the People to alter or to abolish it, and to institute new Government, laying its foundation on such principles and organizing its power in such form, as to them shall seem most likely to effect their Safety and Happiness."
from *The Declaration of Independence*
(1776)

"The future of the world depends so much on the American New Left. Nowhere are the social contradictions deeper, and nowhere does a rebel have a greater opportunity to demonstrate the firmness of his convictions than here."
Vladimir Dedijer to
Jean-Paul Sartre
The New York Times
(February 4, 1971)

"A despot, be he the best of men, commits a crime by governing according to his own sweet will. He is a good shepherd who reduces his subjects to the level of animals."
Denis Diderot

"Every revolution, and every war, creates illusions and is conducted in the name of unrealizable ideals."
Milovan Djilas

"There is a political feudalism where a dynasty has the trappings of a parliamentary system but manipulates it for the benefit of the ruling class.... Revolution in the twentieth century means rebellion against another kind of feudalism ... economic feudalism ... and the United States should promote democratic revolution against these conditions of economic feudalism."
Supreme Court Justice
William Douglas

"Like Saturn, the Revolution devours its children."
Jacques Mallet du Pan
Considerations sur la nature de la Révolution (Brussels, 1793)

"The Revolution, by its destructive nature, brings inevitably in its train, a military Republic."
Jacques Mallet du Pan
Considerations sur la nature de la Révolution (Brussels, 1793)

"Revolution is an outrageous and wicked attack upon the people of all countries still more than on their governments, it is much more of a conspiracy against the rights of nations, than in favor of the rights of men."
Jacques Mallet du Pan
Considerations sur la nature de la Révolution (Brussels, 1793)

"Every revolution was first a thought in one man's mind."
Ralph Waldo Emerson

"A revolution is a pure phenomenon of nature, which is led more accordingly to physical laws than according to the rules which in ordinary times determine the development of society."
Friedrich Engels (1851)

"The times of the superstition which attributed revolution to the illwill of a few agitators have long passed away. Everyone knows nowadays that wherever there is a revolutionary convulsion, there must be some social want in the background which is prevented by outworn institutions from satisfying itself."
Friedrich Engels

"They set up the courts; they set up the police; they set up the army; they set up an educational system; they set up the newspaper; they set up all the apparatus to brainwash and to keep in subjugation.... No people in this world have ever achieved independence and freedom through the ballot or having it legislated to them. (They) got their freedom through struggle and through revolution."
William Epton (1964)

"In Nicaragua, an entire people is fighting for its independence. I would condemn revolutionary violence if I thought that a non-violent way existed."
Rev. Miguel D'Escoto (1979)

"The idealists who make a revolution are bound to be disappointed.... For at best their victory never dawns on the shining new world they had dreamed of, cleansed of all meanness. Instead it dawns on a familiar, workaday place, still in need of groceries and sewage disposal. The revolutionary state, under whatever political label, has to be run not by violent romantics but by experts of marketing, sanitary engineering, and the management of bureaucracies. For the Byrons among us, this discovery is a fate worse than death."
John Fischer
Natural Enemies

A SEMI-REVOLUTION
I advocate a semi-revolution.
The trouble with a total revolution
(Ask any reputable Rosicrucian)
Is that it brings the same class up on top.
Executives of skillful execution
Will therefore plan to go half-way and stop.
Yes, revolutions are the only salves.
But they're one thing that should be done by halves.
                         Robert Frost

"A true revolution is almost always violent and usually it is extremely violent. Its essence is the destruction of the social fabric and institutions of a society, and an attempt, not necessarily successful, to create a new society with a new social fabric and new institutions."
              J. W. Fulbright (1966)

"No revolution can ever succeed as a factor of liberation unless the MEANS used to further it be identical in spirit and tendency with the purposes to be achieved."
              Emma Goldman
              My Further Disillusionment in Russia
              (1924)

"Revolutions come only when a 'boiling point' has been reached, when man has so altered the structures of his communal life that the future becomes radically open. Such periods are never quiet, nor do they automatically produce good."
              W. Fred Graham
              The Constructive Revolutionary:
              John Calvin (1971)

"True revolutionaries—those who wish to humanize life by freeing captives, healing the ill, opening blind eyes, and bringing justice to society—know that history discloses how men make their own future."
              W. Fred Graham
              The Constructive Revolutionary:
              John Calvin (1971)

"The right of Revolution is an inherent one. When people are oppressed by their government, it is a natural right they enjoy to relieve themselves of the oppression if they are strong enough, either by withdrawing from it, or by overthrowing it and substituting a government more acceptable."
                         U. S. Grant

"Each guerrilla [revolutionist] must be ready to die, not to defend an ideal, but to transform it into a reality."
                         Che Guevara

"In the arduous profession of the revolutionary, death is a frequent occurrence."
                         Che Guevara

"It indeed seems doubtful whether revolutionaries can revolutionize their own country. The fateful effects of a revolution are usually felt elsewhere. The French Revolution altered France relatively little but it created Germany. Similarly, the fateful effects of the Russian Revolution will be a United Europe and a new China."
              Eric Hoffer
              The New York Times Magazine
              (April 25, 1971)

"We are usually told that revolutions are set in motion to realize radical changes. Actually, it is drastic change which sets the stage for revolution. The revolutionary mood and temper are generated by the irritations, difficulties, hungers, and frustrations inherent in the realization of drastic change. Where things have not changed at all, there is the least likelihood of revolution."
                        Eric Hoffer
                        The Ordeal of Change (1964)

"Revolution is the point at which individual psychology connects itself to universal history. Because of this the study of objective factors alone can never yield a knowledge of when or how revolutionary transformations take place."
                        Said of Georges Sorel in
                        Radicalism and the Revolt Against
                        Reason by Irving L. Horowitz.

"In the grave is the corpse,/The idea lives."
                        Victor Hugo

"Revolution is the larva of civilization."
                        Victor Hugo

"As the sun never rises from the west, so no revolution past or present has ever come from the upper class."
                        Kita Ikki (1906)

"Revolution is not the outcome of the fires of battle, but a war of ideas. . . . So no matter how much blood is spilled or how many corpses pile up, if the same system of thought continues it is called a war and is not a revolution.
                        Kita Ikki (1906)

"Revolution means the death of an old society and the birth of a new society."
                        Kita Ikki (1906)

"We cannot ignore the fact that our own government originated in revolution, and is legitimate only if overthrow by force can sometimes be justified. That circumstances sometimes justify it is not Communist doctrine, but an old American belief. The men who led the struggle forcibly to overthrow lawfully constituted British authority found moral support by asserting a natural law under which their revolution was justified, and they bravely proclaimed their belief in the document basic to our freedom. Such sentiments have also been given ardent and rather extravagant expression by Americans of undoubted patriotism."
                        Supreme Court Justice
                        Robert Houghwout Jackson (1950)

"The stream of revolution, once started, could not be confined within narrow banks, but spread abroad upon the land."
                        J. Franklin Jameson
                        The American Revolution Considered as
                        a Social Movement (1926)

"Uprisings are to be answered by reform, by attacking the 'disease' that lies behind them rather than by suppressing its 'Symptoms.'"
                        John Jay (October 27, 1786)

"The generation which commences a revolution rarely completes it."
                        Thomas Jefferson

"God forbid we should be twenty years without a rebellion. What country can preserve its liberties if the rulers are not warned from time to time that their people preserve the spirit of resistance?"
                        Thomas Jefferson, Letter to
                        General William S. Smith
                        (November 13, 1787)

"God is just and his justice cannot sleep forever."
Thomas Jefferson
Notes on Virginia (1782)

"The tree of liberty must be refreshed from time to time with the blood of patriots and tyrants. It is their natural manure."
Thomas Jefferson (1787)

"We can't have education without revolution. We have tried peace education for 1,900 years and it has failed. Let us try revolution and see what it will do now."
Helen Keller (1916)

"Those who make peaceful revolution impossible will make violent revolution inevitable."
John F. Kennedy

[The Iranian Revolution] is a revolution that took place in a country that was eaten alive like a field of wheat infested with locusts. We are at the beginning of our road. What do you expect of a child that is six months old, born in a field filled with locusts, after 2,500 years of bad harvests and 50 years of poisonous harvests. That past cannot be wiped out in a few months, not even in a few years. We need time."
Ayato'llah Rehu'llah Khomeini
September 12, 1979

"If exasperation often drives men to revolt, it is always hope, the hope of victory, which makes revolution."
Peter Kropotkin
The Spirit of Revolt (1880)

"Revolutionary propaganda selects symbols which are calculated to detach the affections of the masses from the existing symbols of authority, to attach these affections to challenging symbols, and to direct hostilities toward existing symbols of authority. This is infinitely more complex than the psychological problem of war propaganda, since in war the destructive energies of the community are drained along familiar channels. Most of those who have a hand in revolution must face a crisis of conscience. Constituted authority perpetuates itself by shaping the consciences of those who are born within its sphere of control. Hence the great revolutions are in defiance of emotions which have been directed by nurses, teachers, guardians, and parents along 'accredited' channels of expression. Revolutions are ruptures of conscience."
Harold D. Lasswell
*World Politics and
Personal Insecurity* (1965)

"A revolution occurs when the upper class cannot and the lower class will not continue the old system."
V. I. Lenin

"For a revolution to break out it is not enough for the 'lower classes to refuse' to live in the old way; it is necessary also that the 'upper classes should be unable' to live in the old way."
V. I. Lenin

"The key question of every revolution is undoubtedly the question of state power. Which class holds power decides everything."
V. I. Lenin
*One of the Fundamental
Questions of the Revolution*

"Revolution is impossible without a national crisis affecting both the exploited and the exploiters."
V. I. Lenin
*Left-Wing Communism, An Infantile
Disorder* (1920)

"Revolutions are festivals of the oppressed and the exploited."
V. I. Lenin
Two Tactics of Social Democracy in the Democratic Revolution (1905)

"Without a revolutionary theory there can be no revolutionary movement."
V. I. Lenin
What Is To Be Done (1902)

"You have convinced us that equality and justice were inviolable concepts, and we must have taken you seriously."
Weldon Levine (student)
Harvard Law School Commencement (1969)

"Any people anywhere being inclined and having the power, have the right to rise up and shake off the existing government, and form a new one that suits them better. This is a most valuable and sacred right, a right we hope and believe is to liberate the world."
Abraham Lincoln (1848)

"If by the mere force of numbers a majority should deprive a minority of any clearly written constitutional rights, it might, in a moral point of view, justify revolution—certainly would if such a right were a vital one."
Abraham Lincoln (1861)

"This country, with its institutions, belongs to the people who inhabit it. Whenever they shall grow weary of the existing government, they can exercise their constitutional right of amending it, or their revolutionary right to dismember, or overthrow it."
Abraham Lincoln
First Inaugural Address (1861)

"The last recourse against wrongful and unauthorized force is opposition to it."
John Locke
Two Treatises on Government

"History shows that no master class is ever willing to let go without a quarrel."
Jack London (1923)

"Unless you go out among the masses to study, analyse and judge their traditions and customs, setting up standards for keeping or doing away with them, and finding a way of making a careful selection, any reform whatsoever will be crushed under the dead weight of tradition."
Lu Hsun
On Custom and Reform (1930)

"A true revolutionary can see farther than other men, as in the case of Mr. Lenin, who looks upon tradition and custom as part of 'culture' and that to change them will be very hard. But to my mind unless these are changed the revolution can last no longer than a sandcastle."
Lu Hsun
On Custom and Reform (1930)

"I suppose that writers in this centre of the revolution like to claim that literature plays a big part in revolution. It can be used, for instance, as propaganda to encourage, spur on, speed up and accomplish revolution. But to my mind, such writing lacks vigour, for few good works have been written to order; they flow naturally from a man's heart with no regard for their possible effect."
Lu Hsun
Literature of a Revolutionary Period (1927)

"For revolution we need revolutionaries, but revolutionary literature can wait, for only when revolutionaries start writing can there be revolutionary literature. So to my mind it is revolution which plays a big part in literature."
  Lu Hsun
  Literature of a Revolutionary Period (1927)

"Those who once had power want to go back to the past. Those in power now want to remain as they are. Those who have not yet had power want reforms."
  Lu Hsun
  Odd Fancies (1927)

"If the peasant is in open rebellion, then he is outside the law of God.... Therefore, let everyone who can, smite, slay, and stab [the peasants], secretly or openly, remembering that nothing can be more poisonous, hurtful, or devilish than a rebel. It is just as when one must kill a mad dog; if you don't strike him, he will strike you, and the whole land with you."
  Martin Luther
  Against the Thievish, Murderous Hordes of Peasants (1525)

"One cannot argue reasonably with a rebel.... One must answer him with the fist so that blood flows from his nose."
  Martin Luther
  Against the Thievish, Murderous Hordes of Peasants (1525)

"Revolutions are like earthquakes. They are tragic, they cannot be predicted, they do not require justification, they cannot really be organized. Revolutions occur when they occur. They are not caused by conspiracies but ... by the indifference and inhumanity and inflexibility of existing institutions."
  David McReynolds
  The New York Times Magazine (May 1970)

"We deplore the outrages which accompany revolutions but the more violent the outrages, the more assured we feel that a revolution was necessary. The violence of these outrages will always be proportioned to the ferocity and ignorance of the people; and the ferocity and ignorance of the people will be proportionate to the oppression and degradation under which they have been accustomed to live."
  Thomas Babington Macaulay

"Liberalism, indiscipline and the easy life are incompatible with the revolution. They are subtle means through which the enemy infiltrates our ranks. Our fight is a fight for the creation of the new man, of a new mentality. Whoever wants to grow fruit trees must constantly struggle to get rid of the pests."
  Samora Machel
  President of Mozambique (1977)

"You don't have a revolution in which you love your enemy. And you don't have a revolution in which you are begging the system of exploitation to integrate you into it."
  Malcolm X (1964)

"A revolution is not the same as inviting people to dinner, or writing an essay, or painting a picture ... ; it cannot be anything so refined, so calm, and gentle.... A revolution is an act of violence whereby one class overthrows another."
  Mao Tse-tung (1927)

"China's ... people have two remarkable peculiarities; they are, first of all, poor, and secondly blank. That may seem to be a bad thing, but it is really a good thing. Poor people want change, want to do things, want revolution. A blank sheet of paper has no blotches, and so the newest and most beautiful words can be written on it."
  Mao Tse-tung (1958)

"Humanity left to its own does not necessarily re-establish capitalism, but it does re-establish inequality."
Mao Tse-tung (1965)

"If there were no contradictions and no struggle, there would be no world, no progress, no life, and there would be nothing at all."
Mao Tse-tung
"On the Correct Handling of Contradictions Among the People" (1957)

"Marxism consists of a thousand truths but they all boil down to one sentence: It is right to rebel."
Mao Tse-tung

"Once class struggle is grasped, miracles are possible."
Mao Tse-tung (1965)

"Political power grows out of the barrel of a gun. Our principle is that the Party commands the gun; the gun shall never be allowed to command the Party."
Mao Tse-tung (1938)

"Revolution and children have to be trained if they are to be properly brought up."
Mao Tse-tung (1965)

"There is no such thing as abstract Marxism, but only concrete Marxism. What we call concrete Marxism is Marxism that has taken on a national form."
Mao Tse-tung (1942)

"The philosophers have only *interpreted* the world, in various ways; the point is to *change* it."
Karl Marx
Theses on Feuerbach (1845)

"Revolutions are the locomotives of history."
Karl Marx,
The Class Struggle in France, 1848-50

"The tradition of all the dead generations weighs like a nightmare on the brain of the living. And just when they seem engaged in revolutionizing themselves and things, in creating something that has never yet existed ... they anxiously conjure up the spirits of the past to their service, and borrow from them names, battle cries and costumes, to present the new scene of world history in time-honored disguise and borrowed language."
Karl Marx
The Eighteenth Brumaire of Louis Bonaparte (1852)

"Late capitalist society is the richest and technically most advanced society in history. It offers—or should offer—the greatest and most realistic possibilities for a pacified and liberated human existence. And at the same time it is the society which very effectively suppresses these possibilities of pacification and liberation. Today this suppression totally controls society as a whole and, therefore, can be abolished only by a radical transformation of the structure of this society."
Herbert Marcuse (1971)

"Today, it [i.e., revolution] merits celebrating, not merely by pious clichés, but by sustained effort to achieve deeper understanding of what we are celebrating—the right of revolution as the last resort in the endless pursuit of happiness."
Alpheus T. Mason
Los Angeles Times
(July 4, 1976)

"Revolutions can no more be made without bringing suffering to many people than wars can be fought without sacrificing lives. But at least, revolution is a mechanism by which tyranny, corruption and injustice are overthrown—almost the only mechanism known to modern man in the underdeveloped two-thirds of the world."
Herbert L. Matthews
Fidel Castro (1969)

"We revolutionaries aren't just chasing a scarlet flag. What we pursue is an awakening of liberty, old or new. It is the ancient communes of France; it is 1793; it is June 1848; it is 1871. Most especially it is the next revolution, which is advancing under this dawn. Revenge is the Revolution, which will sow liberty and peace over the entire earth."
Louise Michel

"Revolution [is] the advent of law, the resurrection of human rights and the revival of justice."
Jules Michelet
Histoire de la Révolution française

"Wherever one goes in this civilized world, one always finds the same set-up. The little man, the man who does the dirty work, the producer is of no importance, receives no consideration and is always being asked to make the greatest sacrifice. Yet everything depends on this forgotten man. Not a wheel could turn without his support and co-operation. It is this man, whose number is legion, who has no voice in world affairs . . . he knows that he has been robbed and cheated from time immemorial. He is suffocated with all this bitter knowledge. He waits and waits hoping that time will alter things. And slowly he realizes that time alters nothing. That with time things only grow worse. One day, he will decide to act. 'Wait!' he will be told. 'Wait just a little longer.' But he will refuse to wait another second."
Henry Miller (1947)

"A revolution is an historical process which leads not to the gates of paradise but to a world similar to the one we know except that many of the things in it, including the psyche itself, have changed."
Jules Monnerot
Sociology of Communism

"All revolutions begin with the land. Men are born on the earth, every man has his one spot, it is his birthright, and men must claim their portion of the earth in brotherhood and harmony."
James Ahmed
in *Guerrillas* (1975)
by V. S. Naipaul

"Revolutions are not made; they occur. Discontent with government there always is; still, even when grievous and well-founded, it seldom engenders revolution till the moral bases of government have rotted away: the feeling of community between the masses and their rulers, and in the rulers a consciousness of their right and capacity to rule."
Sir Lewis Namier
Vanished Supremacies (1962)

"A revolution can be neither made nor stopped. The only thing that can be done is . . . to give it a direction . . . go along with the opinions of the masses and with events. . . . What the people want is almost never what the people say. Their will and needs ought to be found not . . . in the people's mouth as [much as] in the ruler's heart."
Napoleon

"The process of revolution, the process of change, the new struggling against the old to produce some synthesis, does not necessarily have to be a destructive thing."
Huey P. Newton (1971)

412 / Quotations on Revolution

"[It is] far less dangerous to the Freedom of a State [to allow] the laws to be trampled upon, by the licence among the rabble . . . than to dispence with their force by an act of power."
New York Journal Supplement
(January 4, 1770)

"It is not hunger that makes revolutions but the fact that the people's appetite was growing *en mangeant*—in the process of eating."
Nietzsche

"Revolutions do not take place in velvet boxes. They never have. It is only the poets who make them lovely."
Carl Oglesby (1965)

"As revolutions have begun, it is natural to expect that other revolutions will follow."
Thomas Paine (1791)

"We have it in our power to begin the world over again. . . ."
Thomas Paine

"When they hear someone posit the greatness of revolution, as something that is supposed to enable one to speak openly and think daringly, they are impelled to pronounce such a view practically counterrevolutionary."
Boris Pasternak (1936)

"Bloodshed is a cleansing and sanctifying thing, and the nation which regards it as the final horror has lost its manhood. There are many things more horrible than bloodshed, and slavery is one of them."
Padriac Peace
Irish Nationalist

"Insurrection of thought always precedes insurrection of arms."
Wendell Phillips (1859)

"Revolution is the only thing, the only power, that ever worked out freedom for any people, The powers that have ruled long, and learned to love ruling, will never give up that prerogative till they find they must, till they see the certainty of overthrow and destruction if they do not! . . . To plant—to revolutionize—those are the twin stars that have ruled our pathway. What have we then to dread in the word Revolution—we, the children of rebels! We were born to be rebels—it runs in the blood.
Wendell Phillips (1848)

"Revolutions are not made; they come. A revolution is as natural a growth as an oak. It comes out of the past. Its foundations are far back."
Wendell Phillips

"In revolution, hope and horror go hand in hand."
J. H. Plumb

"Of all political ideas, perhaps the most dangerous is the wish to make people perfect and happy. The attempt to realize heaven on earth has always produced a hell."
Karl Popper (1971)

"A revolution is, in the moral sphere, an act of sovereign justice that results from the force of circumstances. Consequently it is its own justification."
P.-J. Proudhon
General Idea of Revolution in the
19th Century (1851)

"One cannot stem the tide of revolution. . . . The more you repress it, the more you are tightening its spring, and the more irresistible you are making its action."
P.-J. Proudhon
General Idea of Revolution in the
19th Century (1851)

Quotations on Revolution / 413

"A revolution is when the masses make the revolution. The popular revolution. But even when a revolution is brought up by others in the name of the masses, it is revolution because it is the expression of what the masses want. I mean, it is popular revolution because it has the support of the people and expresses the will of the masses."
        Col. Muammar el-Qadhafi
        Revolutionary Moslem leader
        of Libya, November 23, 1979

"No revolution was ever spearheaded by wriggling, chanting drug addicts who are boastfully antirational, who have no program to offer, yet propose to take over a nation of 200 million, and who spend their time manufacturing grievances, since they cannot tap any authentic source of popular discontent."
        Ayn Rand (1970)

"... society, like a great river, usually meanders slowly across the gently sloping plains of change, quickening for a brisker flow in response to shifts in basic technology and to special crises, such as wars.... Only very occasionally do the streams of social change go plunging over a great waterfall of revolution. Such drastic changes occur when the underlying realities of society grow too remote from an overly rigid social system and bring a widespread alienation and despair."
        Edwin O. Reischauer
        "Expanding the Limits of History"
        Saturday Review (May 29, 1976)

"Nothing has been accomplished so long as anything remains to be accomplished."
        Maximilien Robespierre

"Revolution is liberty's war against its enemies."
        Maximilien Robespierre (1793)

"Revolution is the war waged by liberty against its enemies.... The revolutionary government has to summon extraordinary activity to its aid precisely because it is at war."
        Maximilien Robespierre
        Speech to the National Convention
        (December 25, 1793)

"Being a revolutionary is like being in love. The characteristic of people in love is that they do not believe that anybody else in their lifetime has also been in love. So they do not learn from other people's mistakes and repeat all the same errors."
        Paul N. Rosenstein Rodan
        The New York Times
        (June 16, 1974)

"[Revolutions] do not break out until the old state of affairs is already ended, until the old order of things has died and is no longer believed in by its own beneficiaries."
        Eugen Rosenstock-Huessy
        Out of Revolution

"We assume that revolutions happen because they are planned. But this supposition is without foundation in reality. Announced revolutions do not happen.... A revolution must overwhelm us as other passions do."
        Eugen Rosenstock-Huessy
        Out of Revolution

"There is nowhere so much talk of liberty as in a state where it has ceased to exist."
        J. J. Rousseau

"Revolution is not what you believe, what organization you belong to, or who you vote for—it's what you do all day, how you live."
        Jerry Rubin
        Do It! (1970)

"There is nothing more common than to confound the terms of the American Revolution with those of the late American War. The American War is over but this is far from being the case with the American Revolution. On the contrary, nothing but the first act of the great drama is closed."
Benjamin Rush (1787)

"Those who make revolution by half measures are only digging a grave for themselves."
Saint-Just

"The word 'revolution' can only apply to revolutions whose goal is liberty."
Saint-Just (1791)

"The recent revolution would not have reached this point had the people had bread. And the people would have forgotten freedom and the hope of freedom if they had been able to forget their stomachs."
Friedrich Schulz
Über Paris and die Pariser

"America and other countries of the advanced capitalist world *are* in revolution. Revolutions do not begin with the thunderclap of a seizure of power—that is their culmination. They start with attacks on the moral-political order and the traditional hierarchy of class statuses. They succeed when the power structure, beset by its own irresolvable contradictions, can no longer perform legitimately and effectively."
Franz Schurmann
"System, Contradictions, and Revolution in America" in R. Aya and N. Miller (eds.) *The New American Revolution* (1971)

"Revolutions are profoundly influenced by the character of ruling classes."
Franz Schurmann

"The only true law is that which leads to freedom."
Jonathan Livingston Seagull (1970)

"It is not for the revolutionaries to sit in the doorways of their houses waiting for the corpse of imperialism to be carried by. . . . It is the duty of every revolutionary to make the revolution."
Second Declaration of Havana
February, 1962

"Give absolute power . . . to a tightly disciplined clique of professional revolutionaries who claim to possess the final scientific truth about human society, who regard men and women as clay to be moulded to the purposes of history, and who have consciously abandoned . . . all absolutes and moral standards, and you can get only one result—totalitarianism."
Hugh Seton-Watson
Encounter (April 1954)

"The revolution is not disposed either to pity or to bury its dead."
Joseph Stalin

"With the assumption of temporal power, the Revolution, like the Church, enters into a state of sin."
I. F. Stone (1967)

"The most awe-inspiring lesson of the French Revolution is not that men with their deliberating reason can make a revolution, but that revolution plays havoc with men."
J. L. Talmon
Political Messianism

"Revolution is for society what a passionate love is for the individual; those who experience it are marked forever, separated from their own past and from the rest of mankind. Some writers have captured the ecstasy of love; hardly any have rekindled the soul-purging fires

of revolution. The writer of genius lives, for the most part, in a private world; it is not surprising that he deals usually with private passions. There have been some good observers of revolution—the best of them . . . observe from outside; it is like reading about the love-affair of the man next door. . . . Revolution calls in question the foundations of social life; it can be grasped only by one who has experienced it and yet possesses the detachment of a political psychologist."
       A. J. P. Taylor
       From Napoleon to Lenin

"All men recognize the right of revolution, that is the right to refuse allegiance and to resist the government where its tyranny or its inefficiency are great and unendurable."
       Henry D. Thoreau (1849)

"Revolutions . . . occurred and always will occur so long as human nature remains the same."
       Thucydides
       History of the Peloponnesian War

"Experience teaches us that, generally speaking, the most perilous moment for a bad government is when it seeks to mend its ways."
       Alexis de Tocqueville

"I am weary of seeing the shore in each successive mirage [of each revolution since 1789], and I often ask myself whether the terra firma we are seeking does really exist, and whether we are doomed to rove upon the seas for ever."
       The Recollections of
       Alexis de Tocqueville

"In a revolution, as in a novel, the most difficult part to invent is the end."
       Alexis de Tocqueville

"Our revolutionaries had the same fondness for broad generalizations, cut and dried legislative systems, and a pedantic symmetry; the same contempt for hard facts; the same taste for reshaping institutions on novel, ingenious, original lines; the same desire to reconstruct the entire constitution according to the rules of logic and a preconceived system instead of trying to rectify its faulty parts. The result was nothing short of disastrous."
       Alexis de Tocqueville

"We can see how it was that a successful revolution could tear down the whole social structure almost in the twinkling of an eye."
       Alexis de Tocqueville

"The duty of every Catholic is to be a revolutionary, the duty of every revolutionary is to make the revolution. The Catholic who is not a revolutionary is living in mortal sin."
       Camilo Torres

"Revolutions have always in history been followed by counterrevolutions. Counterrevolutions have always thrown society back, but never as far back as the starting point of the revolution."
       Leon Trotsky
       Diary (1926)

"Every successful revolution puts on in time the robes of the tyrant it has deposed."
       Barbara Tuchman

"Novus Ordo Seclorum" (1776) ("A New Order of the Ages [is Born]")
       Vergil
       Back of U.S. dollar (American
       Revolution as beginning of a
       world revolution)

"Never will twenty folio volumes bring about a revolution. Little books are the ones to fear, the pocket-size, portable ones that sell [cheaply]. If the Gospels had been [expensive], the Christian religion could never have been established."
    Voltaire (1765)

"Our cruel and unrelenting enemy leaves us only the choice of a brave resistance, or the most abject submission. We have, therefore, to resolve to conquer or to die."
    George Washington
    August, 1776

"... kid's culture is one of respect for human life and a deep belief in peace. We have learned though that to be honest we must live outside the law, to be free we must fight."
    The Weatherman Underground
    (January 1971)

"Our revolution (1776–1783) has ended the need for revolution forever."
    General William C. Westmoreland
    to The Daughters of the American
    Revolution (April 20, 1970)

"A TOTAL REVOLUTION
(*An Answer for Robert Frost*)
I advocate a total revolution.
The trouble with a semi-revolution,
It's likely to be slow as evolution.
Who wants to spend the ages in collusion
With Compromise, Complacence and Confusion?
As for the same class coming up on top
That's wholecloth from the propaganda shop;
The old saw says there's loads of room on top,
That's where the poor should really plan to stop.
And speaking of those people called the "haves",
Who own the whole cow and must have the calves
(And plant the wounds so they can sell the salves)
They won't be stopped by doing things by halves.
I say that for a permanent solution
There's nothing like a total revolution!
P.S. And need I add by way of a conclusion
I wouldn't dream to ask a Rosicrucian.
    Oscar Williams

"The great virtue of revolutions is that they create the circumstances in which a society's problems *can* be solved."
    William Appleman Williams
    The Contours of American History (1961)

"We have forgotten the very principle of our origin if we have forgotten how to object, how to resist, how to agitate, how to pull down and build up, even to the extent of revolutionary practices, if it is necessary to readjust matters."
    Woodrow Wilson

"A time of revolution ... is the season of free liberty. Alas! The obstinacy and perversion of men is such that she is too often obliged to borrow the very arms of despotism to overthrow him, and in order to reign in peace must establish herself by violence. She deplores such stern necessity, but the safety of the people, her supreme law, is her consolation ... But is this a sufficient reason to reprobate a convulsion from which is to spring a fairer order of things?"
    William Wordsworth
    A Letter to the Bishop of Llandaff
    (February 1793)

"We were not born violent. We do not enjoy killing people. We just want peace and freedom. But our daily lives are violent. The country is violent. The enemy leaves us no choice. Either we sit by saying 'ay bendito' as our nation dies, or we stand up, organize, prepare for the revolution we know is coming."
            Young Lords Party

"Revolution in its full sense cannot be achieved by force of arms. It must be prepared in the minds and behavior of men, even *before* institutions have radically changed. It is not an act, but a process."
            Howard Zinn
            "The Art of Revolution" (1970)

Author-Editor Index

References are to entry numbers

Aaron, Richard I., 1786
Abbott, Wilbur C., 1701, 1703
Abcarian, Gilbert, 788
Abend, Hallett Edward, 4755
Abidi, A., 6199
Abramovich, Raphael R., 2538
Abramson, Michael, 3225
Abray, Jane, 2063
Acomb, E.M., 2337
Acton, Edward, 2206
Acton, H.B., 937–38
Acton, John E., 1890
Aczél, Tamás, 3110
Adair, D., 3314
Adamolekun, 'Ladipo, 5544
Adams, Arthur E., 2509, 2562, 2599
Adams, Brooks, 92
Adams, H.P., 939
Adams, Nina S., 5112
Adams, Randolph G., 3388
Adams, Richard N., 3843, 4097, 4109
Adams, Samuel, 3554
Adams, Thomas R., 3463, 6100
Adamson, Walter L., 2495
Adas, Michael, 368
Adelman, Jonathan R., 417
Adeniran, Tunde, 686
Ader, Emile B., 1112, 1176
Adie, I.W.A.C., 4820
Adie, Robert F., 3844
Adkins, Nelson F., 3589
Adler, Douglas D., 6051
Ado, Anatolii V., 5997
Adorno, Theodore W., 1230, 1426
Adu-Shumays, Mary D., 3464
Africa Information Service, 5675
African Bibliographic Center, 5330
Agpalo, R.E., 5309
Aguilar, Luis E., 3801, 3845–46
Agyeman, Opoku, 5345, 5563
Ahlstrom, Sydney E., 3494
Ahmad, Eqbal, 396–97, 5758, 5856
Ahmad, S.H., 4918
Ahmed, A.S., 369
Ahn, Byung-joon, 4919, 4958
Aidit, D.M, 5129

Aiken, Henry David, 293
Ajala, Adekunle, 5373, 6175
Akamatsu, Paul, 4580
Ake, Claude, 5374
Akenson, Donald H., 2920
Akers, Charles W., 3550
Akhavi, Shadragh, 5883
Akintoye, S.A., 5375–76
Al-Afif, Ibrahim Massaud, 5681
Alavi, Hamza, 687
Alba, Victor, 3847, 3878, 4007
Albert, Michael, 294
Alberts, D.J., 517
Albertson, Dean, 750
Albornoz, Oswaldo, 6133
Alden, John, 3262–63, 3534
Alder, J.H., 530
Aldred, Guy A., 877
Aldridge, A.O., 3581
Alexander, John T., 2169
Alexander, Horace, 5194, 5230
Alexander, Robert J., 3848–51, 4100, 4111, 4293, 4440–41
Alexander, Yonah, 529, 563–66, 5855
Ali, Bashir Hadj, 5447
Ali, Tariq, 3640, 4564
Alinsky, Saul, 789
Alkan, M. Turker, 6174
Allan, Graham, 359
Allardt, Erik, 276–77
Allen, Harry C., 6101
Allen, Henry E., 5298
Allen, Mary B., 905–06
Allen, William Sheridan, 2988
Allende, Salvador, 4294
Almond, G.A., 1177, 2880
Alperovitz, Gar, 3207
Alpert, Jane, 6124
AlRoy, Gil Carl, 702, 3802, 4189–91
Altbach, Philip G., 716, 718, 741, 770
Althusser, Louis, 940
Alves, Marcio Moreira, 4378
Amado, Janaína, 6150
Amalrik, Andrei A., 2207
Amann, Peter, 11, 1855, 2343, 2382
Ambler, John S., 3126

419

American Enterprise Institute for Public
   Policy Research, 3212
Amery, Leopold, 5195
Ammerman, David, 3324
An, Tai Sung, 4959
Ancheta, Celedonio A., 5310
Andelman, David A., 5645
Anderson, Andy, 3111
Anderson, Benedict R., 5130
Anderson, Charles F., 5196
Anderson, Donald W., 1231
Anderson, E.N., 2175
Anderson, Lady Flavia C., 4615
Anderson, Perry, 4259
Anderson, Rodney D., 4054
Anderson, Thomas P., 3852
Anderson, William A., 484
Andics, Helmut, 2759
Andrade, Mario de, 5646
Andrade, Victor, 4112
Andreski, Stanislav, 3641
Andrews, C.F., 5231
Andrews, Charles M., 3254, 3325
Andrews, I., 1487
Andrews, William, 336
Andrews, William G., 5457
Andrews, William R., 5041
Angress, Werner T., 2881
Ansari, S., 5726
Ansell, Meredith O., 5681
Antonius, George, 5805
Antony, Jonquil, 2445
Anweiler, Oskar, 2626, 2660
Apple, R.W., Jr., 5857
Applebaum, David A., 2375
Appleby, Joyce, 3359
Applewhite, Harriet B., 1981
Apter, David E., 295, 3618, 5421
Aptheker, Herbert, 235, 3213–14, 3264
Archdeacon, Thomas J., 6102
Archer, George D., 5684
Archer, Jules, 2819, 4854
Arciniegas, German, 12
Ardagh, John, 3138
Arendt, Hannah, 12, 93–94, 225, 278,
   453, 485, 1431, 3108
Aris, Stephen, 531
Aristotle, 1476
Armentrout, L. Eve, 4470
Armstrong, George, 532
Arnade, Charles W., 4113
Arnade, Kurt Conrad, 328, 3803
Arnold, Oren, 4080
Aron, Raymond, 486, 941, 3127, 3139
Aronde, Julio, 4264
Arrighhi, Giovanni, 5346
Arriola, Jorge Luis, 6131
Artz, Frederick B., 2208, 2322, 2328

Artzt, E., 507
Asante, S.K.B., 5422
Ascher, Abraham, 2539–40
Ascherson, Neal, 4273
Ascoli, Peter, 6103
Ash, Roberta, 3215
Ashby, Joe C., 4056
Ashe, Geoffrey, 5232
Ashley, Maurice, 1604–06, 1662, 1688,
   1704–07, 1759
Ashton, Robert, 1607, 1689
Asprey, Robert B., 429
Aston, Trevor, 1514
Atiyeh, George N., 5783
The Atlantic, Editors of, 757
Atkins, Ronald, 4008
Atmore, Anthony, 6186
Atwood, Rodney, 6104
Aubéry, Pierre, 3128–29
Augur, Helen, 3445
Aulard, Alphonse, 1891, 2019
Avakian, Bob, 4855–56
Avakumovich, Ivan, 3093
Aveling, Eleanor Marx, 1038
Avineri, Shlomo, 942–43, 1113
Avishai, Bernard, 533
Avrich, Paul, 824-26, 874, 1515, 2594,
   2627, 2661–62
Axelos, Kostas, 944
Aya, Roderick, 1, 701, 727, 1454, 3642,
   5757, 5774
Ayela, Nega, 5708, 5719
Aylmer, Gerald E., 1608, 1736
Ayoob, Mohammed, 6197
Azad, Abul Kalam, 5197
Azicri, Max, 4126
Azmon, Yael, 1132

Bacciocco, Edward J., 3643
Badaev, A.E., 2600
Baechler, Jean, 95–96, 398
Baerlein, Henry, 4009
Baerwald, H., 4701
Bahadurke, Syed Ahmed Khan, 5155
Bahlman, Dudley, 1760
Bailey, David C., 3984
Bailyn, Bernard, 465, 3240, 3255, 3360,
   3372
Bain, Chester A., 5042
Baines, John M., 4407, 4422
Baird, Leonard L., 719
Bak, James, 1554
Baker, Anthony S., 2476
Baker, Raymond William, 5838
Bako, Elemer, 2869, 3106
Bakunin, Mikhail, 878
Balabanova, Angelica, 2760
Baldwin, Alice, 3501

Author-Editor Index / 421

Baldwin, Roger N., 896, 900
Ball, Terence, 5993
Ball, W.M., 4581
Balsama, George D., 1972
Balta, Paul, 5884
Ba Maw, U., 4582
Band, Claire, 4756
Band, William, 4756
Bandyopadhyaya, Jayantanuja, 1381
Banerjee, D.N., 279
Banks, Robert, 1273
Banning, Lance, 1353, 1986
Baradat, Leon P., 296
Baraheni, Reza, 5858, 5885
Baran, Paul A., 4127
Barber, B., 360, 1259
Barber, Benjamin R., 1816, 3644
Barber, Elinor G., 2007
Barber, Noel, 3112
Barbour, Floyd B., 3753
Barcata, Louis, 4960
Barclay, Glen St. J., 1260
Barea, Arturo, 3025
Barent, C.R., 4172
Barfield, Rodney, 2750
Baritz, L., 3645
Barka, Mehdi Ben, 5755
Barkan, Elliott R., 3241
Barker, Ernest, 1708, 2140
Barkin, David P., 4142
Barkun, Michael, 370
Barnard, F.M., 3161
Barnes, Eric W., 3446
Barnes, Jack, 3646
Barnes, Thomas G., 1516
Barnet, Richard J., 5759
Barnett, A. Doak, 4583-84, 4710-11
Barnett, Charles, 5577
Barnett, Clifford, 4174
Baron, Samuel H., 2589, 2663
Barrow, Thomas C., 3471, 3513
Barry, Tom, 2921
Barzun, Jacques, 945, 1335
Basalla, George, 1796
Bascio, P., 14
Basil, John D., 2595
Bassiouni, M. Cheriff, 567, 5811
Basso, Lelio, 2882
Bastid, Marianne, 4492
Basu, A.R., 6176
Baszkiewicz, Jan, 1944, 5998
Batatu, Hanna, 5806
Bauer, Alice H., 618
Bauer, Arthur, 97
Bauer, Otto, 2367
Bauer, Raymond A., 618
Baum, Richard, 4915, 4920-21, 4961
Bauman, Zygmunt, 1114

Baumann, Carol Edler, 568
Baumont, Maurice, 2989
Bax, Ernest Belfort, 1555, 2076
Baxandall, Lee, 913
Bayitch, S.A., 3792
Baynham, Simon, 6177
Bazant, Jan, 4010, 4048
Bazillion, Richard J., 2398
Beach, Stewart, 3555
Beach, Vincent W., 2309
Beal, M.F., 1296
Beals, Carleton, 98, 3853, 4074
Bearman, Graham, 1892, 2700
Beaslai, P., 2922
Beauvois, Daniel, 5999
Beck, Carl, 1232
Becker, Carl, 3326, 3373
Becker, Francis Bennett, 2751
Becker, George J., 2446
Becker, Jillian, 569
Becker, Robert A., 3472
Beckett, J.C., 2923
Beckett, Paul A., 5486-87
Bedeski, Robert E., 4471, 4565
Beer, Max, 1115-16
Beesly, Augustus Henry, 2040
Beezley, William H., 4071, 4077
Begin, Menachim, 5807
Behr, Edward, 5458
Behrens, C.B.A., 1964, 1967
Beik, Paul H., 2077
Béjar, Héctor, 4423
Belaunde, Victor A., 3948
Belcher, Henry, 3447
Belden, Jack, 4712
Bell, Belden, 4351
Bell, Daniel, 297, 751, 790
Bell, David V.J., 99
Bell, J. Bowyer, 430, 534, 570-72, 2924, 5760
Bell, John Patrick, 3854
Bell, Susan Groag, 5951
Bell, Wendell, 3855
Belloc, Hilaire, 1893, 2106
Belnap, David F., 4274
Beloff, Max, 3231
Benard, Cheryl, 6200
Ben-Dak, Joseph, 487
Bender, Frederic L., 946
Bender, Gerald J., 5578
Bendiner, Robert, 535
Bendix, Reinhard, 100-01, 1432
Benecke, Gerhard, 1562
Benjamin, Thomas, 6135
Benningsen, Alexandre A., 5761
Benson, Frederick R., 3026
Beqiraj, Mehmet, 703
Berciamo, Modesto, 6127

Berdyaev, Nicholas, 1178, 2664
Berens, John F., 1274
Beres, Louis René, 5923
Berg, Lasse, 5198
Berg, Lisa, 5198
Berger, Martin, 1092, 1095, 5946
Berger, Peter, 102
Bergère, Marie-Claire, 4491-92, 4795
Bergmann, G., 280
Berkeley, George F.H., 2427
Berkhofer, Robert F., Jr., 3265
Berki, Robert, 1117
Berkin, Carol R., 1297, 3507
Berkman, Alexander, 884-86
Berle, Adolph A., 103, 3804
Berlin, Isaiah, 947
Berman, Marshal, 1823
Berman, Paul, 5043, 6125
Berman, Sanford, 5331
Bernal, Martin, 1118
Bernet, Jacques, 6000
Bernstein, Alvin H., 1485
Bernstein, B. J., 3400
Bernstein, Eduard, 1119, 1709
Bernstein, Harry, 3856
Bernstein, Samuel, 2447, 6070
Bernstein, Thomas P., 1354
Berque, Jacques, 5839
Berrigan, Daniel, 3599-600
Berrigan, Philip, 3606
Bertaud, Jean-Paul, 6001
Berthoff, Rowland, 3396
Bertin, P., 6046
Berton, Peter, 4448
Beshah, Teferra-Worq, 5685
Beshir, Mohamed Omer, 5377
Beslay, Charles, 2448
Best, Heinrich, 2408
Best, Mary A., 3582
Bestor, Arthur R., 3514
Betsworth, Roger G., 6126
Bettelheim, Bruno, 784
Bettelheim, Charles, 1163, 2601, 2665, 4962
Beyme, K. von, 104
Bezucha, Robert J., 2310, 2312
Bhattracharyya, Jhanabrata, 5188
Bhuyan, Arun, 5199
Bialer, S., 783, 791, 1423
Bianchi, Eugene C., 1281
Bianco, Lucien, 4484, 4796-97, 4821
Bienen, Henry, 449, 5647
Bienvenu, Richard T., 1845, 2107
Bill, J., 5859
Billias, George A., 3232, 3266
Billington, James H., 1282, 2628
Billington, Ray A., 3237
Binder, Leonard, 5808

Binkley, Robert C., 15, 2209
Birch, R.C., 3267
Birch, Una, 2078
Bird, Thomas E., 2504
Birla, G.D., 5233
Birn, Raymond, 1517
Birnbaum, Eleazar, 4446
Birns, Laurence R., 4332
Biswas, S.C., 5234
Bithell, Jethro, 2883, 2990
Bittner, Egon, 785
Black, Cyril E., 1179
Blackburn, Robin, 948, 4167, 4259
Blackey, Robert, 2, 105, 194, 1355, 4275, 5488, 5547, 5648
Blackman, Morris J., 3857
Blackmer, Donald L., 1180
Blackwood, B.G., 1646, 5989
Blair, Leon B., 792
Blaiser, Cole, 3805
Blake, J. Herman, 3740
Blakemore, Harold, 3806
Blanc, Louis, 668, 2383
Blanchard, Calvin, 3583
Blanchard, William H., 1824
Blanksten, G., 3807
Blanning, T.C.W., 1518
Blanqui, Auguste, 329
Blaquierre, Edward, 2854
Blauvelt, Mary Taylor, 1710
Blecher, Marc J., 4922
Bleiber, Helmut, 2399
Blickle, Peter, 5979-80
Blinkhorn, Martin, 3019, 3027
Block, Fred, 921-22
Block, J.H., 720
Bloom, Solomon F., 949
Bloomfield, Jon, 6052
Bluhm, William T., 298
Blum, Jerome, 2368
Blumberg, Arnold, 6067
Blumenberg, Werner, 950
Blumenstock, Dorothy, 1416
Boahen, A.A., 5418
Boardman, Eugene Powers, 4616
Boas, Marie, 1797
Boatner, Mark M., III, 3252
Bober, M.M., 951
Bobroff, Anne, 5952
Bocheński, Joseph M., 914, 1172
Bodde, Derk, 4757
Body, Paul, 1846
Boggs, James, 1313, 3724
Boizard, René, 6047
Boll, Michael M., 2529, 2541
Bolloten, Burnett, 3028-29
Bolton, Glorney, 5235
Bomani, Paul, 5730

Bonachea, Ramon L., 4143
Bonachea, Rolando E., 4203, 4217
Bonavia, David, 4923
Bonazzi, Tiziano, 5958
Bond, James E., 350
Bondurant, Joan V., 488, 624, 5236
Bone, Christopher, 3647
Bongie, Laurence L., 669
Bonilla, Frank, 4439, 4442
Bonnett, Nicole, 4260
Bonney, Richard J., 1584
Bonomi, Patricia U., 6105
Bonwick, Colin, 793, 3473
Boogs, Carl, Jr., 226
Bookchin, Murray, 827–28
Boorman, Scott A., 4857
Boorstein, Edward, 4295
Boorstin, Daniel J., 794, 3327, 3389
Booth, Sally S., 3328
Bordewich, F., 6201
Borg, Dorothy, 4813
Borkenau, Franz, 1181–82, 2179, 3030
Borowsky, Peter, 6086
Borrás Llop, José María, 6091
Borton, Hugh, 704
Bose, Arun Coomer, 5200
Bose, Atindranath, 829
Bose, Nirmal Kumar, 5237–40
Bose, Subhas Chandra, 5201–02
Bosher, J.F., 1973
Boskin, Joseph, 3648, 3741
Botsford, Keith, 2180
Bottomore, T.B., 795, 1233
Bouc, Alain, 4858
Bouchier, David, 299
Boudon, Raymond, 721
Bourdieu, Pierre, 5459–60
Bourgeault, Guy, 3784
Bourges, Hervé, 3140
Bourgi, A.C., 5489
Bourgin, Georges, 2449
Bourguina, Anna M., 2526
Bourne, Henry Eldridge, 1856
Bouvier, Pierre, 5518
Bowden, Tom, 403, 1382
Bowen, Catherine D., 3427
Bowen, Don R., 514
Bowers, Claude Gernade, 2079, 3565
Bown, Colin, 4485
Boyce, D.G., 2926
Boyd, Herbert, 5564
Boyer, Richard E., 1711–12
Boyle, John, 2911
Brace, Joan, 5461
Brace, Richard M., 2038, 5378, 5461
Bracey, John H., Jr., 3754–55
Braddy, Haldeen, 4081
Bradford, M.E., 3268

Brading, D.A., 4061, 4082
Bradley, John, 2666
Bradshaw, Jon, 537
Braesch, Frédéric, 1952
Braga de Macedo, J., 6098
Braganca-Cunha, Vincente, 3197
Brailsford, H.N., 1737, 5283
Brancourt, Jean-Pierre, 5995
Brandenburg, Frank R., 4050
Brandes, Paul D., 1319
Brandt, Conrad, 4697
Bratton, Michael, 5731
Brauer, Jerald C., 3502
Braun, Frank H., 5791
Braungart, R., 748–49
Braunthal, Julius, 371
Bray, Robert, 3448
Braybrooke, David, 923
Brea, Juan, 3056
Breines, P., 3712
Brenan, Gerald, 3031
Brennan, Ray, 4215
Brenner, Anita, 4011
Brent, Harry, 172
Brereton, J.M., 5153
Breshkovsky, Catherine, 6077
Brett, Sidney Reed, 1663
Breunig, Charles, 2210
Brewer, Anthony, 952
Breytenbach, W.J., 5565
Bridenbaugh, Carl, 3329
Bridenthal, Renate, 5935, 5953, 6017, 6082
Bridge, S., 3162
Bridges, Thomas, 3808
Bridgham, Philip, 4911, 4924–25
Bridgman, Jon M., 6178
Brietzke, Paul, 5686, 5722
Brimmell, Jack H., 1183
Brine, Lindesay, 4617
Brink, William, 3756
Brinkman, Carl, 106
Brinton, Crane, 107, 1857, 2108
Brisbane, Robert H., 3757–58
Britton, John A., 3809
Brockway, A. Fenner, 625, 5379
Broderick, Walter J., 4397
Brodie, Fawn, 3566
Brogan, D.W., 108, 722, 907
Brogan, Hugh, 2294
Broido, Eva, 2569
Broido, Vera, 1298, 2569
Bromage, Mary C., 2912, 2927
Bromley, John Selwyn, 1500
Broszat, Martin, 2991
Broué, Pierre, 3032
Browder, Robert, 2527
Brower, Daniel R., 2667–68
Brown, Arthur, 4659

Brown, Bernard E., 3141-42
Brown, Bruce, 953
Brown, Clifford W., Jr., 1415, 3133
Brown, Emily C., 5762
Brown, H. Haines, 924
Brown, Judith M., 5241-42, 6172
Brown, Lyle C., 4068
Brown, M.L., 2337
Brown, MacAlister, 4608
Brown, Mark, 2311
Brown, Richard, 3390, 3522
Brown, Richard Maxwell, 451, 489-90, 3269
Brown, Robert E., 3391
Brown, Stuart Gerry, 109
Browne, Edward G., 5809
Browning, Andrew, 1747
Browning, Frank 3208
Browning, Tatiana, 2546
Brownlie, Ian, 5343
Brugger, Bill, 4963, 6152
Brunel, François, 6002
Brutents, K.N., 1383
Bruton, James K., 5732
Bruun, Geoffrey, 2109
Brzezinski, Zbigniew, 281, 657, 3216
Buchan, John, 1713
Buchanan, George, 2542
Buchanan, John G., 3584
Buckingham, Peter, 110
Buckley, William F., Jr., 658
Buckman, Peter, 796
Budenz, Louis F., 1184
Buechler, Hans C., 4115
Buel, Richard, Jr., 3374, 3380
Buell, Hal, 5044
Buhl, W.L., 1312
Buijtenhuija, Rob, 5347
Bukharin, Nikolai, 1433, 2761, 5947
Bulgakov, Sergei, 954
Bulhan, Hussein Abdilahi, 5490
Bulletin of the Atomic Scientists, 5010
Bullock, Alan, 2171, 2992
Bullough, Vern L., 1798
Bumsted, J.M., 3523
Bunge, William, 3759
Bunting, Brian, 5741
Bunyan, James, 2565
Bunzel, John H., 16
Buonarroti, Fillippo Michele, 2080
Burchett, Wilfred, 431, 4585, 5045-47, 5380
Burdick, Charles B., 2884
Burggraaff, Winfield J., 4438
Burke, Edmund, 2148-49
Burke, Edmund, III, 5491
Burke, Peter, 46, 691, 1794
Burks, R.V., 1185

Burlingame, Anne Elizabeth, 1993
Burnett, Ben G., 3858
Burns, C.D., 111
Burns, Edward McNall, 300
Burns, Emile, 919, 955
Burns, James MacGregor, 1234
Burns, Richard Dean, 5016
Burr, Robert N., 3810
Burridge, Kenelm, 372
Burton, Anthony M., 491, 573
Bury, J.P.T., 2211
Bushnell, Paul, 3448
Busi, Frederick, 2437
Butler, Ed., 1434
Butler, Jeffrey E., 5337
Butterfield, Herbert, 1799
Buttinger, Joseph, 1120, 5048-50
Button, James W., 3760
Buve, Raymond Th. J., 4062
Byrne, F.J., 2960

Cabral, Amilcar, 5649-61, 5674-76
Cabral, Luis, 5612
Cabrera, Luis, 3986
Cáceres Prendes, Jorge Rafael, 6132
Caffi, A., 492
Cahill, Holgel, 4618
Cairns, Trevor, 1894
Calhoon, Robert McCluer, 3270
Calhoun, Craig, 5933
Califano, Joseph A., Jr., 752
Calkins, Kenneth R., 2885
Call, Tomme Clark, 4012
Callery, Joseph M., 4619
Calvert, Peter, 17, 112-13, 3987, 4064
Câmara, Dom Hélder, 4379
Camejo, Pedro, 4352
Camejo, Peter, 351, 3649
Cameron, Allan W., 5018
Cameron, Charlotte, 4013
Cameron, J.M., 454
Cameron, James, 5381
Cameron, Kenneth N., 956
Cameron, Wm. Bruce, 114
Cammett, John M., 1186
Camp, Roderic A., 3988
Campbell, Leon G., 3811, 4408-10, 4424
Camus, Albert, 115-16
Canavan, Francis P., 2150
Canfield, Cass, 3556
Cannon, Terry, 5051
Cantacuzene, Princess, 2543
Cantlie, James, 4673
Cantor, Milton, 797
Cantor, Norman F., 236
Cantril, Hadley, 266
Capino, Diosdado G., 5311-12
Caplan, Nathan S., 3742

Caponigri, A. Robert, 256
Capouya, Emile, 897
Capp, Bernard, 373
Cappon, Lester J., 3253
Cardozo, Harold G., 3033
Carlson, Andrew R., 830
Carlton, David, 574, 589
Carlton, G., 1096
Carlyle, Thomas, 1895
Carmichael, Joel, 957, 2593, 2820
Carmichael, Stokely, 3725, 5423
Caroll, Walter F., 5793
Carr, Barry, 3989
Carr, Edward H., 879, 958, 1121, 2602, 2629, 2669–71
Carr, Raymond, 3034–36
Carrier, Fred, 5763
Carroll, Kevin K., 1486
Carson, Clayborne, 6128
Carson, George B., Jr., 2563
Carsten, F.L., 2212
Carswell, John, 1519, 1761
Carter, April, 831
Carter, G.M., 5382
Carter, Gwendolen M., 5742
Carter, Peter, 4859
Carver, George, 5022
Carver, Terrell, 1097
Casanova, J.C., 52
Case, Clarence Marsh, 626
Case, Margaret H., 4459
Cash, Anthony, 2672, 2762
Cassinelli, C.W., 1384
Castro, Fidel, 4216–17, 4296
Casuso, Teresa, 4218
Cattell, David T., 3037
Catton, Bruce, 3271
Catton, William B., 3271
Caudet, Francisco, 6092
Caulfield, Max, 2928
Caute, David, 2213, 5519
Cavanaugh, Gerald J., 1873
Cavendish, Patrick, 4973
Cell, Charles P., 4713
Censer, Jack Richard, 2025, 6003
Center for Black Education, 5743
Cerati, Marie, 6004
Césaire, Aimé, 5383
Chadwick, Owen, 1283
Chaffin, Robert J., 3524
Chai, Winberg, 4486, 4698
Chailiand, Gérard, 5613, 5638, 5662–63, 5764
Chalmers, Douglas A., 3859
Chalmers, George, 3272, 3585
Chamberlain, Bobby, 4371
Chamberlain, William Henry, 2530, 2673
Chan, F. Gilbert, 4472, 4788, 4805, 6165

Chan, Sylvia, 4912
Chandler, Robert W., 5052
Chang Kuo-T'ao, 4765
Chang, Maria Hsia, 1363, 4651
Chang, Y.C., 5011
Chapel, Robert T., 3321
Chapelle, Dickey, 4210
Chaplin, David, 4411, 4425
Chapman, H., 4714
Chapman, John W., 860, 1825
Charques, Richard, 2544
Chassin, Lionel Max, 4715
Chattopadhyaya, Haraprasad, 5156
Chaudhuri, Sashi Bhusan, 5157–58
Chaudury, P.C. Ray, 5243
Chauhan, D.S., 5224
Chavran, R.S., 4586
Chege, Michael, 5687
Chen Ch'ang-feng, 4783
Chen, Jack, 4964
Chen, James K., 4456
Ch'en, Jerome, 4487, 4818, 4860–61
Chen, King C., 4566, 5095
Ch'en, Kung-Po, 4488, 4789
Chen, Percy, 4758
Ch'en Pōta, 4716, 4759, 4862
Chen, Yu-Shih, 4473
Cheng, J.C., 4610
Cheng, Peter P., 4822
Cheng, Ronald Ye-lin, 117
Cherniavsky, Michael, 2674
Chernov, Victor, 2570
Cherry, George L., 1749
Chesneaux, Jean, 4489–92, 4717
Chick, N.A., 5167
Chilcote, Ronald H., 1385, 3793, 5546, 5560, 5579, 5614–15, 5644, 5664
Childs, David, 959
Childs, John, 1762
Chiou, C.L., 4965
Cholvy, Gérard, 6005
Chomsky, Noam, 237
Chopra, P.N., 5203
Chorley, Katharine, 418
Chow Tse-tung, 4493
Christenson, Reo M., 301
Christianson, Paul, 1629
Christie, Ian R., 3233, 3465, 3474–75
Christman, Henry M., 2746
Christofferson, Thomas R., 6068
Chu, Franklin D., 3125
Chuang, H.C., 4966
Chubb, O. Edmund, 4494
Church, Clive H., 2214, 2308
Church, William F., 1994
Ciardi, John, 3620
CIDAC, 5639
Ciria, Alberto, 4357

Clarence-Smith, W.G., 5566
Clarendon, Edward, Earl of, 1599
Clark, Ann B., 4695
Clark, George, 1763
Clark, John P., 891
Clark, Joseph, 18
Clark, Kenneth B., 3743
Clark, Martin, 2496
Clark, Michael K., 5462
Clark, R.E., 5420
Clark, Ramsey, 455
Claudin, Fernando, 1187
Claudin-Urondo, Carmen, 2763
Cleaver, Eldridge, 3726-27
Clecak, Peter, 798, 3621, 3650
Clement, Alain, 5962
Clements, Barbara Evans, 1299
Clements, Frank, 5784
Clements, Paul H., 4634
Cliff, Tony, 2764
Cline, Howard F., 3990, 4014, 4065
Clissold, Stephen, 3860
Clouse, Robert G., 374
Clutterbuck, Richard, 432, 575-76
Coast, John, 5131
Coatman, John, 5204
Cobb, Richard C., 1293, 2024, 2026, 2032, 2052, 2060, 2064, 2081, 2097, 2110, 2128-29, 2181
Cobban, Alfred, 1356, 1817, 1826, 1847, 1896-98, 1953, 1974, 2098-99, 2151
Cochin, Augustin, 2082, 6006-07
Cockcroft, James D., 3861, 4015
Coffey, Thomas M., 2929
Cohan, A.S., 118
Cohen, Arthur A., 4863
Cohen, Carl, 1188
Cohen, G.A., 960
Cohen, John M., 5683, 5688, 5715
Cohen, Leonard, 1189
Cohen, Lester H., 3242, 3361
Cohen, Mitchell, 753
Cohen, Norman S., 493
Cohen, Stephen F., 2603
Cohler, Anne M., 1827
Cohn, Henry J., 1546
Cohn, Norman, 375
Cohn-Bendit, Daniel, 3143-44
Cohn-Bendit, Gabriel, 3143
Coiffard, Aimé, 6042
Colbourn, H. Trevor, 3362, 3375, 3424
Cole, Allan Burnett, 4694, 4699
Cole, G.D.H., 961-62, 1122, 2215
Cole, Hubert, 3949
Coles, Robert, 3600
Colletti, Lucio, 302, 963
Collier, Bernard, 4278
Collier, Daniel M., 206

Collier, Elsie, 4718
Collier, John, 4718
Collier, Simon, 3862, 3950
Collins, M.E., 2930
Collins, Michael, 2931
Collins, Randall, 119
Colodny, Robert G., 3038-39
Coltman, Irene, 1654
Colton, Ethan T., 120, 2216
Comerford, Anthony, 2932
Cometti, Elizabeth, 3508
Commager, Henry Steele, 1386, 3567
Committee on Internal Security, United States House of Representatives, 577
Compton, Boyd, 4700
Conant, Ralph W., 494
Conde, Roberto Cortes, 3863
Cone, Carl B., 2152-53
Confino, Michael, 832
Congdon, Lee, 6085
Conine, Ernest, 4412
Connelly, James L., 2017
Connelly, Owen, 1899
Connery, Robert H., 495
Conniff, Michael L., 4372
Connolly, James, 1123, 2908
Connolly, William E., 303
Connor, James E., 2747
Connor, Walter D., 1124
Conquest, Robert, 2765
Constandse, A.L., 815
Constantino, Renato, 5323
Conway, Moncure D., 3586
Conze, Edward, 3040
Cook, Blanche, 1300-01
Cook, Don, 3181
Cooley, John K., 5384
Cooper, Bert, 5053
Coper, Rudolf, 2886
Corbett, Patrick, 304
Corbitt, Duvon C., 4128
Cornforth, Maurice, 1435
Cornwall, Julian, 1520
Corrigan, Philip, 964
Cosenza, Mario E., 1492
Coser, Lewis A., 78, 121, 456
Costeloe, M.P., 4048
Costigan, Giovanni, 2913, 2933
Cottam, Richard W., 5860, 5886, 6202
Cotter, Michael, 5014
Countryman, Edward, 3381, 6106
Coupland, Reginald, 3476
Courrière, Yves, 5463
Cousin, Bernard, 6008
Coverdale, John F., 3041
Cowan, Paul, 3607
Cowell, F.R., 1488

Cowie, Leonard W., 1672
Coyle, Wallace, 3277, 3425, 3507
Coyne, John R., 3651
Crahan, Margaret E., 1275, 4187
Crane, Robert I., 4466-67
Crankshaw, Edward, 2217
Cranston, Maurice, 1787, 1818, 3652-53
Craven, Wesley F., 3234
Crawley, Eduardo, 4353
Creelman, James, 4075
Crétineau-Joly, J., 668, 2131
Crew, Phyllis Mack, 1572
Croce, Benedetto, 965
Crocker, Lester G., 1828, 1995
Crook, David, 4495
Crook, Isabel, 4495
Crook, W.H., 2477
Crosland, C.A.R., 1125
Cross, James Eliot, 433
Cross, Truman B., 2630
Crossley, Robert N., 5981
Crossman, R.H.S., 1126
Crough, Colin, 754
Crow, Jeffrey J., 3535
Crowley, James B., 4786
Crozier, Brian, 122, 401
Cruickshank, A.A., 1002
Cruse, Harold, 3744, 3761
Cullman, L., 4967
Cumberland, Charles C., 4016-19
Cumming, William F., 3536
Cummins, Ian, 5938
Cunha, Euclides da, 4380
Cunhal, Alvaro, 3183, 3198
Curran, Joseph M., 2934
Currey, Cecil B., 3330
Currie, Elliott, 19
Curtin, Philip, 5385
Curtis, Eugene, 2111
Curtis, Michael, 2482
Curwen, C.A., 4620
Cusack, David, 4297
Cushing, Harry A., 3554

Dabney, Virginius, 3428
Dahl, Robert A., 238, 1387
Dakin, Douglas, 1968
Dalrymple, Willard, 3622
Daly, William T., 1235
Dan, Theodore, 2604
Dandler, Jorge, 3864
Dangerfield, George, 2935, 5159
Daniels, Robert V., 1190, 1357, 2596, 2605, 2631-32, 2675-77, 2752
Dann, John C., 3243
Danziger, Raphael, 5464
Darby, John, 2936
Darrell, Trent, 578

Dash, Leon, 5580
Datta, Dhirendra Mohan, 5244
Daubier, Jean, 4968
Davenport, Gary T., 2914
Davids, Jules, 4611
Davidson, Basil, 5348, 5386-87, 5430, 5548, 5567-68, 5581, 5593, 5616-21, 5640, 5733, 6192
Davidson, James West, 376
Davidson, Philip, 3537
Davidson, Sara, 4279
Davies, Alun, 688, 2012
Davies, Godfrey, 1594, 1609, 1733, 1744
Davies, James C., 20-22, 73, 123, 227, 239, 479
Davies, John Paton, 3184
Davies, K.G., 3244
Davin, Delia, 4719
Davis, Angela Y., 3728
Davis, Burke, 3429
Davis, Daniel S., 6093
Davis, Fei-Ling, 4496
Davis, Harold E., 3807, 3865-66
Davis, Horace B., 966, 1127, 2896
Davis, John A., 2497
Davis, Richard, 1422, 2915
Davison, Roderic Hollett, 5299, 5788
Dawson, Christopher, 1411, 2083
Dawson, Philip, 1900, 2008, 2084
Day, Richard B., 2821
Deak, Istvan, 2366, 2420-21, 2424, 2871
Deakin, F.W., 1191
Dean, Thomas, 1065, 1290
Deas, Malcolm, 3812
Debo, Richard K., 2678
DeBonis, J., 5448
Debray, Regis, 4242, 4265-68, 4298
Decalo, S., 5388
deCastro, Josue, 3883, 4381
Decker, Jane Elizabeth, 3130
Decouflé, André, 124
deCrespigny, Anthony, 305, 619
Deeb, Marius K., 5677
DeFrancis, John, 4864
DeGiorgio, Fulvio, 2290
DeGrazia, Sebastian, 337
Degrood, David H., 1436
De Jong, Rudolf, 816-17
Dekemejian, R. Hrair, 5835
Delaney, Robert Finley, 1192
DeLeon, Daniel, 125
DeLeon, David, 833
DeLigt, Barthelemy, 627
Dellinger, David, 628
Delpar, Helen, 4393
DeLuna, Frederick A., 2384
DelVasto, Lanza, 629
Delyusin, Lev, 4865

Demaris, Ovid, 579
Deme, László, 2422-23
Demier, Francis, 6062
Deming, Barbara, 620, 630
Denholm, Anthony, 2385
Denisoff, R. Serge, 126, 205
Denitch, Bogdan Denis, 3092, 3094
Dennis, Lawrence, 402
Denton, Charles F., 3813
Depauw, Linda Grant, 3425
Depelchin, Jacques, 5349
DePoncins, Leon V., 1236
Derfler, Leslie, 1128
DeRomilly, Jacqueline, 1477
Derry, John, 3477
Desai, A.R., 5205
DeSaint-Armand, Imbert, 2344
Deschuytter, Joseph, 6009, 6043
DeSeve, Micheline, 3785
DesForges, Roger V., 4660
Desfosses, Helen, 1129
Detweiler, Robert, 1388
Deutsch, Karl, 400, 1255
Deutscher, Isaac, 925, 1193, 1358, 2633, 2679, 2814, 2822-24
DeValera, Eamonn, 2937
Devanesen, Chandran D.S., 5245
Devereux, Robert, 5792
Devillers, Philippe, 4866
Devlin, Kevin, 4211
DeVylder, Stefan, 4327
Dewart, Leslie, 4188
Dhawan, Gopinath, 5246
D'Hoop, Jean-Marie, 4823
Diamond, Martin, 3363
Dickerson, O.M., 3331
Dickinson, G. Lowes, 2218
Diederich, Bernard, 6147
Diggins, John P., 3654
Dillon, E.J., 4020
Dimock, Martha McHutchison, 3273
Dingeman, Jim, 6191
Dinges, John, 4299
Dingle, E.J., 4645, 4661
Dion, Leon, 3785
Dipadova, Theodore A., 2054
Dippel, Horst, 1858, 5960
Dirlik, Arif, 659, 4474-75, 4720
Disch, Arne, 689
Dittmer, Lowell, 4824, 4913, 4926, 4969
Diwakar, Ranganath R., 5181, 5247
Dix, Robert H., 4398
Djilas, Milovan, 1194, 2219, 3095
Djordjevic, Dimitrije, 6053-54
Doan Van Toai, 5023
Dobson, Christopher, 580
Dodge, Guy H., 1829
Doeppers, Daniel F., 5313
Dohrn, Bernardine, 3601

Dolgoff, Samuel, 880, 3042
Dombroski, Robert S., 2199
Domes, Jürgen, 4497, 5000, 5012
Domínguez, Jorge I., 3951, 4144, 4192
Dominique, Michel, 6010
Donaghay, Marie, 1945
Donaldson, Robert H., 1237
Doolin, Dennis J., 755
Doolin, Paul Rice, 1589
Dormon, James H., 3315
Dorr, Rheta Childe, 2571
Dorrill, William F., 4927, 4970
Dorschner, John, 4145
Doty, C. Stewart, 670
Douglas, Jack, 723
Douglas, William O., 127, 3209
Douglass, Elisha P., 3430
Douglass, James W., 240
Dowd, David L., 2220
Downton, James V., 1238
Doyle, Edward, 6170
Doyle, William, 1954, 1965-66
Dozier, Robort R., 1848
Drachkovitch, Milorad M., 967-69
Draper, Hal, 756, 970
Draper, Theodore, 3762, 4129, 4219-20
Drescher, Seymour, 2295
Dreyer, Frederick, 2141-42, 2154
Drinnon, Richard, 887
Drucker, H.M., 306
Dubois, Jules, 4221
Duff, Ernest A., 3867
Duff, Peggy, 3131
Duffett, W.E., 5206
Duggett, Michael, 926
Duhet, Paule-Marie, 6011
Duignan, Peter, 5332-33, 5389, 5744
Duiker, William J., 4635, 5054-56
Dukes, Paul, 6078
Dukore, Bernard F., 1320
Dulles, John W.F., 4021, 4382
Duly, Leslie Clement, 1258, 5734
Dumont, René, 1130, 4146
Dunayevskaya, Raya, 258, 1437
Duncan, W. Raymond, 3868
Duncanson, Dennis J., 5057
Dung, Van Tien, 5058
Dunlop, John B., 2221
Dunn, D. Elwood, 5594
Dunn, H.H., 4085
Dunn, John, 128, 1423
Dunn, John M., 1788
Dupee, F.W., 2842
Dupré, Louis, 971
Dupuy, R. Ernest, 3274, 3449
Dupuy, Trevor N., 3274
Durden-Smith, Jo, 3763
Dutt, Gargi, 4971
Dutt, R. Palme, 273, 2766

Author-Editor Index / 429

Dutt, V.P., 4971
Duveau, Georges, 2345, 2450
Dworkin, A.P., 1338
Dyer, Nancy A., 4819
Dynes, Russell R., 484
Dziewanowski, M.K., 2680, 3525

Earnshaw, Graham, 6168
Easterbrook, David L., 5334
Eastlake, William, 1321
Eastman, Lloyd E., 4721
Eastman, Max, 972, 1131, 1389, 2222, 2815, 2825
Eastwood, J., 2346
Easwaran, Eknath, 5248
Eaton, Jeanette, 5249
Ebenstein, William, 1195-96
Eberstein, Alfred, freiherr von, 2409
Ebert, Theodor, 5189
Ebinger, Charles K., 5569
Ebon, Martin, 4244
Ebony, Editors of, 3764
Eckstein, Harry, 23, 27, 129, 399
Eckstein, Susan, 3814, 3869, 4057
Eddy, W.H.C., 973
Edie, Carolyn A., 1750
Edelman, Robert, 2681
Edelmann, Alexander T., 3870
Edwardes, Michael, 4556-57, 5160-61, 5207
Edwards, Harry, 3729
Edwards, Jill, 3043
Edwards, Lyford P., 24, 130
Edwards, Owen Dudley, 6107
Edwards, Ruth Dudley, 2938
Edwards, Stewart, 2436, 2451
Edwards, Tony, 4485
Egbert, Donald Drew, 1107
Egerton, H.E., 3355
Egnal, Marc, 3414
Egret, Jean, 1955
Ehrenreich, Barbara, 758
Ehrenreich, John, 758
Ehrmann, Henry, 3132
Ehrmann, Jacques, 1322
Eichel, Lawrence, 759
Eidelberg, Philip Gabriel, 2223
Eimerl, Sarel, 1901
Eisen, Jonathan, 724
Eisenberg, A., 631
Eisenstadt, S.N., 25, 1132, 1350, 1390, 1438, 1652
Eisenstein, Elizabeth L., 1946, 2000, 2224
Elegant, Robert S., 4722, 4772, 4928
Elkin, Boris, 2634
Elkins, Stanley, 3426, 3431
Ellemers, J.E., 1565
Ellenburg, Stephen, 1830
Elliott, Emory, 3495

Elliott, J.H., 1502, 1809-10
Elliott-Bateman, Michael, 403, 2225
Ellis, Gene, 1359
Ellis, Geoffrey, 1884
Ellis, John, 403, 419, 434
Ellis, Joseph J., 3538
Ellul, Jacques, 131, 496, 3133
Ellwood, Charles A., 262
Ellwood, Ralph C., 2682
El-Rayyes, Riad, 435
Elton, Godfrey, 1987, 2226, 2906
Eltzbacher, Paul, 834
Elvin, Mark, 4498
Elwis, P.B., 2908
Embree, Ainslee T., 5162
Emerson, Rupert, 5765
Emin, Ahmed, 5300
Engel, Barbara, 5953
Engels, Friedrich, 497, 1098, 1556, 2227, 2465
Engle, Paul, 3510
Enos, John L., 4147
Epstein, Israel, 4723, 4777
Epstein, Jason, 3655
Erasmus, Charles J., 4115
Ericson, Edward E., Jr., 760
Erikson, Erik H., 5250
Erlich, John, 761
Erlich, Susan, 761
Ernst, Joseph A., 3382, 3414, 6108
Esch, P.A.M. van Der, 3044
Esedebe, P. Olisanwuche, 5350, 6179-80
Esherick, Joseph W., 4662, 4742, 4825
Esler, Anthony, 2312, 3656
Esmein, Jean, 4972
Esquenazi-Mayo, Roberto, 3798
Estañol, Jorge Vera, 4072
Ettinger, Elzbieta, 2887
Ettinghausen, Richard, 5785
Etzold, Thomas H., 4805
Eubanks, Cecil L., 915, 1091
Eudin, S.J., 4643
Evans, Alona E., 581
Evans, David P., 5965
Evans, Elizabeth, 3511
Evans, Ernest, 582
Evans, Les, 3165, 4300
Evans, Michael, 974
Evans, Peter, 6181
Evans, R.E., 3450
Ewing, Thomas E., 4646
Eyck, Frank, 2347, 2410
Ezergailis, A., 2228

Faber, Karl-Georg, 2411
Fabricio, Roberto, 4145
Fage, J.D., 5390, 5406
Fagen, Richard R., 26, 4280
Fagg, John Edwin, 3871

Fairbairn, Geoffrey, 4587
Fairbank, John K., 4468, 4499-500, 4697, 4826
Falcoff, Mark, 4281
Falcón, Romana, 3991, 6136
Falk, Richard A., 228
Fall, Bernard B., 4603, 5059-61, 5099
Fallaci, Oriana, 4260, 5861-62
Fanon, Frantz, 1336-37, 5520-23
Far, K.H., 4909
Farber, Samuel, 4173
Fariqi, Khwaja A., 5163
Faris, Ralph M., 975
Farjenel, F., 4647
Farmer, Paul, 2376
Farnsworth, Beatrice, 1302
Farrell, Robert, 1200
Farsoun, Samih K., 5793
Fasel, George, 2348, 2377
Fathi, Asghar, 5863
Fatima, S., 4567
Faucheux, Marcel, 2132
Faúndez, Julio, 4282, 6145
Fauvet, Paul, 3185
Fay, Bernard, 1521, 1859
Feagin, Joe R., 498
Fedyshyn, O.S., 2864
Fehrenbacher, Don E., 3269
Feierabend, Ivo K., 264, 457, 499
Feierabend, Rosalind L., 264, 457, 499
Feigelson, Naomi, 3657
Feinberg, Richard E., 4301
Feinstein, Alan, 5391
Feis, Herbert, 4814
Feit, E., 4213
Fejto, François, 2349, 3113
Feld, M.D., 1503
Feldman, Arnold S., 27
Feldman, Gerald D., 1516
Feldman, Herbert, 4588
Fenn, Charles, 5100
Fennessy, R.R., 1392
Ferguson, E. James, 3275
Ferguson, J. Halcro, 3872, 4193
Fernandes, Florestan, 4383
Ferns, H.S., 4358
Fernsworth, Lawrence, 3045
Ferreira, Eduardo, 5665
Ferrero, G., 1902
Ferro, Marc, 414, 2545, 2635, 2683
Fessehatzion, Tekie, 5689
Fest, Joachim C., 2993
Festa-McCormick, Diana, 2378
Fetscher, Irving, 976
Feuer, Lewis S., 28, 307, 762, 1034
Feuerwerker, Albert, 4476, 4501, 4621, 4827
Field, Henry Martyn, 1860

Fieldhouse, D.K., 6182
Fields, Rona M., 3199
Figgis, Darrell, 2939
Figner, Vera, 2229
Filatov, V.P., 6084
Fincher, John, 4648
Fine, Ben, 977
Finer, Samuel Edward, 338, 420
Finlay, George, 2855
Finn, James, 632
First, Ruth, 5682
Firth, C.H., 1610, 1714
Fisch, Harold, 5810
Fischer, Ernst, 978
Fischer, George, 2510, 2644
Fischer, John, 2027
Fischer, Louis, 2767, 5251-52
Fischer, Michael M.J., 5887
Fischer-Galati, Stephen, 690, 6054
Fišera, Vladimir, 3158, 6055
Fisher, Eugene M., 5811
Fisher, Harold Henry, 1197, 2565
Fisher, L.E., 3952, 4426
Fisher, Sydney George, 3451
Fisher, Sydney N., 5812
Fitch, John S., III, 339
Fitzgerald, C.P., 4724-26, 4867
Fitzgerald, E.V.K., 4424
Fitz Gerald, Frances, 5062
Fitzgibbon, Russell H., 3815-16, 4130
Fitzlyon, Kyril, 2546
Fitzpatrick, David, 2940
Fitzpatrick, John C., 3539
Fitzpatrick, Sheila, 2684
Fizaine, Jean-Claude, 6063
Flacks, Richard, 725-28, 742, 784
Flaissier, Sabine, 1933
Flakser, David, 979
Flanigan, William H., 458
Fleisher, Helmut, 980
Fleming, Donald, 465
Fleming, Marie, 835
Fleming, Peter, 4636
Fleming, Thomas, 3276
Fletcher, Anthony, 1522
Fletcher, Roger, 1110
Flexner, James T., 3432
Flores Caballero, Romeo, 671, 3953
Florinsky, Michael T., 2547, 2685
Floyd, David, 2511
Fluharty, Vernon Lee, 4399
Flynn, Peter, 4384
Fogelman, Edwin, 458
Fogelson, Robert M., 500-01, 3765
Foley, John P., 3569
Foltz, William J., 400
Foner, Eric, 3587
Foner, Philip S., 3730

Footman, David, 2686-87
Forbis, William H., 5888
Ford, Franklin L., 1885, 2005
Foreign Policy Association, 538
Foreman, James, 3731
Forman, James D., 836, 1133, 1198, 2994
Foronda, Marceline A., Jr., 5314
Forrest, Alan, 1975, 6012
Forstenzer, Thomas R., 2386
Forster, Robert, 1523, 1571, 1586, 1809, 2003, 2006, 2168, 2182
Forsythe, Dennis, 5492
Fort, Gilberto V., 4122
Fortuny, José Manuel, 3817
Foster, Julian, 719, 728-29, 744, 763, 3748
Fourquin, Guy, 1493
Fowler, William M., Jr., 3277, 3425, 3507
Fox, George, 660
Foy, Colm, 6194
Fraina, Louis C., 1134
France, Anatole, 2085
Franda, Marcus W., 5756
Frank, Andre Gunder, 3873
Frank, Joseph, 1738
Franke, Wolfgang, 4502
Frankel, Boris, 927
Frankel, Harry, 3557
Frankle, Robert, 1751
Franklin, J.H., 1789
Franqui, Carlos, 4179
Franz, Günther, 1557-58
Fraser, Antonia, 1715
Fraser, Ronald, 3046
Frazee, Charles A., 2850
Freeman, Michael, 3, 2143-44, 6050
Freemantle, A., 4880
French, Allen P., 1673
Frey, Linda, 2085
Frey, Marsha, 2085
Fried, Albert, 1109
Friedel, Frank, 3226
Friedland, Elaine A., 5595
Friedland, William H., 5392
Friedman, Edward, 1372, 4766
Friedrich, Carl J., 132, 228, 230, 287, 332, 923, 1348, 2292
Fritz, Jean, 3433
Frolic, B. Michael, 4811, 4929
Frölich, Paul, 2888
Fromm, Erich, 308
Fry, John, 3713
Fryer, D.W., 5132
Fuentes, Carlos, 4086
Fuks, A., 1473
Fuller, J.F.C., 5208
Fülöp-Miller, René, 1393, 2606
Fulton, Richard M., 6109

Funck-Brentano, Frantz, 1969
Fund for the Republic, 1166
Fung, Edmund S.K., 4649
Furet, François, 1903-04, 2065, 6013
Fursenko, A.A., 1360
Furtado, Celso, 3874
Fusi, Juan Pablo, 3036

Gabriel, Phyllis S., 1361
Gage, Nicholas, 5864
Gall, Norman, 4237, 4283
Gallaher, John G., 2387
Gallo, Ezequiel, 4359
Gallo, Max, 2112
Galtung, Johan, 459
Galula, David, 672
Gamson, William A., 133
Gandhi, Mohandas K., 633, 5253-59
Gandy, Clara I., 2139
Gandy, Ross, 4024
Gann, Lewis, 436, 5333, 5389, 5744
Garaudy, Roger, 981
Garces, Joan E., 4294
García Basauri, Mercedes, 6094
García Márquez, Gabriel, 4284
Gardiner, S.R., 1595, 1611-13, 1716-17
Gardner, George H., 5790
Garibaldi, Giuseppe, 2498
Garratt, G.T., 5178
Garrett, Clark, 377
Garrett, Michell B., 1956
Garson, G. David, 729
Garvey, J.E., 4790
Gasster, Michael, 4663
Gaulton, Richard, 4568
Gauthier, Florence, 6014
Gaxotte, Pierre, 1905
Gay, Peter, 1135, 1813, 2066, 3364
Geertz, Clifford, 1259
Geismar, Peter, 5493, 5525
Gelder, Stuart, 4727
Gellner, Ernest, 282
Gemkow, Heinrich, 982, 1099
Gendron, François, 2028
Gendzier, Irene L., 5494-95, 5526
Genovese, Eugene D., 3954
Gentles, Ian, 5990
Gentz, F., 1394
George, Brian T., 4650
George, C.H., 2230
George, Margaret, 2047
Geras, Norman, 2889
Gerassi, John, 1439-40, 3818, 3883, 4245, 4400
Gerberding, William P., 3658
Gerhart, Gail, 5745
Gerhart, John D., 5351
Gerlach, Larry, 3515, 3540

Gershoy, Leo, 1861, 1906-07
Gervasio, Antonio, 3186
Geschwender, James A., 29, 3766
Gettleman, Marvin E., 3217, 5063-64
Gettleman, Susan, 5064
Getzler, Israel, 2531, 2636
Geyl, Pieter, 1573-74
Ghosh, P.C., 5260
Ghosh, Prodyot Kumar, 6153
Gibbon, Peter, 2941
Gibbs, Jack, 3047
Gibney, Frank, 3103
Gibson, Charles, 3943
Gibson, Richard, 5393
Gibson, W., 2452
Gidney, J.B., 2573
Gil, Federico A., 3920, 4168, 4302-03
Gilam, Abraham, 2400
Gilbert, Alan, 983
Gilbert, F., 30
Gilio, Maria Esther, 4338
Gilkes, Patrick, 5690-92, 5716
Gill, Graeme J., 2688
Gillespie, David, 66
Gillespie, Joan, 5465
Gillin, Donald G., 4477
Gillis, John R., 2183
Gillispie, G.C., 1800
Gilly, Adolfo, 4180
Gilmore, Susan, 776
Gilpin, W. Clark, 378
Ginsborg, Paul, 2426, 2428
Gipson, Lawrence H., 3332-33
Girault de Coursac, Pierrette, 6048
Girling, John L.S., 1441, 4589
Gist, N.P., 1338
Gitlin, Todd, 3659
Gittings, John, 4238, 4778
Gjerstad, Ole, 5582, 5611, 5642
Glantz, Michael H., 5622
Glazer, Nathan, 764
Glazier, Kenneth M., 5335-36
Glazunov, Y., 5024
Gleason, Abbott, 799
Godechot, Jacques, 673, 1849, 1862, 1908, 1957, 2133, 5996, 6015
Godfrey, James Logan, 2113
Godoy, Jose F., 4076
Godwin, William, 892
Goertz, Hans-Jürgen, 1547
Golan, Galia, 3166
Golden, Richard M., 1585, 5987
Goldenberg, Boris, 4131, 4194
Goldendach, David B., 984
Golder, Frank A., 2528
Goldfrank, Walter L., 1368, 3992
Goldie, L.F.E., 539
Goldman, Emma, 888-89, 2572

Goldman, Merle, 4930
Goldman, Peter, 3767
Goldstein, Steven M., 4704
Goldston, Robert, 2689, 3048, 3452, 3768, 4728, 5065, 5261
Goldwater, Walter, 781
Goldwert, Marvin, 4360
Golin, Steve, 2184
Gombin, Richard, 5917
Gómez Cafarenel, José, 3707
Gonzáles, Luis J., 4246
Gonzalez, Edward, 4222
Gooch, G.P., 1655, 2334
Good, Robert C., 5746
Goode, Stephen, 583, 3660
Goodey, Chris, 2690
Goodman, Mitchell, 3661
Goodman, Paul, 134, 818
Goodrich, Carter, 4101
Goodsell, Charles T., 4413
Goodsell, James Nelson, 3868, 4223
Goodspeed, D.J., 340
Goodwin, Albert, 1395, 1863, 1875, 1886, 1909, 2004
Gordon, David C., 5466, 5766
Gordon, Leonard A., 4553
Gorky, Maxim, 2607, 2768
Gorrow, Bernard J., 1362
Gorz, André, 1136
Gosselin, Louis L.T., 1958
Gosztony, Peter, 3109
Gotesky, Rubin, 1315
Gott, Richard, 3819, 3875
Gottfried, Paul, 379, 2335
Gottheil, F.M., 5496
Gottschalk, Louis, 31, 65, 1864-65, 1910, 2041, 2816
Goubert, Pierre, 5988
Gough, Hugh, 6016
Gough, John, 1790
Gough, Kathleen, 4590
Gough, Robert, 6110
Gould, James A., 309
Gouldner, Alvin W., 1226, 1478
Goulet, Denis, 32
Gouré, Leon, 4290
Gourfinkle, Nina, 2769
Goylisolo, Juan, 4212
Grady, Robert C., Jr., 1784
Graham, Hugh Davis, 21, 460, 474, 502
Graham, Lawrence S., 3200, 6096
Graham, Marcus, 1323
Graham, Richard, 3955
Graham, Robert, 5889
Graham, Ruth, 6017
Graham, W. Fred, 1524
Gramont, Sanche de, 3745, 4373
Grampp, William D., 3526

Gramsci, Antonio, 2499
Granier, Jean, 6018
Granqvist, Hans, 5006
Gray, Alexander, 1137
Gray, Jack, 4828, 4868, 4973
Grayson, George W., Jr., 3820
Grayson, J.C., 5986
Greaves, C. Desmond, 2942
Greaves, Richard L., 1504
Greeman, Richard, 2438
Green, Frederick C., 1831
Green, Gil, 584, 800, 3201, 4148
Green, Martin, 5262
Greenberg, Martin H., 527
Greene, Evarts Boutell, 3408
Greene, Felix, 135
Greene, Jack P., 1523, 1571, 1586, 1809, 2168, 3235–36, 3245, 3278–79, 3316–18, 3334, 3397–98, 3503, 3541, 3579, 6111
Greene, Thomas H., 1396
Greenlaw, Ralph W., 1911–12
Greenstein, F.I., 478
Greenup, Leonard, 4361
Greenup, Ruth, 4361
Greer, Donald, 2086, 2114
Gregg, Richard B., 634, 5263
Gregoire, R., 3145
Gregor, A. James, 310, 801, 985, 1363, 4651
Gregory, David, 928
Gregory, Dick, 5865
Gregory, James S., 4622
Greig, Ian, 1442
Grieb, Kenneth J., 4092
Grieder, Jerome B., 4503
Grierson, Edward, 1575
Grierson, Philip 2560
Griewank, Karl, 136
Griffin, Charles C., 3794, 3945, 3956
Griffin, Patricia E., 4729
Griffith, J.A.G., 33
Griffith, Samuel B., II, 4779
Griffiths, Brian, 1443
Griffiths, Gordon, 1566
Grimes, Alan P., 311, 3365
Grimshaw, Allen D., 461
Grimwood-Jones, Diana, 5786
Grob, G.N., 3232
Grohs, G.K., 5497
Grose, Clyde, 1745
Gross, Feliks, 137, 241, 312, 1239
Groth, Alexander J., 313, 1240
Gruber, Helmut, 1174
Gruening, Ernest, 4022
Grundy, Kenneth W., 503, 5394
Gudoshnikov, L.M., 5013
Guéhenno, Jean, 1832

Guerin, Daniel, 837
Guerman, Mikhail, 2691
Guevara, Ernesto Che, 4239, 4247–51
Guha, Arun C., 5209–10
Guillermaz, Jacques, 4767
Guizot, François, 1664
Gungwu, Wang, 4504
Gunter, Elizabeth Ellington, 6057
Gupta, Maya, 5190
Gupta, Vijay, 5693
Gurian, Waldemar, 2608–09
Gurley, John G., 1397
Gurr, Ted Robert, 21, 34, 138, 264, 462, 477, 499, 502, 504–05, 1364–65, 1412, 1424, 2145
Gusfield, Joseph R., 139, 730
Gush, George, 1614
Guthier, Steven L., 2863
Gutierrez, Alberto Ostra, 4114
Gutierrez, Jose A., 3218
Gutteridge, George H., 3478
Gutting, Gary, 5966
Guttman, Allen, 3049
Guzman, German, 4401
Gwynn, Denis Rolleston, 2943–44
Gyorgy, Andrew, 1199

Haan, N., 720
Haas, Arthur, 5974
Hachey, Thomas, 1324
Hacker, Frederick J., 585
Hacker, Louis M., 3319, 3415
Hackl, Ursula, 5972
Haddad, George M., 5813
Haffner, Sebastian, 2890
Hagopian, Mark N., 140, 314
Hahm, Ben, 4272
Hahn, Harlan, 498
Hail, William J., 4623
Haim, Sylvia G., 5898
Haimson, Leopold H., 2548, 2610
Haithcox, John P., 5211
Hakes, Jay E., 341
Halasz de Beky, I.L., 3107
Halberstam, David, 5101
Hale, Dennis, 753
Hale, Oron J., 2231
Hales, E.E.Y., 1284
Hall, A. Rupert, 1801
Hall, D.G.E., 6154
Hall, J.C., 1833
Hall, Linda B., 3993, 6137–38
Hall, Walter Phelps, 2232
Halle, L.J., 315
Haller, William, 1596, 1656, 1733
Halliday, Fred, 1366, 5866–67, 5890
Halperin, E., 586
Halperin, Maurice, 4224–25

Halperin, Morton H., 4829
Halperin, Samuel William, 2891
Halperin-Donghi, Tulio, 3876, 4362
Halpern, Manfred, 35, 1348, 5814
Hamalainen, Pekka K., 2859, 2861
Hamburg, G.M., 2505
Hamburger, Joseph, 2233
Hamerow, Theodore S., 2234, 2336, 2401, 2412
Hamill, H.M., Jr., 3957
Hamilton, Charles V., 3725
Hamilton, David, 5694
Hamlin, D.L.B., 3837
Hammen, Oscar J., 2350
Hammond, N., 277, 1229
Hammond, Thomas T., 1167, 1200, 2770
Hamnett, Brian R., 6134
Hampden-Turner, Charles, 802
Hampson, Norman, 1886, 1913, 1976, 2042, 2115
Han, Sin Fong, 5143
Handal, Schafik, 3821
Handelman, Howard, 4128
Handlin, Mary, 3366
Handlin, Oscar, 3366
Handman, Max, 229
Hangen, Welles, 2235
Hanke, Lewis, 3998, 4101, 4103
Hanley, J., 506
Hanley, Thomas, 3504
Hanna, Sami A., 5790
Hanna, William John, 731
Hanrahan, Gene Z., 437, 3985, 4832
Hansen, E., 2478
Hansen, Emmanuel, 5485, 5498–99, 5527
Hansen, Joseph, 2826, 3877, 4149
Hanser, Richard, 2995
Hansis, Randall, 3994
Han Suyin, 4869–70
Harbeson, John W., 5685, 5695–98
Harcave, Sidney S., 2512
Hardacre, Paul H., 1677, 1702
Harding, Neil, 2771
Hardy, Jack, 3280
Haring, C.E., 3822
Harlow, Ralph V., 3558
Harmon, Ronald, 4371
Harrington, Michael, 1138
Harris, Christina P., 5840
Harris, David, 3608
Harris, George S., 5301
Harris, H.S., 2067
Harris, Janet, 765
Harris, Jean-Pierre, 6019
Harris, Louis K., 3756, 3878
Harris, Nigel, 1398, 4791

Harris, Richard, 4252, 5767
Harris, Richard, 4450
Harrison, J.F.C., 380
Harrison, James P., 4768, 4802, 6171
Harrison, Royden, 2453
Harrison, Royden, 2453
Harsgor, M., 3202
Hart, John M., 838, 4058–59
Hart, Thomas G., 4730
Hartmut, T., 141
Hartog, Hendrik, 6112
Hartogs, Renatus, 507
Hartz, Louis, 3383
Harvey, Albert, 5577
Harvey, Bernard, 1793
Harvey, Robert, 6097
Hasbrouck, Alfred, 4356
Hasegawa, Tsuyoshi, 2532–34, 6075
Haskins, Caryl, 1802
Haskins, James, 142
Hastings, Adrian, 5352, 5596
Hatch, John, 5395
Hatch, Nathan O., 381
Hatto, Arthur, 36–37
Hauberg, C.A., 4102
Haupt, Georges, 2567
Haupt, Heinz-Gerhard, 6071
Hauser, George, 5666
Hauss, Charles, 3146
Havel, Hippolyte, 839
Hawgood, John A., 2402
Hawke, David, 3392, 3588
Hay, Edward, 2945
Haycock, Ronald, 421
Hayden, Tom, 3602, 3609
Hayes, Carlton J.H., 1261, 2236
Hayes, J.J., 2396
Hayes, T. Wilson, 1739
Haywood, Max, 1325
Hazard, Paul, 1996
Hazen, Charles Downer, 1914
Hazlett, J. Stephen, 2185
Headrick, Daniel R., 2435
Heald, Edward T., 2573
Healy, Ann E., 2513
Heath, Dwight B., 4103, 4115
Heath, G. Louis, 3732, 3769
Heaton, John Wesley, 1489
Heder, Stephen, 4569
Hedlin, Myron W., 2637
Heer, Friedrich, 2237
Heer, N., 2589
Heggoy, Alf Andrew, 5445, 5467
Heiden, Konrad, 2996
Heiden, Linda, 5699
Heilbroner, Robert L., 986
Heimann, Peter M., 1794

Author-Editor Index / 435

Heimert, Alan, 3505
Heinl, Nancy G., 3958
Heinl, Robert D., Jr., 3958
Hejzlar, Zdenek, 3159
Heller, Michael, 2753
Hellman, Judith A., 4023
Hellman, Ronald G., 3857
Helms, Cynthia, 5891
Henderson, A.J., 1850
Henderson, Ernest F., 2087
Henderson, Lawrence W., 5583, 5666
Henderson, Martha T., 4689
Henderson, Peter V.N., 6139
Henderson, William, 4544
Henderson, William Darryl, 5066
Henderson, W.O., 1100
Hendin, Herbert, 732
Henissart, Paul, 5468
Hennessy, C.A.M., 4169
Henningham, Stephen, 6155
Henretta, James A., 3479
Henriksen, Thomas H., 5549–53, 5597–98, 5607
Hensman, Charles R., 1444, 4677
Hentoff, Nat, 3624–25
Hepburn, A.C., 2909, 2978
Herberle, Rudolf, 143, 2997
Hercules, Frank, 3770
Hérissay, Jacques, 6044
Herman, Valentine, 5924
Hermassi, Elbaki, 1367
Herod, Charles C., 3746, 6129
Herr, Richard, 1811, 2296
Herrick, Paul B., Jr., 3823
Hervey, Maurice H., 3879
Herzog, Jesús Silva, 3995
Hexter, J.H., 1639, 1665
Heyman, Neil M., 2817
Heymann, Frederick, 1494
Hibbert, Christopher, 1915, 5164
Hibbs, Douglas A., Jr., 508
Hicks, Granville, 1445
Hicks, John, 2454
Higginbotham, Don, 3453–54
Higgins, E.L., 1877
Higgins, W. Robert, 3455
Higham, John, 3234
Higonnet, Patrice L.R., 2068, 6020–21
Hildebrand, George C., 5119
Hill, Christopher, 1603, 1615, 1640, 1657–58, 1669, 1684, 1718–19,1728, 1740, 2772
Hill, Larry D., 4066
Hilliker, Grant, 4429
Hillquit, Morris, 2238
Hills, F., 361
Hilton, Major-General Richard, 5165

Hindley, Donald, 5133
Hiniker, Paul J., 4974
Hinshaw, Cecil E., 5212
Hinton, Harold C., 4910, 6156
Hinton, William, 4808, 4812, 4975–76
Hirsch, Herbert, 509
Hirsch, Walter, 86
Hirschfield, Burt, 4637
Hirst, David, 587
Hirst, Derek, 1630
Hiwer, Addis, 5717
Hoang Van Chi, 5067
Hoare, Q., 2499
Hobbs, Cecil C., 4463
Hobbes, Thomas, 1600–01
Hobsbawm, Eric J., 144, 382, 705, 2239, 4394, 5939
Ho Chi Minh, 5102–03
Hodges, Donald C., 1093, 3880–81, 4024, 4235, 4363, 5768
Hodges, Tony, 5570, 5623
Hodgkin, Thomas, 5068, 5794
Hoerder, Dirk, 3399, 3409, 6113
Hoeven, Johan Van Der, 987
Hoffer, Eric, 145–46, 3210
Hoffman, Abbie, 3610–12
Hoffman, George W., 3096
Hoffman, John, 988
Hoffman, Robert, 840, 908
Hofheinz, Roy, Jr., 4803
Hofstadter, Dan, 5841–43
Hofstadter, Richard, 452
Ho Kan-Chih, 4731
Holborn, Hajo, 2998
Holcombe, Arthur N., 4505
Hollingworth, Clare, 5795
Holmes, George, 1495
Holmes, T. Rice, 5166
Holorenshaw, H., 1741
Holt, Edgar, 2429, 2946
Holt, Peter, 2280
Holtmann, Robert B., 2088
Holzapfel, Kurt, 6022
Holzer, Hans, 3542
Homan, Roger, 6203
Honderich, Ted, 511
Hood, James N., 2069–70
Hook, Sidney, 463, 989–91, 1201
Hooker, James R., 3771
Hooker, Richard J., 3281
Hoover, Calvin B., 38, 2999
Hope, Marjorie, 635, 3662, 4395–96
Hopkins, James K., 5919
Hopkins, P., 267
Hopper, Rex D., 39, 137
Hordynski, Jozef, 2329
Horecky, Paul, 2561

Horne, Alistair, 2455–56, 4304, 5469
Horowitz, David, 147–48, 3626, 3663
Horowitz, H., 1752
Horowitz, Irving Louis, 242, 841, 2483, 3882–83, 4150, 4385
Horvat, Branko, 5948
Horwitz, R.H., 311
Horsburgh, H.J.N., 5264
Horward, Donald D., 2240
Hosford, David H., 1764
Hosmer, James K., 3559
Hottinger, Arnold, 5796
Hough, Richard A., 2514
Houn, Franklin W., 4792
Houtart, François, 3884
Hoveyda, Fereydoun, 5892
How, Julie, 4644
Howard, Dick, 992, 2899
Howard, Donald D., 1525
Howard, Harry N., 5302
Howard, Roger, 4871
Howe, Irving, 1139, 2827, 3664–65
Howe, John R., Jr., 1278, 3364, 3371, 3376
Howe, Russell Warren, 5396
Howe, Samuel Bridley, 2856
Howell, Roger, Jr., 1632, 1685
Howell, Thomas A., 5432
Howes, Robert C., 881
Hsia, Adrian, 4977
Hsiao, Gene T., 4931
Hsiao Tso-liang, 4732, 4773
Hsieh, Winston, 4642
Hsiung, James C., 4872, 4875
Hsüeh, Chün-tu, 4506–07, 4690–91, 4932
Hsuing, James C., 4508
Huang Sung Kang, 6157
Hubbard, Maryinez L., 5667
Huber, Thomas M., 6158
Huberman, Leo, 1140, 3840, 4151, 4269
Hu Chang-tu, 4509
Hu Chiao-mu, 4769
Hucker, Charles O., 4451–52
Hudson, G.F., 1202, 4591
Hudson, Rexford A., 4285
Hufton, Owen, 6023
Hughes, Merritt Y., 1730
Hughes, Richard T., 1668
Huizer, Gerrit, 3885
Hulbrook, Francis X., 3828
Hull, Richard W., 5735–36
Hulse, James W., 1141
Humbaraci, Arslan, 5470, 5561
Humphrey, Richard D., 2484
Humphreys, Robert A., 3417, 3795, 3886–87, 3944, 3959
Hunczak, Taras, 2865
Hunt, James D., 5265

Hunt, Lynn A., 1947–48, 1982, 2056, 2089
Hunt, Richard N., 993
Hunt, Robert Nigel Carew, 994, 1203
Hunter, Neale, 4997
Hunter, Robert, 149
Huntington, Samuel, 243, 464
Hunton, W. Alphaeus, 5353
Hussain, Mehmood, 5815
Hutchins, Francis G., 5266
Hutchings, Frank, 40
Hutchinson, David, 5167
Hutchinson, Martha Crenshaw, 540, 5471
Hutchinson, Paul, 1285
Hutchinson, Thomas, 3313
Hutson, James H., 3255, 3283, 3318, 3396, 3434, 3443, 3498, 3522
Hutton, Patrick H., 6056
Hutton, William H., 1559
Huyen, N. Khac, 5104
Hyams, Edward, 588, 1142, 1420
Hyes, Peter V., 2379
Hyman, Anthony, 5291
Hyndman, H.M., 1316
Hyslop, Beatrice, 1887, 2023

Ibanez, V. Blasco, 4025
Ibrahim, Youssef M., 5868
Idzerda, Stanley J., 1874, 2039, 3246
Iglitzin, Lynn B., 3666
I-Kua Chou, 4830
Ilardo, J., 631
Illich, Ivan, 41
Illick, Joseph E., 733
Ilyichov, L.F., 1101
Ingraham, Barton, 1399
Inkeles, A., 1259
Inlow, E. Burke, 5893
Inman, Samuel Guy, 4098
International Mass Media Research Center, 916
Isaacman, Allen F., 5599, 5608
Isaacs, Harold R., 1339, 4733
Isichei, Elizabeth, 5397
Isono, Fujiko, 2186, 4570
Israel, John, 4692, 4806, 5001
Israeli, Raphael, 5959
Issawi, Charles P., 5844
Ito, Kikuzo, 4933
Itoh, Hiroshi, 4568
Ives, E.W., 1616
Iyer, Raghavan, 5267

Jack, H.A., 5268
Jackman, R.W., 330
Jackson, D. Bruce, 3888
Jackson, Gabriel, 3050–53
Jackson, Sir Geoffrey, 4339
Jackson, George L., 3733

Jackson, Henry F., 5472, 5500
Jackson, James, 1446
Jackson, James C., 5132
Jackson, Karl D., 5134
Jackson, T.A., 2947
Jacob, J.R., 1690
Jacob, Margaret C., 362
Jacobs, Dan N., 1175, 4701
Jacobs, Harold, 3667
Jacobs, Jane, 3788
Jacobs, Paul, 3668
Jacobs, Wilbur R., 3247
Jaeggi, U., 150
Jaegher, Raymond J. de, 5007
James, C.L.R., 3960, 5398
James, Cyril L., 1413, 1916
James, Daniel, 4253-54
James, Margaret, 1647
James, Sydney V., 3496
Jameson, J. Franklin, 3410
Jancar, Barbara Wolfe, 1303
Jankowski, James P., 5845
Janos, Andrew C., 404, 2874
Jansen, G.H., 5816
Janzow, M. Theophil, 1548
Japhet, M., 331
Jarrett, Derek, 1867
Jaszi, Oscar, 2875
Jaurès, Jean, 1143, 1917
Jay, Douglas, 1144
Jaynes, Gregory, 5872
Jazani, Bizhan, 5894
Jeanneret, Georges, 2457
Jefferson, Thomas, 3568-69
Jeffreys-Jones, Rhodri, 465, 512
Jehlen, Myra J., 3527
Jellinek, Frank, 2458, 3054
Jencks, Christopher, 3627
Jenkins, Brian, 590, 5930
Jenkins, Robin, 1340
Jennings, Lawrence C., 2351
Jensen, DeLamar, 1581
Jensen, Merrill, 3237, 3248, 3282, 3384, 3421, 3543
Jen Yu-Wen, 4624
Jervis, William H., 2020
Jessop, Bob, 151
Jessup, F.W., 1633
Jezer, Martin, 42
Jezierski, John V., 3320
Jinadu, L. Adele, 5501-03, 6183
Joesten, Joachim, 5846
Joffe, Ellis, 4934
Johnpoll, Bernard K., 6099
Johnson, Chalmers, 152-53, 426, 438, 706, 4478, 4807, 4831, 4935
Johnson, Christopher H., 2313
Johnson, Dale L., 4305

Johnson, Douglas, 1918-19
Johnson, Gail, 5895
Johnson, John J., 342, 422-23, 3889, 3961
Johnson, Kenneth F., 3858
Johnson, Oakley C., 995
Johnson, Olive M., 154
Johnson, Richard, 3147
Johnson, Richard A., 3890
Johnson, Ross, 3097
Johnson, William Weber, 4026
Johnston, Robert H., 2241, 2692
Johnstone, Monty, 2439
Joll, James, 843
Jonas, A., 5108
Jónás, Paul, 3115
Jones, Alice Hanson, 3335
Jones, C., 4676
Jones, David R., 2638
Jones, Ernest, 1312
Jones, Francis P., 2948
Jones, Howard Mumford, 155, 3544
Jones, I. Deane, 1617, 1765
Jones, J.R., 1766-68
Jones, Kirby, 4228
Jones, Larry Eugene, 2187
Jones, Thomas M., 5973
Jones, W., 5700
Jordan, Donald A., 4510
Jordan, K., 5737
Jordan, W.K., 1691
Jordan, Z.A., 996
Jordon, David P., 2035
Joseph, Gilbert M., 3996
Joughin, Jean T., 2459
Joussain, André, 156
Jouvenel, Bertrand de, 157
Jubran, Glenn M., 5817
Judson, Margaret A., 1659, 1692
Judt, Tony, 2242
Jumper, Roy, 5015
Jureidini, Paul A., 405
Jussila, Osmo, 2860

Kabir, Humayun, 5225
Kahin, Audrey, 5127
Kahin, George Mc T., 5135
Kahn, Roger, 766
Kaiser, A., 1868
Kaiser, Robert B., 43
Kaiser, Thomas E., 6024
Kaledin, Arthur O., 179
Kamenka, Eugene, 44, 230, 929, 997, 1273, 1414, 1425, 2352, 4708, 5949
Kaminsky, Howard, 1496
Kamm, Henry, 5116
Kammen, Michael G., 3480, 3545
Kaniki, Martin H.Y., 5354

Kann, R.A., 674
Kantor, Harry, 4430
Kanza, Thomas, 5399
Kaplan, A., 247
Kaplan, B.H., 921, 1410, 5793
Kaplan, Carol, 5064
Kaplan, Frank L., 3167
Kaplan, Lawrence, 1400, 1693, 5064
Kaplan, Lawrence S., 3518
Kaplan, Morton A., 244, 1204
Kaplan, Temma, 5934-35
Kaplow, Jeffry, 1920, 1959, 2000
Karanjia, R.K., 5896
Karnow, Stanley, 4873
Karol, K.S., 4152, 4198, 4978
Karpat, Kemal H., 5295
Karunakaran, K.P., 5269
Kasslow, E.M., 4100
Kataoka, Tetsuya, 4734
Katkov, George, 2549, 2773, 6076
Katope, Christopher, 1326
Katsiaficas, George, 3134
Katz, Donald R., 5701-02
Katz, Friedrich, 4082-83, 6140
Katz, Robert, 591
Katz, Stanley Nider, 3481
Katzanbach, Edward L., 4832
Kau, M.Y.M., 343
Kaufman, Robert R., 3897
Kaufmann, W.W., 3962
Kautsky, John H., 1227, 1351, 5769
Kautsky, Karl, 592, 1145-47
Kavich, Martin, 3482
Kay, Cristobal, 4331
Kazziha, Walid W., 5818
Kearney, Hugh F., 1795, 1803
Kecskemeti, Paul, 3114
Keddie, Nikki R., 5873, 5897, 6204-05
Kedourie, Elie, 5770, 5898
Kedward, Roderick, 844
Keeler, Mary F., 1666
Keen, Benjamin, 3800, 3891, 4364
Keep, John L.H., 2589, 2693
Keer, Dhananjay, 5270
Keesing's Research Report, 4979
Kehde, Ned, 3597
Keller, Elke, 6087
Keller, Theodore, 2639
Kelley, Dean M., 1276
Kelley, Jonathan, 4116
Kellner, Douglas, 1447
Kelly, Donald R., 1526
Kelly, George A., 158, 1415, 3133, 6045
Kelly, J.B., 5797
Kelman, Steve, 767
Kemmerer, Edwin Walter, 4051
Kendell, Jonathan, 4278
Kenez, Peter, 415

Keniston, Kenneth, 717, 734-35, 3669-70
Kennedy, Emmet, 6025
Kennedy, Michael L., 2048, 6026-27
Kennett, Lee, 6114
Kenski, Henry C., Jr., 231, 1421
Kent, Edward, 245
Kent, J.H.S., 1277
Kent, Percy Horace, 4664
Kenyon, Cecelia M., 3385
Kenyon, J.P., 1597, 1748, 1753, 1769-70
Kerber, Linda K., 1304, 3509
Kerensky, Alexander, 2527, 2535, 2550, 2574
Kerkvliet, Benedict J., 5324
Kern, Robert, 5956
Kern, Robert W., 845
Kerner, Robert J., 4465
Kerpelman, L.C., 736
Kerry, Tom, 4874
Kessle, Gun, 4987
Kesteloot, Lilyan, 5400
Ketchum, Richard M., 3466
Keyes, Charles F., 363
Khadduri, Majid, 5819
Khaled, Leila, 5820
Khan, M. Afzal, 5292
Khomeini, Ayato'llah Rehu'llah, 5899
Khrushchev, Nikita S., 593
Kieniewicz, Stefan, 2188
Kiernan, B., 45
Kiernan, T., 2774
Kiernan, Victor G., 46, 930, 2243, 5940
Kifner, John, 5875
Kileff, Clive, 5738
Killian, Lewis M., 218, 3747, 3772
Kilroy-Silk, Robert, 1148
Kim Byong Sik, 5150
Kim Il Sung, 5151
Kim, Kyung-Won, 2090
Kim, Sung Bok, 3515
Kimball, Marie, 3570
Kimmel, Michael, 1368
Kinderman, Katharine S., 4984
Kindersley, Richard, 2694
King, David, 2849
King, Frank H.H., 5145
King, Martin Luther, Jr., 3734
King, Richard, 803, 3671
Kingdon, Robert M., 1505, 1527
Kingston-Mann, Esther, 2640, 2754
Kinnaird, Lawrence, 3825
Kinross, Lord, 5303
Kinsbruner, Jay, 3963-64, 4306
Király, Béla K., 3115
Kirby, D.G., 2641
Kirby, E. Stuart, 4453
Kirchheimer, Otto, 47

Kirchner, Hubert, 1560
Kirk, G.E., 5821
Kirkland, John D., 2071
Kirkwood, David, 2244
Kishlansky, Mark, 1679–80, 1735
Kissin, S.F., 998
Kitagawa, Joseph M., 4833
Kitchen, Martin, 1094
Klaiber, Jeffrey L., 4414, 4431
Klaren, P.F., 4432
Klassen, John M., 1497
Klassen, Walter, 1561
Klehr, Harvey E., 1241
Klein, A. Norman, 466
Klein, Donald W., 4695
Klein, Fritz, 6088
Klein, Herbert S., 4104, 4116–17
Klein, Jean, 5449
Klein, Martin A., 5401
Klein, Randolph Shipley, 3528
Kline, Harvey F., 3813, 3841–42, 3940, 4002, 4095, 4107, 4132, 4213, 4291, 4337, 4349, 4418
Kling, Merle, 4133
Knachel, Paul, 1590
Knapton, Ernest John, 1921
Knei-paz, Baruch, 2828
Knibiehler, Yvonne, 6064
Knight, Amy, 1294
Knoles, Thelma Cox, 4084
Knollenberg, Bernhard, 3336–37
Knox, A.J. Graham, 6141
Knox, Gregory H.C., 737
Knudson, Jerry W., 4078, 4105
Koch, Adrienne, 3377, 3571
Koberdova, I., 6072
Kochan, Lionel, 2515, 2695
Kochanek, Stanley A., 48
Koehn, Peter, 5703
Koenigsberg, Richard A., 1262, 1341
Koenigsberger, H.G., 1506–07, 1528, 1567
Koenker, Diane, 2696
Koepcke, C., 159
Kohl, James V., 3892, 4106
Kohn, Hans, 160, 1242, 1263–64, 3000
Kohout, Pavel, 675
Kolakowski, Leszek, 999
Kolarz, Walter, 1168
Kolb, Robert, 1549
Konrad, George, 1149
Koonz, Claudia, 5935, 5953, 6017, 6082
Kopkind, Andrew, 541, 804, 3628–29
Korn, H.A., 778
Korngold, Ralph, 3965
Kornhauser, William, 49, 232, 246, 3001
Korotkov, I., 2755
Korsch, Karl, 1000–01

Korshin, Paul J., 1448
Kort, Fred, 1474
Koser, Konstantin, 2473
Kossman, E.H., 1564, 1591
Kossok, Manfred, 161, 5941
Koury, Enver M., 5822
Kousovlas, D. George, 2857
Kovrig, Bennett, 2245
Ko Wang Mei, 446
Koyré, Alexandre, 1804
Kraft, Joseph, 5473, 5704
Kramer, Jane, 542
Kramnick, Isaac, 4, 316, 893, 1508, 2155–56
Kranzberg, Melvin, 2353, 2460
Krieger, L., 2336
Kriesberg, L., 25
Krimerman, Leonard I., 846
Kripalani, Krishna, 5271
Kristol, I., 751
Kropotkin, Peter A., 898–901, 1922
Krout, M.H., 786
Krugman, Paul, 6098
Krupskaya, Nadezhda, 2775
Kubalkova, V., 1002
Kuhn, Thomas S., 1805–06
Kuhn, Philip A., 4511, 4612
Kumar, Krishan, 162
Kun, Miklos, 875
Kunen, James S., 768
Kuper, Leo, 636, 1334, 1342
Kupperman, Robert, 578
Kurtz, Stephen G., 3255, 3283, 3318, 3396, 3443, 3498, 3522
Kusin, Vladimir V., 3159, 3168
Kwang-Ching, Liu, 4500
Kwong, Julia, 4916
Ky Son, 5117

Labadie, Joseph A., 847
Labaree, Benjamin W., 3284, 3338, 3467, 3475
Labedz, Leopold, 1003
Labrousse, C.E., 1977
Lacerte, Robert K., 3946
Lach, Donald, 1865
Lachs, John, 917
Lackner, Bede K., 2246
Lacouture, Jean, 5105, 5771
Lacy, Dan, 3285, 3304
La Dany, L., 4936
Ladd, D.M., 3961
Ladendorf, Janice M., 5168
Lader, Lawrence, 805, 3672
Ladis, Fondas, 2851
Ladurie, Emmanuel Le Roy, 691
Laffey, Ella S., 4613
Laffin, John, 5823

LaFrance, David G., 6142
Lahiry, Ashutosh, 5272
Laidler, Harry W., 1150
Lajpat Rai, Lala, 5213
Lakey, George, 163
Lamartine, Alphonse M., 2388
Lamberg, Robert F., 4240
Lambert, Robert D., 6130
Lamont, William, 1618, 1694
Lampert, Evgeny, 2697–98
Landau, Saul, 3668, 4299
Landauer, Carl, 1151
Landis, Arthur H., 3055
Landon, Kenneth P., 5126
Landon, M., 1771
Landor, Alfred, 5537
Landsberger, Henry A., 692, 707, 3893–94, 4090, 4093
Lane, David, 1205
Lane, Robert E., 317
Lane, Roger, 513
Langer, Paul F., 5113
Langer, William L., 2247, 2337, 2354
Langford, Paul, 2157, 3386, 3468
Langguth, A.J., 594
Langley, J. Ayo, 5344
Lanne, Bernard, 5571
Lansdale, Edward G., 5025
Lanternari, Vittorio, 383
LaPorte, Robert, Jr., 3918
Lapwood, Nancy, 4735
Lapwood, Ralph, 4735
Laqueur, Walter, 50, 439–40, 543, 595–96, 738, 2699, 2985
Large, David, 2338
Large, Stephen S., 4571
Larrain, Jorge, 318
Larsen, O.N., 78
Larsson, Reidar, 5
Lartéguy, Jean, 3895
Lasch, Christopher, 3673
Laski, Harold J., 164, 1206
Lasky, Melvin J., 51–52, 1449, 3116
Laslett, Peter, 1785
Lasswell, Harold D., 247, 1243, 1416, 2987
Laszlo, Ervin, 1315
Latham, R.C., 1650
Latouche, P., 848
Lattimore, Owen, 4512, 4592
Lauerhass, Ludwig, 3796
Launitz-Schurer, Leopold S., Jr., 3339
Laurent, Marcel, 6028
Lavine, Harold, 4134
Lawless, Richard I., 5446
Lawson, Alan, 3301
Lazar, Arpad von, 3897
Leach, Edward, 597

Leader, Shelah Gilbert, 5002
Leamer, Lawrence, 3674
Le Barbier, Françoise, 4491
Lebedz, Leopold, 1325
Lebel, Phillip, 5705
Le Bon, Gustave, 268–69
Ledeen, Michael, 544, 5900
Leder, Lawrence H., 3286–87
Lederer, E., 53
Le Duan, 5026, 5069–70
Lee, Grace, 1313
Lee, Hong Yung, 4937, 4980, 5003
Lee, Ming T., 4771
Lee, Peter, 2700
Lee, Ta-Ling, 4665
Lefebvre, Georges, 1923–24, 1960–61, 2014
Lefebvre, Henri, 1004, 3148
Leff, Gordon, 1005
Lefort, Claude, 6029
Legg, Wickham, 1878
Legge, J.G., 2413
Leggett, George, 2701
Leggett, John, 739
Leguineche, Manuel, 6095
Legum, Colin, 5355, 5706, 5718
Leiden, Carl, 165
Leifer, Michael, 4593
Leitenberg, Milton, 5016
Leites, Nathan, 406, 2611
Leith, James A., 598, 2461
Lemarchand, René, 5532
Lemisch, Jesse, 3400–01
Lemos, Ramon M., 1791, 1834
Lenczowski, George, 5678, 5901
Leng, Shao-chuan, 4678
Lengyel, Emil, 1265
Lenin, V.I., 1006–07, 2776–82
Lenk, K., 166
Lenotre, G., 2029
Lens, Sidney, 806
Lensen, G.A., 2575
Lent, John A., 5315
LeoGrande, William M., 4199, 4342
Leonard, Thomas C., 6115
Leonhard, Wolfgang, 1008
Lerner, Daniel, 1243, 2987
Lerner, Michael P., 717, 735, 3675
Lerner, Warren, 2702, 5961
Lernoux, Penny, 3898
Leslie, R.F., 2330
Leśnodorski, Boguslaw, 2049
Lesser, Charles H., 3230, 3546
Lessner, F., 1009
Lester, Jules, 3735
Levenson, Joseph R., 4513–14
Levesque, Jacques, 1129, 4195
Levine, Daniel H., 4187, 4443

Levine, Norman, 1010
Levine, Robert M., 3997
Levy, Darline Gay, 1305
Levy, Richard, 4705
Lew, Roland, 4834
Lewes, George Henry, 2116
Lewin, Moshe, 2783
Lewis, Anthony, 3676
Lewis, Arthur, 2485
Lewis, Bernard, 5304
Lewis, Charlton M., 4515
Lewis, Flora, 545-46
Lewis, Geoffrey, 5305
Lewis, Gordon K., 3899, 4261
Lewis, Gwynne, 2015, 2134
Lewis, J.D., 2339
Lewis, John, 1011-12
Lewis, John Wilson, 68, 699, 4595, 4709, 4774-75, 4836, 4938, 5039, 5144
Lewis, Martin Deming, 5273
Lewis, Oscar, 4181-83
Lewis, Paul, 3560
Lewis, Theodore B., 1509
Lewis, William, 5900
Lewy, Guenter, 1286
Leys, Simon, 4981
Liang, C.T., 4666
Liberation, Editors of, 6195
Libiszowska, Zofia, 5967
Li Chien-nung, 4516
Lichter, S. Robert, 5932
Lichtheim, George, 931, 1013, 1152-53, 3135
Lida, Clara, 5936
Lidove, Marcel, 2135
Lieberthal, Kenneth G., 4736
Liebman, Arthur, 740
Liebman, Marcel, 2703
Lieuwen, Edwin, 416, 3900, 4027, 4125
Liew, K.S., 4667
Lifshultz, Lawrence, 4595
Lifton, Robett Jay, 270, 4596, 4982
Ligt, Bart de, 5214
Li Jui, 4875
Lilly, W.S., 167
Lin, Robert H.T., 4625
Lindbeck, John M.H., 4776, 4990
Lindemann, Albert S., 2248
Linden, Ian, 5402
Lindley, Augustus F., 4626
Lindner, C., 168
Lindsay, A.D., 1014
Lindsay, Jack, 1619
Lindsay, Michael, 4517
Linebarger, Paul M., 4679-80, 6159
Lineberry, William P., 599
Lin Piao, 4780, 4883
Linteau, Paul-André, 3789

Lipset, Seymour Martin, 101, 248, 676, 741, 769-71, 3901
Lipshires, Sidney, 3714
Lipsky, William E., 1352
Lissagaray, P.O., 2462
Liston, Robert A., 600
Litt, John, 3892
Littell, Robert, 3169
Little, David, 1529
Little, Richard W., 49, 352
Little, Tom, 5847
Liu, Alan P., 4983
Liu, Frederick Fu, 4781
Lively, Jack, 2297
Lively, J.F., 283
Livingston, Donald W., 1369
Livingston, Marius H., 601
Llanos, M.A., 4286
Llerena, Mario, 4226
Lloyd, G.E.R., 1479
Lloyd, Roger B., 1287
Lo, Ruth Earnshaw, 4984
Lobban, Richard, 5624
Lobkowicz, Nikolaus, 169, 1015
Locke, Don, 894
Locke, John, 1792
Lockhart, Robert H. Bruce, 2576
Lockridge, Kenneth A., 3393, 3402
Lockwood, Lee, 3773, 4227
Lockwood, T.D., 284
Lodge, Juliet, 5925
Lodge, Richard, 1772
Loewenstein, Julius I., 1016
Loewenstein, K., 285
Lofchie, Michael F., 5534
Lomax, Bill, 3117
Lomax, Louis E., 3774
Lomax, William, 3180
London, Ivan D., 5004
London, Jack, 170
London, Kurt, 2652
London, Miriam, 5004
Long, Durward, 719, 728-29, 744, 763, 3748
Long, Priscilla, 3677
Longworth, Philip, 2167
Loomis, Stanley, 2117
Lopes, Agostinhe, 3190
López, Adalberto, 3902
Loria, Achille, 1017
Lothstein, Arthur, 3678
Lotta, Raymond, 4985
Lotveit, Trygve, 4793
Loubère, L.A., 2100
Lougee, Carolyn C., 1989
Lougee, Robert W., 2355
L'Ouverture, Toussaint, 3966
Love, Robert S., 5707

Loveman, Brian, 4307
Lovett, Clara M., 1297, 2500
Low, Mary, 3056
Lowell, Edward J., 1962
Lowenfels, Walter, 1328
Lowenthal, Abraham F., 3903, 4415, 4433
Lowenthal, Richard, 54, 4835
Lowry, Bullitt, 6057
Lowy, Michael, 4255
LSM, 5728, 5747
Lu Hsun, 6160
Lu, S.Y., 909
Luard, Evan, 353
Lubac, Henri de, 910
Lubasz, Heinz, 2249
Lucas, Colin, 2001, 2118
Lucas, Philippe, 5528
Lucas, Stephen E., 3340
Luccioni, Jean, 1480
Luce, Paul A., 171
Luce, Phillip Abbott, 3679
Lukács, Georg, 1018–19, 2784
Lukas, J. Anthony, 3680
Luke, Louise E., 5954
Lumpkin, Henry, 6116
Lunacharsky, Anatoly V., 1450
Lunn, Alfred, 1207
Lunn, Arnold, 3057
Lupsha, Peter A., 467
Luraghi, Raimondo, 6030
Lutnick, Solomon, 3483
Luttwak, Edward, 344
Lutz, Ralph H., 2884, 2892–94
Lutz, William, 172
Luxemburg, Rosa, 2577, 2895–99
Lyashchenko, Peter I., 2590
Lynch, John, 3959, 3967
Lynd, Staughton, 617, 3630
Lynn, Kenneth S., 3547
Lyons, Eugene, 2704
Lyons, F.S.L., 2949
Lyons, Martyn, 2057

McAlister, John T., Jr., 5027, 5071–72
Macardle, Dorothy, 2910
Macaulay, Neill, 4354, 4386
Macaulay, Thomas Babington, 1773
McBride, William Leon, 5942
McCaffrey, Lawrence J., 2950–51
McCain, James A., 5356
McCamant, John F., 3867
McCants, David A., 3529
McCarger, J., 3188
McCarthy, Joseph M., 5610
McCauley, Martin, 2566
McClellan, Woodford, 2189, 2463
McClelland, James C., 6079
MacCoby, Simon, 807

McColl, Robert W., 4572
McCollester, Charles, 5668
McColley, Robert, 3387
McConahay, John B., 522
McConville, Maureen, 3154
MacCormack, John R., 1695
McCormack, T.H., 787
McCoy, Alfred W., 5112
McCreary, Guy Weddington, 4028
McCuen, John J., 667
McCullagh, Francis, 4029
MacCurtain, Margaret, 1295
McDaniel, Robert, 5824
MacDonagh, Michael, 2952
MacDonagh, Oliver, 2953–54
McDonald, Angus W., Jr., 4798, 4804
McDonald, Joan, 1835
McDowell, R.B., 1869, 2955
MacEoin, Gary, 3904
McEvoy, J., 772
MacEwan, Arthur, 6144
McFadden, Thomas, 1288
McFarlane, Bruce, 4996
MacFarlane, Charles, 4627
MacFarquhar, Roderick, 4917, 4939
MacGaffey, Wyatt, 4174
MacGregor-Hastie, Roy, 4876
McHugh, Roger, 2956
McIlwain, Charles H., 3422
MacIntyre, Alasdair, 286, 3715
MacIntyre, Stuart, 5943
Mack, A., 661
Mack, Raymond W., 55
McKay, Donald C., 2389
MacKay, John Henry, 849
McKeel, Arthur J., 3506
McKendrick, Neil, 1753
McKenzie, Kermit E., 1417
MacKenzie, Norman, 1154
MacKerras, Colin, 4518
Mackesy, Piers, 3456
McKitrick, Eric, 3426, 3431
McKnight, Gerald, 602
McLane, Charles B., 4815
McLane, John R., 5169
McLaughlin, Barry, 271
McLean, H., 2644
McLean, John, 1451
McLeish, John L., 4030
McLellan, David, 1020–24, 1102
MacLeod, Duncan J., 3411
McLoughlin, William G., 3497–98, 3503
MacLysaght, Edward, 2957
McManners, John, 1836–37, 1875
McManus, Doyle, 5876
MacNair, Harley F., 4668
McNeal, Robert H., 2516, 2612–13, 2785, 5955

Author-Editor Index / 443

McNeil, G.H., 1819-20
McPhee, Peter, 2380
Macpherson, C.B., 287, 1531, 2158
McReynolds, David, 3631, 3681
McVey, Ruth T., 4597
Macciocchi, Maria Antoinetta, 4998
Machiavelli, Niccolo, 1530
Maciás, Anna, 3998, 6143
Maciu, Vasile, 2434
Madelin, Louis, 1925, 2043-44
Maenchen-Helfen, Otto, 1048
Magdoff, Harry, 4323
Magon, Ricardo F., 4031
Magubane, Bernard M., 5669, 5748
Maguire, J.J., 259
Maguire, John M., 1025
Mahadevan, T.K., 637, 5274-76
Mahar, J. Michael, 5182
Maier, Hans, 1289
Maier, J., 4001
Maier, Pauline, 468, 3341, 3435, 3541, 3551
Mailer, Paul, 3203
Main, Jackson T., 3288, 3418
Maitan, Livio, 4416, 4519
Major, Reginald, 3775
Majul, Cesar Adib, 5325
Majumdar, Ramesh Chandra, 4558, 5170
Makey, Walter, 1532
Makler, Harry M., 3200
Malaparte, Curzio, 345
Malcolm X, 3736
Malefakis, Edward E., 3058
Malia, M., 2644
Mallet du Pan, Jacques, 1926
Mallin, Jay, 395, 4236, 5073
Mallison, George B., 5171
Malloy, James M., 4107, 4118-19
Malone, Dumas, 3572-73
Malraux, Andre, 4737
Mamalakis, M.J., 4328
Mar ashe, Louis, 2756
Mancall, Mark, 662
Manceron, Claude, 1927-28, 6031
Mandel, Ernest, 173-76, 773, 1026-27
Mandelbaum, David G., 5226
Mander, John, 3905
Manheim, Jarol B., 450
Manitzas, Nita R., 4142
Mankiewicz, Frank, 4228
Mankoff, Milton, 742
Mann, Eric, 3776
Mannheim, Karl, 319
Manning, Brian, 1641, 1648
Mansergh, Nicholas, 2958
Manuel, Frank E., 1452, 3059
Manuel, Fritzie P., 1452
Mao Tse-tung, 4877-83

Maravall, J.M., 56
March, James G., 79
March, Thomas, 2464
Marcos, Ferdinand E., 5326
Marcu, Valeriu, 2786
Marcum, John, 5572-73, 5584-85
Marcus, Steven, 1103
Marcuse, Herbert, 678, 1028, 3708-10, 3716-20
Mardin, S., 5296
Marek, Franz, 260
Margadant, Ted W., 2250, 2440
Marie, Jean-Jacques, 2567
Marighella, Carlos, 427
Marina, William, 3403
Marine, Gene, 3777
Markakis, John, 5708, 5719
Markov, Walter M., 2119
Marks, Robert B., 4799
Marks, Robert W., 3721
Marquez, Robert, 1329
Marr, David G., 5028, 5074-75
Marr, Phebe Ann, 5798
Marriott, J., 2390
Marsh, Margaret, 850
Marshall, Terence, 1821
Martello, William E., 5337
Marti, Jose, 3906
Martic, Milos, 1453
Martin, Benjamin F., 663
Martin, Bernard, 4681
Martin, Esmond G., 5535
Martin, Everett Dean, 177
Martin, Francis X., 2959-60, 2963
Martin, Guy, 5504-05
Martin, James Kirby, 3289-90, 3436
Martin, Kingsley, 1997
Martin, Lionel, 4229
Martin, Marta S., 4143
Martin, William A., 4638
Marton, Endre, 3119
Martz, John D., 3907, 4402
Marx, Karl, 851, 1029-39, 2356, 2465, 4628
Masilela, Ntongela, 5506
Mason, Alpheus T., 57
Mason, Edward S., 2466
Masotti, Louis H., 514
Massell, Gregory J., 1306
Massie, Robert K., 2551
Masson, David, 1729
Mast, Herman, III, 4573
Masters, Anthony, 882
Masters, Roger D., 1838
Masur, Gerhard, 3968
Mathews, Shailer, 1929
Mathiez, Albert, 1930, 2120-21
Matrat, Jean, 2122

Matteos, Salahudin, 5625
Mattheisen, Donald J., 2403
Matthews, Herbert L., 178, 3060-62, 4184-85, 4230
Matthews, Tanya, 5474
Matthewson, Timothy, 3947
Mattick, Paul, 1208
Maullin, Richard, 4403
Mauny, Michel de, 5926
Maupas, Charlmegne Emilie De', 346
Maurer, Charles B., 852
Maurice, C. Edmund, 2357
Mauss, Armand L., 3632
Mawdsley, Evan, 2705
Maxey, Kees, 5749
Maximoff, G.P., 883
Maxton, James, 2787
Maxwell, Kenneth, 3187
May, Gita, 2091, 2190
Mayer, Arno J., 679
Mayer, Gustav, 1104
Mayer, J.P., 2298-99, 2397
Mayer, Milton, 3002
Mayer, Peter, 1209
Maynard, John, 2552
Mayo, Henry B., 1040
Mayo, L.S., 3313
Mazgaj, Paul, 2486
Mazlish, Bruce, 179, 1244
Mazour, Anatole G., 2251
Mazrui, Ali A., 1370, 5357, 5412
Mbeki, Gowan, 708
Mbengo, F., 5358
M'Bou-Yembi, Léon, 5425
Meadows, Paul, 58
Meadows, Thomas Taylor, 4520
Meaker, Gerald H., 3063
Meaney, Neville, 3291
Mecham, J.L., 3908
Medhurst, Kenneth, 4308
Medlicott, W.N., 2172
Medlin, Virgil, 2706
Medvedev, Roy A., 1155, 2707
Mehlinger, Howard, 2517
Mehnert, Klaus, 774
Mehring, Franz, 1041
Mehta, Ved, 5277
Meier, August, 3755
Meier, Paul, 2252
Meijer, J.M., 6080
Meinecke, Friedrich, 2404
Meisel, James, 680
Meiselas, Susan, 6148
Meisler, Stanley, 4343
Meisner, Maurice, 4521, 4738, 4785-86, 4836
Mekeel, Arthur J., 6117
Meldrum, A.N., 1807

Meleish, Andrew, 3482
Melgunov, S.P., 2578
Mellink, A.F., 1564
Mellon, Stanley, 2191
Melo, Father Antônio, 4387
Melotti, Umberto, 180, 5772
Melvin, Peter H., 2146
Mende, Tiber, 4522
Mendel, Arthur P., 1042, 3136
Mendels, Doron, 5971
Mendizabal Villalba, Alfredo, 3064
Meneses, Enrique, 4231
Menges, Constantine C., 547
Mennell, Stephen, 2303
Menon, V.P., 5215
Mercier Vega, Luis, 3909
Merino, Hugo Zemelman, 4315
Merkx, Gilbert W., 3925
Merriman, John M., 2310, 2313-15, 2318, 2323, 2327, 2331, 2391
Merriman, Roger B., 1533
Merritt, Richard L., 3321
Mesa-Lago, Carmelo, 4204-05
Mészáres, János, 59
Meszaros, Istuan, 1043
Metallo, Michael V., 4652
Metcalf, Thomas R., 5172
Metford, J.C.J., 3969
Methvin, Eugene H., 808
Meusel, Alfred, 60, 664
Meyer, Alfred G., 1044-45, 1210, 2788
Meyer, Edith P., 3512
Meyer, Jean, 6118
Meyer, Jean A., 4032-33
Meyer, Michael C., 3798, 4034
Meyer, P.H., 1990
Mezerik, Avrahm G., 3170, 5475
Michael, Franz, 4629, 4884
Michaels, Albert L., 4046
Michelena, Jose A., 4439, 4442
Michelet, Jules, 1931
Mickolus, Edward F., 5927
Midlarsky, Manus, 80, 3826
Migdal, Joel S., 5773
Mignet, F.A.M., 1932
Mikes, Georges, 3120
Milazzo, Matteo J., 3098
Mllene, Charles, 6184
Miles, Michael W., 775
Milibrand, Ralph, 932, 1046
Miliukov, Pavel N., 2553, 2614
Miller, A., 772
Miller, Abraham H., 5928
Miller, Alice P., 2159
Miller, David, 2961-62
Miller, Glenn T., 364
Miller, John C., 3292, 3342, 3561
Miller, Joseph C., 5554

Author-Editor Index / 445

Miller, Lillian, 3343
Miller, Linda B., 158
Miller, Martin A., 901-02
Miller, Michael V., 776
Miller, Norman, 701, 727, 1454, 3642, 5403, 5757, 5774
Miller, Perry, 1278
Miller, William Robert, 638
Millett, Allan R., 5076
Millett, Richard, 4344, 4355
Millon, Robert P., 4087
Mills, C. Wright, 1047, 4153
Milton, David, 4986, 4999
Milton, John, 1730
Milton, Nancy, 4986, 4999
Minar, D.W., 288
Minter, William, 5562, 5574, 5626
Misra, B.B., 4559
Misra, D.K., 5278
Misselwitz, Maurice, 4739
Mitchell, Allan, 2900
Mitchell, Broadus, 3293
Mitchell, Christopher, 4120
Mitchell, Harvey, 2072, 2130, 2192
Mitrani, Barbara, 3910
Mittelman, James, 3188
Mlynar, Zdenek, 3171
Mmbaga, J.K., 5670
Mohanty, Manoranjan, 4885
Mohr, Charles, 548, 5555
Mohrenschildt, Dmitri von, 2579
Mollat, M., 1498
Möller, Horst, 6032
Molnar, Thomas, 681
Momboisse, Raymond M., 407
Mondlane, Eduardo, 5609
Monnerot, Jules, 181, 1211
Montalva, Eduardo Frei, 3827
Monteiro, Anthony, 5709
Moody, Joseph N., 1277
Moody, Peter R., Jr., 665
Moody, T.W., 2916, 2963, 6089
Moolman, J.H., 5627
Moon, S. Joan, 2193
Moore, Barrington, Jr., 61, 182-83, 249, 3633
Moore, Harriet L., 4816
Moore, John Norton, 354
Moore, Marie-France, 3786
Moorehead, Alan, 2708
Moote, A. Lloyd, 1510, 1592
Moraes, Dom, 4554
Morell, David, 5121
Moreno, Francisco J., 3910
Moreno, José A., 4241
Morf, Gustave, 603
Morgado, Michael S., 5671
Morgan, David W., 1111, 2901

Morgan, Edmund S., 3238, 3256-57, 3294-95, 3344, 3367, 3404, 3437, 3499
Morgan, Michael, 2789
Morgan, Ted, 4200
Morgenthaler, Eric, 5878
Morison, Samuel E., 3249
Morley, John, 1720, 1839, 2160
Morley, Morris, 4334
Mornet, Daniel, 1998
Morosini, Giuseppe, 6193
Morray, J.P., 4154
Morrill, J.S., 1696, 5991
Morris, Bernard S., 184
Morris, David J., 4309
Morris, Gouverneur, 1882
Morris, James, 3322
Morris, Richard B., 3258, 3296-97, 3438-39, 3519
Morrow, Felix, 3065
Mortimer, Robert A., 5450
Morton, A.L., 1697
Mosca, Gaetano, 1245
Moses, Bernard, 3970-71
Mosk, Sanford A., 4052
Moss, Bernard H., 2315, 2479
Moss, Robert, 549, 4310
Mosse, George L., 3003
Motley, John Lothrop, 1576
Motyl, Alexander J., 2866
Mouffe, Chantal, 2501
Moulton, Phillips P., 639
Mountjoy, Alan B., 5775
Mousnier, Roland, 709, 1586
Mowat, C.L., 2253, 2633
Mowry, A.M., 3219
Mpakati, Attati, 5359
Mubako, Simbi V., 5739
Muchnik, N., 5561
Mueller, R.H., 3598
Mugomba, Agrippah T., 5600
Mukherjee, Subrata, 5994
Muller, Edward N., 469
Mullett, Charles F., 1754, 3368, 3419, 3423
Mulvey, Helen F., 2907
Mungo, Raymond, 3613
Munro, Ion S., 2502
Munro, Robin, 6169
Murkland, H.B., 4135
Murphy, Fred, 4352
Murphy, John F., 581
Murphy, William J., Jr., 2291
Murray, Robert Henry, 2161
Murray, Roger, 5451
Murrin, John M., 3396
Mus, Paul, 5072
Muse, Benjamin, 3778

Mutchler, David E., 3911
Mwansasu, Bismarck U., 5405
Myerhoff, Barbara G., 743
Myerson, Michael, 3614
Myrdal, Jan, 4987

Nachman, Robert G., 4374
Nadal, George, 1568
Nadelson, Regina, 3779
Naess, Arne, 621
Nair, Pyarelai, 6173
Nairn, Tom, 3152
Nalbandian, Louis Z., 1455, 2254
Namier, Lewis B., 2358, 3484
Nanda, B.R., 5279
Nanes, Allan, 5855
Naquin, Susan, 384
Narayan, Jayaprakash, 4560-61
Nardin, Terry, 516
Narkiewicz, Olga A., 5944
Nasaw, David, 2194
Nash, Gary B., 3345, 3412
Nash, June, 3912
Nassar, G.A., 5848
Navarro, Moisés González, 3999
Naylor, Phillip Chivique, 6189
Neal, Fred W., 3096
Nee, Victor, 4523, 4706, 4988
Needler, Martin C., 3913
Neeson, Eoin, 2964
Negaran, Hannah, 5293
Neher-Bernheim, Renée, 6033
Nehru, Jawaharlal, 5216-17, 5280
Nelson, Harvey, 5005
Nelson, Lowry, 4155
Nelson, Truman, 3780
Nelson, William H., 3516
Nesvold, Betty A., 457
Nettlau, Max, 853-57
Nettels, Curtis P., 3440
Nettl, J.P., 2902
Neuhaus, Richard J., 102
Neuhauser, Charles, 4914
Neumann, Franz, 3004
Neumann, Sigmund, 62, 185, 2340
Neumann-Hoditz, R., 5106
Nevins, Lawrence, 5556
Nevinson, Henry W., 2518
New, John F.H., 1721
Newell, Richard S., 5294
Newman, Edgar Leon, 2316-18
Newman, Robert S., 4574-75
Newton, Huey P., 3737
Nezhinsky, L.N., 2872
Nguyen Nghe, 5507
Nicholson, Joe, Jr., 4206
Nickbin, Saber, 5902
Nicolaievsky, Boris, 1048
Nieburg, H.L., 470-72, 515

Niedergang, Marcel, 4417
Niemeyer, E.V., Jr., 4035
Nikol, John, 3828
Niles, Hezekiah, 3548
Nilsson, Nils Åke, 6081
Ninsin, Kwame A., 5426
Nisbet, Robert A., 187-88, 3405
Njoto, 5136
Nkemdirim, Bernard A., 5360
Nkoana, Mathew, 5405
Nkrumah, Kwame, 5433-41
Noakes, Jeremy, 2986
Nobari, Ali-Reza, 5903
Nobile, Philip, 3682
Nogee, Joseph L., 4287
Nollau, Günther, 1212
Nolte, Ernst, 3005
Nomad, Max, 189-90, 1401
Nora, Pierre, 5962
Norbu, Dawa, 4576
Nordheimer, Jon, 4214
Nordlinger, Eric A., 347
Normanby, C.H. Phillips, first Marquis of, 2392
North, Robert C., 4643, 4817
North American Congress on Latin America, 4311
Norton, Augustus R., 527
Norton, Mary Beth, 1307
Nottingham, John, 5410
Noumoff, S.J., 5149
Nova, Fritz, 1105
Novack, George, 176, 250, 3220
Novak, D., 819
Novak, Steven J., 777
Nowlan, Kevin B., 2965
Noyes, Paul, 2414
Nozick, Robert, 858
Ntalaja, Nzongola, 5361, 5740
Nucleus Group of the First Ministry of Machine Building, 4837
Nun, Jose, 3914
Nunes, Albano, 3189
Nuñez, Carlos, 4336
Nunn, Frederick M., 3829, 4312
Nunn, G. Raymond, 4447
Nursey-Bray, Paul, 6190
Nussbaumer, Heinz, 5904
Nutt, Katharine F., 5154
Nwafor, Azinna, 5575
Nyandoro, G.M.K., 5729
Nyang, Sulayman Sheih, 5672
Nyangoni, C.K., 5729
Nyangoni, Wellington W., 5750
Nyerere, Julius, 5538-41
Nzongola, Georges N., 5362

O'Ballance, Edgar, 4782, 5077, 5476, 5825

Obear, Frederick W., 744
Oberling, Pierre, 5790
Obermann, Karl, 2405
Oberschall, Anthony R., 63, 191
Obichere, Boniface L., 5628
Obiechina, Emmanuel, 5508
Obinani, F. Chuckwuma, 5363
Obinyan, Tom Uwa, 5364
Obolensky, D., 385
O'Brien, Conor Cruise, 550, 2966
O'Brien, J., 3683
O'Brien, James P., 3634
O'Brien, Jay, 5557, 5629
O'Brien, Joseph V., 2967
O'Brien, Patrick, 5849
O'Brien, Philip, 4313
Ó Broin, Leon, 2916, 2968–69
Ochberg, Frank, 604
O'Conner, Frank, 2970
O'Conner, Harvey, 3221
O'Conner, James, 4170, 4175
O'Conner, Ulick, 2971
O'Corrain, D., 1295
O'Donnell, Terence, 5905
O'Faolain, Sean, 2972
O'Farrell, Patrick, 2973–74
Ogg, David, 1774–75
Oglesby, Carl, 3603–04, 3684
O'Gorman, Frank, 2162
O'Gorman, Ned, 1330
O'Hegarty, Patrick S., 2975
Ojwok, Omwony, 5365
Okadigbo, Miriam, 5427
Okello, John, 5536
Okoye, F. Nwabueze, 3530
Oksenberg, Michael, 4940, 4989
Okuma, Thomas Masaji, 5586
Ola, Opeyemi, 6185
O'Leary, Daniel Florencio, 3972
Olenik, J. Kenneth, 4653
Olgin, Moissaye J., 2580, 2829
Oliver, B., 5727
Oliver, D., 251
Oliver, Peter, 3314
Oliver, Roland, 5406, 6186
Ollard, Richard, 1620
Ollman, Bertell, 1049
Olsen, Richard, 1050
Olson, Alison Gilbert, 3485
Omar, F., 5800
Omari, T. Peter, 5442
O'Meara, Patrick, 5742
Onate, Andres D., 4886
O'Neill, Bard E., 517, 5929
O'Neill, Brian, 2976
O'Neill, Robert J., 5078
O'Neill, Thomas P. 2977
Onoge, Omafume F., 5428
Opello, Walter C., 5592

Opoku, K., 5673
Oppenheim, Samuel A., 2615
Oppenheimer, Martin, 441
Oren, Nissan, 2255
Ortega y Gasset, José, 408, 3066
Orwell, George, 3067
Osanka, Franklin Mark, 442, 4210
Osborn, Annie, 1534
Osborne, John W., 2256
Osborne, Michael J., 1475
Osborne, Milton, 4598, 5029
Ott, Thomas O., 3973
Ottaway, David, 5477, 5720
Ottaway, Marina, 5477, 5710, 5720
Oury, Raymond, 6034
Overholt, William H., 64, 192
Owen, Launcelot, 2642, 2709
Oxaal, Ivar, 1343

Paden, John N., 5338
Padmore, George, 5407
Padover, Saul K., 1033, 1051–54, 2036
Padula, Alfred, 4316
Page, Benjamin B., 3172
Page, Stanley W., 2757–58, 2790–91
Paget, Julian, 682
Pahlavi, Ashraf, 5906
Pahlavi, Mohammad Reza, 5907
Paige, Jeffrey M., 3742, 5776
Paine, Thomas, 2163, 3589
Paiva, Vasco, 3190
Pakenham, Frank, 2977
Palacios, Jorge, 4314
Paléologue, Maurice, 2554
Palij, Michael, 859, 2867
Palmer, Alan, 2178
Palmer, David Scott, 4418, 4434
Palmer, J.A.B., 5173
Palmer, Norman, 4678
Palmer, R.R., 65, 1851–53, 1870, 1888,
   1983, 2013, 2021, 2061, 2092, 2123
Palmier, Leslie, 5137
Paloczi-Horvath, G., 4887
Palumbo, Michael, 5950
Pan, Stephen, 5007
Pandey, B.N., 5186
Panguene, Armando, 5601
Panikkar, K. Madhu, 5408, 5587
Panofsky, Hans E., 5339
Panter-Brick, Simone, 5281
Papandreou, Andreas, 2852
Papcke, S., 150
Parekh, Bhikhu, 1156
Pares, Bernard, 2555
Paret, Peter, 409, 443, 2136
Pareto, Vilfredo, 1246
Parker, Geoffrey, 1569, 1577–79
Parker, Harold T., 924, 2191
Parkes, Henry B., 1055

Parkin, C., 2164
Parkinson, Roger, 4088
Parrish, W.E., 355
Parry, Albert, 605
Parry, R.H., 1621
Parrington, Vernon, 3552, 3563, 3580
Parsons, Howard L., 1056
Parsons, James B., 710
Partridge, P.H., 1425
Pastor, Peter, 2873, 2876
Patai, Raphael, 1456
Patch, Richard W., 693, 4108–09
Patrick, Alison, 2045, 2050
Pattee, Richard, 5630
Patti, Archimedes L.A., 5079
Paul, Cedar, 193
Paul, David W., 3173
Paul, Eden, 193
Paul, Robert S., 1722
Paulos, Milkias, 5684
Paulson, Ronald, 2147
Paxson, Frederic L., 3974
Payne, James, 4404
Payne, Robert, 1057, 2792, 2830, 3068, 4888–89
Payne, Ronald, 580
Payne, Stanley G., 3069–70
Paynton, Clifford T., 2, 105, 194
Pearl, Valerie, 1698
Pearse, Andrew, 3915, 4110
Pearson, Hesketh, 3590
Pearson, J.D., 4460
Pearson, Michael, 3457
Pearson, Neale J., 4093, 4345
Pearson, Raymond, 2556
Pease, Theodore Calvin, 1742
Pech, Stanley Z., 2374
Peck, Abraham, 2903
Peck, James, 4523, 4988
Peckham, Howard H., 3458
Peers, Edgar A., 3071
Pelenski, Jaroslaw, 1429–30, 1512, 2049, 2182, 2188, 2201, 2204, 2421, 3496, 3509, 3525
Pélissier, René, 5588–89, 5591
Pellicani, L., 195
Pelton, Leroy H., 640
P'eng Shu-tse, 4524
Pennington, Donald, 1667, 1670
Pennock, J. Roland, 860
Penvenne, Jeanne, 5576
Pepper, Curtis Bill, 551
Pepper, Suzanne, 4740, 4809
Peralta, Cresencio, 5316
Peraza, Fermin, 4123
Peretz, Don, 5836
Pérez, Louis A., Jr., 3830, 3916, 4124, 4176

Perinbam, B. Marie, 5509–10
Perkins, Dwight H., 4941
Perlin, Terry M., 861
Perlman, F., 3145
Perlmutter, Amos, 424
Pernoud, Georges, 1933
Péron-Lecouturier, S., 6065
Perrie, Maureen, 2506, 2643
Perry, David C., 509
Perry, Elizabeth J., 4525, 6161–62
Perry, Lewis, 846
Perry, Ronald W., 66
Persons, Stow, 1107
Pessen, Edward, 3211
Petegorsky, David W., 1743
Peterson, Arnold, 154
Peterson, Kessie, 4084
Peterson, Merrill D., 3574–75
Peterson, Patti, 718
Peterson, Suzanne, 2030
Pethick-Lawrence, Lord, 5282
Pethybridge, Roger, 2519, 2710
Petitfrère, Claude, 6049
Petras, James F., 3917–19, 4262, 4315, 4334
Petrie, Charles, 1674
Petrie, W. M. Flinders, 1472
Petros, James, 5030
Petrossian, Vahe, 5879
Pettee, George S., 67, 196
Peyre, Henri, 1991, 2441
Pfaff, William, 552
Pfeffer, Richard M., 4942–43
Phan Thien Chau, 5017
Phelan, John Leddy, 4405
Philip, G.D., 4435
Philipp, Mango Bayat, 5801
Philips, Cyril H., 5187
Phillips, J.F.V., 5443
Phillips, Jill, 4454
Phillips, Leona, 3227, 4454
Phillips, Ruby Hart, 4156
Phillips, W. Alison, 3369
Philp, Kenneth Roy, 2246
Pickles, Dorothy M., 5478
Pierson, Stanley, 1157
Pierson, William W., 3920
Pike, Douglas, 5080–82
Pike, Frederick B., 4436
Pilbeam, Pamela, 2319–20
Pimlott, Ben, 3191–92
Pin, A., 5109
Pinchon, Edgcumb, 4089
Ping-ti Ho, 4946
Pinkham, Lucile, 1776
Pinkney, David H., 2321–23, 2332
Pinner, Frank A., 745
Pinson, Koppel S., 1256

Author-Editor Index / 449

Pinto, Cruz, 5631
Pipes, Richard, 2626, 2634, 2711–13
Pittman, John, 3193
Plamenatz, John, 289, 320, 1058, 2257
Plank, John N., 4137
Plato, 1481
Plattner, Marc F., 1840
Plekhanov, Georgi Valentinovich, 862
Pocock, J.G.A., 1535
Pohl, James W., 1371
Pois, Robert A., 5915
Poitras, Guy E., 3844
Polak, H.S.L., 5282
Pole, J.R., 3250, 3298–99
Polin, Raymond, 1213
Polišenksý, Josef V., 2359
Pollak, Karen, 5727
Pollard, D.E., 4944
Pollock, David H., 3921
Polsby, N.W., 478
Polybius, 1482
Pomeroy, William J., 444, 5447, 5654
Pomper, Philip, 876, 903–04, 2714–15
Ponomarev, Boris N., 1059, 1214
Popkin, Jeremy D., 2093, 2101, 6035
Popper, Karl, 1060, 1426
Porath, Y., 5826
Porch, Douglas, 2258, 3204
Porter, Cathy, 1308
Porter, Gareth, 5119
Portes, Alejandro, 4288
Porzecanski, Arturo C., 4340
Posner, Charles, 3149
Pospelov, P.M., 2793
Possony, Stefan T., 1215, 2748, 2794
Poster, Mark, 2073, 3150
Postgate, Raymond, 197, 2176, 2259, 2360
Potash, Robert A., 4365
Potholm, Christian P., 5409, 5721
Potter, Jim, 6119
Poulantzas, Nicos, 1158
Powell, Edgar, 1499
Powell, John D., 4444
Powell, John R., 1681
Powell, T.G., 5968
Powell, W., 3615
Powelson, John P., 3922
Powers, Paul, 5283
Powers, Thomas, 3685
Prall, Stuart, 1598, 1777
Pratt, Cranford, 5404
Pratt, Helen Gay, 4741
Pravada, Vitezslav, 3163
Preston, Paul, 553, 3020, 3072
Preston, Richard A., 1317
Priaulx, Allan, 3151
Price, Don C., 4669

Price, H. Edward, Jr., 554
Price, Jane L., 1247, 4526
Price, Morgan P., 2581
Price, Roger D., 2324, 2393–95, 2442–43
Pridham, Geoffrey, 2986, 3006
Prince, J.F.T., 198
Prior, Andrew, 1061
Prosper, P.A., Jr., 2478
Proudhon, Pierre-Joseph, 911
Puhle, H.J., 3923
Purcell, Hugh, 3073, 4890
Purcell, Victor W., 4599, 4639
Pushkarev, Sergei G., 2582, 2716
Pustay, John S., 410, 683
Putnam, Robert D., 1248
Puzzo, Dante E., 3074–75
Pye, Lucian W., 399, 4891, 4990, 5146

Qayyum, Shah A., 5850
Quan, Lau-king, 4469
Quandt, W.B., 5479
Quartem, João, 4263
Quataert, Donald, 5297
Quattrocchi, Angelo, 3152
Quellel, Charif, 5511
Quesada, F.M., 4408
Quinana, Segundo V. Linares, 3831
Quinn, Peter A., 2917
Quirk, Robert E., 4036–37, 4049

Ra'anan, Uri, 336
Rabinowitch, Alexander, 2616–17, 2636, 2717
Rabinowitch, Janet, 2636, 2717
Race, Jeffrey, 68, 5083
Rachleff, Peter, 1062
Racz, Elizabeth, 6036
Rader, Daniel L., 2333
Rader, Melvin, 1064
Raddatz, Fritz J., 1063
Raddock, David M., 4945
Radhakrishnan, S., 5284
Radkey, Oliver Henry, 2618, 2644, 2718–19
Radvanyi, James, 3121
Raeburn, Michael, 5751
Raeff, Marc, 2168, 2260
Ragatz, Lowell J., 2173
Raikov, A.V., 5191
Rainbolt, John C., 35l7
Raines, John C., 1065, 1290
Rajasooria, Jeffrey, 5432
Ralston, David B., 179
Ralston, Richard David, 5512
Raman, A.S., 5192
Ramazani, Nesta, 6206
Ramazani, R.K., 6207

Ramm, Hartmut, 4270
Ramos, Roberto, 3983
Ramsaur, Ernest Edmondson, Jr., 5306
Ramsay, David, 3311
Rand, Ayn, 3686
Randall, Margaret, 1249
Ranke, Leopold von, 1622, 2261
Rankin, Hugh H., 3300, 3536
Rankin, Mary B., 4670
Rapoport, David C., 332, 606
Rappoport, Angelo S., 1108
Raptis, Michel, 4316
Rath, R.J., 2369
Ratliff, William, 3924
Rattan, Ram, 5227
Rauch, Georg von, 2720
Rauschning, Herman, 3007-08
Rawding, F.W., 5174, 5285
Rawley, James A., 356
Rawlinson, Frank, 4479
Rea, Kenneth W., 4702
Read, Christopher, 2520
Read, Herbert, 863
Recto, Manuelito M., 4577
Redclift, Michael, 695
Reddaway, Peter, 2795
Redstockings of the Women's Liberation Movement, 1309
Reed, Christopher, 2262
Reed, John, 2583, 4038
Reich, Charles A., 3635, 3687
Reichert, William O., 864
Reid, Anthony, 5138
Reid, John G., 4671
Reid, John Phillip, 3346-47, 6120
Reid, Malcolm, 3790
Reid, W. Stanford, 1536
Reimer, A. James, 5982
Reinermann, Alan J., 2853
Reisch, Michael, 2051
Reissner, Will, 1418
Rejai, Mostafa, 252, 321, 428, 1250, 1402, 4838, 4892
Remington, Robin A., 3160
Remmer, Karen L., 3925
Reshetar, John S., Jr., 2868
Restarick, Henry B., 4682
Resurreccion, Celedonio O., 5317-18
Reszler, André, 820
Revel, Jean-François, 1458, 3636, 3688
Revere, Robert B., 5452
Rey, Lucien, 5533
Reynolds, Barbara, 5865
Rhoads, Edward, 4672, 4693
Rhodes, James M., 3009
Riazanov, David, 1066, 1106
Rice, Edward E., 4991
Rice, G.W., 6037

Rich, Andrea, 1331
Richard, Yann, 6205
Richards, Michael, 1460, 2195, 2325
Richards, Vernon, 3076
Richardson, R.C., 1778
Richet, Denis, 1904
Richmond, Al, 3616
Richmond, Douglas W., 4047, 4068, 4073, 4077, 4083
Richmond, Hugh M., 1731
Richmond, John, 5851
Richter, Melvin, 2292
Rickards, Maurice, 1461
Ricketson, William F., 3593
Ricks, Timothy, 3749
Ridenour, Ron, 4346
Riding, Alan, 3832, 4347-48
Ridley, F.F., 2487
Ridley, Hugh, 2406
Riepe, Dale, 200
Riezler, Kurt, 263
Ripon Society, 201
Riquelme, John Paul, 933
Risjord, Norman, 3413
Ristic, Dragisa N., 3099
Ritcheson, Charles R., 2165, 3469, 3486
Ritter, Alan, 912, 5937
Ritter, Archibald R.M., 3921, 4201, 4207
Ritterberger, V., 2880
Rivera, Charles R., 520
Rizvi, Saiyid Athar Abbas, 5908
Roach, John, 2174
Roback, Leo, 3787
Robe, Stanley L., 3926
Roberts, Adam, 333, 637, 641, 3177
Roberts, Dick, 5031
Roberts, J.M., 1934
Roberts, John, 2263
Roberts, Paul Craig, 1067
Robertson, Priscilla, 2361
Robertson, William S., 3975
Robin, Léon, 1483
Robins, Robert S., 3823
Robinson, Geroid Tanquary, 2557
Robinson, James Harvey, 1550
Robinson, Joan, 4992
Robinson, Leland W., 5738
Robinson, Richard A.H., 3077, 3205
Robinson, Thomas W., 4993
Robiquet, Jean, 2016
Robottom, John, 4527
Robson, Eric, 3259, 3459
Rock, David, 4366, 6149
Rockefeller, John D., III, 3222
Rodnitzky, Jerome, 809
Rogel, Carole, 6058
Roger, Alan, 3301
Rogers, J.A., 899

Rogers, P.G., 386
Rogger, Hans, 2645
Rohdie, S., 5453
Rojo, Ricardo, 4256
Romani, George T., 2503
Romein, J., 4600
Romein, J.E., 4600
Ronalds, Francis Spring, 1537
Ronning, Chester, 4528
Roosevelt, Kermit, 5909
Roots, Ivan, 1623–24, 1723
Ropp, T., 2322
Rosberg, Carl G., Jr., 5392, 5410
Rosdolsky, Roman, 1068
Rose, R.B., 2033, 6038
Rose, Steven, 2074, 2094
Rose, Thomas, 521
Rosen, Milton K., 3689
Rosen, Stanley, 5008
Rosenau, James N., 202
Rosenberg, Arthur, 2619
Rosenberg, William G., 2597, 2721, 5963
Rosenstein-Redan, Paul N., 4289
Rosenstock-Hüssy, E., 203
Rosenstone, Robert A., 1462, 3078, 3648
Rosenthal, Bernice Glatzer, 2264, 6082
Rositzke, Harry, 3690
Ross, Gandy D., 1069
Ross, James R., 3781
Ross, Michael, 2137
Ross, Robert, 5366
Ross, Stanley R., 4000–01, 4039, 4079
Ross, Steven T., 1935
Rossanda, Rossana, 4839
Rossen, John (Johnny [Appleseed]), 3206, 3637
Rossetti, Stephan J., 517
Rossi, Peter H., 5787
Rossie, Jonathan G., 3394
Rossiter, Clinton, 3348, 3395
Roszak, Theodore, 3691
Rotberg, Robert I., 5411–12
Roth, Jack, 2480, 2488
Rothermund, Indira, 5286
Rothfels, Hans, 2341
Rothman, Stanley, 70
Rousseau, Jean Jacques, 1841
Rousset, Pierre, 5032, 5118
Roustan, Marius, 2095
Rowbotham, Sheila, 1310
Rowe, David N., 4529
Rowen, Herbert H., 1511, 1580–81
Rowney, Don Karl, 2818
Roxborough, Ian, 4317
Roy, Jules, 5480
Roy, M.N., 684, 4530
Royal United Services Institute, 607
Royster, Charles, 3420, 3460, 6121

Rubenstein, Richard E., 501, 3692–93
Rubin, Barry, 5910
Rubin, Jerry, 3605, 3617
Rubinoff, Lionel, 204
Rudé, George, 290, 1538, 1871, 1949, 1978, 1984, 2124, 2196, 2265, 5918
Rudebeck, Lars, 5632–33, 5641
Rudwick, Elliot, 3755
Rue, John E., 4893
Ruiz, Ramón Eduardo, 1388, 4040, 4060, 4157
Rule, James, 2326–27
Rulleau, Claudine, 5884
Rumpf, E., 2978
Runkle, Gerald, 865
Rush, Gary, 205
Russell, Bertrand, 1159, 1463, 2620
Russell, Conrad, 1634
Russell, D.E.H., 425
Russell, James, 5945
Russell, William H., 5175
Russell-Wood, A.J.R., 3976
Rutherford, John, 4041
Rutledge, Ian, 3194
Ryan, Alan, 895
Ryan, Dennis P., 6122
Ryder, A.J., 2904
Ryerson, Richard Alan, 3349

Sable, Martin H., 393
Sablinsky, Walter, 2521
Sachse, William L., 1746, 1755
Sacks, I. Milton, 5033
Sadat, Anwar El, 5852
Sagarra, Eda, 1332
Sagay, J.O., 5413
Sagnac, P., 1970
Saibel, Bob, 5911
Said, Abdul A., 206
Said, A.M., 5827
Saikal, Amin, 5912
Salamanca, Bonifacio S., 5319
Salazar, Gustavo A. Sánchez, 4246
Sale, Kirkpatrick, 3638–39, 3694
Salert, Barbara, 6
Salisbury, Harrison E., 2266, 2722, 4994
Salmon, J.H.M., 696, 1539, 1992
Salvadori, Massimo, 1160, 1216
Salvemini, Gaetano, 1936
Sampson, E.E., 746, 778
Samudavanija, Chairanan, 5121
Sanborn, Alvan Francis, 2031
Sanchez, George I., 4042
Sanchez, Jose M., 3079
Sandeen, Ernest R., 387
Sanders, Ronald, 1109
Sanderson, J.B., 1070
Sandhu, Swaram S., 5218

452 / Author-Editor Index

Sanford, Robinson Rojas, 4318
Sanger, R., 786
Sanger, Richard H., 274, 5679
San Juan, E., Jr., 1019
Sankaran, Nair V., 4555
Santos, Gloria M., 5320
Sargent, Lyman T., 3695
Sarkesian, Sam C., 445
Sarkisyanz, E., 4601
Sarrazin, Chantal, 5642
Sartre, Jean-Paul, 4158
Sathyamurthy, T.V., 71
Sattler, Martin J., 411
Satyaprakash, 5184
Saul, John S., 5346, 5367, 5414, 5602–04
Sauvage, Leo, 4257
Savelle, Max, 3350, 3531, 3833
Sayer, Derek, 1071
Sayigh, Rosemary, 5828
Saywell, William G., 4573
Scalapino, Robert A., 4480, 4531, 4602–03
Schaerf, Carlo, 574, 589
Schakovskoy, Zinaida, 2536, 2584
Schama, Simon, 1872
Schanche, Don A., 5880
Schapiro, Leonard, 1217–18, 2795
Scheer, Robert, 1427
Scheiner, Irwin, 697
Schell, Orville, 4533–34, 4742
Schemann, Ludwig, 2300
Schenk, Wilhelm, 1699
Scheven, Yvette, 5340
Schieder, Theodor, 207, 2197
Schiffrin, Harold Z., 4683
Schinz, Albert, 1814
Schleifer, James T., 2293, 2301
Schleunes, Karl A., 2059
Schlesinger, Arthur M., 3260, 3351–52
Schlesinger, Arthur M., Jr., 3367
Schmalhausen, S.D., 208
Schmitt, Bernadotte E., 2342
Schmitt, D., 5777
Schmitt, Karl M., 165, 3927
Schnapp, Alain, 3153
Schneider, Ronald M., 4099, 4388
Schneiderman, Jeremiah, 1072
Schoenbaum, David, 3010
Schöffer, I., 1403, 1570
Scholler, Heinrich, 5722
Schram, Stuart, 4840–41, 4894–95, 4995
Schrecker, Paul, 257
Schreiber, Jan, 608
Schulkind, Eugene, 2467
Schultz, J.A., 3314
Schulz, Gerhard, 2267
Schurer, H., 821

Schurmann, Franz, 72, 4532–34, 4946, 4986, 5096
Schwarcz, Vera, 4947
Schwartz, Benjamin, 4535, 4697, 4707, 4794, 4872, 4948
Schwartz, David C., 73, 264
Schwartz, Harry, 3174
Schwartz, Hillel, 5920
Schwarz, Fred, 209
Schwarz, Solomon M., 2522
Schwoerer, Lois G., 1756, 5992
Scobie, James R., 4367–68
Scott, James C., 698, 711, 4604
Scott, John, 2268
Scott, Robert E., 4043
Scott, Samuel F., 5922
Scott, Tom, 1544–45, 1551, 5983–84
Scott, William, 2125
Scribner, Bob, 1562
Sea, Thomas F., 1552
Seal, Anil, 4562
Seale, Bobby, 3738
Seale, Patrick, 3154
Sears, David O., 522
Seaver, Henry L., 1812
Seaver, Paul, 1700
Sedgwick, P., 2585
Sédillot, René, 5975–76
Sedwick, Ellery, 3591
Sée, Henri, 1979
Seebohm, F., 1540
Seegers, A., 5605
Seers, E. Dudley, 4159
Segal, Howard P., 6061
Segal, Ronald, 1344, 2831, 5368
Seidman, Joel I., 1169
Seifert, Harvey, 642
Seigel, Jerrold, 1073
Se-Jim Kim, 5152
Sekyi, H.V.H., 5369
Selassie, Bereket Habte, 5723
Selden, Mark, 1372, 4703, 4743, 5757
Seliger, Martin, 322–23, 1074
Selsam, Howard, 1161
Selser, Gregorio, 3928
Selucky, Radoslav, 5916
Selznick, Philip, 2621
Semmel, Bernard, 1075, 1280, 1291
Sen, Mohit, 5219
Sen, Surendra Nath, 5176
Sender, Kamon, 3080
Senghor, Léopold-Sédar, 5542–43
Senn, Alfred Erich, 2269
Seretan, L. Glen, 890
Serge, Victor, 2585, 2832
Servan-Schreiber, J.J., 3155
Service, Robert, 2622

Author-Editor Index / 453

Sessions, Kyle C., 1563, 5985
Sethna, D.P., 5097
Seton-Watson, Hugh, 1219-21, 1464, 2198, 2270, 2723
Sewell, Elizabeth, 74
Sewell, William H., Jr., 2271, 2381, 6069
Shaban, M.A., 5829
Shafer, Boyd C., 1257, 1266, 2022
Shaffer, Harry G., 918
Shanab, Robert E.A., 5768
Shanahan, William O., 5950
Shanin, Teodor, 2724
Shapiro, Gilbert, 2000
Shapiro, Jane P., 1189
Shaplen, Robert, 4605-06, 5084, 5098
Sharabi, Hisham B., 5830-31
Sharkey, Stephen R., 2199
Sharma, B.S., 5370
Sharma, Hari P., 4590
Sharma, Jagdish, 5185
Sharma, Nasira, 5914
Sharman, Lyon, 4684
Sharp, Gene, 622-23, 637, 643-45, 5287
Shashko, Philip, 2472
Shatz, Marshall S., 866
Shaull, M. Richard, 210
Shaver, Barbara A., 4286
Shaw, Peter, 3353
Shaw, Robert, 5341
Shaw, William H., 1076
Sheehan, Edward R.F., 5680
Sheehan, Vincent, 5288
Shepherd, George W., 1373
Shepperson, George, 6107
Sheps, Arthur, 3470
Sheridan, James E., 4536
Shibata, Minoru, 4933
Shibata, Shingo, 5085
Shiffren, H., 4480
Shih, Vincent Y.C., 4630
Shimbori, Michiya, 747
Shipley, Peter, 2272
Shirer, William L., 3011, 5289
Shklar, Judith N., 1842
Shore, Herb, 5606
Short, Anthony, 5147
Short, James F., Jr., 473, 523
Shorter, Edward, 2273
Showman, Richard K., 3226
Shridharani, Krishnlal, 5220
Shub, David, 2796
Shuja, Sharif M., 474
Shukman, Harold, 1191, 2773, 2797
Shulim, Joseph I., 1889, 2102-04
Shultz, Richard, 555
Shy, John W., 443, 3228, 3443, 3461
Siao-Yu, 4896

Sibley, Mulford Q., 646-47
Siegel, Jules, 75
Sievers, A.M., 275
Sigel, Roberta, 748
Sigmann, Jean, 2362
Sigmund, Paul E., Jr., 324, 3929, 4319, 5778
Silber, Irwin, 5779
Silj, Alessandro, 609
Silverman, Henry J., 810
Silverman, Kenneth, 3549
Silverman, Saul, 2798
Silvert, Kalman H., 693, 3834, 3930
Simmons, R.C., 3302
Simon, Reeva S., 5789
Simon, Sheldon W., 5120
Simone, Vera, 4537
Simpson, Amos E., 76
Simson, H.J., 5832
Sinclair, Andrew, 4258
Sinclair, Louis, 2813
Singer, Daniel, 3156
Singer, Martin, 5009
Singer, Peter, 648, 1077
Singh, Baljit, 446
Singh, Kusum J., 1374
Singh, Y., 653-54
Singleton, Seth, 2647
Sisson, Dan, 3223
Sithole, Ndabaningi, 5752
Sizwe, No, 5753
Sked, Alan, 2370
Skeffington, F. Sheehy, 2979
Skidmore, T.L., 4389
Skilling, H. Gordon, 3164, 3175
Skinner, Tom, 211
Sklar, Richard, 5341
Skocpol, Theda, 77-78, 1375-77, 1404, 1410
Skolnick, Jerome H., 19, 253, 3696
Skowronek, Jerzy, 1512, 5977
Skurnik, W.A.E., 5712
Slater, Philip, 3697
Slaughter, Jane, 5956
Sloan, John W., 4287
Sloan, Stephen, 5139
Sloane, William Milligan, 2062
Slote, Walter H., 4439
Slottman, William B., 2874
Slovo, Joe, 4271
Slusser, Robert M., 2598
Sluzar, S., 783, 791, 1423
Smail, John R.W., 5140
Smedley, Agnes, 4744
Smelser, Marshall, 3261
Smelser, Neil J., 212
Smirnow, Gabriel, 4320

Smit, J.W., 1571
Smith, Anthony D., 1267-68
Smith, Arthur L., 1331
Smith, Canfield F., 2274, 2725
Smith, Clarence Jay, 2726
Smith, Colin, 610
Smith, Duane E., 3658
Smith, Dwight L., 3229
Smith, Earl, 6187
Smith, Earl E.T., 4186
Smith, Edward Ellis, 2727
Smith, F.B., 2352
Smith, G.N., 2499
Smith, Irving H., 2833
Smith, John David, 349
Smith, L.M., 1569
Smith, M.B., 720
Smith, Myron J., Jr., 528
Smith, Page, 3303, 3576
Smith, Paul H., 3487
Smith, Peter H., 4369
Smith, Robert A., 2166
Smith, Robert B., 5034
Smith, Robert C., 5513
Smith, Robert F., 4067
Smith, Robert Freeman, 1378, 4137, 4177, 4196
Smith, Steven R., 1686
Smith, Tony, 5481
Smith, W.R., 5221
Snell, John L., 3012
Snellgrove, Laurence Ernest, 3081
Snow, Edgar, 4760-62
Snow, Peter G., 4370
Snow, Vernon F., 1651
Synder, David, 2200
Snyder, Louis L., 1269-70, 1345
Snyder, Richard C., 55
Sobel, Lester A., 611, 4321
Sobolev, P.N., 2591
Soboul, Albert, 1937-38, 1980, 2002, 2009-10, 2075, 2105
Soejatno, 5128
Soja, Edward W., 5338
Solari, Aldo, 3901
Solomon, Alan C., 5342
Solomon, Richard H., 4538, 4745
Solt, Leo F., 1682
Solzhenitsyn, Alexander, 2799
Somerville, John, 1056
Sommerfield, John, 3082
Sontag, Raymond, 2275
Sorel, Georges, 524, 2489-91
Sorich, Richard, 4455
Sorokin, Pitirim A., 213-15
Sosin, Jack M., 3488
Southwood, Ken, 475
Southworth, H.R., 3021

Spahn, Janet P., 782, 3595
Spahn, Theodore J., 782, 3595
Spalding, James C., 1379
Spanier, John W., 254
"The Spark," Editors of, 5431
Spence, Jonathan D., 6163
Spencer, H.R., 334
Spencer, Martin E., 934
Sperber, Manès, 476
Sperber, Murray A., 3083
Spielberg, Joseph, 712
Spitzer, Alan B., 867, 2201
Sprigge, C.J.S., 1078
Springer, Philip B., 216, 427
Sproxton, C., 2425
Spurlin, Paul M., 1815
Ssu-yü Teng, 4609, 4631-32
Staar, Richard F., 5930
Stadelmann, Rudolph, 2415
Staël, Madame la Baronne de, 2096
Stage, John L., 3304
Stahl, Friedrich J., 2416
Stalin, Joseph, 2592, 2800-01
Stallings, Barbara, 4329
Stampfer, Judah, 1465
Staniland, Martin, 5514
Stanley, John L., 2489, 6074
Stanley, Peter W., 5321, 5327
Stanlis, Peter J., 2139
Stanwood, Frederick, 5802
Starr, John Bryan, 4819, 4843, 4897
Statera, Gianni, 779
Stavenhagen, Rodolfo, 3931
Stearns, Peter N., 2363, 2492
Stecchini, Livio C., 337
Steenkamp, Willem, 5590
Steenland, Kyle, 4330
Steenson, Gary P., 2276
Steiger, George N., 4640
Stein, David Lewis, 3698
Stein, William W., 6151
Steinbach, Udo, 6208
Steinberg, David, 724
Steinberg, David J., 5328
Steinberg, I.N., 2728
Stempel, John D., 6209
Stenson, Michael, 5144, 5148
Stepan, Alfred, 4390
Stephens, Henry M., 1879, 1939
Stephens, James, 2980
Stephens, Winifred, 6039
Stephenson, Matthew A., 1067
Sterling, Claire, 556, 612
Stern, F., 2336
Stern, T., 365
Sternberg, Fritz, 2729
Sterrenburg, Lee, 265
Steuernagal, Gertrude A., 3722

Stevens, Evelyn P., 4002
Stevenson, David, 1541–42
Stevenson, J., 2338, 3468
Steward, Theophilus G., 3977
Stewart, John Hall, 1876, 1880
Stickter, Jim, 4322
Stiles, William Henry, 2371
Stinchcombe, Arthur L., 79
Stites, Richard, 1311, 2553
Stockhammer, Morris, 920
Stockton, Bayard, 2858
Stokes, E.T., 713
Stone, Glyn, 3022
Stone, John, 2303
Stone, Lawrence, 7, 1635, 1649
Story, D., 2396
Stourzh, Gerald, 5964
Stout, Harry S., 3500
Stout, Neil R., 3462
Strachey, John, 1162
Straka, Gerald M., 1779–81
Strakhovsky, Leonid I., 685, 2648
Strauss, Eric, 2981
Strauss, Harlan J., 2507
Street, John, 3978
Strong, Anna Louise, 4746–47
Stuart, Reginald C., 3239
Stuart, Susan M., 1361
Stuart-Fox, Martin, 5110–11
Stubaus, K.R., 3290
Sturgill, Claude, 1543
Sturtevant, David R., 5329
Suárez Andrés, 4138, 4232
Subrahamanian, N., 5228
Suchlicki, Jaime, 4160–61, 4178, 4290
Suda, Zdeněk L., 6059
Sudama, Trevor, 4844
Sugar, P.F., 1854
Suggs, George G., Jr., 3305
Sukanov, N.N., 2586, 2593
Suleiman, Michael W., 5803
Sullivan, David S., 411
Sully, François, 447
Sun Yat-sen, 4685–86
Suny, Roger G., 2730
Suny, Ronald, 2202
Sutherland, Elizabeth, 4208
Suttmeier, Richard P., 4539
Sutton, Antony, 394
Sutton, Horace, 3835, 5515
Svoboda, George J., 822
Swarup, Shanti, 4748
Sweezy, Paul M., 1140, 1163, 3824, 4151, 4269, 4323
Switzer, K.A., 520
Swomley, John M., Jr., 261
Sworakowski, Witold, 1173
Sydnor, Charles S., 3441

Syme, Ronald, 1490
Symmons-Symonolewicz, Konstantin, 1271
Sydenham, M.J., 1940, 2055
Syrop, Konrad, 3104
Szamuely, Tibar, 2649
Szelenyi, Ivan, 1149
Szilassy, Sander, 2877
Szulc, Tad, 3195, 3750, 3836, 3932

Taber, Robert, 448, 4162
Taburi, P., 2346
Taine, Hippolyte, 1971
Talbott, John, 557, 5454, 5482
Talmadge, D., 217
Talmon, J.L., 2277
Talmon, Y., 366
Tan, Chester C., 4540, 4641
T'ang Leang-li, 4749–50, 4763
Tang, Peter S.H., 4845
Tang Tsou, 4946, 4949–50
Tanham, George K., 5086, 5108
Tannahill, Neal R., 1222
Tannenbaum, Frank, 3837, 3933, 4003, 4044–45, 4053
Tanner, J.R., 1757
Tanter, Raymond, 80, 3826
Tarling, Nicholas, 4898, 5122
Tashjean, John E., 81
Tassi, Aldo, 3378
Tate, Thad W., 3370
Tauber, Gisela, 3564
Taurer, Bernard, 4846
Tawney, R.H., 1642–43
Taylor, A.J.P., 2171, 2278, 2417, 2430, 3013
Taylor, Edmond, 3137
Taylor, F. Jay, 3084
Taylor, George E., 4614
Taylor, George V., 1950–51
Taylor, Philip A.M., 1636
Taylor, Philip B., Jr., 4337
Teiwes, Frederick C., 4951
Témime, Emile, 3032
Temperley, Harold W., 1758
Templin, Ralph T., 649
Teodori, Massimo, 3596
Terrall, Mary, 3125
Terrill, Ross, 4899, 4952
Thackeray, Frank W., 2279
Thaxton, Ralph, 4481, 4800, 4810
Theen, Rolf H.W., 2650, 2802
Thiers, M.A., 1941
Thirion, Andre, 1251
Thomas, Emory M., 357
Thomas, Hugh, 3023, 3085, 4139–40, 4163–64
Thomas, Keith, 1670

Thomas, Norman, 1164
Thomas, Paul, 1079
Thomas, Tony, 3782
Thomis, Malcolm I., 2280
Thompson, Brian, 5724
Thompson, Edward J., 5177-78
Thompson, James M., 1881, 1942, 2046, 2126-27
Thompson, John M., 2517, 6083
Thompson, Robert, 412, 2281, 4578
Thompson, William Irwin, 2982
Thompson, William R., 335, 348
Thoreau, Henry David, 650
Thorn, Richard S., 4119
Thornton, Richard C., 4541-42
Thornton, Thomas P., 1179
Thrupp, Sylvia L., 388
Thucydides, 1484
Thwaites, John, 3309
Tibi, Bassam, 6198
Tierney, Brian, 1963, 2623
Tignor, Robert L., 5804
Tillion, Germaine, 5483-84
Tilly, Charles, 477-78, 666, 699, 1349, 1466, 2138, 2200, 2203, 2273, 2282, 2326-27
Tilly, Louise, 2282
Tilly, Richard, 2282
Timasheff, Nicholas S., 413, 2651
Timberg, Thomas A., 5193
Timothy, Bankole, 5444
Tinker, Hugh, 1346
Tisa, John, 3086
Tise, Larry E., 3535
Toch, Hans, 272
Tocqueville, Alexis de, 1943, 2302-05, 2397
Todorov, Nikolaj, 2474
Tokes, Rudolf L., 2878
Toland, John, 3014
Tolles, Frederick B., 3406
Tolstoy, Leo, 651-52
Tomasevich, Jozo, 3100
Tompkins, Keitha, 897
Tompkins, Stuart R., 2624, 2731
Tongko, Primo L., 5322
Toohey, Robert E., 3489
Toplin, Robert Brent, 3699
Topolski, Jerzy, 1429
Topping, Seymour, 4543
Torbado, Jesús, 6095
Tormay, Cecile, 2587
Torres, Camilo R., 4406
Torres, Simon, 4264
Touraine, Alain, 3157
Touré, Sékou, 5545
Townsend, Peter, 4751
Townsend, William Cameron, 4069

Townshend, Charles, 2918, 6090
Toye, Hugh, 5114
Toynbee, Arnold J., 82, 1419
Toynbee, Philip, 3087
Trager, Frank N., 4544, 4607
Traikov, Veselin, 2475
Trautmann, Frederic, 5931
Treadgold, Donald W., 2803
Treasure, Geoffrey, 1587-88
Tregonning, Kennedy G., 4464
Tremblay, Louis-Marie, 3787
Trenard, Louis, 6066
Trend, J.B., 3979
Trevelyan, George M., 1625, 1782, 2431-32
Trevelyan, George Otto, 3306
Trevelyan, Humphrey, 5833
Treviranus, G.R., 2283, 2732
Trevor-Roper, Hugh R., 1644, 1687
Trimberger, Ellen Kay, 1228, 1405, 1410, 5957
Trollope, Theodosia, 2433
Trotsky, Leon, 2468, 2523, 2804, 2834-45, 3088, 4545
Trotsky, Natalya Sedova, 2832
Truitt, Willis H., 309
Trullinger, James Walker, Jr., 5087
Trusker, Andy, 4375
Truzzi, Marcello, 216, 427
Tsien, Tsuen-Hsuin, 4456
Tucker, Gerald E., 1380
Tucker, Robert, 2454
Tucker, Robert C., 1080-82, 2652, 2733, 2749
Tullis, F.L., 4437
Turley, William S., 5088
Turnbull, Patrick, 3089, 5035
Turner, Ian, 2653
Turner, John B., 3751
Turner, John J., Jr., 513
Turner, Ralph H., 83, 218
Turner, Robert F., 5089
Turner, Thomas, 5372
Turok, Ben, 1467
Turton, Andrew, 5123
Tuveson, E.L., 389

Ubbelohde, Carl, 3490
Udokang, Okon, 5558
Uhalley, Stephen, Jr., 4900
Ulam, Adam B., 325, 1083, 2284-85, 2625, 2654
Uldricks, Ted, 2655
Underdown, David, 1678
Ungar, Sanford J., 3151
Unger, Irwin, 3700
United Kingdom, Foreign Office, 4953
Unnithan, T.K., 653-54

Untermann, Ernest, 219
Upton, Anthony F., 2862
Urdang, Stephanie, 5634
Uribe, Armando, 4335
Urry, John, 220
Urrutia Lleo, Manuel, 4233
Utete, C. Munhamu Botsio, 5754

Valdelin, Jan, 5713
Valdés, Nelson P., 4125, 4203, 4217
Valenta, Jirl, 3176
Valentin, Veit, 2418
Valentinov, Nikolay, 2805
Valenzuela, Arturo, 4291
Valenzuela, J. Samuel, 4291
Vali, Ferenc A., 3122
Vallier, Ivan, 3934
Vallières, Pierre, 3791
Van Alstyne, Richard W., 3323, 3521
Vance, Cyrus R., 560
Vanden, Harry E., 3838
Van Den Berghe, P.L., 1347
Van der Laan Bouma, Rob, 5924
Van Der Wusten, H., 2919
Van Duzer, Charles Hunter, 1988
Van Dyke, Stuart, Jr., 5455
Van Heijenoort, Jean, 2846
Van Kley, Dale, 2018
Van Ness, Peter, 4546, 4847
Van Paassan, Pierre, 3015
Van Slyke, Lyman P., 4752
Van Tyne, Claude H., 3307, 3356, 3491
Vardys, V. Stanley, 1084
Vargas, Florencia, 4324
Vasys, Dalius, 2508
Vatikiotis, P.J., 37, 5834, 5837, 5853–54
Vaughan, C.E., 1843
Vaughan, Robert, 1724
Véliz, Claudio, 3935–36, 3999, 4139
Velli, M., 1252
Venter, Al J., Jr., 5635, 5643
Venturi, Franco, 2734
Vergara, José Manuel, 4324
Vermeil, Edmond, 3016
Vernadsky, George, 2806
Vernon, Richard, 2481, 2493
Ver Steeg, Clarence L., 3416
Veyne, Paul, 291
Vibart, Cononel E., 5179
Vickers, George R., 3701
Vidal-Naquet, Pierre, 3153
Vien, Nguyen Khac, 5036–37, 5090
Viet Nam, Democratic Republic of, 5020–21
Villegas, Daniel Cosío, 3937
Viñas, Angel, 3024
Vincent, David, 811
Viorst, Milton, 3702

Vivarelli, Roberto, 2494
Vivas, Eliseo, 3723
Vivó, Raúl Valdés, 5725
Vizetelly, Ernest Alfred, 868
Voegelin, Eric, 935, 1999
Vogel, Ezra F., 4954
Vohra, Ranbir, 4547
Völgyes, Ivan, 2871, 2879
Voline, 2735
Volskii, N.V., 2807
Volsky, George, 4202
von Albertini, Rudolf, 5415, 6188
Von der Mehden, Fred R., 525
Vo Nguyen Giap, 5091–92
Von Laue, Theodore H., 2656, 2736, 5429
Vossler, Otto, 3577
Vovelle, Michel, 6040
Vucinich, Wayne S., 3101

Wada, George, 479
Wadlow, Joan K., 1258, 5734
Waelder, Robert, 221
Wagandt, Charles L., 3224
Wager, W. Warren, 1406
Wagner, Francis S., 3123
Wahlke, John C., 3319, 3357
Wai, Dunstan M., 5371
Wakeman, Frederic, Jr., 4482, 4901
Walker, Andrew G., 4787, 4848
Walicki, Andrzej, 2204
Walker, Angus, 1085
Walker, Thomas W., 4349–50
Wall, Irwin M., 5456
Wallace, Donald Mackenzie, 2737
Wallace, Melanie, 450
Wallace, Michael, 452, 480
Wallbank, Thomas W., 4563
Waller, Derek J., 4548
Wallerstein, Immanuel, 5416–17
Wallis, W.D., 390
Wallot, Jean-Pierre, 5969
Walsby, Harold, 326
Walsh, James E., 2372
Walter, Eugene Victor, 481–82, 526
Walzer, Michael, 812, 1468, 1652–53, 1660, 2034, 2037
Wandibba, Simiyu, 5516
Wandycz, Piotr S., 1430
Wang Fan-Hsi, 4764
Wang, Gungwu, 4955
Wang, James C., 4907
Wang, Shih, 4770
Ward, Alan J., 2983
Ward, A.W., 1758
Ward, Barbara, 327
Ward, Colin, 869
Warr, Michael, 5714
Warren, Frank A., 1165

Warren, Harris Gaylord, 3839–40
Warren, Mercy Otis, 3312
Warth, Robert D., 2564, 2745, 2808, 2847
Wasserman, Mark, 3891, 4004
Wasserstrom, Robert, 4094
Waterburg, Ronald, 4063
Waters, M., 2898
Watkins, Frederick, 316
Watson, Andrew, 5124
Watson, Francis M., 614
Watson, I. Bruce, 5229
Watt, Richard M., 2905
Watterson, John S., 3442
Waung, W.S., 4549
Weatherbee, Donald E., 5141
Weatherhead, R.W., 4001
Weaver, Gary R., 780
Weaver, James H., 780
Weaver, Jerry L., 4095
Webb, Beatrice, 1223
Webb, Sidney, 1223
Weber, Eugen, 667
Weber, Max, 1253
Weber, Ralph, 1324
Webster, Charles, 1808
Webster, Donald E., 5309
Webster, Graham, 1491
Webster, J.B., 5418
Webster, Nesta, 222, 1985
Wedgwood, Cicely V., 1582, 1626–28, 1725
Weigard, Hermann J., 1553
Weiker, Walter F., 5308
Weinberg, Henry H., 6073
Weiner, Peter H., 4096
Weingraf, Tom, 5451
Weinstein, Donald, 391
Weinstein, James, 3703
Weinstein, Martin, 4197
Weinstein, Michael A., 503
Weinstein, Warren, 5372
Weintraub, Dov, 5715
Weintraub, Stanley, 3090
Weir, Robert M., 3407
Weisser, Michael, 2286
Welch, Claude E., Jr., 223, 483, 1407
Wells, William V., 3562
Welsh, William A., 1254
Wendel, Jacques M., 6123
Werlich, David P., 4420–21
Werner, Jayne, 5075
Werstein, Irving, 3091
Wertheim, W.F., 1318
Weslager, C.A., 3354
Wessell, Leonard P., Jr., 1086
Wesson, Robert G., 1087, 1224
Westby, D., 748–49
Western, J.R., 1783

Westrich, Sal Alexander, 1593
Weydenthal, Jan B. de, 3105
Weyl, Nathaniel, 4070, 4165
Weyl, Sylvia, 4070
Wheaton, Eliot B., 3017
Wheeler, Douglas L., 2205, 5591
Wheeler, Harvey, 255
Wheeler, Lois, 6167
Wheeler, Richard, 3251
Wheelwright, E.L., 4996
Whelan, James, 6146
Whelan, Joseph G., 1170
Whetten, Lawrence L., 1171, 5882
Whitaker, Arthur P., 3799, 3980, 4005
Whitaker, Paul M., 5559
White, Christine Pelzer, 5038–39
White, D. Fedotoff, 2588
White, Gordon, 4922
White, J. Todd, 3230
White, Judy, 4325
White, M.M., 3367
White, Morton, 3379
White, Richard Alan, 3938
White, Robert A., 4090
White, Wayne E., 5787
Whiteford, Scott, 712
Whiteman, Anne, 3233
Whiting, Allen S., 4673
Whyte, Martin King, 4850
Wiarda, Howard J., 3196, 3813, 3841–42, 3939–40, 4002, 4095, 4107, 4132, 4291, 4337, 4349, 4418
Wick, Daniel L., 6041
Wickwire, Franklin B., 3492
Wiener, P., 30
Wigdil, W., 85
Wilbur, Clarence Martin, 4644, 4687, 4696
Widman, Allan K., 2524, 2537, 2558
Wieczynski, Joseph L., 2568
Wilgus, A. Curtis, 3018, 3797
Wilkerson, Loree, 4234
Wilkie, James W., 4046, 4054
Wilkinson, David, 358
Wilkinson, Paul, 615–16
Wilkinson-Latham, Christopher, 5180
Will, George F., 562
Willer, David, 86
Willers, David, 6196
Willetts, H.T., 1191
Williams, Albert Rhys, 2738–39, 2809
Williams, Ann, 5921
Williams, D., 1822
Williams, Desmond, 2984
Williams, E.N., 1501
Williams, Edward J., 3941
Williams, Gwyn A., 2011
Williams, J.-C., 5489
Williams, L., 2738

Williams, Maurice, 4688
Williams, Merryn, 1844
Williams, Roger L., 2469-70
Williams, S.L., 2471
Williams, William Appleman, 3553
Williamson, Audrey, 3592
Wills, Antoinette, 6060
Wills, Garry, 3578
Wilson, Bryan, 392
Wilson, Carlos, 4341
Wilson, Charles, 1583
Wilson, Colin, 224, 1292
Wilson, D.A., 5413
Wilson, David A., 400
Wilson, Derek, 1272
Wilson, Dick, 4550, 4784, 4902-03
Wilson, Edmund, 2740
Wilson, George M., 87
Wilson, Greta O., 5142
Wilson, Henry S., 5419
Wilson, Jerome D., 3593
Wilson, Patrick, 4461-62
Wimbush, S. Enders, 5761
Windrow, Martin, 1614
Windsor, Philip, 3177
Winegarten, Renee, 1333
Wingfield-Stratford, Esmé, 1675-76
Winkler, Heinrich August, 1469
Winn, Peter, 4331
Wint, Guy, 4753-54
Winter, G., 292
Wirth, John D., 4376, 4391
Wishrich, Robert S., 1470, 2848
With, Christopher B., 2407
Wittfogel, Karl A., 1408, 2657, 4483, 4708, 4851
Woddis, Jack, 1471, 5107, 5529
Wolf, Charles, Jr., 406
Wolf, Eric, 700-01, 714
Wolfe, Alan, 3704
Wolfe, Bertram D., 1088, 2658, 2741-43, 2810-11
Wolfe, Don M., 1732, 1734
Wolff, P., 1498
Wolff, Robert Paul, 870
Wolfgang, Marvin E., 473, 523
Wolfskill, George, 4047, 4068, 4073, 4077, 4083
Wolfson, Murray, 936, 1089
Wolfstein, Eugene Victor, 1409, 3783
Wolin, Sheldon S., 234, 771
Woloch, Isser, 715, 2058
Wolpe, Harold, 88
Wolpert, J.F., 89
Wolpert, Stanley A., 5222, 6164
Womack, John, Jr., 4091
Wong, Young-tsu, 4651
Woo, T.C., 4674

Wood, Dennis B., 4171
Wood, Gordon S., 3308, 3371, 3532
Wood, Sidney, 3309
Woodcock, George, 655, 823, 871-72, 2365, 5290
Woods, T.P.S., 1637
Woodside, Alexander B., 5093
Woodward, C. Vann, 3752
Woodward, E.L., 2287
Woodward, William, 3594
Woodrych, A.H., 1683
Woolsey, Theodore D., 1225
Worcester, Donald E., 3981
Worsley, Peter M., 8, 90, 367, 1229, 5493, 5782
Wright, D.G., 2053
Wright, Esmond, 3358, 3493
Wright, Freeman J., 3941
Wright, Mary C., 4648, 4655, 4795
Wright, Tennant C., S.J., 4852
Wriston, Harry M., 5970
Wu, Eugene, 4448, 4457
Wylie, Laurence, 3125
Wylie, Raymond F., 4853, 4904, 4956
Wyndham, Francis, 2849
Wynia, Gary W., 3942

Xuan Khu Dang, 5094

Yang, C.K., 4551
Yarmolinsky, Avrahm, 2744
Ybarra, T.R., 3982
Yeh Chiang, 4905
Yen Chang-Lin, 4906
Yen Ching Hwang, 4675
Yglesias, J., 4209
Ying-Mao Kau, 4709
Yip, Ka-Chef, 4472
Yoder, Dale, 9, 91, 4006
Yoke, Kitazawa, 4579
Yokoyama, Suguru, 4801
York, Neil L., 3444
Young, Alfred F., 813-14, 3310
Young, Arthur, 1883
Young, Ernest P., 4656-57
Young, George M., 1726
Young, James, 635
Young, Jordon M., 4377, 4392
Young Lords Party, 3225
Young, Marilyn B., 5963
Young, Nigel, 3705
Young, Peter, 1727
Young, Stephen B., 5040
Young, Whitney M., Jr., 3751
Yuan-Li Wu, 4957
Yuan Tung-li, 4458
Yule, George S.S., 1671
Yu-Sheng, Lin, 4552

Zabih, Sepher, 5914
Zacek, Joseph F., 5978
Zagorin, Perez, 10, 1513, 1638, 1645, 1661, 2147
Zahar, Renate, 5530-31
Zaidi, A. Moin, 5223
Zaller, Robert, 1631
Zammit, J. Ann, 4326
Zaninovich, M. George, 3102
Zartman, I. William, 3178, 5636-37
Zasloff, Joseph J., 4608, 5013, 5015
Zeitlin, Irving M., 1090, 2306
Zeitlin, Maurice, 3919, 4141, 4166, 4292
Zelnick, Reginald E., 2659
Zeman, Z.A.B., 2288, 3179
Zenker, E.V., 873, 2373

Zetkin, Klara, 2812
Zetlin, Mikhail, 2289
Zetterbaum, Marvin, 2307
Zhang, Kaiyuan, 4658
Zhang, Lei, 6166
Zilliacus, Konni, 2525
Zinner, Paul E., 2177, 3124
Zolberg, Aristide, 5517
Zolbrod, Paul, 1326
Zollschan, George K., 86
Zondag, Cornelius H., 4121
Zorza, Richard, 3706
Zucker, A.E., 2419
Zuckerman, Michael, 3533
Zwiebach, Burton, 656
Zylawy, R., 2085

Subject Index

References are to entry numbers

Abbasid Revolution, 5829
Abd al-Qadir, 5464
Action Française, 2486
Adams, John, 3427, 3434, 3437
Adams, Samuel, 3435, 3550–62, 3574
Adler, Friedrich, 6051
Addis Ababa, 5704
Afghanistan, 1366, 5291–94
Africa, 1355, 1370, 1407, 1437, 5330–754, 5755–56, 5765, 6175–96. *Also see* Pan-Africanism; Southern Africa; and separate listings for African countries
  colonialism in, 5333, 5359, 5366, 5379, 5383, 5389, 5415, 6182, 6188
  East, 5357, 5414
  history of, 5330, 5337, 5374–75, 5379, 5381–82, 5385–87, 5390, 5395–98, 5406, 5408, 5413, 6186
  and ideology, 5344, 5349, 5356, 5428, 5438, 5745, 6185
  liberation movements in, 5331, 5344, 5382, 5393, 5416, 5418, 6176
  and Marxism, 5345, 5349, 5358, 5365
  military coups d'état in, 330–31, 341, 1407, 5388, 5403, 5640, 6177
  nationalism in, 5346, 5361, 5370, 5377, 5410, 5419, 5770, 6176, 6190
  North, 5384, 5814. *Also see* Middle East
  peasants of, 5348, 5361, 5367, 5372, 5401
  politics in, 5341–42, 5344, 5356, 5360, 5376, 5389, 5409, 5416–17, 5505
  religion in, 5352, 5384, 5402
  revolutionary politics in, 5348, 5360, 5365, 5367, 5379, 5381, 5394, 5396, 5399–400, 5408, 5450, 5497, 5522, 5673, 6183
  socialism in, 5392, 5404, 5538, 5540–43
  and Soviet Union, 6184
  student rebellion in, 731, 5412
  Sub-Saharan, 5344, 5347, 5411–12
  terrorism in, 564, 6177

Africa *(continued)*
  and United States, 5368
  West, 5397, 5418–*19*
Agrarian reform. *See* Land reform
Agrarian revolt, 712, 1961, 2286, 2320, 2557, 4053, 4359, 4804, 4810, 5715, 5776. *Also see* Provincial politics
Agriculture, 2368, 2618, 2642, 3058, 3918, 3931, 4330–31, 5776, 6014
Alexander I, 2279
Alexander II, 1298
Algeria, 398, 409, 557, 5378, 5457–62, 5465, 5467, 5469–70, 5473, 5477–79, 5481–84, 5486, 5509, 6176, 6189
  peasants of, 5509
  terrorism in, 5454, 5471
  war in, 5449, 5456, 5463, 5469, 5474, 5480, 5482
Algerian Revolution (1954–1962), 5445–84. *Also see* Abd al-Qadir; Fanon, Frantz; *Front de libération nationale* (FLN)
  and France, 5456–57, 5464, 5475, 5478, 5481, 5484, 6189
  French Algerians in, 5455, 5466, 5468
Algiers, 3745
Algiers, Battle of, 5454, 5512
Alienation, 264, 748, 1043, 1049, 1067, 5530
Allende, Salvador, 4273–74, 4279–81, 4284–87, 4289–90, 4295, 4298, 4300–01, 4304, 4308, 4313–14, 4318–19, 4321–22, 4324, 4327–28, 4330–32, 4334, 6145–46
American Revolution (1776–1783), 1360, 1371, 1378–79, 1394–95, 1430, 1457, 1535, 1858, 2293, 3226–549, 5922, 5958, 5962, 5964–65, 5967, 5969, 6015, 6100–23. *Also see* entries for individual revolutionists
  and Articles of Confederation, 3421
  Boston Tea Party, 3338

461

American Revolution *(continued)*
  clergy during, 3495, 3501, 3503
  Coercive Acts and, 3324
  committees of correspondence in, 3349, 3390
  and Declaration of Independence, 3365, 3369, 3373, 3578
  and Enlightenment, 3360, 3364, 3377, 3567
  Founding Fathers of, 3426, 3431–32, 3439
  and the Great Awakening, 3497, 3505
  and law, 3346, 6112, 6120
  Loyalists during, 1379, 3339, 3487, 3493, 3523
  military in, 3230, 3347, 3401, 3443, 3448, 3453, 3458–61, 5922, 6104, 6122
  and nationalism, 1274, 3239, 3323, 3329, 3353, 3428, 3494, 3512, 3523, 3528, 3531, 3567
  Navigation Acts and, 3331
  press in, 6103, 6115
  Quakers in, 3506, 6117
  relations with Britain during, 793, 3235, 3332, 3341, 3352, 3434, 3463–93, 6100–01, 6119
  and religion, 3494–506, 6117
  revolutionary ideas in, 3359, 3361–63, 3366, 3370–73, 3376, 3499, 6106, 6111, 6113
  in the South, 3455, 3534–35, 6116
  and the Stamp Act, 3344, 3354
  and war, 3227, 3243–62
  women in, 3507–12
Anarchism, 800, 815–912, 1159, 1463, 2867, 3615, 3644, 3651, 5934–37. *Also see* Bakunin, Mikhail; Berkman, Alexander; DeLeon, Daniel; Godwin, William; Goldman, Emma; Kropotkin, Peter; Nechaev, Sergei; Proudhon, Pierre-Joseph
  in Bohemia, 822
  in Brazil, 4382
  in Germany, 830
  history of, 821, 829, 837, 854–57, 873
  in Japan, 4571
  and Karl Marx, 1079, 2215
  in Mexico, 838, 4031
  in Russia, 826, 2627, 2661
  in Spain, 828, 845, 3042, 5934–36
  theories of, 819, 831, 834, 837, 873, 5937
  in the United States, 824–25, 833, 864, 3527
  women and, 832, 850, 5935
Ancien régime. See subentry under French Revolution (1789–1799)

Andalusia, 5934
Andean peasant revolts, 3811, 4428
Angola, 1385, 5380, 5564–73, 5576, 5578–79, 5581, 5583, 5586–91
  warfare in, 5582, 5589
Angolan Revolution (1961–1975), 5548–49, 5551, 5553, 5561, 5563–91, 6191. *Also see* Portuguese Africa
  and liberation, 5548, 5553, 5574–75, 5582, 5617
  nationalism in, 5586, 5588
  politics of, 5569
  and Portugal, 5566, 5576, 5578, 6191
Anticolonialism, 5074, 5359. *Also see* Colonialism; Liberation
Anushilan Samiti, 6153
Aprista, 4429–30, 4432
Arafat, Yasir, 605
Arab World, 335, 5786, 5811, 6191. *Also see* Africa, North; Islam; Middle East; and separate listings for individual Arab countries
  guerrillas in, 5825
  and Marxism, 5818
  and nationalism, 5677, 5784, 5805, 5818, 5826, 5830, 6198
  socialism in, 5790, 5827
Argentina, 4356–70, 6149
  military in, 4360, 4365
  nationalism in, 4360
  politics of, 4357, 4362, 4365–66, 4369–70, 6149
Argentine Revolution (1930), 4356
Aristocracy, 1497, 1764, 1769, 1964, 1966, 2001, 2003–06, 2169, 2188, 2359, 2368, 2505, 6020, 6041
Aristotle, 169, 1474, 1476–77, 1479, 1483
Armenia, 1455, 2202, 2254
Armies. *See* Military
Arnold, Benedict, 3420
Art, 1461, 2691, 3086, 6003, 6081
Asia, 1437, 4445–5329, 5755, 5765. *Also see* Middle East; South Asia; Southeast Asia; and listings for individual Asian countries
  Communism in, 4584, 4602–03
  East, 4446, 4581
  and nationalism, 4586, 4600, 5771
  Northeast, 4465
  peasants of, 4594, 4604
  terrorism in, 564, 4555
  and United States, 4585, 4596
Assassination, 606, 5665
Athens Revolt (287 B.C.), 1475
Austria, 1120
  military in, 2366, 2370
  peasants in, 2368

Subject Index / 463

Austria *(continued)*
and socialism, 1120
Austro-Hungarian Revolution (1848), 2334, 2357, 2366–73
Authority, 239, 406, 1563, 2656, 4995, 5134
Axelrod, Pavel, 2540
Azania, 5753

Baader-Meinhof, 569
Baal, 5384
Ba'athist Revolution, 5795. *Also see* Iraq
Babeuf, Gracchus, 2068, 2080, 2094, 5976
Bakunin, Mikhail, 832, 874–83
Balkans, 385, 690, 2241, 2474–75, 2692, 5974, 6054
Bangladesh, 4595
Barrès, Maurice, 670
Basques, 531, 547, 553. *Also see* Spain
Baumann, Bommi, 613
Bavaria, 379, 2900, 3006
Baxter, Richard, 1694
Bazargan, Mehdi, 5861
Beals, Carleton, 3809
Becker, Carl, 6110
Behavioral theory, 122, 212, 3315
Belgian Revolution (1830), 6066
Bengal, 4553, 5188
Berkeley, University of California, 718, 756, 771, 776. *Also see* Student rebellions
Berkman, Alexander, 884–86
Bernstein, Eduard, 1110–11, 1135
Berrigan, Daniel, 3599
Betancourt, Romulo, 4441
Bihar, 6155
Black Panthers, 3730, 3732, 3769, 3775, 3777
Black power, 772, 3725, 3753, 3772, 3778, 5745
Black Revolution (c. 1954–   ), 522, 772, 3213–14, 3224, 3724–83, 5500, 6128–29. *Also see* Black Panthers; Black power; Cleaver, Eldridge; Davis, Angela; Ghettos; Jackson, George; Malcolm X; Racism
and Black nationalism, 3740, 3744, 3746, 3755, 3762, 6129
protest in, 3748, 3754, 3765
and revolt, 3741, 3753, 3766, 3774
riots in, 3741–43, 3752, 3760, 3766
violence in, 3760, 3765, 3781
Blanqui, Louis Auguste, 867, 2447, 6056
Bloch, Marc, 5982
Blond, 6010
Bogomils, 385

Bohemia, 822
Bolívar, Simon, 3948, 3961, 3968, 3972, 3979, 3981–82
Bolivia, 3864, 4240, 4243, 4246, 4252, 4254
military in, 4120
peasants in, 4106, 4110
politics of, 4117, 4120
Bolivian Revolution (1952), 3805, 3814, 3869, 4100–21
Böll, Heinrich, 613
Bolshevik Revolution. *See* October Revolution; Russian Revolution (1917)
Bolshevism, 1299, 1311, 2248, 2522, 2532, 2543, 2565, 2567, 2574, 2578, 2594–625, 2773, 4072, 5952, 6079, 6086. *Also see* Lenin, V. I.; Menshevism; October Revolution (1917); Russian Revolution (1917); Trotsky, Leon
Boudicca's Revolt (60 A.D.), 1486–87, 1491
Bourbons, 2328
Bourgeoisie, 2001, 2007–08, 2187, 3391, 3690, 4419, 4795, 5362, 5428, 5713. *Also see* Class
Boxer Rebellion (1900), 4528, 4633–41. *Also see* Chinese Revolutions (General)
Boyle, Robert, 1690
Brabant, 6003
Brazil, 1385, 3976, 4263, 4371–92, 5579, 6150
and Communism, 4382
military in, 4377, 4390
politics of, 4375, 4384–85, 4388–90
Prestes Column, 4386
Brazilian Revolution (1930), 4372, 4376–77, 4392
Brezhnev, Leonid, 2612
Britain. *See* England; Great Britain
Buddhism, 363, 365
Bukharin, Nikolai, 5947
Bulgaria, 2255
Bulgarian Revolution (1876), 2472–75
Bunyan, John, 1684
Buonarroti, Filippo Michele, 2080, 2224
Bureaucracy, 229, 1405, 1973, 2214, 4850, 4954, 5628
Burgh, James, 3366
Burke, Edmund, 1369, 1392, 2139–66, 3241, 6050
Burke, Thomas, 3442
Burma, 4582, 4601
Burton, Henry, 1668
Cabral, Amilcar, 1355, 5488, 5613, 5644–48, 5662–73

464 / Subject Index

Calonne, Charles Alexandre de, 2004
Calvin, John, 1524, 1572
Cambodia, 4574-75, 4579, 5116-20
Canada, 3597, 3784-3791, 6108
Canton Rising (1902-1903), 4470
Cape Verde Islands, 5610, 5625, 6194.
  Also see Cabral, Amilcar;
  Guinea-Bissau Revolution
Capital, 977, 1014, 1029, 1068, 1071. Also
  see Marx, Karl
Capitalism, 273, 921, 977, 1014, 1029,
  1049, 1196, 1397, 1410, 1795, 2895,
  4481, 5793, 5894
Cárdenas, Lázaro, 4010, 4068-70
Caribbean, 3792, 3855, 3899
Carlos: Portrait of a Terrorist, 610
Carnot, Lazare, 6022
Carranza, Venustiano, 4071-73
Castro, Fidel, 1400, 3862, 3888, 4122,
  4136, 4161, 4172-74, 4178, 4186,
  4192, 4198, 4210-18, 4220-25,
  4227-31, 4233-34, 4296. Also see
  Castroism; Cuban Revolution (1959)
Castroism, 3924, 4219, 4226, 4232
Catalan Revolt, 1810
Catholic Church, 1282-83, 1289, 1532,
  1585, 2017-18, 2020, 2853, 2920,
  2961, 3021, 3606, 3884, 3893, 3898,
  3908, 3911, 3934, 4048-49, 4397,
  4400, 4409, 6133
Cavaignac, Louis, 2384
Central Europe, 2212, 5974, 5977-78.
  Also see Eastern Europe
Ceylon, 4462
Charisma, 369, 1238, 1438, 4222, 4824,
  5421, 5771. Also see Leadership
Charles I, 1626-28, 1672-76, 1726
Charles X, 2309
Ch'en Pō-ta, 4853, 4904
Chernov, Victor, 2630
Chetnik Movement, 3098, 3100. Also see
  Yugoslavian Revolution (1941-1945)
Chiang Kai-shek, 6159
Chicago, 519, 3628, 3698
Chile, 3864, 3950, 4307, 4312, 4315,
  4328-29
  and Communism, 4286
  military in, 3829, 4312, 4325
  and socialism, 4272, 4282, 4294, 4303,
    4305, 4318, 4326
Chilean Revolution (1891), 3806, 3879,
  6145-46
Chilean Revolution (1924-1925), 3829
Chilean Revolution (1931), 3822
Chilean Revolution (1970-1973),
  4272-335, 6145-46. Also See
  Allende, Salvador
  class conflict in, 4332-35
  Communism in, 4286

Chilean Revolution (continued)
  constitutional politics in, 4285, 4291,
    4301-02, 4307, 4319, 6145
  economics in, 4327-29
  and Marxism, 4276, 4310, 6146
  military during, 4312, 4325
  peasants in, 4315, 4330
  rural conditions and, 4307, 4315,
    4330-31
  socialism in, 4272, 4282, 4294, 4303,
    4305, 4310, 4318, 4326
  and Soviet Union, 4287
  and United States, 4332-35
China, 665, 684, 1354, 1357, 1372,
  1375-77, 1384, 1398, 1404,
  4448-58, 4468, 4470-552,
  4565-66, 4568, 4572, 4579, 4583,
  4589, 5958, 5963, 6152, 6168. Also
  see Boxer Rebellion (1900); Chinese
  Communism; various Chinese
  Revolutions; Mao Tse-tung; Sun
  Yat-sen; Taiping Rebellion
  (1850-1864)
  Communism in, 1247, 4477, 4486,
    4488, 4508, 4519, 4524, 4526,
    4533, 4535, 4644, 4678, 4688,
    4690-91, 4694-701, 4710, 4719,
    4725, 4727, 4748, 4752, 4765-71,
    4773, 4784, 4786, 4788-89,
    4792-94, 4802, 4807, 4815, 4863,
    4878, 4886, 4914-15, 4927, 4948,
    4973, 4978, 5761
  guerrillas in, 428, 437, 4879
  history of, 4491-92, 4494, 4498, 4500,
    4502, 4509, 4512, 4516, 4523,
    4528-29, 4533-34, 4541-42,
    4549, 6152, 6156-57, 6159, 6163,
    6165, 6167
  ideology in, 4486, 4508, 4531-32,
    4535, 4573, 4616, 4630, 4653,
    4920, 4930, 4946, 4957, 4970,
    4974
  leadership in, 1237, 4471, 4507, 4526,
    6168
  and Marxism, 4474-76, 4483, 4521
  military in, 417, 4511, 4519, 4649, 4668,
    4693, 4777-82, 4790, 5000, 5005
  Millenarian Rebellion (1813), 384
  modernization in, 5959
  nationalism in, 4472, 4477, 4533, 4644,
    4651, 4657, 4805-07
  peasants of, 709, 1372, 4477, 4481,
    4490, 4732, 4796-99, 4801, 4803,
    4807, 4915, 6162
  politics of, 4497, 4516-17, 4541, 4548
  rebellions in, 4479, 4482, 4501, 4511,
    4520, 4621, 6161
  and religion, 4551
  and socialism, 1118, 4836, 4996

China *(continued)*
  student protest in, 755
  warfare in, 4533, 4800
  and the West, 4487, 4499, 4504, 4514
Chinese Communism. See China,
  Communism in; Chinese Revolution
  (1927–1949)
Chinese Revolution (1911–1927;
  Nationalist), 4491–92, 4568,
  4642–88, 6165–66. *Also see*
  Chinese Revolutions (General); Sun
  Yat-sen
  Communism during, 4644, 4678, 4688
  ideology of, 4654, 4655
  leadership of, 6165
  military in, 4649, 4668
  nationalism in, 4644, 4651, 4657
  and Soviet Union, 4643–44, 4669, 4673
  and United States, 4650, 4652
Chinese Revolution (1927–1949;
  Communist), 4491, 4566, 4689–817,
  4878, 6152, 6167. *Also see* China,
  Communism in; Chinese Revolutions
  (General); Long March; Maoism; Mao
  Tse-tung
  classes in, 4709, 4717, 4795–803,
    4807, 4877
  Communism in, 4690–91, 4694–99,
    4701, 4710, 4725, 4727, 4748,
    4752, 4773, 4784, 4786, 4788–89,
    4792–94, 4802, 4807, 4815
  leadership of, 4771–76
  and Marxism-Leninism, 4785, 4787,
    4790
  military in, 4693, 4777–82, 4790
  nationalism of, 4805–07
  peasants in, 4796–803, 4807
  and rural activism, 4709, 4732, 4804,
    4808, 4810, 4812
  and Soviet Union, 4815–17
  students in, 4692, 4806
  and United States, 4813–14
  women in, 4719
Chinese Revolution (1966–1969; Cultural)
  4845, 4907–5013, 6156, 6169. *Also
  see* Chinese Revolutions (General);
  Maoism; Mao Tse-tung
  economics and, 4941, 4957, 4996
  education in, 4916, 4975, 5009
  ideology of, 4920–21, 4930, 4946,
    4957, 4970, 4974
  leadership of, 4932, 4948
  and military, 5000, 5005
  peasants in, 4915
  politics of, 4922, 4945, 4949, 4958,
    4969, 4980, 4983, 4986, 5011–12
  power struggle in, 4924–25, 4934, 4970
  and rural activism, 4921, 4967
  youth in, 5001–03, 5009

Chinese Revolutions (General), 4478–79,
  4482, 4484–85, 4491–92, 4500–02,
  4505, 4512, 4520, 4522–23, 4525,
  4527–28, 4530, 4533–34, 4537,
  4545, 4547, 4549, 4572, 4579, 6161
Christianity, 638, 2019, 4188, 5352. *Also
  see* Catholic Church; Religion
Christophe, 3949
Cities. *See* Urban areas
Citizenship, 100, 1468
Civil disobedience, 494, 625–26, 648,
  650, 655–56, 1431, 1468, 5241, 6155.
  Also see Nonviolence
Civil war, 62, 202, 349–58, 1539, 1584,
  2666, 2686, 2859, 2861, 2964, 3447,
  4661, 4715, 4740, 4759, 5565, 5569,
  6204
Clarendon, Edward, Earl of, 1687
Class, 101, 749, 996, 1149, 1194, 1342,
  2000–01, 2724, 2730, 3838, 4171,
  4844, 4877, 5629, 5708, 5719, 5748,
  5806, 6020. *Also see* Aristocracy;
  Bourgeoisie; Peasants; Proletariat
  consciousness, 726, 1018
  ruling, 922, 5514
  struggle, 948, 1030, 1145, 1373, 1636,
    2002, 2665, 4329, 4419, 5358,
    5428, 5434, 5632, 5933
  war, 2370
Cleaver, Eldridge, 3773
Cohn-Bendit, Daniel, 613
Coke, Edward, 3419
Coleridge, Samuel Taylor, 74
Collective behavior, 19, 212, 218, 456, 461,
  473, 477–78, 487, 523, 3315
Collins, Michael, 2922, 2970
Colombia, 4393–406
  Comunero Revolution (1781), 4405
  guerrillas in, 4397, 4403
  military in, 4399, 4403
  politics of, 4398, 4402–03
Colonialism, 3513, 5067, 5333, 5366,
  5379, 5383, 5389, 5495–96,
  5510–11, 5513, 5516, 5521, 5530,
  5631, 5634, 5754, 6176, 6182, 6188
Columbia University, 766, 768. *Also see*
  Student rebellions
Committees of surveillance, 6042
Communism, 983, 1062, 1069, 1083,
  1166–225, 1437, 1709, 2068, 2094,
  5961. *Also see* Marxism; Socialism;
  and individual country listings and
  subentries
  in Asia, 4584
  in East Asia, 4581
  in Europe, 1181, 1185, 1222, 2177
  guerrilla warfare and, 428
  history of, 1174–76, 1182, 1191, 1193,
    1205, 1212, 1214, 1225

466 / Subject Index

Communism *(continued)*
ideology of, 281, 289, 2632
in Latin America, 3848, 3851–52, 3888, 3924, 4286
nationalism and, 1220, 1265, 2711, 3123
parties, 1194, 1214, 1217, 1222, 1232, 1241
in Southeast Asia, 1183, 4587, 4608
terrorism and, 592–93
theory and practice of, 1190, 1195, 1202–03, 1210, 1225
in Third World, 5769
women and, 1303
world, 1170, 1173–74, 1180, 1182, 1191, 1209, 1212, 1219
Communist Manifesto, 1036, 1044, 1198. *Also see* Marx, Karl
Comparative studies, 457–58, 525, 712, 727, 736, 1189, 1222, 1232, 1237, 1248, 1271, 1347, 1352–409, 1513, 1859, 3805, 3814, 3869, 3937, 4565–68, 4574–75, 5401, 5488, 5552, 5965, 5974, 6113, 6176
Comunero Movement (Spain), 1812
Comunero Revolution (1781; Colombia), 4405
Comuñero Revolt (1721–1735; Paraguay), 3902
Condorcet, Marie-Jean, 1992–93, 5960
Confederacy, 349, 351, 355, 357
Conflict, 119, 122, 300, 315, 350, 406, 426, 456, 488, 590, 624, 1209, 1215, 1346, 1412, 1935, 3257, 3269, 3455, 3656, 3666, 3754, 3857, 3910, 3925, 3930, 4171, 4297, 4329, 4369, 4404, 4443, 4983, 5016, 5042, 5064, 5083, 5236, 5360, 5372, 5572, 5583, 5723, 5749, 5895, 6197
Congo, 5362
Conscientism, 5427, 5435. *Also see* Nkrumah, Kwame; Nkrumahism
Conservative, 134, 379, 1696, 1707, 2156, 2442, 2903, 3007, 3365, 3370, 3629, 3905. *Also see* Right wing
Conspiracy, 340, 903, 1636, 1678, 2284, 3053, 3655
Constitution, 109, 1595, 1597, 1692, 1748, 2403, 3346, 3421–22, 3655, 4285, 5325, 5964
Containment, 147
Corporations républicaines, 6069
Cortés, Hernando, 3862
Costa Rica, 3813, 3854
Counter-insurgency, 396, 410, 661, 672, 682–83, 5467, 5552, 5732. *Also see* Counterrevolution
Counterrevolution, 60, 398, 657–85, 1038, 1541, 1793, 2128–30, 2133–34, 2274, 2359, 2386, 2725, 2829, 2875, 3040,

Counterrevolution *(continued)*
3065, 3188, 3716, 3953, 4316, 4323, 4383, 4530, 4580, 4729, 5556, 5793, 5909. *Also see* Counter-insurgency
Coup d'état, 323–48, 1511, 3803, 3914, 4324–25, 5143, 5293, 5388, 5403, 5421, 5909, 6177
Creative Revolution, 193, 198
Crèvecoeur, Hector St. John, 3527
Cripps, Sir Stafford, 5194
Cristero Rebellion (Mexico), 4032
Cromwell, Oliver, 1400, 1688, 1701–27
Crowds, 1489, 1538, 1755, 1978, 2081, 2265, 2318, 2321, 2359, 2655, 3399, 3401, 3409, 6113
Cuba, 425, 428, 1275, 1361, 3871, 3906, 3916, 4144, 4154, 4156, 4158–59, 4163, 4172–78, 4196, 4198–209, 4211–12, 4214–15, 4218, 4222–23, 4227–28, 4232, 6144
Communism in, 4150, 4186, 4232
military in, 3930, 4176
nationalism in, 4166
peasants of, 4191
and socialism, 4146, 4170, 4175
Cuban Revolution (1933), 3830, 3845
Cuban Revolution (1959), 3805, 3837, 3937, 4122–209, 4264, 4343. *Also see* Castro, Fidel; Castroism; Debray, Regis; Guevara, Che
and class, 4139, 4166, 4171, 4189–91
and Communism, 4150, 4186, 4232
economics in, 4136, 4159, 4196, 4207, 6144
guerrillas in, 428, 4133, 4152
and Latin America, 4193–94
military in, 4176
nationalism and, 4166
politics of, 4132, 4139, 4166, 4171, 4176
religion in, 4187–88
socialism and, 4146, 4170, 4175
and Soviet Union, 4165, 4192, 4195
students in, 4160
and United States, 4153, 4196
women in, 4126, 4182
Cultural change, 213–14, 276–77, 298, 670, 1019, 2607, 3173, 3498, 3538, 3549, 3697, 3786, 3878, 4487, 4509, 4635, 4745, 4983, 4995, 5126, 5295, 5650, 5659–60, 5667, 6157
Cultural Revolution, 41, 953, 2684, 2763, 3621, 3690, 4846, 5671, 5868, 6193. *Also see* Chinese Revolution (1966–1969; Cultural)
Curaçao, 484
"Curés," 5987
Czech Revolution (1848), 2374
Czech Revolution (1968), 3159–79
Czechoslovakia, 3159–60, 3163,

Subject Index / 467

Czechoslovakia *(continued)*
  3165-68, 3172-73, 3175, 3178, 5978, 6052
  Communism in, 3160, 3166, 6059
  and socialism, 3171-73

Danton, Georges, 2040, 2042-43, 5999, 6044
Darwin, Charles, 945
Davis, Angela Y., 3779
Davitt, Michael, 2979, 6089
De Abajo, 3926
deBeaumont, Gustave, 2293
Debray, Regis, 4259-71
Decembrist Revolt. *See* Russian Revolution (1825)
Dechristianization, 6040
Declaration of Rights, 5964, 5992
DeCleyre, Voltairine, 824
Decolonization, 5415, 5449, 5486, 5554
De Forest, David Curtis, 4364
DeLeon, David, 890
Democracy, 183, 235, 250, 255, 313, 571, 648-49, 1188, 1201, 1709, 2295, 2303, 2307, 2339, 3582, 6038, 6166
  in Argentina, 4360, 4369
  in Brazil, 4389
  in Chile, 4291
  in China, 4667, 6166
  in Czechoslovakia, 3174
  in Egypt, 5836
  in Ethiopia, 5710
  in France, 1983, 1985, 2382, 3130, 3391, 6038
  in Germany, 2405, 2880, 2891, 2997
  in Great Britain, 2981
  in Latin America, 3865
  in Mexico, 4079
  in Portugal, 6097
  socialism and, 1155
  in Spain, 3036
  terrorism and, 536, 571
  in United States, 2302, 3380, 3384, 3783
Democratic Revolution, 1279, 1844-72, 2362, 2371, 2381, 2851, 3198, 3813, 3855, 3933, 5995
de Mun, Albert, 663
Dependency, 6188
Despotism, 1408
de Tracy, Destutt, 6025
De Valera, Eamonn, 2927, 2972, 2977
Developing nations, 324, 4385, 5777, 6185. *Also see* Third World; Underdeveloped areas
Dialectics, 1018, 1436
Díaz, Félix, 6139
Díaz, Porfirio, 4074-76

Dickinson, John, 3424
Dictatorship, 183, 1242, 1707, 1710, 2049, 2806, 3036, 3866, 4353, 5442, 5890, 6147
Dien Bien Phu, 5035, 5059
Diggers, 1739
Diplomacy, 411, 2269, 2430, 2542, 5569
Directory, 2056-58. *Also see* French Revolution (1789-1799)
di Rienzo, Cola, 1492
Dissent, 126, 236, 734, 782, 814, 3598, 3670
Dominican Republic, 3841, 3871
Dorr Rebellion (1842), 3217, 3219
Dual-revolution thesis, 6110
Dutch Revolt. *See* Netherlands Revolt
Dutch Revolution (1795), 1851, 1872

East Africa. *See* Africa, East
East Anglia Rising, (1381) 1499
Eastern Europe, 2170, 2177, 2188, 2212, 2270, 2559, 5974, 5977
Easter Rising. *See* Irish Revolution
East Germany, 2235
Eastman, Crystal, 1300-01
Eastman, Max, 1301
Economics, 272-75, 965, 977, 996, 1014, 1026, 1067, 1253, 1473, 1524, 1688, 1911, 1950, 1964, 1973, 1977, 1979-80, 2006, 2132, 2187, 2234, 2313, 2390, 2412, 2590, 2821, 3382, 3414-16, 3471-72, 3798, 3814, 3861, 3874, 3922, 3945, 4121, 4136, 4196, 4207, 4255, 4327-29, 4362, 4427, 4828, 4941, 4957, 4996, 5297, 5318, 5496, 5705, 5707, 5748, 5754, 5804, 5849, 5948, 6024, 6098, 6144, 6187
Economic theory, 952, 1067, 1253, 5916, 6187
Ecuador, 339
Education, 2092, 2185, 4809, 4916, 4921, 4975, 5009, 5600. *Also see* Student rebellions; Universities
Egypt, 1405, 5839-43, 5845, 5847, 5849-51, 5854, 5959
  military in, 5843
  nationalism in, 5840
  and socialism, 5849
Egyptian Revolution (1919), 5804
Egyptian Revolution (1952), 5835-54. *Also see* Nasser, Gamal Abdel
Eight Trigrams Uprising (1813), 384
1830 Revolutions, 2308-33, 6062-66
1848 Revolutions, 905, 934, 1030, 1039, 2234, 2247, 2334-435, 6067-69
Elites, 1226-28, 1233, 1237, 1240-41, 1243, 1246, 1248, 1254, 2182, 2987, 3407, 3901, 3988, 4369, 4531, 4804, 5040, 5347, 6176

Elizabeth I, 1583
El Salvador Revolt (1932), 3852
El Salvador Revolution (1948), 6132
Empire, 3469, 3471, 3474–76, 3489, 3521, 5765
Engels, Friedrich, 915, 956, 1009–10, 1066, 1070, 1081, 1091–106, 1640, 2350, 2778, 5938, 5945–46. *Also see* Marx, Karl; Marxism
England, 90, 1391, 1399, 1509, 1519, 1529, 1590, 1848, 1863, 1867, 2265, 2325, 2453. *Also see* Glorious Revolution; Great Britain; Irish Revolution; Puritan Revolution
  Irish relations with, 2910, 2913, 2919, 2926, 2935, 2973–74, 2981
  military in, 1679–83, 1704, 1735, 1762
  millenarianism in, 373, 377, 5919–20
  peasants of, 1641
  radicals in, 793, 807, 893, 1508, 3473
English Civil War. *See* Puritan Revolution
Enlightenment, 1386, 1845, 1854, 1989–99
Les Enragés, 2032–33, 5976. *Also see* French Revolution (1789–99)
Equatorial Guinea, 6177
Eritrea, 5688, 5699, 6195. *Also see* Ethiopian Revolution
Ethics, 261, 997, 1161, 1380, 3361
Ethiopia, 1359, 1366, 5707, 5715–18
  ideology in, 5710
  military in, 5703
  peasants of, 5686, 5715
  and socialism, 5698
Ethiopian Revolution (1974–1977), 5683–725, 6195
  class in, 5708
  and democracy, 5710
  economics in, 5705, 5707
  and land reform, 5688, 5692, 5697, 5715
  military in, 5703
  modernization and, 5716
  peasants in, 5686
  politics of, 5698, 5703, 5722
  women in, 6195
Ethnicity, 2859, 2861, 5144, 5372. *Also see* Racism
Europe, 162, 312, 1128, 1283–84, 1386, 1399, 1429, 1457, 1495, 1500–3205, 3514, 3520, 5974, 5977, 5995–96, 6107. *Also see* 1830 Revolutions; 1848 Revolutions; and separate listings for individual countries
  anarchism in, 835
  Communism in, 1181, 1185, 1222
  counterrevolution in, 679, 685
  ideology in, 312, 1457

Europe *(continued)*
  millenarian movements in, 362, 368, 373, 375, 377, 379–80, 382, 385–88, 391
  peasants of, 688, 690, 696, 709, 715
  and socialism, 1151
  terrorism in, 531–32, 541–42, 544, 547, 549, 553, 564, 569, 591, 609
  violence in, 477
Evolution, 275, 1119, 1312–18, 2516, 3886, 4014, 4135, 4508, 4593, 5373, 5399, 5493, 5669, 5745, 5949, 5956, 6051, 6131
Existentialism, 941, 3150

Fanon, Frantz, 1355, 1380, 5485–531, 5648, 6190
Fanshen, 4804, 4812
Fascism, 273, 801, 1188, 1196, 1287, 1469, 2502, 2985, 2994, 3005, 3020, 3069, 3898, 5198, 6201
Fatalism, 6064
February Revolution (1917), 2533–34, 2536–37, 2541, 2545, 2549, 6075. *Also see* Menshevism; Russian Revolution (1917)
Fedayeen, 5823. *Also see* Palestine
Feminism, 1296, 1299, 1301–02, 1309, 1311, 2063, 5956. *Also see* Women
Ferrari, Giuseppe, 2500
Feudalism, 459, 3396, 5716
Fifth Monarchy Men, 373, 386. *Also see* Puritan Revolution
Finland, 2860
Finnish Revolution (1917–1918), 2859–62
Forest, René, 6047
Fouché, Joseph, 6019
France, 377, 409, 1375, 1377, 1391, 1399, 1404, 1567, 1859, 1861, 1867, 2181–82, 2192, 2196, 2200–01, 2214, 2218, 2226, 2257–58, 2271, 2273, 2287, 2476, 2482, 2486–87, 2492, 6056, 6103. *Also see* French Revolution (1789–1799); French Revolution (1830); French Revolution (1848); French Revolution (1968); Fronde; Paris Commune
  and Algeria, 5456–57, 5464, 5475, 5478, 5481, 5484, 6189
  Communism in, 3136, 3143, 3147, 5456
  ideology in, 284, 1987, 1988, 2018, 2196, 2443, 5926, 6003
  military in, 2110, 2258, 2322, 2324, 6001
  millenarianism in, 5920
  nationalism in, 2021–23
  peasants of, 688, 709, 2250, 5997
  socialism in, 284, 928, 2033, 2100, 2242, 2315, 3146, 5975–76

France *(continued)*
  student rebellion in, 721, 779, 2180, 3144
  terrorism in, 5926
  warfare in, 1539, 2062, 2137
Franco, Francisco, 3077, 3081
Frankfort Parliament, 2402–03, 2410. *Also see* German Revolution (1848)
Franklin, Benjamin, 3330, 5960
Freedom, 61, 235, 803, 864, 1159, 1201, 1288, 1463, 2406, 2931, 2947, 3045, 3112, 3292, 3334, 3644, 3671, 4163, 4567, 5195, 5197, 5223, 5387, 5438, 5441, 5498–99, 5538–39, 5747, 5850, 5916
Freemasonry, 1521
Freethinking, 6007
FRELIMO, 5602, 5605. *Also see* Mozambique Revolution
French Revolution (1789–1799), 377, 1061, 1353, 1358, 1360, 1394–95, 1404, 1820, 1835, 1854, 1864–65, 1873–2138, 2140, 2153, 2181–82, 2196, 2214, 2226, 2265, 2287, 2304, 5922, 5951, 5962, 5964, 5974, 5978, 5997–6049. *Also see* Directory; Girondins; Jacobins; Louis XVI; Napoleon; Reign of Terror; Robespierre, Maximilien; Vendée
  and American Revolution, 1859, 1864, 1928, 1945, 1970, 3246, 6015
  Ancien regime and, 1376–77, 1894, 1927–28, 1943, 1955, 1964–71, 2069, 2271, 2296, 2304
  Bastille in, 1957
  and bourgeoisie, 2001, 2007–08, 2022
  Cahiers, 1951, 2023
  class in, 2000–02, 2031, 6012, 6020
  economics of, 1911, 1950, 1964, 1973, 1977, 1979–80, 2006, 2132, 6012
  and Enlightenment, 1989–99
  enragés in, 2032–33, 5976
  Estates General in, 1956
  foreign relations in, 2059–62, 2090, 5974
  ideologues of, 1988, 6024
  military in, 5922, 6001, 6015
  nationalism and, 2021–23
  nobility during, 1964, 2001, 2003–06, 6020, 6041
  in Paris, 2009, 2024–31, 2051, 2113, 2117, 6009
  parlements in, 1965, 2005
  peasants and, 688, 2012–14, 5997, 6014
  and press, 6026, 6035, 6103
  in provinces, 1947–48, 1975, 2006, 2014, 2026, 2072, 2084, 2089, 6014, 6024, 6068

French Revolution *(continued)*
  religion and, 2017–20, 6005, 6040
  Sans-Culottes of, 2009–11
  September Massacres in, 1958
  social aspects of, 1912, 1917, 1972, 1974–76, 1978–80, 2006, 2031, 2132, 6006, 6037
  women in, 1305, 5951, 6011, 6017, 6023, 6036, 6039
French Revolution (1830), 2181–82, 2196, 2200, 2214, 2218, 2226, 2257–58, 2265, 2271, 2273, 2287, 2309–28, 2331–33, 6062–66
French Revolution (1848), 1030, 2181–82, 2196, 2200, 2214, 2218, 2226, 2257–58, 2265, 2271, 2273, 2287, 2351, 2355, 2375–97, 6068–69
French Revolution (1870–71). *See* Paris Commune
French Revolution (1968), 2181, 3125–58, 6055
Freud, Sigmund, 953, 3714
Frey, les frères, 6033
Fronde (1648–1653), 1368, 1391, 1584–93, 5987–88
Front de libération nationale (FLN), 5471–72. *Also see* Algerian Revolution
Futurism, 2199

Gaismair, Michael, 1561
Gandhi, Mohandas K., 621, 1370, 1374, 1381, 1393, 1409, 1444, 5181–85, 5224–90, 6172–73. *Also see* Civil disobedience; Indian Revolution; Nonviolence; *Satyagraha*
Gang of Four, 665. *Also see* Chinese Revolution (1966–1969)
Gapon, Father, 2521
Garibaldi, Giuseppe, 2431
General Strike, 2477, 2485
Generations, 28, 42, 725, 748, 762, 774, 777, 2312, 3408, 3413, 3428, 3647, 3656, 4938, 4945, 5004, 5853, 5973
Geneva, 1504–05
Gentry, 1639, 1642–43, 1646, 5989, 5991. *Also see* Puritan Revolution
German Revolution (1848), 2234, 2334, 2355, 2357, 2398–419
German Revolution (1918–1919), 2880–81, 2883–86, 2890–94, 2900–01, 2903–05, 6086–88
Germany, 1037, 1384, 1399, 1858, 2187, 2227, 2234, 2864, 2880, 2883, 2891–93, 2901, 2903–05, 2990–91, 2998–3000, 3003, 3011, 3013, 6067. *Also see* German Revolution (1848); German Revolution (1918–1919); Nazi Revolution; Peasants' Revolt

Germany *(continued)*
  anarchism in, 830
  Communism in, 2881
  ideology in, 1037, 3033
  literature of, 1332
  socialism in, 2901, 2904, 2991, 3004
  student rebellions in, 5932
  terrorism in, 569, 613
  warfare in, 2904
Ghana, 5369, 5407, 5432, 5436. *Also see* Nkrumah, Kwame
Ghettos, 498, 500, 3741–42, 3765–66
Girondins, 2054–55. *Also see* French Revolution (1789–1799)
Glorious Revolution (1688–1699), 1535, 1606, 1744–83. *Also see* James II; William III
  army in, 1762
  European background of, 1761
  and law, 1749–50
  mob during, 1755
  and monarchy, 1762, 1767, 1774–75, 1783
  nobility in, 1764, 1769
  politics of, 1752–53, 1771
  propaganda in, 1756
  and religion, 1753, 1780
Godwin, William, 891–95
Goldman, Emma, 887–89
Gorky, Maxim, 2810
Government, 278, 347, 2054, 2169, 2375, 2422, 2517, 2688, 3418, 3639, 3870, 3920, 4333–34, 4434, 5057, 5801, 5899
Gramsci, Antonio, 1186, 2495–97, 2501
Great Britain, 1491, 1535, 1537, 1758, 2011, 2272, 2280, 2906, 3022, 3043. *Also see* England; Ireland; Scotland
  ideology of, 299, 1652–53
  and Marxism, 5943
  millenarianism in, 373, 377, 386–87
  socialism in, 1116, 1141, 1157
  and Third World, 3962, 4064, 4556, 4622, 5122, 5196, 5207, 5802, 5832
  and United States, 793, 3235, 3332, 3341, 3352, 3463–93, 6101, 6119
Greece, 1473–84, 2851–52, 2857–58, 5951, 5971
Greek Communist Party, 2857
Greek Revolution (1821), 2850, 2853–56
Griffith, Arthur, 2915
Guatemala, 3832, 4092, 4099, 6131
Guatemalan Revolution (1944), 4092–99
Guerrilla warfare, 426–48, 483. *Also see* Military; Peasant Revolution; Rebellion; Revolt; Urban guerrillas
  in Africa, 5394
  in Angola, 5585

Guerrilla warfare *(continued)*
  in China, 428, 437, 4879
  in Colombia, 4404
  Communism and, 428, 442, 5146
  in Cuba, 428, 4133, 4152, 4238
  in Guinea-Bissau, 5628, 5638, 5654
  history of, 429, 434, 436, 439–40
  in Ireland, 2918, 2921
  in Latin America, 3812, 3875, 3877, 3892, 3895, 4262, 4397
  in Malaya, 5146
  Marxism and, 444
  in Middle East, 5825
  in Palestine, 435
  in Peru, 4423
  terrorism and, 575, 583, 613
  theory and practice of, 430, 446–47, 4241–42, 4248, 4879–80
  in United States, 3623
  in Vietnam, 428, 5046, 5077
  in Zimbabwe, 5731
Guevara, Che, 1444, 3880, 4235–58, 4270. *Also see* Cuban Revolution
  Bolivian campaign of, 4240, 4243, 4246, 4252, 4254
  and guerrilla warfare, 4238, 4241–42, 4248, 4255
Guillén, Abraham, 3881
Guinea, 5544
Guinea-Bissau, 5548, 5551, 5553, 5561, 5610–43
  warfare in, 5622, 5627, 5635–37, 5643
Guinea-Bissau Revolution (1963–1974), 5610–43, 6194. *Also see* Cabral, Amilcar; Cape Verde Islands; PAIGC
  class in, 5629, 5632
  and colonialism, 5631, 5634
  guerrillas in, 5628, 5638
  liberation of, 5548, 5553, 5616–18, 5625, 5631, 5640, 5658
  political mobilization in, 5633, 5641
  and Portugal, 5561, 5622, 5631
  and Portuguese Africa, 5548, 5551, 5553, 5561, 5610–43, 5658, 5676, 6194
  post-liberation period of, 5623, 5626, 5628, 5639, 5642, 6194
  women in, 5634

Haase, Hugo, 2885
Habsburgs, 822, 2288, 2366, 2370
Haile Selassie, 5718
Haiti, 3871, 3946–47, 3949, 3958, 3973, 3977
Halévy Thesis, 1280
Har Dayal, 5762
Harvard University, 759. *Also see* Student rebellions

Subject Index / 471

Hegel, Georg, 258, 963, 1061, 2067, 2071, 2658, 6018
Henry, Patrick, 3529
Hereros Revolt, 6178
Herzen, Alexander, 325, 2206
Herzen, Natalie, 832
Hessians, 6104
Hidalgo Revolt, 3957. *Also see* Latin American independence revolutions
Hippies, 3657. *Also see* New Left; Student rebellions
Historical Materialism, 965, 1433, 1469, 5136
Hitler, Adolf, 569, 1384, 2992-93, 2995-96, 3006, 3009-10, 3014. *Also see* Nazi Revolution
Hobbes, Thomas, 315, 1531, 1791
Ho Chi Minh, 5095-107
Holland, 1511, 5986. *Also see* Netherlands
Horn of Africa, 5723
Hostages, 5928
Hotman, François, 1526
Hsi-liang, 4660
Huk Rebellion, 5324. *Also see* Philippines
Humanism, 5961
Hume, David, 669
Hungarian Revolution (1848), 2357, 2420-25, 3106, 3110
Hungarian Revolution (1918-1919), 2869-79, 6085
Hungarian Revolution (1956), 2177, 3106-24
Hungary, 875, 1846, 1853-54, 2245, 2869-70, 2874, 2876, 2878
  Communism in, 2245, 5973, 6085
Huang Hsing, 4506
Hunan, 4798, 4801, 4804
Hu Shih, 4503
Hus, Jan, 2230
Hussite Revolution, 1494, 1496-97

Iakhontov, A. N., 2674
Idara Rebellion (1931), 5354
Identity, 1338-39, 5652-53
Ideology, 276-327, 659, 1243, 1342, 2866, 3718, 5778, 5917-18, 6020, 6024-25, 6190. *Also see* subentries under individual country listings
  in Africa, 5344, 5349, 5356, 5428, 5438, 5745, 6185, 6190
  of Communism, 281, 289, 2632, 3097, 4535
  culture and, 276-77, 298
  in Europe, 312, 1457
  in Latin America, 1378, 3857, 3912
  of Marxism, 323, 968, 979, 1071, 1074, 5349
  in Middle East, 5808

Ideology *(continued)*
  of nationalism, 327
  of New Left, 729, 736
  of PLO, 5815
  politics and, 279, 283, 285, 288, 296, 298, 301, 303, 305-06, 309, 311, 316-17, 322, 3374, 3858
  religion and, 1278, 5296
  revolutionary, 276-77, 4974
  of terrorism, 278
Ikki, Kita, 87
Imperialism, 135, 174, 184, 952, 1110, 1219, 1464, 1694, 2777, 3108, 4334, 4590, 5365, 5439, 5557, 5566, 5612, 5740, 5839, 5940, 6101
Independence. *See* Liberation
India, 713, 1398, 1422, 4461-62, 4466, 4553-55, 4560-61. *Also see* Gandhi, Mohandas K.; Indian Revolution; Sepoy Mutiny
  British involvement in, 4556
  Communism in, 5211
  history of, 4557-59, 6164
  nationalism in, 4562-63, 5186, 5191, 5205-06, 5211, 5213, 5221
  peasants of, 713
Indian Revolution (1920-1949), 5186-223, 5241-43, 5266, 5272-73, 5286, 6172-73. *Also see* Gandhi, Mohandas K.
  and British, 5196, 5207
  and Communism, 5211
  Hind Swaraj in, 5256, 5259
  history of, 5194-95, 5197, 5201-02
  nationalism, 5186, 5191, 5205-06, 5211, 5213, 5221
  and nonviolence, 5189, 5212, 5214, 5218, 5220
  and Quit India Movement, 5199, 5203, 5223, 5266
  and religion, 5218
  terrorism in, 5190
Indochina, 398, 409, 4608, 5064, 5077. *Also see* Southeast Asia; Vietnam
Indonesia, 5127-42
Indonesian Communist Party, 5129, 5133, 5137
  ideology of, 5141
  nationalism in, 5135
  politics of, 5131
Industrial Revolution, 2256, 4012, 4052, 5933
Inequality, 1124, 2306, 2423, 3363, 4116
Injustice, 182
Instability, 227
Insurgency. *See* Insurrection
Insurrection, 399, 401, 405-06, 421, 494, 517, 555, 1453, 2250, 2447, 2945, 2980, 2982, 3951, 4143, 4261, 4619,

Insurrection *(continued)*
  5053, 5121, 5147–48, 5189, 5467, 5476, 5929. *Also see* Warfare
Intelligentsia, 726, 1149, 1226, 1304, 1657–58, 1808, 2100, 2206, 2262, 2352, 2358, 2406, 2484, 2520, 2625, 2634, 2715, 2731, 3003, 3019, 3090, 3168, 3362, 3367, 3375, 4015, 4663, 4670, 4912, 5039, 5400, 6085
Internal war, 23, 129, 158, 702, 2136, 5569
International civil war, 62, 202
International order, 228, 5746
International politics. *See* World politics
Internationals, 969, 1174, 1209, 1212, 1439, 2189, 2463, 2702
Intervention, 5759, 6197
IRA. *See* Irish Revolution
Iran, 5855, 5857–61, 5863–66, 5868, 5870–72, 5875–76, 5878, 5882–83, 5885–91, 5893–95, 5897–98, 5900–03, 5908, 5910–11, 6205. *Also see* Persia
  military in, 5877
  nationalism in, 5886
Iranian Revolution (1978–1979), 1366, 5855–914, 6199–6209. *Also see* Khomeini, Ayato'llah Rehu'llah; Pahlavi, Mohammad Reza
  cultural revolution in, 5869
  and Iraq, 6202
  left wing in, 5879
  and nationalism, 5886
  politics of, 5868, 5874, 5883, 5897–98
  and religion, 5870, 5874, 5878, 5881, 5883, 5887, 5897, 5899, 5908, 6208
  and United States, 5855, 5866–67, 5891, 5900, 5910
  women in, 5872, 6200, 6206
Iraq, 5795, 5798, 5806, 5819, 6202
Iraqi Revolution (1958), 5819
Ireland, 2906–07, 2941, 2978
  nationalism in, 2909, 2916–17, 2952, 2978, 2981, 2983
  and socialism, 2978
  warfare in, 2937, 2939–40
Irgun, 570
Irish Rebellion (1798), 1850, 1860, 1869
Irish Revolution (1916–1922), 1382, 1422, 2906–84, 6089–90. *Also see* individual revolutionists
  Black and Tans in, 2925
  Easter Rising of, 2911, 2915, 2928–29, 2932, 2959, 2968, 2976, 2982–83
  Irish Republican Army, 2918, 2924
  Irish Republican Brotherhood, 2916, 2969
  labor and, 2911, 2979

Irish Revolution *(continued)*
  and nationalism, 2909, 2916–17, 2952, 2978, 2981, 2983
  religion in, 2920, 2941, 2961
  Sinn Fein in, 2948
  and Ulster, 2936, 2941, 2962
Irvingite Movement, 359
Islam, 2786, 5786, 5794, 5816, 5869, 5877, 5880–81, 5899, 6200, 6208. *Also see* Arab world; Middle East
Italy, 532, 591, 609, 1180, 1186, 2494–503, 3041
  Communism in, 1180, 1186
  peasants of, 2426
Italian Revolution (1848), 2357, 2426–33

Jackson, George, 3739, 3750, 3763, 3776
Jacobins, 1846, 2030, 2047–51, 2058, 2100, 2105, 2108, 3960, 5926, 6002, 6006, 6016, 6026–27. *Also see* French Revolution (1789–1799)
Jacquerie, 2223
James II, 1773–74
Jansenism, 1585
Japan, 704, 747, 1405, 4472, 4568, 4580, 6158
  Communism in, 4571
Jay, John, 3438
J-curve, 21–22, 152–53
Jean-Jacques, 5975
Jefferson, Thomas, 1353, 1986, 3437, 3563–78
Jesus Christ, 1275, 3636, 3688, 4187, 5384
Jews, 1470, 2400
Jogiches, Leo, 2887. *Also see* Luxemburg, Rosa
Journalists. *See* Press
July Monarchy, 2316–17, 2333. *Also see* French Revolution (1830)

Kádár, János, 2245
Kallias, 1475
Kano, Amino, 5391
Kant, Immanuel, 1428, 2071
Das Kapital. *See Capital*
Kautsky, Karl, 2276
Kemal, Mustafa (Ataturk), 5303, 5307. *Also see* Turkish Revolution (1919–1923)
Kenya, 5410
Kerensky, Alexander, 2550, 6076
Khomeini, Ayato'llah Rehu'llah, 5862, 5865, 5867, 5869, 5873–74, 5881, 5904
Khrushchev, Nikita, 593, 2612
Kim Il Sung, 5151

Kirmâmî, Mîrzâ Âqâ Khân, 5801
Kollontai, Aleksandra, 1299, 1302, 1308
Korea, 5149-52
Korsch, Karl, 1447
Kościuszko, Tadeusz, 3525
Kossuth, Louis, 2424
Kotane, Moses, 5741
Kronstadt Revolt (1921), 2631, 2662
Kropotkin, Peter A., 854, 896-902
Krupskaya, Nadezhda, 2785. *Also see* Lenin, V. I.
Kuhn, Thomas, 5966
Kun, Béla, 2245, 2878
Kuomintang, 4653, 4655, 4674, 4739. *Also see* Chinese Revolution (1911-1927); Chinese Revolutions (General)

Labor, 2271, 2273, 3946, 5916
Lafayette, Marquis de, 2038-39, 3246
Landauer, Gustav, 852
Land reform, 3194, 3918, 4062, 4077, 4082, 4115, 4330-31, 4732, 5310, 5688, 5691, 6014
Language, 6021
Laos, 4585, 5108-15
Latin America, 3018, 3792-4444, 6131-51. *Also see* entries for individual countries; Caribbean
  agrarian problems in, 3918, 3931
  class in, 1373, 3838
  colonial period of, 3943, 3951, 3970-71. *Also see* Latin American independence revolutions
  and Communism, 3848, 3851-52, 3888, 3924
  coups d'état in, 328, 3803, 3914
  economics of, 3861, 3874, 3922
  governments of, 3870, 3920
  guerrillas in, 393, 3812, 3875, 3877, 3881, 3892, 3895
  history of, 3794-95, 3798-800, 3842-44, 3853, 3856-63, 3867-68, 3870, 3872-74, 3876, 3878, 3880, 3886-87, 3889, 3891, 3896-97, 3900, 3903, 3905, 3907-12, 3917, 3919, 3923, 3925, 3929-36, 3939-42
  literature of, 1329
  and Marxism, 3801, 3846, 3880, 3924
  masses in, 3882
  military in, 422, 3828-30, 3889, 3914
  and nationalism, 3810, 3834
  peasants in, 3811, 3820, 3838, 3885, 3894, 3915, 3931
  politics of, 3844, 3857-58, 3861, 3870, 3878, 3880, 3897, 3900, 3903,

Latin America, politics of *(continued)*
  3907-08, 3910-11, 3916-17, 3925, 3929, 3936, 3939-42
  radicals in, 3820, 3836, 3883
  and religion, 3884, 3893, 3898, 3908, 3911, 3934, 6133
  social change in, 3843, 3859, 3868, 3893, 3912, 3925, 3934-35, 3939
  social structure of, 3917, 3922
  terrorism in, 564, 586
  and Trotskyism, 3850
  and United States, 3898-99, 3913, 3918
  violence in, 3967, 3910
Latin American independence revolutions, 671, 3874, 3906, 3943-82, 6133-34. *Also see* Bolívar, Simon; Christophe; L'Ouverture, Toussaint; O'Higgins, Bernardo; San Martín, José de
  in Brazil, 3976
  in Chile, 3950
  economics and, 3945
  and Great Britain, 3962
  in Haiti, 3946-47, 3949, 3958, 3973, 3977
  in Mexico, 3953, 3957, 5986
  religion and, 6133
  in San Domingo, 3960
  social aspects of, 3945
  and Spain, 3953, 3970
  and United States, 3956, 3980
  in Uruguay, 3978
Law, 156, 245, 350, 354, 455, 472, 581, 597, 652, 1529, 1749-50, 3346, 3417, 3423, 3655, 5686, 5722, 6112
Latvia, 2228
Lavrov, Peter, 2714
Leadership, 189-90, 580, 1232, 1234, 1238, 1245, 1247, 1250, 1252, 1254, 1354, 1440, 2046, 2051, 2167, 2567, 2626, 2655, 2959, 3144, 3425, 3436, 3455, 3732, 3849, 4047, 4457, 4486, 4507, 4526, 4656, 4771-76, 4891, 4932, 4948, 5097, 5111, 5121, 5188, 5479, 5771, 5841, 6165, 6168. *Also see* Charisma
Lebanon, 5803
Lee, Light-Horse Harry, 6121
Lefebvre, Georges, 2013
Left wing, 782, 3595, 3640. *Also see* New Left
  in Europe, 1128, 2213
  in France, 2242, 2391, 2467, 3143
  in Germany, 2901
  ideology of, 294
  in Iran, 5878
  in Latin America, 3801, 3818, 4288
  in Spain, 3020, 3029, 3078

Left Wing *(continued)*
  in United States, 797–98, 805,
    3597–98, 3632, 3650, 3654, 3658,
    3672–73, 6099
  women in, 5956–57
Legitimacy, 1981–82, 2142, 3094, 3393,
  3407, 4104, 4927, 6174
Lehl, 570
Lenin, V. I., 302, 1308, 1389, 1393, 1397,
  1409, 2222, 2230, 2238, 2480, 2612,
  2640, 2650, 2658, 2670, 2701, 2736,
  2745–75, 2783–87, 2789–99,
  2802–12, 2876, 4270, 6084. *Also see*
  Bolshevism; Leninism; Russian
  Revolution (1917)
Leninism, 927, 937, 1002, 1059, 2577,
  2776–82, 2788, 2800–01, 2873,
  3877, 4785, 4840. *Also see* Lenin,
  V. I.; Marxism-Leninism
Levellers, 1733–38, 1741–42
Lewy, Guenter, 1276
Liang, Ch'i-ch'ao, 4513
Liberalism, 16, 724, 2398, 2403, 2405,
  2510, 3365, 4503
Liberation, 240, 261, 299, 1370, 1373,
  1383, 1872, 2188, 2913, 2947, 2971,
  3437, 3452, 3713, 3717, 3782, 4128,
  4546, 4549, 4603, 5036, 5058, 5116,
  5162, 5209, 5331, 5344, 5382, 5393,
  5416, 5418, 5447, 5453, 5507,
  5547–48, 5553, 5574–75, 5582,
  5601, 5616–18, 5625, 5631, 5640,
  5652–54, 5658–60, 5689, 5721,
  5726, 5728–30, 5739–40, 5743,
  5754, 5760, 5767, 5774, 5779, 5903,
  5913, 6090, 6133, 6152, 6176. *Also
  see* Anticolonialism; Latin American
  independence revolutions
Libertarianism, 810, 1288, 1829
Liberty, 1534, 1596, 1656, 2306, 3347,
  3432, 3489, 3497–98, 3572, 3655,
  6017
Libya, 5677
Libyan Revolution (1969–1970), 5677–82
Lincoln, Charles H., 6110
Lin Piao, 343
Li Ta-chao, 4521
Literature, 1192, 1319–33, 2316–17, 2378,
  2413, 3026, 3769, 3790, 3794–95,
  3798, 4041, 5913, 6021
Lithuanian Social Democratic Party, 2508
Liu Shao-ch'i, 4824, 4969
Locke, John, 1531, 1784–92
London, 1538, 1686, 1698, 2338, 3468,
  5265
Long March, 4768, 4783–84. *Also see*
  Chinese Revolution (1927–1949)
Louis XVI, 2034–37
L'Ouverture, Toussaint, 3960, 3965–66

Lu Hsun, 6157, 6160
Luther, Martin, 1550, 1560, 5981
Luxemburg, Rosa, 2882, 2887–89, 2902,
  6087

MacNeill, Eoin, 2960
Machado, Gerado, 3830, 4173
Machiavelli, Niccolo, 1380
Machiavellism, 5281
Madero, Francisco I., 4017, 4077–79,
  6142
Mainz, 1518
Makhno, Nestor, 859, 2867
Malaya, 5143–48
  Communism in, 5144, 5146–48
  and nationalism, 5145
Malcolm X, 3736, 3767, 3783
Manchester, 1103
Manchu Dynasty, 4664, 4671. *Also see*
  Chinese Revolution (1911–1927)
Manin, Daniele, 2428, 2432
Maoism, 1008, 1363, 4538, 4785, 4787,
  4821, 4828, 4833–34, 4836, 4838,
  4848–51, 4857, 4865, 4872,
  4877–83, 4885, 4892, 4895, 4897,
  4901, 4904–05, 4965, 4973. *Also see*
  Mao Tse-tung
Mao Tse-tung, 258, 1142, 1175, 1374,
  1381, 1384, 1397, 1401, 1459, 4471,
  4565, 4700, 4722, 4738, 4745, 4753,
  4783, 4791, 4794, 4818–20,
  4822–27, 4829–32, 4835, 4837,
  4839–47, 4852–56, 4858–64,
  4866–71, 4873–76, 4884, 4886–91,
  4893–94, 4896, 4898–900,
  4902–03, 4906, 4911, 4915,
  4924–25, 4927, 4933, 4936–37,
  4939, 4942, 4953, 4959, 4974,
  4981–82, 4985, 4991, 5006, 6168.
  Also see Chinese Revolution
  (1927–1949); Chinese Revolution
  (1966–1969); Chinese Revolutions
  (General); Maoism
Marat, Jean Paul, 2041
Marcuse, Herbert, 1369, 3707–23, 6127
Marian Exiles, 1653. *Also see* Puritan
  Revolution
Mariátegui, José, 4407, 4422, 5506
Marx, Karl, 169, 258, 291, 315, 915, 920,
  923, 926, 928, 930, 932–34, 936,
  938–40, 942, 944–47, 950–51,
  953–54, 956–60, 965, 974, 976, 978,
  981–82, 984, 987, 989, 993, 996,
  1000, 1006, 1009–12, 1015–17,
  1020–26, 1041, 1048, 1050–54, 1057,
  1061, 1063, 1066, 1073, 1077–79,
  1084–86, 1089, 1091, 1106, 1113,
  1135, 1175, 1370, 1389, 1397, 1459,

Marx, Karl *(continued)*
  1470, 1640, 2222, 2238, 2350, 2439,
  2751, 2778, 3636, 3688, 3714, 4187,
  4628, 4791, 5492, 5772, 5835,
  5938–39, 5941–42, 5945, 5975–76.
  Also see Engels, Friedrich; Marxism
Marxism, 800, 890, 913–14, 916–1090,
  1092–93, 1157, 1213, 1363, 1884,
  2202, 2215, 2252, 2276, 2339, 2501,
  2577, 2761, 2778, 2836–37, 4259,
  4270, 4276, 4310, 5916, 5938–45,
  5948, 6127. *Also see* Communism;
  Engels, Friedrich; Marx, Karl;
  Marxism-Leninism; Socialism
  aesthetics and, 913
  in Africa, 5345, 5349, 5358, 5365, 5654
  and alienation, 1043, 1049, 1067
  in Arab world, 5818
  capitalism and, 921, 952, 977, 1014,
    1029, 1049, 1068
  in Chile, 6146
  in China, 4474–76, 4483, 4521, 4787
  class in, 926, 948, 996, 1018, 1030,
    1072, 5358
  economics and, 923, 965, 977, 996,
    1014, 1026, 1029, 1031, 1067, 5948
  ethics and, 997
  in France, 928, 934, 3148, 3150
  in Great Britain, 5943
  and guerrilla warfare, 444, 4255
  history of, 931, 951, 956, 960, 980, 994,
    1013, 1018–19, 1053, 1064, 1069,
    1076
  as humanism, 1008, 1019, 1065, 1084,
    1290, 1437
  ideology of, 291, 323, 968, 979, 1008,
    1037, 1071, 1074
  and imperialism, 952, 5940
  in Latin America, 3801, 3846, 3880,
    4276, 4310
  and Mao Tse-tung, 4839, 4848,
    4852–53
  in Mozambique, 5597
  nationalism and, 966, 5938
  and nonviolence, 925
  and religion, 954, 1065
  and revolution, 935, 970, 1019, 1033,
    1080
  in Russia, 2610, 2636, 2649, 2654,
    2657, 2694, 3720
  in Southeast Asia, 4607
  and state, 921–22, 927, 932, 934
  theory of, 921–22, 927–28, 936, 938,
    942, 944, 952, 960–62, 964, 966,
    970, 981, 987–88, 990, 1002, 1011,
    1021, 1023–27, 1040, 1043, 1045,
    1062, 1076, 1085, 1087, 1092, 1094,
    2501, 4825
  in Third World, 5772

Marxism *(continued)*
  in Vietnam, 5033, 5040
Marxism-Leninism, 937, 1002, 1059, 1209,
  3924, 4234, 4785, 4790, 5423–24.
  Also see Leninism; Marxism
Massachusetts, 3334, 3390–91, 3409,
  6111
Mass movements, 408, 2693, 5822
Mau Mau, 5410
May Fourth Movement, 4493, 4552. *Also
  see* Chinese Revolution (1911–1927);
  Chinese Revolutions (General)
Media, 598, 655, 916, 3659. *Also see*
  Press
Medieval rebellions, 1492–99
Meiji, 4568, 4580. *Also see* Japan
Melanesia, 367
Mellows, Liam, 2942
Menshevism, 2522, 2526, 2530–31,
  2539–40, 2548. *Also see*
  Bolshevism; February Revolution
  (1917); Russian Revolution (1917)
Menzel, Adolph von, 2407
Mercenaries, 6104
Merezhkovsky, D. S., 2264
Meslier, Curé, 5975
Messene, 5971
Messianic movements, 360, 383, 390,
  808, 6033. *Also see* Millennial
  movements
Methodism, 1277, 1280, 1291
Metternich, Count, 2853
Mexican Revolution (1854–1855; Ayutla),
  3890
Mexican Revolution (1910), 3805, 3814,
  3837, 3869, 3937, 3983–4091,
  6135–43. *Also see* Cárdenas,
  Lázaro; Carranza, Venustiano; Díaz,
  Porfirio; Madero, Francisco I.;
  Obregón, Alvaro; Orozco, Pascual;
  Villa, Pancho; Zapata, Emiliano
  anarchism in, 4031
  and Catholic Church, 4048–49
  caudillos in, 4061–62
  diplomacy of, 4064–67
  economics and, 4050–54
  and Europe, 6140
  and institutionalism, 3988, 4002
  labor in, 4055–60
  military in, 3994, 4027
  and nationalism, 4067, 4073
  peasants in, 4061–63, 4082, 4087
  politics of, 3994, 3996, 4027, 4055,
    4077, 6135
  Porfirians in, 6139
  Royalists in, 6134
  in San Luis Potosí, 3991, 6136
  and United States, 6140
  women in, 3997, 6143

476 / Subject Index

Mexico, 1351, 1388, 3809, 3988, 5968, 6134. *Also see* Mexican Revolution
  anarchism in, 838
  Communism in, 3927
  ideology of, 4058, 4087
  independence of, 671, 3953, 3957
  military in, 3994, 4027
  nationalism in, 4067, 4073
  peasants of, 4061–63, 4082, 4087
  student protest in, 740
Michel, Louise, 6057
Middle class. *See* Bourgeoisie
Middle East, 4446, 5756, 5783, 5785, 5787–89, 5793, 5814, 5833–34. *Also see* Arab world; Africa, North; and entries for individual countries
  history of, 5788, 5812, 5821
  ideology in, 5808
  military in, 5813
  terrorism in, 571, 587
Mignet, François, 6064
Military. *Also see* Guerrilla warfare; Militia; Urban guerrillas; Warfare; and subentries under individual country listings
  in Africa, 331, 341, 1407, 5388
  armies, 417–19, 421, 1735, 1762, 2110, 2258, 2323–24, 2366, 2370, 2537, 2558, 3196, 3199, 3204, 3346, 4027, 4176, 4365, 4408, 4519, 4778–79, 4782, 5000, 5066, 5092, 5388, 5798, 5946, 6001, 6015, 6048, 6076, 6122
  coups d'état by, 331, 333, 335, 339, 341, 343, 347–48, 3914, 4325, 5388, 5403
  and government, 331, 347, 1405, 3829, 4120, 4399, 4433–34, 5813
  in Latin America, 422, 3828, 3889, 3914
  in Middle East, 335, 5813
  navies, 1681, 2641, 2705, 3828, 6118, 6122
  officers of, 415, 1704, 2638
  politics and, 338, 347, 420, 424, 4365, 4390, 5295, 5308
  and sailors, 3230, 3401
  and soldiers, 414, 424, 1407, 2558, 2635, 2660, 3192, 3230, 3448, 4403, 5877, 5922, 5965
  in warfare, 342, 409, 414–25, 1371, 2755, 2817, 5965
Militia, 2533, 5986. *Also see* Military
Mill, James, 2233
Millennial movements, 359–92, 1142, 1694, 3009, 5916, 5919–21. *Also see* Messianic movements
Milton, John, 1728–32
Ming Dynasty, 710
Mobs. *See* Crowds

Modernization, 1227, 1348–51, 2295, 2509, 3269, 3863, 3934, 4018, 4388, 4432, 4504, 4539, 4850, 5716, 5958–59
Mohammed, 5384
Monck, General, 1662, 1664
Mondlane, Eduardo, 5598, 5606
Mongolia, 2186, 4570, 4592, 4646
Moore, Barrington, 70, 77
More, Thomas, 1142
Morocco, 5378, 6176
Morris, William, 2252
Most, Johann, 5931
Mozambique, 5380
  nationalism in, 5592, 5595
  warfare in, 5596
Mozambique Revolution (1964–1975), 1361, 5549, 5551, 5553, 5561, 5592–609, 6192–93. *Also see* FRELIMO; Mondlane, Eduardo; Portuguese Africa
  liberation of, 5553, 5601
  Marxism in, 5597
  nationalism in, 5592, 5595
  and Portugal, 5604
"Mucker" revolt, 6150
Mugabe, Robert, 5733
Mussolini, Benito, 2480
Müntzer, Thomas, 1547, 5982
Myth, 89, 282, 544, 820, 979, 1082, 1266, 1456, 1898, 2199, 2322, 3525, 4002, 4220, 4422, 4927, 5410, 5566, 5578, 5764

Namibia, 5380, 5747
Napoleon, 1906, 1914, 5978
Napoleonic Era, 1885, 1899, 2088, 5977
Nasser, Gamal Abdel, 5838, 5841–43, 5846, 5853
Nationalism, 313, 1255–72, 1341, 1437, 1827, 5650, 5924, 5938, 5949–50, 6129, 6176, 6190. *Also see* Patriotism; and subentries under individual country listings
  in Africa, 5346, 5361, 5370, 5377, 5410, 5419, 5546, 5734, 5770, 6176, 6190
  Arab, 5677, 5784, 5805, 5818, 5826, 5830, 6198
  in Asia, 4586, 4600, 5770
  and Communism, 1220, 1265, 2711, 3122, 5761
  in East Asia, 4581
  in Europe, 2209
  ideology of, 327
  in Latin America, 3810, 3834
  Marxism and, 949, 966, 2202, 5938
  in Quebec, 3784, 3787–88, 3790, 6130
  socialism and, 1123, 1127

Nationalism *(continued)*
    in Southeast Asia, 4593
    South Moluccan, 5924
    in Third World, 5769
    in Ukraine, 2863, 2866, 2868
National liberation. *See* Liberation
National liberation fronts, 5768
National Revolution, 693, 2288, 3198, 3810, 5915
Nation building, 100, 400, 712, 1565, 2950, 3282, 3284, 4007, 5327, 5544, 5765
Navy. *See* Military
Nazi Revolution (1933), 2985–3017. *Also see* Fascism; Hitler, Adolf; Nazism
Nazism, 2986, 2997, 3015, 5915
Neapolitan Revolution (1820–1821), 2503. *Also see* Italy
Nechaev, Sergei, 832, 876, 903–04
Negro revolts. *See* Black Revolution
Neocolonialism, 2852, 5439
Netherlands, 2478, 5924, 5986. *Also see* Holland
Netherlands Revolt (1566–1609), 1564–83, 5986. *Also see* Philip II; William the Silent
New England, 376, 381
New Left, 729, 753, 1146, 3595–706, 3708, 3712, 5957, 6124–26. *Also see* Berrigan, Daniel; Hippies; Left wing; Marcuse, Herbert; Students for a Democratic Society; Student rebellions; Weathermen; Yippies
    counter culture and, 3663, 3635, 3682, 3687, 3691
    and Trial of Chicago Eight, 3602, 3628, 3655, 3680, 3698
    underground press and, 3613, 3674
New Life Movement, 659
New Model Army, 1679–80. *Also see* Puritan Revolution
New York, 2291, 3334, 3339, 3381, 3481, 6111
Nicaragua, 4349, 4351, 4353–55
Nicaraguan Revolution (1978–1979), 4342–55, 6147–48. *Also see* Sandino
Nicholas II, 2551
Nien Rebellion, 6161
Nietzsche, Friedrich, 291
Nigeria, 5363, 5391
Nihilism, 1311, 3008
Nkrumah, Kwame, 5420–44
Nkrumahism, 5423, 5424, 5431
Nobility. *See* Aristocracy
Nonviolence, 488, 617–56, 925, 3604, 3778, 3781, 5189, 5212, 5214, 5218, 5220, 5236, 5250, 5257–58, 5263, 5276, 5281. *Also see* Civil disobedience; Gandhi, Mohandas K.

North África. *See* Africa, North; Middle East
North Vietnam. *See* Vietnam
Novelty, 52, 93
Nuclear threat, 5923
Nyerere, Julius, 5537

Obedience, 182
Obregón, Alvaro, 3994, 4020, 6137–38
O'Brien, William, 2952, 2967
O'Connell, Daniel, 2943
October Revolution (1917), 2565, 2578, 2585, 2589, 2591–95, 2598, 2601–05, 2623, 2645, 2670, 2683, 2691, 2707, 5952, 6077–83. *Also see* Russian Revolution (1917)
O'Faolain, Sean, 2914
O'Higgins, Bernardo, 3963
Order, 151, 228, 238, 243, 245, 255, 863, 1529, 4144, 5722, 5986
Organization, 79, 785, 1253, 1567, 2113, 2414, 2476, 3130, 3190, 4077, 4532, 4946, 4962, 5043, 5191, 5738, 6153
Organization of African Unity (OAU), 5594
Orozco, Pascual, 4034

Pacifism. *See* Nonviolence
Padmore, George, 3771
Pahlavi, Mohammad Reza (Shah of Iran), 5875, 5883, 5888, 5892–93, 5896, 5901, 5908, 5912
PAIGC, 5611, 5613, 5622, 5625, 5656. *Also see* Cabral, Amilcar; Guinea-Bissau Revolution
Paine, Thomas, 1392, 3579–94
Pakistan, 4461–62, 4564, 4567, 4588, 5187
Palestine, 570, 1382, 5817, 5826, 5828, 5832
    guerrillas in, 435, 5815, 5831
Palestine Liberation Organization (PLO), 5815
Palmerston, Lord, 2425
Pan-Africanism, 3771, 5345, 5349, 5350, 5353, 5373, 5398, 5422, 5563, 6175, 6179–80, 6185, 6187
Panama Revolution (1903), 3828
Paraguay, 3902, 3938
Paraguayan Revolution (1904), 3839
Paraguayan Revolution (1936–1940), 3840
Paris, 1305, 1538, 1585, 1592, 2009, 2024–31, 2051, 2113, 2117, 2203, 2315, 2323, 2378, 2381–82, 2387, 2392, 2445–46, 2450, 2452, 2455, 2457, 2460, 3142, 5987, 6009, 6038, 6060, 6069, 6091

Paris Commune (1871), 1293, 2179, 2181, 2196, 2200, 2218, 2226, 2257, 2287, 2436-71, 6070-73
Parker, Henry, 1691
Party, 207, 407, 1214, 1217, 1222, 1229, 1237, 1239, 1567, 1770, 2187, 2202, 2254, 3093, 3147, 3191, 3485, 3877, 4002, 4117, 4199, 4429, 4432, 4519, 4774, 5032, 5038, 5472, 6059, 6105
Pasha, Suleyman, 5792
Pathans, 369
Pathet Lao, 4603, 5113, 5115. *Also see* Laos
Patriotism, 391, 414, 1872, 2635, 3323, 3329, 3353, 3428, 3512, 3528. *Also see* Nationalism
Peace, 173, 455, 651, 653, 1056, 2267, 2937, 3189, 4044-45, 4379, 5082, 5212, 5257, 5469, 5744
Pearse, Patrick, 2938
Peasant revolt, 686-715, 1520, 1544-63, 2223, 2250, 2557, 2640, 2754, 3058, 3811, 3885, 4087, 4189-90, 4315, 4330, 4428, 4490, 4594, 4800, 4802, 5188, 5324, 5372, 5979-85, 6053. *Also see* Guerrilla warfare; People's war
  in Andes, 3811, 4428
Peasants, 183, 687, 689-95, 697-99, 702-03. *Also see* Class; Peasant revolt; and subentries under individual country listings
  in Africa, 5348, 5361, 5367, 5401
  in Balkans, 690, 6053
  in Europe, 715, 6053
  in Latin America, 3820, 3838, 3894, 3915, 3931
  Marxism and, 926
  in Palestine, 5828
  in Third World, 5773
  in Vivarais, 696
Peasants' Revolt (1524-1525), 1544-63, 5979-85
Peking, 4636, 4638, 4757, 4994, 5007
Peloponnesian War, 1484
People's war, 438, 706, 1372, 3403, 4589, 4777, 4780, 5092, 5551. *Also see* Guerrilla warfare; Peasant revolt
Permanent Revolution, 141, 185, 953, 2643, 2814, 2840, 4211, 4841, 4843, 4846, 4884
Persia, 5801-02. *Also see* Iran
Persian Revolution (1905-1909), 5809, 5824
Peru, 1359, 1405, 3809, 3864, 4407-37, 6151. *Also see* Aprista; Túpac Amaru Revolt
  Church in, 4409, 4414, 4431

Peru *(continued)*
  during colonial period, 4408-10, 4424, 4426
  ideology in, 4407, 4430
  military in, 4408, 4412, 4424, 4433-35
  and nationalism, 4417, 4425
  peasants of, 4428, 4437
Petrarch, Francesco, 1492
Petrograd, 6075
Petty bourgeoisie, 5365
Phaidros, 1475
Philadelphia, 3340, 3349
Philippine Revolution (1896), 5315, 5323, 5325, 5327, 5329
Philippine Revolution (1972; Democratic), 5310-14, 5316-22, 5326
Philippines, 5309-29
Philip II, 1575
Philosophy, 256-61, 293, 883, 914, 917, 937, 956, 971, 998, 1001, 1034, 1058, 1061, 1082, 1654, 1790, 1830, 1833-34, 1838, 3378-79, 3571, 3678, 3722, 4255, 4885, 5236, 5244, 5246, 5286, 5942, 5966, 6187
Plato, 1401, 1478, 1480-81, 2141, 2162, 2489, 5501-02
Plekhanov, George, 2263
Plug-Uglies, 465
Poetry, 6092
Poland, 1430, 1868, 2177, 2204, 2279, 2311, 2329-30, 3103-05, 5967, 6072
  Communism in, 3103, 3105
Police, 2081, 2386, 2701
Polish Revolution (1956), 3103-05
Political behavior, 288, 3844, 3878, 5012
Political change, 63, 232, 243, 285, 336, 339, 1240, 1339, 2199, 2327, 2354, 2717, 3126, 3173, 3907, 3925, 3929, 3936, 3939, 3940, 3942, 4117, 4385, 4388, 4390, 4398, 4442, 4443, 4958, 5016, 5152, 5416, 5554, 5633, 5641, 5703, 5769, 5773, 5777, 5814, 5867, 5873, 5897-98, 6016, 6174
Political philosophy, 225, 230, 235, 237, 240, 248, 1025, 1034, 1070, 1201, 1431, 1476, 1830, 2152-53, 2747, 2821, 3389, 3626, 5218, 5267, 5281, 5360, 5977, 6024, 6187
Political revolution, 229-31, 252, 274, 3621, 4012, 5322
Political science, 303, 309, 311, 4548, 5341-42, 5503
Political stability, 3826
Political strategy, 226, 252, 306, 3880, 3994, 5286
Political theory, 66, 300, 459, 646, 831, 873, 908, 922, 1002, 1025, 1027,

Political theory *(continued)*
1225, 1355, 1508, 1512, 1531, 1534, 1661, 1788–89, 1817, 1821, 1830, 1833–34, 1838, 1858, 2162, 2164, 2297, 2495, 2620, 2771, 2828, 3374, 3378–79, 3383, 3387–88, 3395, 3645, 3722, 3776, 3826, 4271, 4895, 4897, 5344, 5487, 5489, 5500–02, 5505, 5527, 5530, 5664, 5668, 5672, 5917, 5948, 5961, 5977, 6024, 6029, 6074, 6174, 6187

Politics. *Also see* Power; Provincial politics; Terrorism; Violence
 elite in, 745, 4302, 4369
 history of, 296, 316, 398, 409, 505, 522, 819, 1618, 1654, 1660, 1693, 1695, 1754, 1770, 1823, 1975, 1981, 2066, 2069, 2154, 2169, 2183, 2234, 2412, 2459, 2479, 2967, 3059, 3390, 3394, 3459, 3465, 3477, 3481, 3486, 3830, 3841, 3908, 3916, 3950, 4027, 4176, 4319, 4365, 4491, 4516, 4541, 4740, 5049, 5241, 5242, 5319, 5376, 5389, 5479, 5569, 5819, 6056
 sociology of, 246–48, 279, 298, 338, 424, 499, 1239, 1457, 1685, 1982, 2187, 3001, 3235, 3480, 3485, 3696, 3840, 3857–58, 3910, 3911, 3917, 3941, 4139, 4171, 4370, 4384, 4389, 4402, 4403, 4949, 4983, 5272, 5309, 5409, 5417, 5748, 5883, 5897, 5957, 5986, 6052, 6196

Polybius, 1482
Popper, Karl, 3711
Popular consent, 404
Populism, 2202, 5953
Portugal, 2205, 3018, 3200, 3205, 3797, 5550, 5555, 5557–58, 5561, 5604, 5622, 5631. *Also see* Portuguese Africa
 Communism in, 3189
 military in, 3192, 3196, 3199, 3204
 peasants of, 3190
Portuguese Africa, 5546–47, 5550, 5552, 5554–62, 5566, 5576, 5578, 5604, 5622, 5631, 6190
Portuguese Guinea (Guiné). *See* Guinea-Bissau
Portuguese Revolution (1974), 3180–205, 6096–98
Potemkin Mutiny, 2514. *Also see* Russian Revolution (1905)
Poutiatine, Countess Olga, 2575
Power. *Also see* Black Power
 autocratic, 1408, 1432, 1791
 economic, 103, 4068, 4372, 4807

Power *(continued)*
 moral, 5242, 5287, 5889
 political, 226, 241, 247, 249, 283, 1201, 3381, 4357, 4774, 5215, 5242, 5889, 6016
 seizure of, 241, 404, 481, 1146, 2578, 2616, 2773, 2881, 2988, 2996, 3006, 3909, 4133, 4138, 4542, 4753, 4924, 4925, 4934, 5054, 5137, 5444
 social, 101, 761, 1342, 2025, 3455, 3905, 4097, 5412, 5593, 6016, 6137
 and socialism, 805, 1149, 1158, 2636, 2726, 2741, 2881, 3029, 3672, 4773, 4807, 4934, 5054, 5137, 5944
 theories of, 157, 247, 249, 2741, 3377, 4970
 uses of, 281, 2534, 4152, 4524, 4773, 4970, 5215, 5582, 5889
Power politics, 343, 2502, 5376
Prague, 822, 3160–61, 3164, 3168, 3171, 3174, 3179
Praxis, 292, 988, 5506
Preconditions, 1510, 1523, 3318
Presbyterians, 364
Press, 542, 2101, 2333, 2858, 3060, 3167, 3352, 3463, 3483, 3613, 3674, 4105, 5315, 6026, 6035, 6066, 6103, 6115, 6151. *Also see* Media
Progress, 61, 221, 389, 1992, 2490, 5373
Project Camelot, 242
Proletariat, 176, 838, 1072, 1086, 1103, 1306, 2315–17, 2381, 2414, 2439, 2522, 2524, 2594, 2659–60, 2696, 2839, 3042, 3130, 3145, 3724, 4055–60, 4100, 4166, 4717, 5039, 5943, 6052, 6069, 6079
Propaganda, 1416, 1422, 1756, 2025, 2817, 3021, 3537, 3561, 5052, 6103
Prophecy, 5920–21
Protest, 110, 133, 139, 236, 253, 432, 500, 506, 632, 707, 715, 717, 719, 723, 725, 728, 730–31, 746, 763, 778, 782, 796, 1150, 1385, 1461, 1538, 2081, 2196, 2946, 3142, 3598, 3648, 3696, 3748, 3754, 3765, 5412, 5579, 5918
Protestant Revolution (Reformation), 1505, 1527, 1536, 1540, 5983–84. *Also see* Peasants' Revolt
Proudhon, Pierre-Joseph, 854, 905–12
Provincial politics, 699, 713, 1766, 1947, 1948, 2084, 2089, 2320, 2386, 2681, 2940–41, 3472, 3996, 4077, 4094–95, 4209, 4307, 4368, 4444, 4709, 4804, 4808, 4812, 4921, 4967, 5011, 5697, 5731, 5986, 6016

480 / Subject Index

Psychological theories, 467, 469, 5915, 6188
Psychology, 262-72, 462, 467, 602, 640, 732, 786, 808, 1262, 1341, 1824, 2103, 2112, 3132-33, 3542, 3564, 4473, 5263, 5490, 5495, 5915, 5932
Public opinion, 1821, 2926
Puerto Rico, 3899
Pugachev Rebellion (1773-1774), 2167-69
Pulaski, Kazimierz, 3525
Puritan Revolution (1640-1660), 1368, 1379, 1391, 1535, 5989-91. *Also see* Charles I; Cromwell, Oliver; Diggers; Gentry; Levellers; Milton, John; Monck, General; Pym, John
  intellectual factors in, 1655-61, 1740
  in London, 1686, 1698
  military in, 1679-83, 1735
  and Parliament, 1630-31, 1666-67, 1693, 1695
  peasants in, 1641
  politics of, 1618, 1654, 1660, 1685, 1693, 1695
  and Puritanism, 1652, 1668-71
  religion in, 1618, 1656, 1693, 1697, 1718, 1731
  and Royalists, 1677-78
  social factors in, 1638-49, 1699-700, 5989, 5991
Pym, John, 1663, 1665

Qadhafi, Colonel, 5677, 5680
Quakers, 6117
Quebec, 603, 3784-91, 5969, 6130

Racism, 351, 1262, 1334-47, 3411, 3757, 5748, 6190
Radek, Karl, 2702
Radetzky, Josef, 2370
Radicalism, 184, 737, 760, 781-814, 1823, 3595, 3598, 3640, 3665, 3668-69, 3671, 5917, 5932-33, 5955, 6050, 6126
  in Argentina, 4366
  in Chile, 4288
  in China, 4552, 4663, 4670, 5003
  in Europe, 2230
  in France, 2025, 2041, 2380, 2483
  in Germany, 2903, 5932
  in Great Britain, 793, 807, 893, 1660, 1696-97, 1740, 3473
  in Japan, 747
  in Latin America, 3820, 3836, 3883
  in Peru, 4435
  religion and, 1273, 1508, 1697
  in Russia, 799, 2697, 2744, 5955
  students in, 747, 760, 774-75

Radicalism *(continued)*
  in United States, 781, 783, 790, 792, 795, 797-98, 805-06, 809-10, 813-14, 833, 3310, 3341, 3385, 3387, 3614, 3632, 3639, 3645, 3648, 3650, 3658, 3672, 3750, 6126
Ranters, 1697. *Also see* Puritan Revolution
Rationalism, 1516
La Raza, 3218
Rebellion, 21, 90, 116, 127, 223, 232, 236, 368, 399, 406, 424, 514, 670, 697, 700-01, 710, 713, 751, 769, 772, 775, 1365, 1424, 1493, 1522, 1599, 1624, 2286, 2325, 2498, 2698, 3133, 3213, 3217, 3340, 3347, 3436, 3609, 3648, 3823, 3954, 4032, 4380, 4479, 4482, 4501, 4511, 4520, 4564, 4576, 4604, 5034, 5134, 5157, 5167, 5174, 5360, 5364, 5411, 5455, 5462, 5465, 5606, 5826, 5987, 5989, 5991, 6151, 6161-62
Rebels, 115, 382, 397, 401, 407, 483, 505, 766, 887, 1238, 1292, 1324, 1435, 1515, 3025, 3430, 3693, 4410, 4525, 4615, 4620, 4947, 5292, 5845, 5863, 5932, 6059
Reclus, Elisée, 835
Red Guards, 5001, 5004, 5006-08. *Also see* Chinese Revolution (1966-1969)
Redmond, John, 2944
Reed, John, 1445, 1462
Reform, 125, 139, 151, 505, 512, 990, 1518, 1886, 1992, 2195, 2316, 2420-21, 2897, 3072, 3079, 3126, 3157, 3166-68, 3172, 3177, 3194, 3472, 3643, 3711, 3897, 3918-19, 3923, 3994, 4020, 4024, 4062, 4082-83, 4115, 4234, 4396, 4418, 4429, 4470, 4591, 4657, 4662, 4926, 5142, 5221-22
Reformation. *See* Protestant Revolution
Regicide, 2034-37
Reign of Terror (France), 2052-53, 2097-127, 6042-45. *Also see* French Revolution (1789-1799)
Religion, 1273-92, 1373, 1508, 1529, 1546-47, 1549-50, 1565, 1572, 1585, 1618, 1693-94, 1697, 1731, 1754, 1780, 2017-20, 2262, 2504, 2520, 4414, 4431, 5982, 5987, 5990, 6005, 6041, 6133. *Also see* Catholic Church; Christianity; Methodism; Presbyterians
  in Africa, 5352, 5384, 5402
  in American Revolution, 3494-506, 6117
  in China, 4551

Subject Index / 481

Religion *(continued)*
 and Christianity, 1273, 1283-84, 1287, 1289, 3079, 4188, 4616, 6040
 and Communism, 1287, 4187
 in Cuban Revolution, 4187-88
 ideology of, 1278
 in India, 5218
 in Iran, 5869, 5873, 5877, 5880, 5883, 5887, 5897, 5899, 5908
 and Islam, 5134, 5677, 5761, 5786, 5794, 5816
 and Latin America, 6133
 and Maoism, 4833
 and Marxism, 954, 1275, 1290
 messianic cults of, 383
 millennial movements of, 388, 392
 in Persia, 5801
 in Turkey, 5296, 5298
Renaissance, 391, 1527
Republican thought, 381, 2315, 2377, 2380, 3371, 3385, 3470, 4788, 6004
Resistance, 99, 116, 240, 526, 622, 636, 639, 641-42, 647, 1310, 1385, 1753, 1789, 2072, 2192, 3098, 3177, 3315, 3341, 3728, 3899, 4363, 4734, 4800, 5212, 5258, 5263, 5366, 5464, 5565, 5579, 5589, 5595, 5599, 5608, 5651, 6002, 6005, 6090
Restoration, 674, 1746, 1767, 1772, 2188, 2201, 2234, 2328, 2411-12, 4655
Revisionism, 975, 1003, 1110-11. *Also see* Bernstein, Eduard
Revolt. *Also see* Rebellion; Rebels
 analysis of, 115, 123, 407, 475, 678, 820, 1444, 2483, 2904, 3716, 5094, 5144, 5760
 Black, 3753, 3766, 3774
 history of, 2558, 3214, 3328, 3835, 3852, 3957, 4374, 4749, 5168, 5170, 5172, 5398, 5588-89, 5620, 5807, 5973, 6149-51
 mass, 408, 498, 686, 2177, 3741, 5208
 peasant, 686, 689, 692, 696, 712, 1520, 2250, 3820, 4359, 4490
 psychology of, 269, 1824, 2277
 vs. reform, 139, 1592, 3122, 3157
 and revolution, 2225, 3128, 5294, 5913
 right to, 57, 777, 3272, 5094, 5760, 5807
 student, 726-27, 754, 756, 764-65, 770-71, 777, 2312, 3140-42, 3144
 vs. tradition, 182, 188, 1495, 1809, 1837, 2151, 3887, 5148
Revolution. *Also see* Liberation; Rebellion; Revolt
 causes of, 12, 20-21, 23-25, 27, 31, 39, 48, 54, 56, 59, 67, 131-32, 138, 140, 149, 171, 179, 194, 196-97
 definitions of, 1, 30, 35, 37, 46, 49-50,

Revolution, definitions of *(continued)*
 53, 60, 64, 67, 71, 78, 85, 3708
 dictionary of, 1420
 and happiness, 13, 57
 history of, 18, 36, 44, 51, 93, 95, 104, 107, 112-13, 128, 130, 136, 167, 178, 186, 203, 207, 219, 1459-60, 1467, 5919, 5941, 5970
 sociology of, 229, 234, 239, 242, 3392, 3401, 3653, 3870, 4055, 4166, 4362, 4579, 4668, 4745, 4922, 4945, 4969, 4980, 4986, 5120, 5131, 5295, 5308, 5477, 5585, 5698, 5722, 6006
 theories of, 1-15, 17-18, 20-22, 28-29, 43, 47, 65-69, 72-73, 75-76, 80-82, 86-87, 90, 92-93, 95-98, 102, 104-08, 111, 117-18, 123-24, 130, 137-38, 140, 145-46, 148, 150, 152-54, 156, 159, 161-62, 164-66, 168-70, 172, 179-81, 187, 192, 194-96, 200, 206, 208, 215, 220, 262-63, 430, 459, 867, 970, 1226, 1228, 1425, 1447, 1453, 1471, 1474, 2144-45, 2292, 2818, 3366, 3370, 3710, 3992, 4653, 4800, 5486, 5488, 5529-30, 5648, 5665, 5917, 5960
Revolutionaries. *See* Revolutionists
Revolutionary consciousness, 88
Revolutionary ideal, 105, 3577
Revolutionary process, 39, 58, 67, 91, 120, 196, 209, 226, 1238, 5504, 5963
Revolutionists, 71, 144, 2278, 5961, 6062. *Also see* Rebels
 doctrines of, 216, 1252, 2207, 2694, 2848, 3821, 5801, 5904
 leadership of, 1238, 1240, 1250, 3439, 5355, 5694
 profiles of, 190, 1231, 1235, 1244, 1249, 1442, 1445, 1526, 2219, 2229, 2244, 2569, 2585, 2727, 2802, 2885, 3424, 3438, 3553, 3606, 3616, 3779, 3808, 4439, 4685, 4889, 5351, 5391, 5493, 5515, 5646, 5670, 5680, 5761, 5820, 5904, 6051
 as proselytizers, 189, 5515, 5525
 psychology of, 32, 224, 1230, 1434, 2733, 4373, 4830, 4947, 5490, 5670, 5998
 as social agent, 142, 695, 2639, 3866, 4470, 5628, 5828
 sociology of, 1237, 1243, 1251, 2426, 3435, 3441, 3660, 3662, 4348, 4496, 4525, 4670, 4771, 5142, 5200
Rhetoric, 1319, 1324, 1326, 1331, 2066, 3340, 3365, 3532, 5371

Rhodesia. *See* Zimbabwe
Rights of Man, 1392, 5964, 5992
Right wing, 782, 790, 2077, 2093, 3077, 3595, 3598. *Also see* Conservative
Riot, 350, 475, 479, 493–95, 500, 513–14, 522, 3347, 3742–43, 3760, 3765, 5826
Rising expectations, 21, 63
Robespierre, Maximilien, 2038, 2098–99, 2102–07, 2111–12, 2115–16, 2119–22, 2124, 2126–27, 6020, 6043–44
Robinson, Henry, 1691
Rochambeau, Jean Baptiste, comte de, 5922
Roland, Madame, 2091
Romanoffs, 2543, 2546, 2551, 2555–57. *Also see* Russian Revolution (1917)
Roman Republic, 5972
Romanticism, 155, 2190, 2277, 2362, 6063
Rome, 1485–91, 5972
Rousseau, Jean Jacques, 302, 315, 605, 1534, 1813–43, 2071, 5993–94, 6000
Roy, M. N., 5211
Rulers, 1232, 1234, 1242, 1245, 1432
Rumania, 2223, 2434
Russia. *Also see* February Revolution; October Revolution; Pugachev Rebellion; Russian Revolution (1825); Russian Revolution (1905); Russian Revolution (1917)
 anarchism in, 826, 2627, 2661
 Cheka in, 2701, 2753
 class struggle in, 2665
 and Communism, 1167, 1171, 1178, 1205, 1214, 1217, 1223, 2608, 2615, 2625, 2675, 2711, 5761
 comparative studies of, 1237, 1351, 1354, 1375–77, 1384, 1404, 2170, 2559, 5963
 counterrevolution in, 685
 exiles from, 2189, 2463
 foreign relations of, 2235, 2241, 2269, 2692, 2860, 3024, 3176
 history of, 1376, 1377, 2195, 2217, 2266, 2274, 2283, 2515–16, 2518, 2528, 2552, 2560–61, 2563, 2568, 2576, 2588, 2590, 2595, 2597, 2652, 2684–86, 2699, 2716, 2718, 2720, 2729, 2732, 2742, 2759, 2773, 2779, 6077
 ideology of, 283, 1008, 2626, 2632, 2741, 4195
 Imperial, 2544, 2546–47, 2713, 2723
 literature of, 1325

Russia *(continued)*
 Marxism in, 1028, 2610, 2636, 2649, 2654, 2657, 2663, 2694
 military in, 414–15, 417, 2537, 2558, 2635, 2638, 2641, 2660, 2705, 2817, 6076
 and modernization, 1351, 1354, 2509, 5963
 nationalism in, 2711, 5761
 nobility in, 2505
 peasants of, 709, 2167, 2506, 2557, 2629, 2644, 2660, 2688, 2709, 2724
 perspective from, 1357, 1360
 populism in, 5953
 proletariat in, 1072, 2529, 2659–60, 2779
 radicalism and, 799
 revolutionists in, 1515, 2221, 2284–85, 2525, 2572, 2675, 2717, 2726
 social democracy in, 2510, 2524, 2719, 2744, 2752
 sociology of, 1375, 2737
 terrorism in, 549, 556, 564, 612, 5930
 and Third World, 2186, 4165, 4192, 4195, 4643–44, 4669, 4673, 4815–17, 5761, 5930, 6184
 warfare in, 2588, 2614, 2737
 women in, 1298–99, 5953–55, 6082
Russian Revolution (1825), 2251, 2260, 2285, 2289
Russian Revolution (1905), 2262, 2266, 2283–85, 2504–25
Russian Revolution (1917), 414, 1302, 1358, 2179, 2195, 2217, 2266, 2283–85, 2526–744, 2772, 2797, 2835, 2842, 5963, 6077–83. *Also see* Bolshevism; February Revolution; Lenin, V. I.; Menshevism; October Revolution; Trotsky, Leon
 agrarian activism during, 2618, 2642
 anarchists in, 2627, 2661
 and art, 2691, 6081
 and Baku Commune, 2730
 Bukharin in, 2603
 class struggle of, 2665
 and Constitutional Democratic Party, 2721
 and Duma, 2600
 economics of, 2590
 foreign policy during, 2678
 July Uprising in, 2617
 and Kornilov Rebellion, 2574, 2648, 6076
 military in, 2638, 2641, 2660, 2705, 6076
 and Nationalist Party, 2681

Russian Revolution *(continued)*
  peasants in, 2629, 2644, 2688, 2709, 2724
  and Petrograd Red Guard, 2529, 2541
  and Petrograd Soviet, 2532, 2616–17, 2626, 2738, 6075
  proletariat in, 2529, 2541, 2594, 2659, 2696
  and Provisional Government, 2527, 2535
  and Social Democracy, 2526
  Socialist Revolutionaries in, 2618, 2643–44, 2719
  Stalin in, 2598
  and the West, 2667, 2732, 6078
  women in, 5952, 5954–55
  Zinoviev in, 2637
Rwanda, 5402, 5532
Rykov, A. I., 2615

Sadat, Anwar, 5838, 5959
Saint-Just, 2109, 2111
Saint-Simoniennes, 2193
Sandino, 3928, 4354
San Domingo, 3960
San Martín, José de, 3969
Sartre, Jean-Paul, 258, 2073, 3150, 4158
Satyagraha, 633, 5227, 5229, 5247, 6173. *Also see* Gandhi, Mohandas K.; Indian Revolution
Saudi Arabia, 5796
Savonarola, 391, 5871
Schlöffel, Gustav Adolph, 2406
Science, 362, 1071, 1084, 1098, 1389, 1796, 1799, 1807, 2222, 4539, 5943, 5966
Scientific Revolution, 1793–808
Scotland, 1693, 6107
Scottish Revolution (1637–1651), 1532, 1541–42
SDS. *See* Students for a Democratic Society
Seattle, 3221
Secret societies, 6153
Self-determination, 2758, 5765–66
Separatism, 3766, 3788
Sepoy Mutiny (1857), 5153–80. *Also see* India
Serdán, 6142
Servia, 2261, 6053
Seven Years' War, 3317, 6030
Sexual Revolution, 69
Sian, 5124
Siege of Paris (1870), 2445–46, 2450, 2455, 2460. *Also see* Paris Commune

Sinn Fein. *See* Irish Revolution
Slavery, 618, 3213–14, 3411, 3530
Slovenes, 6058
Smith, Adam, 3526
SNCC. *See* Student Nonviolent Coordinating Committee
Snow, Edgar, 6167
Snyder, Louis L., 5950
Social change, 34, 48, 69, 187, 256, 449, 470, 495, 506, 707, 1229, 1381, 1443, 1448, 1532, 1649, 1690, 2354, 3092, 3345, 3399, 3402–03, 3405, 3412, 3843, 3859, 3868, 3893, 3912, 3925, 3934–35, 3939, 4054, 4437, 4787, 4848, 5773, 5777, 5814, 5982, 6061, 6081, 6106, 6150. *Also see* Society
Social conflict, 55–56, 119, 121–22, 191. *Also see* Conflict
Social Democracy, 1205, 2524, 2526
Socialism, 313, 835, 964, 1098, 1107–65, 1196, 1207, 1463, 1709, 2242, 2352, 2466, 2489, 4251, 5780, 5916, 5947–48, 5961. *Also see* Communism; Marxism; and subentries under individual country listings
  in Africa, 5392, 5404, 5426, 5538, 5540–43
  anarchism and, 835, 862, 898, 910
  Arab, 5790, 5827
  in Europe, 1151, 2215, 2248
  history of, 1109, 1115, 1120, 1122, 1133, 1148, 1150–54, 1225, 5975–76
  nationalism and, 1123, 1127
  in Third World, 1129
  tradition of, 1132
  women in, 1302, 5956
Socialist politics, 1124, 1126, 3703, 4132, 4366
Socialist Revolution, 1134, 1147, 1361, 2591, 2843, 2851, 4132, 4705, 4718, 5069, 5477, 5915
Socialization, 6007
Social movements, 29, 83, 114, 139, 143, 191, 205, 213–14, 266–67, 271–72, 382, 484, 3215, 3406, 3410, 5776
Social order, 100, 151, 5278, 5960
Social revolt, 3214
Social Revolution, 92, 273–74, 853, 1375, 1404, 1473, 2031, 2288, 3010, 3675, 3758, 3805, 3922, 4098, 4104, 4115, 4134, 4159, 4399, 4475, 4708, 5123
Social system, 152
Social theory, 249, 499, 803, 908, 942, 966, 1133, 1253, 1334, 1842, 2483, 2495, 2828, 3671, 4800, 5671, 5948, 5960, 5994, 6074, 6187

Society, 214, 238, 247, 302, 363, 422, 487, 571, 713, 795, 1060, 1069, 1332, 1342, 1365, 1372, 1424, 1700, 1837, 1975, 2078, 2132, 2303, 3334, 3398, 3666, 3718, 3770, 3870, 3889, 3905, 3930, 3945, 4041, 4362, 4385, 4424, 4487, 4509, 4551, 4776, 4877, 4990, 5472, 5532, 5654, 5897–98, 5994, 6081, 6106
Society of Thirty, 6041
Sociological theory, 475, 723, 966, 1127, 4843
Sociology, 45, 79, 106, 117, 119, 124, 126, 181, 195, 215, 475, 653, 1004, 1211, 1239, 1433, 1457, 2143, 2724, 4173, 5528, 5933, 6006, 6074
Soldiers. See Military
Soledad, 3739, 3750. Also see Black Revolution; Jackson, George
Solzhenitsyn, Alexander, 325
Somoza family, 4349, 4353, 4355, 6147. Also see Nicaraguan Revolution
Sorel, Georges, 2480–84, 2488–89, 2493, 6074. Also see General Strike; Myth; Syndicalism
South Africa, 633, 636, 5380, 5737, 5741, 5744–45, 5748, 6196
South America. See Latin America
South Asia, 4459–62, 4467, 4590, 5756
Southcott, Joanna, 5919
Southeast Asia, 474, 1183, 4463–64, 4578, 4587, 4589, 4593, 4597–99, 4604–05, 4607, 6154
Southern Africa, 425, 1373, 5380, 5726, 5734, 5740, 5742–43, 5748, 6196
South Moluccans, 5924
South Vietnam. See Vietnam
South Yemen, 1366
Soviet Union. See Russia
Spain, 553, 1575, 1577, 1579, 1809–12, 2243, 2286, 2435, 3018–20, 3027, 3063, 3797, 3953, 3970, 5323. Also see Spanish Civil War
  anarchism in, 828, 845, 5934–36
  Communism in, 3037
  peasants of, 2286
  and socialism, 3020
  terrorism in, 531, 547, 553
Spanish American Revolutions, 3944–45, 3948, 3951, 3956, 3961, 3964, 3967, 3974–75, 3979. Also see Latin American independence revolutions
Spanish Civil War (1936–1939), 2179, 3018–91, 6091–95
  anarchism in, 3042
  art in, 3086
  and Carlism, 3027
  Falange in, 3069

Spanish Civil War (continued)
  foreign involvement in, 3022, 3024, 3041, 3043–44, 3049, 3053, 3074, 3084, 5968
  and Francisco Franco, 3077, 3081
  intellectuals in, 3090
  Lincoln Battalion in, 3078
  literature in, 3019
  and Mexico, 5968
  women in, 6094
Spanish Guinea, 6177
Spanish Revolution. See Spanish Civil War
Stability, 227
Stalin, Joseph, 593, 1384, 2598, 2612, 2670, 2677, 2727, 2733, 2736, 2759, 4716, 4874
State, 237, 515, 858, 921–22, 927, 932, 934, 1158, 1377, 1404, 1407, 1415, 1469, 1477, 1826, 2018, 2075, 2179, 2566, 2632, 2650, 2731, 2750, 2780, 2961, 3908, 4002, 4057, 4317, 4409, 4427, 4471, 4565, 5414, 5647, 5713, 5731, 5780, 5793, 5883, 5925, 5947
Status, 101, 6206
Stendhal, M. H. B., 2184
Stern, 570
Strategy, 133, 174, 199, 216, 226, 252, 398, 412, 789, 791, 1179, 1197, 1306, 1402, 2281, 2340, 2621, 3646, 3675, 3782, 3821, 3877, 3880, 3994, 4195, 4207, 4239, 4268, 4285, 4300, 4584, 4587, 4829, 4832, 4848, 4857, 4937, 5224, 5263, 5286, 5605, 5760–61, 6015
Stratification, 79
Structural change, 78, 214, 276–77, 326, 459, 461, 1375, 1551, 2118, 2340, 3004, 3793, 3917, 4097, 4328, 4511, 4935, 5655, 5984
Stuarts, 1594, 1597, 1609, 1611, 1625–28, 1763. Also see Charles I; Glorious Revolution; James II; Puritan Revolution
Student Nonviolent Coordinating Committee (SNCC), 6128
Student rebellions, 716–80, 2387, 3127, 3130, 3140, 3144–45, 3147, 3153, 3729, 4160, 4692, 4806, 5003, 5932. Also see French Revolution (1968); New Left; Universities
Students for a Democratic Society (SDS), 3694. Also see New Left
Sudan, 5371, 5377
Sukarno, Achmed, 5141
Sung Chiaojen, 4667
Sun Yat-sen, 4565, 4650–52, 4676–88, 6165–66

Superstition, 1335
SWAPO, 5747. *Also see* Namibia
Swisher, Earl, 4702
Switzerland, 2269
Syndicalism, 851, 1159, 1463, 2476, 2478-79, 2485-87, 2492. *Also see* Sorel, Georges
Systems, 152, 158, 1189, 1194, 1224, 2654, 5916

Tactics, 395, 580, 1197, 2074, 2621, 2637, 2751, 4239, 4602, 6015
Taiping Rebellion (1850-1864), 4609-32. *Also see* Chinese Revolutions (General)
Tambov Revolt (1920-1921), 2647
Tanzania, 5404, 6181
Teachers, 2379. *Also see* Universities
Teng, 5959
Terror, 278, 395, 482, 526, 531, 534, 537, 549, 571, 582, 585, 593-94, 598, 603, 613, 2052-53, 2109, 2114, 2117-18, 2123, 2125, 2759, 4029, 4325, 4637, 5073, 5858, 6177. *Also see* Reign of Terror; Terrorism
Terrorism, 527-616, 5454, 5923-31, 6021
  and democracies, 536, 544, 571, 578, 582, 616
  in Europe, 541-42, 544
  in Germany, 569, 613
  guerrillas and, 575, 583
  and hostage negotiations, 5928
  in India, 4555, 5190
  international, 527-29, 538-39, 556, 563-64, 567-68, 572, 574, 579, 581-82, 589-90, 601, 612, 5923, 5927, 5930
  in Italy, 532, 591, 609
  in Latin America, 586
  in Middle East, 570, 587
  in Netherlands, 5924
  political, 611, 614-15
  in Quebec, 3791
  revolutionary, 540, 554, 584, 5190
  in Russia, 549, 556, 593, 612, 5930
  in Spain, 531, 547, 553
  urban, 573, 613
  in Vietnam, 555, 5073
Thailand, 363, 4572, 5121-26
Theory. *See* Anarchism, theories of; Behaviorial theory; Communism, theory and practice of; Economic theory; Guerrilla warfare, theory and practice of; Marxism, theories of; Nonviolence; Political theory; Power, theories of; Praxis; Psychological theories; Revolutions, theories of; Social theory; Sociological theory

Theory and practice, 446, 448, 565, 647, 661, 672, 773, 837, 964, 990, 1045, 1162, 1195, 1203, 2609, 2620, 2771, 3675, 4219, 4261, 4913, 5234, 5409, 5425, 5629, 5961. *Also see* Praxis
Theory of alienation, 1043, 1067
Theory of history, 960, 1076, 1094, 1822, 2073, 3361
Theory of the state, 922, 927, 1092, 1789, 2049
Thiers, Adolphe, 6064
Third World, 5030, 5037, 5757-58, 5763-67, 5771-78, 5781-82, 6197. *Also see* Developing nations; Underdeveloped areas
  of the Americas, 1441, 3860
  leadership of, 5771
  literature and, 1328
  and Marxism, 5772
  peasants of, 5773
  politics of, 5773, 5777
  religion in, 392
  socialism and, 1129
  and Soviet Union, 5761
  and United States, 5759, 5781
  warfare in, 661
Tibet, 4576
Tito, Josip, 3095
Tkachev, Pyotr, 2650
Tocqueville, Alexis de, 1279, 2290-307, 2397, 6061
Torre, Haya de la, 3808
Torres, Camilo, 4397, 4400-01, 4406
Totalitarianism, 94, 310, 562, 993, 1458, 1825, 3108, 4707
Touré, Sékou, 5544
Tradition, 188, 204, 654, 1132, 1137, 1332, 1504, 1509, 1659, 2241, 2645, 2692, 3269, 3866, 3887, 4736, 5075, 5090, 5535, 5599, 5608, 5698, 5756, 5794, 5917, 6056, 6193
Travot, Jean-Pierre, 6046
Trotsky, Leon, 1409, 1470, 2468, 2650, 2813-49, 3850
Tudor Rebellions (England), 1522
Tunisia, 5378, 6176
Túpac Amaru Revolt (1780-1784), 4408-10, 4424, 4426. *Also see* Peru
Tupamaros, 4336, 4338, 4340-41. *Also see* Uruguay
Turgot, Robert, 1968, 1992, 6123
Turkey, 1405, 5295-308, 6174
Turkish Revolution (1908), 5297, 5306-07
Turkish Revolution (1919-1923), 4567, 5296, 5302, 5304, 5307, 6174. *Also see* Kemal, Mustafa
Turkish Revolution (1960-1961), 5295, 5308

486 / Subject Index

Turner, Nat, 3213
Tyranny, 38, 2122

UDI, 5746, 5749. *Also see* Zimbabwe
Uganda, 5403
Ukrainian Revolution (1917–1921), 859, 2863–68
Underdeveloped areas, 45, 342, 423, 1398, 3861, 3873, 5600, 5731, 5767, 5769, 5776, 6188. *Also see* Developing nations; Third World
Unions, 2770, 5737
United Nations, 539, 1346
United States, 1386, 1388, 1419, 1429, 1509, 1865, 1870, 1928, 2293, 3049, 3084, 3206–783, 6099–126. *Also see* American Revolution; Black Revolution; New Left
  anarchism in, 825, 833, 864, 890
  colonial period of, 3227, 3245, 3271, 3284, 3286, 3299, 3302, 3313, 3320–21, 3323, 3325, 3327–37, 3339–41, 3343, 3348, 3351, 3392–93, 3471–72, 3474–75, 3479–81, 3485, 3488, 3492
  and Communism, 1166, 1169, 1192, 1241, 3771
  ideology of, 299, 1304, 1353, 1378, 1457, 1986, 3359–61, 3371–72, 3374, 3376, 3500
  and Marxism, 995, 3220
  military in, 3230, 3401, 3443, 3448, 3453, 3458–61
  millenarianism in, 364, 376, 381, 387
  and nationalism, 1274, 3239, 3494, 3523, 3567, 3740, 3744, 3746, 3755, 3762
  nonviolence in, 617
  radicalism in, 781, 788–90, 792–98, 805–06, 809–10, 813–14, 3209, 3595, 3597
  socialism in, 1107, 1165, 3646
  student protest in, 716–20, 723–30, 732–39, 741–46, 748–51, 756–72, 774–78
  terrorism in, 564, 582
  and Third World, 45, 1441, 3519, 3898–99, 3913, 3918, 3956, 3980, 4064–67, 4109, 4153, 4196, 4332–35, 4355, 4499, 4585, 4596, 4650, 4652, 4813–14, 5052, 5062, 5079, 5084, 5321, 5327, 5368, 5759, 5781, 5855, 5866, 5891, 5900, 5910, 6147
  violence in, 450–52, 460, 465, 480, 489–90, 493–94, 498, 501–02, 510, 512–13, 518–19, 521–22, 3522, 3760
  and warfare, 3219, 3227, 3243
  women in, 1304, 1307, 3507–12

Universities, 730, 735, 751, 757, 760, 769, 777, 780, 1421, 3126, 4160, 4975. *Also see* French Revolution (1968); Student rebellions
Urban areas, 395, 495, 498, 505, 514, 522, 573, 699, 1552, 1685, 1689, 1948, 2089, 2310, 2337, 3345, 3412, 3741, 3820, 4057–59, 4709, 4798, 4804, 5144
Urban guerrillas, 395, 427, 432, 441, 573, 613, 3820, 3881, 3892, 4338, 4340–41, 4375
Uruguay, 3978, 4336–41
U.S.S.R. *See* Russia
Utopia, 319, 389, 779, 858, 1098, 1114, 1427, 1449, 1452, 2704, 2750, 4836, 5975–76, 6079

Vendée, 2128–38, 6046–49. *Also see* Counterrevolution; French Revolution (1789–1799)
Venetian Revolution. *See* Italian Revolution (1848)
Venezuela, 4438–44
  Communism in, 4440
  peasants of, 4444
  politics of, 4442–44
Venice, 2426, 2428, 2432
Vergennes, Charles, 1945
Vergniaud, Pierre, 2079
Vienna, 2369, 2373
Viet Cong, 555, 5066, 5081–82, 5086. *Also see* Vietnamese Revolution
Viet Minh, 5061, 5086. *Also see* Vietnamese Revolution
Vietnam, 361, 1372, 3466, 5014–16, 5113. *Also see* Vietnamese Revolution
  Communism in, 5017, 5041, 5054, 5067, 5080, 5088–89, 5094
  guerrillas in, 428
  history of, 5042, 5044, 5048–49, 5051, 5055–56, 5071, 6170–71
  ideology in, 5040
  military in, 5016, 5066, 5092, 5965
  nationalism in, 5028, 5055
  peasants of, 1372, 5038–39
  and socialism, 5024
  warfare in, 5053, 5082–83, 5086–87, 5965
Vietnamese Revolution (1945–1973), 1371, 4566, 4572, 4574–75, 4579, 5014–94, 5965, 6170–71. *Also see* Ho Chi Minh; Viet Cong; Viet Minh; Vo Nguyen Giap
  Communism in, 5017, 5041, 5054, 5067, 5080, 5088–89, 5094
  government during, 5057
  guerrillas in, 5046, 5053, 5077, 5086

Subject Index / 487

Vietnamese Revolution *(continued)*
ideology of, 5040
intellectuals in, 5039
and Marxism, 5033, 5040
military in, 5016, 5066, 5092, 5965
nationalism in, 5028, 5055
and North Vietnam, 5067
party in, 5032, 5038
peasants of, 5038–39
politics of, 5016, 5031, 5049
proletariat in, 5039
and socialism, 5024
and South Vietnam, 5022, 5058
and United States, 4585, 5052, 5062, 5079, 5084, 5965
Villa, Pancho, 4080–84
Violence, 27, 449–526, 624, 631, 639, 652, 1380, 1431, 1489, 2488, 2491, 5214, 5220, 6155
in Algeria, 5453
in Asia, 474, 6155
in Brazil, 4375
civil, 231, 456, 462, 504, 514
collective, 461, 473, 477–78, 487, 523, 2200
colonial, 5510, 5513
in Europe, 477
in France, 2200, 2320
ideology of, 503
in India, 5236, 6155
in Indonesia, 5139
in Latin America, 3867
in Mexico, 4026
in Middle East, 587
political, 17, 165, 450, 458, 464, 467, 469, 474–75, 483, 498, 508–09, 511, 513, 516–17, 522, 525–26, 534, 1179, 3638, 3693, 4375, 5139
revolutionary, 466, 468, 491, 571, 3625, 5504
terrorist, 597
in South Africa, 6196
in United States, 450, 452, 460, 465, 480, 489–90, 493–94, 498, 501–02, 510, 512–13, 518–19, 521–22, 3522, 3604, 3620, 3625, 3638, 3666, 3693, 3699, 3760, 3765, 3781
in Yugoslavia, 3092
Virginia, 3334, 6111
Vivarais, 696
Voltaire, 6000
Vo Nguyen Giap, 5078
von Steins, Lorenz, 6032

Wagner, Richard, 945
Walden, 650
Waldshut, 5984
Warfare, 350, 394, 396–413, 528, 561, 632, 1297, 1468, 2232, 2575, 2658,

Warfare *(continued)*
4892, 5220, 5257, 5973, 6030, 6088. *Also see* Civil war; Guerrilla warfare; Internal war; International civil war; Military; People's war; Urban guerrillas; and subentries under individual country listings
in Africa, 5561
in Asia, 4578–79, 4587
class, 2370
counterrevolutionary, 398, 410, 672, 677, 683
and insurgency, 555
Marxism and, 1075
peasant, 714, 4800
race, 1344
revolutionary, 396–98, 400, 405, 409, 411–12, 1356, 2281, 4255, 4578, 4587, 4800, 5053, 5086, 5189, 5437, 6114
Warren, Mercy Otis, 3361
Washington, George, 3429, 3437, 3440, 3947
Watts Riots, 522, 3752. *Also see* Black Revolution
Weathermen, 3599, 3667, 6125. *Also see* New Left
Weber, Max, 1438, 5835
Weimar Republic, 2880
The West, 1424, 1452, 1852, 2235, 2667, 3926, 4487, 4632, 5562, 5958
West Africa. *See* Africa, West
Westernization, 2656
West Indies. *See* Caribbean
Williams, Roger, 378
William the Silent, 1582
William III, 1772, 1774–76
Wilson, Woodrow, 2873, 2876, 4066
Winstanley, Gerrard, 1739, 1743
Witte, Count Sergei, 2517
Women, 832, 1293–311, 5919, 5951–57, 5986. *Also see* Feminism
and anarchism, 850, 5935
in China, 4719
in Cuba, 4126, 4182
in England, 5919
in Ethiopia, 6195
in France, 1293, 1305, 6011, 6017, 6023, 6036, 6039
in Guinea-Bissau, 5634
in Iran, 5873, 6200, 6206
in Mexico, 3998, 6143
Moslem, 1306
in Russia, 1294, 1298–99, 1302, 1311
in Spain, 5935, 6094
in United States, 1304, 1307, 3507–12, 5957
Working class. *See* Proletariat
World politics, 244, 251, 254, 300, 301, 464, 1569, 1802, 4517, 5031, 5746

488 / Subject Index

World Revolution, 160, 173, 175, 222, 228, 260, 1212, 1215, 1285, 1410–19, 2757, 2791, 2819, 2839, 4753
The Wretched of the Earth (Fanon), 5491
Yeats, Samuel Butler, 2917
Yenan, 4704, 4743, 4786. *Also see* Chinese Revolution (1927–1949)
Yippies, 3605, 3657. *Also see* New Left
Yorubaland, 5376
Young Lords, 3208, 3225
Young Turks. *See* Turkish Revolution (1908)
Yugoslavia, 3101–02
   Communism in, 3093, 3096–97

Yugoslavia *(continued)*
   and socialism, 3102
   warfare in, 3100
Yugoslavian Revolution (1941–1945), 3092–102

Zanzibar, 5532–36
Zapata, Emiliano, 4085–91
Zimbabwe, 5727–33, 5735–36, 5738–39, 5746, 5749–52, 5754
   nationalism in, 5738, 5750
Zionist Revolution, 570, 5810
Zizka, John, 1494
Zola, Emile, 6073
Zubatatov, Sergei, 1072